Library

Student Collection
Seven Day Loan

Return date

Search Engine Freedom

Information Law Series

VOLUME 27

General Editor

Prof. P. Bernt Hugenholtz
Institute for Information Law
University of Amsterdam

The titles published in this series are listed at the back of this volume.

Search Engine Freedom

On the Implications of the Right to Freedom of Expression for the Legal Governance of Web Search Engines

Joris van Hoboken

Wolters Kluwer
Law & Business

Published by:
Kluwer Law International
PO Box 316
2400 AH Alphen aan den Rijn
The Netherlands
E-mail: sales@kluwerlaw.com
Website: www.kluwerlaw.com

Sold and distributed in North, Central and South America by:
Aspen Publishers, Inc.
7201 McKinney Circle
Frederick, MD 21704
United States of America
Email: customer.service@aspenpublishers.com

Sold and distributed in all other countries by:
Turpin Distribution Services Ltd.
Stratton Business Park
Pegasus Drive, Biggleswade
Bedfordshire SG18 8TQ
United Kingdom
Email: kluwerlaw@turpin-distribution.com

Printed on acid-free paper.

ISBN 978-90-411-4128-6

Printed and Bound by CPI Group (UK) Ltd, Croydon, CR0 4YY.

Table of Contents

List of Abbreviations

A-G	Advocate-General
BBS	Bulletin Board Service
BGH	Bundesgerichtshof
BPjM	Bundesprüfstelle für jugendgefährdende Medien
BVerfG	Bundesverfassungsgericht
CDA	Communications Decency Act
CoE	Council of Europe
COM	European Commission document number
CPC	Cost per Click
CPM	Cost per Mille
DMCA	Digital Millennium Copyright Act
EC	European Commission
ECD	EU Directive on Electronic Commerce
ECHR	European Convention on Human Rights
ECtHR	European Court of Human Rights
EHRC	European Human Rights Commission
EU	European Union
FCC	Federal Communications Commission
FSM	Freiwillige Selbstkontrolle Multimedia-Diensteanbieter
FTC	Federal Trade Commission
FTP	File Transfer Protocol
HTTP	Hypertext Transfer Protocol
IFLA	International Federation of Library Associations
IP	Internet Protocol
ISP	Internet Service Provider
IWF	Internet Watch Foundation

Acknowledgements

The completion of this book which is the result of my PhD thesis at the Insititute for Information Law (IViR) would not have been possible without the support of many who have been important for my research, my academic development and my personal life. First, I want to acknowledge the intellectual support and patience of my supervisors Prof. Nico van Eijk and Dr. Natali Helberger. I am thankful both for the directions they provided as well as the space they left me to develop my own voice. A special thanks goes out to Prof. Egbert Dommering for his involvement in this project, and his past work and continuing intellectual support for IViR. I would also like to thank the other members of my thesis committee, Prof. Wolfgang Schulz, Prof. Milton Mueller, Prof. Peggy Valcke and Prof. Richard Rogers.

IViR is a wonderful place to conduct research. I feel much indebted to my colleagues for their contributions to the intellectual and social climate there. My gratitude also goes out to all the others at the University of Amsterdam that supported me and showed an interest in my work.

I am grateful to Harvard's Berkman Center for Internet & Society and Yochai Benkler for supporting my stay there in the fall of 2008 and want to thank Urs Gasser, Colin Maclay, Jonathan Zittrain, Eszter Hargittai, Rebecca Tabasky, Amar Ashar, Wendy Seltzer, Ethan Zuckermann, Phil Malone, Lokman Tsui, and Chris Soghoian for their welcome, help, advice, critiques and thoughts that contributed to my stay and my research there and after.

Furthermore, I want to specially mention and thank the following people for their time, friendship, interest and invitations to present my work: Eben Moglen, Ian Brown, James Grimmelmann, Frank Pasquale, Niva Elkin-Koren, Eric Goldman, Tal Zarsky, Dag Elgesem, Miguel Peguera, Biella Coleman, Benjamin Mako Hill, Eddan Katz, Bogdan Manolea, Meryem Marzouki, Rikke Frank Joergensen,

Acknowledgements

Bodo Balasz, Michael Zimmer, Ben Peters, Maria Gomez Rodriguez, Theo Röhle, Malte Ziewitz, Seda Gürses, Gon Zifroni, Konrad Becker and Felix Stalder.

To Peter Robinett I express my appreciation for his patient and witty comments on my use of the English language. To the Bits of Freedom crew and Ot van Daalen, I want to signal my esteem and appreciation for working together. My final words here are in gratitude and love for my friends, the band and my family.

Joris van Hoboken
Amsterdam, June 2012

Chapter 1
Introduction

1.1. GENERAL INTRODUCTION

Over the last two decades, a new type of medium, the Web search engine, has established itself as an essential intermediary of the public networked information environment. The World Wide Web, its sheer abundance of available material and its inherent lack of organization, created the need for this new kind of service, which provides an ordered index to what is available, in terms of its usefulness, quality and attractiveness for different users. Internet users have flocked to search media, thereby turning them into a locus of online marketing activities as well as important platforms to reach an audience for information providers.

In other words, search media can be seen as primary contributors to the 'opening up' of the Web, understood as the process of connecting information and ideas online to their societal use. Not surprisingly, the centrality of search engines for the Web and the effectiveness of search engines in this process of opening up information and ideas online have spurred public debate, litigation and regulatory activity with regard to the proper legal limitations on the provision of search engine services.

China's interference with Google is probably the most popular example of a government's interference with the deployment of search engine technology on the Internet. To be able to run its search engine service in China, *google.cn* has had to obtain a license and censor its search results to prevent references to a variety of topics, including politically sensitive speech. The severe limitation on search services in China is not restricted to Google and is part of a much broader, sophisticated and repressive Internet policy.

China, however, is not the only country where search engine operations are the subject of government pressure or legal restrictions that impact their ability to open up the Web more generally. This happens in constitutional democracies as well.

Search engines in Germany, for instance, block results categorized by public authorities as hate speech, such as the right extremist web forum *stormfront.org*.[1] All over the world, including the United States and Europe, search engines have been ordered and incentivized to remove references to illegal or unlawful content. Sometimes, search engines have had to prevent certain searches from taking place, for instance, the search query 'Maradona' in Argentina.[2] Some specialized search engines have been judged to be illegal altogether, for instance the Dutch search engine *Zoekmp3*, which specialized in finding music files published on websites.[3] And perhaps most strikingly, there are legal developments in Spain where a court, at the request of a public data protection authority, is considering ordering the removal of lawful information from Google, including newspaper articles and official public documents, due to their alleged impact on the privacy of individuals.[4]

It is inevitable that a study about search engines is, also, a study about Google, culturally and commercially the most successful general purpose search engine in the United States, Europe and most other parts of the world. The dominance of Google, and the consolidation of the market for general purpose search engines, has led to a new set of regulatory concerns related to search engine governance. It has been remarked that by operating its service, Google helps establish the winners and losers in the networked information environment. In doing so, it could harm the fundamental communicative interests of certain end-users and information providers. In view of those interests and the political, cultural and economic power that a search engine such as Google has, it is argued that legal restrictions on operating its service may be warranted.[5] For example, some commentators argue in favor of treating dominant search engines as essential facilities or common carriers. This treatment would aim to bring search engine governance back in line with the communicative interests of information providers and end-users.

Information providers on the Web continue to try to hold Google legally responsible for damages as a result of lowered rankings. Interest groups as well as public authorities continue to complain about the lack of responsibility on the part of search engines to deal with questionable and harmful content, such as the anti-semitic website *Jewwatch.com*. And at the time of writing—and only thirteen years after its launch—Google is caught up in a number of lengthy antitrust investigations related to its core product i.e. search. Many have started to compare these investigations with the start of similar battles of antitrust authorities against Microsoft or AT&T. Notably, some of the complaints which have led to the investigation go to the core of the search engine's operations, namely Google's decisions about the selection and ranking of relevant search results for end-users' queries.

---

1. See section 9.2.1.
2. See Soghoian & Valle 2008. See also Van Hoboken 2009c.
3. Gerechtshof [Court of Appeals] Amsterdam, June 15, 2006 (*Zoekmp3.nl*). See also section 9.4.2.
4. See Halliday 2011b.
5. See e.g. Pasquale 2010a.

1.2.   SEARCH ENGINE GOVERNANCE AND FREEDOM
               OF EXPRESSION

In each of the cases referred to above, search engine operators are or could be limited in their freedom to provide a service that makes online information more readily accessible to Internet users. China's Internet information policy is clearly problematic from a constitutional democratic perspective and is an interference with the right to freedom of expression. But how far can constitutional democracies go, when restricting search engines operations? Or more specifically, to what extent can search engines claim protection under the right to freedom of expression in cases of government regulation or with respect to the application of existing law?

It is clear that search engines deserve credit for their contribution to the accessibility to information and ideas online. In Europe, the well-known '*Paperboy*' ruling by the German *Bundesgerichtshof* contains one of the clearest references to the value of search media for end-users. The court stated the following:

> Without the use of search services and their application of hyperlinks (exactly in the form of deep links) the sensible use of the vast abundance of information on the World Wide Web would be practically impossible.[6]

Here, the German Supreme Court clearly recognizes that the availability of search engine services and their use of hyperlink technology, which was the actual point of litigation, help establish the value of the World Wide Web as a source of information in society. Although, in its argumentation, the court does not explicitly refer to freedom of expression, its reference to the 'sensible use' of an information medium implicitly points to values underlying it.[7] Surely, the services that help make the Web a valuable source of information must be a positive thing from the perspective of freedom of expression? This would imply that legal restrictions on their operations should be assessed carefully.

Unfortunately, a proper assessment of the proportionality of a possible interference with the right to freedom of expression will not always take place. The examples of search engine case law mentioned above each show, in their own way, the potential significance of freedom of expression for the legal position of search engines. What they also tend to have in common is the vague manner in which the implications of the right to freedom of expression are qualified. In the Dutch *Zoekmp3* case, for instance, the Amsterdam Court of Appeals, after concluding that the provider was acting unlawfully, did acknowledge that the prohibition of *Zoekmp3* constituted an interference with Article 10 ECHR. However, it did not explain in what manner a search engine is protected by Article 10 ECHR.

---

6.   *Ohne die Inanspruchnahme von Suchdiensten und deren Einsatz von Hyperlinks (gerade in der Form von Deep-Links) wäre die sinnvolle Nutzung de unübersehbaren Informationsfülle im World Wide Web praktisch ausgeslossen.* (Translation by the author), BGH [German High Court] July 17, 2003, I ZR 259/00 (*Paperboy*), § 54.
7.   In more recent judgments that follow the *Paperboy* judgment, explicit reference is being made to the value of search engines for the freedom of expression and information. See OLG Hamburg [Court of Appeals Hamburg], February 20, 2007.

Neither did it elaborate on the interference's justification, which could at least have been questioned. The same music files not only remained available for end-users regardless of the availability of the *Zoekpm3* search engine, but many could also be easily found with the intelligent use of other, general purpose search engines.

European legislatures have yet to properly respond to search engines as a new phenomenon. As will be discussed in this thesis, legislative action could, for instance, be directed at facilitating legal certainty and the space for search engines to operate their service and provide the value for Internet users mentioned above. In comparison with the United States, such legal space for search services to operate, from the perspective of their positive contributions to the free flow of information on the Internet, has not been firmly rooted in legislation.

All the examples of case law above involve the application of generally applicable legal provisions related to the lawfulness of the publication and dissemination of information and ideas or the operation of businesses more generally. In academia, there is a growing body of work about the law, as it relates to the operations of search engines, but the freedom of expression perspective on search engine governance is still far from understood. Considering the ever-growing cultural, political and economic importance of the Internet and the World Wide Web in our societies, and the societal interests involved in the availability of effective search tools, this state of affairs by itself justifies further research. Web search is one of the most intensively used types of services online. Without effective search tools, the Internet would hardly be the valuable source of information it is today. Any speaker on the Internet relies on the help of search intermediaries to reach an audience. This implies that the way search engines function determines to a large extent whether we effectively enjoy our freedom to receive and impart information and ideas on the Web. Thus, if any principle should be high up on the legal and regulatory agenda in relation to search engine governance, freedom of expression is a good candidate.

1.3.   GENERAL RESEARCH QUESTION AND
        SCOPE OF THE STUDY

This thesis will try to bring clarification to the question of freedom of expression as it relates to search engines. It will do so by looking at the search engine medium as it emerged in the networked information environment and will address the regulatory debate about search engine governance from the perspective of freedom of expression. More specifically, the aim of this thesis is to conceptualize the role of search engines in the public networked information environment, the proper boundaries for government involvement following from the right to freedom of expression and the instruments that have been or could be used by the State to promote the right to freedom of expression in the context of search.

As mentioned before, freedom of expression has scarcely been addressed in the context of search engines, while it is clear that the legal governance of web search engines has an impact on the right to freedom of expression, as well as on the effective exercise of this right by online speakers and end-users. The still open question of how the right to freedom of expression applies to the search engine context clearly needs to be addressed in the legal debate about search engine governance.

The ultimate goal of this thesis is to develop an understanding of how freedom of expression doctrine, as well as media and communications law and policy more generally, can successfully incorporate search media. Freedom of expression as a fundamental right, but also as a fundamental legal and normative principle, has been a leading theoretical concept shaping the relationship between legislators and media and telecommunications in constitutional democracies. Press freedom may be the clearest example of this. Freedom of expression limits a government's ability to proscribe certain information flows. It also informs the possible necessity, permissibility, or feasibility of government and legal action aimed at realizing freedom of expression in our societies.

In view of the foregoing, the general research question of this thesis can be formulated as follows:

> What are the implications of the right to freedom of expression for search engine governance and government involvement with regards to search?

Of course there is much that is not the subject of this study. First of all, this is a work of legal scholarship in the field of information law. While the typical architecture and operations of search engines will be explained in Chapter 3, this thesis will not go into the technical details of search engines as an objective in itself. Search media are technically and operationally complex, and they are an active field of study in computer and information science, as well as microeconomics. The results from these fields inform this thesis but are not within the scope of analysis. The same applies for the structure of the search engine market, i.e. the economics of search engines more generally. The business models of search engines, as well as the market developments in the search engine industry, have legal and policy relevance, but a detailed study of the economics of the search engine market is beyond the scope of this research. An overview of market developments will be part of this thesis, but this overview is meant to provide context rather than scientific substance.

This research is legal and encompasses theoretical, conceptual and explorative analyzes. In line with the research question, the emphasis is placed on the formulation of a freedom of expression theory for the Web search medium, the ensuing legal relations between national governments and search media providers on the one hand, and the relations between search media, end-users and information providers on the other hand. Because of the current state of affairs of search engine law, such an endeavor inevitably has a conceptual and explorative character. There is no coherent body of search engine law in Europe,[8] and neither will this thesis propose a general regulatory and legal framework in that direction. The legal status

---

8. See Van Eijk 2006, 7.

of search engines is quite generally unclear and case law at the higher Court levels remains rare or absent.

The fundamental right to freedom of expression is at the center of this study. This fundamental right is laid down in different fashions as a fundamental and constitutional right in international conventions and national constitutions. The legal perspective of this thesis is situated in the triangle of European media and communications law, the European fundamental rights framework of the European Convention of Human Rights, Article 10 ECHR in particular, and the legal developments in various Member States. Notably, these national legal developments will not be addressed in great detail and will mostly serve as examples.

An important restriction on the scope of this study is related to the ways in which search engine operations can be considered relevant from the perspective of copyright law and trademark law. Search engines may use or relate to third-party content in ways restricted by copyright law. For instance, to provide their service search engines obviously have to copy large amounts of copyright-protected works and store them in their index. This raises interesting questions about the implications of a conflict between the fundamental right to freedom of expression and the application of copyright law to search media, but these questions will not be addressed. There is a steady stream of case law about trademark infringement in search engine advertising in Europe as well as the United States, but the question of whether search engines themselves may infringe trademarks with the selection and publication of their search results and advertisements will not be discussed. Competition law and patent law, which are arguably important areas of law for the governance of search engines and competition in the search engine market, are also excluded from the analysis.

Notably, the legal issues arising from trademark and copyright infringements in search results and underlying websites will be included in the analysis to the extent that these issues result in a question of third-party or *indirect* liability of search engines for third-party content and communications. A large part of the available case law about the legal responsibility of search engine providers relates to this question, which does not require a detailed analysis of copyright law in the context of search engines.

This thesis makes a contribution to the legal and regulatory debate about search engines from a European perspective, while mostly focusing on the legal framework at the European level. To add a comparative element to this study and reflect on the European framework, U.S. First Amendment doctrine and relevant elements of U.S. law relating to search engine governance will be discussed. There are several reasons for including U.S. law as a comparative element in this study about search engine governance and freedom of expression. First, U.S. law has strongly influenced global practices in the context of the Internet. Second, the richness of First Amendment doctrine can help explore the possible implications of the right to freedom of expression for the governance of search media, while often allowing for interesting conceptual comparisons due to the existing differences in approach. Third, almost all major search engines are U.S. companies, which has resulted in the situation that law and policy, as related to search, are more developed in the United States than elsewhere.

1.4.   STRUCTURE AND METHODOLOGY

This thesis is divided into three distinct parts. The first part discusses the functioning, background and context of the search engine medium, thereby providing a foundation for the subsequent legal analysis. The second part will discuss the right to freedom of expression, its role in the legal governance of other important entities in the public information environment and its general implications in the context of search engine media. The third part discusses a number of more specific regulatory issues related to search engine governance from the perspective of the right to freedom of expression.

The first part of the thesis provides the necessary understanding of Web search and its context for the later parts of this thesis. It is mostly descriptive and divided into two chapters. Chapter 2 provides an overview of the history of the search engine, its emergence in the networked information environment created by the World Wide Web in the early 1990s and the various developments in the market for online search media that have shaped the current offering of search media. Chapter 3 gives a definition of the search medium and explains, in basic terms, the functioning of a typical search engine and the different elements that make it work in practice. In addition, the position and function of the search engine medium in the public networked information environment will be discussed, as well as its functional relationship to information providers and end-users.

The second part consists of five different chapters: a general chapter on freedom of expression (Chapter 4), three chapters with an analysis of the implications of the right to freedom of expression in the context of other entities in the public information environment (Chapters 5 and –7), and building on these analyzes a final chapter on the implications of the right to freedom of expression in the context of search (Chapter 8).

Chapter 4 discusses the dominant rationales underlying the right to freedom of expression as well as the specific legal provisions that will be at the heart of the analysis in this thesis. These are the specific rights to freedom of expression as enshrined in Article 10 of the ECHR and the U.S. First Amendment. The relevant elements from the legal doctrine related to these legal provisions will be discussed in this chapter as well. To be specific, it includes a discussion of the general scope and the possibility of limitations of these provisions. And, it addresses the role of government under the right to freedom of expression, the difference between negative and positive obligations and the possibility of horizontal effect.

Chapters 5–7 analyze the implications of the right to freedom of expression for the governance of the press, Internet access and public libraries, respectively. The subject of these chapters is shortly denoted as press freedom, ISP freedom and library freedom. These three chapters will follow a similar structure and logic, while doing justice to the particular nature of these institutions. By studying the research question in these contexts and by focusing on the way the implications of the right to freedom of expression are related to the particularities and roles of these entities in the public information environment, these chapters lay the foundation to develop a similar theory of search engine freedom in Chapter 8.

In each instance, the answers to the following questions will be addressed: In what ways and on what grounds are legal governance and government involvement with regard to these entities informed by the right to freedom of expression? What is the role of these entities in the public information environment and how has that role informed freedom of expression doctrine? What are the typical actions or issues that have called for an evaluation of the proper role of government under the right to freedom of expression? And what is the position of information providers or speakers on the one hand and end-users, listeners or readers on the other hand, if the entity is conceptualized as a speech intermediating institution?

There are a variety of reasons for the selection of the press, Internet access and public libraries to build an understanding about the ways in which the right to freedom of expression should apply to the context of search media. Most importantly, by selecting the press on the one hand, and Internet access on the other hand, two classic regulatory models for media and communications providers are captured, namely the model focusing on the press as well as the model commonly denoted as common carrier.[9] Both these models are useful in conceptualizing the role of search engines in the public information environment, since search engines may have to be placed somewhere on the axis between non-discriminatory conduit and active and selective communicator. Since the implications of the right to freedom of expression are informed by the role of a certain entity, a study of these models will also help clarify the way freedom of expression should apply in the search engine context.

The analysis of library freedom is best justified by the comparable role that libraries play with regard to the world of information and ideas: to help their patrons navigate and obtain access. The history of search engines is closely related to the library, and early search engines and information retrieval were mostly developed in the context of library and information science. Of special interest is also the positive role of the State in the context of the public library in view of the ideals underlying the right to freedom of expression.

The selection of the press, Internet access and public libraries implies that this thesis will not analyze the constitutional model of broadcasting. It is clear that the broadcasting model could have provided additional insight into freedom of expression doctrine as it applies to different entities in the public information environment. In particular, the dual role of government under the right to freedom of expression in the broadcasting context, as possible infringer and as protector of the right to freedom of expression of the public, would have been of interest.

---

9. Notably, the analysis in Ch. 6 will not presuppose that Internet access providers should be legally treated as common carriers. In the networked information environment, they are simply the entities which, from a functional and regulatory perspective, come closest to this traditional model.

However, due to the need to limit the scope of analysis as well as a number of substantive reasons, broadcasting is not addressed in detail. The dual role, mentioned above, can also be found in the context of public libraries. And the public library is of additional interest due to the historical relation to the organization of information and ideas which is an important aspect of search engines. In addition, broadcasting does not play as important a role in the value chains in which search engines operate, compared to the (electronic) press and Internet access providers.

Chapter 8 will address the general question of the implications of the right to freedom of expression for the legal governance of Web search engines. And it will further conceptualize the role of search engines in the public information environment from a normative perspective, which is one of the main questions addressed in this thesis. It will do so by building on the conclusions in Chapters 2 and 3, and by comparing the role of search engines with the role of the press, Internet access providers and public libraries. Subsequently, the main conclusions from Chapters 5–7, about the way the role of a communications provider informs its protection under the right to freedom of expression, is used to address the question of the implications of the right to freedom of expression in the context of search engine governance. More specifically, Chapter 8 addresses the question of the proper scope of protection under the right to freedom of expression of the search engine provider, the end-users and the information providers. For which decisions and actions should search engines be able to claim protection and on which grounds? How does the active and selective role of search media compare to the editorial control and freedom in other media and what could be considered the duties and responsibilities of search media, which are tied to the exercise of the right to freedom of expression by Article 10 ECHR? And what role do information providers and end-users play in a theory of search engine freedom?

The final part of this thesis (Part III) builds on the conclusions in Chapter 8, while focusing on a number of specific and important regulatory issues in the context of search engine governance. The issues addressed in these final chapters of the thesis have been selected because their proper resolution could contribute from a proper understanding of the right to freedom of expression in the context of search engines. In other words, the final part of the thesis demonstrates the value and relevance of a theory of search engine freedom for the debate about the legal governance of search engines more generally. In addition, the results and conclusions of Chapter 8 are used to discuss the extent to which the right to freedom of expression has been properly taken into account in legal and regulatory practice.

Chapter 9 addresses regulatory issues related to the legal governance of 'access' in search media. More specifically, it focuses on the responsibility of search engines for opening up illegal and unlawful information and ideas and the proper implications of the right to freedom of expression in this context. In Europe in particular, the question of legal obligations for the removal of online material from search engines' indices and the existing self-regulatory frameworks that result in removal of references remain important topics at the European and Member State level. Chapter 9 will address the question of proactive actions and possible duties of care on search engines to police their index in detail, as well as the existing framework of third-party liability of search engines in the networked information environment.

Chapter 10 addresses three specific regulatory issues related to search engine quality and the ranking and selection of search results. First, the fundamental regulatory notions of diversity and pluralism will be discussed. To what extent do the current offerings of search media, and of particularly dominant search engines especially, impact diversity and pluralism? What would be the main concerns when addressing search engines from this perspective and what is needed if legislators or regulatory agencies were to move forward from this perspective, which is after all a fundamental concern for them on the basis of Article 10 ECHR? Second, the regulatory issues relating to the lack of transparency in the ranking and selection of search results will be discussed, in particular the regulatory backgrounds of the separation between sponsored and organic results in search engine result pages. The section will discuss the value for end-users and the underlying assumptions of the labeling of sponsored search results in detail and address the question of how this practice relates and contributes to transparency and search engine quality more generally. Third, and finally, the issue of search engine user privacy and user data processing will be addressed, focusing specifically on the instrumental nature of privacy and data protection laws with regard to the intellectual freedom and autonomy of end-users.

Chapter 11 provides a summary and brings together the main findings in this thesis. On this basis, it provides answers to the general research question and makes a number of recommendations in relation to the proper role of government with regard to search engine governance, the question of whether existing elements of the regulatory framework for search media can be improved, as well as the question of directions for future legal and empirical research in this field. The research for this thesis was concluded in August 2011. After which, only a small number of substantive additions and changes have been made.

Part I

Web Search Engines: Functioning, Background and Context

Chapter 2
A Short History of Search Engines and Related Market Developments

2.1.   THE INTERNET, THE WEB AND THE RISE OF
         NAVIGATIONAL MEDIA

2.1.1.   EARLY VISIONS OF NAVIGATION IN DIGITIZED
         INFORMATION ENVIRONMENTS

The way digital computing would lead to a revolution in information and knowledge navigation was already being explored more than half a century ago, when computers were still a rarity and neither the Internet nor the World Wide Web existed. Most famously, Vannevar Bush, in his article '*As We May Think*', envisioned the 'memex', an electronic device in which individuals would store their books, records and communications on micro-film, and which would be consultable through a system of indices and speedy navigation.[10] The users of the memex would be able to tie different pieces of knowledge together and compose their own trails in the body of information available on the memex. These ties and trails would remain available for later consultation and use.

Bush imagined this memex would help society overcome the limitations of the scientific organization of knowledge through the traditional indexing and storage of paper-bound information. His work was, and still is, part of the scientific literature relating to knowledge and libraries, a scientific field which was actively addressing the issue of how to organize the ever-growing field of human knowledge through the use of new technologies. In the same field, but almost two decades later, Licklider continued this endeavor with a research project on the

---

10. Bush 1945. For a discussion, see Stefik 1996, 15–23. Paul Otlet may have been the first to explore these issues. See Wright 2008; Rayward 1990.

characteristics of 'the future library'—to be precise, 'the library of 2000'.[11] Licklider, mentioning Vannevar Bush as his main external influence, started with the same assumption: knowledge was growing at a speed beyond society's capacity to make use of it.[12] The primary reasons for this growing discrepancy, he claimed, were the limitations of paper-bound knowledge from the perspective of the user's need to retrieve relevant information. The only solution, according to Licklider's team, would be a fusion of the computer and the library into what they would end up calling a 'precognitive system'. Their work considered the feasibility of such a system on the one hand and the criteria it would have to fulfill on the other.[13] For instance, they concluded that the system would have to make the body of knowledge available when and where needed, foster the improvement of its organization through its use and converse and negotiate with the user when he or she formulates requests.

These early theoretical developments related to the use of digital technology to consult digital collections of information gave birth to the field of information retrieval, the science or field of information engineering relating to the search and retrieval of electronic materials and of the information within such materials.[14] The scientific roots of current Web search engines lie in this field of information retrieval.[15] But already, more than fifty years ago, many seemingly obvious but fundamental improvements were conceptualized and tested for information retrieval more generally, which realized the promise of the computer not only as a basic storage unit for information but also for making this information more easily accessible. In the 1950s, for instance, information scientists proposed the use of statistical text measures for the relevance of documents. Maron and Kuhns conceptualized the use of words as indexing units for documents and the measuring of word overlap, i.e. the similarity of the entered search query to the set of indexed words in available documents, as a criterion for retrieval relevance.[16] These and related ideas caused a paradigm shift in thinking about the problem of information retrieval: relevance in information retrieval systems would no longer be a binary affair, meaning that a document was simply relevant or not, but would become a prediction of how valuable a document would be for a user of the system. This prediction would be based on an inference of the searcher's input and the contents of the documents in the system.[17] The field of information retrieval has made rapid progress ever since and has made a major contribution to the

---

11. See Licklider 1969.
12. See Stefik 1996, 24.
13. See Licklider 1969, 32–39.
14. See Singhal 2001; Lesk 1995.
15. See Röhle 2010, 17.
16. Maron & Kuhns 1960, 216–224. For a discussion of Kuhns work, see Singhal 2001. For a discussion of Luhn's propositions regarding text-statistical measures as a model for relevance, see Röhle 2010, 113–118.
17. See Maron 2008, 971–972.

conceptualization and development of the subsequent search engines for the Internet and the World Wide Web, which this study focuses on.[18]

The following section will shortly explore the historical societal context of search engines by looking at the issue of findability and the state of search technology from the start of the Internet to the current public networked information environment. Notably, a choice has been made to focus on the historical background of Web search engines from the perspective of end-users and to see them as the current end-product of the development of instruments for effective navigation and retrieval which evolved together with the expanding digital information environment.

2.1.2.   THE INTERNET: CONNECTING THE NODES

When the Internet, or to be more precise the 'Advanced Research Projects Agency Network' (ARPANET), was developed in the late 1960s,[19] the network was more about computer resource sharing than about the sharing of knowledge and information. In that sense, it was far from the visions of Bush and Licklider about the use of networked computing to create a 'memex' or 'the future library'. Notwithstanding this primary purpose of sharing computing resources, the issue of findability, i.e. users of the network being able to know what computer resources, documents or other users were available on or connected to the network, was an important one that had to be addressed. It was partly resolved by the funding through ARPA of a Network Information Center (NIC) at the Stanford Research Institute (SRI). The NIC was created by the SRI research group led by Douglas Engelbart, a pioneer in human computer interaction and networked computing. The NIC maintained several directories essential to the use of the network.[20]

Because of their research into the opportunities of better handling of digital resources, Engelbart's research group was an attractive candidate to fulfill the role as envisioned for the NIC. Nonetheless, the NIC was not particularly successful in the task of overseeing the resources that were available on the ARPANET. It proved hard to organize a reliable and complete directory of network resources and capabilities.[21] Ultimately, a lot of information about the network was shared informally or off the network. When the electronic mail protocol was introduced, the newsletter became an important new means of sharing resource information. The *ARPANET News*, for instance, had a special section featuring certain network resources.[22]

---

18.   See Singhal 2001. See also Baeza-Yates & Ribeiro-Neto 2011.
19.   For a history of the Internet, see Abbate 2000. See also Hafner & Lyon 1996, Stefik 1996.
20.   Abbate 2000, 59.
21.   See Abbate 2000, 85–89, 213.
22.   See Hafner & Lyon 1996, 229–230. ARPANET News was edited by the same Stanford Research Institute.

The current Internet grew out of the ARPANET of the 1970s, but besides ARPANET, there were many other computer networks that offered similar possibilities, such as the global network based on the X25 network standard that was widely deployed by the telecommunications industry in the 1980s. Ultimately, various standardization efforts, including the introduction and promotion of the TCP/IP standards in the 1980s, and the switchover of other networks to this defining Internet standard, helped create the global network of networks, the Internet, that we know today.[23]

Public access to the network remained limited until the beginning of the 1990s. Throughout the 1980s, several private networks provided services to meet the popular demand that was shaped by the early personal computer revolution of that time. Dial-in networks such as CompuServe, America Online (AOL), Prodigy, and a variety of smaller Bulletin Board Services (BBSs; accessible for computer users by calling in over regular phone lines), offered the possibility to access information and entertainment, post messages and play early network-based computer games. These BBSs were very popular in the beginning of the 1990s and many of the early legal issues related to the Internet involved BBSs.[24]

Notably, the ARPANET was not a public resource; access to the network was restricted. This remained the case until the Internet became publicly accessible in the 1990s. As a consequence, the resources that were available on the network were not part of the public information environment either. And those who had access to the network could, in principle, not freely access all the information on the Internet, unless they had (implied) permission to do so. It is clear that these features of the ARPANET had important implications for the state of findability on the network, as not all the material on the network was freely accessible to all the users, let alone potential directory and/or search engine providers. This excerpt from a set of guidelines about the use of ARPANET from the Defense Communications Agency (DCA) in an ARPANET Newsletter from 1981 shows the restrictions on the accessibility and further use of information on the ARPANET:

> Files should not be FTPed by anyone unless they are files that have been announced as ARPANET-public or unless permission has been obtained from the owner. Public files on the ARPANET are not to be considered public files outside of the ARPANET, and should not be transferred, or their contents

---

23. Abbate 2000. On the general engineering aspects of computer networking, see Kurose & Ross 2009.
24. Examples are the raid of the Private Sector BBS of Hacker Magazine 2600. See '2600' 1985. For a discussion of the German CompuServe battle against access for German citizens to illegal content which started in 1995 (Germany), see Determann 1999. See also *Playboy Enterprises Inc. v. Frena*, 839 F. Supp. 1552 (M.D. Fla. 1993); *Religious Technology Center v. Netcom On-Line Communication Services, Inc.*, 907 F. Supp. 1361 (N.D. Cal. 1995).

given or sold to the general public without permission of DCA or the ARPA-NET sponsors.[25]

In addition, even though users of the early Internet of the 1970s and 1980s may have been able to access material hosted elsewhere, before the introduction of browsers and the World Wide Web, it was relatively hard to find (unknown) content on the Internet. There were no search engines as yet and files in remote locations were typically accessed by using the file transfer protocol (FTP) protocol. This protocol was designed to transfer files over the network and not to find them effectively. The Domain Name System (DNS), which added a human understandable address space to the numerical Internet address space did help Internet users remember the locations of known organizations and hosts, but its value from the perspective of effective navigation online, particularly in view of the potential of information retrieval in digital information collections, was (and remains) limited.[26]

As the amount of resources available on the network grew steadily, effective retrieval became more and more of an issue, and specialized services were developed to keep track of resources and provide network users the means to find materials. The first Internet search engine, Archie, was the first service to provide a searchable index of the titles of files available on anonymous[27] FTP servers on the network. It was developed by McGill University students in Montreal in 1990.[28]

As mentioned above, the FTP protocol had its limitations due to its focus on transferring materials over the network. These limitations of the Internet around 1990, in terms of the organization of content on the network to allow for the effective retrieval of material and its effective dissemination more generally, spurred the development and implementation of systems of additional protocols relating to the publication and organization of information on the Internet.[29] One of these sets of protocols was Gopher, which entailed a different way of organizing electronic materials on host sites on the network and ways of communicating with them from remote locations. The other and more famous one was the World Wide Web hypertext system, which will be discussed in the next section.

The Gopher system, which was released in 1991, relied on directory-based hierarchies for the storage and retrieval of information on the Internet.[30] In a Gopher environment, Internet users would be presented with directories of content

---

25. Haugney 1981. The Defense Communications Agency was responsible for the legal management of ARPANET and with its guidelines it addressed the typical variety of legal issues related to the opportunities that the network offered to access and distribute information.
26. For a more recent discussion of the navigational value of domain names, see Committee on Internet Navigation 2005.
27. Anonymous FTP was commonly used to make material generally accessible for remote users, while not requiring users to log into the host server.
28. See Sonnenreich & Macinta 1998, 1–2.
29. See Schatz & Harding 1994.
30. Anklesaria et al. 1993.

available on the network much like they were used to in the typical text-based computer interfaces at the time.[31]

The Gopher system for the publication of information on the Internet is of special interest from the perspective of the history of search engines because it had search and the effective retrieval of material designed into the system. Gopher involved so-called structured directory formats, calling for the organizing of online material in tree-like hierarchies, and moreover its design included the possibility of special full-text search servers which would help users of the network locate documents in specific domains. A second early search engine, Veronica, developed in 1992 at the University of Reno, focused on this new Gopher protocol and provided a directory of the hierarchies of Gopher servers available on the Internet. Like Archie, Veronica was limited to titles and did not offer full-text search.[32]

Notably, the specific focus on search and the organization of material on the network in the Gopher protocols was absent in the hypertext environment as was introduced with the World Wide Web. Or perhaps, it is better to say it was deliberately left open. The World Wide Web, unlike Gopher, revolutionized the way the Internet was used as a public information environment. In combination with newly introduced browser technology, it marked a new phase in the use of the Internet for the sharing of information and ideas. And it also signified the real start of the development of search engine services and technology.

2.1.3. THE WORLD WIDE WEB: BROWSERS, HYPERLINKS AND SPIDERS

The World Wide Web hypertext system was developed by Tim Berners-Lee and his colleagues at CERN (the European Organization for Nuclear Research), as a new way to organize information on the Internet. Building on existing ideas about hypertext and the memex vision of Vanevar Bush, the proposal for a World Wide Web in 1990 aimed to make online information more easily accessible in a universal format that would potentially link all online information together as a network of hypermedia nodes. As the first proposal for the World Wide Web stated:

> The current incompatibilities of the platforms and tools make it impossible to access existing information through a common interface, leading to waste of time, frustration and obsolete answers to simple data lookup. There is a potential large benefit from the integration of a variety of systems in a way which allows a user to follow links pointing from one piece of information to another one. This forming of a web of information nodes rather than a hierarchical tree or an ordered list is the basic concept behind HyperText.[33]

---

31. Media theorist Florian Cramer offers his website in Gopherspace. See Cramer http://cramer. pleintekst.nl:70/.
32. See Sonnenreich & Macinta 1998, 2–3.
33. Berners-Lee & Cailliau 1990.

In other words, the World Wide Web hypertext system offered network users the opportunity to organize online information themselves by linking it together, instead of relying on more rigid hierarchical tree-structures such as in the Gopher system. Any contributor to online information, when using the hypertext markup language (HTML), would be able to link to any other available hypertext online resource, thereby integrating the new material with the rest in a universal 'web' of online materials. Network users would access the online environment with 'browsers', which would interpret the hypertext world and allow users to navigate it by going from node to node across the hypertext structured material on the Web. The nodes were to be identified by Uniform Resource Locators (URLs), which were based on the Internet host name space (DNS) and which would provide for a World Wide Web address space.

The World Wide Web hypertext system proved an enormous success and is generally seen as the application of the Internet that made it attractive to the masses.[34] Developed and first implemented in the global community of high-energy physicists, its use grew very rapidly after the release of Mosaic, an early publicly available graphical Web browser that had more advanced capabilities such as allowing images to be shown as part of a Web page. Soon after, other commercial browsers became available on the market, such as the commercial Mosaic release called Netscape.

The organization of online information through a dynamic web of hyperlinked nodes, instead of a preconceived hierarchical structure, implies much more freedom for both users and contributors of the network than the hierarchical organization of materials in the Gopher system. The World Wide Web places emphasis on the ability of end-users to navigate online material effectively and relies on the knowledge of users—of all sorts—about the network and on their resourcefulness to provide the links to other available valuable materials on the network. Hence, this initial lack of organization of the hypertext environment implied an enormous opportunity for users to help 'organize' the World Wide Web and the navigation of information and ideas it made potentially possible. On the one hand, the World Wide Web design implicitly assumed that end-users and third parties would actually organize the Web. On the other hand, the demand for this organizing activity inclined steeply as the Web started to grow: there was more and more demand for 'useful link' web pages, directories and search services which would help users find material located elsewhere.

The first Web search engines which responded to the demand for organized findability were, like Archie and Veronica, developed in the scientific community. The first crawler-based search engine, a search engine that uses a piece of software called a 'crawler' to access, analyze and index the World Wide Web automatically by following links from page to page, was the World Wide Web Wanderer, developed at MIT in the early 1990s.[35] Its main purpose was to analyze and report on the growth of the Web. The Wanderer automatically looked on the Web for available

---

34. See Abbate 2000, 216–218. See also Berners-Lee 2000.
35. See Sonnenreich & Macinta 1998, 3.

material and systematically stored data about this material, including its location, in a central index which was called the Wandex.

Not everyone on the network welcomed the arrival of crawlers, also called bots or spiders, which automatically navigated the network to analyze its content. The network load caused by the Wanderer or similar software by repeatedly looking up material online to refresh their indices, soon led to complaints and discussions about the ethical use of and proper restrictions on the deployment of crawlers. Notably, this discussion did not result in a ban on crawling activity, assuming that such a ban would be possible or enforceable. It did spur the development of an unofficial industry standard that allowed website hosts to give instructions to the crawlers indexing their sites. This *robots.txt* de facto standard, which is still generally followed today, was developed by Martijn Koster along with an index of the World Wide Web called ALIWEB. Instead of crawling the Web, ALIWEB relied on webmasters to create and submit a special indexing file outlining the material they were publishing.[36] ALIWEB's 'anti-spider' model did not succeed in mobilizing webmasters enough to be able to create an index large enough to compete with other search engines. Instead, the crawler-based search engine model, in which the service would simply look for the available material on its own, was actively pursued and soon a growing number of spiders began crawling the Web.[37]

In terms of the model of how to create an index of online material necessary to provide useful Web search services for end-users, the main rivaling model for the crawler-based search engine was the human-edited directory, of which the Virtual Library, Yahoo!, Looksmart and Magellan were all examples. Besides the Wandex, important early examples of crawler-based search engines were Excite and WebCrawler, the latter being the first to index the complete documents on the Web and the first to provide a full-text search capability. Yahoo!, the most popular directory in the World Wide Web's history, grew out of a manually organized set of hyperlinks created by two Stanford students.[38] When it became more and more popular, they made their index of hyperlinks searchable.

Over the years, the directory-based model for offering organized findability has slowly declined and the crawler-based model has become the standard for general purpose search engine services.[39] However, even today, the leading crawler-based search engine, Google, does still offer a directory as a part of its offerings to its users. In addition, some of their operations with regard to their crawler-based service increasingly rely on other directories,[40] or the kind of human judgment and intervention with regard to the relevance of online material which

---

36. Sonnenreich & Macinta 1998, 4.
37. The idea that the different crawlers may be duplicating the same effort spurred the project Commoncrawl, a project to 'maintain and make widely available a comprehensive crawl of the Internet for the purpose of enabling a new wave of innovation, education and research'. See http://www.commoncrawl.org.
38. See Sonnenreich & Macinta 1998, 6–7.
39. See Rogers 2009b.
40. Crawler-based search engines can also use existing directories to help them organize their index and rank references.

could be seen as a principal characteristic of human-edited directory-based services. As a result, the traditional distinction between crawler-based and human-edited directories has been blurred over the years.

2.2. THE WEB SEARCH ENGINE

2.2.1. WEB SEARCH ENGINES: THE BIRTH OF AN INDUSTRY—1993–1998

Similar to the case of browsers, the market soon picked up in the field of search engines, and commercial search engine providers and directories have been dominant ever since. As a result of the commercial nature of search engine services, the further development of search engine services and the innovations in this field are, to a considerable extent, a matter of business innovation, rather than only innovation in the scientific or technical sense of the word. Early search engine developers explored the various business opportunities related to Web search engines, developed new advertising models or licensing schemes, and explored strategic alliances with media conglomerates, the telecommunications and the ICT industry. Despite such activity, fundamental improvements to Web search technology continue to be made. Dominant Web search engines such as Google heavily rely on cutting edge research in the fields of computer science and electrical engineering, language processing and network economics, and have also themselves been at the forefront of fundamental improvements in Internet and Web service engineering. For the purposes of this chapter, we will provide a general overview of the main developments in the search engine industry and the various business models that were invented and pursued by search engine entrepreneurs. The business model of search engines will not be analyzed in detail as a goal in itself.

Soon after the first web search services developed by researchers in the academic realm gained visibility, some of them acquired venture capital and went commercial. This is the first phase of the Web search industry, which political economist Van Couvering in her research on search engine bias, denotes as the phase of 'technical entrepreneurship'.[41] The dominant crawler-based search engine in this period, ranging roughly from 1993 until 1998, was AltaVista. Yahoo! was the most important directory online. It is interesting to note that AltaVista provided Yahoo! with crawler-based organic search results, complementing Yahoo!'s directory. Competition between different Web search services mostly focused on the size of the index—or directory—and the speed of response to user queries.

In this first stage, the business case for early search engines, similar to many new online services, was not clear. The most common revenue stream was advertising, which on the early Web typically involved the placement of advertisements in the form of banners on a cost-per-view basis. Search engines and directories

41. See Van Couvering 2009.

were attractive real estate for the placement of such advertisements as they attracted large numbers of Internet users. But apart from advertising, which linked search engines to the media industry, search engine providers started to rely on licensing, a long-established business model for software and related technology. By licensing their search engine software to destination websites or other services with high traffic, such as America Online (AOL) or Netscape, search engine technology companies could increase their distribution and secure revenue. These and other types of distribution deals became and remain an important field of competition between different search engine providers. These revenue sources were important because subscription-based business models, such as those introduced by Infoseek in 1995, proved unsuccessful in the face of free services of comparable quality.[42]

Of special interest in the first stage of development of the search engine industry is the advertisement-based business model that was developed in late 1997 by business entrepreneur Bill Gross and implemented in the service GoTo. com.[43] Instead of crawling the World Wide Web, GoTo.com relied on the auctioning of keywords to the highest bidding online information provider. These bidders would not have to pay per view of their advertisement, which was the common way to sell advertisement space and is typically denoted by CPM (Cost per mille). Instead, bidders would only pay if a user would actually follow the advertised link to the bidder's site, a model denoted by CPC (Cost per click). This resulted in a shift from monetization of audiences to the monetization of actual traffic to destinations. GoTo.com was very successful and pioneered the syndication of paid search listings; around the year 2000 it had become the industry leader in the paid search market.

Table 2.1: A Selection of Notable Web Search Engines

AltaVista	Crawler-based search engine (1995), market leader around 1996–1997, under ownership of Compaq (1998), CMGI (2000), Overture (2003) and Yahoo! (2003).
Archie	First Internet search engine (1990), provided a searchable index of titles of online resources.
Ask	Formerly known as Ask Jeeves (1996), initially modeled around concept of answering everyday questions of users. It was renamed Ask.com in 2005, is currently owned by IAC. It is said to have stopped producing its own organic results.
BING (Microsoft)	General purpose search engine service, formerly named MSN and Live.com, in which Microsoft invested billions of dollars to be able to compete with Google.

---

42. See Van Couvering 2009. See also Infoseek 1995.
43. For a discussion, see Battelle 2006, 101–104.

Blekko	New general purpose Web search engine, developed in California, went in closed alpha since July 2010 and has become publicly available in 2011.
Exalead	French search technology company (2004), participated in the Quaero project and is mostly focused on enterprise search.
Excite	Early crawler-based search engine which went the portal route with its merger with @Home in 1999.
Google	Web search provider (1998) coming out of Stanford; current market leader in the Web (search) services industry; made important improvements to the Web search experience for end-users since the end of the 1990s and implemented very successful paid listings program for search listings and the Web more generally.
Ilse	Early crawler-based search engine in the Netherlands, which stopped producing its own Web index and is now owned by Sanoma.
Inktomi (HotBot)	Early crawler-based search engine software company coming out of UC Berkeley (1995), implemented into HotBot service which was the U.S. market leader in the late 1990s. Acquired in 2002 by Yahoo!.
Lycos	Popular portal in the end of the 1990s, separate companies for U.S. and Europe (owned by Bertellsmann and Telefonica). In Europe, Lycos portal included Web search Fireball and news search Paperball.
MetaCrawler	The first *meta* search engine (1995), searching various genuine search engines simultaneously and presenting those results to its users.
Open Directory Project	An open content volunteer-edited Web directory (1998), also known as 'dmoz', owned by Netscape (Oct 1998), which was in turn acquired by AOL (Nov 1998).
Overture (GoTo.com)	Founded by Bill Gross, pioneer of pay-per-click (CPC), auctioning model and paid listings syndication.
Quaero	Politically inspired Franco-German search engine project that turned into two separate Research & Development industry investment programs for search technology in the broader sense.

Table 2.1 *(cont'd)*	
Veronica	Early Internet search engine based on the Gopher protocol (1992).
Yahoo!	Early popular and commercially successful Web directory (1994), coming out of Stanford, branched off into various other personal services and advertisement products and acquired several Web search engines throughout its history. Stopped producing its own organic search results in 2010.
WebCrawler	Early Web search engine.
World Wide Web Wanderer	First crawler-based Web search engine.

2.2.2.   THE BIRTH OF GOOGLE

Van Couvering lets the period of technical entrepreneurship end shortly after the first public offerings, amongst which Yahoo!'s IPO in 1996 was one of the most significant ones in the Internet industry. The period that starts after that is a period in which one sees a tendency towards vertical integration and a focus on the creation of, and partnerships in, so-called portals. Most search engine companies in this period had a directory or a search engine at their core, but became focused on the presentation of all sorts of featured content and other services to their visitors. As Van Couvering shows, the featured content partnerships were seen as a way businesses could attract audiences to their content and services by paying these steadily growing portals for prominence. These vertical partnerships culminated in the vision of the 'fully-integrated portal' of the late 1990s, which amongst other things promised renewed control of the user's online experience for media conglomerates and telecommunications providers.[44] In line with the related tendency to vertical integration, several major deals were made that involved early search engine companies, such as the deals in 1999 between Infoseek and Disney and between Excite and @Home, which also involved AT&T.

    As a result of the creation of portals and vertical partnerships involving featured content and services, the search engine was slowly downgraded in importance from being the core business to just a requirement or even an impediment to the portal's business model.[45] While the fully-integrated portal's focus was on keeping the user on the portal's sites, Web search engines in the strict sense tended to direct users away to other destinations online.

---

44. See Van Couvering 2009. See also, Meisel & Sullivan 2000.
45. See Ince 2000. See also Edwards 2011.

In hindsight, these developments opened up the space for Google to start its remarkable rise to dominance in the search engine industry. Google, similar to the early search engines, was developed in the academic realm, by computer science doctoral candidates Sergey Brin and Lawrence Page who were focusing on information retrieval science.[46] Google started as an experiment with a new ranking algorithm (PageRank) based on the network topology of hyperlinks on the World Wide Web.[47] PageRank was a global relevancy measure that assigned relevance to a document based on the weighted sum of incoming links to that document. The weight of the each link was determined by the relevance of that document itself and the amount of other links from that document.[48] At first, the Google search service was clearly focused on providing the best search results possible, instead of seeing search engines as a means to a business end. Apart from venture capital and some important first distribution deals, for instance its deal with Netscape, the early Google did not have an advertisement-based business model and also no partnerships that involved featured content on their site. Instead, Google offered search results only, with a remarkably clean user interface that in no way resembled the cluttered portals and directories which were so common at that time.

By the time Google was introduced, existing search engines had also increasingly suffered from third-party manipulation of their relevance and selection criteria, and innovations and better business practices in this field were badly needed from the perspective of Internet users.[49] The typical selection and ranking of entries in the index in response to user queries by early search engines such as AltaVista proceeded in two steps. First, the query led to a subset of documents in the index that contained at least one of the query terms. This incentivized the use of irrelevant terms on websites in order to reach larger audiences in search engines. Second, the subset would be ranked according to basic information retrieval measures such as the amount of times that certain terms appeared on the website, the URL, and different hypertext meta-data, such as the field for the description of the content of the website. In response, other search engine optimization techniques were developed, such as various uses of meta-tags which would ensure better ranking in search results. As a consequence, the overall quality of search engines for users declined, whereas the need for effective navigational media grew alongside the rapidly growing World Wide Web.

Google's PageRank algorithm, which relied on a global measure for the relevance of websites, was in many ways motivated as a response to the growing

---

46. For a history of Google, see Vise & Malseed 2005; Battelle 2006; Levy 2011, Edwards 2011, Röhle 2010.
47. Brin & Page 1998.
48. See Brin & Page 1998. See also Langville & Meyer 2006.
49. This manipulation of search results also soon led to various legal issues. See Nathenson 1998. For a discussion, see Ch. 8 and Ch. 10.

infoglut and the manipulation of search engine results.[50] And in those early years after its launch, Google's focus on the quality of the search experience for its users gave it a competitive advantage. In 2000, after having displaced one of its main competitors, Inktomi, as the source of organic search results at Yahoo!, Google founder Larry Page was confident enough to state Google's superiority in terms of the relevance of Google's search results:

> We have very complex software that constantly analyses search results and can adapt itself to provide users with web pages that are more relevant to their search than from any other search engine.[51]

At the same time, the operational costs of general purpose search engines were steadily growing. Around the year 2000, the Web was estimated to already consist of more than 1 billion indexable pages. The crawling, indexing and speedy response to user queries on this scale demanded more and more fundamental innovations, knowledge and financial investment from search engine providers. In addition to its focus on improved ranking algorithms and the clean user interface, the success of Google in addressing these demands can help explain its remarkable rise as the dominant search engine at the beginning of the twenty-first century.[52]

Over the years, Google let go of their initial objection to an advertisement-based business model. It introduced the 'self-service ad program' Adwords in October 2000.[53] Since then, Adwords has been improved and perfected. Notably, in February 2002 the initial pay-per-view model was replaced by a pay-per-click model similar to the one used by Overture, the former GoTo.com. In May 2002, Google took over industry leader Overture's most important customer, AOL, with a major distribution deal which paved the way for Google's dominance in paid search listings.[54] Together with the extension of Adwords into the realm of general web publishing, i.e. the contextual advertising service AdSense, it solidified tremendous revenue streams for the company that it has used to finance additional free services for end-users, research and development and a range of acquisitions. These acquisitions include video platform YouTube in 2006, the online display advertising network DoubleClick in 2007, and the recent acquisition of ITA, a dominant search software and technology company in the travel industry.

---

50. See Brin & Page 1998.
51. See Foremski 2000.
52. For accounts of the rise to dominance of Google, see Battelle 2006; Vise & Malseed 2005; Olsthoorn 2010; Vaidhyanathan 2011; Auletta 2009; Levy 2011; Edwards 2011.
53. See Battelle 2006, 125–127.
54. See Gallagher 2002.

2.2.3.   Consolidation of the Web Search Industry: 2000–2011

Over the first decade of the twenty-first century, the search industry has gradually consolidated further and only a few global market players dominate the market for general purpose search results in the European countries and the Americas. This current period in the history of the search engine industry, is the one Van Couvering denotes with 'syndication and consolidation'.[55]

Consolidation has taken place on a number of levels.[56] First, many independent search engine providers were bought by other companies. The bursting of the dot-com bubble contributed to some of these acquisitions. Around the year 2000, Yahoo, for example, bought the search engine companies Overture, Inktomi and AlltheWeb. At the time when Yahoo! established ownership of Overture, the latter had already acquired AltaVista.

Second, many crawler-based search engines made the decision to stop producing search results themselves and enter into syndication deals with dedicated search engine providers instead. This means that the amount of search result producers has declined correspondingly. Google proved particularly successful in establishing syndication deals, both for its organic results as well as for its paid listings.[57] These deals effectively secured access to the majority of Internet users for Google.

Third, general purpose search engines services started to offer more and more specialized services for their users, which implied that a simple Web search engine became less and less sustainable as a stand-alone business. Again, Google is best used as an example in this regard. It started to introduce more and more language specific services, it introduced image search in 2001, news search and product search in 2002, book search in 2003 (Google Print), geographic search in 2004 (Google Local) and ultimately the fully-integrated 'universal search' service in 2007. Many of these new features and services were made possible by the acquisition of smaller companies which had developed successful technologies enabling these specialized services. Whereas many of these new additions could be seen as extensions of finding information, dominant providers in the Web search industry also started to offer different kinds of services to Internet users and thereby compete in other markets. Google, for instance, now offers a web-based email service (Gmail), an operating system for mobile devices (Android), and a cloud-based solution for document creation (Google Docs).

For the dominant search engine providers today search is only part of their business, but it remains one of the most important drivers in the industry. This may be illustrated most clearly by the decision of Microsoft to invest billions of dollars into the development of a search engine with its own organic and paid listings. Microsoft's MSN portal used to deliver search results of other search engine providers, including Google, but in 2011, after an investment of billions of dollars and two

---

55. See Van Couvering 2009.
56. For figures, see Van Couvering 2009.
57. For a discussion, see Levy 2011; Edwards 2011.

Table 2.2: Current Search Engine Market Share in terms of Query Volume[58]

	Google (%)	Bing (%)	Yahoo! (%)	Ask (%)	Other (%)[59]
The Netherlands (June 2010)[60]	94	1	1	0	4
Germany (May 18, 2011)[61]	89	4	2	1	4
France (March 2011)[62]	92	4	1	0	3
United Kingdom (May 14, 2011)[63]	90	4	3	1	2
United States[64]	65	14	16	3	1

changes in names, Microsoft's Bing is now the second search engine in the western world as measured in search query volume. In fact, Microsoft has replaced Yahoo! as Google's main competitor in the web search industry, since Yahoo! has given up the competition in the field of organic search results. More specifically, in 2009 Yahoo! and Microsoft entered into a partnership which ended Yahoo!'s production of search results after a deal between Google and Yahoo! fell through because of the alleged anticompetitive nature as a result of Google's already dominant market position.

2.2.4.   THE WEB SEARCH INDUSTRY IN EUROPE

If we look more closely at the search industry in Europe, the most important development has been the almost complete extinction of European-based search engines in terms of market share. Historically, in Europe similar phases of development can be found as described above, but European search engines have never successfully competed with the Web search giants from the Unites States. Since the

---

58. These figures are derived from different public reports of net statistic providers and are meant to serve as an indication of market share.
59. In the Netherlands, meta-search engine Vinden.nl (3%), and Ilse.nl (1%); In Germany, T-Online (owned by T-Mobile but search results by Google) (2%), and others (2%); for France, SFR (1%) Orange (1%) and non-specified (1%); for the United Kingdom, non-specified (2%); for the United States, AOL (1%).
60. See Checkit.nl 2010.
61. See Webhits 2011.
62. See AT Internet 2011.
63. See Hitwise 2011.
64. See Comscore 2011.

second half of the 1990s, one can find a range of early Internet entrepreneurs in European countries who started local search and directory businesses.[65] But ultimately, most popular European crawler-based search engines stopped producing their own search results, went bankrupt, or only remained as brand destinations and domain-names in the hands of other companies.

In the Netherlands, for example, the crawler-based search engine Ilse had significant market share for some years. This service was launched back in 1996 by computer science student Wiebe Weikamp with two of his friends and was primarily focused on search results of particular interest for the Dutch population. In 2000, it was acquired by a large media company (VNU Uitgevers), and it stopped producing its own search results under the subsequent ownership of media company Sanoma. In Germany, Fireball and Web.de were strong local competitors. Web.de no longer produces its own search results, whereas Fireball shut down in 2002 after having been integrated with Lycos Europe in 2000. Lycos Europe's assets, after having been acquired by Telefonica and Bertelsmann and after having seen its search engine market share decline sharply since the end of the 1990s, were separately offered for sale in 2008. Fast, a successful Norwegian technology company with a strong search technology portfolio, was bought by Microsoft in 2008.[66] Exalead, a search engine technology company founded in 2004 in France, still exists as an independent European crawler-based search engine but is largely focusing on enterprise search services and business information management solutions. A notable example of a Web search engine that remains competitive at the national level is Yandex in Russia.

The dominance of U.S. companies in the sphere of the organization of information and ideas has not gone unnoticed and continues to spur political activity at the highest levels.[67] The most famous example of a European counter-initiative is Quaero, the European search engine project that never actually materialized into a service. Quaero was announced publicly in 2005 by both French president Chirac and German chancellor Schroeder as a public Franco-German initiative to create a competitive European search engine.[68] The Quaero project, which included, amongst other members of the European ICT and telecommunications industry, the companies Thomson, France Télécom and Exalead, soon lived on as separate German and French public research investment programs, for which State aid was approved by the European Commission in 2007.[69]

2.2.5.   ALTERNATIVES AND THE FUTURE OF WEB SEARCH SERVICES

The consolidation of the Web search industry into an oligopoly or quasi-monopoly of services in the west, does not imply that no alternatives exist or that the dominant

---

65. See also Halavais 2009, 25–26.
66. See Pandia Search Engine News 2006.
67. On the French perspective of mobilization against Google, see Jeanneney 2007.
68. For the speech of the French President, see Chirac 2006. See also Chrisafis 2006.
69. For the German program THESEUS, see European Commission 2007b. For the French program Quaero, see European Commission 2008a.

services have become the only destination available for Internet users to search for online material. It also does not imply that research and development in relation to Web search only takes place behind the closed doors of a handful of dominant companies. In fact, many small search engine service providers have been developed, many of which still exist. There is a variety of alternatives to the dominant search engines provided by Google or Microsoft for locating online material. And if one takes a closer look at these alternatives, one can also often discern competing models for the production of references to online material to Internet users.

First, amongst the alternatives for the dominant search engines there are many so-called vertical or niche search engine providers. These verticals specialize in references to certain types of online destinations. Examples can be found in the context of many specific consumer markets, such as housing, travel or shopping, or with regard to certain types of information, such as medical, legal, financial or geographical data. The ongoing success of many of these vertical search engines is typically attributed to their greater focus in comparison to general, horizontal search engines, and their resulting ability to select references of high quality for their users on the one hand, and the specific commercial opportunities tied to the matchmaker role between providers of certain goods, services or information and potential users or customers in specific markets on the other hand. Many of these verticals are commercial, but in the public sector we can also find a range of specialized search engines that make specific documents and publicly available information more easily accessible for Internet users. The importance and success of vertical search engines can also be recognized by the various ways in which both Google and Microsoft have acquired, launched and integrated specialized search services into their offering.

Second, there are still alternative horizontal search engines other than Google and Microsoft that have only a limited market share. The most recent example, which emerged after a three-year long phase of development, is California-based search engine Blekko. Blekko offers end-users a service which is quite similar to the one offered by Google. As mentioned above, in some countries, such as in Russia (Yandex), Czech Republic (Seznam), and further away in South-Korea and China (Baidu), there are strong local competitors.

Third, both academic researchers and entrepreneurs are still actively exploring various alternative models to offer effective means to find online material for Internet end-users. Just one of the interesting alternatives that has been conceptualized over the last decade is a peer-to-peer model for a Web search engine. There are several academic, commercial, and free and open source software projects that have pursued this model for the production of online references for Internet users. Second, the way people use the World Wide Web keeps shifting considerably due to the successful launch of new types of services, such as social network sites (Facebook) and microblogging sites (Twitter). These services offer Internet users a different way to select access material in the online environment.

Finally, there are ways in which developments related to online publishing practices more generally could change the search engine environment significantly. An important strand of research and development in the field of Internet information engineering that is strongly related to the thinking about improved search for the Web, is the work on the so-called Semantic Web. The Semantic Web project could be described as an attempt to develop methods and technologies that increase the possibilities for machines to interpret the contents or meaning of online material directly. As a consequence, this research focuses more on the improved organization of material on the World Wide Web itself than on improving models to build and operate search engines. It is interesting to note that the inventor of the Web, Tim Berners-Lee, is one of the driving forces behind the Semantic Web project, in which researchers and developers have been participating since 1999.

From the perspective of Web search engines, the Semantic Web project is fascinating for a number of reasons. First, the lack of semantics in the World Wide Web's technical design may have been one of the strongest drivers for the emergence of the Web search industry as we know it. The Web and the hypertext protocols allow any Web publisher to link to anything else. This makes an open online universal document space possible, which is precisely one of the major strengths of the World Wide Web. As we noted earlier in this chapter, the designers of the Web implicitly assumed that Web users would organize the Web. This design philosophy created a strong demand for third-party 'useful links' web pages, directories and search services which would help Internet users find material located elsewhere.

Second, if we turn to the search engines of today, one could argue that they have, in fact, developed a kind of Semantic Web overlay, in the sense that search engines have specialized in making recommendations about the relevance, content and meaning of online material based on their own analysis of that material.[70] The big difference is that most of this meta-information about online material is kept behind the closed doors of the server farms that host their version of the annotated index of the Web.

To conclude, the semantic web project, understood as the extension of the current Web, in which information is given well-defined meaning, better enabling computers and people to work in cooperation,[71] could potentially have a significant impact on the search engine industry if it were to be implemented openly and successfully.[72] While it would allow all search engines to improve their offerings, it could also take some of the power of dominant search engines—the part which is based on their *exclusive* understanding of the material on Web—away from them by opening up similar or even improved meta-data to the Internet community as a whole.

---

70. See e.g. Arnold 2010.
71. See Berners-Lee et al. 2001. The THESEUS Research and Development investment program in Germany is specifically focused on the development of semantic Web technologies. See THESEUS.
72. The Semantic Web project has been quite unsuccessful in making the Web evolve into a semantic web. For a discussion of the utopian project of exhaustive reliable metadata, see e.g. Doctorow, 2001. However, if one understands the semantic Web project as a variety of related methods and technologies that increase the possibilities for machines to interpret the meaning of online material, the Semantic Web project has produced various successes which have been adopted in different contexts. See e.g. W3C, W3C Semantic Web Activity, http://www.w3.org/2001/sw/.

2.3.   CONCLUSION

This chapter has offered a short overview of the history of search engines, starting from the early ideas about the opportunities of improved navigation of information in digital information systems to the rise of search engines as one of the most important media of the public networked information environment made possible by the World Wide Web. In particular, it shows how the design of the World Wide Web, which has become the universal platform for online publication since its launch in the early 1990s, implied a natural demand for navigational media and services that would help users find valuable online material. It is interesting although not necessarily surprising to note that most of these services were initially developed in the academic realm. Later on, the business opportunities related to search engines became an important driver for the further development of the search engine industry and the innovations that have taken place since then, such as the pay-per-click advertisement models that the market leaders use today.

The eventual consolidation of the search engine market can be historically tracked to a number of contributing factors. Some of those factors are inherent in the operation of a general purpose search engine, such as the growing, evolved expectations of search services by end-users or the increased barriers to entry into the market. Other contributing factors include the integration of the search engine as an important business asset in the digital media and ICT industry, thereby reproducing existing consolidation in related markets in the search engine context. Of the many search companies that started offering their service in the 1990s, only Google remains a mature independent company with its own search engine at its heart.

This points to one of the most remarkable aspects in the history of search engines, namely the fast rise of Google as the dominant global player in the search engine market. In 2011, in many countries, including the Netherlands, Google controls more than 90% of the market in terms of user share and the amount of searches performed on the Web. It is not surprising that this has attracted a steady stream of commentary over the last decade and has meant that Google has become synonymous with Web search for the better part of the general audience. But, although Google has had and continues to have an enormous impact on the search engine industry and the way Internet users access information on the Web more generally, it is important to look beyond this single company's commercial search service. There are still competitors to Google's search service in the market for general purpose web search, such as Microsoft's Bing. In some jurisdictions, strong national alternatives exist, such as in Russia. More importantly, there are numerous other publicly and privately funded services with specific focuses which contribute to the findability of online information for end-users. In addition, research and development in search continue to offer new insights into alternatives to current search engines and the ways in which online information can be organized to enhance effective retrieval of online resources.

Chapter 3

Web Search Engines in the Public Networked Information Environment

3.1. WEB SEARCH ENGINES: BASICS

3.1.1. DEFINITION

As a legal category in information law, the search engine is not well defined. There are a number of legal categories that include search engines, for example 'information location tool',[73] but these definitions only serve specific legal contexts. In fact, it is unclear, and an interesting general question to which this research contributes, whether search engines should be a separate legal category altogether.

The search engine can be more easily defined from a functional perspective, in which case the following definition could be given for the search engine that is the subject of this study:

an information retrieval system for the public networked information environment.

Throughout this study, the term 'public networked information environment' is used to denote the collection of information which is publicly available on the Internet, and on the World Wide Web in particular.[74] Broadly speaking, search engines help end-users find and effectively retrieve this information. In the following chapter, the questions of what search engines are, what they do and how they do it, will be answered in more detail to have a better understanding of search engines for the remainder of this study.

---

73. See section 9.3.2 for the legal context and discussion of the 'information location tool' category.
74. The term 'networked information environment' is commonly used in the legal and scientific literature to denote the Internet as an information environment more generally. See Benkler 2006. See also Lynch 2001, 12–17.

The goal of this chapter is to properly conceptualize search engines from a functional perspective. The next section will present (1) the basic information flows between search engines, their users and information providers, (2) the typical architecture of a commercial search engine and (3) its user interface. In the section after that, the broader context in which search engines exist and operate will be discussed with reference to the layered model for networked communications and the value chains in which they play an important role. In the final section, the two different functional roles which search engines perform in these value chains will be discussed in more depth, namely their role with regard to the end-users of search engines on the one hand and with regard to information providers and advertisers on the other hand.

3.1.2.   BASIC INFORMATION FLOWS

Figure 3.1 shows the typical and most basic information flows induced by the operation of a search engine on the Web. The search engine is positioned in its intermediary position between the online information provider on the one hand and the Internet user on the other hand. It aggregates information and stores it in its index (2), typically with the use of sophisticated crawling software that makes automatic requests for the available online material (1). On the basis of that index and its subsequent analysis, it provides a service to end-users, whose input, in the form of search queries and other data (3) results in an output by the search engine, in the form of a ranked selection of references to and descriptions of certain information providers (4). From this selection, the user can follow specific references and make an information request to a specific information provider (5) to receive the information provider's full information offering (6).

Figure 3.1: Basic Information Flows

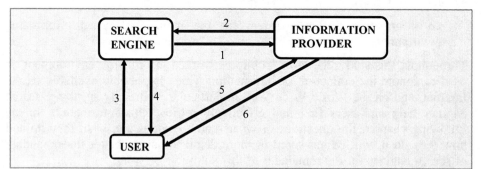

3.1.3.   BASIC ARCHITECTURE

Schematically, the typical basic functional architecture of a search engine consists of a crawler, a parser, an index and a user interface (see Figure 3.2).

The crawler, parser and index together form the technical back office of the search engine. The crawler interacts with the information providers. It is a complex computer program that looks for information on the Internet, according to a set of criteria which tell it where to go and when. Over the years, crawlers have become more sophisticated. They are now able to access more and more of the material that is available online, such as dynamically stored Web content, which used to be part of the so-called hidden Web.[75] The parser is the processing tool between the crawler and the index. It systematically stores the retrieved information in the index. The pieces of content the crawler finds are not the same in size, sort, language, code and other characteristics, so the parser needs to normalize them for the index. It also extracts a number of related data and meta-data that can be useful for the search engine's technology.

Figure 3.2: Basic Search Engine Architecture

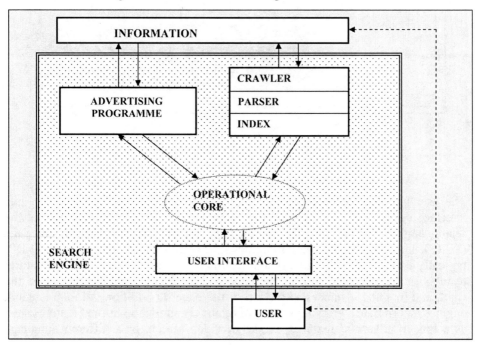

---

75.   See generally, Olston & Najork, 2010, 175–246.

The index is an ordered list of references to pieces of content on the net, but it is also more than that. The index is a large and complex database of which the references and keywords are basic elements. The index also contains information that is needed to apply the ranking algorithms. These lie at the heart of the search engine's technology and determine which references are presented to users and in what order.

Figure 3.3: Search Engine Result Page (SERP)

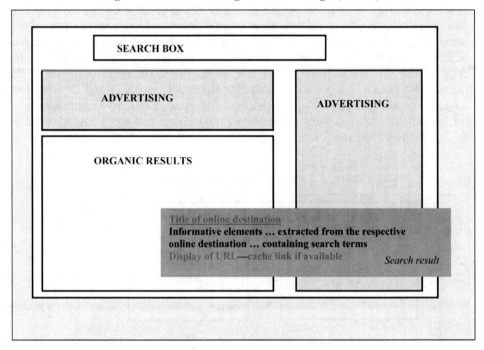

The user interface is the (layout of the) website offered to the user. The user interface design shapes the actual user experience.[76] The basic elements of the search engine interface are the search box and the search engine result page (SERP). For commercial search engines, the search engine result page (SERP) typically consists of a list of organic results, also called algorithmic or natural results, on the left hand side of the page and a list of sponsored results on the right, and in some instances at the top of the page. In addition, all major search engines incorporate a growing variety of relatively similar additional features such as a link to advanced features, image or video search, or a different language

---

76. For a comprehensive and readable account of the various aspects of search engine user design, see Hearst 2009. Hearst does not discuss the optimization of the user interface from the perspective of advertising revenue optimization. See also Manning et al. 2009; Höchstötter & Lewandowski 2009. For a discussion of transparency and advertising, see section 10.3.1.

version. Some of these additional features can have some regulatory relevance, since they can be used to inform users about the ways they can control their search process. Examples of such features are Google's SafeSearch feature, which filters for adult content, or the link to its privacy policy, which Google somewhat recently added to its homepage.[77] Figure 3.3 shows the typical layout of the result page as well as the typical layout of a search result, also called a search hit.[78] The layout of search advertisement has proliferated widely on the Web outside of the context of search engines due to contextual advertisement programs like AdSense, which use partner websites' content to place relevant advertisements on those websites.

3.2.   SEARCH ENGINES IN THEIR CONTEXT

3.2.1.   SEARCH ENGINES AND THE LAYERED MODEL FOR THE NETWORKED COMMUNICATIONS ENVIRONMENT

As discussed in Chapter 2, search engines exist in the context of the World Wide Web, the open hypertext structured information environment made possible by the Internet. Search engines have become central to the functioning of the public networked information environment, but from a technical perspective they are neither essential for this environment to exist nor for online material to be accessible to users. Conversely, it is true that the information flows induced by the use of search engines are made possible by the various protocols of the Internet's application layer, such as the HyperText Transfer Protocol (HTTP) which structures the service as it is made available to users. However, none of the layers of the layered model of networked communication (see Figure 3.4) contain elements specifically designed for search engines, even though these services play such a central role to the organization and navigation of content that is available on the network.

The layered model for the technical design of networked communications systems has inspired a functional layered model for such systems that contains three horizontal functional layers and which has gained some traction in regulatory debates about the networked communications environment.[79] These layers are a layer of physical infrastructure, a transport/logical/code layer and a content layer. Both the technical TCP/IP model and the functional model are shown in Figure 3.4. The horizontal character of this layered model can be contrasted with the traditional vertical regulatory models (silos) for various types of media or forms of communication, and models which have been eroded by the phenomenon of convergence.

If we look at the networked communications environment and the way the various communications network, technology and service providers map onto it,

---

77. See Anderson 2008.
78. For a discussion of search user interface design, see Hearst 2009.
79. For a discussion, see Solum and Chung 2003; See also Benkler 2000; Werbach 2002.

the functional layered model is sometimes used to conceptualize the role of specific entities in the communications environment on the one hand. On the other hand, it is used to frame the different regulatory questions that arise in the context of networked communications, more specifically in which layer-specific legal issues can or should be addressed.

Figure 3.4: TCP/IP Sub-layers and Functional Layered Model for Networked Communications

TCP/IP SUBLAYERS		Functional Layered Model
Application	HTTP, FTP, etc...	Content, Interaction, Communication
Transmission	TCP	Content, Interaction, Communication
Network	IP	Transport, Logical, Code
Link	Ethernet	Physical
Physical	Physical equipment	Physical

However, it should be noted that the functional layers are an abstraction. Most importantly, the market structure and the practices of major players in the net-worked communications environment do not map nicely into the various layers of the model. The recent debate about net neutrality and the preservation of the end-to-end principle is a good example of this.[80] On the other hand, there are various forms of regulatory spillover, such as the enforcement of laws relating to the legality of content by targeting the Domain Name System (DNS) in the application protocol layer or even further down into the functionality of TCP/IP.[81]

If one uses the layered model for networked communications to look at search engines, they would seem to map principally onto the transport/logical/code layer. Web search engines are complex systems of software, typically server-based, made accessible for users of the network. But, search engines have a rather unique link with the content layer as well. First, Web search engines derive their functionality from the existence of publicly accessible content on the World Wide Web. Without the open and unstructured dynamics of content creation on the Web, search engines would not have the pivotal role that they have today. And second, search engines can be argued to consume and pro-duce 'content' on their own, namely information about information, or meta-information.

---

80. For a discussion, see Van Schewick 2010. See also Wu 2003.
81. For a discussion of Internet filtering by access providers, see section 6.5.

Search engines present Internet users with human-readable representations of the networked information environment, while at the same time depending on various forms of machine-readable meta-information offered by other information providers or extracted from them or other places themselves. This relation to the content layer should definitely not be taken as a necessary or even sufficient argument for treating search engines, from a regulatory perspective, as traditional content providers (when they publish references for end-users) or as consumers of content (when they aggregate content for their index). What it does mean is that the conceptualization and regulatory treatment of this category of meta-information or 'meta-content' may be one of the key elements in properly solving the legal issues arising in the context of Web search engines.[82]

3.2.2.   SEARCH ENGINES IN THE INTERNET COMMUNICATIONS 'CHAIN'

Another way to conceptualize search engines in the networked information environment is to position them in the chain or, more accurately, the network of communications on the Internet. From this perspective, a Web search engine, similar to end-users and information providers, lives on the borders of the network, which itself is made up by basic communication services, such as hosting providers, access providers and the Internet backbone at the highest level. Major search engines such as Google have more than one location from which they provide their search service and typically connect to the Internet in multiple ways at a much higher level than a basic website. Yet, this does not change the basics of this representation of the search engine in the network of Internet communications in Figure 3.5.

If anything, this representation clarifies the relation of the principal actors, in the context of search engines, to the Internet as a whole. But apart from that, it does not clarify the actual importance of search engines in terms of what is happening on the network. To really understand the role and importance of search engines in the public information environment, it is more useful to modify this representation of search engines in the network of communication and focus on the flow of value instead of the flow of actual data.

Over the last fifteen years, Web search engines have become central brokers in many of the partly overlapping value chains in the networked online information environment. For instance, search engines connect end-users to informative online publications, political groups and various forms of electronic commerce (e-commerce). These value chains in which the search engine operates can be broadly summarized from two different perspectives, namely a value chain flowing from content and service providers towards end-users and a partly corresponding but opposite value chain from end-users to information providers, both with search engines somewhere in the middle. In addition to clarifying the function of various

---

82. Compare Winkler 1997, 35–36.

entities in the information environment, the value chain perspective can be useful from a regulatory and policy perspective, because it helps clarify the reasons for many of the conflicts between different entities in the value chain, conflicts that often arise because of the interest in control over such value.

The value chains in Figure 3.6 are generalizations and simplifications. First, many entities that perform an important role in the current networked information environment are left out, such as hosting providers. In addition, a search engine provider may be accessible through the use of its website but it can also be built into the end-user's equipment's operating system, which is common in the case of mobile devices. Notably, the generalized flow of value does not necessarily represent the way money flows between the various entities in the chains. An in-depth analysis of the economic dynamics of these value chains is beyond the scope of this study.

Figure 3.5: Search Engines in the Network/Chain of Internet Communication

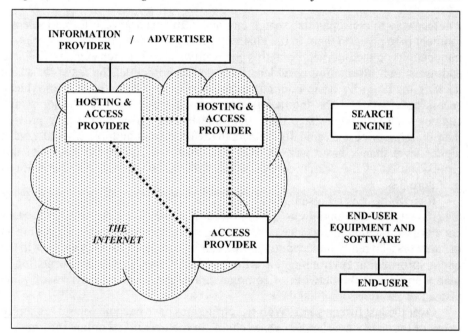

Finally, the search engine category in the value chain can be generalized into a broader category of 'selection intermediaries' which organize—or in the spirit of the Web's open information structure, let end-users organize—online materials and destinations by mapping, ordering, ranking, selecting, excluding, validating and valuating them.[83] These selection intermediaries shape the relative accessibility of online material. As a category, it includes not only search engines and directories, but

---

83. See Chandler 2008. See also Van Hoboken 2009.

also other phenomena such as portals, recommendation and bookmarking tools and services (delicious, StumbleUpon), social networking sites (Facebook), microblogging sites (Twitter) and news aggregators (Digg).

The first of the two value chains (I) in Figure 3.6 is a generalization for the usual value chain for the flow of content, information and data to end-users. On the left, content is produced and published or made available online, services are offered and goods are sold on specific locations on the Web. All of these partly rely on the operations of search engines to find their way to the end-user. Between the end-user and the search engines, the access providers provide the essential service for end-users of enabling them to go online in the first place. In addition, user equipment and software operating on this equipment can have an impact on the consumption of 'content' by end-users. Internet filters are a good example, as well as browsers, toolbars and operating systems. Similar to this, in the case of the mobile Internet the user equipment and mobile operating systems have been an important point of control in the value chain.

Figure 3.6: Search Engine in Generalized Value Chain(s) of Networked Communication

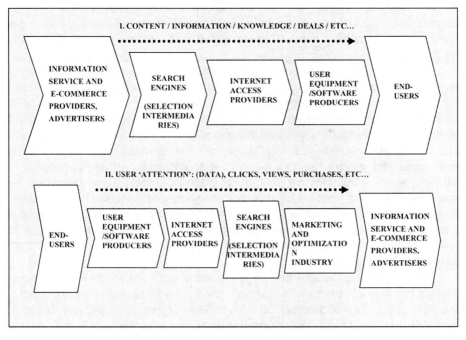

The second value chain (II) is meant to illustrate the way the user represents the value that various information and service providers are competing for.[84] Search

---

84.   See Van Couvering 2009. See also Bermejo 2007; Röhle 2007; Elmer 2004.

engines such as Google and related advertisement networks such as AdSense are amongst the primary services to structure and sell the end-user's attention to those who are willing to pay for it. The portals we discussed in the last chapter play a similar role. Search engines have established a highly effective and lucrative monetization stream for end-user traffic, on which information, service, and e-commerce providers as well as advertisers have come to depend. Search engines auction the targeted user attention and information needs on their platforms, effectively selling the clicks of users in combination with other data about users and their activity.

As a result of the existence of this second opposite value chain, the search engine marketing (SEM) industry and the search engine optimization (SEO) industry play an important role between the search engines and the information providers and advertisers. They help optimize the traffic to their clients' websites by structuring search advertising campaigns and optimizing their presence in organic results. User attention and user data in the form of click streams have become a basic value flow on the Web, and search engines are amongst the big players and amongst the big targets in the growing Internet marketing industry. Simply put, a website with sufficient traffic can make money on the Internet and search engines are important means to provide such traffic. This reality has had a major impact on the search engine industry as a whole, since search engines have not always been successful in discerning between genuinely or just seemingly useful destinations for their users.

To summarize, the competition for search engine users induces information providers, including other search services, to pay for search engine advertising on the one hand and to invest in optimization of their ranking in natural search results on the other hand. However, some information providers will be, quite predictably, willing to optimize traffic from search engines to their sites for less benign reasons. This includes information providers that do not have genuine information offerings themselves and merely function as real estate for optimization instruments and advertisements. It includes information providers that offer information or services that would not have been selected by the search engine or ranked as prominently for particular queries if the search providers would have carefully evaluated the relevance manually. To give just one example, adult content providers can lure end-users to their website by wrongly suggesting they have adult content relating to often-searched celebrities.[85]

The existence of related and opposite value chains illustrates well the basic conflict of interest between information providers and end-users that a commercial search engine, as a matchmaker between different types of supply and demand in the public networked information environment, has to reconcile. On the one hand, user demand for information, knowledge and attractive e-commerce offers must be met by search engines in their competition to satisfy end-users. On the other hand,

---

85. See Ch. 8 and Ch. 10 for further discussion of the legal issues related to so-called search engine spam and search engine manipulation from the perspective of search engine regulation and freedom of expression.

the profitability of the search platform is directly related to its ability to draw attention to those who are willing to invest in reaching an audience. As is obvious, such willingness is not always a good predictor for the ultimate value of references for end-users.

To summarize, in this section three perspectives on search engines in their context have been presented to come to a better understanding of the role of search engines in the public networked information environment. The next section will discuss the different functions the search engine performs with regard to end-users and information providers, the direct stakeholders in communications through search engines, in more detail.

3.3. WEB SEARCH ENGINES: A FUNCTIONAL PERSPECTIVE

3.3.1. END-USERS: INFORMATION, NAVIGATION AND TRANSACTION

The information retrieval literature has developed several models to understand human interaction with search engines, generally focusing on people's reasons for using information retrieval systems and their strategies to arrive at satisfactory results when interacting with these systems.[86] From the perspective of search engine operations, these models play a crucial role in the interpretation of user queries, the design of search engines and the way further interaction, such as query reformulation and evaluation, is facilitated.

An important general conclusion from this literature, that can help in understanding the role of search engines in the networked information environment, is that there are many different situations in which Internet users choose to use a search engine in the first place.[87] Classic information retrieval systems, such as those offered in the academic realm or by libraries, had mostly focused on facilitating information needs of specialized users. The typical model for the interactive search process between users and the search engine in such information retrieval systems is shown in Figure 3.7. The information needs of the users in the classic information retrieval system could be broadly categorized as *informational*: a user wanted to find certain information that was presumed to be present in the corpus of information which the information retrieval system was providing access to.

However, in the context of Web search engines it was observed that as a consequence of the open and more varied nature of the Web as an information environment, the information needs of end-users when engaging in a search process were more varied as well. More specifically, Broder concluded that Web search engines were dealing with two additional types of frequent information

---

86. See Hearst 2009.
87. See Broder 2002. For a discussion, see Hearst 2009.

Figure 3.7: Classic Model of the (Interactive) Search Process

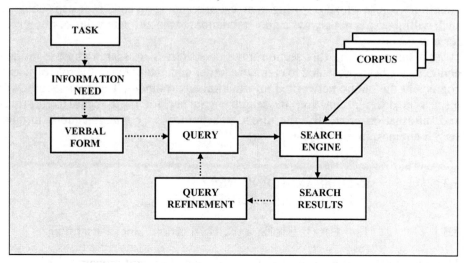

needs, which he categorized as *navigational* and *transactional*.[88] He called a query navigational if a user wanted to find a specific website which he knew or assumed to be present on the Web. He called a query *transactional* if the user aimed to reach a destination where further interaction would take place, such as making a purchase or obtaining a resource. Further research has offered additional insight into these different categories and the way search engines could respond more effectively to the different reasons end-users had for interacting with search engines online.[89]

The broad categorization of user needs in the information retrieval literature helps clarify the rather broad societal role which search engines have come to fulfill.[90] First, in responding to the navigational needs of end-users search engines help users navigate to specific online locations. They respond to these navigational queries by directing users to the 'home page' of various organizations, institutions, companies or persons. Importantly, if the user's information need is known to be navigational, for example the query 'University of Amsterdam', there is only one right answer that the search engine should give, namely the website of the University of Amsterdam. As is evident, search engines are the primary online destination for gaining access to this simple type of navigational information.

Second, search engines help end-users find information about specific topics. They do so by returning search results directing to websites that have information about these topics, in the form of general information, specific answers, advice or lists of other relevant sources of information. In this category of informational queries, search engines help users learn something about a topic, say 'freedom of

---

88. See Broder 2002.
89. See e.g. Rose & Levinson 2004. See also Jansen et al. 2008.
90. Examples are loosely based on Rose & Levinson 2004.

expression' or 'Barbie'. They steer users to websites that help them find answers to specific questions, such as 'European Union Member States' and 'gold price' or obtain representative lists of certain entities 'Amsterdam universities'. Finally, they help users gain advice before making decisions or advice with regard to their problems, underlying queries such as 'stop smoking', 'vote Obama', 'cheap tickets', or 'cure headache'.

Third, search engines direct users to purchasing opportunities, services and resources online, in the form of e-commerce sites 'flowers delivery', 'batelle the search', online services and entertainment, 'malcolm gladwell', 'south park', 'french anthem mp3', 'el clasico streaming link', and other resources 'weather report', 'map Amsterdam', 'apple pie recipe', 'material girl lyrics'. This type of queries is directly related to the presence of directly available resources on the Web, which search engines help place at their users' fingertips. The information need of the user is not related to reaching a specific defined destination (navigational) or generally obtaining further information on a topic (informational), but in reaching a destination that allows for the interaction he or she is interested in.

As is hopefully apparent from the examples given above, search engines will have to guess the actual information needs of their users as expressed in different queries. The same query 'Barbie' could be navigational: the user wants to access the Barbie home page of Mattel; informational: (the user wants to read about the history of Barbie or get information about product safety and quality for an article in a parent magazine; or transactional: the user wants to find a picture of a Barbie for a presentation about the history of toys or to simply buy a Barbie online. To a large extent, this type of intelligent guessing is precisely what offering a search engine is all about: to select and rank a list of online resources that has a good—or better, as high as possible—chance of satisfying the demand of the user as imperfectly expressed in a search query.

The basic model of information needs described above implies, for instance, that search engines will typically want to treat queries consisting of the name of an entity as navigational, returning the authoritative result in the first place.[91] For other types of queries, similar strategies can be observed and expected. The availability of the online collaborative encyclopedia Wikipedia has most likely been a particular blessing for satisfying informational queries. However, these are anecdotal characterizations of industry practices. The actual practices of general purpose search engines such as Google are a lot more complicated and, for various reasons, remain largely undocumented. What has become clear is that over the last decade, the analysis of historic user data has come to play a very important role for search engines in making informed guesses that satisfy their users and optimize themselves as marketing platforms. The legal issues that arise from the often opaque use of large amounts of user data from the perspective of freedom of expression will be discussed in detail in Chapter 10.

---

91. See e.g. the leaked document relating to Google's human search quality evaluation program, Google 2007b. For a discussion, see Sullivan 2010a.

The value chains in which search engines operate may help clarify some of the ways in which search engines have developed overarching strategies of discerning and responding to the various information needs of their users. For instance, the commercial nature of search engines has had an obvious impact on the way search engines would like to satisfy certain information needs of users. For example, transactional information needs may be more likely to attract advertiser bidding. More specifically, commercial search engines as well as advertisers can be expected to be particularly interested in optimizing their strategies with regard to queries with high consumer intent.[92] At the same time, navigational queries are attractive because they still allow search engines to present end-users with alternatives, the reference to which search engines can easily justify with reference to query purpose ambiguity. Finally, the position of search engines in various value chains of online resources can also explain specific vertical integration strategies by search engines. Seeing that they direct users' attention away to popular third-party resource collections, search engines may come to the conclusion that they would be better off developing their own competing resources. Google's search service, Google Maps (launched in 2004 to compete with AOL's MapQuest), Youtube and the unsuccessful project called 'knol' (commonly interpreted as a means to compete with Wikipedia), may all serve as examples.

In summary, search engines go well beyond the function of what could be seen as a simple telephone directory for the Web. They help users with a large variety of rather different information needs by actively selecting and ranking lists of online destinations. These information needs of users range from political, medical and educational to commercial, domestic and recreational. This clearly shows not only the societal breadth of the function of search engines in our information environment but also hints at the variety of important public and private interests that are tied to their operation. The fundamental legal questions relating to the role of search engines in providing access will be discussed in detail in Chapters 8–10.

On a more fundamental level, the way search engines end up selecting and ranking results for their users can be characterized as the expression of a range of underlying judgments about the relevance of various kinds of information and destinations in relation to the relative importance of the perceived needs of their users. Hence, on the one hand, the search medium is a facilitator to the communicative process between end-users and information providers. It does not itself, in its role as a search engine, publish information on the Web, but merely provides ranked collections of references to third-party content to end-users. On the other hand, the search engine does have to make a variety of choices about the way 'relevant' Web destinations will be selected, ranked and presented to its users on the basis of its analysis of the material on the Web and its interpretation of the perceived information needs as expressed by the users' queries. In the chapters that follow, the important question will be addressed regarding the extent to which these type of choices, the existence of which gives some of the search engine's

---

92. For a discussion of the way search engines can strategically respond to such queries, see Dai et al. 2006.

operations an *editorial* character, must be qualified under the right to freedom of expression.

3.3.2. SEARCH ENGINES AS FORUMS FOR INFORMATION PROVIDERS AND MARKETING PLATFORMS

As previously stated, the search engine is one of the most important ways for information providers to reach an audience online. Information providers, online services, e-commerce providers and advertisers have come to depend on general purpose search engines to establish an online presence and/or be successful as a business. As is understandable information providers and search engines each have their own preferred terms and conditions for carriage.

From the perspective of the information provider, one can discern three ways in which they tend to end up in the index of general purpose search engines. The first and standard way is that they simply allow their publicly available website to be indexed and ranked by the search engine in the organic or natural results. The information provider just puts his content online and waits for the search engine's crawlers to come by and include it. In this context, it is important to mention that information providers can instruct search engines with the use of the *robots.txt* protocol, a de facto standard in the industry, whether or not they want to be indexed in the first place.

There are several services that can help speed up the process of being included in search engines and major directories, and some search engines, including Google, offer a special set of tools for webmasters with which they can monitor the way they are included in the index. Whereas some information providers will simply sit back and let search engines include them in their service, others will use all the available means to optimize the way search engines help them reach end-users through their organic listings. Notably, the most important aspect to optimize for information providers is not their plain inclusion in the index but their selection as relevant and receiving optimal ranking in response to relevant user queries.

The second way information providers end up in search engine listings is through participation in paid placement programs. As discussed in Chapter 2, most search engines are commercial and have developed a monetization strategy that is based on the auctioning of targeted advertising space tied to specific end-user queries. Search engines cater to the information needs of users, who are not simply looking for the location of a website or information about a topic, but also as the starting point to make a purchase. In addition, the granularity of targeting which search engines can provide is highly attractive. Google's AdWords program has been the most successful paid listing program online and includes a growing range of additional choices to select and optimize paid placement of advertisements in response to particular queries by particular groups and types of users.

The third way search engines could end up referencing certain information is by contracting with information providers to be able to include them in their index, or to include them more effectively. The deals between Google and Twitter about (more) effective retrieval of tweets by Google users can serve as an example.

Notably, search engines are themselves examples of information providers that sell their information to be included in other search engines. Many search services and portals contract with other search engines for search results and provide their own information service with them. Ask stopped producing its own search results in 2010 and is said to pay Google for its organic search results.[93] Yahoo! has contracted with Microsoft for organic results. In general, there are hundreds of search engines but only a small percentage create their own index. Many vertical search engines operate in this manner. How often general purpose search engines enter into these kinds of arrangements is not well documented. Most commonly, search engines such as Google would simply buy the owner of this exclusive set of information and related technology and integrate it into its service.[94]

3.4.   CONCLUSION

This chapter has first clarified the basic elements of the search engine architecture, most notably the crawler, the index and the user interface. Furthermore, the role of search engines in the networked communications environment has been discussed, with reference to the layered model for networked communications and in respect to two interdependent and partly opposite value chains. And finally, the different functions the search engine performs with regard to end-users and information providers, and the direct stakeholders in the communications through search engines, have been discussed in more detail.

The analysis of the position of search media in the layered model of networked communications, clarifies that search engines map both to the top of the application and services layer as well as to the content layer.[95] On the one hand, Web search engines are complex systems of software, typically server-based, made accessible for users of the network in their Web browsers. On the other hand, search engines have a rather unique link with the content layer. Search engines can be argued to consume and produce a specific 'content' of their own, namely information about information, or meta-information.

The representation of the search engine in view of the essential value chains in the public networked information environment offers more insight into the important position search media find themselves in. The first value chain in which the search engine plays an important role is the flow and control over knowledge, information, data, news, offers, etc., from all sorts of online information and

---

93. It is notable that the Ask website does not refer to the actual producer of the references it shows to its users and it refused to clarify the actual source of organic results when asked for it by specialized media. See Sullivan 2010b.
94. See Ch. 2 for an overview of business developments in the search engine industry.
95. See also Wu 2010, 279–289.

service providers to end-users. The second value chain, which is of greater importance from a business perspective, represents the flow and control over user attention and activity, in the form of their page views, clicks, purchases and personal data. In both of these value chains, search media, and what can be denoted as selection intermediaries more generally, have established themselves as one of the central mediating institutions. More specifically, search media are uniquely situated to negotiate between these different kinds of value, a position from which they derive most of their power.[96] Search engine users retrieve value flowing through them as well as through search engines, in the first chain, in return for which they subject themselves to the extraction of value flowing away from them to information providers in the second value chain.

In comparison to traditional information retrieval systems, in which the information needs of users were typically restricted to the *informational*, Web search media tend to serve two additional types of user needs, namely *navigational* and *transactional*. Navigational queries are the type of queries with which users aim to reach a specific online destination which they know or simply assume to exist. By satisfying navigational queries, search engines help Internet users reach the home page of various institutions, organizations, companies or persons. Informational queries represent the user needs that are directed at learning something about a certain topic. Transactional queries represent the type of user needs which are directed at reaching a destination where the user will be able to use or consume a resource.

The conclusion follows that the function of search media goes well beyond the function of what could be seen as a simple telephone directory for the Web. They help users with a large variety of rather different information needs, by selecting and ranking lists of online destinations. These information needs range from political, medical and educational to commercial, domestic and recreational. This shows not only the societal breadth of the function of search engines in our public networked information environment but also hints at the large variety of public and private interests that are tied to their operation.

Finally, search engines end up selecting and ranking results for their users. The choices of how to do that can be seen as the expression of a range of underlying judgments about the relevance of various kinds of information and destinations in relation to the relative importance of the perceived needs of their users. To perform its function as matchmaker between information providers and end-users, the search engine has to make a variety of choices about the way 'relevant' Web destinations will be selected, ranked and presented to its users on the basis of its analysis of the material on the Web and its interpretation of the perceived information needs as expressed by the users' queries. This type of choices may give some of the search engine's operations an *editorial* character. In the chapters that follow, the question will be addressed, amongst others, of what that means from the perspective of the right to freedom of expression.

---

96. See Röhle 2009. See also Wu 2010, 279–289.

Part II

Freedom of Expression Theories

Chapter 4

The Right to Freedom of Expression

4.1.   INTRODUCTION

Whereas 'freedom' is accepted as a cornerstone of western constitutional democracies, it is also one of the most debated concepts in society. In these more general debates, some scholars have tried to highlight the commonalities between different conceptions of freedom, such as negative freedom and positive freedom.[97] One of the most successful attempts to come to a generally acceptable conception of freedom is the definition of freedom as a triadic relationship by MacCallum.[98] He took the position that all discussions about the meaning of freedom could be captured by a common conception of freedom of *something* (an actor; X), *from* something (a preventing condition; Y), *to* do, not do, become or not become something (an action, or condition of circumstance or character; Z).[99] In his seminal paper, which received general recognition by political philosophers,[100] MacCallum clarifies that different conceptions of freedom correspond to differences about what are the actors, what counts as relevant preventing conditions or what are the actions or conditions of circumstance or character that should be taken into account.

MacCallum's definition of the concept of freedom will serve as a background framework to discuss the implications of the right to freedom of expression in this study for the actors in the public information environment. If this concept of freedom is taken to the legal field, in particular to the field of fundamental and constitutional rights to freedom of expression, an additional 'actor' arises, namely the State and all other actors invested with public authority. Constitutional and

97. For a general discussion of positive and negative liberty, see Berlin 2002.
98. MacCallum 1967.
99. MacCallum 1967, 314.
100. For a discussion, see Blokland 1995, 126.

fundamental liberties such as the right to freedom of expression can then be seen as ordering mechanisms, guaranteeing fundamental liberties in terms of legal relations, vertically between public authorities and private actors, and to some extent horizontally, to be discussed below, between private actors themselves.

When asking the question about the implications of the fundamental right to freedom of expression for the governance of search engines and government involvement with search engines in particular, a number of questions naturally arise. First, what does *freedom of expression* entail or imply in general? Second, what is *the proper role of government* under freedom of expression? Third, since we are interested in the proper role of government with regard to a specific medium under freedom of expression doctrine, what is this proper role *with regard to different media*? Fourth, does this role *depend on the means of communication and its context and on which grounds*? And fifth, *with regard to what actions and which conflicts* should we evaluate the proper role of government under freedom of expression in the context of search engines? Before considering these general questions (Section 4.4), the legal provisions guaranteeing freedom of expression in their respective contexts that will provide the basis of the analysis will be discussed (Section 4.03), as well as the dominant theories providing a rationale for the fundamental right to freedom of expression (Section 4.2).

4.2.   FREEDOM OF EXPRESSION THEORIES

An important aspect of freedom of expression doctrine is the underlying theoretical justification for having freedom of expression in the first place. The theoretical arguments underlying freedom of expression are often invoked by legislatures and justices and have helped give the right to freedom of expression its current meaning. Without reference to the underlying justifications, some of the specific directions freedom of expression doctrine has taken cannot be fully understood, since they typically serve to delineate the right's scope or to assess the gravity of a particular interference and its societal effects. For this reason, the three dominant justifications for a right to freedom of expression are presented here for later reference. To be sure, there are other, sometimes more specific, theoretical justifications that have been given for freedom of expression.[101] However, the three dominant justifications are the argument from democracy, the argument from truth and the argument from autonomy or self-fulfillment. Whereas these arguments could be used as independent justifications, in practice one often finds a mixture of these theories.

The starting point of a theoretical justification of freedom of expression is to single out a class of acts that is privileged on the grounds of the right to freedom of

---

101.   For a systematic analysis of the justifications underlying freedom of expression, see Schauer 1983. See also Stone et al. 2008; Scanlon, 1972; Barendt 2005, 1–38.

expression, in the sense that these acts are subject to different, less restrictive—thus more favorable—legal treatment than acts that are not part of that class.[102] More specifically, to make sense as a separate principle, freedom of expression has to entail the protection of acts that would justify the imposition of sanctions absent a right to freedom of expression. One could, for instance, read the consideration of the European Court that freedom of expression is applicable not only to information or ideas that cause no harm, but also to those that 'offend, shock or disturb the State or any sector of the population' in this light.[103]

4.2.1.   DEMOCRACY

The argument which bases the right to freedom of expression on democracy considers freedom of expression as a prerequisite for democratic self-governance. The sovereignty of the people is guaranteed by the freedom to express and receive information and ideas. Freedom of expression underlies public deliberation and ensures the accountability of government. Also, in a representative democracy, freedom of expression makes it possible for the elected to know the opinions of the people. Thus, the right to impart information can be seen as a prerequisite for citizens to be able to participate in public debate, and the right to receive information can be seen in light of the need of the public to inform itself and form an opinion about matters of public concern. The argument from democracy, defended most powerfully by the American philosopher Alexander Meiklejohn, tends to emphasize the free circulation of information and ideas of political and societal relevance.[104] The theory about democracy has sometimes been used to argue that information and ideas unrelated to politics, government or public affairs, such as the information about private individuals have a less protected status.[105]

The argument from democracy has found its way into several of the judgments of the European Court of Justice and the U.S. Supreme Court. The explicit reference to 'democratic society' in the restriction clause of Article 10 ECHR strongly links the argument from democracy to the right to freedom of expression. Restrictions of the right have to respect fundamental principles of a constitutional democracy. In one of its early judgments on Article 10 ECHR, *Handyside v. The United Kingdom*, arising from a complaint by British publisher Handyside over the seizure of 'The Little Red Schoolbook,' which advised schoolchildren about controversial subjects such as sex, drugs and school politics, the Court made a strong connection between democracy and the right to freedom of expression. It stated the following:

> [t]he Court's supervisory functions oblige it to pay the utmost attention to the principles characterising a "democratic society". Freedom of expression

---

102. Scanlon 1972, 1.
103. ECtHR December 7, 1976, *Handyside v. The United Kingdom*, § 49.
104. See Meiklejohn 1948; Meiklejohn 1961.
105. For a critique of this view, see Chafee 1948.

constitutes one of the essential foundations of such a society, one of the basic conditions for its progress and for the development of every man.[106]

Similar to this, references to the principle of democratic government can be found in First Amendment doctrine. In *Terminiello*, for instance, the Supreme Court stated the following:

> it is only through free debate and free exchange of ideas that government remains responsive to the will of the people and peaceful change is effected.[107]

As will become apparent in the next chapters in more detail, there are several specific elements of freedom of expression doctrine that have been linked to the argument from democracy. The right of every person to receive information freely, for instance, has frequently been stated in terms of democratic self-governance. And the idea that the press and the media have a particular societal role in providing a forum for deliberation and a way for the public to inform itself has been clearly linked to the democratic rationale for the right to freedom of expression.

4.2.2.   THE 'MARKETPLACE OF IDEAS' OR THE 'TRUTH THEORY'

A related but different argument for freedom of expression is the argument from truth. This argument, which can be traced back to the work of John Milton[108] and John Stuart Mill,[109] states that freedom of expression and information is the best way to ensure the discovery of truth. It is related to the argument from democracy in the sense that the discovery of political wisdom and truth with regard to public affairs enhances self-governance. The argument from truth was defended in its purest form by Mill. In *On Liberty*, Mill expressed his famous view as follows:

> [. . .] the peculiar evil of silencing an opinion is, that it is robbing the human race; [. . .]; those who dissent from the opinion still more that those who hold it. If the opinion is right they are deprived of the opportunity of exchanging error for truth: if wrong, they lose, what is almost as great a benefit, the clearer perception and livelier expression of truth produced by its collision with error.[110]

Closely related to the discovery of truth rationale is the 'marketplace of ideas' theory, which was introduced by Supreme Court Justice Holmes in his dissenting

---

106. ECtHR December 7, 1976, *Handyside v. The United Kingdom*, § 49.
107. *Terminiello v. Chicago*, 337 U.S. 1, 4 (1949) "The vitality of civil and political institutions in our society depends on free discussion. [. . .] it is only through free debate and free exchange of ideas that government remains responsive to the will of the people and peaceful change is effected. The right to speak freely and to promote diversity of ideas and programs is therefore one of the chief distinctions that sets us apart from totalitarian regimes." See also section 5.3.1.
108. See Milton 1999.
109. See Mill 1863.
110. *Ibid.*

opinion in *Abrams*. Holmes concludes that underlying the First Amendment was the following idea:

> the best test of truth is the power of the thought to get itself accepted in the competition of the market.[111]

This rationale embraces the argument from truth by comparing the search for truth to the economic theory of the invisible hand of the marketplace. Both Mill and Holmes conclude that the suppression of opinions and information for the reason that they are perceived as untrue or otherwise unwanted by government is the wrong approach, because it would stand in the way of testing their truth or value.

Although some scholars have done so, the argument from truth does not have to be taken literally.[112] As a metaphor, it simply emphasizes the need for the exchange and valuation of ideas and information free of State interference. Some have criticized the argument from truth as being too optimistic with regard to the human capacity to discover truth, since the theory provides no evidence that the truth will actually arise as a result of free expression and inquiry. In fact, there is ample empirical evidence that there are structural biases in the functioning of free discourse in groups and society that stand in the way of the discovery of truth.[113] As a result, some have argued in favor of improving the marketplace of ideas, mostly basing their argument on the argument from democracy.[114] Maybe, however, the result of free discourse will simply be a different mix of consensus and disagreement, and not necessarily truth. A more pessimistic version of the 'marketplace of ideas' argument answers this empirical objection by stating that the free marketplace of ideas is simply better than other options.[115]

4.2.3.　　Individual Dignity, Self-fulfillment and Autonomy

While both the argument from truth and the argument from democracy value individual freedom, their emphasis lies on a public or common good. The last argument presented here is different in that sense. It derives from autonomy and self-development and places the emphasis on the fundamental value of freedom of the individual herself, and in particular on the ability of the individual to develop her full capacities to obtain knowledge and to express herself.[116] This theory takes human liberty, freedom of choice, and the value of and respect for diversity as the starting point.

The Handyside judgment, cited above, contains a reference to the self-fulfillment of every man in society:

---

111. *Abrams v. United States*, 250 U.S. 616, 629 (1919).
112. Nieuwenhuis 1991, 31–35.
113. See e.g. Sunstein 2006. See also Baker 2002.
114. See e.g. Sunstein 1993; Fiss 1996. See also Lippmann 1922; Lippmann 1920.
115. See Schauer 1983, 33–34.
116. *Ibid.*, 47–49. See also Baker 1989.

[f]reedom of expression constitutes [. . .] one of the basic conditions for [. . .] the development of every man.[117]

The emphasis on the value of diversity and variety in information and media and the freedom of choice has been of particular interest for European information and media policy. Variety and diversity of ideas and information enhances the autonomy of listeners, because it enhances their ability to reflect and make well-informed choices.

The protection of a right to freedom of expression of organizations and corporate entities is more difficult to reconcile with a theory of freedom of expression that relies on individual autonomy and human dignity.[118] From the perspective of this rationale, such rights should only be granted insofar as they can be derived from the rights of actual people. In practice, both under the ECHR and in the United States, the rights of private legal persons and corporations are protected under the right to freedom of expression. The ECtHR reaffirmed in *Autronic* that Article 10 applies not only to natural persons, but also to profit-making corporations, as follows:

[n]either Autronic AG's legal status as a limited company nor the fact that its activities were commercial nor the intrinsic nature of freedom of expression can deprive Autronic AG of the protection of Article 10 [. . .]. The Article [. . .] applies to "everyone", whether natural or legal persons.[119]

In the United States, the Supreme Court concluded in *Bellotti,* as follows:

[t]here is no support [. . .] for the proposition that such speech loses the protection otherwise afforded it by the First Amendment simply because its source is a corporation that cannot prove, to a court's satisfaction, a material effect on its business.[120]

---

117. ECtHR December 7, 1976, *Handyside v. the United Kingdom,* § 49.
118. See e.g. Benkler 2001, 23. See also Redish 2001.
119. ECtHR May 22. 1990, *Autronic v. Switzerland,* § 47.
120. *First National Bank of Boston v. Bellotti*, 435 U.S. 765, 804-05 (1978). More recently, *Citizens United v. Federal Election Commission*, 558 U.S. 8 (2010). See Justice White's dissent in *Bellotti* for a unambiguous acknowledgement of the inconsistency of this conclusion with the argument from autonomy and self-development: "[i]ndeed, what some have considered to be the principal function of the First Amendment, the use of communication as a means of self-expression, self-realization, and self-fulfillment, is not at all furthered by corporate speech. It is clear that the communications of profitmaking corporations are not 'an integral part of the development of ideas, of mental exploration and of the affirmation of self'. They do not represent a manifestation of individual freedom or choice."

4.3. FREEDOM OF EXPRESSION PROVISIONS

4.3.1. THE RIGHT TO FREEDOM OF EXPRESSION IN INTERNATIONAL HUMAN RIGHTS TREATIES

On the global level, freedom of expression is protected in two UN treaties. Article 19 of the UN Universal Declaration of Human Rights (UDHR) provides the following:

> Everyone has the right to freedom of opinion and expression; this right includes freedom to hold opinions without interference and to seek, receive and impart information and ideas through any media and regardless of frontiers.[121]

And Article 19(2) of the UN International Covenant on Civil and Political Rights (ICCPR) provides the following:

> Everyone shall have the right to freedom of expression; this right shall include freedom to seek, receive and impart information and ideas of all kinds, regardless of frontiers, either orally, in writing or in print, in the form of art, or through any other media of his choice.[122]

Because this study mostly adopts a European perspective, we will not study these international provisions on freedom of expression. They do provide additional guidance on the governance of global communications and the legality under international law of the repression of search engines in countries such as China,[123] but from a European perspective they are of little extra value, and in the transatlantic debates about the right to freedom of expression they tend to play a more limited role as well.

One aspect of Article 19 of the UN UDHR and Article 19(2) of the ICCPR is worth discussing here, namely their explicit reference to the *freedom to seek* information and ideas, regardless of frontiers and through any media. When one looks at the reason for this reference, which is absent in the ECHR and the EU Charter, one finds evidence that this freedom to seek is an implicit reference to a right to gather information, which was included in the UDHR as a result of efforts by the news industry.[124] Recent international human rights documents tend to refer to this right to seek information and ideas as a (limited) right to seek and gain access to government-held information or, in short, 'a right to information'.[125] Although

---

121. United Nations Universal Declaration of Human Rights, adopted and proclaimed by General Assembly resolution 217 A (III) of December 10, 1948.
122. The United Nations International Covenant on Civil and Political Rights, adopted and opened for signature, ratification and accession by General Assembly resolution 2200A (XXI) of December 16, 1966.
123. For a discussion of Internet filtering under the international human rights framework, see e.g. Rundle & Birdling 2008.
124. Hamelink 1994, 155. See also Schiller 1976, 31–32.
125. See e.g. UN Commission on Human Rights 1998.

of possible relevance in specific areas of search engine activity, such as a search engine's right to crawl government information, this right to gather information—related to freedom of information laws such as the Freedom of Information Act in the United States or the *Wet openbaarheid van bestuur* in the Netherlands—is of limited relevance for this study. Above and beyond, a similar right to (state-held) information was also recognized by the ECtHR in a recent judgment concerning a freedom of information request by a Hungarian non-governmental organization.[126] There is no reason to believe that the specific reference to the right to seek information and ideas in the UN context adds substantive value to an implicitly guaranteed right in the European context.

4.3.2.   ARTICLE 10 ECHR AND THE EU CHARTER

Article 10 of the European Convention on Human Rights provides as follows:

Article 10—Freedom of expression

1. Everyone has the right to freedom of expression. This right shall include freedom to hold opinions and to receive and impart information and ideas without interference by public authority and regardless of frontiers. This article shall not prevent States from requiring the licensing of broadcasting, television or cinema enterprises.

2. The exercise of these freedoms, since it carries with it duties and responsibilities, may be subject to such formalities, conditions, restrictions or penalties as are prescribed by law and are necessary in a democratic society, in the interests of national security, territorial integrity or public safety, for the prevention of disorder or crime, for the protection of health or morals, for the protection of the reputation or rights of others, for preventing the disclosure of information received in confidence, or for maintaining the authority and impartiality of the judiciary.[127]

The ECHR is at the heart of the protection of fundamental rights in Europe. The members to the Convention are the forty-seven Member States of the Council of Europe, including all the members of the European Union. The European Court of Human Rights oversees the enforcement of the Convention. The Committee of Ministers and the Parliamentary Assembly provide additional guidance with regard to the obligations under the Convention by adopting recommendations and resolutions. The Convention is not supposed to be static. The Court has concluded time

---

126. ECtHR April 14, 2009, *Társaság a Szabadságjogokért v. Hungary*. See also section 5.5.1.
127. Council of Europe, Convention for the Protection of Human Rights and Fundamental Freedoms, November 4, 1950, Europ. T.S. No. 5.

and again that the Convention is "a living instrument which must be interpreted in the light of present-day conditions".[128]

Formally, the ECHR is a regional international treaty between the sovereign Member States of the Council of Europe, whereas the Member States, by creating the European Communities and later the European Union, introduced a supranational legal order, which limits the sovereignty of the Member States in particular areas of law.[129] For members of the Council of Europe, the ECHR is the most important of international fundamental rights treaties, because of the possibility for individuals to complain about an infringement of their rights and receive a binding judgment. For Dutch law and legal scholarship, the Convention is particularly significant because of the combination of primacy and direct effect granted to international rights and obligations such as Article 10 ECHR by the Dutch Constitution (Articles 93 and 94) on the one hand, and the absence of (judicial) constitutional review of primary Dutch legislation on the basis of constitutional rights provided for in the Dutch Constitution (Article 120) on the other hand.

The relation of the European Union to the Council of Europe and the ECHR is still relatively complex. The European Union has not acceded to the ECHR (yet),[130] but the ECHR is still understood to be binding on the European Union indirectly, because of what was provided for in Article 6(2) of the European Union Treaty.[131] More generally, the adherence of the European Union to the Convention is illustrated by the fact that to be eligible for membership to the European Union, candidates must be members of the Council of Europe and ratify the Convention.

Since the Lisbon Treaty came into force on December 1, 2009, Article 6 of the EU Treaty contains a stronger reference to the EU's own fundamental rights instrument, namely the European Charter on Fundamental Rights,[132] next to a recognition of the rights, freedoms and principles in the ECHR. The Article also contains an obligation on the EU to accede to the Convention, as follows:

Article 6 Treaty on European Union (ex Article 6 TEU)

1. The Union recognizes the rights, freedoms and principles set out in the Charter of Fundamental Rights of the European Union of 7 December 2000 [. . .] which shall have the same legal value as the Treaties.

The provisions of the Charter shall not extend in any way the competences of the Union as defined in the Treaties.

---

128. See e.g. ECtHR April 25, 1978, *Tyrer v. the United Kingdom*, § 31.
129. See ECJ February 5, 1963, *Van Gend & Loos v. Netherlands*, C-26-62; ECJ July 15, 1964, *Flaminio Costa v. E.N.E.L.*, C-6/64.
130. In the ECJ's view, the European Community failed the requirements to accession to the ECHR. See ECJ, *Opinion 2/94* [1996] ECR I-1759. The EU Constitutional Treaty, and later the Lisbon Treaty, make future accession possible.
131. For the old Article 6 TEU, see Consolidated version of the Treaty on European Union, OJ C 325, December 24, 2002.
132. Charter on Fundamental rights of the European Union, December 18, 2000, OJ 2000/C 364/01.

The rights, freedoms and principles in the Charter shall be interpreted in accordance with the general provisions in Title VII of the Charter governing its interpretation and application and with due regard to the explanations referred to in the Charter, that set out the sources of those provisions.

2. The Union shall accede to the European Convention for the Protection of Human Rights and Fundamental Freedoms. Such accession shall not affect the Union's competences as defined in the Treaties.

3. Fundamental rights, as guaranteed by the European Convention for the Protection of Human Rights and Fundamental Freedoms and as they result from the constitutional traditions common to the Member States, shall constitute general principles of the Union's law.[133]

The legal significance of both the Convention and EU law for the legal order of the Member States results in a rather complex triangular relationship of national law, international fundamental rights law and supranational EU law. This triangular relationship is of particular importance for law and policy fields such as information law, in which the protection of fundamental rights is a dominant concern. As a result, EU secondary law in the field of information law and policy also regularly refers to the Member States' obligations under the Convention, and the various Council of Europe institutions tend to take note of legal developments in the European Union.

Article 52(3) of the EU Charter on Fundamental Rights provides that the meaning and scope of the rights in the Charter which correspond to rights in the ECHR shall be the same as those laid down by the Convention. But, it also clarifies that this is not to prevent EU law from providing more extensive protection. At the judicial level, the European Court of Justice regularly refers to Article 10 ECHR or other provisions in its judgments and allows for challenges on the basis of the rights and freedoms guaranteed by the Convention.[134] More recently, the Court and its Advocate-Generals are increasingly arguing cases on the basis of the rights and freedoms as provided for in the Charter.

The relevant provision in the Charter on Fundamental Rights of the European Union on 'freedom of expression and information' is Article 11:

Article 11 Freedom of Expression and Information

1. Everyone has the right to freedom of expression. This right shall include freedom to hold opinions and to receive and impart information and ideas without interference by public authority and regardless of frontiers.

2. The freedom and pluralism of the media shall be respected.

---

133. Consolidated versions of the Treaty on European Union and the Treaty on the Functioning of the European Union, OJ C 83, March 30, 2010.
134. See e.g. ECJ March 6, 2001, *Connolly v. Commission*, C-274/99P. See generally Lawson 1994, 219–252.

It is only logical that the relative importance of the Charter's provisions in comparison with the Convention will rise in the European Union legal context, since the right has been officially recognized by the EU Treaty. At present, however, Article 11 of the Charter is only of relatively limited additional substantive value to an analysis of the right to freedom of expression at the European level. We will, therefore, mostly restrict our discussion of the right to freedom of expression in Europe to Article 10 ECHR based on the case law of the ECtHR.

[1] ECHR Limitation Clause

Except for the freedom from torture in Article 3 ECHR, all rights and liberties in the ECHR contain specific limitation clauses.[135] The relevant rights and freedoms for the field of information law, including Articles 8 and 10 ECHR, all have a similar structure, delineating the scope of the right in the first paragraph and the possibility for limitations in the second paragraph. The Court has interpreted this limitation clause in its case law throughout the years and developed a set of criteria to test the permissibility of interferences. Interferences must be 'prescribed by law', have a 'legitimate aim' corresponding to one or more of the explicitly and exhaustively listed legitimate grounds for interference, and be 'necessary in a democratic society'.[136]

The standard that interferences need to be 'prescribed by law' or, in different words, be 'in accordance with the law', contains both a formal and a substantive element. It means that an interfering measure must have some legal basis in national law, reflecting the principle of legality.[137] But it also relates to the 'quality of law'. The law must be both accessible and foreseeable.[138] In the ECtHR's case law, this test is linked to the overarching principles of the rule of law that one has to be able to know one's rights and obligations, and arbitrariness is prohibited.[139]

The 'legitimate aim' test is the least substantive in practice. The list of legitimate aims that are mentioned in Article 10, second paragraph—national security, territorial integrity or public safety, the prevention of disorder and crime, the protection of health and morals, the protection of the rights of others, the prevention of the disclosure of information received in confidence and the maintenance of the authority and impartiality of the judiciary—covers most restrictions and the Court tends to scrutinize the weight that can be attached to the aim of a particular restriction in view of the third standard, whether the interference is 'necessary in a democratic society'.

In its case law on the permissibility of interference, the Court tends to place the emphasis on the standard that an interfering measure must be 'necessary in a

---

135. A general limitation clause for Article 11 EU Charter can be found in Article 52, first paragraph.
136. For a general overview, see van Dijk et al. 2006, 334–350.
137. ECtHR March 25, 1983, *Silver and others v. the United Kingdom*, § 86.
138. ECtHR September 25, 2001, *P.G. and J.H v. the United Kingdom*, § 44.
139. Van Dijk et al. 2006, 336–337.

democratic society'. The application of this standard involves a balancing on the basis of proportionality between the aims and effects on the one hand, and the weight and character of the interference on the other hand. In this context, the Court has clarified that "the adjective 'necessary' is not synonymous with 'indispensable', neither has it the flexibility of such expressions as 'admissible', 'ordinary', 'useful', 'reasonable' or 'desirable'".[140] The test implies the existence of a 'pressing social need' and that the measure must be 'relevant and sufficient'.[141]

It is important to note that in its assessment of the necessity of interferences in a democratic society, the Court leaves a 'margin of appreciation' to the Member States "to make the initial assessment of the reality of the pressing social need implied by the notion of 'necessity' in this context".[142] The margin of appreciation that is granted to the Member States varies. In some contexts, such as prior restraints on publications about current events, or in cases in which the Court concludes that there is relative consensus about the weight that should be attached to the rights and interests in questions, the Court deploys a limited margin of appreciation, whereas in other contexts, the margin of appreciation can be wider.[143]

Finally, in the context of the right to freedom of expression, the Court also takes into account the possible deterrent effects of restrictive measures on the exercise of the right to freedom of expression in society more generally. This deterrent effect, which can be unintended, is called the 'chilling effect' doctrine.[144]

4.3.3. THE FIRST AMENDMENT

The relevant part of the First Amendment of the U.S. Bill of Rights[145] provides as follows:

> Congress shall make no law [. . .] abridging the freedom of speech, or of the press [. . .][146]

---

140. ECtHR March 25, 1983, *Silver and others v. the United Kingdom*, § 97.
141. ECtHR December 7, 1976, *Handyside v. the United Kingdom*, § 50.
142. ECtHR December 7, 1976, *Handyside v. the United Kingdom*, § 48.
143. For a wide margin of appreciation, see e.g. ECtHR November 20, 1989, *Markt Intern Verlag v. Germany*. For an example of a limited margin of appreciation, see e.g. ECtHR November 26, 1991, *Observer and Guardian v. the United Kingdom*.
144. See most recently, ECtHR May 10, 2011, *Mosley v. the United Kingdom*, §§ 125–132 (rejecting the idea of a pre-notification requirement for privacy-interfering publications with reference to the chilling effect a similar requirement would give rise to). See also ECtHR March 27, 1996, *Goodwin v. United Kingdom*, § 39 (addressing the deterrent effect of a legal obligation for journalists to reveal the source of their information).
145. United States Constitution, Bill of Rights, Adopted 1791.
146. The First Amendment also establishes freedom of assembly, religious freedom and the right to petition government.

The Bill of Rights is a part of the U.S. Constitution[147] and subject to judicial review by the U.S. Supreme Court. A discussion of the particularities of U.S. constitutional law and constitutional review of State and federal laws is beyond the scope of this study.[148] Important issues will be mentioned when necessary. First Amendment case law is known for its complexity and inconsistencies. But the aim here is not to deliver an authoritative interpretation of the First Amendment. Instead, we are mostly interested in learning from First Amendment doctrine without taking an independent position on the precise meaning of the U.S. Constitution. The analysis in the next chapters will also draw important elements from the richness of the debates about the implications of the First Amendment, present some of the relevant leading cases and opinions, and discuss the different arguments that have been put forward to argue in favor of and against particular interpretations.

[1] The First Amendment: Limitations and Level of Scrutiny

The First Amendment lacks a provision legitimizing interferences as in Article 10 of the Convention. This has made the First Amendment powerful but judicial review complex. The free speech absolutists have argued that the provision should be taken literally, in the sense that speech and, in particular, the press cannot be the legitimate object of government restrictions at all.[149] Others have claimed, on historical grounds, that the First Amendment does nothing more than forbidding press licensing and abolishing the doctrine of seditious libel.[150] The Supreme Court has accepted neither of these positions. Over time, it has developed a complex set of criteria determining the scope of the right to free speech and conditions under which different types of government interference can be legitimate.

---

147. United States Constitution, Adopted 1787.
148. The Fourteenth Amendment, section 1, is of special importance for the U.S. federal system of constitutional review. It was adopted in 1868, just after the Civil War. The Fourteenth Amendment contains the so-called due process' clause, as follows: "[. . .] nor shall any State deprive any person of life, liberty, or property, without due process of law; nor deny to any person within its jurisdiction the equal protection of the laws." The definition of liberty under the due process clause of the Fourteenth Amendment includes the First Amendment. See *Gitlow v. People*, 268 U.S. 652, 666 (1925) ("Assumed, for the purposes of the case, that freedom of speech and of the press are among the personal rights and liberties protected by the due process clause of the Fourteenth Amendment from impairment by the States"), *Stromberg v. California*, 283 U.S. 359, 368 (1931). ("The principles to be applied have been clearly set forth in our former decisions. It has been determined that the conception of liberty under the due process clause of the Fourteenth Amendment embraces the right of free speech.")
149. Justice Black is known for defending this position in a number of dissenting opinions and his legal scholarship. See e.g. *New York Times Co. v. United States*, 403 U.S. 713, 714 (1971). (Black: "In my view, it is unfortunate that some of my Brethren are apparently willing to hold that the publication of news may sometimes be enjoined. Such a holding would make a shambles of the First Amendment.") See also *Smith v. California*, 361 U.S. 147, 157 (1959) (Black, J. Concurring). See also Black 1960.
150. Stone et al. 2008, 3–8 and cited references. See also Levy 1985, 3–15.

Two distinctions as regards the legitimacy of restrictions of free speech in U.S. constitutional law are of general importance in the Court's case law, namely the distinction between protected and unprotected speech and the distinction between content-based and content-neutral (time, place and manner) restrictions on speech.[151] The distinction between protected and unprotected speech, i.e. the so-called two-level theory of speech, was adopted by the Supreme Court in *Chaplinsky*. In this judgment, involving the constitutionality of a prosecution for the utterance of offensive language by a Jehovah's witness against a police officer, the Supreme Court clarified that some categories of expression and information are not (or hardly) protected and can thus be the legitimate subject of government interference.[152]

The distinction between content-neutral or (time, place and manner) and content-based restrictions is relevant for the level of scrutiny by the Court. If the Court considers a restriction to be content-based, it applies strict scrutiny. Specific examples of strict scrutiny include the doctrines relating to overbreadth and vagueness, and the Court's case law relating to prior restraints. A content-based restriction of protected speech can only be legitimate if it is narrowly targeted and if it furthers a compelling State interest.[153] Content-neutral restrictions are subject to a lower standard of constitutional review, i.e. intermediate scrutiny, than content-based restriction. A content-neutral restriction must further an important governmental interest, unrelated to the suppression of speech and whose incidental restriction of protected speech is not greater than is necessary to further that interest.[154] The review of content-neutral restrictions thereby involves a mode of balancing, whereas the scrutiny of content-based restrictions of protected speech involves a presumption that restrictions are not legitimate.

As explained in the introduction, First Amendment doctrine will be prominently addressed as a comparative element in this study. Because of the differences between the structure and the substance of freedom of expression doctrine in the United States and in Europe, the choice to prominently address the First Amendment deserves some further explanation here. After all, the First Amendment is widely portrayed as unique and exceptional.[155] This would imply that any attempt to draw from First Amendment doctrine for the European legal context would be

---

151. For a discussion on the proper First Amendment level of scrutiny in the context of the application of private laws of general applicability, see Solove & Richards 2009. See also O'Neil 2001.
152. *Chaplinsky v. New Hampshire*, 315 U.S. 568, 571 (1942): "There are certain well-defined and narrowly limited classes of speech, the prevention and punishment of which has never been thought to raise any Constitutional problem. These include the lewd and obscene, the profane, the libelous, and the insulting or 'fighting' words—those which by their very utterance inflict injury or tend to incite an immediate breach of the peace. It has been well observed that such utterances are no essential part of any exposition of ideas, and are of such slight social value as a step to truth that any benefit that may be derived from them is clearly outweighed by the social interest in order and morality." For a discussion, see Kalven 1960.
153. See e.g. *New York v. Ferber* 458 U.S. 747 (1982).
154. See *Turner Broadcasting System, Inc. v. FCC*, 512 U.S. 622, 662 (1994).
155. For an overview of this debate, see Schauer 2005a.

hopeless. However, considering the purpose and legal context of this study, this point of view has to be rejected.

First, the structural differences between Article 10 ECHR and the First Amendment can make direct comparison much harder, but both provisions are really about the same (contested) concept, the special constitutional status of a set of communicative freedoms. One striking difference has been already discussed above, namely the difference in the way the possibilities of restrictions of the right to freedom of expression are dealt with. Another difference between the protection of fundamental freedoms between the United States and Europe is commonly attached to the level of protection of the freedom of speech. U.S. law is widely considered to be exceptional because of the high value the U.S. Constitution attributes to expressive liberties.[156] But throughout the following chapters, it will become apparent that there are many similarities as well. Most importantly, however, it is not the purpose of this study to debate or understand the differences between First Amendment and European freedom of expression doctrine as a goal in itself. But, First Amendment doctrine will be used to establish a better understanding of what is at stake, as well as the way freedom of expression can be understood to be implicated in the context of search engine governance.

Perhaps one of the best explanations for the structural differences between the ECHR and the U.S. doctrine on freedom of expression is, as Frederick Schauer has argued, the fact that the First Amendment has existed for more than two hundred years and has led to intense judicial engagement at the level of the U.S. Supreme Court since 1919. The ECtHR's case law on freedom of expression only dates back to the second half on the 1970s.[157] This means that it made a late and a fresh start on some of the most pressing legal and societal questions arising in the freedom of expression context. It is much rarer for the U.S. Supreme Court to touch upon a fundamental question relating to the right to freedom of expression that it has not already dealt with in the past in some manner. The implied richness of free speech doctrine in the U.S., however, is precisely a reason to study it and draw from it.

Moreover, in the field of the governance of Internet communications, the United States has had a decisive impact on global and European law and policy. This influence can be found in specific instances of law making, such as the concept of safe harbors to regulate intermediary liability, which will be discussed in more detail in Chapters 6, 8 and 10. But its influence extends more generally. Although the Internet and its governance were privatized in the 1990s, the United States never really gave up its sovereign stake in this network of networks that had been predominantly developed since the 1960s in the United States.[158] Optimistically speaking, a transatlantic dialogue on Internet governance and Internet regulation in general is important for both the United States and for Europe. The question of the implications of the right to freedom of expression for Internet

---

156. See e.g. Schauer 2005a; Gardbaum 2008. See also, critically, Blanchard 1992.
157. See Schauer 2005b, 49–69.
158. See e.g. Mueller 2002, 154–162.

governance and regulation will and should, of course, be part of this dialogue. It is this dialogue to which this study aims to make a contribution as well.

And finally, in the context of Web search engines, all Web search services dominant in Europe have their headquarters on U.S. soil. This has implications for the regulatory and legal debate. First, not only the industry but also the legal debate about search engine governance seems more mature in the United States.[159] This does not necessarily mean that it has come up with the best answers, but it has been more intense and generally better informed. Second, there is an obvious incentive for U.S.-based online services to design their policies in view of their local law and subsequently raise these policies, as much as possible, to a global level. This influence of legal solutions from the United States can take different forms, such as standard contractual agreements and choice of law, or engagement with European policy makers on different levels. Thus, search engine governance in Europe is, and will probably remain, heavily influenced by the U.S. search industry and U.S. law and policy. If Europe is to develop its own views, laws and policies about the implications of the right to freedom of expression for the governance of search, it is essential to understand and valuable to learn from the American debate about this pressing question and put the possibly different answers in perspective.

4.4.   FREEDOM OF EXPRESSION DOCTRINE: FURTHER CLARIFICATIONS

4.4.1.   THE PROPER ROLE OF GOVERNMENT UNDER FREEDOM OF EXPRESSION

The question of the proper role of the State and the different branches of government under freedom of expression doctrine lies at the root of most debates about the implications of the right to freedom of expression. There are two main lines of thought which, in simplified terms, map relatively well to the current legal mainstream in the United States and Europe respectively. The first is that freedom of expression is a negative right, to be invoked against government interference: government may not restrict the free circulation of information and ideas. Freedom of expression, like other classic fundamental rights, is about creating a sphere free of State influence or the exercise of State power. This view is popular in America.

A different conception of freedom of expression with regard to the role of the State sees, apart from the right to freedom of expression as a negative right, protecting against undue government interference, also a positive role and under some circumstances even a positive obligation for governments under the right to freedom of expression. In this view, the State should promote the free exercise of

---

159. See in particular Grimmelmann 2010b; Grimmelmann 2007a; Bracha & Pasquale 2008; Goldman 2006; Gasser 2006; Elkin-Koren 2001.

the right to freedom of expression and provide for the societal conditions in which this free exercise can prosper.

At the heart of this debate lies a difference in opinion about the character of rights and liberties and the role of the State in that regard. In continental Europe, the constitutional rights framework developed further since the Second World War and incorporates social welfare rights, It contains positive obligations with regard to the exercise of classic fundamental rights such as freedom of expression[160] and the protection of private life,[161] as well as horizontal obligations or *Drittwirkung* in Germany.[162] The U.S. constitutional mainstream, with some notable exceptions,[163] remains strongly attached to a negative rights interpretation of the First Amendment and other fundamental rights.

The way the character of relationship between different parties is constitutive for the implications of the right to freedom of expression for the legal governance of these relationships can be illustrated using a quadrant with two interdependent axes: vertical and horizontal relations on one axis and a negative or positive role of government on the other axis.

First, different implications arise in the context of vertical relations, meaning relations between public authorities and private parties, and that of horizontal relations, meaning relations between private parties amongst each other. For instance, the prohibition of censorship is a typical example of the way the right to freedom of expression serves as a constraint on the role of government in vertical relations, whereas defamation law tends to deal, either directly or indirectly, with the implications of the right to freedom of expression in horizontal relations.

As is directly apparent from the formulation of Article 10 ECHR, as well as that of the First Amendment, the right to freedom of expression is first and foremost concerned with restricting government action in vertical relations between public authorities and private parties. However, due to various developments at the European level, as well as the level of some of the Member States, it has become accepted that fundamental rights can have implications for the legal governance of horizontal relations. This theory of horizontal effect of fundamental rights is called 'third-party effect' or is denoted by its German name, *Drittwirkung*.[164]

---

160. In particular, the positive obligation as regards pluralism in the context of the media. See sections 5.5.1, 10.2.2.
161. See recently ECtHR December 2, 2008, *K.U. v. Finland.*
162. For an overview, see van Dijk et al. 2006, 28–32 and cited references.
163. See e.g. *Marsh v. Alabama*, 326 U.S. 501 (1946). In *Marsh* the Supreme Court finds state action of a corporate town.
164. The third-party effect of basic rights and freedoms in the German Basic Law was an implication of the *Lueth* ruling of the German Constitutional Court in 1958, which declared that the Basic Law contained an objective system of values, which "must apply as a constitutional axiom throughout the whole legal system," BVerfGE 7, 198 (Lueth). For a discussion, see Kommers 1997, 48–49; Prueb 2005, 23–32.

Figure 4.1: The Right to Freedom of Expression and the Role of Government

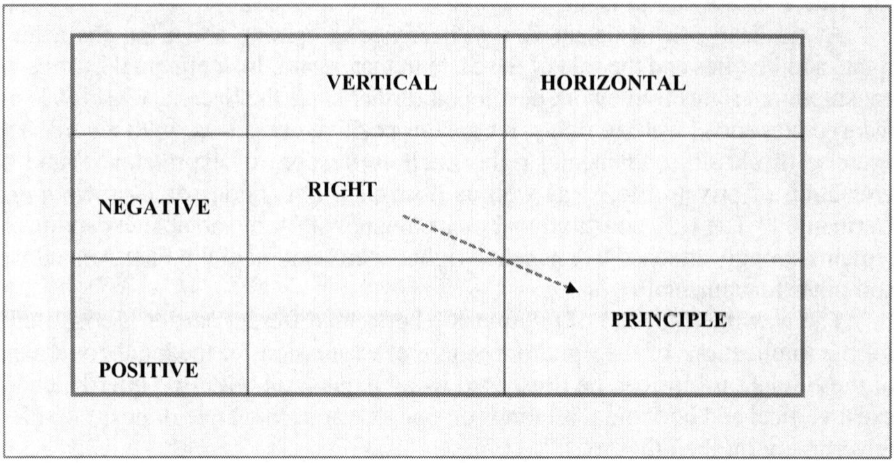

	VERTICAL	HORIZONTAL
NEGATIVE	**RIGHT**	
POSITIVE		**PRINCIPLE**

The doctrine of horizontal effect is complex and the subject of extensive legal debate.[165]

The horizontal effect of fundamental rights can be either indirect or direct. Direct horizontal effect means that the fundamental right would directly function in relations between private parties in a way that allows a private party to enforce the right against the other private party directly. This type of horizontal effect is generally rare and is absent at the level of the ECHR. The right not to be discriminated against by other members of society on grounds such as race or sexual orientation could be seen as an example of a fundamental right with direct effect, namely the fundamental right to equal treatment. But, typically, one would still rely on specific anti-discrimination legislation to effectuate this right. A better example of direct effect is found in Irish law, where the Irish Supreme Court has interpreted the Irish Constitution to create an independent action for breach of constitutionally protected rights against persons other than the State and its officials.[166] The ECHR only provides for the possibility to complain about the violation of the rights set forth in the Convention by one of the state parties (Article 34 ECHR), which excludes the possibility of direct horizontal effect of the Convention.

Indirect horizontal effect entails the interpretation of the law governing private relations in light of the existence of fundamental rights. At the national level, this indirect effect is often effectuated in the context of adjudication through the filling-in of open norms, such as general duties of care, fault requirements, equity and fairness, or of the interpretation of other norms in light of constitutional guarantees. In the context of the ECHR, indirect horizontal effect is typically effectuated

---

165. For a general overview, see van Dijk et al. 2006, 28–32, and cited references. See also Sajó & Uitz 2005.
166. See Gardbaum 2003, 396.

through the recognition of positive obligations on the State to protect the enjoyment of fundamental rights in the sphere of relations between individuals or in cases in which a complaint relates to a conflict between private parties and competing fundamental rights are at stake. In the latter situation, the ECHR's case law calls for a balance to be struck between the right to freedom of expression and a counterbalancing right or interest on the other side, such as the right to private life[167] or the right to property and economic freedom more generally.[168]

The ECtHR's case law relating to Article 8 ECHR contains strong positive obligations to protect the right to private life between individuals. But also in the context of Article 10 ECHR, the Court has recognized positive obligations with regard to the legal governance of horizontal relations. This has come from the recognition of the demands of the 'effective exercise' of the right to freedom of expression, for instance with the following consideration in *Özgür Gündem v. Turkey*:

> Genuine, effective exercise of [the right to freedom of expression] does not depend merely on the State's duty not to interfere, but may require positive measures of protection, even in the sphere of relations between individuals [...].[169]

The most important example of a positive obligation in the European context of freedom of expression is the obligation to promote pluralism, which will be discussed in more detail later in this thesis. This positive obligation is rather general and leaves a lot of room for Member States' interpretations. It can thereby hardly be used to effectuate specific rights in particular contexts. In general, the Court has emphasized the following in its case law relating to the possible existence of positive obligations:

> In determining whether or not a positive obligation exists, regard must be had to the fair balance that has to be struck between the general interest of the community and the interests of the individual, the search for which is inherent throughout the Convention. The scope of this obligation will inevitably vary, having regard to the diversity of situations obtaining in Contracting States, the difficulties involved in policing modern societies and the choices which must be made in terms of priorities and resources. Nor must such an obligation be interpreted in such a way as to impose an impossible or disproportionate burden on the authorities [...].[170]

A specific or strictly delineated positive obligation is absent in the context of Article 10 ECHR. It may therefore be more appropriate in the context of positive obligations under Article 10 ECHR to speak of a fundamental legal principle than a legal obligation. The doctrine of positive obligations to safeguard the effective

---

167. See e.g. ECtHR June 24, 2004, *von Hannover v. Germany*.
168. See e.g. ECtHR May 6, 2003, *Appleby and Others v. the United Kingdom*.
169. ECtHR March 16, 2000, *Özgür Gündem v. Turkey*, § 43.
170. *Ibid.*

exercise of the rights and freedoms under the ECHR thereby also implies that in general, the ECHR can be seen as a set of fundamental legislative principles for the national legislatures. In contrast, the ECtHR's case law on the right to private life as enshrined in Article 8 ECHR does contain more strict positive obligations with regard to horizontal relations. In its recent judgment in *K.U. v. Finland*, for instance, the Court came to the conclusion that a positive obligation existed to facilitate effective criminal procedure against the infringement of Article 8—in the relation between private parties—that had given rise to the complaint.[171] More generally, data privacy regulations in the EU, harmonized in the Privacy Directive (95/46/EC), are sometimes seen as an example of the State fulfilling its positive obligations under Article 8 ECHR to ensure the protection of constitutional guarantees in vertical *and* horizontal relations.[172]

As mentioned above, the horizontal effect of fundamental rights under the ECHR can be translated back to a vertical relationship. It is the State which is ultimately held responsible for the way the application of the 'normal' national law to relations between private parties could interfere with the genuine and effective exercise of the fundamental rights of any of the parties involved.[173] In other words, the question is whether the application of national laws, not directly related to the right to freedom of expression—such as laws giving effect to privacy or property— must be seen as a State act which requires justification.

In other words, both the question of horizontal effect and the question of the possible existence of positive obligations can be seen as an answer to the question of the way public authorities need to be implicated to trigger the protection of fundamental rights and constitutional norms.[174] The U.S.'s answer to this question is the State Action Doctrine. This doctrine, similar in complexity to the doctrine of positive obligations and horizontal effect in Europe, holds that U.S. constitutional rights, in the standard view, do not have direct or indirect horizontal effect. Yet, there are certain exceptions to this general view and United States constitutional law does contain some elements that imply indirect horizontal effect of constitutional guarantees. In *Shelley v. Kraemer*, for instance, the U.S. Supreme Court held that the State court had to be considered a State actor and that an injunction to enforce a contractual agreement not to sell property to African Americans would violate the Equal Protection Clause of the Constitution. The holding is controversial precisely because of its logical implications of indirect horizontal effect; constitutionalism in private law runs counter to the American commitment to the functioning of the free market in the broad sense.[175]

The debate about the role of the State in light of the right to freedom of expression can also be framed as a debate about formal expressive liberty and

---

171. ECtHR December 2, 2008, *K.U. v. Finland*.
172. See Recitals 10 and 11, Directive 95/46/EC, OJ L 281, November 23, 1995.
173. See Tushnet 2003.
174. *Ibid.*, 79–80.
175. *Ibid.*, 81.

equality on the one hand and substantive expressive liberty and equality on the other hand.[176] If one adopts a negative rights conception, substantive differences in expressive liberty, for instance as a result of inequalities of financial means or education, are irrelevant. Both Rupert Murdoch and a homeless person in Paris have similar rights to freedom of expression: If they do publish their views or attempt to access information, public authorities are not allowed to interfere, in the absence of specific exceptional circumstances. If one defends a substantive notion of expressive liberty, pre-existing differences in the ability of parties to enjoy their rights and liberties effectively do matter, to some debatable extent, and should, to that extent, be considered when legally sanctioning conflicts about information flows.

In the rich debates about access to the modern means of communication, many have precisely argued in terms of a more substantive conception of expressive liberty.[177] The ownership of the means of communications in the hands of a few can be seen as a threat to democracy and the effective exercise of the fundamental rights of the great majority of individuals. The privileged few will be able to control and access such means effectively, while others will not. The negative rights conception tends to largely ignore these aspects of the actual state of affairs in society, the baseline allocation, in the context of constitutional review, or considers them as a given. It could be argued that this is exactly what should happen, because of the State's obligation to treat everyone equally before the law. However, the State could, at the same time, be said to be responsible for the substantive material and immaterial inequalities in society because of the assignment and enforcement of other legal entitlements such as property rights and its educational policy. It is the State itself that helps create, further develops and enforces the baseline allocation in society through its general laws and policies.[178]

The question of the proper role of government under freedom of expression will either explicitly or implicitly involve an answer to this fundamental debate about the character of the right to freedom of expression. Hence in the chapters that follow, the discussion about the implications of the right to freedom of expression will be tied to these differences from time to time.[179] In particular, the analysis will not be restricted to freedom of expression as a negative right but will also consider arguments that point to a possible or even necessary positive role of government.

The reasons for this are threefold. First, the law itself does go beyond freedom of expression as a negative right, in particular in the European context. Second, the

---

176. For a discussion, see Balkin 1990.
177. See e.g. Barron 1967.
178. See e.g. Tushnet 2008, 101. In U.S. legal theory, this line of reasoning goes back to legal realist Hale. See Hale 1923.
179. There is another reason why the question about the attribution and scrutiny of the baseline allocation is of particular relevance in the context of search engines. This reason is that search engine law mostly takes place through the application of the general applicable laws which are typically associated with baseline conditions, thereby obscuring the possible restrictive impact on communicative liberties.

predominantly private law context of the Internet raises the question about substantive expressive liberties and a possible positive, facilitative role of government and the need to recognize the importance of a sphere free of undue State interference. Finally, a more substantive view of expressive rights and liberties does take these rights and liberties more seriously and does not seek to do justice by declaring the proper context in which the relevant actors operate irrelevant.

4.4.2.   THE ROLE OF GOVERNMENT UNDER FREEDOM OF EXPRESSION AND
            DIFFERENT 'MEANS OF COMMUNICATION'

Rather than studying the implications of freedom of expression in isolated instances of speech and communication more generally, the analysis that follows will focus on the role of certain providers of communications and information services in the public information environment. Central to this focus is the conceptualization of this public information environment as consisting of a range of communicative processes between speakers and audiences. These communicative processes are mediated through various communication infrastructures and the entities that provide or control them. For instance, print technology gave rise to publishers, newspapers and distributing entities such as the postal services, libraries or book sellers. The Internet and the World Wide Web gave rise to a range of new intermediaries, such as Internet access providers, message board operators, hosting providers, social networks and search engines.

By studying and analyzing freedom of expression doctrine for traditional or more established means of communication, the foundation for an answer regarding the implications of freedom of expression for the governance of search engines will be laid down. Hence, the following chapters will study the implications of freedom of expression for the communicative processes in the context of three distinct speech-carrying intermediaries, namely the press, the Internet access provider and the library. The reasons for this selection will be discussed below. In each instance, the answers to the following questions will be addressed: In what ways and on what grounds is the governance and government involvement with regard to these entities informed by the right to freedom of expression? What are the typical actions or issues that have called for an evaluation of the proper role of government under freedom of expression doctrine? And what is the position of information providers/speakers and end-users/listeners/readers if the entity is conceptualized as a speech intermediating institution?

4.4.3.   WHAT ACTIONS AND WHICH ISSUES ARE (STILL) RELEVANT UNDER
            FREEDOM OF EXPRESSION?

If one looks at the history of freedom of expression doctrine, it has developed from a normative theory about specific types of restrictive State actions such as licensing and censorship to a more general theory about the right to express, impart, receive information and ideas and the governance of information flows in society.[180] As such, the right to freedom of expression not only informs the legitimacy of certain legal restrictions on speakers and publishers, but also the rights of audiences and distributors and the rights and obligations between non-government entities. The analysis of the typical implications of freedom of expression for the press, Internet access providers and libraries, and of the primary stakeholders in these contexts will help reveal the extent to which certain actions and related conflicts are relevant from the perspective of freedom of expression and how the different freedom of expression interests of the parties involved have shaped this answer.

In a linguistic sense, Article 10 ECHR delineates quite literally the type of actions which are protected, namely the freedom to receive and impart information and ideas. Freedom of expression and information in the broad sense protects all kinds of communicative actions, including the right to transmit information freely. The same is true for the First Amendment.[181] This focus on the freedom to communicate in different ways and capacities means that one could simply zoom in on the various communications that are taking place, identify the typical restrictions on these communications and discuss their legal legitimacy. But such an endeavor would be too limited for a number of reasons.

First, not all kinds of communications are protected by the right to freedom of expression, and certainly not in the same way. Freedom of expression tends to protect the actions which have come to be seen as legally meaningful from the perspective of freedom of expression theory.[182] Typical examples of such actions which are considered to be of particular importance are the right of citizens to speak about matters of public concern, the editorial freedom of newspapers to decide which articles to print on the front page, the right to publish information without asking the authorities for permission, or the right of the citizen to read and inform himself. Thus, to conceptualize the scope of freedom of expression in the context of search engine governance, it will be most fruitful to try to reach a characterization of the 'typical' scope of what is actually protected under the right to freedom of expression.

Second, not only communicative actions but also actions that are indirectly linked to communication can be protected under the right to freedom of expression. For instance, the right to freedom of expression also protects the freedom to decide how to use the means to communicate. For example, a restriction on the freedom to decide to whom a theatre can be rented for public performances can be an infringement.[183] As we will see in Chapter 5, it can also protect media against

---

180. For historic background of the ECHR, see e.g. Matscher & Petzold 1988. For the United States, see Stone et al. 2008, 3–8.
181. For a discussion of *Griswold*, see also section 5.5.1.
182. See e.g. Schauer 2004.
183. It is interesting to note that the legal protection of the substance of theatre performances under the right to freedom of expression in the Netherlands is only a relatively recent phenomenon. Before 1977, the municipal authorities could censor theatre performances. See de Meij 1996, 26–27.

special restrictive legal treatment, such as discriminatory taxation.[184] In other words, the scope of freedom of expression includes actions that are only indirectly related to communication but facilitate its exercise or are a necessary part for various actors to exercise it.

Third, what ends up being protected under the right to freedom of expression will, in many ways, be connected to the normative theories underlying the right to freedom of expression. The end-user's freedom to receive information and ideas freely and become an informed citizen is considered to be worth protecting because of the importance of informed citizens in a democratic society and their autonomy as human beings. In a similar vein, as the analysis of press freedom, ISP freedom and library freedom in Chapters 5 to 7 will show, the protection of these entities under Article 10 ECHR strongly takes into account their 'societal role'. For instance, the function of the press as a public watchdog and as a platform for debate about matters of public concern implies strong protection for the press: producing and selecting the conversations that are to be part of the public debate, in a manner that is 'uninhibited, robust and wide-open' as formulated by the U.S. Supreme Court in *Sullivan*.[185] In the case of ISPs, freedom of expression theory emphasizes the protection of the interests of end-users and information providers precisely because of the relatively passive intermediary role of ISPs. In sum, the right to freedom of expression helps protect the 'public freedom of expression interest' in the free dissemination of information and ideas. To the extent that new institutions and players, such as search engines, act according to a societal interest in their functioning relating to the underlying ideals of freedom of expression theory, they should receive proper protection. The question is how this public freedom of expression interest in the context of search engines should be conceptualized.

When answering the question about such public interest, it should also be kept in mind that it would be wrong to make freedom of expression fully instrumental to a particular conception of the public interest in the free circulation of information, knowledge and ideas. There is no agreement between legal theorists, or others for that matter, as to the definition of such a conception. The law, in turn, has referred to different public interests, derived from the theories discussed above, underlying freedom of expression, but it has also protected the right to freedom of expression independently. To state it differently, freedom of expression can be seen as having both a public interest component, which takes the fundamental right as a societal ordering principle in view of high order public interests such as the functioning of democracy, and a state-free sphere for the individual perspective, in which individuals and other private actors should, to some debatable extent, be allowed to exercise their rights freely, without reference to a public good.

---

184. See section 5.2.
185. *New York Times Co. v. Sullivan*, 376 U.S. 254 (1964).

4.4.4.   SELECTION OF THE PRESS, INTERNET ACCESS PROVIDERS
              AND LIBRARIES

There are a number of traditional regulatory models and relating theories of freedom of expression for different media and modes of communications. These
include, for instance, the model for the press, the model for common carriers
such as post and telephony communications and the model for broadcasting. Freedom of expression has played an important role in the development of these regulatory models. As we will see in more detail below, the distinction in particular
between distributors and publishers has important consequences for freedom of
expression.

Of special importance in media and telecommunications policy research is the
traditional layered mode, consisting of infrastructure, transmission/distribution
and content. As discussed in Chapter 3, these layers have also served as a conceptual regulatory model in the context of the Internet and the World Wide Web. If we
look at the role of Web search engines in the communicative process, they are
information services themselves, providing information *about information*, so they
can be studied from the perspective of regulatory models in the content layer. But
because they are meta-media and a functional prerequisite for effective navigation
online, they intimately relate to the transport layer as well. The principal value of
search engines is that they mediate effectively between searchers and information
providers, making up for the lack of navigational structure in the hyperlinked
environment that is the World Wide Web.

By selecting the press and Internet access providers both perspectives are taken
into account: transport and content. Since from the perspective of information flows
search engines seem to have characteristics of distributors as well as those of publishers or editors, a publishing intermediary as well as a distributing and transport-related
intermediary have been selected for further analysis. The press and press freedom
serves as the subject for studying the implications of freedom of expression for
publishers. Internet access providers and the discussion about their role with regard
to the regulation of content flows and the question of filtering have been selected as
the subject for studying the implications of freedom of expression for distributors
and common carriers.

The study of the implications of the right to freedom of expression for Internet
access providers is also used to provide insight into the regulatory model for media
and communications on the Internet more generally. For the same reason, some of
the recent developments with regard to the press and libraries that are related to the
particular dynamics of the Internet and digitization will be addressed in Chapters 5
and 7. Although the emergence of new communication technologies does not
necessarily imply that fundamental starting points of media and telecommunications law and policy have to be changed, the Internet has been the cause of a
number of shifts and particular regulatory and conceptual problems. Convergence,
self-publishing opportunities and the exponential growth of publicly accessible
material, new applications such as peer-to-peer, automation and governance
through technology, and the absence of effective points of control for traditional

77

modes of content regulation, are amongst those issues that call for a reassessment of existing starting points. These developments have left governments and others in search of new ideas about and effective modes of fulfilling their proper role.[186]

The implications of the right to freedom of expression for the legal governance of public libraries is also studied for a different reason. They have been a dominant institution in making accessible the existing knowledge products in our society. In fact, it is in the context of the library and library science in the broad sense that most of the ideas about the ordering and cataloguing of knowledge have been developed. Web search engines are newcomers in this field. They provide extremely successful services in a field where the library has held a relatively dominant societal position for a long time.

The strong degree of government involvement in the establishment, functioning and governance of public libraries makes it interesting to contrast with the situation of Web search services. The public library is a public organization, publicly funded for reasons that suggest a strong role of government in providing access to ideas and information and educating the public. By studying the governance of libraries, the freedom of expression implications that relate to a government- funded information institution can be revealed. These are mostly absent when looking at the press and Internet access providers, because their provision does not depend on the State and has been left to the market.

---

186. Independent of the governmental regulatory reorientation relating to the arrival of the global networked information facilitated by the Internet, the role of government as a regulator and policy maker has shifted more generally over the last two decades through privatization, globalization and a strong focus on market ordering.

Chapter 5

Press Freedom

5.1. INTRODUCTION

In this chapter, the legal concept of press freedom—the implications of the right to freedom of expression for the governance of the press—will be discussed, as will as some of the elements of press freedom doctrine that are of particular interest for this study about the governance of Web search engines. The analysis is mostly focused on the press, understood as the newspaper industry, and the legal arrangements relating to the societal production and organization of a public debate about matters of public concern. Sometimes, mass media more generally and broadcasting will be discussed in passing, but the particular regulatory model for broadcast media will not be addressed. The reason for this exclusion is partly found in the need to restrict the analysis, but also in the extraordinary constitutional position of broadcasting regulation and the application of the regulatory model for the press for online media.

This chapter will first address the following general questions relating to press freedom: What is the proper role of government with regard to the press given freedom of expression and on what grounds? And how is that proper role reflected in the regulatory framework of the press, which tends to rely on the professional ethics of journalism and self-regulation? The analysis will discuss these issues in relation to Article 10 ECHR and in relation to the First Amendment. In addition to the question about the position of the press under the right to freedom of expression and about the way press freedom has been (partly) construed as an instrumental freedom to serve citizens and potential speakers, section 5.3 will discuss the doctrine of prior restraints on the press and the duties and responsibilities of the media. In section 5.4, the debate about the possibility to grant access rights to the press for potential speakers will be discussed, as well as the concept and protection of the press' editorial freedom. Section 5.5 will discuss the relationship between the press and its readers by looking more closely at the public's right to inform itself, the protection of commercial publications and advertising in the media, and the issue of readers' privacy.

If there is any institution that is historically linked to the fundamental right to freedom of expression, it is the press. To a considerable extent, the right to freedom of expression in its current form is the result of centuries-long struggles about the legal governance of the press and about the evolved uses and societal practices of it with regard to the publication of information and ideas after the invention of print technology in the fifteenth century.[187] The printing press helped lower the barriers for the dissemination of information and ideas enormously and ultimately offered opportunities to much broader groups of people than just the clergy previously, to publish and distribute Bibles, books, pamphlets, posters, newspapers, journals and other printed materials.

In the context of press freedom, the focus is usually placed on the periodical press and newspapers in particular and, to a lesser extent, on the publication of books. As the platform for political debate about matters of public concern, the periodical press occupies a central political and cultural position in society, a position which has earned it the title 'the Fourth Estate'. And more than any other institution in the public information environment, the press has contributed to freedom of expression doctrine. The wide circulation of newspapers began after the inventions of offset printing around 1800. Large-scale advertising arrived later in the nineteenth century. Advertising would provide significant additional income to the press beyond the revenues it previously received merely from subscriptions and news-stand sales to readers. The industrialization of the press turned news-papers into a mass medium and led to significant concentration of the market due to high entry barriers.

As the periodical press never functioned in isolation, the governance of other links in the chain of getting news from the press and its sources to its reader has always mattered a great deal to the functioning of the press. Historically, the postal services and the telegraph were of particular importance for the functioning of the press and newspapers. Postal services were used to distribute publications and the telegraph was a primary means for gathering news and making it possible to print in multiple locations. More recently, the Internet has reshaped the news industry and continues to do so. The electronic publishing industry depends on being carried by Internet access providers and other online intermediaries such as search engines to reach an audience.

Over the last decade, digitization and convergence of media on the Internet have had disruptive effects on the press and its business models. Notable developments include a decline in subscription-based journalism online and offline, heavy competition for advertisements, and the rise of self-publishing, citizen journalism and blogging. Online newspapers now publish a continuously updated set of articles and include audio-visual material. They can personalize their offering

---

187. See Starr 2004, Eisenstein 1979, McLuhan 1962, de Sola Pool 1983, Barendt 2005, Nieuwenhuis 1991, Hemels 1969.

according to the interests of particular readers, target the advertisements that are being placed next to their editorial content, facilitate interaction with and between readers, and make the material available not only on a website but also through other means such as email, RSS-feeds (Really Simple Syndication) and mobile applications. Wikileaks is an important and widely debated example of a new journalistic phenomenon, in which people who are not journalists in the strict sense aggressively publish secrets and which also presents a particularly interesting perspective on the attitude of the traditional news industry towards new journalistic models and practices that have arisen in the networked information environment.[188]

The traditional press' transition to the digital environment has not been a success for all. An oft-heard concern, from the perspective of the quality of the news environment, is the mass lay-off of journalists by newspapers.[189] Convergence between different media means that traditionally separated markets for news are increasingly overlapping. The same news reports, whether in text, images or audio-visual content, are published on online newspapers, websites of broadcasters and other online destinations, all of which compete for audiences as a result. New players have emerged in the value chain, including news aggregators and search engines, which both help electronic publishers reach an audience but also compete with them—rather successfully—for advertising revenue. As a result of the decreased barriers to entry, access to worldwide publishing for information providers has probably never been as widespread as it is now. At the same time, some of the bottlenecks in communication have simply shifted to other places, because not everyone can communicate to everyone.

5.2.   THE REGULATORY FRAMEWORK FOR THE PRESS

Compared to other media and means of communication, regulatory involvement with the press is now minimal.[190] This was not always the case. In fact, the concept of freedom of expression is intimately tied to historical instances of government involvement with the press and print media in general. Its progressive acknowledgement in national constitutions and international fundamental right instruments has come to shield the press against different types of involvement by public authorities. The motives for government involvement with the press include not only the interest to control public debate, the will to influence public opinion, the protection of general State interests such as State secrets, the protection against negative publicity, the protection of specific private interests, the protection of the impartiality of the judiciary and the upholding of respect for the courts and public authority more generally, but also the support of the institutional structure for public debate in line with the ideal of democracy.

---

188. See Benkler 2011.
189. See e.g. Baker 2009a, Baker 2009b.
190. For an overview, see Nieuwenhuis 1991.

After the abolishment of the practice of press licensing and systematic censorship of the press, other measures such as the taxation of press-related services have been used to influence the press. There are examples of tax exemption for publishers and the press, and the regulation of tariffs for the necessary use of transport and distribution channels, which were often in the hands of State monopolies. It is notable that the traditional State monopolies earlier found in radio and television broadcasting throughout Europe, or in relation to postal mail, telegraphy and telephone services, are absent in the case of the press. An early example of special press taxation is the stamp tax introduced by the British Government in 1712. This tax on printed items was a replacement of the licensing scheme for printing presses and structured in a way that would be a heavy burden on the newspaper press.[191]

In the nineteenth century, the opposite became public policy in the United States. The U.S. exempted publishers and newspapers from certain taxes and the press' use of the postal system was subsidized.[192] Such positive State aid with regard to the press and media in general became commonplace in the twentieth century. However, positive State involvement has to be carefully structured to be compatible with the demands of a free press. Subsidization of the press, for instance, is not in line with the freedom of the press if it subsidizes discriminatorily, in terms of viewpoints and content in particular.[193] The recent discussions about the government's role with regard to the failing newspaper industry have again brought the limitations on possible government involvement to the fore.[194]

In the second half of the twentieth century, it became accepted that the State may have a role in preventing too much concentration in the press and the media in general.[195] In the interest of pluralism, media, including print media, are usually not only subject to general competition law, as any other commercial undertaking, but also to special media concentration and cross-ownership rules and policies.[196] Concentration of media outlets in the hands of a few would undermine pluralism and diversity, of which, according to the ECtHR, the State is the ultimate guarantor.[197] Therefore, a press and media policy aimed at preserving the conditions necessary for a pluralist press can be seen as a reflection of the right to freedom of expression and not as an interference with the press' constitutionally protected freedom.[198]

The current regulatory model for the press consists of a framework of generally applicable laws in combination with self-regulation. Relevant said laws for the press are for instance defamation law, privacy law and copyright law. Sector-specific press laws are rare. Exceptions are anti-concentration regulation in

---

191. See Starr 2004, 38–39.
192. See *ibid.*, 125–126.
193. See Nieuwenhuis 1991, 157–161.
194. For a discussion, in the context of the Netherlands, see Nieuwenhuis 2009.
195. See Nieuwenhuis 1991.
196. See Nieuwenhuis 1991. For a discussion of pluralism and diversity, see Valcke 2003; Nieuwenhuis 2007.
197. ECtHR November 24, 1993, *Informationsverein Lentia v. Austria*, § 38. See also section 5.5.1.
198. See Nieuwenhuis 1991.

view of preserving pluralism in the public information environment and, in some countries, right of reply statutes.[199]

The self-regulation of the press can be subdivided into a professional ethics component on the one hand, and—in some countries—a formalized component on the other hand. In the journalistic profession and the governance of the press activities, the professional ethics of journalism have an important role. The responsibility for ethical treatment of sources, subjects, targets and the public are considered to be part of this.[200] In many countries, self-regulation through the professional ethics of journalism is complemented with a formalized self-regulatory structure for the press, sometimes in the form of codes of conduct, either for specific newspapers or industry-wide. Self-regulation for the press can also include the establishment of a press council dealing with complaints regarding publications. Historically, press self-regulation in Europe was formalized in the first decades after World War II, mostly as a reaction to threats from governments that legislation would be passed otherwise.[201]

It is important to note that journalistic ethics are not carved in stone and have always been the subject of debate, because journalistic ethics vary across media and between individual journalists. Because of new and uncontrolled entry into the publishing market on the Internet, online publishers are a diverse crowd. This has put the existing self-regulatory structures under pressure and incidentally given rise to new self-regulatory initiatives such as a blogger code of conduct. Some new publishers are precisely motivated by a perceived failing in the functioning of the traditional press. Other newcomers seem to denounce journalistic ethics completely. As Yochai Benkler argues, after a detailed analysis of the media storm surrounding Wikileaks in 2010 and early 2011, "'professionalism' and 'responsibility' can be found on both sides of the divide, as can unprofessionalism and irresponsibility."[202] Finally, it is important to note that some new online journalistic practices arise from completely different professional backgrounds. Platforms for collaborative filtering, such as Reddit, fulfill some of the filtering functions that used to be performed by journalists. The same may, in some ways, be said for the phenomenon of Web search engines. However, these services are staffed with engineers, writing and tweaking algorithms to support their services instead of journalists chasing stories, and they act in rather different professional traditions.

For these reasons, attempts to *legally* define who can or should be viewed as a journalist on the basis of a certain set of professional standards are difficult and tend to be controversial, because of the freedom of expression and the need for free

---

199. For a discussion of right of reply statutes and their permissibility under the right to freedom of expression in the United States and Europe, see section 5.4.2.
200. See Ward 2006. See also Verdoodt 2007.
201. See Tambini et al. 2008, 64–89, and cited references.
202. Benkler 2011.

entry to journalistic practice.[203] In the context of Article 10 ECHR, the duties and responsibilities tied to the exercise of the right to freedom of expression are linked to journalistic ethics. The doctrine of duties and responsibilities will be discussed later in this chapter, as well as the question of a possible privileged position of the press and journalists under the right to freedom of expression.

The EU's regulatory involvement with the press is minimal. EU media policy is mostly directed at audio-visual media through internal market regulations. Involvement in the field of the press is mostly limited to concerns over pluralism and diversity. Notably, the difficulties of continuing to make a defendable distinction between regulated and unregulated services on the basis of traditional broadcasting regulation are starting to show in the European context of the audio-visual media services directive's treatment of online on-demand services.[204] Convergence between different types of media and the rapidly changing realities of audio-visual media production and consumption raise fundamental questions about the way the degree of legitimate regulatory involvement under the right to freedom of expression depends upon the type of media involved.

As mentioned, in the subject of media pluralism, more generally, some activity takes place in the European context which touches upon the press as well. The legal basis for EU activity in the field of media pluralism is found in the positive obligation of the State to guarantee media pluralism. Quite specifically, the European Parliament has repeatedly expressed its concern over media ownership and control in Italy. In addition, the European Commission recently launched an initiative regarding media pluralism in the Member States,[205] which has resulted in a study on indicators for media pluralism,[206] and the establishment of a High Level Group on Media Freedom and Pluralism.[207] The study on indicators for media pluralism will be discussed in more detail in Chapter 10, since it contains a reference to the question of making Web search engines part of an analysis of media pluralism.[208]

5.3.   FREEDOM OF EXPRESSION AND THE PRESS

The judgments of the ECtHR and the U.S. Supreme Court on the implications of the right to freedom of expression for the press are amongst their most famous judgments. Whereas freedom of expression applies to natural persons, the press and others alike, the ECtHR has emphasized the protection of the press under

---

203. In the Netherlands, for instance, the recent delineation of the media exception in the context of the data protection laws by the Dutch Data Protection Authority and the delineation of the group of persons to be able to claim protection of confidentiality of sources led to such a debate. See Dutch Data Protection Authority 2007.
204. See Valcke & Stevens 2007, 285–302.
205. European Commission 2007a.
206. Valcke et al. 2009.
207. European Commission 2011.
208. See section 10.2 in particular.

Article 10, underlining the role of the press in a democratic society. In particular, the ECtHR has tied the protection of the press to its task of informing the public. The following section is a short overview of the case law of the ECtHR and the U.S. Supreme Court on press freedom. The questions that will be answered are the following: What is the scope of Article 10 ECHR and the First Amendment in the context of the press? Is there any special protection of the press and, if so, on what grounds is this extra protection afforded? More specifically, the way press freedom is informed by the freedom of expression interests of its readers and possible speakers will be addressed. There will also be a discussion of the doctrine of prior restraint on the press and on the duties and responsibilities tied to the exercise of the right to freedom of expression by Article 10, second paragraph.

5.3.1.   STATUS OF THE PRESS UNDER THE RIGHT
           TO FREEDOM OF EXPRESSION

In the context of Article 10 ECHR, the European Court of Human Rights has consistently tied the special status of the press not to a particular institutional delineation of the press or journalists, but to their role in society and their contributions to ideals underlying freedom of expression. The decisive factor for any special protection or status under Article 10 ECHR is that there is a contribution to the public debate on matters of general public interest.[209] Whereas a newspaper or a professional journalist might more easily claim to be making such a contribution because of its widely accepted role in society, there is no reason why ordinary citizens or other entities would not be entitled to claim a similar contribution, as long as they have contributed to the underlying goals of Article 10 ECHR. In line with this inclusive interpretation of press freedom as public debate freedom, the Court has applied the special standards it developed for the press to other parties such as 'small and informal campaign groups,' or 'groups and individuals outside the mainstream.'[210]

The special status of—but not restricted to—the press and journalists under Article 10 ECHR plays out in particular in the context of the admissibility of interferences. The level of judicial scrutiny will be high and the margin of appreciation of the Member States in the context of the press is limited.[211] In general, when dealing with the press, the test of Article 10, second paragraph will be applied most restrictively by the Court, as follows:

> The most careful scrutiny on the part of the Court is called for when, as in the present case, the measures taken or sanctions imposed by the national

209. For a discussion, see Voorhoof 2008a.
210. ECtHR February 15, 2005, *Steel and Morris v. the United Kingdom*, § 89. See also ECtHR April 14, 2009, *Társaság a Szabadságjogokért v. Hungary*.
211. See ECtHR December 10, 2007, *Stoll v. Switzerland*, § 105 ("Where freedom of the 'press' is at stake, the authorities have only a limited margin of appreciation to decide whether a 'pressing social need' exists").

authority are capable of discouraging the participation of the press in debates over matters of legitimate public concern [. . .].[212]

This will be different in the case of interferences with publications of ideas and information which do not contribute to the public debate about matters of general public interest, such as communications of a commercial nature, or about the private life of individuals.[213]

It can be concluded from the Court's case law on the protection of publications under the right to freedom of expression that hardly anything is excluded from the scope of Article 10 ECHR, first paragraph. The actual legal protection under Article 10 ECHR will depend on the weight that is contributed to the protected matter or action, which will subsequently play out in the context of the permissibility of interferences under Article 10, second paragraph. As mentioned, restrictions of publications on matters of public concern result in stricter scrutiny by the Court as well as a strictly limited margin of appreciation. However, one should note that in many cases the right to freedom of expression will have to be balanced against a countervailing fundamental right, such as the right to private life of Article 8 ECHR.

Information, ideas, facts and value judgments are all protected under Article 10, as well as the form in and means by which they are being communicated. But in terms of their protection, the Court tends to make a distinction between facts and value judgments, because the latter cannot be proven right or wrong. This also implies that a legal requirement to prove an opinion can by itself be an infringement of Article 10.[214] Notwithstanding this general difference, value statements without some factual support for them can be excessive, in which case they may be legitimately restricted if called for.[215] The Court has acknowledged the difficulty of making a strict distinction.[216]

That Article 10 ECHR does provide additional protection of information and ideas in general can be seen in the ECtHR's judgment in *Sunday Times*. Here, the Court restated its conclusions from *Handyside* that freedom of expression constitutes one of the essential foundations of a democratic society and is applicable "not only to information or ideas that are favorably received or regarded as inoffensive or as a matter of indifference, but also to those that offend, shock or disturb the State or any sector of the population."[217] It went on to conclude that "[t]hese principles are of particular importance as far as the press is concerned."[218]

The reference to 'legitimate public concern' in the Court's case law, also denoted by 'public interest' or 'general interest', raises the question about the

---

212. See ECtHR May 20, 1999, *Bladet Tromsø and Stansaas v. Norway*, § 64.
213. For a discussion of the protection of commercial speech under Article 10 ECHR, see Randall 2006. See also Van Dijk et al. 2006, 800–801; Sakulin 2010, 122–126, 144–151.
214. See ECtHR February 15, 2005, *Steel and Morris v. United Kingdom*, § 87.
215. *Ibid.*, § 87.
216. See e.g. ECtHR May 27, 2004, *Vides Aizsardzibas Klubs v. Lettonie*, § 43.
217. ECtHR April 26, 1979, *Sunday Times v. the United Kingdom*, § 65.
218. *Ibid.*

scope of this concept. The Court has addressed this question mostly parenthetically, without providing much substantive guidance. It has made distinctions between the substantive merits of types of speech, such as commercial speech and political speech, of which the latter carries more weight under the Convention. It has delineated the reporting about public officials from the reporting of details about private individuals, because in the former case the press exercises its vital role of *watchdog* whereas it does not in the latter. This sometimes necessitates a substantive judgment on the merits of particular publications, such as in the case of *Von Hannover* about the balancing of privacy and speech interests. There the Court declared that the publications about the Princess of Monaco were insufficient from its public interest perspective, which is strongly linked to democratic ideals, as follows:

> the publication [. . .] in question, the sole purpose of which was to satisfy the curiosity of a particular readership regarding the details of the applicant's private life, cannot be deemed to contribute to any debate of general interest to society despite the applicant being known to the public [. . .].[219]

The best suggestion for a general guiding principle underlying the general or public interest in the context of Article 10 ECHR, and the press more generally, is provided by the democratic theory discussed in Chapter 4. However, the notion of public interest or general interest under Article 10 ECHR remains relatively undefined.[220]

In contrast to Article 10 ECHR, the text of the First Amendment contains an explicit reference to the protection of the press, apart from the more general freedom of speech. Some have read this as meaning that the organized press should receive special protection under the First Amendment.[221] The explicit reference to freedom of the press in the First Amendment would be redundant otherwise and the freedom of the press is argued to be a structural provision guaranteeing that the press as an institution, independent of government, would serve as an additional check on the three branches of government.[222]

The U.S. Supreme Court has never endorsed the view that the organized press holds special constitutional privileges and has construed the right to free speech and the freedom of the press in the First Amendment to exist irrespective of whether the circumstances concerned a member of the organized press or another organization or individual.[223] It decided most clearly against special constitutional privileges of the organized press in *Hayes*, wherein it decided that there is no special guarantee for access to information for the organized press that is not

---

219. ECtHR June 24, 2004, *Von Hannover v. Germany*, § 65.
220. See e.g. Sanderson 2004.
221. See Stewart 1975, Lange 1975, Nimmer 1975.
222. Stewart 1975, 633–634.
223. The view was explicitly denounced by Justice Burger in his Concurring Opinion in *National Bank of Boston*. See *First National Bank of Boston v. Bellotti*, 435 U.S. 765, 796 (1978).

available to the public generally.[224] The organized press also receives no special immunity from the application of general laws.[225] If we look at the Court's case law, some First Amendment's standards for the press, such as the 'Times-Gertz-standard' for defamation, typically involve the highest scrutiny. They do not necessarily require that the publication originates from the press, but that it involves matters of public concern.[226] The Supreme Court concluded that speech "concerning public affairs is more than self-expression; it is the essence of self-government" and occupies the "highest rung of the hierarchy of First Amendment values."[227] Thus, insofar as the periodical press reports on public affairs it can claim the highest protection possible, which is comparable to the situation under Article 10 ECHR. As mentioned above, the organized press is, in practice, most likely to be able to claim protection under this standard.

One substantive difference between press freedom under the First Amendment and Article 10 ECHR is the priority of free speech under the American Constitution in comparison with other values. As a result, under certain conditions the First Amendment provides speakers, publishers and the press with significantly more protection, for instance against defamatory false statements of fact.[228] In *New York Times Co. v. Sullivan*, a police chief sued the New York Times newspaper for false statements of fact in an editorial advertisement by an African American civil rights group.[229] The police chief asserted that the advertisement contained several falsehoods regarding his role in civil rights protests. The Supreme Court concluded that the First Amendment required that there must be proof that a false statement relating to the conduct of a public official must be

---

224. *Branzburg v. Hayes*, 408 U.S. 665 (1972). For a recent discussion of the journalist's privilege under the First Amendment, see Papandrea 2007.

225. *Associated Press v. NLRB*, 301 U.S. 103 (1937) (mentioning libel laws, contempt of court, antitrust laws, taxation, and applying laws relating to organized labor). See also *Cohen v. Cowles* 501 U.S. 663, 670 (1991). In particular, the First Amendment does not protect news agencies against an antitrust action if they violate the Sherman Act by restricting the dissemination of news and reports by members and non-members. See *Associated Press v. United States*, 326 U.S. 1, 20 (1945). ("[The First] Amendment rests on the assumption that the widest possible dissemination of information from diverse and antagonistic sources is essential to the welfare of the public, that a free press is a condition of a free society. Surely a command that the government itself shall not impede the free flow of ideas does not afford nongovernmental combinations a refuge if they impose restraints upon that constitutionally guaranteed freedom. Freedom to publish means freedom for all, and not for some. Freedom to publish is guaranteed by the Constitution, but freedom to combine to keep others from publishing is not. Freedom of the press from governmental interference under the First Amendment does not sanction repression of that freedom by private interests. The First Amendment affords not the slightest support for the contention that a combination to restrain trade in news and views has any constitutional immunity.") See also Citizen *Publishing Co. v. United States*, 394 U.S. 131, 139–140 (1969).

226. *Dun & Bradstreet, Inc. v. Greenmoss Builders*, 472 U.S. 749 (1985) (Concluding that the Gertz standard does not apply to publications that are not of public concern, such as credit reporting about businesses).

227. *Dun & Bradstreet, Inc. v. Greenmoss Builders*, 472 U.S. 749, 759 (1985).

228. See Anderson 1975.

229. It is worth noting that the paid-for nature of the publication was not of concern. See also section 5.3.2 and section 8.4.3.

"made with 'actual malice'—that is, with knowledge that it is false or with reckless disregard of whether it was false or not" for it to be constitutionally permissible to punish its publication.[230] In its opinion, the Court relied on a variety of fundamental concerns underlying freedom of expression, and in particular referred to the dangers of chilling effects and self-censorship that would arise from a weaker standard for defamatory publications. It stated that "debate on public issues should be uninhibited, robust, and wide-open."[231] It also concluded that "[e]rroneous speech is inevitable, if the First Amendment freedoms are to have the breathing space they need to survive."[232] This willingness to err in favor of free speech, which is also implied by the chilling effect doctrine, is characteristic of First Amendment doctrine.[233]

The standard was later extended to speech about public figures.[234] In *Gertz*, the Supreme Court clarified that the strict 'actual malice' standard for false statements of fact does not apply to statements about private parties. Such speech does not relate to matters of public concern, and for this reason the state's interest to protect individuals against defamatory falsehood is greater.[235] Under the First Amendment there is no such thing as a false idea, but false statements of fact are low-level speech.[236] The reason for the protection of false statements of fact against punishment under an actual malice standard is found in the importance of robust debate. Again, the possible chilling effects of legal interferences with unprotected or low-level speech can make them impermissible under the First Amendment.[237] Relying on *Sullivan*, the Supreme Court has concluded that speech concerning public figures and officials may be provocative and intended to cause emotional distress but cannot be punished in the absence of 'actual malice'.[238] For these reasons, parodies which involve false statements of facts that cannot reasonably be believed to involve the subject of parody, receive First Amendment

---

230. *New York Times v. Sullivan*, 376 U.S. 254, 265–292 (1964).
231. *New York Times v. Sullivan*, 376 U.S. 254, 270 (1964).
232. *New York Times v. Sullivan*, 376 U.S. 254, 271 (1964).
233. See also Schauer 1978.
234. *Curtis Publishing Co. v. Butts, Associated Press v. Walker*, 388 U.S. 130 (1967).
235. *Gertz v. Robert Welch, Inc.*, 418 U.S. 323, 347–348 (1974). ("So long as states do not impose liability without fault, the states may define for themselves the appropriate standard of liability for a publisher or broadcaster of defamatory falsehood injurious to a private individual and whose substance makes substantial danger to reputation apparent.")
236. See *Gertz v. Robert Welch, Inc.*, 418 U.S. 323, 339–340 (1974). (Clarifying that "under the First Amendment, there is no such thing as a false idea. However pernicious an opinion may seem, we depend for its correction not on the conscience of judges and juries, but on the competition of other ideas." And "although the erroneous statement of fact is not worthy of constitutional protection, it is nevertheless inevitable in free debate.")
237. For a discussion of the proper boundaries of judicial review in these contexts, see Note 1969, Note 1970.
238. *Hustler Magazine v. Falwell*, 485 U.S. 46 (1988). ("The sort of robust political debate encouraged by the First Amendment is bound to produce speech that is critical of [public officials and public figures]. Such criticism, inevitably, will not always be reasoned or moderate; public figures as well as public officials will be subject to 'vehement, caustic, and sometimes unpleasantly sharp attacks.'")

protection even if the speech is patently offensive and is intended to inflict emotional injury.[239]

The 'Times-Gertz' standard is a characteristic feature of the U.S. free speech doctrine and much stronger than the protection afforded by Article 10 ECHR. Under Article 10 ECHR, it is permitted for national law to require that statements of fact must be substantiated and consistent emphasis is placed on 'reliability' in the context of the media's duties and responsibilities. The notion of duties and responsibilities tied to the exercise of the right to freedom of expression, which will be discussed below, is completely absent in U.S. freedom of expression doctrine.

5.3.2.　　　Article 10 ECHR and the Press' Role in Serving the Interests of Speakers and Readers

Although the press can be seen as the actual source of publicity, meaning that the press is of course a speaker itself, it is at the same time a mediating institution between other possible speakers and readers. The question is to what extent press freedom takes into account the contribution of the press to the realization of the communicative interests of these other stakeholders. The answer is that it does so to a considerable extent both under Article 10 ECHR and also in the U.S. context.

Press doctrine under Article 10 ECHR refers to the communicative interests of all three primary stakeholders: the press itself, its readers, and to possible speakers who can find an audience through the press. First and foremost, the Court has tied the special status of the press under Article 10 ECHR to the interests of readers and the public in general. In addition, the Court has also emphasized the importance of press freedom because of the press' intermediary role in disseminating the statements and ideas of others to an audience. Both lines of reasoning imply that press freedom under Article 10 ECHR serves the interests of others than the press itself. The protection of the press against government interference is construed around a particular idea of the press and its role in a constitutional democracy. This does not imply that the press is subordinate to the interests of readers if there may be a conflict of interest. The horizontal protection of readers and speakers under the right to freedom of expression vis-à-vis the press will be discussed in more detail in the subsequent sections.

With regard to the interests of readers, the ECtHR concluded in *Sunday Times* that freedom of expression protects the press against government interferences in reporting about an ongoing judicial proceeding, because it is the press' task to inform the public about these matters of public interest:

> [W]hilst the mass media must not overstep the bounds imposed in the interests of the proper administration of justice, it is incumbent on them to impart information and ideas concerning matters that come before the courts just as in other areas of public interest. Not only do the media have the task of

---

239. *Hustler Magazine v. Falwell*, 485 U.S. 46 (1988).

imparting such information and ideas: the public also has a right to receive them [...].[240]

In this and other judgments, the Court has added that the press plays a "vital role of 'public watchdog'"[241] and that freedom of the press "affords the public one of the best means of discovering and forming an opinion of the ideas and attitudes of political leaders."[242] In *Guerra*, stated "that the public has a right to receive information as a corollary of the specific function of journalists, which is to impart information and ideas on matters of public interest."[243] Thus, the Court has time and again connected the special status of the press to its function and task of informing the public.

To a lesser extent, the Court has tied freedom of the press to its role in providing a forum to others. In its *Jersild* judgment, which dealt with the prosecution of a Danish journalist for including racist statements by a right-extremist in a television documentary, the Court restated that news reporting receives special protection under Article 10 ECHR and journalists should not be unduly restricted in reporting statements of others, which is one of their primary roles and tasks:

> News reporting based on interviews, whether edited or not, constitutes one of the most important means whereby the press is able to play its vital role of "public watchdog" [...]. The punishment of a journalist for assisting in the dissemination of statements made by another person in an interview would seriously hamper the contribution of the press to discussion of matters of public interest and should not be envisaged unless there are particularly strong reasons for doing so.[244]

There are references tying the protection of the press under the First Amendment to the interests of possible speakers through the press and its readers, although more than the ECtHR, the Supreme Court emphasizes the freedom of the press from government interference independent of a particular designated role. Even though First Amendment doctrine does contain references to an institutional democratic theory for press freedom, it places more emphasis on a free market for information and ideas, and in general entails a less instrumental notion of press freedom than press freedom under Article 10 ECHR.[245]

This does not mean that First Amendment case law does not contain ample references to the interests of an informed public, the interest of the public

---

240. ECtHR April 26, 1979, *Sunday Times v. the United Kingdom*, § 65.
241. ECtHR November 26, 1991, *Observer and Guardian v. The United Kingdom*, § 59. See also ECtHR July 8, 1986, *Lingens v. Austria*, § 44 ("a sanction such as this is liable to hamper the press in performing its task as purveyor of information and public watchdog"); ECtHR March 25, 1985, *Barthold v. Germany*, § 58 ("a criterion such as this is liable to hamper the press in the performance of its task of purveyor of information and public watchdog").
242. ECtHR July 8, 1986, *Lingens v. Austria*, § 42.
243. ECtHR February 19, 1998, *Guerra and others v. Italy*, § 53.
244. ECtHR September 23, 1994, *Jersild v. Denmark*, § 35.
245. Strong references to a constitutionally established role of the press can be found in certain dissenting opinions. For references and a critical discussion, see Bevier 1980.

in self-governance and the interests of the speakers to reach an audience through the press.[246] The Supreme Court made its most famous reference to the interests of the receiving end of communications in the context of broadcast media. In *Red Lion*, the Court declared the following:

> [I]t is the right of the viewers and listeners, not the right of the broadcasters, which is paramount. [. . .] It is the right of the public to receive suitable access to social, political, esthetic, moral, and other ideas and experiences which is crucial here.[247]

Of course, particularly in the broadcasting context, the interests of the audience serve as an argument to regulate media, restricting the freedom of broadcasters to act self-interestedly. First Amendment doctrine provides that under certain conditions, government has a legitimate interest to restrict the dissemination of information in the interest of the 'captive audience' and uniquely pervasive media.[248]

In *Sullivan*, there is a particularly strong reference to the interests of speakers to reach an audience through the press. Rebecca Tushnet has recently argued that *Sullivan* was precisely about First Amendment protection of the intermediary role of the press.[249] The idea is that the 'actual malice' standard, discussed above, did not aim to protect the speech of the Times in this case as such, but the possibility of the press as an intermediary to publish third-party material without extensive fact-checking. In addition, Tushnet shows that *Sullivan* can be interpreted as an endorsement of the newspaper business model on the grounds of First Amendment values relating to the press as an intermediary. The publication for which the New York Times was sued was an advertisement, and commercial speech had been termed 'low-level speech' in *Chaplinsky*. The Supreme Court, however, dismissed any claim that the paid-for nature of the publication should be of any concern, in particular because it would "shut off an important outlet for the promulgation of information and ideas by persons who do not themselves have access to publishing facilities—who wish to exercise their freedom of speech even though they are not members of the press."[250] Hence, the implication of *Sullivan* could be that when the business model of a certain entity that claims protection under the First Amendment is in line with the values underlying freedom of expression, there

---

246. See e.g. *Grosjean v. American Press Co., Inc.*, 297 U.S. 233, 250 (1936) ("The predominant purpose of the grant of immunity [against special taxation of the press] was to preserve an untrammelled press as a vital source of public information."); *Zurcher v. Stanford Daily*, 436 U.S. 547, 572 (1972) (Stewart, J., dissenting); *Mills v. Alabama*, 384 U.S. 214, 218 (1966).
247. *Red Lion Broadcasting Co. v. FCC*, 395 U.S. 367 (1969) (deciding on the Constitutionality of the FCC's fairness doctrine for broadcasters. "Differences in the characteristics of new media justify differences in the First Amendment standards applied to them [. . .]." The Court acknowledges the scarcity of frequencies in the context of broadcasting as a legitimate ground for regulation. "But the people as a whole retain their interest in free speech by radio and their collective right to have the medium function consistently with the ends and purposes of the First Amendment.").
248. See section 5.5.2.
249. See Tushnet 2008, 120–124.
250. *New York Times v. Sullivan*, 376 U.S. 254, 266 (1964).

is no reason to separately scrutinize the commercial for-profit motives which are inherent in its operation.

5.3.3. PRESS FREEDOM AND THE DUTIES AND RESPONSIBILITIES UNDER ARTICLE 10

As mentioned above, the protection of the press under Article 10 of the Convention supposes certain commitments. In general, the strong emphasis on the societal role of the press, which gives it extra status and protection under Article 10 ECHR, raises the question whether a conception of this role is also used to confine its freedom. If the press were to function in a way that is not in accordance with its perceived role in a democratic society envisaged by the ECtHR, there would be less reason to protect it against interferences.

This question leads to a discussion of the duties and responsibilities which are inherent in the exercise of the right to freedom of expression as enshrined in Article 10.[251] By exercising one's right to freedom of expression, one undertakes specific duties and responsibilities depending on context, profession, impact and the technical means used for communicating. In *Hachette Filipacchi*, the Court formulated this as follows:

> [W]hoever exercises his freedom of expression undertakes "duties and responsibilities" the scope of which depends on his situation and the technical means he uses. The potential impact of those means must be taken into account when considering the proportionality of the interference. The safeguard afforded by Article 10 to journalists is subject, because of those very "duties and responsibilities", to the proviso that they provide reliable information in accordance with the ethics of journalism [...].[252]

Thus, the protection of the press under Article 10 ECHR could be called a double-edged sword. It implies the application of stricter scrutiny with regard to interferences on the one hand, but involves special duties and responsibilities tied to the profession and the medium on the other hand.[253] More specifically, the protection under Article 10 ECHR of the press' statement of facts and opinions is colored by the ethics of journalism.

The Court has rejected overly strict requirements on the press, for instance the "general requirement for journalists systematically and formally to distance themselves from the content of a quotation that might insult or provoke others or damage their reputation."[254] The Court has concluded on a number of occasions

---

251. See ECtHR May 20, 1999, *Bladet Tromsø and Stansaas v. Norway*, § 65; ECtHR July 29, 2008, *Flux v. Moldavia (No. 6)*, § 22.
252. ECtHR June 14, 2007, *Hachette Filipacchi Associees v. France*, § 42.
253. See also Council of Europe, Parliamentary Assembly, Resolution 1003 (1993) on the ethics of journalism.
254. ECtHR December 14, 2006, *Verlagsgruppe News Gmbh v. Austria*, § 33.

that this requirement is not reconcilable with the press' role of providing information on current events, opinions and ideas.[255] But the double-edged nature of freedom of expression under Article 10 ECHR remains. Whereas the press and journalists are allowed to provoke and exaggerate,[256] they also have to be careful, accurate and act in good faith, as the Court recently concluded in *Stoll*:

> [T]he safeguard afforded by Article 10 to journalists in relation to reporting on issues of general interest is subject to the proviso that they are acting in good faith and on an accurate factual basis and provide "reliable and precise" information in accordance with the ethics of journalism.[257]

The *Stoll* judgment is also of interest because the Court reflects on the duties and responsibilities of the press in the light of present-day conditions.[258] These present-day conditions, in the Court's eyes, have strengthened the importance of journalists abiding by their professional ethics, as follows:

> [T]hese considerations play a particularly important role nowadays, given the influence wielded by the media in contemporary society: not only do they inform, they can also suggest by the way in which they present the information how it is to be assessed. In a world in which the individual is confronted with vast quantities of information circulated via traditional and electronic media and involving an ever-growing number of players, monitoring compliance with journalistic ethics takes on added importance.[259]

Thus, the influence and impact of media as well as the risk they pose in terms of misinforming the public increase the duties and responsibilities of the media. However, the Court's judgment in *Stoll* has been criticized for relying too much on the judgment of the Swiss press council and placing too much emphasis on duties and responsibilities.[260]

The problem is that the duties and responsibilities tied to the exercise of freedom of expression in Article 10 and linked to the ethics of journalism by the Court in its case law, consistently mirror the actual freedom of expression which Article 10 ECHR aims to provide. Thus on the one hand, the right to freedom to expression not only applies to the substance, but also extends to the *means of*

---

255. *Ibid.* See also ECtHR March 29, 2001, *Thoma v. Luxembourg*, § 64.
256. See ECtHR April 26, 1995, *Prager and Oberschlick v. Austria*, § 38. ("Journalistic freedom also covers possible recourse to a degree of exaggeration, or even provocation.") It is interesting to note that the Court has never considered provocation and exaggeration to be a duty or responsibility.
257. ECtHR December 10, 2007, *Stoll v. Switzerland*, § 103.
258. The need to interpret the Convention in light of present-day conditions was established in ECtHR April 25, 1978, *Tyrer v. the United Kingdom*, § 31. See also section 4.3.2.
259. ECtHR December 10, 2007, *Stoll v. Switzerland*, § 104.
260. See Judge Zagrebelesky, dissenting, in ECtHR December 10, 2007, *Stoll v. Switzerland*. See also Voorhof 2008, 197–203.

communications and *the form* in which information and ideas are made public.[261] On the other hand, the duties and responsibilities include the responsible use of media and means of communication, in light of their respective impact and influence, and the form in which information and ideas are being presented in view of the difference in suggestive capabilities of different forms of communications and media.

What is missing in the Court's recent case law is a consistent acknowledgement of the importance of giving the press and others leeway with regard to the definition and fulfillment of their duties and responsibilities, which in addition tend to be presented as generally accepted standards, instead of the contested ones they really often are in their practical application.[262] In 1994, the Court still referred to this leeway with regard to reporting techniques in *Jersild*, when it concluded that "[i]t is not for this Court, nor for the national courts for that matter, to substitute their own views for those of the press as to what technique of reporting should be adopted by journalists."[263] More recently, however, there is a tendency in the Court's case law wherein duties and responsibilities consistently serve to legitimize limitations on the right to freedom of expression, thereby providing an extra line of defense for public authorities to limit expressive liberties. A perceived disregard for certain media ethics standards may lead to a lower level of scrutiny and a higher margin of appreciation for the State, thereby making it less likely that the interference will be considered unnecessary in a democratic society.

This emphasis on duties and responsibilities is problematic and difficult to reconcile with the principle that freedom of expression provides something extra in terms of protection.[264] In addition, how one should actually assess the influence and impact of different media or other related non-legal standards remains unanswered in *Stoll* and in the ECtHR's case law in general. Media is everywhere in contemporary society, but its impact and influence are hard to measure, let alone in terms of negative or positive contributions. If left unqualified, the perceived impact

---

261. See ECtHR April 26, 1995, *Prager and Oberschlick v. Austria*, § 57, and ECtHR May 22, 1990, *Autronic v. Switzerland*, § 47.
262. There are references to this leeway but they are rather weak, such as in ECtHR January 21, 1999, *Fressoz and Roire v. France*. ("In essence, [Article 10] leaves it for journalists to decide whether or not it is necessary to reproduce such documents to ensure credibility. It protects journalists' right to divulge information on issues of general interest provided that they are acting in good faith and on an accurate factual basis and provide 'reliable and precise' information in accordance with the ethics of journalism.") In theory, the deterrent effect doctrine could provide such an answer. See the dissenting opinions in ECtHR June 14, 2007, *Hachette Filipacchi Associees v. France*.
263. ECtHR September 23, 1994, *Jersild v. Denmark*, § 31.
264. This extra line of defense for the authorities defending an interference can be identified in ECtHR October 22, 2007, *Lindon and others v. France*. ("Nonetheless, novelists—like other creators—[. . .] are certainly not immune from the possibility of limitations as provided for in paragraph 2 of Article 10. Whoever exercises his freedom of expression undertakes, in accordance with the express terms of that paragraph, 'duties and responsibilities'.") Recent dissents in the Court's case law show an internal conflict at the ECtHR about the emphasis on duties and responsibilities and journalistic ethics. For a discussion, see e.g. Voorhoof 2008bm Voorhoof 2008c.

of the media and the perceived 'present-day conditions' remain hypothetical and can serve as an excuse for restricting the right to freedom of expression. The doctrine of duties and responsibilities may, in some cases, even result in a shift of the Court from scrutinizing the actual interferences with the media by public authorities to scrutinizing the actions of the media.[265]

Such possible critiques notwithstanding, it is clear that the considerations of the Court as regards duties and responsibilities will have to be taken into account in the context of the Internet, the Web and dominant search engines. Since the duties and responsibilities in the Court's case law tend to emphasize professionalism, maybe not too much should be expected from the ECtHR in the context of unorganized, often irresponsible, self-publications on the Internet. And in particular, since duties and responsibilities consistently mirror the actual freedoms in specific contexts, duties and responsibilities for Web search, as a means of communication and having a distinct impact or influence and way of presentation, should be formulated.

5.3.4.   PRESS FREEDOM AND THE PERMISSIBILITY OF PRIOR RESTRAINTS

Of all interferences with the freedom of expression, prior restraints are consistently considered the most problematic, both under Article 10 of the Convention as well as under the First Amendment.

The ECtHR concludes in *Guardian and Observer v. United Kingdom* that Article 10 ECHR "does not in terms prohibit the imposition of prior restraints on publication, as such."[266] The Court does, however, assert that prior restraints "call for the most careful scrutiny on the part of the Court," in particular when the press is concerned because: "news is a perishable commodity and to delay its publication, even for a short period, may well deprive it of all its value and interest."[267]

This specific case is also interesting because it bases the impermissibility of the prior restraint upon the factual availability of the material. This could be argued to be important in the context of obligations to remove references to content on Web search engines, since they are not able to remove the material from the Web.

---

265.   See e.g. ECtHR July 29, 2008, *Flux v. Moldova (No. 6)*, § 26. ("The Court will examine whether the journalist who wrote the impugned article acted in good faith and in accordance with the ethics of the profession of journalist. In the Court's view, this depends in particular on the nature and degree of the defamation at hand, the manner in which the impugned article was written and the extent to which the applicant newspaper could reasonably regard its sources as reliable with respect to the allegations in question." Three of the seven justices joined a strong dissenting opinion, concluding that "in the Court's view the social need to fight poor journalism is more pressing than that of fighting rich corruption. The 'chilling effect' of sanctions against press freedom dreaded by the Court's old case-law has materialised through the Court's new one.")

266.   ECtHR November 26, 1991, *Observer and Guardian v. the United Kingdom*, § 60.

267.   *Ibid.*

The case cited above dealt with a prior restraint imposed by a Court in the United Kingdom on *Spycatcher*, a book documenting sensitive dealings of British national security agencies. The court held that the wide availability of the publication—it had been rather successfully published abroad and the United Kingdom had not sought an import ban—rendered the prior restraints imposed on the U.K. publication disproportionate. Hence, the matter-of-fact availability of information imposes further restrictions on the permissibility of prior restraints, in particular if government does not seek restrictions immediately.[268]

First Amendment doctrine contains a heavy presumption against the constitutional permissibility of prior restraint on the press.[269] Prior restraints are "the most serious and the least tolerable infringement on First Amendment rights."[270] The press is protected against prior restraints on publications, but not against being punished for them after publication if the publication is found to be illegal. In *Nebraska*, the U.S. Supreme Court explained this difference as follows:

> If it can be said that a threat of criminal or civil sanctions after publication "chills" speech, prior restraint "freezes" it at least for the time.

The damage of prior restraints can be particularly great when it restricts the communication of news, and commentary on current events brings in extra weight, since "the element of time is not unimportant if press coverage is to fulfill its traditional function of bringing news to the public promptly."[271]

The restrictions on prior restraints and on licensing as a form of prior constraint go beyond restrictions on the act of publication. They also protect against city laws requiring prior permission for the distribution of printed materials.[272] Such standardless licensing laws would restore a system of censorship and licensing which were abolished by the First Amendment. When dealing with standardless licensing laws, the Supreme Court tends to declare these laws invalid on their face, instead of looking into the application of the law in the particular case at hand. The problem with standardless licensing from the perspective of the First Amendment, even of laws that merely aim to restrict littering, is that control over the circulation of information and ideas is vested in a government agent without appropriate standards to guide his actions.[273]

To some extent, First Amendment safeguards against prior restraints are procedural. In a case involving a prior restraint on the issuance of films to prevent

---

268. ECtHR November 26, 1991, *Observer and Guardian v. The United Kingdom*, § 66–70.
269. *Nebraska Press Association v. Stuart*, 427 U.S. 539 (1976). See also *New York Times Co. v. United States*, 403 U.S. 713 (1971).
270. *Nebraska Press Association v. Stuart*, 427 U.S. 539, 559 (1976).
271. *Nebraska Press Association v. Stuart*, 427 U.S. 539, 561 (1976).
272. *Lovell v. Griffin*, 303 U.S. 444 (1938). (Concluding that such an ordinance is void on its face because its character strikes at the very foundation of the freedom of the press by subjecting it to license and censorship. Liberty of the press started initially a right to publish "without a license what formerly could be published only with one.")
273. *Kunz v. New York*, 340 U.S. 290 (1951). For an overview of the objections against licensing and prior restraints, see Emerson 1955, 656–660.

(unprotected) obscene speech, the Supreme Court established that under appropriate procedural safeguards eliminating the dangers of censorship the prior restraint would have been constitutional.[274] These procedural safeguards require that the burden of proof for the unprotected status of speech must lie on the censor, that before judicial review prior restraints must be limited to the preservation of a status quo for the shortest period possible, that they are compatible with sound judicial procedure and that a prompt final judicial determination of obscenity must be assured.[275] The Supreme Court has recently distinguished cases with a content-neutral licensing scheme from prior restraint cases. The latter can be considered permissible time, place and manner regulation if they serve legitimate interests and do not restrict speech disproportionally.[276]

5.4. THE PRESS AS GATEKEEPER: EDITORIAL FREEDOM AND ACCESS TO THE PRESS

5.4.1. BACKGROUND TO THE DEBATE ABOUT ACCESS TO THE PRESS

Due to the power of the press in its intermediary role between speakers and potential sources of information and the general public, access to the press and the media as a gatekeeper more generally is a hotly debated topic related to press freedom.[277] The press is modern society's town hall and is characteristically seen as one of the primary places for public debate and shaping of public opinion. Hence, it is problematic if the press, as a whole, is generally biased in its coverage or does not offer the opportunity for certain views or facts to be published and subsequently received by an audience at all.

Of course, it is important to acknowledge the various alternatives for a speaker or a source of information more generally if a newspaper would decide to not publish it. If one newspaper does not want to publish, there may be other outlets that will. In practice, national and international news agencies have a great influence on what information will be published by the press, so their access policies are important as well. Another option for speakers in search of an audience for particular information or ideas would be to pay for publication, in other words to self-publish or advertise. Access for advertisers, whether editorial or commercial, is usually restricted as well, but in a different fashion. Finally, and in the current situation perhaps most importantly, the speaker could decide to self-publish on the Web.

---

274. *Freedman v. Maryland*, 380 U.S. 51 (1965).
275. *Ibid.*
276. See *Thomas v. Chicago Park District*, 534 U.S. 316 (2002). (Stating that *Freedman* is "*inapposite because the licensing scheme at issue here is not subject-matter censorship but content-neutral time, place, and manner regulation of the use of a public forum.*")
277. See Barron 1967; Lange 1973; Lichtenberg 1987, 329–350; Nieuwenhuis 1991, 146 and cited references.

Taking into account the range of alternatives and keeping in mind the low barriers to entry to publish information and ideas on the World Wide Web, the discussion about access rights in the context of the press may seem awkward. It is not surprising that the discussion about access rights was most prominent at a time when entry barriers were higher, the media were quite concentrated, and were considered by many to be too biased in their coverage and selection, and not sufficiently open for a wide range of speakers to be heard. One interesting account of the power of traditional mass media in defining the boundaries of public debate has been offered by media scholar Hallin.[278] He analyzed in detail how the press can systematically undermine the recognition of certain points of view in society by systematically excluding them or exposing them as unacceptable.

Those who lamented the power of traditional mass media as the gatekeepers of public debate have welcomed the lower entry barriers to publishing that the net-worked information environment offers.[279] As a result, the discussion about access rights to the mass media may now have partly shifted to different intermediaries, such as search engines.[280] For this reason, the debate about access regulation of the press remains of great interest, and it will therefore be revisited here. Access regulation under the First Amendment and the Article 10 framework will be addressed together.

From the perspective of the right to freedom of expression, the relation between speakers and important speech forums such as the press raises a number of issues. The issue that will be discussed here is the possibility to legally guarantee the opportunity of certain speakers to have information and ideas published in a particular news outlet against the will of the publisher. The analysis will be based on an analysis of the constitutionality of right of reply statutes under the right to freedom of expression.

It is clear that access rights for speakers to the press interfere with the editorial freedom of the press, since they would affect the press' freedom to choose which information and ideas to carry and which to exclude from its publications. From an economic viewpoint, it would also interfere with the operation of the press in the sense that it would have to dedicate resources to the publication of information and ideas, resources which it would otherwise have dedicated to other information and ideas. Hence, an access right for speakers also affects the economic freedom of the media. This economic freedom of the media, in turn, indirectly impacts the media's editorial freedom, since it means that particular economic incentives arise in the context of the exercise of its editorial function.[281] To summarize, access regulation of the press sharply raises the question about the protection of the editorial freedom of the press under the right to freedom of expression. After looking at its

---

278. Hallin 1986. For studies in communications science on the gatekeeping role of the mass media, see White 1950, Innis et al. 1991, Shoemaker 2001.
279. For a discussion of the power of the press in defining the legitimate spheres of debate in society and the way the Internet may have reduced that power, see Rosen 2009. See also Aikens 1996.
280. Pariser 2011; Introna and Nissenbaum 2000; Chandler 2007; Pasquale 2010; Kreimer 2001. See also section 10.2.1.
281. See *Miami Herald Publishing Co. v. Tornillo*, 418 U.S. 241 (1974).

(un)constitutionality, this section will conclude with a discussion of the editorial freedom of the press more generally.

5.4.2.   ACCESS REGULATION AND EDITORIAL FREEDOM

The most common access right in the press context, which exists in some European jurisdictions, is a reactive right, namely a right of reply. The idea behind the right of reply is that it offers the opportunity to have an opposing view published, to correct false statements of fact, or to present an opportunity to reach an audience by someone who has been negatively affected by a publication. Such a right to access a media outlet can be seen to be based on the right to freedom of expression of the particular speaker, as a corollary of the audience's right to inform itself or as a remedy for an infringement of other protected interests such as the right to private life or the speaker's reputation.[282]

Many countries do not have a right of reply at all, for instance the Netherlands and the United States, because of the limitation it implies for the press' editorial freedom. Access rights in the context of the press are unconstitutional under the First Amendment. The unconstitutional status of access regulation of the press can be contrasted with the U.S. broadcasting framework, in which access regulation is generally more common and the FCC was committed to the so-called fairness doctrine for decades.[283] This doctrine imposed an obligation on broadcasters to guarantee balanced reporting with regard to different points of view.

The consensus is that Article 10 ECHR does not imply a right to access the press and in particular, no right of reply or right to rectification.[284,285] However, under the appropriate circumstances, the right of reply or rectification is not seen as an undue interference with the right to freedom of expression of the press under Article 10 ECHR.[286] The decision by the press regarding what to publish is an editorial decision and thereby protected under Article 10 ECHR. An access right, granted by the law, is an interference with the protected interests of the press under Article 10 ECHR and needs to satisfy the test of Article 10 ECHR, second paragraph. This interference could be based on the possibility to restrict the right to freedom of expression of the press in the interests of the 'protection of

---

282. Van Dijk et al. 2006, 786–787. See also Barendt 2005, 422–427.
283. For an overview of the debates about the fairness doctrine, which was applied by the FCC as a condition for broadcasting licensing, approved by the U.S. Supreme Court in *Red Lion*, and finally abolished during the Reagan presidency in the 1980s, see Benjamin et al. 2006, 197–240.
284. See Barendt 2005, 425–427.
285. See Council of Europe, 'Recommendation of the Committee of Ministers to Member States on the right of reply in the new media environment', Rec(2004)16. See also Recommendation of the European Parliament and of the Council of December 20, 2006 on the protection of minors and human dignity and on the right of reply in relation to the competitiveness of the European audiovisual and on-line information services industry', OJ L 378, December 27, 2006, 72–77.
286. See e.g. ECtHR June 14, 2007, *Hachette Filipacchi Associees v. France*.

the reputation or rights of others'. If viewed as a vertical freedom of expression issue between the State and the press, the interference would need to be 'necessary in a democratic society'. However, to the extent that the State could be seen to act under its positive obligation to protect the fundamental rights of others by granting a right to access the press, a mere balancing of interests would be taking place.

The European Human Rights Commission has rejected a challenge to a right of reply provision.[287] Also, the German Constitutional Court has concluded that right of reply provisions do not interfere with press freedom as enshrined in the German Constitution. It is interesting to note that the German Court concluded that these provisions not only protected the personality rights of individuals but also the right to freedom of expression, specifically the rights of readers to be better informed about a dispute.[288] Finally, the ECtHR's interpretation of duties and responsibilities under Article 10 ECHR colors the editorial freedom of the press under the Convention. From the perspective of Article 10 ECHR, the editorial freedom of the press goes hand in hand with the responsible use of the freedom to select information and ideas for publication.

Under the First Amendment, a right of reply in the context of the press is plainly unconstitutional, as the Supreme Court's judgment in *Miami Herald v. Tornillo* clarified. *Tornillo* sets a strict standard in the First Amendment's protection of editorial freedom.[289] The Court addressed the issue of whether a State statute granting a political candidate a right to equal space to reply to criticism and attacks by a newspaper violated the guarantees of a free press in the First Amendment. After a discussion of the arguments in favor of and against access rights to the press,[290] the Court pointed to the necessary implementation of a governmental or consensual mechanism to enforce these kind of rights. The Court concluded that no such mechanism could be imagined that would be consistent with the First Amendment's protection of a free press and held the Florida statute unconstitutional. First of all, it asserted that what was at stake was "whether editors and publishers can be compelled to publish which reason tells them should not be published."[291] After this first reference to editorial freedom, it concluded that access rights function as an economic penalty—taking up space—and might lead editors to avoid controversy. In the final paragraph of its judgment, the Court addressed the press' editorial freedom, which according to the Court ultimately bars access rights to the press. Because of its clarity and continuing influence on the U.S. freedom of expression doctrine, it is cited here in full, as follows:

---

287. European Human Rights Commission, 13010/87, *Ediciones Tiempo v. Spain* (1989) 62 *D&R* 247.
288. BVerfG January 14, 1998, 1 BvR 1861/93. See Barendt, 457.
289. *Miami Herald Publishing Co. v. Tornillo*, 418 U.S. 241 (1974).
290. See Barron 1967; Lange 1973.
291. *Miami Herald Publishing Co. v. Tornillo*, 418 U.S. 241, 256 (1974).

[T]he Florida statute fails to clear the barriers of the First Amendment because of its intrusion into the function of editors. A newspaper is more than a passive receptacle or conduit for news, comment, and advertising. The choice of material to go into a new paper, and the decisions made as to limitations on the size and content of the paper, and treatment of public issues and public officials—whether fair or unfair—constitute the exercise of editorial control and judgment. It has yet to be demonstrated how governmental regulation of this crucial process can be exercised consistent with First Amendment guarantees of a free press as they have evolved to this time.[292]

Thus, the editorial freedom of a newspaper consists of the freedom to decide what material goes into the newspaper, the content, form and size of the articles and the way the newspaper treats the issues it chooses to report. Even if this treatment may be unfair, biased or wrong, the First Amendment does not allow government to encroach upon it, for instance by granting rights to speak through the newspaper for specific individuals.

A question that remains unanswered in *Tornillo* is when and on which grounds an intermediary should be considered a passive receptacle or conduit and when it should not. This is an important question as the freedom to exercise editorial control and judgment about information flows is typically used to delineate the press from passive receptacles or conduits. It is also important because of the different modalities of control and selection one finds in the networked information environment. Finally, since the exercise of editorial control and judgment is linked to strong First Amendment protection against regulation, this also implies that other intermediaries that want to defend a certain level of discretion in their intermediation policies may invoke the *Tornillo* standard against government interference.

Moreover, *Tornillo* does not provide for a clear distinction between the exercise of the right to freedom of expression by a journalist or editor or a news organization as a whole. This implies that the economic freedom of news organizations is further strengthened by the organization's First Amendment claims against government interference.[293] In fact, First Amendment doctrine seems increasingly hostile to any distinction between the economic freedom of speech intermediaries in society and their possible right to freedom of expression.[294] This discussion and the possible distinction between editorial media and passive conduits, and the way search engines should be positioned between these two models, will be further addressed in the subsequent chapters.

---

292. *Miami Herald Publishing Co. v. Tornillo*, 418 U.S. 241, 259 (1974) [footnotes omitted].
293. For a critical discussion of the use of free speech claims as disguised property claims, see Lichtenberg 1987, 329–350.
294. See *Citizens United v. Federal Election Commission*, 558 U.S. 8 (2010).

5.5.   THE PRESS AND ITS AUDIENCE: THE RIGHT TO BE
            INFORMED, THE ROLE OF ADVERTISING AND THE
            READER'S PRIVACY

5.5.1.   PRESS FREEDOM AND THE RIGHT TO BE INFORMED

Section 5.3 showed that to a considerable extent, the rationale of press freedom is linked to the interest of the public to inform itself. In fact, the ECtHR has consistently spoken of *a right* of the public to inform itself. In this section, the question will be addressed as to what extent this right can be invoked against the press itself or serve as the basis of legitimate government interference with the functioning of the press.

Notably, the freedom of expression under Article 10 ECHR, as well as under the First Amendment, implies the freedom to gather and receive information without undue interference by public authorities. This right to gather and receive information freely is the least of what can be expected from this right to be informed. Freedom of expression doctrine gives no reason to believe that there is something such as a right to be informed by a particular news outlet about particular issues.[295] Such a right to gain access to information by the press would amount to a rather grave interference with the press' freedom, which actually allows the press to not be transparent in its functioning, for example by protecting the confidentiality of journalistic sources. Yet, under Article 10 ECHR, the Court has provided some further qualifications to the right to be informed that will be discussed below.

In practice, the reader's or end-user's freedom to receive information is guaranteed by a free market in information products. Potential readers can freely choose which of them to patronize and whether or not to read them. Public libraries and public broadcasting are often legitimized with reference to a market failing from the perspective of the interests of the public. The idea is that certain information products will not be produced in large enough quantities or in certain qualities from a public policy perspective. In metaphorical terms, such interventions by public authorities could be said to aim to improve the marketplace of ideas.

Even in relation to government, Article 10 ECHR does not, in general, imply a right to access specific information, or what is sometimes called a right to know or a right to information. In recent times, the ECtHR came close to acknowledging such a right, which would reflect the rights granted in freedom of information laws, but it still considers the right of the public to access government information freely as a negative right.[296] In *Guerra*, where the issue was first brought before the

---

295. For an in-depth analysis of a possible 'right to information' from the media, see Helberger 2005, 67–89.
296. See ECtHR, April 14, 2009, *Társaság a Szabadságjogokért v. Hungary*. The Court recognizes "that the public has a right to receive information of general interest", and declared restrictions on access to information held by the Hungarian Constitutional Court unconstitutional. However, the Court does not conclude that there is a positive obligation for the state to actively

Court, the Court recognized that it had "recognized that the public has a right to receive information as a corollary of the specific function of journalists, which is to impart information and ideas on matters of public interest."[297] After naming a few of the specific circumstances of the case, the Court clarified the following:

> [Article 10] basically prohibits a government from restricting a person from receiving information that others wish or may be willing to impart to him. [...] That freedom cannot be construed as imposing on a State, in circumstances such as those of the present case, positive obligations to collect and disseminate information of its own motion.[298]

It is possible, but improbable, that under different circumstances, a positive obligation to actively impart information might exist. In *Guerra*, the ECtHR overturned the Commission's decision, which had construed a positive obligation, based on Article 10 ECHR, to make the information in question available to the public.[299]

The Court has further qualified the right to receive information and ideas as a corollary to press freedom in *Lentia* and in cases involving publicity of private individuals such as *Von Hannover*. The *Lentia* judgment contains the following complex argument:

> The Court has frequently stressed the fundamental role of freedom of expression in a democratic society, in particular where, through the press, it serves to impart information and ideas of general interest, which the public is moreover entitled to receive [...]. Such an undertaking cannot be successfully accomplished unless it is grounded in the principle of pluralism, of which the State is the ultimate guarantor.[300]

In other words, the audience has a right to receive information and ideas freely, and more specifically it has a right to a diverse, pluralist media offering. The State itself has the obligation to promote and even guarantee pluralism, but in the way it pursues this objective it can restrict media freedom disproportionately.[301] A closer look at *Lentia*, in which a State monopoly on broadcasting was declared to be incompatible with the demands of Article 10 ECHR, further shows that the Court, from the perspective of freedom of expression and media pluralism, prefers

---

produce or impart information. It considered the restrictions on the possibility to gain access to the government-held information to be an interference, which could not be justified under the second paragraph: "In view of the interest protected by Article 10, the law cannot allow arbitrary restrictions which may become a form of indirect censorship should the authorities create obstacles to the gathering of information. For example, the latter activity is an essential preparatory step in journalism and is an inherent, protected part of press freedom."

297. ECtHR February 19, 1998, *Guerra v. Italy*, § 53.
298. *Ibid.*
299. *Ibid.*, §§ 52–53.
300. ECtHR November 24, 1993, *Informationsverein Lentia v. Austria*, § 38.
301. See Nieuwenhuis 200, 367–384.

wider access of different channels over a constrained environment with guarantees for diversity.[302]

Finally, under Article 10 ECHR the weight that must be attached to the right to receive information and ideas freely depends upon the subject matter. It must be interpreted more narrowly, in situations in which publicity does not serve the democratic ideal of public debate, such as when it merely serves the curiosity of readers in the details about the private life of individuals.[303]

First Amendment doctrine contains many of the same doctrinal elements as have been discussed above. However, a positive obligation to promote pluralism in the interest of the public to inform itself is absent. In general, the First Amendment can be seen as protecting the individual's informational self-governance. In situations in which the media audience is 'captive', in the sense that it may be presented with certain media contents unwillingly, the government is, under certain circumstances, allowed to regulate media and protect these interests without breaching the First Amendment.

The text of the First Amendment does not specifically mention the right to receive information freely, but the First Amendment certainly implies such a right. In *Griswold*, the Supreme Court clarified that the fundamental rights from the Bill of Rights have to be thought of as creating a 'penumbra of rights'.[304] In particular, the right of freedom of speech and press includes not only the right to *utter or to print*, but also the right to distribute, receive and read, the freedom of inquiry and thought, and the freedom to teach, because without these 'peripheral rights' the specific rights would be less secure.[305] The First Amendment does not establish a right to access information or a right to know.[306] In certain contexts, such as in the case of judicial proceedings, government cannot withhold certain information from the public or restrict its publication.[307]

More generally, the right to freedom of expression on the receiving end of communications can be seen as a form of self-governance with regard to the information flows an individual decides to engage in. In that sense, the right goes beyond a right not to be hindered by the State when one attempts to access available information. First Amendment case law involves a number of interesting additional elements relating to this self-governance of incoming communications, which are worthy of discussion here, namely the idea of the captive audience in media regulation, more generally the right to choose freely what to read and listen to, and the presumption against paternalism in the case law about commercial speech. In comparison with the European framework, these elements place much more emphasis on free speech as a guarantee of a State-free zone,

---

302. ECtHR November 24, 1993, *Informationsverein Lentia v. Austria*, § 39.
303. See ECtHR June 24, 2004, *Von Hannover v. Germany*.
304. Compare Chandler 2008, 4.
305. *Griswold v. Connecticut*, 381 U.S. 479, 482–483 (1965).
306. For a skeptical discussion of any 'right to know' under the First Amendment, see BeVier 1980.
307. *Richmond Newspapers v. Virginia*, 448 U.S. 555 (1980); *Globe Newspaper Co. v. Superior Court*, 457 U.S. 596 (1982).

independent in its protection of other higher values such as a well-informed public in a democracy.

The idea of the captive audience can be found in a number of rulings of the Supreme Court. The idea is that restrictions on the right to impart information and ideas can be legitimate when communications would intrude upon the fundamental interest of the audience in its informational self-governance. It is worth noting that in the context of the press, the captive audience doctrine cannot legitimize interferences. In the broadcast context, however, the Supreme Court accepted that there is a stronger case for regulation, because of the "uniquely pervasive presence of the broadcast medium in the lives of the public."[308] Thus, protection of the public against over-intrusive (indecent) speech can be constitutional, particularly if it is capable of intruding upon the privacy of unwilling listeners.[309] In *Martin*, the Court made it clear that the First Amendment protects the freedom of the unwilling audience not to receive information, but this does not imply that the house-to-house distribution of material (literature) can be prohibited in general, as follows:

> [T]he city may make it an offense to ring the bell of a householder who has appropriately indicated that he is unwilling to be disturbed. This or any similar regulation leaves the decision as to whether distributors of literature may lawfully call at a home where it belongs—with the homeowner himself.[310]

The doctrine of the captive audience is interesting in the context of the Internet and the intermediary role of search engines precisely because there seems no reason at all to assume a captive audience in this context. The interactive nature of the public networked information environment strongly enhances the possibility of Internet users in the self-governance of their information intake. As is obvious, search engines play an important role in that regard, since they help Internet users select and access the material they themselves find worthy of their attention.

---

308. *FCC v. Pacifica Foundation*, 438 U.S. 726, 747–750 (1978). More in particular, indecency can be regulated, in contrast to the press medium, because broadcasts extend into the privacy of the home, and it is impossible completely to avoid those that are patently offensive. Broadcasting, moreover, is uniquely accessible to children. Ironically, *Pacifica* involved the broadcasting of a satire about the indecency regulation of the FCC.

309. See also *Stanley v. Georgia* 394 U.S. 557 (1969) (additional protection of speech in the private sphere); *United States v. Reidel* 402 U.S. 351 (1971) (Stanley does not imply a right to distribute the obscene material that could not be penalized constitutionally under Stanley.); *Osbourne v. Ohio*, 495 U.S. 103 (1990) (*Stanley* inapplicable to child pornography.); *Paris Adult Theatre I v. Slaton* 413 U.S. 49 (1973); *Rowan v. Post Office Department*, 397 U.S. 728 (1970), (government may act to prevent intrusion into the privacy of the home of offensive speech. It may even acknowledge a request not to receive any more communications by a certain other party over the mail. "A man's home is his castle" into which "not even the king may enter."); *Cohen v. California*, 403 U.S. 15 (1971) ('Fuck the Draft' utterance in Court and captive audience). See also Stone 1974, 262–272; *Erznoznik v. Jacksonville*, 422 U.S. 204 (1975).

310. *Martin v. City of Struthers*, 319 U.S. 141 (1943).

5.5.2.   PRESS FREEDOM AND COMMERCIAL COMMUNICATIONS

Many of the regulatory interferences by public authorities in the relation between the public and entities that impart information and ideas are legitimized with reference to the interests of readers and the readers' right to receive information and ideas in particular. One interesting example of this is the way the right to receive information freely has informed the constitutional status of commercial communications under the First Amendment and Article 10 ECHR. Of special interest in the context of commercial communications and press freedom is the triangular relationship between the media, its audience and its advertisers. These two topics will be discussed below.

Both the U.S. Supreme Court and the ECtHR have granted commercial speech significant protection, in view of the rights of the public to receive such communications. In both cases, commercial communications are protected but enjoy a lesser status and can be regulated.[311]

The Supreme Court's gradual extension ofFirst Amendment protection for commercial speech is worth recounting here because of its strong dependence on a specific interpretation of the right to receive information freely. Under the First Amendment, commercial speech was first considered to be low-level speech and could therefore be regulated.[312] In the 1970s, the Court started narrowing the unprotected status of commercial advertising. Advertisements that did more than just propose a commercial transaction, but provided factual information on a matter of public interest, became protected speech.[313] In *Virginia Pharmacy*, the Supreme Court went further and concluded that commercial intent could not render speech wholly unprotected.[314] Thus, even speech that solely proposes a commercial transaction does not lack protection under the First Amendment. The core argument for this conclusion is basically a very strict argument against paternalism: suppression of truthful non-deceptive advertising is unconstitutional because it denies the audience the right to decide for themselves what is in their best interest.[315]

---

311. On government regulation of commercial speech under the First Amendment, see Stone 2008, 161–186.
312. *Valentine v. Chrestensen*, 316 U.S. 52 (1942) (Commercial advertising is added to the list of low-level speech in *Chaplinsky*).
313. *Bigelow v. Virginia*, 421 U.S. 809 (1975).
314. *Virginia State Board of Pharmacy v. Virginia Citizens Consumer Council*, 425 U.S. 748 (1976).
315. *Virginia State Board of Pharmacy v. Virginia Citizens Consumer Council*, 425 U.S. 748, 770 (1976). ("The alternative is to assume that this information is not in itself harmful, that people will perceive their own best interests if only they are well enough informed, and that the best means to that end is to open the channels of communication rather than to close them. [. . .] It is precisely this kind of choice between the dangers of suppressing information and the dangers of its misuse if it is freely available, that the First Amendment makes for us [. . .].").

Hence *Virginia Pharmacy* establishes that truthful, non-deceptive commercial advertising is protected under the First Amendment.[316] Finally, in *Liquormart* the Supreme Court concluded that the fact that an activity, e.g. gambling, could be constitutionally banned in its entirety, does not imply that if it is not, the non-misleading advertising about the activity can be banned or unduly restricted. This is because such bans usually "rest solely on the offensive assumption that the public will respond 'irrationally' to the truth" and, in fact, the First Amendment "presumes that attempts to regulate speech are more dangerous than attempts to regulate conduct."[317] Thus, the First Amendment seems to contain a heavy presumption in favor of the rationality of the audience.[318] The public may not be protected by government against its possible inclinations to act unwisely in response to advertising.[319]

The European Court of Human Rights has made a similar gradual move towards a protected status of commercial speech under Article 10 ECHR.[320] And more generally, the idea of an informed media consumer who can decide, or at least be allowed to decide, what media to engage in, has firmly established itself in European media law and policy. We will come back to this debate in the context of search engines and their end-users in Chapter 8.[321]

Of specific interest in the context of the press and the status of advertising under the right to freedom of expression is the triangular relationship between commercial media, their audiences and their advertisers. Commercial media that make profits through advertising have to strike some kind of balance between the interests of readers and their potential advertisers.[322] Income through advertisements has been a primary source of revenue of the periodical press since the nineteenth century and remains a primary source of income for the newspaper industry.

In the press context, we find some of the more advanced ways of dealing with the tensions that media face when having to balance advertising and their audience interests. Over the years, the more serious newspaper outlets have developed a range of voluntary institutional guarantees with respect to the quality of newspaper journalism in relation to the profit-making motives of their employers. The most important of these guarantees is the wall of separation between the editorial processes and advertising in the news industry. In the United States, this separation

---

316. For the four-step test for the constitutionality of regulation of commercial advertising see *Central Hudson Gas v. Public Service Commission of New York*, 447 U.S. 557 (1980).
317. *Liquormart Inc. v. Rhode Island*, 517 U.S. 484 (1996).
318. Or, one can say critically, it is indifferent to the rationality of the audience's reaction. Compare Lippmann 1920, 27–28.
319. For a critical overview of the effects of the Supreme Court's treatment of laws regulating commercial advertising on the public sphere, see Collins & Skover 1996 (Claiming for instance that "America's marketplace of ideas has largely become a junkyard of commodity ideology"). See also Redish 2001.
320. See Sakulin 2010, 144, Randall 2006.
321. See section 8.6.2.
322. See Baker 2002.

took place in the beginning of the twentieth century.[323] Related to this, around the same time the rule was developed that advertisements in the news media should be clearly recognizable by readers. This was a response to the proliferation of so-called reading notices, i.e. advertisements that read like news stories.[324]

It is clear that the editorial independence from commercial motivations is under more pressure in the context of media which are completely paid for through advertisements.[325] A commercial enterprise offering a free newspaper will need to focus on optimizing advertising revenue. It has been noted that this can have distorting effects on the quality of information being offered, since the interests of readers and advertisers do not necessarily align.[326] In addition, when the reader can access news freely the economic signaling function in the market between publishers and readers deteriorates; readers are no longer capable of expressing their willingness to the publisher to pay for (greater) quality. At present, an increasing amount of news, particularly the offering of electronic media, is entirely paid for through advertising. The free nature of many information products online may increase the focus on advertisers as the primary constituency. This leads to the practice in which the popularity of stories is really the only measure for the performance of journalists.[327] In Chapter 8, and in more depth in Chapter 10, the question will be addressed as to how search engines have responded to the incentives arising out of their advertisement-based business models and the ideal of independence, expressed through a separation between editorial and advertising processes.[328]

5.5.3.   PRESS FREEDOM AND THE READER'S PRIVACY

The discussion above shows how the press' business model can impact the audience's ability to inform itself freely. This points to a final aspect of the legal relation between readers and the press which is relevant from the perspective of the right of media users to receive information and ideas freely, namely communications privacy or reader privacy. Especially in the digital environment, the reader's privacy may come under increased pressure due to the ways in which reading habits are used to profile audiences and support the optimization of revenues.[329]

Privacy is instrumental to the freedom of citizens to inform themselves freely. Moreover, the concept of privacy itself is strongly linked to the prevalence of the written word, the enjoyment of which happens to take place in private. It can be

---

323. See Nerone & Barnhurst 2003, 435–449.
324. See Lawson 1993, 25–44.
325. For a discussion, see Baker 2002.
326. *Ibid.*, 24–26, 88–89.
327. See McGrath 2010; Peters 2010. See also Pariser 2011.
328. See section 10.3.1.
329. See Richards 2008.

seen as a normative outcome of print culture in modern societies, as a range of communications scientists have shown.[330] As Felix Stalder states it:

> While the separation between the private and the public was never without its own set of contentions, print's physical nature has ensured that the gap between the two domains was maintained fairly reliable and unproblematic. There was simply no efficient way for authors to observe readers, even if they wanted to. As print culture became more deeply entrenched in Western culture, privacy, its unintended effect, became seen as one of society's central virtues.[331]

This classic communications model, in which publishing (public) and reading (private) are neatly separated, has been broken. The way communications between the electronic press and its readers are currently structured online has strongly individualized the communications between the press and its readers. In contrast to print, digital technologies allow for the continuous surveillance of reading and information-accessing habits. Web publishing supports the personalization of the press offering in view of the specific interests of individual readers. Why would an online newspaper continue to serve sports news to the reader who tends to read reports about local politics and literature reviews? And why would it continue to serve local news to the reader who is consistently looking for recent market developments? The strongest driver for personalization in the news industry may, ultimately, be the need to compete for advertising revenue online. The personalization and underlying profiling of readers can strongly serve the media's interest in optimizing its advertising revenues. In fact, it is now commonly suggested that the only way for the newspaper industry to survive will be to make use of the behavioral targeting offerings of the Internet advertising industry.[332]

When looking at the classic communications model from a constitutional perspective, it was mentioned that the First Amendment protects against intrusion by the government into the right to freely receive information in the context of the home.[333] Since the right to respect for private life of Article 8 ECHR extends to informational privacy and communications traffic data, it can also be invoked to grant protection in this context. But Article 10 ECHR may strengthen the value that is attached to the protection of privacy in this context. If one is free to access information, but such access is registered and subsequently accessible to public authorities, this would amount to an interference with freedom of expression. In addition, the registration of media use could be a deterring factor to engage in the media. Thus, through the doctrine of chilling effects, Article 10 ECHR could

---

330. For a short overview of this discussion, see Stalder 2002.
331. See Stalder 2002.
332. See Pariser 2011.
333. *Rowan v. Post Office Department*, 397 U.S. 728 (1970). See also *Lamont v. Postmaster General*, 381 U.S. 301 (1965). A state court recently held that access to bookstore records intrudes upon First Amendment rights, *Tattered Cover, Inc. v. City of Thornton*, 44 P.3d 1044, 1053 (Colo. 2002). For a discussion, see Richards 2008, footnote 189 and accompanying text. But see Stone 2005 (pointing to the lack of protection of confidentiality of bookstore records).

take into account the need for privacy safeguards in the context of individualized media use.

To conclude, the importance of readers' privacy in the context of electronic press access is increasing because of the way the communications between publishers and readers are structured online. Internet communications happen one-to-one and interactively, and as a consequence online information providers, including newspapers, can and increasingly choose to keep detailed logs on the consumption of their publications by end-users. These logs are extremely useful, because they can be used to improve and personalize editorial content and to better target advertising, resulting in higher revenues. These logs can also be used in ways that the reader of online media may not suspect. They can be used to identify particular readers and discriminate between them. Although some commentators have raised the issue of the tension between a free press and extensive profiling of readers, these developments, and particularly the practices of behavioral targeting in the context of online media have not yet led to new legislation or constitutional case law in the United States or Europe.[334] It is notable that the issue has been prominently addressed in the context of Web search engines. Of all entities in the networked information environment they know the most about information-accessing behavior.[335]

5.6.   CONCLUSION

Both the European Court of Human Rights and the United States have dedicated some of their most significant judgments to the press and its freedom under the ECHR and the American Constitution respectively. What stands out, in particular in the considerations of the European Court of Human Rights as regards the protection of the press, is that the press is considered to have an important role in our constitutional democracy. The right to freedom of expression sanctions the freedom of the press partly because of its role in informing the public and contributing to the dissemination of information and ideas. A free press also implies that the regulatory role of the State with regard to the affairs of the press is minimal. Press governance is mostly dealt with through self-regulation. We have also identified a general development as regards the role of the State in the European context, in which positive involvement, such as indiscriminatory subsidization, media concentration rules and media pluralism policies more generally, are permissible means to safeguard a healthy media environment. Of course, examples of restrictive legal pressure remain, and in this context Article 10 ECHR and the First Amendment call for compelling justifications.

---

334. See Richards 2008; Cohen 1996; Solove 2007.
335. See sections 8.6.4 and 10.4.2 for the discussion of privacy and access to information in the context of search engines. See section 7.4.7 for a discussion of the value of the patron's privacy in the context of the library.

The press can claim the highest available protection under the ECHR and the First Amendment but does not have a specially protected status which is unavailable to others who are not part of the organized press. Hence, other institutions, groups and individuals should be able to claim similar protection if they contribute to publications on matters of public concern as well as their selection and dissemination. It is important to note that under Article 10 ECHR, everyone engaged in their protected expressive liberties also commits themselves to certain duties and responsibilities. The self-regulation of the press, the ethics of journalism and their context, their impact and the technical means used by them for communicating ideas and information are relevant in this context. In *Stoll* and other recent judgments the European Court of Human Rights has signaled that it takes these duties and responsibilities seriously. The press has to ensure accuracy, precision, reliability and sometimes even prudence and reasonableness. The duties and responsibilities are inherent limitations on the exercise of one's expressive liberties and need to be interpreted in the present-day conditions with regard to the new media environment, in which, in the ECtHR's view, they have taken on added importance.

The instrumental character of press freedom standards, which seems to weigh most heavily in the European context, is limited by the independent protection of the press and its editorial freedom in particular. In this context, U.S. free speech doctrines seem to attach more weight to the protection of the press independent from the interests of the public to inform itself or the interests of possible speakers to reach an audience. It thereby arguably entails a less instrumental notion of press freedom. In fact, the editorial freedom of the press vis-à-vis possible speakers is absolute in the United States, as follows from *Tornillo*. The First Amendment completely bars access regulation of the press. The Supreme Court refers to editorial freedom as the exercise of editorial control and judgment. It includes discretion regarding the choice of material to go into a newspaper, the decisions made as to limitations on the size and content of the newspaper, and its treatment of (public) issues and officials. Under the ECHR, editorial freedom of the press is also protected but it is possible that certain interferences can be legitimate, for instance with reference to the rights and freedom of others. In addition, the press has to exercise its editorial freedom in accordance with the duties and responsibilities mentioned above. Both Courts do not rule out the permissibility of prior restraints, an absolute restriction on editorial freedom, but apply heavy presumptions against its permissibility under the right to freedom of expression.

First Amendment law contains a number of additional interesting doctrinal elements which reflect on the protected interests of potential speakers to reach an audience and the interests of the audience with regard to receiving information freely. First, under the First Amendment overbreadth doctrine the Supreme Court can scrutinize the effects of legal restrictions on unprotected speech on the free flow of protected matter. If there is a mere possibility of chilling effects of the regulation of unprotected speech it can make a restriction on unprotected matter impermissible under the First Amendment. The regulation of speech to protect against unwilling exposure can be legitimate if the means of communications used would impose upon the self-governance of the audience. Finally, the First Amendment also contains a heavy presumption in favor of the rationality of the audience, which is illustrated most clearly in the Supreme Court's case law about the protected status of commercial communications and the public's right to receive them.

As was noted in the beginning of this chapter, the organized press is subject to disruptive change, as a result of a range of developments, such as convergence, digitization and the entry of new players such as search engines, news aggregators and amateur journalists. These developments will have a lasting effect on the press' business model. In this light, it is all the more important to conceptualize the values underlying the right to freedom of expression and the freedom of the press and the various entities in the emerging networked information environment that could be the inheritors of its freedoms.

about the responsibility of search engine providers has been the subject of a similar conflict of interests and arguments, this analysis in this Chapter is particularly useful for the purposes of this study.

The chapter starts (section 6.2) with some general background to the regulation of communications network providers. More specifically, the notions of common carrier and universal access will be discussed, as well as the way these notions reflect the public interest in the governance of access to communications networks. The next section (section 6.3) will discuss the question of the general implications of the right to freedom of expression for the governance of access in the context of Internet access providers. Of specific concern is the question of the implications of the right to freedom of expression for the governance of horizontal conflicts over access between broadband providers and Internet users. Two different and conflicting views on these implications will be presented. The first view bases the protection of Internet access providers under the right to freedom of expression on the communicative liberties of Internet users and points to the possibility of regulating access providers in the interest of freedom of expression. The other view grants Internet access providers their own right to exercise editorial discretion over third-party communications.

These general points of view will be illustrated in more detail by analyzing the way the right to freedom of expression has helped shape the existing legal framework with regard to the responsibility of Internet access providers for illegal and unlawful third-party communications (section 6.4). This framework consists of safe harbors for liability on the one hand, and the self-regulatory paradigm on the other hand. In the section 6.5, the legal governance related to filtering by access providers will be addressed. Internet filters have been consistently promoted as a way to restrict illegal information flows on the Internet. In the debate about Internet filters, concerns over the right to freedom of expression have played a prominent role.

In this chapter, the non-legal term Internet Service Provider (ISP) will be used to denote the basic Internet-related services, such as Internet access, transmission and hosting. This chapter focuses almost exclusively on ISP activity that consists of providing access to the Internet for end-users (Internet access providers). Of special relevance is the legal status of ISP activity that goes beyond mere conduit and interferes at the level of content. The role of access providers is somewhat shifting in this regard, in the direction of more and more involvement, because of a complex interplay of economic, legal and technological developments. This chapter is not concerned with the precise scope of various legal provisions, e.g. the hosting or mere conduit safe harbors in the Directive on Electronic Commerce or the Digital Millennium Copyright Act, or the definition of electronic communications networks and services. Instead, the focus is placed on the way these provisions and the regulatory framework applying to the involvement of access providers with content and third-party communications, have been shaped by restrictions by or concerns over the right to freedom of communication.

Chapter 6

ISP Freedom

6.1.   INTRODUCTION

This chapter will address the way the right to freedom of expression applies to the legal governance of 'access' to the public networked information environment by analyzing its proper application to the legal framework for Internet access providers. The latter are an essential element in the value chains of the Internet, since they provide the connection of Internet users to the rest of the network. In regulatory debates, the role of Internet access providers in the information environment is often compared to traditional conduits such as the postal and telecommunications services. From the perspective of the right to freedom of expression, the role of access providers can intuitively be considered facilitative. They provide the means to exercise one's right to freedom of expression.

However, the analysis of the implications of the right to freedom of expression for Internet access providers is complicated by the fact that the relatively clear regulatory model for traditional conduits has not yet found its way to the digital environment. In addition, regulatory debates about the legal responsibility of Internet access providers are partly shaped by the anxiety that they may facilitate too much. Information access providers are sometimes considered points of control, placing the facilitative role of access providers with regard to the communicative interests of end-users and online information providers under pressure.[336] In other words, there is a clash between the resulting regulatory and legal pressure on Internet access providers to restrict communications and access to online information on the one hand, and their continuing role in providing unrestricted access to the Internet for end-users on the other hand. This makes an analysis of the implications of the right to freedom of expression for the legal governance of Internet access providers complex but all the more interesting. Since the debate

---

336.   See e.g. Lichtman & Posner 2005.

The nature of online communications means one has to consider the possible ramifications of Article 8 ECHR, which protects the right to private life and correspondence, or similar constitutional safeguards.[337] It is notable that restrictions on into communications can run into the protection of both Articles 8 and 10 ECHR.[338] There are similar (but different) safeguards under the U.S. constitution, such as the Fourth Amendment. First Amendment doctrine contains some elements relating to the private sphere as well. For instance, the impact of media on the private sphere of individuals can have an impact on the protection under the First Amendment.[339] Regulation may be permissible if it protects citizens against unwanted exposure to indecent communications in their private sphere.[340] The mere possession of indecent and even obscene material cannot be punished because of their private nature.[341] To restrict the scope of the analysis, the implications of the right to private life and the confidentiality of communications will not be addressed in detail. Sometimes, the term 'freedom of communication' will be used to refer to the communicative freedoms in the context of the Internet, including the right to respect for private life and the confidentiality of private communications. This is in line with the terminology used in this context in the Council of Europe Committee of Ministers, Declaration on freedom of communication on the Internet.

---

337. ECtHR March 25, 1983, *Silver and others v. the United Kingdom*, § 85 ("the two provisions overlap as regards freedom of expression through correspondence"). See also ECtHR November 25, 1997, *Grigoriadis v. Greece*. (The punishment of a soldier for his utterances in a letter to a superior that was not disseminated more widely constitutes a breach of Article 10. The Court holds that the non-public nature of the utterances weighed against the necessity of the punishment.)
338. ECtHR February 21, 1975, *Golder v. U.K.*
339. Some courts have concluded that the First and Fourth Amendment are exclusive. See e.g. *ACLU v. NSA*, 493 F.3d 644 (6th Cir. 2007). See also Richards 2008, note 94.
340. See e.g. *Rowan v. Post Office Dept.*, 397 U.S. 728 (1970) (The law may grant addressees "a mailer's right to communicate must stop at the mailbox of an unreceptive addressee", citing "the ancient concept 'that a man's home is his castle'" into which "not even the king may enter"); *FCC v. Pacifica Foundation*, 438 U.S. 726 (1978). (Indecency regulation of broadcast media—FCC declaratory order with regard to the seven indecent words—constitutional because these media "have established a uniquely pervasive presence in the lives of all Americans.").
341. See e.g. *Stanley v. Georgia* 394 U.S. 557 (1969) ("obscenity statute is unconstitutional insofar as it punishes mere private possession of obscene matter"). The implications of *Stanley* for restrictions on distribution are limited: *United States v. Reidel*, 402 U.S. 351 (1971) (*Stanley* does not imply a right to deliver or distribute the obscene material whose mere private possession cannot be constitutionally be penalized under *Stanley*), *Osbourne v. Ohio*, 495 U.S. 103 (1990) (holding that *Stanley* is inapplicable to criminalization of possession of child pornography, because the underlying rationale was found not to be paternalistic but aims to prevent actual harm to children).

6.2.   REGULATION OF COMMUNICATIONS NETWORK
           PROVIDERS AND FREEDOM OF EXPRESSION

6.2.1.   BACKGROUND

The freedom to deploy and use communications networks is essential for the exercise of the right to freedom of expression and the freedom of communication more generally. The ability to receive and impart information and ideas has always to a considerable extent depended on effective carriage across different communications networks. Recognizing the enormous public utility of communications networks, states have established and facilitated postal services, telephony, telegraphy and electronic communication networks such as the Internet. On the other hand, throughout history, states have controlled, used or called upon communication network providers to suppress access to information and particular modes of distribution. Postal services,[342] telegraph[343] and telephone companies,[344] and more recently Internet Service Providers (ISPs)[345] have been asked or put under legal obligations to ban certain communications from their networks. In other

---

342. For the U.S. postal context, see generally, See John 1998; Fowler 1977; Deutsch 1938. The Supreme Court has ruled several times on the discretionary power of Congress to restrict access to the postal services. See e.g. *Ex Parte Jackson*; 96 U.S. 727 (1878); *Public Clearing House v. Coyne*, 194 U.S. 497 (1904) ("Congress may designate what may be carried in, and what excluded from, the mails, and the exclusion of articles equally prohibited to all does not deny to the owners thereof any of their constitutional rights."); *Milwaukee Social Democratic Pub. Co. v. Burleson*, 255 U.S. 407 (1921) (The order of Postmaster General revoking second class mail privilege for newspaper due to repeated publication of nonmailable matter is constitutional); *Leach v. Carlile*, 258 U.S. 138 (1922) (Postmaster General granted considerable discretion to conclude whether material in the mail is postal fraud, i.e. overstated advertising of medicinal preparation); *Lamont v. Postmaster General*, 381 U.S. 301 (1965) (Scheme involving the delay of delivery of foreign publication, the Peking Press, until addressee reacts on notice, "is unconstitutional, since it imposes on the addressee an affirmative obligation which amounts to an unconstitutional limitation of his rights under the First Amendment."); *Blount v. Rizzi*, 400 U.S. 410 (1971) (administrative censorship scheme for the postal mail violates the First Amendment since "it lacks adequate safeguards against undue inhibition of protected expression"). See also Justice Learned Hand's famous test for incitement in *Masses Publishing Co. v. Patten*, 244 F. 535 (S.D.N.Y. 1917) (concluding that the refusal of the Postmaster General to carry a revolutionary journal violated the First Amendment).
343. Western Union reportedly used to cut off certain newspapers (thereby running them out of business) if they criticized the telegraph company or its business partner, the Associated Press. See e.g. Czitrom 1982, 26–28.
344. See e.g. de Sola Pool 1983, 106. Typically, Information services over telephone are regulated to restrict access to certain content such as indecency. For the Dutch context, see Hoge Raad February 26, 1999, *Antelecom.* (Conceptualizing a restriction on the possibility to use certain call-back services by the Antillian telecommunications monopolist as an interference with Article 10 ECHR.)
345. See e.g. ECJ, Conclusions of Advocate General M. Pedro Cruz Villalón, April 14, 2011, Case C-70/10 (*Scarlet v. SABAM*).

cases, communication networks have acted voluntarily, to restrict access and block and filter out information flows they did not wish to carry.[346]

Restrictions on carriage of content over communications networks raise issues under the right to freedom of communication. Restrictions on the newspaper's use of telegraphy, or the stipulation of special postal and tax rates for the press are examples of how restrictions and regulation of communication networks can undermine free public debate. More recently, concerns about freedom of communication on the Internet have arisen in the context of filtering by ISPs and the disconnection of Internet users from the network as a sanction for alleged copyright infringement.[347]

In contrast to the regulatory framework for the press, with its emphasis on non-interference and self-regulation, the regulation of postal services, telegraphy, telephony and electronic communication networks has been extensive. However, such regulation was traditionally mostly content neutral.[348] In Europe, the classical transport and communications services were nationalized relatively soon after the societal adoption of the underlying technologies. In the United States, the postal services are organized by the State due to the constitution, whereas telephony and telegraphy were always privately owned, but regulated industries.[349]

6.2.2.   REGULATION: RATIONALES, UNIVERSAL SERVICE
          AND COMMON CARRIAGE

The extensive regulation of communication networks, which continues today, is informed by their general public interest on the one hand and legitimized by their particular economics—economies of scale and network effects—on the other hand. The market for communications networks brings about interconnection issues and the infrastructure tends to be an essential facility. In addition, regulation of communications networks contains elements of consumer and privacy protection. This chapter will not focus on these general characteristics of the regulatory framework for communications service providers but look more closely at a number of specific issues relating to the role of the right to freedom of communications in the regulatory framework and the ongoing discussions about the proper responsibility of Internet access providers with regard to third-party communications.

---

346. For examples, see Nunziato 2009. See also Barron 1993.
347. For a discussion of the disconnection of end-users by access providers and the right to freedom of expression, see UN 2011. See also Lucchi 2011.
348. Telecommunications and postal regulation for national monopolies used to contain specific provisions for the stoppage or interruption of communications. See e.g. Article 14 of the (former) Dutch Telegraphy and Telephony Act 1904. The justification of this Dutch provision was found in the obligation for civil servants to report criminal acts when they become aware of them.
349. U.S. Constitution, Section 8: Powers of Congress: "The Congress shall have Power [. . .] To establish Post Offices and Post Roads."

Before looking at more specific issues relating to freedom of expression and access providers, it is helpful to shortly address two central concepts in the regulatory framework for communications networks with regard to the governance of access, namely the 'universal service obligation' and 'common carriage'.

The 'universal service obligation' can be generally defined as a regulatory guarantee for all citizens to be able to get access to a service without discrimination—in particular regardless of geographic location—and with certain guarantees of basic quality.[350] United States law contains a universal service obligation in the Telecommunications Act 1996, 47 U.S. section 254. The European Union's Universal Service Directive, which is part of the regulatory framework for the electronic communications network and services, contains universal service obligations in Chapter II.[351] At present, fixed telephony is a universal service— Article 4(1) of the Universal Services Directive—and specific minimal guarantees as regards quality, capabilities and price are prescribed. It is notable that the object of the universal service obligation is dynamic, as can be seen from the provisions themselves. The European Commission regularly reviews what should be considered part of the universal service obligation. In line with this dynamic interpretation, there is currently a debate whether or not end-user access to Internet broadband should be included in the universal service obligation.

The legal concept of 'common carriage' can be traced as far back as Roman law. It was developed further in English common law and became an important part of the U.S. common law system relating to transportation and communications services. In the twentieth century, the common carrier obligations were included in the administrative legal frameworks for communications network providers.

Common carriage can be seen as a distinctive regulatory model for service providers in the information and communications environment, distinctive from the model for the press and the broadcasting model. It applies to communications service providers, offering transmission or conduit services to the public. Common carriage ties access and equal treatment obligations to transportation and communications service providers invested with the public interest. It is important to note that common carriage also implies a limitation on liability.[352] The common carriage requirement of non-interference and non-discrimination is usually understood only to apply to lawful communications.

Due to the rise of the Internet as the dominant communications network and the multiplicity of roles of the Internet in the networked communications environment (convergence), the discussion about the proper application of the 'common carriage' model has become more complex. In the early 1990s, telecommunications law scholar Eli Noam aptly called the issue "content interconnection in an

---

350. On the (history of the) notion of 'universal service' in the U.S. context, see Mueller 1997.
351. Council Directive 2002/22, 2002 OJ (L 108), 51 (EC).
352. For the U.S. context, see e.g. Perrit 1992; Nuziato 2009; Barron 1993. See also Koelman 2000, note 165 cited references.

intermedia environment."[353] Of late, the discussion about common carriage in the Internet environment has mostly taken place under a new flag, namely the principle of 'net neutrality'. This principle refers to the principle of non-interference of Internet service providers with the way the network is actually being used. Net neutrality is often defended with reference to the economic and public interest value of the so-called end-to-end principle in the Internet's design.[354] The non-interference standard is discussed with regard to blocking or prioritization, in relation to content, destinations, applications and end-user equipment. Access providers carry communications of websites directed at the general public and facilitate private communications such as email or voice communications. Audio-visual material, the mass distribution of which is historically governed by broadcasting regulation, is flowing over the Internet in unprecedented quantities as well. In other words, access providers carry one-to-one, one-to-many, and many-to-many types of communications at the same time. They are the new gateways to online media and basic information services. In addition, broadband services facilitate the use of user-driven software applications, such as peer-to-peer filesharing, Internet telephony and email.

Although it may seem logical to see a link between the role of the State to promote the effective exercise of one's right to freedom of communication on the one hand and the existence of common carrier and universal service obligations on the other hand, this link is not always made by regulators in practice. In fact, historically, the link between these fundamental regulatory concepts for communications regulation and the right to freedom of expression and democratic and societal participation more generally was not made at all and has only quite recently been made in the United States during the Clinton's administration and later in the European context. The European Commission now links universal service obligations to the question whether the respective services (and service levels) are essential for *social inclusion*.[355] It is clear that the effective basic communicative freedoms can be considered a prerequisite for social inclusion as well. A more explicit link between freedom of communication and a fundamental right to Internet access has recently been made in the context of proposals to disconnect users from the Internet. The link between freedom of communications and common carriage types of obligation is typically made in the context of restrictions by ISPs on access to content through filtering technology, not controlled by the end-user.[356]

---

353. See Noam 1992, 426–428. See also Barron 1993.
354. See Wu 2003. See also van Schewick 2010.
355. EC, http://ec.europa.eu/information_society/policy/ecomm/current/consumer_rights/universal_service.
356. See section 6.5.

6.3.   FREEDOM OF EXPRESSION AND INTERNET
             ACCESS PROVIDERS

6.3.1.   STATUS OF INTERNET ACCESS PROVIDERS UNDER
             THE RIGHT TO FREEDOM OF EXPRESSION

From the perspective of Article 10 ECHR, access providers can claim protection
under the right to freedom of expression in cases where public authorities would
prevent them from offering their services on the market, or oblige them to block or
filter content. In *Autronic*, in which the Court first clarified that also companies
enjoy protection under Article 10 ECHR, the Court concluded the following:

> Article 10 [. . .] applies not only to the content of information but also to the
> means of transmission or reception since any restriction imposed on the means
> necessarily interferes with the right to receive and impart information.[357]

Thus, Internet access providers can claim protection under Article 10 ECHR for
interferences (in vertical relations) with their role in transmitting information and
ideas, irrespective of the actual content. Interferences would have to satisfy the test
of Article 10, second paragraph. As can be seen from the citation above, the
interference with the means of transmission and reception offered by communications providers is derived from the interests of others to impart and receive information and ideas freely. It also follows from the ECtHR's case law that users of
communications services can sometimes themselves complain against restrictions
(at least by public authorities) on the use of such means which affect them
directly.[358] Notably, the requirement that restrictions have to affect applicants
to the Court directly delineates this possibility to claim protection under Article 10
ECHR, from an *actio pupolaris*.

6.3.2.   ACCESS REGULATION AND THE RIGHT TO FREEDOM OF EXPRESSION

The most difficult questions about the implications of the right to freedom of
expression for the legal governance of access in electronic communications networks arise in the context of horizontal relations between communications service
providers and the users of the network. First, does the right to freedom of expression impact the legal governance of horizontal conflicts over access? What is the
proper role of the State is in this regard? If, all of a sudden, all access providers
would decide to block access to a certain controversial but legal website, would this
information provider have to be able to complain about this due to its right to
freedom of expression protected by Article 10 ECHR? And, more generally, does
the right to freedom of expression point to a role for public authorities to prevent

---

357. ECtHR May 22, 1990, *Autronic v. Switzerland*. See also ECtHR May 24, 1988 *Mueller and
      others v. Switzerland*.
358. See e.g. ECtHR October 29, 1992, *Open Door v. Ireland*.

access providers from exercising undue interference with communications on the network? As will become clear in this chapter, the views on this issue diverge and there may not be a generally accepted set of implications of the right to freedom of expression to answer these questions. Below, a general overview of the debate will be offered by contrasting two generalized points of view.

One point of view would consider the protection of access providers under the right to freedom of expression to be derived from the communicative liberties of end-users.[359] This view would hold that Internet access providers can claim protection under the right to freedom of expression to the extent that they can base their claim on the interests of their users to impart and receive information and ideas freely. This line of thought directly implies that it is possible for access providers to act in conflict with the communicative interests of their users. In other words, this view could inform the State to consider regulating access providers to guarantee the protection of these interests through legal requirements.[360] Some would go further and claim that the State has a proper legal obligation to restrict access providers from interfering with the free flow of information on their networks. In the European context, this positive obligation on the State can be linked to the positive obligation on the State to promote pluralism and the role of the State to protect the *effective exercise* of the right to freedom of expression.[361]

The other point of view, which is mostly found in the United States, does not make the connection between the protection of access providers under the right to freedom of expression and the rights and freedoms of the users of the network. Instead, it conceptualizes the right to freedom of expression as a negative right which prevents government from regulating the way the free exercise of the right to freedom of expression plays out in private relations. The right to freedom of expression protects legal entities and actual individuals alike. In this view, the right to freedom of expression protects the discretion over communicative means that a particular entity controls, be it a natural person, the owner of a nation-wide broadband network or an online news outlet.[362] This protection would be granted in vertical relations against regulation and government interference. With regard to horizontal conflicts over access, the right to freedom of expression would simply require that government would leave the resolution to the functioning of the market. Hence, this view denies the possibility of government to be positively involved in the protection of freedom of expression in society, since freedom of expression is both seen as a negative constraint on government involvement as well as not restricted to proper individuals.

These two different points of view and their implications for the status of access regulation under the right to freedom of expression can be illustrated by

---

359. See e.g. CoE, Committee of Ministers, "Declaration on Freedom of communication on the Internet," May 28, 2003. See also Balkin 1990; Balkin 2004; Benkler 2001; Nunziato 2009; De Sola Pool 1983; Carter 1984; Barron 1993.
360. See e.g. Berman & Weitzner 1995. See also Krattenmaker & Powe 1995.
361. See section 4.4.1.
362. See e.g. Yoo 2010. See also Tribe & Goldstein 2009.

contrasting the status of 'common carriage' with the status of access regulation for the press. Common carriage can be seen as the strongest possible form of access regulation. It basically nullifies the editorial freedom of the entities it is applied to and would, as a result, be incompatible with the right to freedom of expression if applied to the press. As discussed in Chapter 5, the editorial freedom of the press, is partly informed by the public interest and the communicative interests of the public and possible speakers. It also protects the press, as a speaker, in relation to possible interferences by public authorities to promote the communicative interests of users and possible speakers.

In the context of traditional conduits, such as the postal services and telephony, the public interest is typically considered to entail universal access, and indiscriminate and non-interference with communications. Common carriage obligations, which were explicitly based on these public interests, ensured that communications services were acting in this public interest. As pointed out above, universal access and common carriage, amongst other regulatory requirements, ensure the widest possible exercise of communicative liberties by Internet users.

Now the question is to what extent access providers, such as the press, assert a right to freedom of expression to defend a possible decision to restrict certain information flows on their networks?[363] There are two contexts in which one could imagine such claims to be made: vertically, in the context of common carrier obligations and horizontally, with respect to access claims by possible users of their networks in reaction to voluntary decisions to restrict information flows for instance through blocking and filtering.

The case law of the European Court of Human Rights does not resolve whether Article 10 ECHR protects the decision of the owner of a communications network *not to* use those means for certain communications. Under Article 10 there is a right to remain silent,[364] but it is highly questionable whether this right—that has been construed in specific circumstances relating to individual liberty—would apply to a corporate entity that merely provides the means to communicate. The fact that Article 10 ECHR applies to individuals and corporations alike could be used to argue that the right not to communicate—in the case of conduits, the right *not to transmit*—is also protected by Article 10 ECHR. However, it is unlikely that the Court would be willing to come to this conclusion.

It is more likely that the Court would respond to horizontal access issues under the right to freedom of expression between access providers and users of the network, by balancing the interest of the free exercise of the right to freedom of expression of users on the one hand, with the right to the free exercise of the provider's property on the other hand. An access provider's right *not to transmit* third-party communications would be based on the economic freedom of

---

363. One of the reasons I ask this question is because of the developments under United States First Amendment doctrine, which increasingly point to a positive answer to this question.
364. See Van Dijk et al. 2006, 783.

communications service providers.[365] This freedom is not necessarily less protected than the freedom of communication of end-users.[366]

The ECtHR had to deal with a comparable issue involving restrictions on the use of private property for expressive purposes in the case *Appleby* and it did not refer to any right not to speak in this case. The decision to refuse access for expressive purposes was considered to be based on the economic freedom of the owner of the means of communication, not on its freedom not to use those means for the expressive purposes of applicants, sanctioned by the right to freedom of expression.[367] In *Appleby*, the ECtHR took account of the Supreme Court's jurisprudence on access to a private forum to speak and protest[368] and concluded that "while freedom of expression is an important right, it is not unlimited. [...] Regard must also be had to the property rights of the owner of the shopping center under Article 1 of Protocol No. 1."[369] The Court concluded that Article 10 ECHR "does not bestow any freedom of forum for the exercise of that right. While it is true that demographic, social, economic and technological developments are changing the ways in which people move around and come into contact with each other, the Court is not persuaded that this requires the automatic creation of rights of entry to private property, or even, necessarily, to all publicly owned property [...]." In other words, under the Convention there is no such thing as a right to access private property to effectively impart ideas. The Court left room for an exception if "the bar on access to property has the effect of preventing any effective exercise of freedom of expression or it can be said that the essence of the right has been destroyed." In such cases, "a positive obligation could arise for the State to protect the enjoyment of the Convention rights by regulating property rights." It is notable that the Court explicitly referred to Marsh *v.* Alabama, the U.S. Supreme Court's judgment affirming speech rights in a corporate town, as an example of such circumstances.[370]

6.3.3.   First Amendment

Like Article 10 ECHR, the First Amendment not only protects the freedom of speech or of the press, but also the freedom to receive and distribute information and ideas.[371] There is a rich history of case law relating to the constitutionality of the publicly owned postal services under the First Amendment dealing with restrictions on the ability to have information distributed or to receive it freely through the

---

365. For example in the Netherlands, see Hoge Raad [Dutch Supreme Court] March 12, 2004 (*XS4all/Abfab*).
366. This could be different in the United States.
367. See ECtHR May 6, 2003, Appleby and Others, § 43.
368. *Ibid.*, § 7.
369. *Ibid.*, § 43.
370. *Ibid.*, § 47.
371. *Griswold v. Connecticut*, 381 U.S. 479 (1965). See also section 5.5.1.

mail.[372] Privately owned communications networks can assert the protection of the First Amendment against State actions restricting the free flow of communications on their networks. It is worth noting that the distribution of unprotected material, such as obscenity, is itself not protected by the First Amendment.[373] However, regulations targeting unprotected speech are still scrutinized for their effects on constitutionally protected communications.[374]

The First Amendment, as applied by U.S. Courts today, arguably implies a broader right not to speak than freedom of expression in the European context.[375] This right has been argued to be available to the owners of the means of communications such as broadcasters, cable companies and Internet access providers.[376] Thus the owner of the means of communication would receive protection of the First Amendment against restrictions (not) to use their property for certain speech, on top of the constitutional protection of their property rights.[377] As mentioned above, this theory equates the exercise of the right to freedom of expression to a considerable extent with the exclusive right over the use of one's property. Property distribution, including the ownership of communicative means, is taken for granted and is its use for communicative means is considered in line with the free market place of information and ideas.

Although in the United States, the constitutional law mainstream is open to this view, and increasingly, the Supreme Court's First Amendment doctrine seems to support it, it is not generally accepted and remains controversial. One of the main lines of criticism emphasizes the incompatibility of this view with the ideal of individual liberty and autonomy underlying the right to freedom of expression, as well as democratic ideal of self-governance.[378] From the ideal of democracy, access providers and the entities that merely act as the gateways to public debate more generally should be prevented from exercising undue interference with the public network information environment. Arguably, the right not to speak only plays a role in cases of compelled speech involving individual liberty. It's the intellectual freedom of individuals that is worthy of protection against compelled speech.

Another way of looking at the question about the legitimacy of interferences of access providers that would harm the communicative liberties of end-users and information providers is to take as a starting point that the 'normal' practice for

---

372. See section 6.2.1.
373. *United States v. Reidel*, 402 U.S. 351 (1971).
374. See e.g. *New York Times Co. v. Sullivan, 376 U.S. 254 (1964)*; *Smith v. California*, 361 U.S. 147 (1959).
375. See e.g. *West Virginia State Board of Education v. Barnette*, 319 U.S. 624 (1943) (State law that requires all children to salute to the flag unconstitutional; distinguished in *Pruneyard*.) *Wooley v. Maynard*, 430 U.S. 705 (1977) (law punishing covering up of motto 'Live free or die' on New Hampshire license plate unconstitutional.) See also *Harper & Row Publishers, Inc. v. Nation Enters*, 471 U.S. 539, 559 (1985).
376. See Balkin 2004, 17–21. See also Benkler 2001; Chandler 2008; Seidman 2008.
377. Property rights are protected by the Fifth Amendment and Fourteenth Amendment.
378. See e.g. Baker 1994.

ISPs would be to provide access to all. General obligations not to do something, namely restrict access to certain users of a communication network, should be distinguished from obligations to use the networks for particular expressive purposes. The U.S. common law theory as regards common carriers functioned in this way.[379] The communications service provider, through its manifestation to the public, 'chose' whether it was a conduit or a publisher. If it opted for the conduit option, it would have no First Amendment rights itself, in terms of the ability to control and discriminate between communications and different sources. If it opted for a publisher status, it would get its own First Amendment rights.[380] This choice also had an impact on third-party liability standards for the service provider. Common carriers received tort immunity in return for equal access obligations, whereas entities that exercised editorial discretion could be held accountable. It is interesting to note that in the United States, these tort standards no longer govern the behavior of Internet intermediaries, as will be shown below.

6.4.   ISP INTERMEDIARY LIABILITY AND THE RIGHT
            TO FREEDOM OF EXPRESSION

6.4.1.   BACKGROUND

The debate about the responsibility of ISPs for their role in providing access to the Internet started in the 1990s in two different legal contexts, namely content regulation on the one hand, and the protection of intellectual property rights on the other hand. Traditional content regulation focusing on publishers and the mass media and the enforcement of national laws were becoming problematic, unfeasible, and unpractical in the context the Internet, since many new information providers entered the public networked information environment and could reach global audiences from locations all over the world. A shift in focus led regulators, litigants and the creative industries to focus on the responsibility and possible role of different types of ISPs to enforce existing rules with regard to illegal and unlawful information flows.[381] In the absence of specific legislation for ISP responsibility, the question whether ISPs could and should be held liable for illegal and/or harmful activities of end-users and online information providers and what could be expected of the different types of services in terms of policing the

---

379. See Perrit 1992, 66–67. Perrit warns that these conclusions are far from clear. See also Barron 1993.
380. See Perrit 1992.
381. Early examples of the targeting of Internet access providers by public authorities can be found in Germany. In a case involving the accessibility of child pornography on Compuserve, the employee Felix Somm was convicted by a Court in Munich and CompuServe was ordered to block the material for German subscribers. In another case, involving the radical-left online publication 'Radikal' hosted in the Netherlands, prosecutors threatened to prosecute Internet access providers if they would fail to block the allegedly terrorist material for their users in Germany. See e.g. European Commission 1996b, 15.

Internet and their users, was not easily answered.[382] The subsequent legal uncertainty that was the result of this first wave of litigation ran counter to the efforts to facilitate e-commerce and the development of the Internet and the Web more generally. This led legislatures in the United States and Europe to enact specific rules about the legal responsibility of ISPs.[383]

The regulatory response with regard to ISP responsibility had two interdependent branches. On the one hand, so-called safe harbors for Internet and online intermediaries were introduces into the law, first in the U.S. and several European countries, and later also at the level of the European Union.[384] These safe harbors were to provide legal certainty for ISPs and establish the proper boundaries of ISP liability for the illegal or infringing activities of third parties.

On the other hand, legislatures called for further self-regulation and a continuing dialogue between the various stakeholders. In other words, the safe harbor regulation established the legal boundaries with regard to the responsibility of Internet intermediaries in the law. Within these boundaries, the industry was expected to establish self-regulatory practices to help address the circulation of unlawful, infringing and also harmful communications. This second branch of the regulatory response, namely self- and co-regulation, became a new paradigm for dealing with information flows on the Internet. Self-regulation was argued to be a better way to reach public policy goals than command and control types of regulation.[385]

The self-regulatory paradigm for ISPs and information services more generally was first established in the EU with the 1998 Council Recommendation for the European audio-visual and information services industry.[386] The 1998 Council Recommendation calls upon the Member States to promote, at the national level, the voluntary establishment of self-regulatory frameworks for the protection of minors and human dignity on the Internet. In the United States, perhaps the best example of the self-regulatory paradigm is one of the limited liability provisions itself, namely CDA, Section 230.[387]

Both the self-regulatory paradigm and the drafting of liability standards lead to concerns over the right to freedom of expression, which will be discussed in this section. First, the liability standards for Internet intermediaries are directly related to the possible chilling effects of these standards on online information flows. Too weak a standard would incentivize Internet intermediaries to be more restrictive

---

382. For a discussion of access to communications networks, tort liability principles and the right to freedom of expression, for the European context, see Koelman 2000 and for the U.S. context, see Perrit 1992.
383. For a discussion and legal comparison of the two frameworks, see Koelman 2000.
384. A number of Member States, including Sweden and Germany had already introduced safe harbors at the national level before the EU harmonized intermediary liability for ISPs.
385. See Price & Verhulst 2005, 135–162. See also Hans-Bredow Institut 2006. Self-regulation has long been promoted beyond the context of Internet regulation. See Baldwin & Cave 1999.
386. Council Recommendation 98/560, 1998 OJ (L 270), 48 (EC).
387. See section 6.4.4.

and possibly too restrictive, thereby obstructing legitimate information flows in the networked information environment.

Second, Internet content self-regulation was directly meant to result in the removal, filtering and blocking of information by the industry. Of specific concern are the possible effects of self-regulation on legitimate content flows and the lack of substantive and procedural safeguards. The question arises whether overly restrictive practices by access providers, resulting from self-regulation, are in line with the right to freedom of communication and to what extent the State itself can be held accountable in its role of promoting, cooperating and shaping self-regulatory frameworks for content regulation on the Internet.[388]

6.4.2. INTERMEDIARY LIABILITY: EU AND THE UNITED STATES

The European legal developments with regard to ISP liability and responsibility took place in the context of illegal and harmful content on the Internet and the protection of minors on the one hand,[389] and the enforcement of copyright law on the Internet on the other hand.[390] These two perspectives met in the discussion leading to the Directive on Electronic Commerce (ECD).[391] The ECD contains provisions which state that basic Internet intermediaries are under certain conditions not to be held liable for the information flows they facilitate. This framework of limited liability consists of three horizontal liability exemptions in the ECD (Articles 12–14), as well as ban on preventive monitoring obligations for these types of intermediaries (Article 15).[392] To be more precise, the Directive protects information society services[393] acting as intermediaries for their 'mere conduit' (Article 12), 'caching' (Article 13), and 'hosting' (Article 14) activities. Article 15 prevents the Member States from imposing general obligations on the providers of the services falling under any of the safe harbors to monitor the information that they transmit or store, or to seek facts or circumstances indicating illegal activity.

---

388. See Tambini et al. 2008. See also Kreimer 2006; Bambauer 2011.
389. See in particular European Commission 1996b; European Commission 1996c; Council Recommendation 98/560, 1998 OJ (L 270), 48 (EC); European Parliament and Council Recommendation, 2006/952, 2006 OJ (L 378), 72 (EC). See also European Commission 1997b, 5 ("in the absence of an accepted classification of operators and functions, the question of liability for operators who merely provide access to services or communications networks remains open. However, a majority came out in favour of an absence of liability for these operators, which however does not me that they have no role to play, for example in informing consumers").
390. See European Commission 1995; European Commission 1996a.
391. European Commission 1997a; European Union Ministers 1997, and the Directive on Electronic Commerce (ECD): Council Directive 2000/31, 2000 OJ (L 178) 1 (EC).
392. Council Directive 2000/31, 2000 OJ (L 178) 1 (EC).
393. Article 2(a) ECD refers to Article 1(2) Directive 98/34/EC as amended by Directive 98/48/EC for a definition of 'information society service': "any service normally provided for remuneration, at a distance, by electronic means and at the individual request of a recipient of services."

An information society service acting as mere conduit, such as an Internet access provider connecting end-users to the Internet, is protected under Article 12 ECD if it does not initiate the transmission, select the receiver of the transmission, or select or modify the information contained in the transmission. Under Articles 13 and 14 ECD, the proxy caching and hosting activities of information society services are conditionally exempted from liability. Notably, the safe harbors do not affect the possibility to claim injunctive relief. They explicitly leave open the possibility for a court or administrative authority to require an ISP to terminate or prevent an infringement. This also applies to information society services acting as mere conduits. Moreover, exemptions do not affect the lawfulness of the processing of information by providers of any of these types of intermediary services. The lawfulness has to be determined by applying the relevant laws of the Member States.[394] Hence, the exemptions do not protect the providers of exempted services against litigation which is aimed at an injunction. Although controversial, judges have ordered Internet access providers to disconnect a specific end-user or to block access to specific online information.[395]

In the United States, the liability of Internet intermediaries for copyright infringements and the responsibility for illegal content such as indecency or defamation has been dealt with separately. The fragmentation of safe harbors along the lines of different underlying legal concerns, which is called a vertical approach, is one of the main differences with the European framework of Internet safe harbors, which has adopted a horizontal solution. The Digital Millennium Copyright Act introduced a safe harbor for liability of access providers for copyright infringement in Section 512(a). It provides that no general monitoring obligations can be imposed upon access providers. Injunctive relief with regard to possible copyright infringement by access providers is further restricted to orders blocking access to subscribers or orders to block access, to a specific, identified, online location outside the United States.[396] An intermediary liability exemption for defamation and other illegal content, except for criminal law, intellectual property law, and communications privacy law, can be found in CDA, section 230. This provision, introduced by the Communications Decency Act in 1996, restricts the liability of so-called interactive computer services. Courts have interpreted it as an absolute safe harbor for ISPs with regard to third-party content. In the next section, the legal developments that led to the current liability regime based on CDA, section 230 will be discussed in detail, as they are intrinsically linked to the implications of the First Amendment for speech carrying intermediaries and the distinction in First Amendment doctrine between different types of speech

---

394. In civil law terms, the safe harbors do not affect the lawfulness of certain actions but they harmonize the requirements for finding fault and/or negligence. See Koelman 2000, 52.
395. See e.g. Chavannes 2007, 174–178. See also Jakobsen 2010.
396. Section 512 (j)(1)(B) of the U.S. Copyright Act. It is notable that this restriction on possible injunctions is absent in the final text of the Directive on Electronic Commerce. For a discussion, see Koelman 2000.

intermediaries.[397] Another difference between United States and the European law, is the scope of the safe harbor framework. The safe harbors in the DMCA, section 512, and the CDA, section 230, both extent to third-party liability of search engines, whereas the European framework did not include this type of service. We will address this difference in more detail in Chapter 9.[398]

The Council of Europe and its Committee of Ministers have addressed ISP responsibility in a number of legal instruments, the most important of which are the Convention on Cybercrime, the Recommendation on self-regulation concerning cyber content, the Declaration on Freedom of communication on the Internet and the Recommendation on freedom of expression and information with regard to Internet filters.[399] The Recommendation on freedom of expression and information with regard to Internet filters will be addressed in more detail in section 6.5.

As will become clear shortly, the safe harbors and the self-regulatory framework for ISPs, take into account freedom of expression concerns. Below we will address the way this has happened in more detail. As the safe harbors in the ECD were inspired by similar legislation in the United States, ISP liability regulation in the United States will be addressed first.

6.4.3. THE DMCA SAFE HARBORS AND THE FIRST AMENDMENT

Before going into detail it is worth noting that the First Amendment applies differently in the context of intermediary liability for copyright infringement and other unlawful activity in the United States.[400] In copyright cases U.S. Courts usually refuse to admit a separate freedom of expression defense, since free speech concerns are considered to be internalized into copyright law itself and copyright law is content neutral.[401] In cases of liability for defamation and otherwise illegal content, the Courts have always needed to balance restrictions on free speech and distributor liability with the requirements of the First Amendment, which sets limitations on liability standards of distributors.[402]

The DMCA safe harbors clarify the responsibility of online intermediaries with regard to third-party copyright infringements. In particular, the due process guarantees tied to the elaborate provision with regard to notice and takedown for

---

397. See Freiwald 2001, Cannon 1996, Myerson 1995.
398. See section 9.3.
399. CoE, Convention on Cybercrime, 2001; CoE, Committee of Ministers, Recommendation Rec(2001)8 of the Committee of Ministers to Member States on self-regulation concerning cyber content, 2001; CoE, Freedom of communication on the Internet, 2003; CoE, Committee of Ministers, Recommendation CM/Rec(2008)6 on measures to promote the respect for freedom of expression and information with regard to Internet filters, 2008.
400. Koelman 2000, 42–44.
401. See generally Hugenholtz 2001. See also Stone et al. 2008, 504. For the relation between the First Amendment and Copyright law, see *Eldred v. Ashcroft*, 537 U.S. 186 (2003) (upholding copyright term extension and concluding that copyright law internalizes First Amendment concerns in idea-expression dichotomy and availability of fair use defense.).
402. See Myerson 1995.

hosting providers can be seen to be informed by freedom of expression concerns. A hosting provider has to notify their customers if they decide to remove or disable access to material (Section 512 (g)(2)). In addition, the DMCA contains a disincentive to issue unjust notifications of infringement. It is unclear to what extent these guarantees were *necessary* from the perspective of the First Amendment. As mentioned above, unlike in the case of distributor liability for defamation, references to the First Amendment in copyright infringement cases are rare. The *Netcom* case, a case before the adoption of the DMCA safe harbors about the responsibility of the provider of a BBS for copyright infringements by its users, contains such a reference. The First Amendment plays a role in the consideration of the fair use defense.[403]

Those protected by the DMCA safe harbors do have to implement a policy that provides for the termination of access of repeat infringers.[404] Nimmer concludes that one can only be considered a repeat infringer—in contrast to an *alleged* repeated infringer—when there is actual proof of infringements in multiple occasions. Hence, a reasonable policy for a broadband provider can place be relatively strict requirements on what is needed before it terminates an Internet subscription. Intermediaries also have to accommodate and not interfere with standard technical measures to prevent infringements from taking place, which is a reference to the anticipated improvements in filtering technology. The DMCA allows and expects ISPs to disable access to material or activity claimed to be infringing as long as it acts in good faith in response to a claim or based on facts of circumstances that the material or activity is infringing (512 (g)(1)). Thus, Internet access providers could, in fact, decide to block access to certain material on the Internet they consider to be infringing.[405]

The DMCA safe harbors for ISPs have been shown to have a chilling effect on legitimate third-party communications, in particular in the context of the hosting safe harbor and the safe harbor for information location tools (search engines).[406] There is—to my knowledge—no case law about the constitutionality under the First Amendment of the possible incentives the DMCA places on ISPs to block

---

403. See *Religious Technology Center v. Netcom*, 907 F. Supp. 1361 (N.D. Cal. 1995). See also Koelman 2000, 41.
404. See Nimmer & Nimmer looseleaf, § 12B.10. Nimmer does not discuss the communicative interests of subscribers not to have a subscription terminated. U.S. courts have held that service providers do not have to implement privacy invasive policies to ensure the impossibility of continuation of service (in the context of free email services) of the repeat infringer. See *Io Group v. Veoh Networks*, 586 F.Supp.2d 1132, 1145 (N.D. Cal. 2008). ("[S]ection 512(i) does not require service providers to track users in a particular way or to affirmatively police users [. . .].") The provision's reference to account holders or customers raises the question as to what intermediaries such as search engines should do with repeat infringers who they do not have a contractual relationship with. See also Ginsberg 2008, note 81 and accompanying text.
405. See also FCC's proposed standards relating to an open Internet, which include the following statement: "[t]he draft rules would not prohibit broadband Internet access service providers from taking reasonable action to prevent the transfer of unlawful content, such as the unlawful distribution of copyrighted works." See Federal Communications Commission 2009.
406. See Berkman Center for Internet & Society, Chilling Effects Clearinghouse.

constitutionally protected speech or to disconnect users. The issue remains hotly debated, currently in the context of the proposal of a new bill relating to copyright enforcement online, the PROTECT IP ACT, which foresees DNS filtering by access providers of websites that contribute to copyright infringements.

6.4.4.   COMMUNICATIONS DECENCY ACT 230 AND THE FIRST AMENDMENT

Outside of copyright law, in the areas of defamation and indecency regulation, the legal developments with regard to intermediary liability took quite another direction. In the twentieth century, U.S. legal practice had developed a rich body of case law dealing with publisher, distributor and carrier tort liability and the First Amendment.[407] A standard case for distributor liability under the First Amendment, for instance, is *Smith v. California*. The Supreme Court ruled that a law establishing strict liability for booksellers selling obscene material is unconstitutional, because it would inhibit freedom of expression by making booksellers reluctant to exercise it.[408] More particularly, the Court emphasized that strict liability on distributors would impose an unconstitutional restriction on the public's access to constitutionally protected material. As mentioned above, common carriers invested with the public interest received immunity for defamation and other torts in return for equal access obligations.[409]

The first ISP defamation cases in the 1990s were dealt with in the absence of specific rules for the liability of different kinds of Internet intermediaries. In *Cubby*, a New York district court determined that the provider of the bulletin board service CompuServe, should be viewed as "the functional equivalent of a more traditional news vendor."[410] The Court considered several print analogies before coming to this conclusion. Even though CompuServe had the contractual right to refuse to carry a particular publication, "in reality, once it does decide to carry a publication, it will have little or no editorial control over that publication's contents."[411] CompuServe had "no more editorial control over such a publication than [...] a public library, book store, or newsstand, and it would be no more feasible for CompuServe to examine every publication it carries for potentially

---

407. For an overview, see Ardia 2010; Perrit 1992.
408. *Smith v. California*, 361 U.S. 147 (1959) (arguing, with regard to the contents of an ordinance imposing liability on booksellers, that the absence of a requirement of knowledge of the contents of the book on the part of the seller implied that the ordinance would tend to impose a severe limitation on the public's access to constitutionally protected matter).
409. See Ardia 2010, 398–401. See also Perrit 1992. Perrit also explains that the precise contours of common carriage status on liability and First Amendment rights have become unclear due to fact that since a century common carriers had become a heavily regulated industry, thereby pushing the common law standards for common carriers to the background in favor of administrative law. See also Perritt 2010, 436–460 (arguing for the free market approach in combination with the development of common law standards through litigation, as well as the combination of tort immunity and equal access obligations.).
410. *Cubby, Inc. v. CompuServe Inc.*, 776 F. Supp. 135 (S.D.N.Y. 1991).
411. *Ibid.*

defamatory statements than it would be for any other distributor to do so."[412] The Court subsequently established the distributor standard for an Internet intermediary like CompuServe to be liable for illegal content:; it would only be liable if it "knew or had reason to know of the allegedly defamatory [...] statements."[413] Hence, a passive, unknowing conduit would not be liable for unlawful third-party communications.

In *Prodigy*,[414] the New York Supreme Court reversed the causal connection between editorial oversight and distributor liability and ruled that an online bulletin board operator is liable if it does exercise such control over the selection of content. Prodigy had been offering online bulletin boards, while actively removing messages it deemed offensive by using technical filtering products and content screening guidelines for its moderators. The *Prodigy* judgment was argued to be bad law, both by proponents of more robust protection of speech online and proponents of more effective regulation of illegal and harmful content. The former argued that if intermediaries such as Prodigy were to be treated analogously to speakers in the print world, this would result in chilling effects on speech, since they would start to monitor and police all communications on their platforms. The latter argued that the Court should not punish the good faith efforts of intermediaries to combat illegal and harmful content by increasing their liability for material that would slip through. This would induce them to be more passive and do nothing about illegal and harmful content.

Acting on the concern that *Prodigy*'s liability standard could cause intermediaries not to assist in restricting access to illegal or harmful content, Congress overruled *Prodigy* and introduced a 'Good Samaritan' blocking and screening of offensive material exemption for Internet intermediaries in the Communications Decency Act.[415] CDA, section 230(c)(1) now provides as follows:

> No provider or user of an interactive computer service shall be treated as the publisher or speaker of any information provided by another information content provider.[416]

Moreover, CDA, section 230(c)(2) limits the civil liability of interactive computer services that do decide to restrict access or availability to content. It provides as follows:

> No provider or user of an interactive computer service shall be held liable on account of—(A) any action voluntarily taken in good faith to restrict access to or availability of material that the provider or user considers to be obscene, lewd, lascivious, filthy, excessively violent, harassing, or otherwise objectionable,

---

412. *Ibid.*
413. For a discussion of *Cubby* and the different liability standards for publishers and distributors because of the First Amendment, see Myerson 1995.
414. *Stratton Oakmont, Inc. v. Prodigy Services Co.* No. 31063/94, 1995, WL 323710 (N.Y. Sup. Ct. May 1995).
415. See Cannon 1996; see also Koelman 2000, 35.
416. 47 U.S.C. § 230 (c)(1).

whether or not such material is constitutionally protected; or (B) any action taken to enable or make available to information content providers or others the technical means to restrict access to material described in paragraph (1).[417]

These provisions were primarily meant to remove possible incentives for online intermediaries not to remove or block access to certain information and to prevent claims against Internet filtering products.[418] In practice, CDA, section 230, is most famous for having been interpreted by the Courts as an absolute safe harbor for hosting or providing access to third-party defamation and indecency for a range of Internet intermediaries, including access providers, hosting providers and search engines.[419]

The CDA did more than introduce section 230. This provision started as a legislative side-note, but gained prominence while some of the CDA's core provisions were struck down on constitutional grounds. The main goal of the Act was to restrict the availability of indecent content on the Internet by making it illegal for information providers to provide access to obscene and indecent content to minors. This part of the CDA was contested on First Amendment grounds and struck down by the Supreme Court in *ACLU v. Reno*.[420] The sequel to the CDA, i.e. Child Online Protection Act (COPA) was passed in 1998, was also struck down on constitutional grounds.[421] *Reno* is an important judgment since it (partly) answers the question about the constitutional protection for speech on the Internet. It establishes that Internet speech receives the highest possible protection under the First Amendment relative to other media, i.e. similar to the press.[422] It is important to note that a more extreme position, in terms of protection against government interference with internet media is possible. Some have argued in favor of no legal restrictions content whatsoever because of the interactive nature of the Internet and the highly supportive features of the Internet in terms of self-governance by the users of the network.[423]

---

417. 47 U.S.C. § 230 (2).
418. See Tushnet 2008.
419. See e.g. *Zeran v. America Online*, 129 F.3d 327 (4th Cir. 1997). For a discussion, see Freiwald 2001.
420. *Reno v. ACLU*, 521 U.S. 844 (1997).
421. *ACLU v. Mukasey*, cert. denied (Sup Ct. January 21, 2009), *ACLU v. Mukasey*, No. 07-2539 (3d Cir. July 22, 2008); *Ashcroft v. ACLU*, 542 U.S. 656 (2004), 322 F.3d 240 (2003); *Ashcroft v. ACLU*, 535 U.S. 564 (2002), *ACLU v. Reno*, 217 F.3d 162 (3rd Cir. 2000); *ACLU v. Reno*, 31 F. Supp. 2d 473 (ED Pa. 1999).
422. *Reno v. ACLU*, 521 U.S. 844 (1997) (CDA provision 223 (a) and (d). The Court ruled that "the risk of encountering indecent material [on the Internet] by accident is remote because a series of affirmative steps is required to access specific material." The Court also considered the lack of precision and the subsequent burden on protected speech. And it considered that the legislation enacted was not the least restrictive means.
423. See e.g. Berman & Weitzner 1995. See also *Sable Communications, Inc. v. FCC*, 492 U.S. 115 (1989). (Holding that the First Amendment bars federal statute prohibiting indecent telephone messages; Telephone must be distinguished from broadcasting because affirmative steps need be taken by the audience.) See also Barlow 1996.

The most interesting aspect of the absolute safe harbor for Internet intermediaries in CDA, section 230 for this discussion is that it gives Internet intermediaries, acting as distributors but also those acting as Internet access providers and search engines,[424] considerable discretion over third-party communications. In fact, this provision is in many ways the opposite of a common carrier obligation. It legally permits Internet access providers to—in good faith—restrict access to or the availability of material that it considers to be *"otherwise objectionable, whether or not such material is constitutionally protected."*[425] Hence, it facilitates filtering at the network level by Internet access providers and expressly legitimates interferences with lawful content. On top of this, the first paragraph is an absolute defense against liability for providing access to unlawful material, sanctioning the decision to act as a passive mere conduit. In other words, in the digital era, the U.S. legislature granted the typical common carrier, i.e. the Internet access provider, tort immunity without corresponding equal access provisions.[426]

The legal discretion offered to ISPs by CDA section 230(c)(2) is also a reflection of the self-regulatory paradigm for Internet regulation. The service provider's choice between voluntary common carriage or restrictive access is left to the industry. The State places itself at a distance, providing the legal space for ISPs to act in and establish the market for information and communications services, within which they are allowed and expected to self-regulate in view of certain public interest objectives. The legislative history of the Communications Decency Act clearly shows that the U.S. legislature meant the Communications Decency Act to provide the space for ISPs to be restrictive, envisaging a role of suppressing objectionable information. In practice, it is mostly used to protect against liability for providing access to illegal material.[427]

But what can be said about the question of the way in which section 230 of the CDA is linked to the First Amendment? More specifically, what do its enactment and survival reveal about the dominant view of the implications of the First Amendment for access governance in horizontal relations between Internet access providers and end-users?

CDA section 230 itself directly refers to the protection of communications by the First Amendment. It expressly legitimizes restrictions by a broad category of Internet service providers, including access providers, hosting providers and search engines, on obscene, lewd, lascivious, filthy, excessively violent, harassing or otherwise objectionable material, *whether or not such material is constitutionally protected*. In other words, the implications of the First Amendment in this context is exclusively vertical.[428]

---

424. See section 9.3.3.
425. There is limited case law about the scope of CDA, section (c)(2). See e.g. *Zango, Inc. v. Kaspersky Lab*, Inc., 2009 WL 1796746 (9th Cir. June 25, 2009).
426. See Tushnet 2008.
427. For empirical data on the application of CDA, Section 230, see Ardia 2010.
428. It can be argued that the Congressional Findings in 47 U.S.C. § 230 (a)(1–5) incorporate free speech values, for instance: "(3) The Internet and other interactive computer services offer a forum for a true diversity of political discourse[. . .]." The Congressional Policy statements in

Furthermore, the provision has had another effect on First Amendment doctrine and case law. If it applies, there is no need for consideration of the First Amendment for the liability standard for third-party communications, since the protection is absolute. In other words, it often blocks the First Amendment from coming into play. This means that the First Amendment, which has had a tremendous impact on U.S. defamation and tort law, has been of small direct value in some of the most important legal decisions about the legal governance of defamatory information flows on the Internet.

If the argument is taken seriously that CDA section 230 codifies free speech values, as is popularly claimed or assumed,[429] this implies that the First Amendment also sanctions the discretion of on-line intermediaries to decide which communications to carry over their networks and on their platforms, because that is what this provision also does. This is mostly in line with the interpretation of the First Amendment in the United States outlined above, which focuses on the protection of the discretion of the owners of the means of communication in the networked information environment.[430] This could also mean that the Federal Communications Commission, which recently started to develop policies to promote Internet freedom, including content and application interconnection for Internet end-users, is fighting an uphill battle. It is interesting to note that the FCC defends these policies to promote open Internet access and end-to-end connectivity of content and applications in the context of broadband, by referring to generally recognized free speech principles as well as the general policy statements included in CDA, section 230(b)(1–5). It seems to take the moderate view that free speech values do not legally require but do allow government regulation to promote them. Remarkably, however, the FCC fails to take into account the wide discretion that is offered to broadband providers in CDA, section 230(c)(2), even though it is basing its ancillary authority to impose the open Internet standards on CDA, section 230, and this authority is contested from the start by large American broadband providers. In 2011, a U.S. Court of Appeals denied the FCC its claimed authority to restrict broadband provider's ability to interfere with communications on its networks. The issue can be expected to be further addressed by American courts in the future.[431]

To conclude this discussion of CDA section 230, a final general observation is in place. It could be argued that the most significant result of this blanket immunity for Internet intermediaries is that it abolished the relevance of the traditional connection between the intermediaries' (editorial) control over third-party communications on the one hand and the legal responsibility for these communications on the other hand. In the press and paper age, the notion of editorial control seems to have functioned mostly intuitively. These intuitions did not readily translate to

---

47 U.S.C. § 230 (b), however, do not contain statements that could be interpreted as a reference to the promotion of free speech values.
429. See e.g. Stone 2010.
430. See section 6.3.3.
431. See Speta 2010.

the online context, in which the functional interference with content flows by different types of entities was taking a different form, for instance through third-party editors or the application of filtering and selection software.

More broadly, the functional interference of different players in the networked information environment can relate to access, selection, navigation, creation, aggregation and transport of content in the network. The proper role and responsibility of the various entities that are carrying out these functions is complex, while the public interests are considered to be great. Considering the (initial) lack of understanding by the Courts how to translate these notions to the online context, combined with the willingness to ensure the unhindered developments of a strong Internet industry, it may have been justified to pass the provisions in CDA, section 230. This provision is, however, a rather simplistic answer to the fundamental questions about the way control and discretion by intermediaries should bring some degree of responsibility, as well as reflect implications for the protection of these intermediaries under the First Amendment. It has, until now, blocked more nuanced legal developments in this field. In addition, it may have strengthened the view that the First Amendment stands in the way of—instead of pointing towards the need for—equal access regulation in the context of Internet access providers to safeguard the effective exercise of the right to freedom of expression in the networked information environment.

6.4.5.   EU Directive on Electronic Commerce and
          Freedom of Expression

In Europe, the Ministerial Bonn Declaration from 1997, which predates the ECD, was one of the first official texts to address the relation between intermediary liability standards and the principle of freedom of expression. The Bonn Declaration asserts that the rules on responsibility "should give effect to the principle of freedom of speech, respect public and private interests and not impose disproportionate burdens on actors."[432] The ECD, in turn, refers to the right to freedom of expression in the context of the freedoms of the European Internal Market, namely the free movement of goods, services and the freedom of establishment. It guarantees these economic internal market freedoms, amongst other things, by introducing the country of origin principle for Information society services.

Recital 9 ECD ties the free movement of information society services to the right to freedom of expression as enshrined in Article 10 ECHR. Compared to the DMCA, the safe harbors in the Directive are not very precise and do not reflect the principle of due process if material is taken down after a notice. The lack of precision is left to the Member States and self-regulatory codes of conduct, to be discussed further below. Recital 46 ECD does provide that "the removal or disabling of access has to be undertaken in the observance of the principle of freedom of expression and of procedures established for this purpose at national

---

432. See European Union Ministers 1997.

level."[433] This recital reflects the view that freedom of expression imposes some restrictions on ISPs in view of the expressive interests of users of their network and communications services.

The precise relation between the right to freedom of expression and the safe harbors depends on the law of the Member States. In general, it is important to note that the ECD *harmonizes* aspects of the internal market for information society services. As always, such harmonization efforts have to respect the EU's constitutional principles of proportionality and subsidiarity. Notably, the harmonization of the liability of intermediary activities relating to the Internet was not complete. The ECD mirrors the safe harbors in the DMCA adopted two years earlier in 1998, but did not address the liability for linking and information location tools. This will be discussed in more depth in Chapter 9. Notwithstanding the room for different choices with regard to the implementation of the safe harbors, most Member States have implemented Articles 12–15 ECD quite literally. In particular, no Member State has introduced additional legal safeguards in line with Recital 46 to respect freedom of expression, for instance by codifying a notice and takedown process and a put back option. Typically, self-regulatory codes of conduct that address ISP notice and takedown practices, such as the latest notice and takedown code of conduct in the Netherlands, do not contain a reference to the right to freedom of expression, assuming the unproblematic status of these types of private self-governance under constitutional guarantees.[434]

6.4.6.   SELF-REGULATORY PARADIGM FOR ISPs IN THE EU
            AND THE RIGHT TO FREEDOM OF EXPRESSION

As mentioned earlier in this chapter, the primary concern with the self-regulatory paradigm from the perspective of freedom of expression is that it turns ISPs into the (private) censors of the Internet. This concern seems to be understood in the European context.[435] Its consistent implementation in existing regulation and policy, however, is less successful.[436]

In general, the notion of self-regulation stands for to the regulatory practice in which private entities are entrusted with some of the elements of regulation, in particular norm formation, adjudication, and enforcement.[437] It is usually contrasted with command and control types of regulation, in which the law seeks to directly define and enforce the legal boundaries of lawful acts in a certain sector of the industry.[438] The related notion of 'co-regulation' or what is also called

---

433. Council Directive 2000/31, 2000 OJ (L 178) 1 (EC).
434. See Van Hoboken 2008b.
435. See e.g. Hans-Bredow Institut 2006, 149–152. Tambini et al. 2008. For the U.S. context, see Bambauer 2011 forthcoming.
436. For a critical overview of the threat of the self-regulatory paradigm for the right to freedom of expression, see European Digital Rights 2011.
437. See Price & Verhulst 2005, 3–4. For a detailed discussion, see Hans-Bredow Institut 2006.
438. On regulation more generally, see Baldwin & Cave 1999.

'regulated self-regulation' refers to the involvement of the State in self-regulatory frameworks.[439] Co-regulation is the more appropriate term for regulatory activity in which the State is not absent but establishes the basis for self-regulation in the law, for instance in its general media and communication policies. The term co-regulation is usually restricted to self-regulation in which there is a legally formalized role of public authorities.

From the perspective of the right to freedom of expression, an important question with regard to the choice for self-regulation is whether an informal, but still active, government role aimed at the restriction and removal of certain content or communications on the network is consistent with the demands of Article 10 ECHR. Interferences with the right to freedom of expression by public authorities must be prescribed by law. This means, first of all, that interferences must have a legal basis. Second, it means that interferences must fulfill the quality of law standards: they must be foreseeable and accessible. In other words, the framework of Article 10 ECHR attaches value to the way interferences by public authorities are legally grounded and delineated. An act by public authorities that constitutes an interference, but is without legal basis, would not survive the test of Article 10.

At the same time, it is clear that an informal role of public authorities in self-regulatory frameworks makes it harder to argue that actual interferences with the free exercise of the right to freedom of expression that result from the application of this framework in practice should be attributed to these public authorities. If the framework is, legally speaking, voluntary, the responsibility for restrictions on information flows lies primarily with private actors. Moreover, this state of affairs is, in many ways, consistent with the implications of the right to freedom of expression in vertical relations. However, it also points to the need to keep in mind that the characterization and structuring of restrictive State action as self-regulation, could be used to obscure the public authorities' role and circumvent the applicable constitutional safeguards: Safeguards that would apply more clearly in case of a formalized role.[440] ISP codes of conduct with regard to illegal, infringing and harmful third-party content and communications are often drafted at the initiative and under supervision of public bodies, and are heavily influenced in their content by government officials. Moreover, in what is sometimes called the 'raised eyebrow tactic', public authorities or the legislature sometimes gives a (last) chance to the industry to fix 'the problems' themselves. More generally, industry codes of conduct are typically drafted not in the absence of the law but within the existing legal boundaries, which already serve to incentivize certain types of private governance in view of public policy objectives. And whereas in the case of press governance, there is no extensive regulation of the 'services' provided to the public, in the case of access providers, the existence of detailed

---

439. See generally Hans-Bredow Institut 2006. See also Tambini et al. 2008.
440. On the impermissibility of this under the Convention, see ECtHR March 25, 1993, *Costello-Roberts v. United Kingdom*. See also Hans-Bredow 2006, 152.

sector-specific regulation implies that the regulatory relation between industry and the State is much more intense from the start.

So, to what extent, and in what ways have these considerations with regard to implications of the right to freedom of expression for self-regulation played a role in the EU regulatory and legislative context? The establishment of the self-regulatory paradigm for online media and information services can be traced back to the 1998 Council Recommendation on the protection of minors and human dignity, which carried the full title: "on the development of the competitiveness of the European audiovisual and information services industry by promoting national frameworks aimed at achieving a comparable and effective level of protection of minors and human dignity."[441] The earlier European Commission green paper on the protection of minors and the communication on illegal and harmful material online, which resulted in this Council Recommendation, contained many explicit references—as well as a detailed overview in the annex—of the demands of Article 10 ECHR in the context of content regulation for media and information services, even though it remains rather vague on the implications for self-regulatory frameworks in particular.[442] The 1998 Council Recommendation, however, mainly refers to the general principle of freedom of expression. The included 'indicative guidelines for the implementation of the self-regulation framework', state "that the proportionality of the rules drawn up should be assessed in the light of: the principles of freedom of expression" and other fundamental interests.[443] However, the way this complex undertaking should take place is left to the stakeholder process at the national level. The recommendation does not introduce or mention any specific restrictions on the self-regulatory codes of conduct which could be seen to follow from the right (and principle) to freedom of expression. In particular, it does not address the question about the possible restrictions following from Article 10 ECHR for the proper role of public authorities in self-and co-regulatory frameworks.

The lack of stipulation of freedom of expression implications for the role of the State in self-regulation of information flows in light of traditional public policy perspectives is somewhat perplexing. From the perspective of the right to freedom of expression and the general obligation on the State to ensure the effective exercise of the rights and freedoms under the Convention, it is clear that the State should not contribute or promote a self-regulatory framework which results in extensive private censoring of legitimate information flows online. It would also be inconsistent with the state's obligations under the right to freedom of expression to deliberately incentivize private parties to do what it would not be allowed to do itself.

In the following section, one of the most controversial self-regulatory developments in the context of Internet access providers will be discussed in more detail, namely the filtering and blocking of parts of the Internet or communications on the network by Internet access providers. The topic of filtering by Internet access

---

441. Council Recommendation 98/560, 1998 OJ (L 270), 48 (EC).
442. See European Commission 1996c.
443. Council Recommendation 98/560, 1998 OJ (L 270), 48 (EC).

providers is chosen for a number of reasons. First, it has raised an intense debate about the proper role of government with regard to Internet regulation and the right to freedom of expression. Second, it relates to the basic questions about the proper boundaries of access regulation in the ISP context. Third, it is not only generally accepted that freedom of expression should be taken into consideration in these contexts, but also that official legal documents contain strong references to the right to freedom of expression. Fourth, the legal and legislative debate about filtering by Internet access providers is relatively mature. There is even a case before the ECJ about the filtering of communications by access providers. And finally, Internet content filters in many ways perform a function similar to search engines. Together, they could be seen to fall into the broader category of selection intermediaries. The discussion will be mostly restricted to the European context.

6.5. INTERNET FILTERING BY ACCESS PROVIDERS

6.5.1. BACKGROUND

The development and application of Internet content filters (hereinafter: 'Internet filters') is a central issue in the regulatory debates about freedom of expression on the Internet and the role of ISPs in providing access to content.[444] There are many types of Internet filters and they are deployed in a variety of circumstances. This section will address the type of Internet filter that limits the accessibility of material on the Internet for end-users and discuss one case relating to the possible filtering by access providers of copyright infringing communications between end-users. The application of filters by hosting providers or online service providers such as YouTube will not be discussed as well as questions relating to the technical aspects of Internet filters.

Internet filters can raise issues under the right to freedom of expression, but generally filtering technology can perform legitimate functions. They are important from the perspective of the broader function of the selection of content in the public networked information environment and thereby fall in the broader category of what could be called selection intermediaries.[445] Selection intermediaries govern the accessibility, i.e. relative reachability of material on the Internet. Examples of selection intermediaries include Internet filters, search engines, recommendation services, and Internet Service Providers ('ISPs') that block or filter content on the basis of their contents.[446] Selection intermediaries fulfill an important function in our information environment, which is characterized by abundance. They help

---

444. See e.g. Sieber & Nolde 2008; McIntyre & Scott 2008; Tambini et al. 2008; Dommering 2009; Dommering & Asscher 2006; Heise Online 2009; Heins et al. 2006; Deibert et al. 2007; CoE, Committee of Ministers, Recommendation CM/Rec(2008)6 on measures to promote the respect for freedom of expression and information with regard to Internet filters, 2008.
445. See section 3.2.2.
446. See Van Hoboken 2009.

end-users to find and select the information they consider relevant or useful, and can exclude information that they are not willing or allowed to access, for instance because it is harmful or illegal.

Internet filters are quite commonly used and installed by end-users, for instance by parents to prevent access to content by their children. They are also widely deployed by private actors on their networks, for instance by employers or Internet cafes. They can be installed in the public sector to restrict access to content or applications.[447] In public institutions such as schools and libraries, which fulfill a particular function or serve an audience that may warrant stronger selection of the accessibility of information, the application of Internet filters is quite common.[448]

Internet access provider can use, be asked to use, or legally ordered their intermediary position to establish gatekeeper control over information flows on the Internet by using Internet filters. The typical context of these measures would be the prevention of access to illegal material on the basis of lists of such material kept and maintained in the context of enforcement of child pornography legislation by criminal law enforcement agencies and special private or private-public entities.[449] In Europe and the United States, the issue of child pornography, has led to a range of regulatory and self-regulatory activity, to use blacklisting of web destinations. In Europe, such blacklisting was first introduced in the United Kingdom and Norway. A European Commission proposal for a new Directive includes an explicit reference to this kind of framework. In a number of countries in and outside of Europe, ISPs have agreed with public authorities to filter child pornography at the network level, for instance in the United Kingdom. In some jurisdictions public authorities require access providers by law to use filtering products at the network level.[450] Proposals for similar legislation or regulatory practices have been discussed in Germany and the Netherlands. At the level of the EU, there have been ongoing discussions about a Directive that would establish the EU regulatory framework for the filtering of child pornography at the European level.

6.5.2.   INTERNET FILTERS AND THE RIGHT TO FREEDOM OF EXPRESSION

The application of Internet filters raises a number of concerns under the right to freedom of expression. The first concern is related to the interests of end-users under the right to freedom of expression, and can be expressed most aptly in terms

---

447. In the United States, some of the government funding to public libraries has been made conditional on the installation of such filtering software. See *U.S. v. American Library Association*, 539 U.S. 194 (2003).
448. For a discussion on Internet filters and libraries, see section 7.4.5. Schools often restrict access to information online with Internet filters.
449. See e.g. Schafer 2010, 535–538. For a discussion of the technical aspects of the U.K. Cleanfeed system and the possibility to reverse engineer the list of blocked illegal content, see Clayton 2006.
450. For a comprehensive overview and discussion of global Internet filtering, see Deibert et al. 2007.

of end-user autonomy. If Internet filters are deployed, without the end-user's consent, knowledge or control over the filtering of content, the end-user is prevented from accessing information freely. In addition, the deployment of certain filtering products by access providers, for instance those that are aimed at blocking the distribution of unauthorized copies of copyright-protected works, would imply that all communications would be screened and monitored with the use of deep packet inspection (dpi) technology. A second concern is related to the interests of online information and service providers, and information sources more generally, to reach an audience. A third concern, which directly impacts the weight of the first two concerns is related to the actual functioning and imperfection of Internet filters in relation to the goals for which they are often being promoted.

Although Internet filters are quite imperfect and ineffective in preventing access to content, they are still widely promoted as a solution for suppressing access to or the communication of illegal or infringing material.[451] In light of the guarantees relating to freedom of communication, it is questionable whether the current Internet filtering products could be an acceptable solution.[452] It is well known that Internet filters applied by access providers based on DNS filtering can be easily circumvented and the same is true for more advanced types of filtering at the network level. In fact, Western democracies, the United States in particular, are actively promoting the development of effective filtering and blocking circumvention software to support political dissidents and activism in countries such as China and Iran.[453] Moreover, the imperfection of blocking and Internet filters in terms of their effect on legitimate content has always posed significant restrictions on the possibility of requiring filtering by access providers. Existing products are notoriously inaccurate, often preventing access to sites that should not be blocked while failing to block many that should.

The capabilities of different kinds of Internet filters that access providers could deploy on their network plays a role in the discussion about the proper responsibility of Internet access providers for facilitating access to illegal content and infringing communications. Under general principles of law, one cannot be required to do the impossible.[454] However, the safe harbor legislation in the E-Commerce Directive anticipated increased technological efficacy. Recital 40 of the E-Commerce directive provides as follows:

> [...] the provisions [...] relating to liability should not preclude the development and effective operation, by the different interested parties, of technical systems of protection and identification and of technical surveillance instruments made possible by digital technology within the limits laid down by Directives 95/46/EC and 97/66/EC.[455]

---

451. See European Commission 2009.
452. Stol et al. 2008.
453. See Figliola et al. 2010.
454. See e.g. Koelman 2000.
455. Council Directive 2000/31, 2000 OJ (L 178) 1 (EC).

Hence, the development of increasingly sophisticated network management and filtering technologies for access providers could make filtering obligations on Internet access providers appropriate in the view of the EU legislature. Article 21(2) of the E-Commerce Directive instructs the European Commission to "analyse the need for additional conditions for the exemption from liability, provided for in Articles 12 and 13, in the light of technical developments", in its evaluations of the Directive.[456]

Fundamentally, however, the issues raised by the imperfection of Internet filters may not be a technological one. Internet filters are inherently imperfect, at least if one takes content and copyright-related legal restrictions on the freedom to communicate seriously. Automated filters will always filter too little and too much at the same time. The reason is that they try to build complicated context dependent norms about the lawfulness of communications into technology. Of course, it is possible that these imperfections would be accepted by the law, but this would simply cause the distinction between lawful and unlawful communications to change from a legal distinction, ultimately requiring a judgment by a court, to a distinction governed by technology.[457]

The mandatory application of Internet filters ordered by public authorities is also considered problematic because they can be seen as prior restraints with regard to the source of the blocked material.[458] As we discussed in the Chapter 5, both Article 10 ECHR and the First Amendment contain a heavy presumption against the permissibility of prior restraints. And as mentioned above, the possibility to circumvent the filters implies that the material itself remains accessible, at least for more savvy end-users. For illegal material, such as child pornography, the fact that the material itself remains online, whereas public authorities should pursue those responsible for the publication and the abuse has been one of the strongest arguments against filtering. It is clear that these circumstances also make the prior restraint all the more problematic.

Because of these problems relating to mandatory Internet filtering from the perspective of freedom of expression, the application of Internet filters has mostly been left to the market and policy has focused on stimulating the market for Internet filtering products, thereby ensuring that end-users have effective means to prevent access to content, for themselves and their children in particular. CDA section 230 can be argued to have this aim and allows for the use of Internet filters by access providers and other intermediaries. It did not imply that ISPs ought not to restrict access to material online, but granted ISPs discretionary power needed to deploy filtering technology voluntarily without risking liability.[459] In the European context, the situation is different, since the safe harbor for Internet

---

456. The first report did not address this possibility, which may be explained by the fact that it mostly focused on whether the Directive was implemented (properly) in the Member States. See European Commission 2003.
457. For a general discussion of the desirability of 'codifying' regulation into software, see Dommering & Asscher 2006. See also Grimmelmann 2005; Lessig 1999; Reidenberg 1998.
458. See Dommering 2009.
459. See European Commission 1996b, 14.

access providers in Article 12 ECD does not contain a provision that protects them against third-party claims if they would be actively interfering with traffic on their networks. In fact, in the European context, by installing Internet filters aiming to restrict access to child pornography or other online destinations, access providers may run the risk of increased liability and injunctions, since other interested parties may have lists of websites that should be filtered also.[460]

In 2008, the Committee of Ministers of the Council of Europe issued as recommendation on freedom of expression and Internet filters, which addresses some of the concerns regarding Internet content filters from the perspective of Article 10 ECHR.[461] The recommendation and the underlying report acknowledge both the legitimate function of Internet filters and the ways in which Internet filters can impact freedom of expression and information. It explicitly addresses some of the perceived requirements of Article 10 ECHR in this context,[462] and addresses the fundamental interests of information providers and end-users. The recommendation calls upon the Member States of the CoE to take measures with regard to Internet filters in line with a set of guidelines promoting user notification, user awareness and user control of Internet filters and accountability of the private and public parties involved. The recommendation makes a difference between mandatory filtering and the use of Internet filters by public entities, such as public libraries and schools on the one hand, and their use by private entities, such as enterprises in the context of Internet access in the workplace on the other hand and addresses the implications of freedom of expression for both situations.

6.5.3.   MANDATORY FILTERING AND THE INTERESTS
              OF INFORMATION PROVIDERS

Internet content filtering, in the form of blacklisting by access providers, deprives the information providers that are being filtered from being received by significant parts of the population. To what extent are these interests of information providers protected under Article 10 ECHR?

If the filtering is mandatory, the access provider could assert the protection of Article 10 ECHR. This protection is partly informed by the interests of speakers to reach an audience.[463] First of all, for any source to be blocked which would not be judged illegal by a proper authority, it could contest the validity of blocking it for its end-users. It would also be able to argue that mandatory filtering would cause it to sometimes block legitimate information sources which would be accessible

---

460. This is the subject of ongoing legal debate and litigation across Europe.
461. CoE, Committee of Ministers, Recommendation CM/Rec(2008)6 on measures to promote the respect for freedom of expression and information with regard to Internet filters, 2008. See also CoE, Report of the Group of Specialists on human rights in the information society (MC-S-IS) on the use and impact of technical filtering measures for various types of content in the online environment, CM(2008)37 add, February 26, 2008.
462. The recommendation of the CoE's Committee of Ministers is not binding.
463. See section 6.3. See also section 5.5.

otherwise. It is possible that the access provider does not protest against mandatory filtering. In these cases, (lawful) information providers that would be blocked could assert their right to impart information and ideas freely. The information provider itself would also be able to claim that the filtering amounts to an interference with its right to impart information and ideas freely as protected under Article 10 ECHR.

The question is whether this interference would be proportional and how the proportionality test should be applied. The U.S. Supreme Court has made it clear in a number of rulings relating to legislation aimed to protect children from accessing harmful content, that the First Amendment involves strict scrutiny, if it targets the publicity of material at the source and requires the measure to be "narrowly tailored to serve a compelling Government interest, the least restrictive means available for the Government to serve the interest of preventing minors from using the Internet to gain access to materials that are harmful to them."[464] The alternative, considered by the Court, was the availability of filtering software, which could be installed and controlled by end-users themselves.

The Council of Europe recommendation qualifies the use of Internet filters in the public sector as an interference with the right to freedom of expression and makes the test of Article 10, second paragraph more explicit. It demands that filtering of Internet content in electronic communications networks operated by public actors or mandatory filtering at the ISP level has to concern "specific and clearly identifiable content", "a competent national authority should have taken a decision on its illegality" and "there should be an opportunity to have this decision reviewed by an independent and impartial tribunal or regulatory body, in accordance with the requirements of Article 6 of the European Convention on Human Rights."[465] Furthermore, the guidelines stipulate that Member States have to ensure that there is an evaluation of the proportionality of filters before and during their implementation in terms of their possible effects on the unreasonable blocking of content. As regards the interests of information providers, the Recommendation states that Member States "should [...] provide for effective and readily accessible means of recourse and remedy, including suspension of filters, in cases where users and/or authors of content claim that content has been blocked

---

464. *ACLU v. Mukasey*, cert. denied (S. Ct. January 21, 2009), *ACLU v. Mukasey*, No. 07-2539 (3d Cir. July 22, 2008); *Ashcroft v. ACLU*, 542 U.S. 656 (2004), 322 F.3d 240 (2003); *Ashcroft v. ACLU*, 535 U.S. 564 (2002), 217 F.3d 162 (3rd Cir. 2000); *ACLU v. Reno* 31 F. Supp. 2d 473 (ED Pa. 1999).
465. Article 6 ECHR, first paragraph: "In the determination of his civil rights and obligations or of any criminal charge against him, everyone is entitled to a fair and public hearing within a reasonable time by an independent and impartial tribunal established by law. Judgement shall be pronounced publicly by the press and public may be excluded from all or part of the trial in the interest of morals, public order or national security in a democratic society, where the interests of juveniles or the protection of the private life of the parties so require, or the extent strictly necessary in the opinion of the court in special circumstances where publicity would prejudice the interests of justice."

unreasonably." This last obligation is also applicable to the use and application of filters in the private sector.

6.5.4.   VOLUNTARY FILTERING BY ACCESS PROVIDERS AND THE
         INTERESTS OF INFORMATION PROVIDERS

The situation changes if the filtering by access providers is voluntary. In these cases, there remains a de facto horizontal conflict between the ISP that imposes filtering and the information providers it is blocking. The legislative resolution for these conflict of interests in the United States is laid down in CDA, section 230(c)(2), which was discussed in section 6.4. This provision grants access providers and other intermediaries wide discretion to decide to block—in good faith—indecent or otherwise objectionable content, even if it is constitutionally protected.

In the European context, this horizontal conflict would lead to a balancing of interests of information providers under Article 10 ECHR (leaving aside possible other interests unrelated to the right to freedom of expression such as economic freedom and unfair competition) with the right to the free exercise of private property of the ISP. Typically, there will be a wide margin of appreciation with regard to the way a positive obligation on the State to guarantee the effective exercise of the right to freedom of expression in horizontal relations, if it exists, will have be fulfilled. Normally, the protection of the interests of information providers in the context of filtering access providers to use filtering will have to be considered to lie in the realm of discretion of the state. National law may place more stringent obligations on the State to protect information providers from being blocked by access providers.[466] Mandatory positive obligations would only arise when individuals would be prevented to effectively exercise their freedom of expression or when pluralism of the information environment would be clearly at stake. In cases in which blocking by access providers would lead to a situation that would deprive a legitimate online speaker from reaching an audience completely, the best argument for a strict positive obligation on the State could be made.[467] Pluralism could be argued to be endangered when over-blocking by Internet filters shows structural biases with regard to certain types or sources of speech or certain types of issues.

It could be argued that the interests of information providers can be easily safeguarded by introducing certain levels of transparency and accountability into

---

466. Which is not the case in, for instance, the Netherlands. See HR 12 maart 2004, *XS4all v. Ab.Fab* (Rejecting the Amsterdam Court of Appeal's argument that Internet access provider XS4all had to permit restrictions on its free exercise of its property rights in its computer and transmission capacity, because of the nature of the services it was offering and in particular the public interests involved in its services, and arguing that Article 10 ECHR, in principle, could not be invoked in defense of an infringement of someone's (free exercise of its) property rights. XS4all sought an injunction to prevent Ab.Fab from sending unsolicited advertising to its customers.)

467. See discussion of *Appleby* in section 6.3.1.

the filtering regimes. With that in mind, the Council of Europe Recommendation calls on the Member States to safeguard the interests of Internet content providers, by providing for effective and readily accessible means of recourse and remedy, including suspension of filters, in cases where content has been blocked unreasonably.[468]

A final question is whether the law could and/or should require Internet access providers not to filter at all. In general, this is probably not the case. It is generally accepted that there are good reasons for Internet access providers to interfere with communications on their networks, for instance in the context of unsolicited communications. As regards content, there seems a growing consensus that it is important to keep the Internet as a platform to reach audiences and consumers open for everyone. Access providers have not yet started to block content on a wider scale than the child pornography context, although it must be noted that also in this context there are many examples of websites, the blocking of which, raises serious questions.[469]

6.5.5.   INTERNET FILTERS AND THE INTERESTS OF END-USERS

Internet filters could implicate the interests of end-users, in particular if they are deployed outside of their control. In these cases, Internet filters would interfere with the freedom of end-users to receive information and ideas, in other words the end-user's autonomy. If Internet filters are deployed by end-users, for instance to prevent their children from accessing certain types of material, and end-users have control over what is being filters, most of the concerns over freedom of expression disappear.[470] One hypothetical conflict remains, namely between a speaker that wants to reach an end-user which decides to block that particular source. In such cases, the protected interests of the end-user carry more weight, for at least two reasons. First, Internet access involves a computer terminal that simply allows for the ability to select what information to access and what to block. This freedom is not only protected under Article 10 CEHR, but the way it is exercised is typically part of the private sphere as well.[471] Second, in this private sphere, the end-user cannot be forced or even expected to listen.[472]

Of course, end-users, when deploying filters, might have control in practice, but in reality the Internet filters are created and maintained by others. Internet filtering products aimed to promote child safety are often opaque—the blocking lists can for instance be protected as trade secrets—and have limited options of

---

468. CoE, Committee of Ministers, Recommendation CM/Rec(2008)6 on measures to promote the respect for freedom of expression and information with regard to Internet filters, 2008.
469. For an overview of controversially blocked sites in the United Kingdom, see Clayton 2009.
470. For instance, if a child would be prevented from accessing the Internet in the parent's home at all, the law would not interfere with this governance of the private sphere. See generally Benkler 2001.
471. See e.g. in the United States, *Stanley v. Georgia*, 394 U.S. 557 (1969).
472. See section 5.5.1.

redress. And the deployment of Internet content filters often does not fully respect end-user autonomy. In fact, Internet filters are typically promoted by public authorities as a solution for problems that are the result of the freedom of end-users, namely the *possibility* to access illegal information. The filtering of content by ISPs does not respect end-user autonomy by definition, since this would give the choice to access the material to the user. Hence, there remains room for public policy to enhance end-user autonomy in the context of Internet filters. It is logical for such public policy to be aimed at end-user autonomy with regard to lawful and legal material.

The respect for end-user autonomy seems to have been the dominant concern underlying the CoE Recommendation on Internet filters and freedom of expression.[473] First of all, the guidelines provide that end-users, where appropriate, must be able to control the level of filtering. The guidelines further stipulate that end-users should have the possibility to challenge the blocking or filtering of content and to seek clarifications and remedies. With respect to the end-user's ability, where appropriate,[474] to activate and deactivate filters and to be assisted in varying the level of filtering in operation, the guidelines call upon the Member States to ensure, in cooperation with the private sector and civil society, the existence of a number of more detailed guarantees. It is provided that end-users should receive guidance regarding the manual overriding of an activated filter, more specifically whom to contact when it appears that content has been unreasonably blocked and the reasons which may allow a filter to be overridden for a specific type of content or Uniform Resource Locator (URL). Furthermore, the recommendation states that content that is filtered by mistake or because of an error has to be accessible without undue difficulty and within a reasonable time. With regard to the use and application of Internet filters by the public sector, Member States have to avoid the universal and general blocking of offensive or harmful content for users who are not part of the group which a filter has been activated to protect, and of illegal content for users who justifiably demonstrate a legitimate interest or need to access such content under exceptional circumstances, particularly for research purposes.

Of course, Internet end-users cannot simply be placed at the receiving end of the communicative process. In the networked information environment, the end-user are also the source of illegal and infringing communications or material. Peer-to-peer distribution technology has harnessed the potential of the Internet for end-users to distribute content between end-users. The sharing of copyright-protected material, such as music, films and software, with the use of such peer-to-peer technology has led to a discussion about the imposition of filtering obligations on ISPs to filter out infringing communications.[475]

---

473. CoE, Committee of Ministers, Recommendation CM/Rec(2008)6 on measures to promote the respect for freedom of expression and information with regard to Internet filters, 2008.
474. The Recommendation does not clarify when this would be appropriate.
475. For an overview of filtering by ISPs in light of copyright infringements, see Angelopoulos 2009.

In Belgium, the rights holders organization SABAM has legally pursued this option most aggressively. It sued Internet access provider Tiscali in 2004 for injunctive relief. It asked the Belgium Court to order Tiscali to stop the infringing communications on its network. The Court of first instance ordered the Internet provider "to mak[e] impossible any form of sending or receipt by its clients, by means of 'peer to peer' software, of electronic files containing musical works that are part of the SABAM repertoire."[476] Tiscali appealed the Court's judgment, and the Belgium Court of Appeals has referred questions about the permissibility of the injunction under European law and the fundamental rights to freedom of expression and private life to the European Court of Justice. More specifically, the Court has to address the question, whether an injunction on access providers that obligates them to identify and block all copyright infringing communications by its subscribers is permissible under Articles 12 and 15 of the E-Commerce Directive and the right to freedom of expression.[477]

The European Court of Justice (ECJ) still has to hand down its judgment, which will be of great significance for the question about the limitations on the possibility to require filtering by access providers that follow from the right to freedom of expression of end-users. If the Court follows that Advocate-General's opinion, these limitations would stand in the way of the kind of filtering as was sought by rights holders in this context. The Advocate-General clarifies that what is presented as a simple injunction in civil proceedings would in effect amount to the permanent imposition of systematic and universal filtering of all the communications on the network, which would eventually have to be extended to all ISPs in the future to be effective.[478] This general and far-reaching character of the sought measure leads the Advocate-General to the conclusion that a specific legal basis would be needed to impose such a system, which was lacking in Belgium Law. In the Advocate-General's view, the measure would apparently be disproportionate, both from the perspective of the rights and interests of the access provider, as well as its end-users.[479]

6.6.   CONCLUSION

In contrast with the regulatory model for the press, traditionally, there has always been extensive regulation of communications network providers. However, content regulation tends to be either absent or minimal and raises issues under the right to freedom of expression. In vertical relations, the owners of the means of

---

476. District Court of Brussels, June 29, 2007, No. 04/8975/A, *SABAM v. Tiscali (Scarlet)*, published in CAELJ Translation Series #001, 25 Cardozo Arts & Entertainment Law Journal, 2008.
477. ECJ, Reference from the Cour d'appel de Bruxelles, February 5, 2010, *Scarlet v. SABAM*, Case C-70/10.
478. ECJ, Conclusions of Advocate General M. Pedro Cruz Villalón, April 14, 2011, *Scarlet v. SABAM*, Case C-70/10, paragraph 66.
479. *Ibid.*, § 67, 68, 87, 113.

communications such as Internet access providers can assert their own right to 'freedom of expression' against government interference, and this right includes the right to access, receive and transmit. Even more than in the case of the press, these rights are informed by the communicative interests of the users of such communications networks. These interests in communicating freely with the use of steadily improving communications techniques (postal mail, telegraphy, telephony and the Internet) were clearly served by a practice in which the network owners would not restrict communications over the network. In that respect, the regulatory concepts of 'common carrier' and 'universal service' which have helped shape the regulatory models for communications network providers, can also be seen as informed by the right to freedom of expression users of the communications network. Universal service requirements acknowledge the way access to communications networks is essential to societal participation. The common carrier requirement guarantees equal treatment of users of the networks, thereby limiting the discretion of network providers to restrict information flows.

Convergence of media and communications has complicated the regulatory environment for communications providers significantly. Internet users, can use one and the same Internet connection, to correspond privately, watch 'television' or broadcast their views for a global audience. The facilitating role of Internet access providers with regard to the *public* networked information environment means that the normative role of the right to freedom of expression for the governance of communications networks has increased in importance. Traditionally, the constitutional right to privacy and confidentiality of private correspondence, such as protected by Article 8 ECHR, were of relatively greater importance.

In this Chapter, the way Internet access providers have been involved in content regulation in the networked information environment was used to study the implications of the right to freedom of expression in this context. This regulatory framework was shown to consist of safe harbors setting the legal boundaries for the liability of ISPs for third-party communications on the one hand, in combination with an emphasis on further self-regulatory or co-regulatory action on the other hand. The case law relating to these laws as well as their legislative history show that freedom of expression has been taken into account in this framework but it remains strongly debated to what extent this has been done properly.

When thought through, legal obligations on access providers to prevent the use of their communications networks for illegal purposes, or the possibility to access illegal material, lead to clear problems under the right to freedom of expression, in particular the conditions set out in Article 10 second paragraph and possibly Article 8, second paragraph. Such general obligations could only be adhered to with the application of Internet filters, the mandatory application of which is more than constitutionality doubtful. Although the pressure to move towards stricter legal responsibility of Internet access providers remains and proposals to require blacklisting by access providers are debated in European Parliament and elsewhere, the right to freedom of expression has been one of the reasons these government interferences with the right to freedom of communication have mostly not materialized into actual laws.

While there are hardly any legal obligations on access providers to interfere with the communications on their network, the self-regulatory paradigm has informed public authorities to seek voluntary cooperation of access providers to regulate content nonetheless. For the most part, public policy aimed to restrict the accessibility of content by access providers has not led to command and control types of regulation but has sought to minimize the official role of the State while at the same time still aiming to achieve more restrictive practices by ISPs. This may partly be the case, as in the case of the governance of the press, precisely because of the right to freedom of expression. However, the relation between access providers and Internet users is quite a different one compared to the press, looking at the press as an intermediary in the public communicative process. Whereas for the press the selection of information and ideas for publication is sanctioned by the right to freedom of expression *because* of the importance of editorial freedom and the fact that this is what the press is supposed to be doing all along, the exclusion or blocking of communications by access providers is hard to harmonize with the ideals underlying freedom of expression, in particular when taking stock of the impact this would have on lawful communications over the network.

This leads to the most complicated issue touched upon in this chapter: how should the impact of the current legal framework on the horizontal relations between access providers and Internet users be evaluated from the perspective of the right to freedom of expression. Or to put it differently, what are the proper implications of the right to freedom of expression for the legal discretion of access providers to restrict communication over their networks? Two different general points of view on this debate emerged in the analysis.

The first, which we may best call the user freedom theory, tends to equate the right to freedom of expression in these potential conflicts of interests between access providers and users to the communicative interests of Internet users. In this theory, if freedom of expression legally requires anything with regard to the legal governance of horizontal relations between access providers and end-users, it would be that government would have to protect the user's interest against undue interferences by Internet access providers, for instance through the establishment of new types of common carrier and universal service rules and through the establishment of due process guarantees in case of specific legitimate interferences with the flow of content or use of the network. In other words, the role of the law should be aimed at the realization of the free exercise of the right to freedom of expression by Internet users. The various Council of Europe recommendations touching upon these issues testify of the dominant nature of this perspective in European freedom of expression doctrine. Within the boundaries of this theory, much debate remains about the nature of the implications of the right to freedom of expression in this context, in particular whether there is a real obligation for the State to act or if it is better to speak of freedom of expression in this context as a regulatory principle.

The second perspective, for which support—and opposition, to be clear—can be found in the United States, tends to equate the right to freedom of expression with the discretion over the use over communicative means as established by the free market. This theory may be best called the ownership discretion theory of freedom of expression. From this perspective, the right to freedom of expression protects the owners of the means of communications (and media more generally) against legal interferences with the freedom to decide how to use those means in the free market. The result of this theory is that the possibility of the government to regulate the horizontal relations between Internet access providers and Internet users to safeguard the communicative interests of the users of the network is actually restricted by the right to freedom of expression of Internet access providers, more specifically a right not to transmit or to exclude.

From a European perspective, it could be concluded that Article 10 ECHR would most probably not support a claim of the network owners not to transmit, but that any such claim would have to be based on the right to private property. In the United States, the legal mainstream may actually be moving in the direction of allowing a similar claim of Internet access providers not to transmit under the First Amendment. This could have significant implications for the political and legal feasibility of network neutrality regulation.

In the safe harbor framework for Internet service providers, the right to freedom of expression could also be shown to be understood by the legislature as relating to the communicative interests of Internet users. It is important to note that the way freedom of expression has been internalized into the EU intermediary liability regime leaves much room for criticism. No due process guarantees have been prescribed, such as one can find in the U.S. Digital Millennium Copyright Act, the room for injunctions is left wide open, and the hosting safe harbor, the scope of which may be less clear than ever, may incentivize intermediaries to restrict lawful communications. In addition, the role of public authorities in the design of self-regulation has been questionable.

The specific analysis of the internalization of the right to freedom of expression in the U.S. legal safe harbor framework showed a mixed picture. Some elements in the regulatory framework seem to sanction the discretion of ISPs to disregard the interests of information providers and end-users in horizontal relations. Section 230 of the Communications Decency Act (which is also applicable to search engines) is possibly most striking in this regard. It not only shields against liability, but also provides far-reaching discretion for interactive computer services with regard to third-party communications. By studying the background of this provision, which was enacted in 1996, it was further shown how this provision has in many ways prevented freedom of expression doctrine from having a further impact on the proper legal regime for various kinds of Internet service providers in the United States, including search engines. The different legal standards for carrier, distributor and publisher liability as they applied in defamation cases before the Internet, and the way editorial freedom and control had played a role in the formation of these standards in a rich set of court decisions have been replaced by a double-edged sword for Internet intermediaries: a shield against liability and legal discretion to block various kinds of content, including constitutionally protected communications.

The two theories mentioned above reflect perspectives on the right to freedom of expression with implications that go well beyond the context of Internet access providers or search engines for that matter. For some, the application of the ownership discretion theory of freedom of expression to the context of the press may be less strikingly absurd than to the context of Internet access providers. In the networked communications environment, however, control over communications with the use of various technologies of control has provided the means for traditionally passive conduits to be more actively involved in the selection and prioritization of content flows on the network, whereas it may have provided others, that tended to be more active with the means to be more passive. Chapter 6 shed some light on the fundamental questions this raises about the way freedom relates to discretion and control relates to responsibility, and the way those answers could ultimately find their ways into properly informed laws and regulation for various entities in the public networked information environment.

Chapter 7
Library Freedom

7.1. INTRODUCTION

This chapter will address the way the right to freedom of expression applies to the legal governance of libraries and public libraries in particular. The position of the library in the public networked information environment from the perspective of this study is interesting for a number of reasons. First, the library combines an active selective role with a relatively passive role. The public library may be the purely intermediary speaker, it selects those worthy of selection while not actively speaking itself. In that sense, the library seen as an intermediary in the networked information environment is different from the press and publishers on the one hand, as well as different from conduits such as Internet access providers. Second, one of the dominant conceptualizations of the Web and the Internet more generally is linked to a vision of the digital library.[480] Search engines help fulfill the potential of the World Wide Web as a globally and publicly accessible library. And finally, library governance offers an example in which the State has fulfilled a prominent and generally facilitative role.

For these reasons, the way the right to freedom of expression has informed the legal governance of libraries, as well as the way public libraries, seen as intermediaries, have dealt with the communicative interests of information providers and library patrons can be expected to contribute to an answer to the main research question. James Grimmelmann, for instance, recently stated:

> A good search engine is more exquisitely sensitive to a user's interests than any other communications technology. [...] Except, perhaps, the library reference desk.[481]

---

480. See section 2.1.1. See also Stefik 1996.
481. Grimmelmann 2010. (Grimmelmann adds that librarians do not scale.)

This chapter will take a closer look at the way public library governance has struck a balance between the different and possibly conflicting communicative interests involved. It will focus on the legal governance of information flows facilitated by the public library from the perspective of freedom of expression and the proper role of government in this context. Section 7.2 will shortly discuss the historic background of the library as well as some of the recent developments related to libraries in the digital environment. Section 7.3 will discuss the normative principles underlying the governance of public libraries, including the right to freedom of expression. What are the general ideas and principles underlying library governance and the library's mission and in what way are those ideas and principles informed by the right to freedom of expression? In section 7.4, a number of specific issues related to the right to freedom of expression in the context of the public library will be discussed, such as the question of the library's independence from government, possible conflicts relating to its collection policy and library censorship, and the value of privacy in the context of access to library materials.

7.2.	THE LIBRARY: HISTORY AND RECENT DEVELOPMENTS

Libraries have existed since the Antiquity and even before that. Old empires erected the first libraries some five thousand years ago. These libraries contained the first collections of written materials.[482] One of the oldest known libraries is the Library of Ashurbanipal, a collection of tens of thousands of clay tablets, in a library named after the king, who ordered the collection of these materials to be stored in a central location. For sure the most famous ancient library is the *Library of Alexandria*, which allegedly construed its collection by confiscating all written materials from incoming ships and travelers.[483] The scarcity of information sources was one of the driving forces behind the creation of libraries. The storage and classification of these materials in one place provided the best access to these valuable materials. Library collections had considerable political importance as well. This is perhaps best reflected in the tragic fate of many of the most famous libraries of the ancient world. New empires and dynasties destroyed them and the cultural and political heritage they represented.[484]

A library can be defined as an organization keeping a systematic collection of information sources in a place.[485] The information sources are selected, classified and ordered for the purpose of facilitating access to them. The material can be classified in terms of the type of medium, such as clay, print, digital storage or the

---

482. On the earliest libraries, see Casson 2001. See also Staikos 2004.
483. Wright 2007.
484. See Wright 2007, 50–51. And still, libraries are deliberately destroyed because of political reasons, such as the national and university library in Sarajevo and various libraries in Iraq. See e.g. Zećo & Tomljanovich 1996.
485. Miksa & Doty 1994.

type of content.[486] A library is also an organization in which library professionals maintain the collection and work to fulfill its mission. Finally, the library used to be a physical place where the collection would be kept and made accessible to the community. The digitization of information sources and the introduction of electronic access and the Internet has transformed this last aspect of libraries and given rise to the phenomenon of the 'digital library', access to which, from a technological or functional perspective, is not necessarily restricted to a specific location.[487]

Throughout history, a large variety of libraries emerged, such as the research library, the national library, the private library and the public library. Naturally, these different types of libraries are different in terms of their collections, functions, funding and governance. A national library typically has strong national archiving and cultural heritage functions. There is a wide variety of private libraries. The academic or research library facilitates the access to research materials and is primarily focused on the scientific community. A public library's primary role is to serve the general public and its collection can be relatively limited. In the remainder of this chapter, the focus is placed on public libraries, including public research libraries.

The roots of the modern library and the public library in particular lie in the period after the invention of the printing press and the Enlightenment. The widespread use of the printing press caused an enormous increase in the amount of publications the library could facilitate access to. The ideal of general literacy of the Enlightenment gave rise to reading societies and public reading rooms. In the Netherlands, these reading societies and public reading rooms became a widespread phenomenon in the nineteenth century. Out of these reading societies and reading rooms, the modern public library emerged.

In recent times, the digitization of information sources and the introduction of the Internet and electronic access have had implications for the library. First, the Internet and the World Wide Web is a tremendous new resource of easily accessible material. Second, digitization has also removed the library's collection from its physical premises into an electronic realm.[488] There are no physical restraints on where to access the collection, if material is digitized. This has made the precise physical location of a library for its users irrelevant, at least from the perspective of access to digitized information. It is unclear to what extent the digital library should replicate some of the boundaries traditional physical libraries would have in terms of their collections. A physical public library would serve a specific community of people in its area and have a collection that reflected its financial

---

486. Knight 1981. On the new opportunities of ordering in the digital world, see Weinberger 2008. For a discussion of the more problematic aspects and consequences of classification, see Bowker & Leigh Star 2000. See also Hacking 1999.
487. About the digital library see generally Pace 2003; Earhshaw & Vince 2008. For a famous early account of the possibility of the digital library, see Licklider 1969.
488. It is worth noting that this also means that the library no longer necessarily controls the materials it provides access to. Digitized materials are often licensed to libraries. Subscriptions to electronic journals are a good example of this. If the publisher discontinue access, the library loses access to 'its' copies.

means and societal goals. If we ignore the current legal limitations on electronic access to digital library materials stemming from copyright law, which introduces superficial scarcity in view of the rights of authors and the encouragement of creative production, one public digital library could easily satisfy the demands for access to written materials for the whole population. In fact, such a library could serve the global population as well. It is this type of library of everything, accessible from everywhere, that is one of the most compelling, be it unfulfilled promises of the digital revolution. It is also this type of library whose abundance would make the development of proper search tools particularly important.

And of course, the Internet and the World Wide Web in particular are often characterized as a 'library' itself.[489] The Internet and the Web may generally lack the professional standards for selection and classification present in the context of libraries. Yet, online platforms to buy books such as Amazon, and online collections of digitized books such as those provided by the Internet Archive or Google Books have made the Internet a major competitor for libraries, satisfying significant parts of information needs that would traditionally be served by libraries.[490] It is worth noting, that general search engines in particular turn the Web into a library for their users.[491] They provide the navigation function for the Web, similar to (but different from) the function of the library's index and collection classification system. In addition, various specific search services for library types of materials are freely offered on the Web, such as Google Scholar and Google Books.

7.3. LIBRARY GOVERNANCE, MISSION AND NORMATIVE PRINCIPLES

7.3.1. REGULATORY MODELS FOR THE PUBLIC LIBRARY

Public library policy and regulation can be seen from the perspective of media and communications law and policy and from the perspective of a more general social welfare policy which includes cultural and educational policy. In the following section, the general regulatory framework for the governance of public libraries will be addressed, mostly from the first perspective, seeing the library as a societal institution contributing to the public information environment. In the following section, a distinction will be made between two general models for communications and media regulation and the role of public institutions in these different models. These models are linked to differences in ideas about the meaning of freedom of expression and differences in the tasks and mission of public libraries.

As with the media in general, the public library not only has a particular role in a society, but its organization and governance also reflects the type of society it

---

489. For an early account of the library metaphor for the Internet, see Stefik 1996, 1–108. On the way Internet discourse shapes law and culture more generally, see Jørgensen 2011.
490. Pessach 2007. See also Darnton 2009.
491. Compare Grimmelmann 2007.

exists in.[492] Following Hallin and Mancini, one can discern three types of media systems in Western societies, namely the North Atlantic liberal model, the North European democratic-corporatist model and the Mediterranean politicized-pluralist model.[493] The organization of the public library reflects the characteristics of these different models, two of which will be shortly addressed here.

The liberal model for media and communications, the model in the United States, is characterized by a dominance of the free market mechanism. Taking a free market perspective, it can be considered the government's role to provide the goods and services (with strong public interests attached to them, or what are also called merit goods) that the market would not provide in sufficient quantities or qualities. General examples are health, security-related services (police, fire-fighters) and education. In the liberal model, a typical example of government provision in the sphere of media and information goods and services is the public library. In comparison, media is left to the market and are predominantly offered by commercial enterprises. A minimal role of government, and the professional quality and independence of media from the State are seen as essential. It is notable that besides the possibility of providing the service itself, the government can also regulate the market in the public interest. The regulation of communication networks and regulatory concepts tied to the public interest in this context such as universal access and common carriage are good examples of this approach, in which the provision of certain goods and services are left to the market, but the public interest is served through regulation.[494]

The democratic-corporatist model, the model one generally finds in the Netherlands and Germany, is a mixed model of media that are tied to specific subsets of the population on the one hand and commercial media on the other hand. In this model, the media are seen as important social institutions, for which the State carries a certain responsibility. The role of government with regard to media, libraries and culture, is not primarily based on market considerations, although they may play a role, and increasingly so, but is based on the idea that the public interest is best served by some involvement of public institutions. In general, public broadcasting, the public library and the State monopolies in communications networks are examples of this approach. In Germany, this approach is called *Grundversorgung*, i.e. a basic duty of care on government to make sure that certain service levels are guaranteed by government for the entire population. Again, it is possible that those guarantees are not met through government funding, but through market regulation.

The differences between the two models are also reflected in the way the right to freedom of expression has informed the governance of media and information services and, for our purposes here, the public library. In the democratic-corporatist model, if there is a reference to freedom of expression, it is usually a reference to a positive obligation under the right to freedom of expression and information, an obligation to safeguard the *effective and equal exercise* of fundamental rights in

---

492. Huysmans 2006.
493. Hallin & Mancini 2004.
494. See section 6.2.

society.[495] The public library in particular is the place where those who may not have the financial means to access knowledge, culture and news in the free market, can do so. In the liberal model, more emphasis is placed on freedom of expression as a negative right, guaranteeing individual liberty and a state-free sphere, the functional independence of public libraries from government,[496] and the prohibition of censorship in the context of libraries. In fact, in the liberal model, one finds more reference to the normative role of fundamental rights in the context of libraries. Freedom of expression and the right to privacy have surfaced prominently in the debates about library governance and related case law in the United States.[497] In the democratic-corporatist model, issues related to fundamental rights are less prominently addressed in the regulatory debates about public library governance. Fundamental rights and the social welfare state have blended together into a mix of publicly funded culture, media and information access support in which the public library occupies an important position. The enabling role of government with regard to providing basic access to knowledge and culture stands at the foreground.

On a different level, the distinction between the liberal and the corporatist model reflects the distinction between individual, free-market based pluralism on the one hand, and organized regulated pluralism on the other hand.[498] A classic example of organized pluralism is the Netherlands, in which the pillared organization of society along the lines of different social groups was reflected by the organization of the media and public libraries. By now, the pillared structure of Dutch society may have lost much of its relevance. And more generally, as result of liberalization of information law and policy as well as European harmonization focusing on the Internal market since the 1980s, the emphasis has shifted in the direction of a free market based approach. But on the European continent, the notion of pluralism, in general and in the media in particular, is still seen primarily as relating to the interests of different societal groups, more than to the interests of individuals.[499] This stands in stark contrast with the notion of individual pluralism in the North Atlantic liberal model. In this model, the individual, invested with political liberties such as the freedom of speech and the freedom of association, is the basic element of political organization in relation to the State and its democratically organized institutions. Pluralism is organized by the free marketplace of ideas, instead of being monitored, facilitated or even regulated by the state.

7.3.2.   THE TASK AND MISSION OF THE PUBLIC LIBRARY

The core mission of the public library can be summarized as the mission to provide a publicly accessible place (possibly digital) where people can access knowledge,

---

495. See Schuijt 2006.
496. But see section 7.4.6.
497. See e.g. Bosmajian 1983.
498. See Hallin and Mancini 2004, p. 53–55.
499. See e.g. Nieuwenhuis 2007.

culture, information and ideas. The public library is still argued to be one of the cornerstones of a western democratic information society as can, for instance, be seen from the international library community's 'Public Library Manifesto' as follows:

> Freedom, prosperity and the development of society and of individuals are fundamental human values. They will only be attained through the ability of well-informed citizens to exercise their democratic rights and to play an active role in society. Constructive participation and the development of democracy depend on satisfactory education as well as on free and unlimited access to knowledge, thought, culture and information. The public library, the local gateway to knowledge, provides a basic condition for lifelong learning, independent decision-making and cultural development of the individual and social groups.[500]

In an age of deregulation, privatization and commercial alternatives for library services, the demarcation of the tasks of public libraries is not an easy undertaking. The mission of the public library is the basis of its funding by the government, but the actual use of libraries may have shifted drastically. The question about the proper role of the State is particularly complex, because of the variety of public purposes the library tends to serve. Is the library simply a place to freely access information, knowledge and culture without financial or other barriers or is it also a city community centre and even a supplier of special courses and education? Is the library the place of last resort to access information and ideas for the least well-off in our societies or should the library focus instead on the qualitative aspects of what is offered by a library, such as the way access is offered?

Because of some of the normative principles inherent in the offering of public libraries, such as independence from commercial influences, it is quite unlikely for market and commercial parties to satisfy those qualitative public interests that are at stake. It is hard to see how a private library, offering the same as public libraries in the same manner, could be sustainable without significant financial support. It can be argued that by focusing on the demand side of its community, which is a natural thing to do for libraries in their mission to serve the public, public libraries can undermine their own legitimacy. If libraries do what the market can do itself, such as making extensive profiles of reading habits to personalize their services for instance, and do not do it differently from the way the market would do it, there may be less reason to fund them.

The public library does, of course, satisfy certain existing market demands, thereby making those markets potentially less attractive for commercial parties. Some of the things the public library has to offer might well be served without subsidies by the state, as in the case of public and commercial broadcasting. Compared to public broadcasting, however, there is still relatively little pressure on library funding from this perspective. At present, there are simply no

---

500. IFLA/UNESCO 1994. IFLA is the International Federation of Library Associations, an international organization representing libraries and their users.

comparable commercial services available, although new services such as Google Books might change this rapidly. The differences in the development of mass digitization projects shows again quite well the different ideas about the role of government in Europe and the United States. Whereas the general opinion in the United States seems, with some notable exceptions, to approve the free market based solution that is emerging in the sphere of digitization projects, In Europe, there is a clear tendency to see a natural role of government in the digitization of the corpus of knowledge and the cultural heritage.[501] Digitization and the creation of search portals for digitized materials in Europe is taking place through public policy and funding and public institutions such as national libraries play a leading role.

From a normative perspective on the mission and legal position of the public library, the right to freedom of expression plays a role alongside other fundamental societal values. Dutch public library scholar Huysmans discerns four general values that together can be seen to provide the normative groundwork for the public library, namely freedom, equality, order/solidarity/cohesion and quality. He connects these four abstract values with nine guiding and more specific normative principles for the public library, namely accessibility and availability, diversity and multiformity, independence and objectivity, solidarity and protection of the vulnerable, social control and integration, cultural (symbolic) environment, reliability and precision, professionalism, and topicality. It is clear that these four values and nine principles do not always align and need to be balanced against each other in different contexts. For instance, information quality or social cohesion could easily be a reason to reject materials from a library, thereby restricting the availability and accessibility. Therefore, these values and principles have to be considered in their totality and in the context of a specific library and its policy. With regard to specific issues relating to the governance of selection of and access to library material, these normative principles do contain useful considerations.

It is notable that the normative principles of Huysmans reflect that public libraries are much more than a place or portal to access information. In particular, the 'protection of the vulnerable', 'social control and integration' and the 'cultural (symbolic) environment' go beyond the governance of selection of and access to information and ideas. The library is seen as a primary meeting place and as well as an accessible center for cultural activities. It is also a place where the groups that have the least means available to access information and knowledge can come. Public libraries tend to play an important role in literacy programs.

From a regulatory perspective, library regulation is mostly restricted to the regulation of funding through subsidies and library administration.[502] In Western-European social welfare states such as the Netherlands, there is a trend since the 1980's, in which the funding of public libraries has been cut down and public

---

501. See Jeanneney 2007.
502. In the Netherlands, the law on public library works (Wet op het openbare bibliotheekwerk, 1975) introduced a legal basis in the law for public library funding. The Welzijnswet 1985 decentralized library funding.

libraries have been deregulated like many other sectors in society. Regulation in such countries is tied to educational and cultural (subsidization) policies. The detailed sector-specific regulation one finds in media and communications law is absent. Library policy and soft law demarcates the functional boundaries of the library and sets certain key targets, mostly qualitative. In the regulatory framework for the public library in the Netherlands, mostly soft law for which regional government carries responsibility, one finds a reflection of the various normative principles named above.[503] The formulation of those principles by Huysmans may, in fact, be seen as a reflection of the role these qualitative standards are meant to play in the 'regulation' of the public library.

The reality of a strongly developed body of professional and ethical standards amongst librarians and a history of information and library science pre-empt legal regulation of the library practice. Library practice with regard to the selection of materials and the organization of access to the collection, is mostly self-governed by the library institutions and community itself. In addition, this practice is informed by the results of the library and information science and tradition.[504] Notwithstanding the principle of self-governance of libraries, there are certainly examples of stricter legal conditions tied to public library subsidies, which directly relate to the selection of and access to information and ideas. In the Netherlands, there has been some case law declaring a certain licensing scheme on the municipal level in the context of libraries unconstitutional, because it infringed the right to freedom of expression.[505] In the United States, there is a more recent example, namely the Internet content filter installation obligation for public libraries. We will address these issues which raise questions about the implications of the right to freedom of expression for the governance of libraries in the next section.

Finally, it should be noted that library law, policy and practice is heavily influenced by copyright law.[506] First, copyright law restrict the types of material libraries can provide access to. For example, European intellectual property law limits the possibility that libraries include certain new materials in their collections, such as proprietary software. Second, it restricts the way access can be provided, such as online access to digital material. The success of public libraries in terms of their use since the 1960s caused a conflict between publishers and authors on the one hand and public libraries on the other hand about the losses of revenue. Ultimately, in many countries a public lending right was introduced, which would guarantee some form of remuneration for right holders. Lending rights and rental rights were harmonized by the European Community in 1992.[507] Copyright law includes rules on how the library can make its collection available and accessible to

---

503. See VNG, Richtlijn voor basisbibliotheken, 2005.
504. See e.g. VNG 1990; VNG 2007.
505. See Hoge Raad [Dutch Supreme Court] November 9, 1960, NJ 1961, 206 (*Vestigingsbesluit leesbibliotheekbedrijf 1958*) System of permits for the provision of public reading rooms is found unconstitutional, i.e. in breach of the freedom of expression provision of Article 7 of the Dutch Constitution.
506. For an overview, see Krikke 1999.
507. Council Directive 92/100, 1992 OJ (L 346) 27 (EEC).

the public, and prescribes an equitable remuneration for publishers related to lending of materials.[508] The European Directive on lending and rental rights introduced a harmonized lending right and rental right which served as a guarantee for such remuneration for the dissemination of copyright and related right protected works through libraries and rental establishments.[509] The public lending right in the Directive is subject to the possibility for broad exceptions by the Member States. As a result, there are considerable differences between European countries in practice.[510]

7.4. SPECIFIC FREEDOM OF EXPRESSION ISSUES IN THE CONTEXT OF LIBRARIES

7.4.1. THE LIBRARY AND FREEDOM OF EXPRESSION

Freedom as a normative value at the core of public library governance, reflects an array of liberties, including the fundamental right to freedom of expression, freedom of religion and freedom of education. In several of its declarations and its Library Manifesto in particular, the International Federation of Library Associations and Institutions (IFLA) has tied the public library's mission to the fundamental right to freedom of expression, and Article 19 of the United Nations Universal Declaration of Human Rights in particular. IFLA also has a specific program, Free Access to Information and Freedom of Expression (FAIFE), to promote freedom of expression in the context of libraries.[511] Freedom of expression in the context of libraries can be best related to the theory of self-fulfillment of the individual, and the democratic ideal of self-governance.

Freedom of expression in the context of libraries has implications for the relation between the publicly funded library and the state, the relation between libraries and potential information sources for their collection, and most importantly, between libraries and their users. In the following section, a number of issues with regard to library governance and freedom of expression will be discussed. First, the implications of freedom of expression for library funding will be addressed. Second, several issues in the relation between libraries and users will be discussed, namely the issue of censorship in the context of libraries, the governance of access to materials and the question about the privacy of library users. This section will conclude with a discussion of the idea of the library as a public forum.

---

508. Von Lewinski 1992, 3–83; Reinbothe & Von Lewinski 1993.
509. See European Commission 2002 (stating that "[. . .] from an economic point of view, the public lending right complements the rental right. In some cases, public lending might even replace rental. Therefore, it was felt necessary to include a [public lending right] in the draft Directive in order to ensure the proper functioning of the Internal Market in this field.").
510. *Ibid.*, 11.
511. IFLA 1999.

7.4.2.   PUBLIC FUNDING OF LIBRARIES AND FREEDOM OF EXPRESSION

In the European context, freedom of expression is seen to entail a positive obligation on public authorities to guarantee a certain basic level of access to information resources. Thus, the public library is a particular instance of the government acting under its positive obligations under Article 10 ECHR.[512] It can be argued that by funding public libraries, the State goes further than is required under Article 10 ECHR. As was noted in previous chapters, the State generally has considerable amount of freedom to choose the way it fulfils its positive obligations under Article 10 ECHR. The actual level of basic access, the ways in which access is granted and organized and most other specific public library governance issues do not follow from this general positive obligation. The positive obligation does entail the general guarantee of pluralism, also in libraries. The diversity and multiformity principles mentioned above reflect this value of pluralism in the library context.

The emphasis on the positive role of the State in the contexts of public libraries in Europe has placed freedom of expression as a negative right to the background. In the United States, by contrast, many public libraries have a (declaratory) library bill of rights as a part of their collection policy, informing the public about their rights with regard to collection governance.[513] From a negative rights perspective, the funding of libraries by public authorities poses the question about the appropriate degree of political involvement with library governance. The independence of public libraries from the government, not in terms of their funding but in terms of their actual governance, could be based on the principle of freedom of expression.[514]

7.4.3.   COLLECTION MANAGEMENT AND ACCESS TO MATERIALS

The library users and their interests in informing and educating themselves is central to all library policy. The library provides access to knowledge and provides tools and services to the library user to search for information in its collection. The normative principles of availability and accessibility have implications for the library's collection policy and the library as a place to discover the existence of materials through metadata systems and a guide to find access to the materials in the library and elsewhere. The findability of material is a key element in library governance.

Library collection management is a complex phenomenon, in which libraries, public and private library services, various types of publishers and review media each play their role.[515] First, the resources of the library in terms of its physical

---

512. See Schuijt 2006, 28. See also Arnbak et al. 1990.
513. See e.g. Santa Clara County Library.
514. But see the decision of *U.S. v. American Library Association* discussed below, section 7.4.6.
515. For an overview of library collection management, see Gardner 1981.

capacity and financial resources to manage a collection play a fundamental role. The selection and collection decisions will have to serve the respective local and possibly regional community. The quality of material is an important concern, although at the same time, a local library's collection will have to be biased towards material that is intellectually accessible for the various groups in that community. It is important to note that the actual selection of books and library materials by public libraries is not an autonomous practice of librarians. In practice, the publishing industry plays an important role in facilitating—and thereby influencing—selection decisions by the public library community. If we look at the Netherlands, for instance, nowadays most public libraries use the services of one privatized organization called NBD|Biblion B.V. for their purchasing decisions. NBD Biblion monitors new publications and has packages tailored to the needs of different types of public libraries. The bulk of books enter the public libraries because of such arrangements.[516]

Because most public libraries have a rather limited collection, the principles of availability and accessibility imply that the ideal situation would be that at least one library should have a copy of a book or other potential library material and that it should be findable and accessible for library users elsewhere. If a book is available elsewhere, there are usually special inter-library traffic arrangements between libraries that are considered crucial for providing access to information. There are similar but less developed international arrangements for gaining access to materials in public libraries abroad which are promoted by IFLA. There can be some legal restriction on such access, for instance that the foreign material has to be legal in the receiving country.[517]

One of the most ambitious—and failed—examples of inter-library arrangements, aiming to provide access to all published material, is the Farmington plan in the United States.[518] The Farmington plan was started in 1942 as an attempt by a group of major university and research libraries to make sure that at least one copy of every valuable publication from each country in the world would be available in some library in the United States. The responsibility for collecting between participating libraries was divided by subject and geographic area of publication. Combined with an inter-library loan system, the Farmington plan would have turned each library into the universal library, in the sense of access and availability. However, for various reasons, including the lack of coordination and the emphasis on availability without consideration of demand, the plan was not a success and was formally dissolved in 1972.[519]

---

516. It is interesting to note that NBD Biblion has made itself somewhat accountable for the reviews it publishes (20,000 a year), with 'guidelines for reviewers' in combination with an appeal procedure. See NBD Biblion 2011. The decision on the merits of an appeal is based on NBD Biblion's guidelines for reviewers and is only accessible to the reviewers themselves.
517. See Gardner 1981.
518. See Gardner 1981, 248–249.
519. See Gardner 1981.

7.4.4.   THE LIBRARY AND ITS RELATION TO THE LIBRARY USER

The relation of the public library's collection management with regard to the user is a complex one. The public library aims to serve the needs of the public so the collection is arranged in view of the library user. This does not mean that library users decide what will be inside the library or that public libraries are completely governed by community demand.[520] The library user might be able to suggest acquisition of certain materials, but the library institutions makes the collection decisions itself. It is possible that the increased emphasis on satisfying popular demand and the use of popularity metrics in collection governance may have changed this slightly. Below, two more specific issues related to collection management and the interests of library users will be addressed. First, the role of libraries in confronting library users with materials they might not have selected themselves and second, the issue of library censorship.

In terms of its offering of a collection of knowledge and culture to its users, a public library is not merely passive in its relation to its users. Historically, the public library has had an emancipator and educational role with regard to the library user. As a result, in the ideal world, a public library is a place where the public, when browsing through the library stacks and catalogues, will be confronted with a carefully selected body of knowledge and information materials they would not have come across otherwise, in a context in which professionals can advice them. The ideal is that this professional has to be passive in the sense that the library user makes the choices of how he navigates the collection.[521] He cannot be forced to read or access certain materials but has to accept the fact that he will be confronted with materials that might upset him.

The confrontational role of libraries, which sees the library's collection of materials as a shared public space that is more than the sum of the individual needs of its users, fits well with the critique of personalization of the public information environment by the American constitutional scholar Cass Sunstein. Personalization is increasingly taking place in the library's accessibility infrastructure. Technology and user data can be used to build a profile of interests on the basis of a library user's lending history and searching behavior. Personalization is attractive for libraries, because it strengthens their relationship with the library user. But it implies a shift as regards accessibility governance from being supply-driven to demand-driven.

Sunstein argues, with reference to the ideals underlying the First Amendment, that personalization of the information environment into a 'daily me' for each citizen stands in the way of the shared experiences that are a prerequisite for a functioning democratic society.[522] It must be noted that Sunstein does not provide much empirical backing for his claims that existing personalization developments are actually having the effects he warns against. As a result, Sunstein's argument

---

520. See Gardner 1981; Osburn & Atkinson 1991.
521. See VNB 1990.
522. See Sunstein 2002; Sunstein 2007.

should be understood as a contribution to the discussion of the normative ideals that should inform selection practices by mediating institutions in the public information environment. In the library context, personalization of accessibility could weaken the ideal of the confrontational role of the library. This is particularly true if there is no possibility to browse the stacks of books and confrontation with material takes place through a search engine. In the United States in particular, this confrontational role of publicly funded information providers is sometimes contested because of the alleged paternalistic role of the State and the positive notion of political liberty it entails. In the context of library collection management, it is generally accepted that the public library should be more than the sum of the wishes of its users. The extreme example of a library failing to adhere to this is the practice of library censorship, which typically entails the removal of material at the request of certain members of parts of the public. Before discussing library censorship, the question of access and collection governance will be addressed through a discussion of the public forum doctrine in U.S. constitutional law as applied to the public library context.[523]

As is obvious, from the perspective of the library materials, there are some hurdles to be taken for them to enter a library.[524] First, recognized publishers are a very important proxy for library collection management. Unpublished material does not usually enter a library, unless it is of local or historic interest. Local libraries might be interested in archiving material relating to the history and culture of the local community. Products of vanity publishers, i.e. publishers that make profits by charging the author for publication, are usually disregarded. Certain independent and alternative publishers could be included, but clearly have a special position.[525] It is important to note that commercial communications are not included in a library. Furthermore, there could be a standard relating to type of material and its format, and for books there could be standards such as the number of pages.

The fact that the library's collection policy mostly relies on publishers implies that the issue of possible illegal material does not arise often. In most cases, the library can rely on publishers to have taken responsibility for the publication of the material. It is possible that a publication turns out to be illegal afterwards. In these circumstances, the library has to make a choice regarding what it will do with the illegal material in its collection. It can destroy the material, or it can make it inaccessible or restrict access but keep it archived. If a public library has archival functions as well, the latter option is preferable. The digital library presents a set of new issues in this context, since publishers often keep control over the materials in the collection and the library does not have a physical copy of the material itself.[526]

The question of whether a library should be seen as a public forum was explicitly answered negatively by the Supreme Court in its heavily divided ruling

---

523. See e.g. Stone 1974; Bevier 2003; Nunziato 2005.
524. For a discussion, see Gardner 1981.
525. See Gardner 1981.
526. See e.g. Besek & Loengard 2008.

on the Children's Internet Protection Act (CIPA), which tied restrictions to library funding to the libraries' freedom to provide access to the Internet, as follows:

> A public library does not acquire Internet terminals in order to create a public forum for Web publishers to express themselves, any more than it collects books in order to provide a public forum for the authors of books to speak. It provides Internet access, not to "encourage a diversity of views from private speakers [...]."[527]

The public forum doctrine, the practical implications of which are rather limited because the Court has restricted its application to traditional public fora, i.e. public parks and streets,[528] was first introduced in *Hague*,[529] which overturned *Davis*.[530] Hague clarified that the government was not allowed full discretion with regard to the regulation of expressive activity in streets and parks, because of their historical function. Streets and parks were considered to function like the public information space per se, the metaphorical town hall. The Court complicated matters in *Adderley*, in which it introduces the concept of a semi-public forum, i.e. a designated public forum for specific purposes, thereby possibly limiting expressive liberties.[531] Since then, the Court has expressly dismissed a range of public forum claims, including claims for utility poles[532] and airports.[533] If public property is not a public forum, the government has much more leeway to impose restrictions on expressive liberties: restrictions only need to be reasonable, as long as they are not viewpoint-based.[534]

---

527. *United States v. American Library Association*, 539 U.S. 194, 207 (2003).
528. The Supreme Court has limited the public function doctrine to functions that are traditionally an exclusive function of the State, *Hudgens v. National Labor Relations Board*, 424 U.S. 527 (1974). See also Stone 2009, 1550.
529. *Hague v. CIO*, 307 U.S. 496 (1939) (famous dictum by Justice Roberts, limiting the possibility the government to restrict speech in streets in parks on the basis of their historical function).
530. *Davis v. Massachusetts*, 167 U.S. 43 (1897) (concluding that the government may limit the use for speech purposes because it may even end the use for public purposes altogether).
531. *Adderley v. Florida*, 385 U.S. 39 (1966), ("The State, no less than a private owner of property, has power to preserve the property under its control for the use to which it is lawfully dedicated.")
532. *Members of the City Council of Los Angeles v. Taxpayers for Vincent*, 466 U.S. 789 (1984) (arguing that "[t]he mere fact that public property can be used as a vehicle for communication does not mean that the Constitution requires such uses to be permitted").
533. *International Society for Krishna Consciousness v. Lee*, 505 U.S. 672 (1992) (deciding in a complicated set of opinions of a heavily divided Court that publicly owned airport terminals are not public fora, because they, having made a late appearance in society "cannot be said have immemorially [...] time out of mind been held in the public trust and used for purposes of expressive activity").
534. See *Perry Educators' Association v. Perry Local Educators' Association*, 460 U.S. 37 (1983). With regard to a public forum content-related speech restrictions must be serving a compelling state interest and must be narrowly tailored. Content-neutral restrictions must be reasonable. If public property is merely designated for speech purposes (voluntarily) it is bound by the same standards. The public owner can, however, withdraw the designation for speech purposes. A third category is property that is neither a forum for speech by tradition (streets and parks) or by designation.

7.4.5.   Censorship in the Context of Libraries

Censorship of materials in the context of libraries is an interesting issue which illustrates the possible conflicts between the selection governance of libraries on the one hand and the demands and expectations of the various elements in the served community on the other hand. It has renewed relevance in the context of Internet content filters on library Internet access points.[535] Library censorship, a non-legal notion, should not be conflated with the notion of prior restraints with regard to publications discussed in Chapters 5 and 6. In the context of libraries, censorship is typically understood as the suppression, removal or deletion of material from a library's collection because it is considered objectionable. The discussion about library censorship often includes the discussion of systematic biases in the decisions to *include* materials in the collection for the apparent reason that the non-selected materials are considered objectionable.

A central complexity in the context of library censorship stems from the fact that the selection of materials for the library's collection is exactly a daily task of librarians. Therefore, library censorship, i.e. the undue suppression, removal or deletion of materials from the collection, has to be differentiated in one way or another, from the normal selection decisions. This distinction is not easily made. The normal selection decisions are informed by the library profession and practice, but what this selection should be is not carved in stone.[536] A classic explanation of the example by Asheim is as follows: "The all-important difference seems to me to be this: that the selector's approach is positive, while that of the censor is negative."[537] In practice, librarians have considerable leeway in selecting the material they want to include in their selection. First, they are considered to be the experts as regards the proper selection of materials. Second, they have to select quite restrictively simply because of the limited resources available. In other words, an effective safeguard against censorship—undue interference with library collections—should, first and foremost, be part of the professional ethics of librarians.

As mentioned above, the primary reason for the suppression of material is its controversial or objectionable nature in the eyes of the library's constituency, which could include the librarians themselves. The fact that public libraries typically have educational purposes and their collections should be suitable for children is a more specific reason for the suppression of materials. The complexity is that the constituency should also inform the selection process; the library is supposed to take the needs and wishes of its constituency into account. Of course, these

---

535. *United States v. American Library Association*, 539 U.S. 194 (2003), 201 F. Supp. 2d 401 (ED Pa. 2002).
536. See Gardner 1981; Osburn and Atkinson 1991.
537. Asheim 1953.

needs could be seriously biased.[538] If the constituency and the librarians of a particular library are predominantly evangelical Christians, this will probably be reflected in that library's collection decisions. Although some bias in terms of selection is acceptable, the collection policy of public libraries in the European context should always take account of the demand of pluralism.

It is worth noting that there are different ways library censorship takes place in practice. One of them would be the intentional suppression or exclusion of material from the collection because of its origin, background or expressed views. Another would be the removal of such material from the collection after protests by members of the user community. Both these forms of library censorship can be the result of actions by individual librarians or the library's management. A different, but quite common, form of undue interference with library collections is the removal or destruction of materials by library visitors.[539]

The classical examples of censorship in libraries in the Netherlands and elsewhere relate to sex, politics or religion. In the Netherlands, public libraries with a certain religious background would bring their collections in accordance with religious views. For instance, catholic libraries in the Netherlands used to censor their collections. In particular, there have been many attempts to censor information about homosexuality and homosexual lifestyle.[540] The selection of books by public libraries which inform young adults about homosexuality remains a very controversial issue in U.S. local communities. In the Netherlands, both the code of conduct for public libraries and the code of conduct for librarians mention censorship as a forbidden practice. Both codes lack a definition of censorship but seem to understand it as the undue interference with the library collection by the government and third parties. There does not seem to be a formalized framework for tracking library censorship.

In the United States, censorship in the context of public libraries is a more hotly debated topic and the library community has developed several instruments to deal with the issue.[541] First of all, the American Library Association (ALA)'s library bill of rights, which deals with public library collection governance, specifically addresses the censorship of materials. The prohibition of censorship in libraries in the library bill of rights was heavily debated around 1950 when there was strong pressure on libraries to label and censor communist materials.[542] In the United States, some libraries have come up with a special procedure for removing material from a library collection, and a special office for intellectual freedom of the IFLA collects and publishes data on such challenges each year, thereby providing some transparency. The library bill of rights provides that "[m]aterials

---

538. See Gardner 1981. The third normative value of Huysmans also reflects this. A bias stemming from a biased constituency will still have to respect the limits placed by the principle of diversity.
539. van Dijk 1994.
540. For an overview of censorship issues in the public library in the Netherlands, see van Dijk 1994; Dingemans 1980.
541. See Bosmajian 1983.
542. See Robbins 1993.

should not be excluded because of the origin, background, or views of those contributing to their creation, [. . .] should not be proscribed or removed because of partisan or doctrinal disapproval."[543] The guidelines also envisage a role of the library to "challenge censorship in the fulfilment of their responsibility to provide information and enlightenment [. . .] and cooperate with all persons and groups concerned with resisting abridgment of free expression and free access to ideas.[. . .]".[544]

Although library censorship was hotly debated in the United States throughout the twentieth century and around 1950 in particular, it took until 1983 for the first case relating to public library censorship to reach the U.S. Supreme Court.[545] In *Pico*, the Supreme Court addressed the right to access books in a public school's library after the local school board decided to exclude nine books from its collection and the permitted school curriculum for its teachers. Reportedly, the school board had based its decision, which it took after having been provided with a list of objectionable books by a conservative parents' group in New York State, amongst other considerations, on the view that the books were *anti-American*.[546] According to the Supreme Court, the First Amendment did "impose limitations upon a local school board's exercise of its discretion to remove books from high school and junior high school libraries."[547] The local school boards' "broad discretion in the management of school affairs [including the decision to remove books from the school library's collection, JvH] must be exercised in a manner that comports with the transcendent imperatives of the First Amendment."[548] In other words, whether or not an action of removal of books from the school's library violated the First Amendment depends on the motivation for removal. The discretion of the school board to remove books ends where it is exercised in "in a narrowly partisan or political manner."[549] It is important to note that the majority opinion explicitly excluded the issue related to the acquisition of books. The Court based its conclusion with regard to the discretion of the school boards on their discretion with regard to educational affairs. Public school students do have some First Amendment liberties in the context of schools but they are colored by the educational environment.

Pico restricts the possibility of legal action against library censorship as defined above. First, although the Court recognizes a right to receive information in the context of a public institution, a school board does not have a general positive obligation to guarantee substantive civil liberties of students through the management of its library. The right to receive information freely in this context, as acknowledged by the Court in *Pico*, may be better understood as an exception:

---

543. American Library Association 1996.
544. *Ibid.*
545. *Board of Education, Island Trees Union Free School District v. Pico*, 457 U.S. 853 (1982).
546. Notably, the excluded books included Pulitzer prize winners: *Laughing Boy*, by Oliver LaFarge and *The Fixer, by* Bernard Malamud.
547. *Board of Education, Island Trees Union Free School District v. Pico*, 457 U.S. 853 (1982).
548. *Ibid.*
549. *Ibid.*

a right not to be the subject of a strict orthodox collection policy. The school board's discretion is not absolute but can be exercised without problems as long as it is not clearly displaying a willingness to act in a narrowly partisan or political manner.[550]

7.4.6. LIBRARIES AS ACCESS POINTS TO THE INTERNET

Libraries do not only offer access to materials that are available in their own collections but also information about and access to materials elsewhere. Nowadays, public libraries also tend to provide Internet access. In addition to their own material, the Internet and the World Wide Web provide a wealth of information for library users. Both in the United States and Europe, the library is also a typical place for the promotion of Internet access through public Internet access terminals.

Of course, the Internet and the Web, because of the uncontrolled nature of these environments, also contain material which used to be absent in library collections, such as commercial communications, pornography and possibly even plainly illegal material. In particular, the fact that Internet access terminals could also be used to gain access to indecency has led to controversial regulatory action and litigation in the United States.[551]

After the initial attempt of the U.S. legislature to suppress access to indecency online through the Communications Decency Act (CDA) and the Child Online Protection Act (COPA), Congress passed the Children's Internet Protection Act (CIPA).[552] CIPA tied an obligation for public libraries to install Internet content filters to library funding. The American Library Association contested the constitutionality of this obligation on First Amendment grounds and the case was finally dealt with by the Supreme Court. The Court concluded, unlike the Court of Appeals, that libraries are not a public forum and have always had to exclude material from their collections.[553] The Court started by linking the way Internet access was being provided to the traditional role of libraries, as follows:

> A public library [. . .] provides Internet access, [. . .] for the same reasons it offers other library resources: to facilitate research, learning, and recreational pursuits by furnishing materials of requisite and appropriate quality.[554]

In other words, restrictions on the availability of material in a public library simply follow from the library's task to pre-select suitable material, i.e. of *requisite and appropriate quality*, and make it systematically available to its users. As a result, it was clear for the Court that the First Amendment could not have the implication

---

550. For further discussion, see also Bosmajian 1983.
551. Filtering by public libraries is also common in the Netherlands. See also section 6.5.
552. See also section 6.4.4.
553. *United States v. American Library Association*, 539 U.S. 194 (2003), 201 F. Supp. 2d 401 (ED Pa. 2002).
554. *Ibid.*

that public libraries were obliged to provide access to all the material online. Hence, they were entitled to deploy filtering on their Internet access points. The Supreme Court reasoned as follows:

> A library's need to exercise judgment in making collection decisions depends on its traditional role in identifying suitable and worthwhile material; it is no less entitled to play that role when it collects material from the Internet than when it collects material from any other source. Most libraries already exclude pornography from their print collections because they deem it inappropriate for inclusion. We do not subject these decisions to heightened scrutiny; it would make little sense to treat libraries' judgments to block online pornography any differently, when these judgments are made for just the same reason.[555]

There would be more to say for this reasoning,[556] if it were not the case that the public libraries themselves, represented by their national association, expressed their discomfort with the de facto *obligation* to install filters. The conflict was not whether or not the libraries were entitled to select access to material, or install filters on Internet access terminals, but whether the government was allowed to compel them to do so. The Court answered this question by first casting doubt on whether libraries could *themselves* claim protection under the First Amendment in their relation to Congress (because they were public entities themselves). It then distinguished a First Amendment case, in which it had concluded that government-funded legal aids could assert the protection the First Amendment in the following manner:

> Public libraries, by contrast, have no comparable role that pits them against the Government, and there is no comparable assumption that they must be free of any conditions that their benefactors might attach to the use of donated funds or other assistance.[557]

The Court finally resolved the issue by its conclusion that the restrictions must be qualified as normal collection decisions and that CIPA did not *require libraries* to install the filters. It merely made government funding for Internet access terminals conditional on the application of filters. The Court did attach weight to the fact that the filtering would be accompanied with a procedure to request access to unduly blocked material.

---

555. *Ibid.*
556. See Bevier 2003. BeVier praises the plurality for its opinion and laments the divergence of opinions about the implications of the First Amendment for the constitutionality of CIPA, and in particular the attempt of a number of dissenting Judges to extent the protection of the First Amendment to anything that would look like a positive obligation in the context of libraries. See also Gardbaum 2003; Gardbaum 2008; Sullivan 1989; Schauer 2004.
557. *United States v. American Library Association*, 539 U.S. 194, 213 (2003). The Court distinguishes *Legal Services Corporation v. Velazquez*, 531 U.S. 533 (2001). This conclusion is remarkable in light of the history of well-documented attempts by public officials to remove material from libraries for politically motivated reasons.

The Court's view, cited above, is not only remarkable in its disregard of the actual sentiments of the American public library community but also in view of our discussion in section 7.3.2, where we concluded that freedom of expression implied independence of the publicly funded library from its funders in terms of its collection and accessibility governance. More generally, it is inconsistent with the right to freedom of expression as a constitutional check against undue interference by the legislative and executive branch, one of the primary reasons for constitutional safeguards to exist in the first place. The wide margin of discretion that is offered to the legislature to influence the library's collection policy, does not fit very well from an information law and policy perspective, in which freedom of expression implies a minimal amount of government involvement in terms of restricting content flows. It fits the sphere of cultural educational and welfare policies of the State much better, in which the State is granted a much wider margin of discretion.[558]

7.4.7. UNMONITORED ACCESS

Public libraries provide access to its collection in a public space and the way access is provided will affect actual library usage. Depending on the architecture of the library and its collection, accessibility and governance, the library users may be able to, as well as actually feel free to, use the library for their personal inquiries. The architecture and spatial management of the library will affect its use and tends to reflect ideas about accessibility governance. The library catalogues, its usability and the availability of assistance will decide whether users will actually find resources. In a similar vein, the extent to which the library users' movements in, browsing through, searching in and lending from the library without being specifically registered, will undoubtedly affect the behavior of its users. The digital library in particular and the subsequent introduction of electronic information retrieval and library management systems presents libraries with the question of how to protect the privacy of their users.

The privacy of library users is considered an essential part of the freedom of expression and information in the context of public libraries.[559] The right to freedom of expression and information may be of lesser value if there can be no legitimate expectation of privacy when searching for and accessing information and ideas.[560] Since the library is typically seen as a place for intellectual activity worthy of protection, the public library sector has repeatedly stood up against government interference into their user's privacy and anonymity.[561] Of specific

---

558. The Supreme Court's case law on the limited First Amendment implications for government spending discretion is controversial. For a discussion, see Sunstein 1993, 36–41.
559. On Privacy in the context of libraries, see e.g. Sommer 1966. See also Nissenbaum 2010, 195–196.
560. For a discussion, see Richards 2008.
561. See Schepman et al. 2008.

concern for libraries has been the possibility for other government agencies to access personally identifiable data on the use and lending data of library materials by individual library users.[562] The U.S. Patriot Act, introduced shortly after the attacks on the World Trade Center in 2001, contained several provisions that allowed law enforcement and national security agencies to gain access to library user data. In 2006, the Dutch legislature passed a law to override personal data protection and facilitate access to personal data held by entities in the public and private sector. The law contains no exceptions for data on intellectual activity, such as data held by public libraries.

It has to be noted that libraries are not completely consistent in their appeal for user privacy. From the library's perspective, the collection of data on lending behavior and the use of databases and catalogues is relevant because libraries would like to recommend to users certain books based on their lending histories, thereby better satisfying the needs of their users. Precisely because of the possibilities to improve their service to library users, libraries are inclined to store more and more personal data on the use of their resources. Hence, it is clear that the electronic environment increases the challenge to protect the privacy of library users. These issues in the context of search engine user privacy are dealt with in more detail in Chapters 8 and 10.

7.5.   CONCLUSION

Libraries may be the oldest societal institution dealing with the selection and accessibility governance of sources of information and ideas. This chapter has provided a short overview of their background and looked more closely into the implications of the right to freedom of expression for the governance of the selection of and access to collections in the context of the public library. Public libraries, like the press and many other traditional knowledge institutions, are going through a transition phase related to digitization and the Internet, which could have a considerable impact on the public libraries' role and future in the information society.

There is a considerable difference with regard to the understanding of freedom of expression in the context of libraries between European countries and the United States. In the American context, much more emphasis is placed on the freedom of speech and individual rights in the library context. This is probably best illustrated with the fact that most public libraries have a bill of rights. This could be explained by the continuing pressure on public libraries in the United States to suppress controversial material. One of such library censorship cases at the level of the U.S. Supreme Court, *Pico*, was addressed in more detail. The Court concluded that the First Amendment does not restrict public libraries from removing

---

562. In the United States, there are several library-specific laws (state level) that protect the privacy of library users. See Richards 2008, note 190 and accompanying text.

controversial content from the library collection as long as they do not act "in a narrowly partisan or political manner."[563]

European scholars argue that by funding public libraries, the State is acting under its positive obligation to promote basic levels of access to information, ideas, culture and knowledge. The collection, classification and accessibility governance in the public library is a matter left to the library profession, and independence from undue interference by public authorities and other external influences is considered a fundamental value.

In the United States, the Supreme Court is unwilling to accept any such positive obligations for the State to promote the substantive liberties of its citizens or interpret State funding to promote access to information in this light. In fact, in its last ruling on public libraries, which involved the constitutionality of CIPA, the Supreme Court ruled that public libraries have "no [. . .] role that pits them against the Government, and there is no comparable assumption that they must be free of any conditions that their benefactors might attach to the use of donated funds or other assistance."[564] It is striking that precisely in the United States, where individual political liberties have had such an impact on library governance, the value of political independence of libraries from the State in the context of collection and accessibility governance is disregarded by the Supreme Court.

It was shown that many of the normative principles developed in the context of the public library can be linked to the underlying ideals of the right to freedom of expression. Public libraries are supposed to provide their constituencies with a collection that respects the principles of pluralism and diversity. As such, they will sometimes confront library users with material they might not have selected themselves. It was noted that due to their role of making selection decisions with regard to the collection, library censorship, understood as the undue suppression or removal of material in public libraries can be hard to distinguish from normal selection decisions. Once libraries have selected material for inclusion in their collection, the governance of accessibility is focused on facilitating access for its users. It was noted how access to material and references to material elsewhere, the Internet in particular, will affect library usage considerably. In addition, it puts pressure on the traditional role of libraries only to provide access to material of a basic quality. Finally, from the perspective of free access to information, the unmonitored access to library materials is of particular concern in the context of libraries.

---

563. *Board of Education, Island Trees Union Free School District v. Pico*, 457 U.S. 853 (1982).
564. *United States v. American Library Association*, 539 U.S. 194, 213 (2003).

Chapter 8

Search Engine Freedom

8.1.   INTRODUCTION

The aim of this chapter is to develop a general framework for the implications of the right to freedom of expression for the governance of search engines, a framework that is shortly denoted as 'search engine freedom'. Drawing on the conclusions in the previous chapter, the analysis will focus on the ways in which the right to freedom of expression may be invoked in the context of search engines by a search engine provider, on the one hand, and the information providers and end-users it mediates between, on the other hand.

Search engine governance involves a great variety of public and private interests related to the effective and free dissemination of information and ideas, and the restrictions on such free dissemination. The three primary stakeholders, namely search engine providers, information providers and end-users, have competing interests in the governance of information flows through the medium. And amongst information providers and end-users, the types of interests vary as well. Moreover, third parties, such as private individuals, rights holders or public authorities have demonstrated their interests in the governance of search media through litigation and calls for regulation.

A complexity arises from the character of the decisions made by a search engine provider. A search engine combines a passive instrumental role with a role of independent communicator of information. It facilitates accessibility and mediates between information providers and end-users, but it does so by adding value through its selection and ranking decisions, which have considerable impact on what ends up being found by end-users. Most search engines, and selection intermediaries more generally, do not make individual determinations of the value of each source of online information in their index but predominantly use automated procedures, web data mining, and end-user data processing and modeling to decide which sources of information to prioritize over others.

This chapter will mostly focus on the question about the scope of the right to freedom of expression for the governance of search. This scope of the right to freedom of expression and information will be addressed in relation to the existing and possible restrictions that could stand in the way of the freedom of expression interests of the primary stakeholders to materialize. A range of existing, proposed or hypothetical legal restrictions on any of the communications between the primary stakeholders aimed at the governance of accessibility will be discussed to develop the argument in this chapter. Whenever feasible, reference will be made to specific proposals for the adoption of a specific type of restriction on search engine operations. Some of the legal restrictions on the right to freedom of expression in the context of search will be addressed in much more detail in the third part of this thesis, which focuses on specific regulatory issues relating to access and quality in search engines.

The focus will be placed on restrictions of a legal nature, and the role of the State or of government is of central concern. Moreover, the analysis is, as in the rest of this study, restricted to issues that are relevant from the perspective of the free circulation of information and ideas, and in particular the governance of accessibility, which lies at the core of governance of information flows in the Web search context. The discussion of the scope of freedom of expression will be tied to the question about the implications of Article 10 ECHR. The ECtHR has not addressed search engines in any of its rulings yet, so we have to draw analogies to other contexts to be able to address the implications of Article 10 ECHR for the possible legal governance of search engines. This has informed the analysis of freedom of expression in the context of the press, access providers and libraries in Chapters 5–7. These chapters have provided a broader picture of the way the implications of the right to freedom of expression are informed by the role of media and communication providers in the public information environment. The conclusions of these chapters about the relevant elements of freedom of expression doctrine will be used in this chapter and in the next part of this thesis.

Article 10 ECHR literally describes the freedom to receive and impart information and ideas as communicative actions which are protected. However, as was demonstrated in the previous chapters, it protects a broader range of communicative actions, including the right to transmit information freely and the right to use communicative means. The same is true for the First Amendment. Article 10 ECHR also implies a right to be able to effectively exercise one's freedom to impart or receive information and ideas, a right that can become relevant in horizontal relations. This focus on the freedom to communicate in different ways and capacities implies that to study the implications of the right to freedom of expression, one could zoom in on the various communications that are taking place, identify the possible interferences with these communications and discuss their legal legitimacy under the ECHR. However, such an endeavor would be both too limited and too broad for a number of reasons.

First, not only communicative actions but also actions that are indirectly linked to communication can be protected under the right to freedom of expression. For instance, the right to freedom of expression also protects the freedom to decide how to use the means to communicate. For example, a restriction on the freedom of a theatre proprietor to decide to whom the theatre will be rented for public performances can be seen as an infringement. It can also protect media against special restrictive legal treatment, such as discriminatory taxation. In other words, the scope of freedom of expression also includes actions that are only indirectly related to communication but facilitate, or are a necessary part for, various actors to exercise it. Trying to discuss all these possibilities does not seem to be a valuable approach.

Second, not all kinds of communicative actions are meaningfully protected by the right to freedom of expression. The right to freedom of expression tends to protect the actions that have come to be seen as legally meaningful from the perspective of the ideals underlying the right to freedom of expression.[565] Typical examples of such actions that are considered to be of particular importance are the right of citizens to speak publicly about matters of public concern, the editorial freedom of newspapers to decide which articles to print, the right to publish information without asking the authorities for permission or the right of citizens to use electronic communications networks freely. Thus, conceptualizing the scope of freedom of expression in the context of search, it may be more productive to look for a characterization of search engine freedom that encapsulates the 'typical' scope in the context of search.

As mentioned, the typical scope of the right to freedom of expression is connected to the normative theories underlying the right to freedom of expression. The end-user's freedom to receive information and ideas freely and become an informed citizen is considered to be worth protecting because of the importance of informed citizens in a democratic society and their individual autonomy. In a similar vein, the analysis of freedom of expression theories for the press, ISPs and libraries in Chapters 5–7 demonstrate that the protection of these entities under Article 10 ECHR strongly takes into account the 'societal role' of these media. For instance, the function of the press as public watchdog and as platform for debate about matters of public concern informs strong protection of the press. This freedom related to the production and selection of information and ideas is meant to guarantee that public debate can be 'uninhibited, robust and wide-open', as formulated by the U.S. Supreme Court in *Sullivan*.[566] In the case of Internet access providers, freedom of expression theory emphasizes the protection of the interests of end-users and information providers, precisely because of the relatively passive intermediary role of ISPs, to provide access. In short, the right to freedom of expression helps protect the 'public freedom of expression interest' in the free dissemination of information and ideas. And similar to the case of access providers, the press and libraries, if search engines can be demonstrated to have a particular role related to thesepublic interests in freedom of expression, they could receive more protection.

---

565. See e.g. Schauer 2004.
566. *New York Times Co. v. Sullivan*, 376 U.S. 254 (1964).

When answering the question about such public interest, it has to be borne in mind that it would be wrong to make freedom of expression fully instrumental to a particular conception of the public interest in the free circulation of information, knowledge and ideas. There is no agreement about the definition of such a conception in freedom of expression theory. The discussion in Chapter 6 of the possible claim of access providers under the right to freedom of expression in the United States, when asked to act as common carriers, may serve as an example of this disagreement. The law and freedom of expression doctrine have referred to different public interests underlying freedom of expression, but have also protected the right to freedom of expression independently. In the search engine context, this protection independent of the public interest means that freedom of expression simply protects the communications between the information provider and the search engine and the communications between the search engine and the end-user against undue interference by public authorities or as a result of other legal restrictions.

The chapter will proceed in the following order. First, a number of general starting points for a discussion of the implications of the right to freedom of expression in the context of search engines will be discussed (section 8.2). Drawing on a comparison between the entities discussed in Chapters 5–7, section 8.3 develops a conceptualization of the societal role of search engines, in which the implications of the fundamental right to freedom of expression can be incorporated. Section 8.4 discusses the implications of the right to freedom of expression for the most important communicative actions of search engine providers. After this, sections 8.5 and 8.6 provide additional perspectives on search engine freedom, from the perspective of information providers and end-users respectively.

8.2.   SEARCH ENGINE GOVERNANCE: STARTING POINTS

8.2.1.   INTRODUCTION

The Web search medium is a new and complex phenomenon in information law and policy. To be able to address the implications of the right to freedom of expression for the governance of search in this chapter, this section will first address some of the general characteristics of Web search governance. The following characteristics will shortly be addressed, as well as the way and the extent to which they will be addressed later in this and the next chapters: First, the structure of the search engine market and the prevailing business model for general purpose search engines. Second, the fact that online search services tend to be publicly accessible on the one hand and could be argued to be part of the public information environment accordingly, though they operate close to and often in the private realm of the end-user, on the other hand. Third, the existing legal and regulatory environment search engines act in is in its infancy. And finally, search engines like many online services act in the global information environment made possible by the Internet, thereby presenting a number of issues relating to legal jurisdiction.

8.2.2.   THE SEARCH ENGINE MARKET AND ITS BUSINESS MODEL

In the first part of the thesis, the general structure of the search engine market was analyzed and the prevailing business model for general purpose search engines was discussed. Monetization strategies can vary, but most services have an advertisement-based business model. This entails the auction of sponsored search results, which are placed next to organic search results. Publicly funded general purpose search engines are absent and over the last two decades, the market has developed into an oligopoly of a few globally operating services, in which Google is by all measures the dominant player. Nonetheless, it was observed in the first part of this study that there remain many other entities, including specialized search portals, directories, Web publishers and new phenomenon such as microblogging sites and social networks, which strongly contribute to the function of facilitating access to, and the findability of, information online. It has to be acknowledged that linking and referencing is a core function of the web environment more generally, which cannot be monopolized by a single search engine or a single type of service.

Most search engines and other selection intermediaries are provided by private actors on a commercial basis. The dominant business model, discussed in more detail in Chapters 2 and 3, involves the sale of targeted reference space. The commercial nature of the services implies that they operate in a vertical relation with the State and a horizontal relation with end-users and information providers. As publicly funded search engines remain the exception, the analysis will focus primarily on the legal governance of commercial search services. A publicly funded search engine would have a comparable relation with the State as the public library. It would act in a vertical relationship with end-users and information providers, which would imply that the latter could have a more straightforward claim under freedom of expression with regard to the governance of information flows.

The advertisement-based business model brings with it a number of regulatory issues relating to the law and regulation with regard to commercial advertising and the possible impact of advertising on the governance of the medium. The separation of advertising and editorial content in print media has served as a model for the legal governance of search media in the context of the demarcation of organic and spon-sored results. The resulting regulatory framework will be more thoroughly discussed in Chapter 10. Further below in this Chapter, the connection to the development of a body of professional ethics of search engine governance and its relation to the right to freedom of expression will be explored.

Search media provide findability in the public networked information environ-ment which provides for access not only to sources of knowledge, information and ideas, but also to a variety of other service providers and e-commerce sites. As a result, search engines not only play an important role in the market place for infor-mation and ideas but also, and not in the least, in actual markets for actual goods and services. The commercial nature of many of the communications in the search engine context can become relevant for the protection under the right to freedom of expression. The right to freedom of expression does not protect commercial and non-commercial communications to the same degree. In general, governments have more leeway to regulate commercial communications. It could be argued that the persuasive presence of commercial communications in general purpose search results, both in sponsored and natural results, gives more room for an active regulatory role and specific restrictions on the freedom of search engine providers. For example, in a recent judgment, the U.S. Ninth Circuit characterized the selection decisions of specialized service for finding housing opportunities as commercial speech. This meant that it could apply the less restrictive test for restrictions of commercial speech to a legal restriction on the operation of search engines pursuant to the Fair Housing Act.[567]

8.2.3.   PUBLIC AND PRIVATE NATURE OF WEB SEARCH COMMUNICATIONS

This study has focused on Web search services which are offered to the public at large through a publicly accessible location on the Internet. Moreover, they index and refer their users to publicly accessible online destinations. Thus, search engines can be said to operate in the public networked information environment, alongside others such as online publishers. However, it is clear that the use of search engines often takes place in the privacy of the home, or in the relative privacy of the workplace. In addition, the interactive nature of the service implies that the actual communications that are taking place between end-users and search engine providers are primarily of a private nature.

To summarize, search media are arguably public, in the sense that the service is offered to the public and its search results refer to publicly accessible destinations. But their actual offerings are quite private, since the actual output of search engine consists of a specific individualized set of search results offered to a particular end-user, in response to a particular query at a certain place and time. The increased personalization of search engine services shifts the nature of these services and their offerings more into the private, individualized sphere.[568] There is no longer such a thing as 'the' references offered by a search engine. The offering of ranked collections of search results have started to depend so much on private interaction with specific end-users that the output of search engines becomes ill-defined without reference to their specific queries under specific circumstances.[569]

From a constitutional perspective, and particularly from the perspective of the important constitutional dichotomy between public and private communications, the private nature of the actual output to end-users, and the dependency of the output on particular end-users, could have implications for the role of government with regard to the communications that are taking place in the context of search. It could be argued that the reading of a newspaper or a book is also of a private nature. The difference, however, is that the actual output of search engines has become

---

567. For further discussion, see section 8.4.3.
568. On the questions, from a German Constitutional perspective not addressed in this thesis, see Schulz et al. 2005a, 26.
569. See Zuckerman 2011, in reaction to Feuz et al. 2011.

hard to define, without taking into consideration the actual user behavior. A newspaper or a book does not change its content depending on the choices of its specific reader.[570] The relative private nature of the communications between end-users and search engines constitute an additional barrier for involvement by public authorities, as the communications are taking place in the private realm, where it would be less appropriate to regulate. As in the case of Internet access providers, not only Article 10 ECHR but also Article 8 ECHR is relevant.

8.2.4. A LEGAL AND REGULATORY FRAMEWORK IN ITS INFANCY

Search engines operate in a regulatory framework that is still in its infancy.[571] Search engine law and regulation consists of a mix of the maturing application of general applicable laws, a growing body of self-regulation, and in some jurisdictions a few search engine specific legal provisions such as the DMCA safe harbor for search engines mentioned in Chapter 6. This mix of different elements of search engines makes it much harder to tackle search engine law and regulation as a whole.

As mentioned, for the most part, search engine law consists of the application of generally applicable laws. Hence, when restricted to issues relating to the free dissemination of information and ideas, the study of search engine law consists of the study of tort law (including defamation law, privacy law and unfair competition law), property law, copyright and database law, trademark law, advertising law, consumer protection law and data privacy laws as they apply to the search engine context.[572] This does not mean that the application of these general laws does not involve issues that are specifically related to search engines, but it simply means that the specific rules that have been applied in this process are judge-made.[573] As will become clear in greater detail throughout the remainder of this study, the right to freedom of expression—through the doctrines of direct or indirect horizontal effect of fundamental rights—has sometimes played a significant role in the debates about the proper application of these general laws and there are several judgments that specifically address this question.[574]

The statutory safe harbors for third-party liability are currently the only example of search engine specific regulation. And these search engine specific

---

570. Due to personalization, a somewhat similar development can be observed in the context of in electronic media more generally. See also section 10.2.1.
571. For an overview of the absence of European search engine law, see van Eijk 2006. See also Jakubowicz 2009; Van Eijk 2009; Van Hoboken 2009; Valcke 2008. For an overview of U.S. search engine law, see Grimmelmann 2007.
572. For an overview, see Grimmelmann 2007. See also Gasser 2006.
573. For an (unconvincing) argument that search engine law should be further developed through a specialized judicial forum, building and extending the judge-made character of search engine law, see Moffat 2009.
574. Such as the BGH *Paperboy* judgment and related rulings in Germany, BGH July 17, 2003, I ZR 259/00 (*Paperboy*).

safe harbors only exist in the United States and not at the EU level.[575] As was shown in Chapter 6, these safe harbor provisions internalize the right to freedom of expression into the standard for intermediary liability for third-party activity to some extent. Except for these safe harbors, specific government involvement with search engines has mostly followed the self-regulatory paradigm for Internet content regulation, which was discussed in Chapter 6.[576] Many of these proposals will be discussed in detail below, particularly how they relate to the right to freedom of expression.

It is important to note here that the call for search engine specific self-regulation often overlaps with the debate about the proper application of generally applicable laws. Generally applicable tort law, for instance, is indeterminate enough to argue both ways. It may be argued on the one hand that search engines should remove illegal information from their index upon request to escape general tort liability. On the other hand, it may be argued that search engines have no such obligation and that any removal of sources of information is thereby voluntary.[577] Moreover, what could be considered self-regulation at one point in time could become an expected duty of care under general tort law principles if it is widely adopted. As was discussed in more depth in Chapter 6, Internet self-regulation often involves a high level of involvement by public authorities, which warrants the question of the extent to which self-regulation merely informalizes the regulatory role of the State instead of minimizing it.[578] This question is particularly relevant for the legitimacy of interferences with the right to freedom of expression under Article 10 ECHR. Any interference by public authorities with the right to freedom of expression, including informal ones, has to be 'prescribed by law'.

8.2.5.   SEARCH ENGINE GOVERNANCE, A GLOBAL INTERNET
           AND JURISDICTION

The establishment of jurisdiction over online services and information providers is an important and complex issue. Compared to Internet access providers, most Web search engines have relatively weak jurisdictional ties. General purpose Web search engines such as the one provided by Google operate on a global scale and, unlike access providers, can easily be provided from abroad like any other website. Increasingly, Web search providers tend to diversify their services into country—or language—based versions. In addition, geo-location software is used to target search results based on location, implying that search engines tend to know the location of specific users. Yet, end-users typically remain free to choose

---

575. Some EU Member States, for instance Austria and Spain, have also adopted search engine specific safe harbors. For a discussion, see section 9.3.4.
576. See section 6.4.1.
577. See Schulz & Held 2007.
578. See Tambini at al 2008, discussed in more detail in section 6.4.6. See also Bambauer forthcoming 2011.

which of the language- or country-specific services to use. This presents a number of problems for any type of country-specific search engine law and policy.

To be able to regulate or apply existing general laws to search engines in specific circumstances, the State should be able to claim jurisdiction in a way that is in line with fundamental principles of international law. These principles include the right to freedom of expression and information which specifically protects the free flow of information between jurisdictions.[579] Considering the international nature of the offering of Web search providers, and the design and the general governance of the Internet as a universal network of interconnected networks more generally, it is likely that different countries only have a limited claim of jurisdiction over the infrastructure and communications of a specific search engine provider. This means that the scope of national law is only applicable or regulation could only be adopted with regard to that 'part' of the service.

The limitations this implies with regard to the effectiveness of any type of country-specific regulation that tries to restrict accessibility of content through search engines are obvious. Laws and policies which would aim to facilitate accessibility may end up being more effective. The search engine laws and policies that are finally adopted should not only respect the accepted principles of jurisdiction, but should also be enforceable. The enforceability of laws on the Internet used to be seen as *the* major obstacle for effective regulation of content flows by national law. It is now generally accepted that well-designed rules and policies can be enforced, even with regard to services and information providers on the Internet.[580]

8.3. BETWEEN ACCESS AND QUALITY: THE SOCIETAL ROLE OF SEARCH MEDIA

8.3.1. THE ROLE OF SEARCH ENGINES IN THE NETWORKED INFORMATION ENVIRONMENT: A COMPARISON

As noted above, search engines combine an intermediary function, between information providers and end-users, with an independent function of communicator of information about information. In their capacity as intermediaries, search engines are perhaps better qualified as a *meta-medium*. In their capacity as independent communicators, search engines act as content (references) providers themselves, making choices about their communicative actions independent of information providers, end-users and others. As will become apparent in the following sections, both perspectives have their own merits and can help properly answer the questions about the implications of the right to freedom of expression for the governance of search.

Search engines do more than just providing references to the information and ideas which are available online in response to user queries. This can be clarified by

---

579. See section 4.3.1.
580. See generally, Goldsmith & Wu 2006.

comparing the function of Internet access providers in the networked information environment, as discussed in Chapter 6, with the function of search engines. An Internet access provider is an essential but invisible part of any attempt of an end-user to access information online. In principle, an access provider—that does not block or discriminate[581]—makes every online destination similarly accessible to its subscribers.

The function of search engines is different from Internet access providers in two fundamental ways. First, they are not a necessary part in the communicative process between online information and end-users. An online destination can be reached without the use of a particular search engine, either directly by using its address on the Web or indirectly by using another search or recommendation service or following a hyperlink elsewhere.

Second, search engines do not facilitate equal access to everything on the Web. They do not connect all end-users to all online destinations but mediate between the two sides on the basis of range of content, destination, and end-user and query-specific characteristics. This mediation is carried out by its decisions and algorithms about the crawling of online material and their selection, ranking and presentation of references. In other words, search engines are not neutral by nature.[582] They actively match information providers (including advertisers) and end-users, and this active role with regard to the valuation of different online destinations for its users is what helps make one search engine more valuable than another.

While search engines do more than providing access, they also do less—as regards the valuation and selection of content—than an actual content provider. This can be clarified with a comparison of the function and the strength of editorial control that is asserted over information flows in the search engine context with the function of the press or the mass media more generally.

The function of search engines is different in two important ways. First, the press not only selects which information and ideas to present to its users, but also actually publishes the information itself, thereby turning itself into the source of publicity. While the press takes the responsibility for the publicity of information and ideas (as well as the non-publicity of what it decided not to print), search engines merely refer to what is already published. In Chapter 5, it was shown that while the press has also been recognized as a platform for information and ideas to find their way to an audience, its primary role is considered to be to actively select what information to publish, using and relying on some and discarding others. By deciding about the trustworthiness of sources and the newsworthiness of the events

---

581. But as was discussed in Ch. 6, even ISPs sometimes make decisions that impact the (relative) accessibility of information. For instance, ISPs could decide to block access to material. ISPs can also have a less direct impact through the caching of material and the reservation of special capacity for certain content providers. See sections 6.4.2 and 6.5.1.
582. See Grimmelmann 2010b.

they report on, they actively help construct the boundaries of public debate—a role that has given them the name 'gatekeepers'.[583]

Second and in relation, because of its role of facilitating the navigation of the online information environment, a search engine's value greatly depends on the comprehensiveness of its index. As a consequence, search engines tend to be far less restrictive in their selection decisions than content providers such as news media. Search engines simply cannot be very restrictive in terms of crawling and indexing, because they would simply lose their navigational function for the Web if they were to discard sources of online information that end-users are, or might be, looking for. 'Recall', one of the two traditional criteria for the quality of information retrieval systems, demands that the index of information retrieval systems should be as comprehensive as possible. On top of that, the sheer amount of available resources online makes it attractive and possibly commercially imperative to rely on others, including information providers, to decide what to index. In practice, the control over indexing and selection is, therefore, de facto shared and distributed. The power of search engines lies not in the exclusion of material but in making material more readily accessible, i.e. matching specific end-users with specific sources of information based on decisions made by search engine providers and, to some extent, programmed into the search engines' architectures. To conclude, whereas a search engine does try to help end-users find the most valuable or relevant online destinations, it does not, except in certain circumstances, try to prevent its users from accessing online information and ideas of low quality or other undesirable characteristics.

To better understand the role of search engines in the public networked information environment, it is useful to compare the accessibility governance of search engines, with the collection and decisions about availability and accessibility that are made in the context of libraries and which were discussed in Chapter 7. Both the search engine and the library combine an intermediary function and an active function with regard to the selection of sources of information and ideas, but they do so in different ways. Simply put, libraries first select information and ideas which are allowed to enter their collections. These collection decisions reflect criteria relating to quality. Hence, decisions about quality are part of the governance of availability. This selective role of libraries is informed by their mission: public libraries, amongst other things, provide basic access to knowledge and our cultural heritage. A lot of media and information in the public information environment, such as commercial communications, illegal material or self-published content are typically not included in library collections in the first place. After the collections have been established, libraries provide an accessibility infrastructure for their patrons that makes everything *in the collection* findable. The library collection is made transparent for end-users through an accessibility architecture that is comprehensive and aims to follow scientific criteria for the organization of material.

---

583. See White 1950; Bass 1969; Shoemaker 1991; Gladney 1996; Sturges 2001.

Like newspapers or libraries, Web search engines could pre-select and exclude information and ideas from their indices. In particular, they could do so *on the basis of quality*. In general, search engines do exclude large amounts of material from their index, but they do so for reasons different from those of newspapers or libraries. For instance, all general purpose search engines exclude material because of legal restrictions, because of search engine manipulation and because of crawling instructions by information providers. All general purpose search engines have serious and ongoing problems with illegal or harmful publications by third parties in their indices. The same search engine that can be used for looking up information about seventeenth century pre-industrial production processes or finding tickets for the 2010 World Cup in South Africa provides access to hardcore pornography, racial hatred and illegal advertising. Most search engines have standard optional filters to prevent indecency from entering their search results. There are several possible legal restrictions on the lawfulness of including material in the index, for instance because of the existence of exclusive rights with regard to the underlying information, such as copyright law, database law, or content-specific restrictions such as defamation law, privacy law, data protection law and child pornography law. The legal regime for search engine intermediary liability as well as their involvement in content regulation will be discussed in Chapter 9.

8.3.2. SEARCH ENGINE GOVERNANCE: BETWEEN ACCESS AND QUALITY

It must be concluded from the above that search engines are more actively involved with content than access providers because of their role in selecting and valuating sources of information and ideas online. At the same time, they are less actively involved as content providers such as the press, because their selection decisions are relatively passive and merely refer to online destinations without taking responsibility for their existence. Moreover, search engines facilitate and exert power over the relative accessibility of information and ideas, not over its availability.

In one of the most thoughtful attempts to conceptualize the societal role of search media in the networked information environment, Dutch philosophers of science, Marres and De Vries, pointed out that search engines have to reconcile two conflicting ideals: the ideal of *universal access* on the one hand and the ideal of *information quality* on the other hand.[584] The first ideal is to help end-users to navigate the *entire Web*, by ordering it and making the material that is available, transparent and universally accessible. The second ideal is to prioritize valuable and accurate information and ideas over lesser ones and to exclude illegal or harmful material. Marres and De Vries point out that the resolution of these conflicting ideals in the 'old' public information environment used to be based on the conceptual separation between the production and legitimization of information and ideas on the one hand and the subsequent use of it on the other hand.

---

584. Marres & De Vries 2002.

For instance, the New York Times traditionally claims to include "all that is fit to print."[585] This implies the exclusion of stories that could not be confirmed by reliable sources, irrelevant information and opinion of low quality. In other words, the legitimacy of the material ending up in a newspaper was, at least in theory, carefully guarded. The ideal of (universal) access was restricted to everything fit to print, and the freedom and responsibility of newspapers to decide what was fit to print, i.e. their editorial freedom, was seen as an essential element of a free press.

Likewise, a library first selects the sources it subsequently makes accessible.[586] Libraries apply quality criteria in the context of these selection decisions. They used to rely on established sources of information and ideas, and everything below a certain quality and relevancy threshold would and could be discarded. After having established a collection, a transparent accessibility infrastructure, informed by professional principles for the organization of knowledge, would ensure universal access to the materials that had been selected.[587] Of course, library accessibility infrastructures such as their classification systems also have their biases, and accessibility is not always guaranteed in practice.[588] The important point, however, is that in the print-based public information environment, access and quality were separated: libraries did not have to worry about quality standards in the context of accessibility, because the simple fact that the book is available in the library means that it is a legitimate source of information for library patrons. Moreover, in their collection selection decisions, libraries could rely on publishers who would only publish what they considered to be of high enough quality. It is notable that the provision of Internet access in libraries, addressed in Chapter 7, has broken down the traditional separation of the governance of quality and access in libraries. Internet access in libraries extends the library collection beyond the sphere of materials with institutional guarantees relating to information quality.

Marres and De Vries point out that the traditional separation between the production and legitimization of knowledge and its use no longer exists in the context of the Web.[589] Furthermore, and more fundamentally, they assert that *the legitimization of sources of information and ideas no longer takes place through the governance of availability but through the governance of accessibility.* In other words, competition in the marketplace of information and ideas has partly shifted from competition in the context of the platforms of publishing media to competition in the context of search media and selection intermediaries.

In general, the ideals of universal access and information quality lie at the core of many of the debates about the governance of information flows on the

---

585. See e.g. The New York Times 1901. ('Only the news that is "fit" to print finds place in its columns.')
586. See section 7.4.
587. Although libraries may sometimes place restrictions on access to certain books, such as rare, valuable or pornographic books. See Bowker & Leigh Star 2000, 11.
588. On the social and political consequences of classification as a phenomenon, see Bowker & Leigh Star 2000.
589. Marres & De Vries 2002.

Internet.[590] The networked information environment and the related possibility of self-publication and further dissemination to the public, unrestricted by traditional knowledge institutions and the mass media, has broken down the institutional encirclement of certain sources of information for societal consumption.[591] This 'disintermediation' is seen as one of the central promises of the Internet and the Web by those who lamented the gatekeeping power of mass media and traditional knowledge institutions.[592] At the same time, this may be seen as the central flaw of the Internet by those who place more emphasis on the public interest in restricting access to uncontrolled flows of information and ideas, and on the value of shared platforms for debate and circulation of information and ideas which guarantee minimal levels of quality.

Freedom of expression theory also reflects these conflicting ideals of quality and universal access. Meiklejohn, for instance, has argued that the value of freedom of speech does not lie in everyone's freedom to speak but that "everything worth saying shall be said."[593] In other words, freedom of expression law and theory should place emphasis on the creation of a framework that helps foster a public debate of high accessibility *and* quality. Selection decisions with regard to information flows would be protected because they contribute to this ideal. Early in the twentieth century, Walter Lippmann made a particularly strong argument in favor of information quality on the basis of the freedom of expression theory related to democratic self-governance.[594] In *Liberty and the News*, Lippmann dismissed some of the most famous arguments for the freedom of the press as the expression of indifference over information quality and the formation of public opinion. He considered this indifference with regard to the functioning of the press wholly irrational:

> In a few generations it will seem ludicrous to historians that a people professing government by the will of the people should have made no serious effort to guarantee the news without which a governing opinion cannot exist.[595]

At least as prominent in freedom of expression law and theory, however, is the principle that government through its laws and policies should not be allowed to restrict access to information or access to audiences but should leave this to the 'marketplace of information and ideas' and the free choices of individuals instead.

---

590. See Marres & De Vries, 188 on the so-called garage box paradox. They compare this paradox to the classic paradox, debated by Lippmann and others, between the ideal of accurate representation of science and facts on the one hand, and political democratic representation and public opinion on the other hand.
591. On the dynamics of encircling and uncircling, from a perspective of search engines, see Duguid 2009.
592. See e.g. Shirky 2008; Gillmore 2004.
593. Meklejohn 1948, 25.
594. Lippmann's work also helped shape the twentieth century ideal of separating the governance of the selection and legitimization of information in the public information environment on the one hand (quality) and its societal use on the one hand (access).
595. See Lippmann 1920.

More speech is better, because it increases competition between speakers and exposes end-users to a wider range of information and ideas. In addition, choices about the relative value of information and ideas should be left to the free market. In the context of the press, controlling and restricting the media in view of information quality is considered an infringement with the press' editorial freedom, which strongly protects the press against access regulation. As was discussed in Chapter 5 with regard to the implications of the right to freedom of expression for commercial communications, First Amendment doctrine contains a particularly strong assumption in favor of the public's rationality.

The breaking down of the separation between quality and access governance in the networked information environment leads Marres and De Vries to conclude that the societal legitimization of knowledge now de facto takes place through processes of opening up. This opening up of the networked information environment, understood as the process of connecting information and ideas online to their societal use, is not a technical undertaking but must be understood as a *societal and political process*.[596] Web search engines, in particular, help construct the boundaries of accessibility in the new networked public information environment. It is interesting to note that Marres and De Vries express particular interest in the possible role of government to resolve these competing ideals, and they point to the importance of considering a facilitative role of government. In their view, the opening up of the Web is a process to which the government and public institutions could contribute.

If we follow this logic, the overarching public interest lies in the establishment of a rich and robust societal infrastructure for the opening up of the Web, one which fosters the societal project of the legitimization and contestation of information and ideas in the public networked information environment. This characterization of the public interest in the governance of accessibility of the Web is attractive precisely because it captures both perspectives, i.e. access *and* quality, which lie at the core of search engine governance. This conception clarifies that search engine providers have to make non-trivial choices with regard to the balance between access and quality. These non-trivial choices are a direct result of the dynamics in the public networked information environment they are acting in. Publicity is no longer restricted to entities that offer a priori institutional legitimacy to the information and ideas they make public. More fundamentally, the choices are not only non-trivial, but also of a political nature and involve the complex balancing of different public and private interests, including the interests of end-users and information providers.

Of course, an important underlying question is how various Web search engines have finally deal with the tension between the ideals of access and quality, which is inherent in the governance of their service. From a legal and normative perspective, the question is in what way search engines can and should be able to assert the right to freedom of expression in view of possible restrictions on the freedom to decide about information flows through their services. In the next

---

596. Marres & De Vries 2002.

section, these questions will be addressed in more depth. A general distinction will be made between two types of decisions a search engine has to make about its governance of accessibility. The first type is about the inclusion and exclusion of information providers in its index, while the second type is about the selection, ranking and presentation of references from its index to an end-user in response to a query. Further in this chapter, the implications of the right to freedom of expression for the communicative liberties of end-users and information providers will be discussed in relation to the freedom of search engine providers.

| 8.4. | SEARCH ENGINE PROVIDERS AND THE RIGHT TO FREEDOM OF EXPRESSION |

| 8.4.1. | INTRODUCTION |

Van Eijk has already noted the difficulties of qualifying search engines in light of the right to freedom of expression because of the complex role discussed above.[597] For reasons related to this double role of search engines with regard to online communications, Van Eijk asserts that the freedoms to impart or receive information, as explicitly mentioned in Article 10 ECHR, are not the main aim of search engines since the information is already present and accessible directly.[598] A search engine does not and cannot change that. Van Eijk concludes that a search engine *facilitates access* to information and does not offer access to information itself. He asserts that this activity of *making accessible* should have a similar status under Article 10 ECHR as the activity of disclosing or disseminating information and ideas. In other words, it is the function of search engines to make specific information, out of the abundance of information online, more readily accessible.[599] Web search engines impact the relative *accessibility* of information which is already publicly available for Internet end-users. Therefore, an analysis of the implications of freedom of expression in the context of search engines should focus on the governance of such accessibility.

| 8.4.2. | THE FREEDOM TO PUBLISH REFERENCING INFORMATION AND THE FREEDOM TO CRAWL |

If we turn to the question about the implications of the right to freedom of expression as protected by Article 10 ECHR for search engine providers, an important starting point is that the publication of search results by a publicly accessible search

---

597. Van Eijk 2006, 5.
598. *Ibid.*
599. The shift of accessibility governance from availability governance runs parallel with a shift from a publisher economy to an attention economy. See van Hoboken 2009c; Goldhaber 1997; Bermejo 2007. See also section 10.2.1.

engine is clearly protected under Article 10 ECHR. The publication of search results itself constitutes a publication of the search engine provider for its end-users. In other words, a search engine not only facilitates access to information of third parties, but also produces information itself, namely information about information. The most important question in this context is not whether the function of referencing by search engines is protected under the right to freedom of expression, but what level of protection should be attributed to search engines' practices of referring to information elsewhere. It is possible that the weight of protection differs because of the type of communication. Referencing information might receive its own level of protection. This status could depend on the public interest in the publication of these references, and the status of the Internet more generally. Linking lies at the heart of the networked information environment. The fact that search engines, in particular, rely on hyperlinking to others can play a role in the assessment of the weight that should be attributed to their freedom to do so. In contrast, the types of content the search engine refers to may play a role in the assessment as well.

In *Times v. United Kingdom*, a case about the protection of publications against defamation lawsuits after a considerable lapse of time, the ECtHR for the first time qualified the importance of the Internet for the promotion of the values protected by Article 10 ECHR.

> In light of its accessibility and its capacity to store and communicate vast amounts of information, the Internet plays an important role in enhancing the public's access to news and facilitating the dissemination of information generally. The maintenance of Internet archives is a critical aspect of this role and the Court therefore considers that such archives fall within the ambit of the protection afforded by Article 10.[600]

But in the same ruling, the Court also lowered the protection for the publication of old newspaper articles on the World Wide Web. It did so by, on the one hand, stating an undefined but seemingly large margin of appreciation for the Member States to impose restrictions on the publication of news archives online, and on the other hand heightening the duties and responsibilities tied to such 'ongoing' publications.

> [T]he margin of appreciation [. . .] is likely to be greater where news archives of past events, rather than news reporting of current affairs, are concerned. In particular, the duty of the press to act in accordance with the principles of responsible journalism by ensuring the accuracy of historical, rather than perishable, information published is likely to be more stringent in the absence of any urgency in publishing the material.[601]

---

600. ECtHR March 10, 2009, *Times v. United Kingdom*, § 27 (adding that "[t]he maintenance of Internet archives is a critical aspect of this role and the Court therefore considers that such archives fall within the ambit of the protection afforded by Article 10").
601. *Ibid.*, § 45.

Referencing information does not, in general, qualify as a publication of public concern or as current affairs. At the same time, it could be argued that referencing information in search engines has become as necessary for end-users to inform themselves about matters of public concern as the underlying stories themselves. Without the appropriate freedoms to reference to stories about matters of public concern, many of those stories would not be effectively accessible.

In *Open Door*, the Court touched more closely on the legality of restrictions on referencing information under Article 10 ECHR.[602] The Court's considerations contain a number of elements that are useful for discussing the implications of Article 10 ECHR in the context of search engines. The case involved an absolute prohibition under Irish Law against providing information about abortion facilities abroad. The Court concluded that the measures in question were disproportionate and were an infringement of Article 10 ECHR. The Court based its judgment on a variety of circumstances. First, it asserted that it was not illegal under Irish law to act on the information in question: it was legal under Irish law to travel abroad to receive an abortion.[603] The Court further noted that the restrictions could have a negative impact on women's health and called for careful scrutiny because other ECHR countries tolerated these activities.[604] Above all, the Court pointed to the absolute nature of the ban on referencing information about abortion facilities, which was therefore overbroad and disproportionate.[605]

The Court's conclusion in *Open Door* was strengthened further by a number of other factors. First, the counselors who were informing pregnant women about abortion facilities were not advocating or encouraging abortion, but merely informing women about the available options:

> [t]he decision as to whether or not to act on the information so provided was that of the woman concerned.[606]

This circumstance, and the fact that some women were likely to decide not to have an abortion on the basis of the information provided, meant that the link between the referencing information and the decision of certain women to act on this information was not as definite as presented by the Irish authorities, according to the Court. The Court also took into account the fact that the information was not provided to the public at large. Moreover, the Court considered that the referencing information was also available through other means, such as in magazines and telephone directories, and that these other means contained lower professional guarantees with regard to the health interests of the women involved.[607] Perhaps, in the present day, the Court would have added a reference to Web search engines

---

602. ECtHR October 29, 1992, *Open Door v. Ireland*.
603. *Ibid.*, § 72.
604. *Ibid.*, § 72. Note that the margin of appreciation in this case would normally have been wide because of the moral nature of the restrictions, in which Member States have more leeway than in other domains.
605. *Ibid.*, § 73.
606. *Ibid.*, § 75.
607. *Ibid.*, § 76.

or the Internet to this list. Finally, the Court deemed the ban ineffective in pre-venting abortions abroad from taking place and, in fact, suggested that this particular restriction on *reliable* information about abortion facilities abroad was likely to have an adverse effect on the health of women.[608]

Open Door shows that absolute restrictions on the publication of certain infor-mation should at least be consistent to be legitimate. The fact that banned infor-mation can still be accessed through other legal means can render a ban dispropor-tionate. This conclusion of the Court is consistent with its considerations with regard to the illegal nature of the prior restraint in *Spycatcher*.[609] These conclu-sions also resonate in the search engine context, for the simple reason that a search engine cannot prevent Internet users from accessing the information directly. This leaves open the possibility that it would be illegal to access the information directly. But at the very least, it raises questions about the proportionality of legal restrictions on referencing information without action being taken against the actual source of the material. More generally, legal restrictions on providing references to certain types or sources of information could incentivize search engines to exclude material the indexing of which would be lawful. Through the doctrine of chilling effects, such restrictions are also relevant under the right to freedom of expression.

The prohibition on search engine providers of publishing references to certain specific types of content or specific online destinations comes closest to what we would call a prior restraint. This is a common phenomenon in countries such as Saudi Arabia and China.[610] In China, for instance, it is apparently prohibited to communicate references to publications relating to the Tiananmen Square protests in Beijing in 1989. In countries more democratic than China, including Germany and Argentina, there are court rulings in which search engines were ordered not to communicate any references to information about specific individuals.[611] It goes beyond the scope of this chapter to discuss in depth the legitimacy of legal inter-ferences on the search engine's freedom to publish references or the possible liability of search engines for referring to illegal or unlawful content. This will be addressed in Chapter 9.

Before discussing the protection of the communication of referencing infor-mation by search engines in more depth, it is important to address the commu-nications that are necessary to publish references on the basis of an index of online content in the first place, namely the crawling of the Web. Without crawling, the type of full-text search engines that have become the standard navigational tool in the networked information environment could not be offered.

Crawling consists of the use of specialized software that harvests the infor-mation which is available on the Internet through automated requests. In view of

---

608. *Ibid.*, §§ 76–77.
609. See section 5.3.4.
610. See Deibert et al. 2007. See also Villeneuve 2008.
611. See Soghoian & Valle 2008; Bonim 2008. See also Van Hoboken 2009c.

the ECtHR's decision in *Autronic*,[612] this kind of automated requests can be considered to be an important and specialized means of reception in the context of the Internet, protected by Article 10 ECHR. The search engine's crawlers are a means of receiving information, in some ways a modern automated version of the researcher or journalist delving for sources of information by making phone calls, talking to people directly or looking through printed material. Article 10 ECHR does not explicitly refer to a right to gather information, but these communicative processes are generally understood to be included in its scope.[613]

The automated and complex nature of crawling technology is directly related to the abundance of publicly accessible sources of online information. Crawling consists of the automated and repeated requests for content available online. The importance of search engines for the dissemination of information and ideas, and the possibility of the public to inform itself, could be one of the determining elements for the extent to which crawling and the subsequent indexing of references is protected and the question of whether possible interferences are in accordance with Article 10 ECHR, second paragraph. Thus, the protection against interferences with crawling by search engines could possibly be enhanced because of the importance of search engines in our information society.

8.4.3.   SEARCH ENGINE FREEDOM: SELECTION AND RANKING

Up to this point, the analysis has focused on the protection of the search engine's freedom to control the composition of its index and to publish references. But the governance of the composition of the index and of the freedom to crawl and publish references is only half the story when it comes to the governance of accessibility of information and ideas by search media. The real impact of these media stems from their selection and ranking technology, and their interaction with information providers and end-users: the selection, ranking and presentation of references in response to particular queries. To what extent can search engines claim protection under the right to freedom of expression for their decisions to select a particular set of references as relevant in relation to a query? And to what extent can search engines claim protection for the way they rank these references once they present them to their users? Before discussing the answers to these questions, it is important to discuss the character of decisions about selection and ranking more detail.

The very fact that search engines select and rank the references for end-users implies that they do make decisions that entail a valuation of information and ideas.[614] As a result, search media impose specific hierarchies on the relative accessibility of information and ideas through their services. It may be important

---

612. See section 6.3.1.
613. See section 4.4.3.
614. See Finkelstein 2008 (pointing out that Google's ranking decisions are driven by popularity metrics). See also Rogers 2009a. Google tends to compliment itself for the disruptive but 'democratizing' impact of its services. See also Caldas et al. 2008.

to realize that a full understanding of the way search engines impose such hierarchies on accessibility and the impact this has on our public networked information environment is currently beyond our grasp. It seems that these hierarchies tend to be informed by a mindset different from traditional ordering mechanisms for knowledge, information and ideas, such as the ones would find in a library. Metrics of quality assurance by human editors have been automated and supplanted by relevancy and popularity algorithms. Moreover, commercial motivations have entered the domain of the organization of information and ideas on the Web due to the function of the Web in facilitating e-commerce and advertising. The incentives and subsequent strategies related to governance of the search platform are partly a result of its business model, i.e. a targeted marketing platform, where organic results are offered alongside sponsored results that provide for income.[615]

Google's search engine algorithms, and its PageRank algorithm in particular, which was the core of Google's search engine when it was launched, are the best known example of the imposition of a particular hierarchy on the ranking of search results. Before Google, and in traditional information retrieval systems, the selection of a relevant set of search results from the index, before ranking, used to take place by imposing a binary measure of relevance between the query and the websites stored in the index. The subsequent ranking of these websites would take place by looking at the similarity between the query and the relevant websites. A website mentioning the University of Amsterdam, for instance, would be considered relevant for a user entering the queries 'University of Amsterdam', 'university' or 'Amsterdam'. A website mentioning the University of Amsterdam a hundred times would be considered, by the typical early Web search engine, to be more relevant than a website only mentioning it once. Not surprisingly, this did not always produce desirable results.

Google's PageRank algorithm was one of the early inventions about the way search engines could use the Web environment as a whole to statistically predict the relative value of different websites in the index. The reputational and commercial economies of hyperlinks were already present before the development of PageRank by Google's founders, as linking between websites was establishing the navigational paths of the visitors of the Web. Google cleverly harvested the value of information that was present in the linking structure of the Web by turning these links into the building blocks of a global ranking metric, in which online popularity and reputation is taken as a relevancy measure, and in which those websites that are more relevant are considered more likely to point to other relevant websites as well.

More than a decade later, in the year 2011, Google's selection and ranking algorithms have undergone major changes. While the linking structure of the Web may still play an important role in its selection and ranking, new ideas of how to improve ranking or establish baseline relevance have been developed. For instance, the choice of users for particular websites, expressed by their clicking

---

615.   See Marres & de Vries 2002. See also Finkelstein 2008.

behavior, now plays an important role in the ranking of search results. Most importantly, the actual selection and ranking does not follow from the use of a single smart algorithm but the combination of a large variety of algorithms and algorithmic corrections, which together produce a search engine's output.

The seemingly dominant criteria for the valuation of information and ideas in commercial Web search engines, namely relevancy, popularity and marketing, can be contrasted with quality, independence and institutional legitimacy, i.e. the traditional professional standards for the ordering of knowledge, information and ideas.[616] As a consequence of their ranking and selection criteria, search engines are helping disrupt the traditional boundaries between different spheres and hierarchies of information, such as the difference between independent information about commercial products and advertising, publications by experts and non-experts, relevant facts and research, and related fantasies and pseudo-science. General purpose search engines do relatively little to discern between these categories.[617] Experts or laymen, politicians or activists, professional journalists or amateur bloggers, well-known or little-known people, companies or non-profit organizations, advertisers and independent product reviewers, all seem to enter the search index on the same footing and are allowed to acquire prominence on search engine results pages.[618]

Although the centrality of major search engines in the networked information environment might lead one to conclude that they are a new type of powerful gatekeeper, search engines hardly exert strict gatekeeping power over the accessibility of information and ideas *independently* of information providers and end-users.[619] The search engine is an interactive navigational tool, both in relation to information providers who want to reach an audience as well as in relation to its end-users who are entering and reformulating their queries. The communicative process between a search engine and an end-user is, to a large extent, shaped by the end-user's input and choices. Search engines tend to rely on end-users to decide for themselves what to search for and where to go. The statistical character of the predictions of relevance also implies that they must be characterized as the mere *suggestion* of possible relevance, not a statement that these references *are* in fact relevant to the user.

Search engines usually rely a great deal on the information providers they reference. Information providers tend to control whether they are included in the first place and can influence their ranking in major search engines in various ways and degrees. Webmasters receive specific guidelines how to optimize their rankings in Web search services. The somewhat open nature of the private governance of search engine selection and ranking decisions, and the possibility to influence

---

616. See Marres & de Vries 2002, 188.
617. See e.g. Zittrain 2008, 131. It has to be noted that the erosion of these categories is a broader societal phenomenon. On top of that, many of these categories are simply replicated in the hierarchies in search media, with or without the help of search engine providers.
618. Willingly or unwillingly.
619. See Röhle 2010.

and manipulate rankings has also given birth to a thriving industry of SEO. As a result, the accessibility of online destinations in a particular search engine is all but carved in stone and the result of a variety of interrelated streams of communications flowing in and out of the search engine's service.

In view of the complexity of selection and ranking decisions by Web search engines, it may not be a surprise that information law and policy have not yet developed a proper understanding of the legal status of these decisions, let alone their protection under the right to freedom of expression. Most of the discussion of the proper legal treatment of these decisions by search engines in view of their impact on public and private interests has taken place in academia. Yet, there are some legal cases and regulatory developments which directly implicate the protection of selection and ranking decisions under the right to freedom of expression, some of which will be discussed in the remainder of this chapter and the next chapters and which start to give an answer about the implications of the right to freedom of expression for their legal governance.

What is at stake in this discussion is the freedom of search engines to decide which selection and ranking algorithms to apply to the material in their index and their legal accountability for making specific decisions. Even if one accepts that there may not, and should not, be a legally correct way to select and rank references, it is possible that there are unethical as well as legally problematic ways of selecting and ranking search results.

There is very little case law or legal material to analyzes these questions in a European context, but it is probable that general applicable law, such as tort law, privacy law or competition law, does limit search engines in their ability to apply certain selection and ranking algorithms at will. At the same time, the status of selection and ranking decisions under the right to freedom of expression should inform the proper application of these laws. Tort law, for instance, would probably prevent search engines from deliberately ranking results in a way that damages certain parties without any proper justification, for example by not selecting or devaluating a particular e-commerce provider while treating its direct competitors quite favorably. European data privacy and anti-discrimination laws probably may restrict the deliberate selection and ranking of results on the basis of sensitive personal characteristics, such as the ethnic background of the targets of search engine queries.[620] More specifically, image search engines that would allow end-users to search for material on the basis of images of people, applying facial recognition technology, may be legally problematic in Europe.[621]

Competition law may restrict the freedom to rank and select material in an anticompetitive fashion. In particular, dominant search engines have a great impact on the underlying markets as well as the markets they operate in themselves. They could use their dominant position to harm competitors. Google, for instance, has been argued to have foreclosed competition in the market for online geographic

---

620. See Article 29 Data Protection Working Party 2008, 13. For Google's reaction, see Fleischer (Google) 2008, 3–5.
621. See van Hoboken 2008a.

services by starting to integrate its own service into its search engine (Google maps). In 2010, the European Commission has started to investigate a similar complaint relating to anticompetitive behavior with respect to other (vertical) search engines.[622] There are a variety of other ways in which Google could compete assertively in the way it ranks and selects search results. It could, for instance, promote the millions of websites in its search results which are using the AdSense service, thereby impacting the broader market for online advertising services, or prioritize YouTube in video search.

In the United States, there have been a few cases involving the application of general laws in which the defending search engine claimed, and in one of them won, wide discretion over its selection and ranking decisions on First Amendment grounds.[623] These cases, including a case about the refusal to run particular advertisements in sponsored search results,[624] sparked debate about fairness and access in the search context, issues which will be discussed in more depth in section 8.5.[625] Although it is questionable as to how much weight should be attached to these particular decisions, a discussion of them can help clarify the issues at stake.

The most famous of these decisions involved a conflict between Google and SearchKing, an online intermediary that seems to have been a relatively successful business because of a particularly good ranking in Google's search results. SearchKing was not an e-commerce provider itself, but a paid inclusion directory for local Oklahoma businesses. Sometime in 2002, SearchKing dropped in Google's results, leading to significantly decreasing revenues for its clients, and a blow to its business model. SearchKing reacted by suing Google for tortuous interference with contractual relations, seeking injunctive relief. Google defended the deliberate devaluation of SearchKing in its rankings by referring to manipulative interference and the low quality of the information offering of SearchKing and its network of websites. Google also claimed that its rankings represented protected speech under the First Amendment. The U.S. District Court for the Western of Oklahoma agreed that ranking decisions were protected under the First Amendment. It concluded, with reference to a Tenth Circuit case (*Jefferson County*[626]) as follows:

---

622. See Dakanalis & van Rooijen 2011.
623. *Search King, Inc. v. Google Tech.*, Inc., No. CIV-02-1457-M, at 6–12 (W.D. Okla. May 27, 2003). *KinderStart.com, LLC v. Google, Inc.*, No. C 06-2057 JF (RS), 2007 U.S. Dist. LEXIS 22648, at 13–15 (N.D. Cal. March 16, 2007). In *KinderStart*, the court did not have to address Google's First Amendment defense. More recently *Habush v. Cannon*, Case No, 09-CV-18149 (Wis. Cir. Ct. June 8, 2011). In *Habush* the Wisconcin court concludes that *the use of a computerized system to sequence search results is not speech*. This is based on its consideration that "the hidden process which causes the link to appear at all [. . .] is content neutral", which is unconvincing considering the way search results ranking and selection is triggered by content.
624. *Langdon v. Google*, Inc., 474 F. Supp. 2d 622, 629–30 (D. Del. 2007).
625. See Bracha & Pasquale 2008; Grimmelmann 2008; Pasquale 2008, 83–84.
626. *Jefferson County Sch. Dist. No. R-1 v. Moody's Investor's Services, Inc.*, 175 F.3d 848 (1999).

A PageRank is an opinion—an opinion of the significance of a particular web site as it corresponds to a search query. Other search engines express different opinions, as each search engine's method of determining relative significance is unique. There is no question that the opinion relates to a matter of public concern. [. . .] 150 million search queries occur every day on Google's search engine alone. [. . .] PageRanks do not contain false factual connotations. While Google's decision to intentionally deviate from its mathematical algorithm in decreasing SearchKing's PageRank may raise questions about the "truth" of the PageRank system, there is no conceivable way to prove that the relative significance assigned to a given website is false. A statement of relative significance, as represented by the PageRank is inherently subjective in nature. Accordingly, the Court concludes that Google's PageRanks are entitled to First Amendment protection.[627]

The Court subsequently concluded that the sought injunction would chill protected speech and would be adverse to the public interest. In fact, it went even further. It concluded that search engine rankings cannot give rise to a claim for tortuous interference with contractual relations because they cannot be considered wrongful, even if the speech is motivated by hatred or ill will. Hence, the central premise of the Oklahoma Court seems to be that because there is no correct way to select and rank references there can also be no legally incorrect way.[628] Hence, the decision on how to select and rank references is seen as the expression of an opinion, which is strongly protected by the First Amendment. The societal impact and possible damage should play out in the free marketplace of ideas. This reasoning is similar to that in *Tornillo*, in which the Supreme Court established the First Amendment protection of newspapers' editorial freedom. The Oklahoma Court could have added that it has yet to be demonstrated how government interference on the crucial process of selecting and ranking websites by search engines could be exercised in consistence with First Amendment guarantees.

The legal consequences of the *SearchKing* judgment's conclusion of bringing selection and ranking decisions under the scope of the First Amendment may obscure the fact that to do so may be quite reasonable. Leaving the predominantly technological and statistical nature of search engine selection and ranking decisions aside, the selection and ranking of references from the index in return to a user's query seems highly comparable to an editorial activity, in many ways comparable to the decision of newspapers regarding what to put in the paper and in which place. This may imply that these decisions should in fact be similarly protected, also in the European context under Article 10 ECHR. It is important to note that bringing these decisions under the scope of the editorial freedom of the media protected by Article 10 ECHR, would in no way have the same implications for the possibility to limit this freedom to select and rank at will in specific

---

627. *Search King, Inc. v. Google Tech., Inc.*, No. CIV-02-1457-M, at 9 (W.D. Okla. May 27, 2003).
628. *Ibid.*, at 6–12.

circumstances, for instance when a search engine provably ranks a website lower for the sole reason that it wants to harm the respective information provider.

Another interesting aspect of the *SearchKing* decision is that despite automating most of its selection and ranking decisions, Google did not to give up its right to select and rank individual sites manually and differently. More generally, the technological nature of the decisions about which selection and ranking algorithms to apply may lead some to conclude that these decisions are of a different nature than those made by humans and that this difference should impact the legal protection of these decisions under the right to freedom of expression.[629] Search engines themselves tend to contribute to the view by claiming that their search results are mechanical, neutral and objective. Newspapers may have been expected to rely on certain well-respected organizational mechanisms for editorial decision-making, in line with the ethics of journalism. However, the real criteria for the newspaper's contents often remained equally unknown. In fact, it would be considered an interference with the newspaper's editorial freedom, if the law were to mandate complete transparency in these matters. Moreover, automation in Web search engine governance is to some extent a result of the massiveness of the Web and the related massiveness of the index. It is simply humanly and economically impossible to provide human evaluations of the relevance of websites for all the queries search engines respond to. And automated decision-making about the value of information is not only economical. Digital technologies have made it possible to incorporate the daily feedback from over a billion websites in the editorial processes of a search engine. As a result, the automated nature of the selection and ranking decisions are directly related to the societal benefits of having modern accessibility technologies and services that are able to keep up with the abundance of information online.

A major problem in discussing the protection of ranking and selection decisions is that the actual ranking and selection criteria that search engines use are rather opaque and thereby impossible to evaluate specifically. As discussed in Chapters 2 and 3, search engines tend to keep details about their algorithms secret. Because of the lack of transparency in the operation of search engines, it is unclear whether the underlying principles for the governance of accessibility of particular search engines are informed by commercial, ideological or scientific principles. It can be argued that by refusing to be transparent about the underlying principles for the selection and ranking of references, search engines refuse to publicly take responsibility for the search results they offer to their users. Thus, it could be argued that search engines can hardly claim particular protection for the kind of selection and ranking decisions they make, unless they were to be more explicit about those decisions.

It can be argued that the comparison of the editorial freedom of the Web search engine to the editorial freedom of the press is problematic due to the commercial nature of search engines as well as the speech they facilitate. This leads to another

---

629. On the question about protection of software under the First Amendment more generally, see Halpern 2000.

case about the First Amendment status of selection and ranking decisions, which involved the application of a generally applicable law to the selection and ranking mechanism of *Roommates.com*, a platform and search engine for housing opportunities. The selection mechanisms were considered to be in violation of the anti-discrimination provisions of the Fair Housing Act (FHA). Roommates' interactive service was facilitating its users' individual and sometimes discriminatory sexual and racial housemate preferences by allowing them to express these preferences and subsequently matching users on the basis of these preferences. Roommates defended itself against the claimed breach of the Fair Housing Act by asserting the Communications Decency Act, section 230, and its First Amendments rights to free speech and intimate association.

The *Roommates* case is best known because of the Ninth Circuit's dismissal of Roommates' CDA 230 defense, on the basis that the service was considered a speaker itself as regards the selection technology.[630] The next line of defense, a First Amendment claim against the application of the FHA, was addressed by the U.S. District Court for the Central District of California after remand. The District Court argued as follows about the status of selection decisions of the service:

> it is far less obvious that Roommate's prompting of its users to provide personal characteristics in order to use its service, or its use of that information in its search and matching functions, is "speech" protected by the First Amendment. Instead, those functions performed by Roommate, and the questions it prompts its users to answer, could be considered mere conduct rather than either speech or a communicative act expressing a viewpoint to which the First Amendment applies. [. . .] However, even if Roommate's prompts for discriminatory information, searches, and matches could be considered speech, it would be, like Roommate's publication of its users' discriminatory preferences, speech of a commercial nature.[631]

After this conclusion, the Court proceeded by applying the test for the regulation of commercial speech,[632] which ended up in favor of the constitutionality of the application of the Fair Housing Act on the Roommates service.

It seems questionable whether the application of the standard for commercial speech is warranted on selection decisions by referencing services. Why would the commercial nature of a search engine as well as that of many of the websites in its index have to implicate its protection under the right to freedom of expression in principle? The U.S. District Court's conclusion seems at least inconsistent with the conclusion about the same questions in the context of the press. In *Sullivan*, the Court explicitly considered that the paid-for nature of the advertisement did not matter for First Amendment purposes, while pointing to the contribution of the commercial business model to the ideals underlying the right to freedom of

---

630. On CDA, Section 230, see section 6.4.4. See also section 9.3.3.
631. *Fair Housing Council v. Roommate.com*, LLC, CV 03-9386 PA (C.D. Cal. November 7, 2008).
632. See section 5.5.3.

expression.[633] Hence, the fact that Roommates provided its services for remuneration should not automatically have had implications for the protected status of its communicative actions.[634]

Both the *SearchKing* and the *Roommates* example relate to the application of generally applicable laws to selection and ranking by search engines, and the question about the implications of the right to freedom of expression in such cases. However, legislatures could—in theory—decide to establish ranking obligations, for instance to increase the relative accessibility of certain information and ideas. Broadcasting law already contains obligations with regard to the carriage and minimal representation of certain broadcasting products, such as local broadcasting or programs in the interest of specific national minorities in view of the demands of pluralism. The possible extension of these obligations to minimal rules for representation in electronic program guides for audio-visual media services would amount to sector-specific search engine regulation. Recently, a proposal for a ranking obligation was put forward in France in the context of the issue of online copyright infringement.[635] It would require search engines to promote online services indicated as constituting a legal offering of content online by a new public authority through higher rankings.

It is clear that the selection and ranking of search results by dominant search engines is of major importance in the relation between search engines and end-users on the one hand and information providers and search engines on the other hand. The function of the search medium is to help Internet end-users find valuable websites. They also help information providers reach an audience.

From the perspective of search engines as intermediaries between information providers and end-users, some have expressed concern about the unfair exclusion or unfair treatment of information providers by dominant search providers.[636] This debate has focused on the proper resolution of the conflicting interests of information providers to reach an audience without undue interference by search engines or other selection intermediaries, and the discretion of search engines to decide about the composition of their index and the ranking of results. In section 8.5, the idea of a fair ranking obligation that has been proposed will be discussed in more depth, particularly the extent to which such obligations could be based on the right to freedom of expression of information providers, as for instance in the context of common carriage obligations on Internet access providers.

Other restrictions on the freedom to select and rank at will could be informed by the interests of end-users. The selection and ranking of results is at the basis of making search engines work for end-users. They will evaluate the quality of search engines in light of the information they are presented in response to their queries.

---

633. See section 5.3.2.
634. See also Ardia 2010; Wilemon 2009.
635. See Manara 2009.
636. See e.g. Chandler 2008; Paquale & Bracha 2008; van Eijk 2006; van Couvering 2009; Introna & Nissenbaum 2000. See also Grimmelmann 2007; Goldman 2006. For a discussion of a documented incident of the manipulation of specific rankings, see Rogers 2009a.

Any ranking obligation therefore, if not specifically informed by and enhancing the rights and interests of end-users, runs the risk of harming them in their interest to freely inform themselves. It is possible to imagine several types of obligations with regard to ranking and selection that would be informed by the interests of end-users. Some have argued, with reference to democratic theory, that search engines should become more open and allow end-users to control the ranking of search results.[637] Not the search engine, but the end-user would become the true editor of search results.

End-users do have an indirect impact on the ranking of results. Increasingly, selection intermediaries personalize their offering on the basis of the end-user's location and behavior. They build profiles of their users to facilitate further personalization and better targeting of the advertisements that are sold. In other words, search engines have started to discriminate between end-users. If such discrimination would start to harm certain groups of end-users, this could be another reason for governments to intervene. One of the ways the law could possibly intervene is by granting end-users more control over the personalization of information services and, for instance, offering the opportunity to opt out of profiling or to edit and share their profiles. At the same time, governments can try to use, and courts can take account of, existing personalization based on location to establish jurisdiction over search engines, perhaps even mandating such personalization, thereby limiting end-users' ability to switch between different localized versions of search.[638]

There is already one legal obligation with regard to the ranking and presentation of search results which is widely accepted, namely the obligation to delineate sponsored results from organic search results. The typical search results page contains two types of references: on the one hand, references to information providers that are shown without financial reward, and references that are shown for payment, on the other hand. Both in Europe and the United States, it is considered a legal obligation that search engines be transparent about this difference. These and other possible obligations on search engines in view of the communicative freedom of end-users will be discussed in section 8.6 and in more depth in Chapter 10.

8.4.4.   SEARCH ENGINES: EDITORIAL CONTROL, FREEDOM, DUTIES AND RESPONSIBILITIES

The ECtHR's arguments in *Open Door* discussed in section 8.4.2 imply that the reliability of referencing information and the professional context in which information is communicated strengthens the protection a communicator receives under Article 10 ECHR. This is in line with the Court's case law on the duties and

---

637. See Rieder 2009.
638. Several European countries have established specific requirements for country-specific search services but neither of them requires them to block access to other country-specific sites entirely. In China, Google's non-China-specific version was regularly blocked. See also section 9.2.

responsibilities that are tied to the exercise of the right to freedom of expression in Article 10 ECHR and which will be discussed in more detail below. Before asking about the proper duties and responsibilities of search engines when selecting, ranking and publishing references, the question should be addressed as to how much responsibility search engines actually take in the context of the governance of the composition of their index and the selection and ranking of search results. This question can help further qualify the way the selection and ranking decisions of the search engine should be seen as editorial ones.

In the context of the press, the newspaper's decision to include or exclude is conceptualized as editorial and protected by the right to freedom of expression. Editorial freedom is one side of the coin, editorial responsibility the other. By publishing a story, the newspaper not only exercises its control over the contents of its medium, but also takes responsibility for the decision that the story is worth being printed. This kind of responsibility is typically absent in the case of a search engine's inclusion of references. Due to the navigational function of search engines for the Web, the fact that information is available online is itself a reason to include it in the index. Moreover, not only do general purpose search engines not try to control everything that goes into their index, but also do not tend to know or try to monitor everything that can be found with the use of their services.

It is important to note that editorial control by search engines over the contents and optimization practices of the websites they reference is not necessarily absent either. Search engines can easily exert control over inclusion and exclusion of references and actually do so in a number of instances. Search engines have to guard the quality of search results against so-called spam, meaning websites which unduly interfere with the automated processes of indexing and ranking. Spam protection is typically based on the enforcement of webmaster guidelines and minimal standard of relevance. It does have some parallels with the filtering of unsolicited email by Internet access providers. Spam protection in the context of search engines is necessary precisely because of a lack of editorial control by search engines with regard to the inclusion and ranking of websites. If a public library would allow the public to place books on the library shelves and insert references into the library catalogue, it would probably have to assert a similar type of oversight to delete references and manipulation of the system.

Of course, search engines also evaluate the quality of their search results more generally and change their algorithms and search engine rankings accordingly. General purpose search engines systematically analyze the behavior of their users by looking at massive amounts of user data. They also let human evaluation teams look at the quality of search results.[639] Sometimes, the evaluation may lead to direct manual changes to search results, for instance in specific cases of search engine manipulation by content providers. Sometimes, the solution to what is considered a problem of search quality is solved by introducing new algorithms. Reported examples include the degrading of the rank of directories with paid-for references in view of the lack of original content, such as *SearchKing* discussed

---

639. See Google 2007b; Sullivan 2010a. See also section 3.3.1.

above, as well as the defusing of the so-called Google Bomb, where Google used to return the website of the President of the United States, George W. Bush in return to the query 'miserable failure'.[640]

Looking at dominant general search engine practices, they seem to aim for comprehensiveness of their index on the one hand, while on the other hand dealing with matters of information quality through their selection and ranking algorithms, which reflects the observation of Marres and De Vries discussed earlier in this chapter. This does imply that they cannot defend the availability of the references in their index with the argument that they are all carefully selected. Yet, the decision of search engines to include websites in the index should probably be considered an editorial decision as much as specific decisions to change the selection and ranking algorithms. The question about the editorial nature of the decision to include or exclude is not only relevant when assessing the protection against restrictions on the communication of references. It is at least as relevant when addressing the possible conflicts of interest between information providers and search engine providers about access. In the context of Internet access providers this issue was addressed in detail, in particular the question of the extent to which an access provider would be able to claim a right to freedom of expression not to provide access, as is the case with the press. This led to a similar discussion whether the decision of an access provider to block communications between information and end-users could be considered editorial.[641]

Unlike in the case of Internet access providers, the relation between information providers and search engines, while also considering the interests of end-users, arguably entails a genuine conflict of protected interests under the right to freedom of expression. The reason is that there is a variety of reasons to exclude or disregard particular sources of information, based on the role of search engines in the networked information environment. This role does include consideration of the quality and relevance of information.

An example may help illustrate the fact that there may not be a single right way to make these choices. Consider the relatively simple query for 'travel insurance'. There is a variety of actors and types of information that could be argued to deserve representation in the set of results the end-user receives. Of course, travel insurers would like to be found. And if many end-users are using the search engine service, insurers would probably be interested in paying for additional representation in the form of advertising. There are many other sources of information that could be included in search results, such as independent consumer organizations which offer advice about the quality of travel insurance, and independent bloggers and customers who have written something about the current market's offering. Some may argue that the second type of information should be considered more valuable for end-users. Others may respond to that prioritization with the complaint that this would be unfair to the first category, while it would also force insurers to buy advertising to reach end-users at all. And these types of information providers are

---

640. See Lettice 2009. See also Sullivan 2007.
641. On the question of 'editorial freedom' of Internet access providers, see sections 6.3.2 and 6.4.4.

only the beginning of a list of conceivably relevant sources of information that could be selected by a search engine. All sorts of other information related to travel insurance, and insurance more generally, could be included. Notably, some of these information providers can be expected to actively compete for user attention in search engines, whereas other information providers would remain passive.

To be able to make these choices at the scale at which general purpose search engines operate, search engines rely on automated decisions and machine learning involving a variety of statistical predictions about the meaning and value of the queries and the information in the index. This may sometimes produce results that would not have been selected by a human editor and could dissatisfy specific information providers or parts of the general public.[642] However, since the amount and variety of queries can simply not be handled by humans and the Web is constantly changing, Web search engines cannot be expected to make a careful *ex ante* and fair evaluation of the set and ranking of references for each single query, such as the query mentioned above.[643]

To a large extent, the legal debate about the possible obligations of search engines relating to the composition of their index has focused on obligations to remove references to unlawful or harmful material. Some commentators, however, have argued that dominant search engines should be restricted in their freedom to exclude material from their index and should act as common carriers. This issue will be discussed in more depth in the next section.

Like any other entity that would assert protection under Article 10 ECHR, a search engine will carry duties and responsibilities that are tied to the exercise of its rights. The question is what these duties and responsibilities could be argued to entail in the search engine context. As was shown in Chapter 5, according to the ECtHR the duties and responsibilitieson the basis of Article 10 ECHR, depend on the technical means used for expression and dissemination. The Court has stated the following:

> [. . .] whoever exercises his freedom of expression undertakes "duties and responsibilities" the scope of which depends on his situation and the technical means he uses. The potential impact of those means must be taken into account when considering the proportionality of the interference.[644]

To which the Court added the following in its more recent judgment in *Stoll*:

> These considerations play a particularly important role nowadays, given the influence wielded by the media in contemporary society: not only do they inform, they can also suggest by the way in which they present the information how it is to be assessed. In a world in which the individual is confronted with vast quantities of information circulated via traditional and electronic media

---

642. See also section 10.2.2.
643. As mentioned above, major search engines do tend—and acknowledge—to have quality control by human evaluators. See Google 2007b; Sullivan 2010a.
644. ECtHR June 14, 2007, *Hachette Filipacchi Associes v. France*, § 42.

and involving an ever-growing number of players, monitoring compliance with journalistic ethics takes on added importance.[645]

These last considerations do seem to resonate in the context of search engines. In line with the Court's reasoning in *Open Door*, it seems to imply that the more a communicator does to enhance the quality of information, the more it can claim protection. In particular, professional standards with regard to such quality and the mode of communicating serve as an extra line of defense against interferences. Most search engines, as noted above, do fairly little to guarantee a threshold of minimum quality of the information to which they provide references. In general, the lack of editorial control and oversight over the inclusion of references could weaken a search engine's protection against interferences under Article 10 ECHR. And if the average quality of search engine references were to be deemed very low, they could hardly claim any protection against interferences with their right to freedom of expression under Article 10.

But there are good arguments in favor of less stringent duties and responsibilities as regards the quality of references. It is important to note here that the duties and responsibilities can cut both ways. On the one hand, they can be argued to imply responsibility on Web search providers to guarantee the quality of references. On the other hand, they could be argued to entail a duty on search engine providers to be comprehensive and not to exclude references lightly. From the perspective of quality, it can be argued that entities which govern the accessibility of information will have to be the ones to sift the wheat from the chaff through filtering, the exclusion of references and the imposition of hierarchies informed by conceptions about information quality. But from the perspective of access, the entities that govern accessibility should be inclusive instead of restrictive.

In reality, the choices of search engines with regard to the inclusion of references fall somewhere in between the two polarities. Although Web search engines tend towards comprehensiveness, a truly inclusive search engine simply does not exist. Large parts of the Web remain excluded from search engines, because of technical reasons such as file formats, crawling speed, the size of the Web, compliance with webmaster instructions not to crawl their content,[646] the exclusion of manipulative results, various legal reasons and self-regulation with regard to illegal and harmful content. At the same time, none of the major search engines exercise the kind of editorial oversight with regard to the quality of specific references as discussed in the example of the query 'travel insurance' above.

And of course, the important question from a legal perspective is not whether, and in which ways, search engines could start to guarantee the quality of their references but whether they ought to do so. By exercising stronger editorial control over the composition of their indices, search engines would end up being much more restrictive and it would be likely that much of the Web would become harder

---

645. ECtHR December 10, 2007, *Stoll v. Switzerland*, § 104.
646. It is notable that compliance with robots exclusion protocols is sometimes argued to be mandatory. See also section 10.2.3.

to find for end-users. In *Open Door*, the ECtHR referred to the normative principle that a communicator that leaves the decision to act upon its communication to the receiver cannot—in principle—be blamed for those decisions. The more passive— or perhaps it is better to say facilitative—the communicator is with regard to the decisional autonomy of its audience, the more protection it receives against inter- ferences that seek to prevent a certain reaction by the audience. The protection search engines would receive would therefore be enhanced by their facilitative role as regards the interests of end-users.

These two perspectives lead back to the paradox of access and quality. From the perspective of access, search engines should help end-users navigate the entire Web. Any exclusion of references from the index would interfere with this primary function. The ECtHR's case law suggests that search engines can defend a choice for inclusiveness with the argument that it is precisely their societal role, in the interest of facilitating accessibility, to provide references to all the sources of information on the Web. The scale at which general purpose search engines operate implies that they cannot check the lawfulness and quality of all the information they refer their users to. This may, in particular, be the case for the non-dominant search engine providers which most likely have fewer resources to proactively deal with issues of quality in their indices. They could do so by prioritizing websites they consider to be of high quality, while still aiming for comprehensiveness of their indices. That being said, a search engine that put more energy into reviewing websites and limited its index to references of established quality and relevance could arguably claim protection under the right to freedom to expression to defend its choice to exert editorial control over its index.

It is striking that while claiming their freedom of expression right to rank information providers freely, search engines do not readily take responsibility for the subjective nature of some of the decisions they make in the process of determining winners and losers in the networked information environment. For instance, in response to a favorable ranking of the anti-Semitic site *Jewwatch. com* in return to the query 'Jew', Google responded that its:

> search results are generated completely objectively and are independent of the beliefs and preferences of those who work at Google.[647]

Since 2007, the words *completely objectively* in this explanation about Google search results have been omitted. To be fair, in both statements Google does take some responsibility for its choice not to manually interfere with the favorable ranking of *Jewwatch.com*. However, it is striking that the statement now contains an even more sweeping statement of disinterest in the quality of its results:

> The beliefs and preferences of those who work at Google, as well as the opinions of the general public, do not determine or impact our search results.[648]

---

647. See Google 2007c.
648. See Google 2007d.

Considering the dominant position of Google in the search engine market, there may be some room for improvement here. In fact, the potential impact of the medium and the nature of the content that can be found through a search engine are considered relevant for its possible duties and responsibilities which exist in the European context. On several occasions, the ECtHR has clarified that the particular impact of media has to be taken into account when considering the permissibility of interferences by public authorities. For instance, in its *Jersild* judgment, the Court concluded as follows with regard to the nature of audio-visual content:

> In considering the "duties and responsibilities" of a journalist, the potential impact of the medium concerned is an important factor and it is commonly acknowledged that the audiovisual media have often a much more immediate and powerful effect than the print media [...]. The audiovisual media have means of conveying through images meanings which the print media are not able to impart.[649]

While the Court seems to refer to the impact of a certain medium, such as audio-visual media in this case, the question could be asked whether the same logic could be applied to the context of search media, dominant providers such as Google in particular. Looking at Web search media, it could be argued that major general purpose search engines with a particularly strong societal impact, would have enhanced duties and responsibilities based on their widespread use and their impact on the different value chains in which they operate. As a result of particular selection and ranking decisions, dominant search providers such as Google may have a disproportional impact on the governance of accessibility. The need for particular legal restrictions on their freedom to make access, selection and ranking decisions which would harm the legally protected interests of others, including the communicative liberties of information providers and end-users, may be more easily established. Such restrictions could be argued to reflect enhanced duties and responsibilities based on their dominant position. However, the need to respect the freedom of search engine providers to make their mediating choices freely would remain and interferences with their protected freedom would need to be both effective and proportional.

8.5. SEARCH ENGINE FREEDOM AND THE INTERESTS OF INFORMATION PROVIDERS

8.5.1. INTRODUCTION

The interest of information providers in the governance of Web search engines is to be present on the search engine's platform and to find their way to an audience. What is at stake for information providers can also be formulated in terms of representation. If no search engine includes a particular source of information,

---

649. ECtHR September 23, 1994, *Jersild v. Denmark*, § 31.

this would deprive it from an important means to acquire attention and legitimacy. Search engines, dominant ones in particular, help establish the winners and losers in the competition for end-user attention.

The impact of dominant search engine selection and ranking decisions goes beyond the mere accessibility of information and ideas. The impact of Google's search platform means that representation in Google is directly related to the degree of success or failure of many online activities, whether they are economic or political.[650] Moreover, several studies show that end-users consider a high ranking in a popular search engine as an independent sign of information quality.[651] For many, inclusion in Google's results alone has become an important point of reference with regard to the mere 'existence' of online information. This leads to the belief that all that is excluded from Google and other general purpose search engines can be legitimately excluded or disregarded elsewhere. In fact, Google's ultimate goal, according to one if its founders, is to make itself indispensable for anyone interested in anything.[652] The search engine index is marketed to its users as a reliable copy of reality itself.

8.5.2.   Search Engine Freedom and the Ideal of
          Unmediated Mediation

In the previous section, it was argued that the right to freedom of expression may actually protect the search engine operator's right to make selection and ranking decisions freely, thanks to the editorial character of its mediation between information providers and end-users. It was also shown that search engines do not readily take responsibility for the way they make those choices. When justifying those decisions to rank some information providers worse than others, search engines often refer to their role in relation to end-users. This reference to the interests of end-users can also be found in Jennifer Chandler's characterization of the speaker's interest in their relation to search engines and selection intermediaries more generally. Drawing on the ideal of an unmediated public sphere, Chandler emphasizes the following:

> the right to reach an audience free from the influence of extraneous criteria of discrimination imposed by selection intermediaries. If selection intermediaries block or discriminate against a speaker on grounds that listeners would not have selected, that speaker's ability to speak freely has been undermined.[653]

The freedom of information providers to reach an audience thereby becomes based on the freedom to select of (specific) end-users. This principle, as formulated by Chandler, comes closest to the ideal of universal access: if discrimination or

---

650. See the discussion of *SearchKing* in section 8.4.3.
651. See Hargittai 2007b.
652. See Levy 2011, 66–67.
653. See Chandler 2008.

blocking of sources takes place, it should be transparent and end-users should be able to control it. The filters for adult content that are typically installed on major search services are an example of the adherence to this principle as formulated by Chandler.

But a number of objections can be raised against the application of this principle to the governance of search engines more generally. First, the role of search engines is to help users find valuable information and ideas. To be able to offer their service, they have to make some choices about the relative value of information and ideas for end-users. Second, it is debatable whether selection intermediaries should not be allowed to prioritize information and ideas in a way that does not directly reflect end-user preferences. Why would it be wrong for selection intermediaries to try to represent a variety of different speakers and sources of information in their search results and *not allow* end-users to block or discriminate between results? In other words, it is possible for selection intermediaries to add value by making a determination independent of end-user preferences. The ideal that the public library adds value by confronting its patrons with its entire collection and presents its patrons with a carefully selected corpus of knowledge and cultural heritage which may not always reflect their preferences are examples of this.

Overall, search engines may be in a better position to decide which information is useful, relevant or valuable than end-users themselves, not excluding the end-users' possibility to critically evaluate these decision afterwards. In fact, this is what search engines are doing all the time. If research on information searching behavior is to be taken seriously, end-users are looking for relatively easy answers, not an incredible range of choices of high quality for every specific search.[654] In general, it seems fair to assume that end-users are relying on search engines to make intelligent selection and ranking decisions for them, instead of having to make all those decisions themselves. From the perspective of the public interests in the opening up of the Web, understood as the process of connecting information and ideas online to their societal use, it may be better to focus on the quality of the decisions Web search engines end up making, than to deny them the freedom to make these choices in the first place.

8.5.3.   INFORMATION PROVIDERS' CONTROL OVER SEARCH
ENGINE GOVERNANCE

With regard to the interests of information providers to reach an audience through search engines, it is important to acknowledge the amount of control they have over search engine governance in practice. Dominant search engines have given information providers a lot of control over their indexing, ranking and the content of references. Information providers can typically control whether they are indexed in

---

654. Research on information-seeking behavior shows that most users stop searching when they find a satisfactory answer, not the best answer. See section 3.3.1.

the first place by using instructions such as robots.txt. They can influence how they and others are ranked by following 'white hat' SEO guidelines, for instance by integrating their information offering through the establishment of links with the rest of the Web. They can control how they are presented when they are included by stipulating a title of their page or offering a so-called site map.

In fact, search engine governance currently entails a degree of control for information providers over the governance of accessibility by Web search engines which may be antithetical to the interests of end-users.[655] As mentioned above, webmasters de facto have complete control over inclusion of information in search results. Even a popular publicly accessible website can exclude itself from all major search engines with the simple placement of an instruction to search engines on its website. And the SEO industry, which is a direct result of the reliance of search engine rankings on third-party signals, is paid by information providers to reach end-users, not to enhance the fair representation of sources of information and ideas in search results.

This begs the question of possible legal restrictions on information providers to compete unfairly—for attention—through Web search engines. At present, the formulation and enforcement of SEO guidelines is left to search engine providers. The public interest in search engine quality may warrant regulation of so-called Web spam, i.e. websites exerting undue influence on search results through their deceptive publications. Web spam is perhaps not as visible as email spam but it is a major problem.[656] The possibility to influence search engine results and rankings is the main driver of the SEO industry.[657] The problem is that unlike in the case of email, the distinction between Web spam and legitimate publications is hard to make without restricting the right to freely publish on the Web. In general, there is no such thing as an unsolicited online publication. Of course, there are a range of legal restrictions on the lawfulness of online publications, but these are not directly related to the context of search engines. Defamation law, trademark law and a range of other laws restrict the freedom of information providers to impart information and ideas online, and they similarly restrict the freedom of information providers to reach an audience through search engines. It may be hard to formulate effective and legitimate additional legal restrictions on publications because of their negative impact in search engines,that do not unduely restrict the publication of lawful material online.[658]

---

655. See e.g. Segal 2010. See also Singhal (Google) 2010.
656. See section 3.3.2. See also sections 10.2.3 and 10.3.1.
657. See e.g. Websense Security Labs 2009.
658. The *Zwartepoorte* case in the Netherlands is a good example of this. A webmaster was ordered to change the legal content of its website because of the resulting suggestive effect of the content in the snippets of Google. Gerechtshof [Court of Appeals] Amsterdam, July 26, 2011 (*Zwartepoorte*).

8.5.4.   RESTRICTING LAWFUL INFORMATION FROM ENTERING THE SEARCH
              ENGINE INDEX

Increasingly, the effectiveness of search engines in opening up information and
ideas online leads to legal and regulatory pressure on the responsibility of the
actual publishers. In general, the global nature of the Internet produces this effect.
If national States would all be allowed to claim jurisdiction over all online publications, we could end up with a global lowest common denominator of legally
permissible online speech.[659] In the context of search engines, a similar tendency
would be observed to have information providers not only carry responsibility for
the decision to publish certain information and ideas, but also for the subsequent
further dissemination of the publication by search engines. The result could be that
in certain cases, it would end up being illegal to publish online what could have
been legally published offline.

From the perspective of the right to freedom of expression, legal restrictions—
on information providers—to allow for the further dissemination of *lawful* publications through search engines are problematic. Nonetheless, there seem to be
some legal proposals and developments in this direction, in Europe in particular.
An example is the restriction on the further dissemination of certain publications
through search engines by the use of robot exclusion protocols. More specifically,
the law would mandate that information providers cannot let certain publications
be indexed, because they are considered unsuitable to be opened up through a
search engine. European data protection authorities have started to interpret data
protection law as posing some limits on the freedom of information providers to
make publications involving personal data crawlable.[660] Under certain circumstances, web publishers are expected to use protocols such as robots.txt to ensure
that certain personal data—a legal category in EU law which includes all information relating to identifiable natural persons—cannot be found in search engines,
except when visiting the actual site on which they are published.[661] The mandatory
standard use of exclusion protocols by social networking sites which guarantee that
the users of such sites cannot be found in search engines is an example of adherence
to this practice. Others have proposed that the safe harbor for third-party material
on websites, such as comment sections on blogs, should be made conditional on the
use of robots exclusion protocols for these parts of the website.[662] It is important to
note that these proposals all rely on the assumption that it would be illegal for
search engines to disobey robot exclusion protocols. Although it is widely accepted
that it is good practice to obey these instructions, it would make a difference if such
good practice is turned into a legal obligation.

The idea that certain sensitive, controversial or possibly illegal information
can be published online but should be excluded from search engines may be

---

659. See Mueller 2010, 186.
660. See Dutch Data Protection Authority 2007. See also van Hoboken 2008a.
661. Dutch Data Protection Authority 2007.
662. Kerr 2007.

understandable from the perspective of the concerns relating to the wide publicity of personal and reputational information. Search engines greatly diminish the practical obscurity of the information they index and can facilitate the accessibility of information and ideas of questionable quality. Information that is traditionally made public mandatorily, such as public records containing personal information, is now more easily accessible. Information which was not traditionally published at all, such as conversations and debate between readers in reaction to news and current affairs, has found permanence on blogs, message boards and comment sections.

The low quality and sometimes illegal nature of such end-user conversations might also warrant leaving these end-user driven conversations, which do not necessarily abide by the standards of responsible journalism, in the obscurity of the unindexed Web. However, a legal regime which would mandate such exclusions would be problematic from the perspective of the right to freedom of expression. To state it mildly, the idea that public authorities have a role in obscuring lawfully published information is difficult to defend.[663]

It is possible that further self-regulatory practices will emerge with regard to the exclusion of information from search engines. Some argue that the press should exclude older material from their Internet archives which could negatively impact the reputation of persons.[664] The line of reasoning could be that through the doctrine of duties and responsibilities undertaken by publishers of information exercising their freedom of expression under Article 10 ECHR, the absence of a robot exclusion instruction could impact the determination of the lawfulness of a restriction on an online publication. There are two related objections to such self-regulatory practices, both grounded in the ideal underlying the right to freedom of expression that the societal circulation of information and ideas be "uninhibited, robust and wide-open."[665] First, it is questionable whether it is good practice for search engines to obey exclusion instructions if information providers use it to try to obscure legal and publicly accessible information which end-users would be interested in reading. Perhaps it is ethical for search engines to do exactly the opposite. Second, there is a lot of pressure on search engines to limit the findability of information in their services, precisely because it is one of the primary effective means to find information and ideas.[666] Information that is excluded is still 'public' in theory, but in many ways it simply ceases to exist. The pressure on search engines to prevent any perceived harm resulting from the opening up of the World Wide Web can easily result in the 'self-censorship' of perfectly valid online sources.[667] To limit risk, information providers would simply exclude controversial information on their site from search engines, and the latter would obey these

---

663. Notably, an exception is the protection of minors against content that is considered harmful. See also section 9.2.
664. See e.g. Hins 2008.
665. *New York Times v. Sullivan*, 376 U.S. 254, 271 (1964).
666. See Van Hoboken 2009b.
667. See Gerhart 2004.

instructions to maintain good relations with the sites they need to crawl and thus escape possible litigation. The results would be a bias towards uncontroversial information and ideas in search engines.

8.6.   SEARCH ENGINES AND THE FREEDOM OF END-USERS

8.6.1.   INTRODUCTION

The freedom of expression interest of the end-user of any kind of information service or medium is typically characterized as the freedom to inform oneself freely. The use of search engines has become a daily activity for end-users. End-users rely on search engines to find information about news, products, services, diseases, travel destinations, political candidates and more. Knowledge workers such as journalists and academic researchers rely on general purpose search engines for their daily activities.[668] Ultimately, it is the fundamental interest of Web search engine users to become informed citizens and consumers that is at stake. It may come as no surprise that there is disagreement about what is needed to facilitate this process.

8.6.2.   SEARCH ENGINES AND THE END-USER'S INTERESTS: ACCESS AND
                QUALITY AS CONFLICTING PERSPECTIVES

The disagreement in the legal and regulatory debate about end-users' interests in the context of search engine governance maps fairly well to the conflicting ideals of universal access and quality discussed earlier in this chapter. The ideals of universal access on the one hand and information quality on the other hand correspond with the following conflicting perspectives on the needs of search engine end-users.

On the one hand, end-users are portrayed as perfectly capable of navigating information and ideas on the Web, precisely because of effective information location tools, which, if possible, should be improved upon to increase the transparency of the corpus of online information for end-users even more. This side would hold that end-users have been liberated from traditional gatekeeping institutions and institutionalized paternalism. They can and should be allowed to decide for themselves what is useful, relevant, harmful, informative or entertaining. More particularly, they should not be hindered by restrictive indexing policies of search engines, possibly as a result of applicable laws and policies, in their freedom to find information online. In line with this perspective, proponents of end-user control have argued that end-users could and should have even more control over their search process, for instance by being able to choose between or completely control the different ranking algorithms and the possible personalization of search results.

---

668.   See Machill & Beiler 2007, 143–242.

On the other hand, end-users are often portrayed as lost, mislead, confused, injured and otherwise negatively affected by the current state of affairs regarding accessibility of information through search engines.[669] This state of affairs is typically portrayed as giving those end-users who want to cause harm or commit crimes the tools to do so. For example, there have been a number of proposals and legal measures to limit the ability of end-users to use certain words and signs as queries. In 2007, European Commissioner for Justice and Home Affairs Frattini sought industry cooperation "to prevent people from using or searching dangerous words like bomb, kill, genocide or terrorism."[670] This particular call for self-regulation was not taken seriously. It is actually hard to imagine how a search for 'genocide' could be considered harmful or dangerous.

It is clear that both characterizations of end-users—one focusing on empowerment and access, the other on quality and harm—are simplistic projections of particular viewpoints. Yet, this might fit the role of listeners, viewers or end-users in media law and regulation more generally, which often remains what Helberger calls *a spiritual one*.[671] The perceived interests of end-users were and remain decisive in regulatory debates about media freedom, but rarely does media law or policy involve them directly.

From a European regulatory perspective, the notion of the 'media-literate viewer', and 'media literacy' more generally, has become the point of reference in the regulatory debate about the interests of end-users of various media, including search engines. The concept of the media-literate end-user incorporates a variety of perspectives on media use, including the citizen and consumer perspective in the relation between end-users and the media.[672] Media literacy is generally defined as "the ability to access the media, to understand and to critically evaluate different aspects of the media and media contents and to create communications in a variety of contexts."[673] While media literacy is being promoted in media law and policy, the rise of the regulatory notion of the media-literate end-user is also a signal of a diminishing role of government in media regulation. Regulators no longer need to decide what is in the interest of the public, but can rely on more active end-users instead. It is notable that the European notion of media literacy is rather ambitious, even with regard to search engines. In the European Commission's view, the said concept specifically includes *feeling comfortable with all existing media, being able to assess information, dealing with advertising on various media, using search engines intelligently* and *understanding the economy of media and the difference between pluralism and media ownership*. Besides placing a focus on end-user choice, the notion thereby also signals a high level of government interest in the end-users' actual use of new media.

---

669. See e.g. Herring 2007.
670. See also section 9.2.3.
671. Helberger 2008, 136.
672. See Helberger 2008. See also Scammel 2000.
673. See European Commission 2007c.

Search engines are used by a wide variety of end-users with different degrees of skills and knowledge. Many professionals use the same search services for their research as laymen do. Journalists have become mass users of Web search services.[674] The Internet, in combination with effective search tools, is a tremendous tool for self-education. It is also a tremendous source of confusion, annoyance and controversy. It is clear that there are groups of end-users who simply lack the education or the necessary skills to turn the abundance of information online into an advantage.[675] What is important to recognize is that many of the problems that the least skilled may experience will not be easily resolved by placing obligations or restrictions on search engine providers. Many of the problems of Internet end-users simply exist at the more fundamental level of education and general knowledge skills[676] or are a direct result of the uncontrolled nature of Web publishing.

And, it must be admitted that almost everyone uses search engines without having a very good idea about their actual functioning. The complexity of Web search technology makes it impossible, even for the best-informed users, to know what is really going on if they type in their search queries in different search services.[677] And most will recognize that when receiving a ranked set of search results, it is quite difficult to judge the relative quality of different search results without considerable background knowledge about the possible sources of information and ideas that the search engine could have referred to. It is easier to find information online than to assess its quality.[678] What remains is a set of functioning hyperlinks, which can be used or discarded. Simply put: every search of the Web in a search engine such as Google is a new experiment.[679] While this may be said from the perspective of end-users, it is similarly true from the perspective of search engines themselves. At Google, "[e]ssentially all queries are involved in some test."[680]

8.6.3.   The End-User: Consumer or Citizen?

The freedom of expression interests of end-users in the context of the governance of search engines involves both consumer as well as citizen aspects. It includes the typical civic engagement with media, particularly with an eye on forming an

---

674. See e.g. Machill & Beiler 2007; Machill & Beiler 2008.
675. See e.g. Kodagoda & Wong 2008.
676. Of particular interest in this regard is the work of Eszter Hargittai. See Hargittai 2004; Hargittai & Hinnant 2005; Hargittai 2007a; Hargittai 2007b.
677. On the way people see and understand Web search engines, see e.g. Hendry & Efthimiadis 2008.
678. Bowker and Leigh Star 2000, 7.
679. I owe this characterization to a talk by David Gugerli at the 2009 Society of the Query conference in Amsterdam. Gugerli has explored the way search engines turn our world into a database. See Gugerli 2009. On the need for critical engagement with Google's offering, see Lovink 2008.
680. See Levy 2011, 61.

opinion about matters of public concern. The heavy use of search engines during political campaigns may serve as an example from this context.[681] But it also includes the freedom to become an informed consumer. In free-market based societies, consumer freedom has become a fundamental aspect of informational autonomy. It is clear that the consumer and citizen aspects of media users do not always align. In the context of mass media, it is generally accepted that commercial motivations can create biases with regard to the editorial content.[682] To prevent commercial motivations from dominating editorial decisions, newspapers tend to have a formalized separation between editorial and commercial governance of the organization. European audio-visual media regulation still contains a number of restrictions on advertising, sponsoring and product placement, such as the legal constraint that news broadcasts cannot be sponsored.

The tension between editorial and commercial motivations and the parallel citizen and consumer aspects of end-users is quite present in the context of Web search services and possibly unresolved. It may simply be hard for search engines to balance the competition for consumers in their services with their role in facilitating culture and knowledge. The advertisement-based business model of major search engine providers may lead to additional tension between these two different value chains, since it will incentivize search engines to focus on the consumer needs of their user.

Most early search services, and search engine portals in particular, used to place quite some emphasis on commercial interests. The user-friendly search engine that Google started offering in 1998, with its improved ranking algorithms, could be seen as placing emphasis again on the interests of end-users to find online information. In their well-known academic research paper about the PageRank algorithm, Larry Page and Segey Brin, at that point still working at Stanford University, wrote a special appendix about the tension between end-user interests and commercial incentives, which was in their view inherent in an advertisement-based business model:

> [W]e expect that advertising funded search engines will be inherently biased towards the advertisers and away from the needs of the consumers.
>
> Since it is very difficult even for experts to evaluate search engines, search engine bias is particularly insidious. [. . .] [L]ess blatant bias [is] likely to be tolerated by the market. For example, a search engine could add a small factor to search results from "friendly" companies, and subtract a factor from results from competitors. [. . .] Furthermore, advertising income often provides an incentive to provide poor quality search results. [. . .] In general, it could be argued from the consumer point of view that the better the search engine is, the fewer advertisements will be needed for the consumer to find what they want. This of course erodes the advertising supported business model of the existing search engines. However, there will always be money

---

681. See Oldham & Leach (Google) 2008. See also Zeller 2006.
682. For an overview, see Baker 2002.

from advertisers who want a customer to switch products, or have something that is genuinely new. But we believe the issue of advertising causes enough mixed incentives that it is crucial to have a competitive search engine that is transparent and in the academic realm.[683]

According to some sources, Google's founders remained reluctant to introduce advertising on their service. Reportedly, they were in general quite negative about the value of marketing and considered industry practices around the year 2000 unethical and contrary to the interests of the end-user.[684] When they did introduce targeted advertising and perfected it into the 'AdWords' program, it turned Google into a revolutionary business success.[685]

It is fair to state that it is more commercially compelling for search providers to satisfy end-users with advertisements than with results that are not paid for. Google's advertisement space has been expanded and advertisement prominence has been improved ever since. Moreover, Google seems to aim for the perfect advertisement: one that actually satisfies the end-user better than any other search result. In a similar vein, when Microsoft stopped the development of search products for academic materials in 2008, it pointed out that it would focus on search with high consumer intent.[686] The debate about search engine quality and advertising will be discussed in more detail in Chapter 10.

8.6.4.   END-USER PRIVACY

The ambiguity of commercial search providers towards the end-user's interest in accessing information freely may be most striking when it comes to end-user privacy. All major Web search engines are offered for free, but they make their users 'pay' with unprecedented amounts of personal data.[687] Search engine providers, like most other Web based services for end-users to be fair, tend to log every single detail about the use of their services. The educated end-user who has an idea of what is going on in terms of user data processing is still presented with a give-or-take with regard to their user data when it comes to searching the Web. If a person chooses to use any of the major search services without taking precautions to limit the possibility to track themselves, they have no access to or control over the data that is being collected, nor are they able to limit its subsequent use in significant ways. This data is usually stored in various unidentified locations, accessible to national security agencies, law enforcement agencies, and third parties in accordance with a variety of local laws. Google's Chief Executive Officer (CEO) at

---

683. Brin & Page, 1998.
684. For a discussion, see Edwards 2011, 68, 307–308. See also Levy 2011, 89, 145.
685. See sections 2.2.2 and 2.2.3.
686. See Microsoft 2008.
687. See e.g. Zimmer 2008.

some point even defended the extensive collection of user data with the argument that it can help government agencies combat crime and terrorism.[688]

The unparalleled amounts of data that are being recorded by a handful of search companies and the special role of search engines as the first points to access information online, led privacy regulators across the world to express concerns about the data collection and processing practices of major search engines. In 2006, two international policy documents on privacy and search engines were adopted, containing statements and recommendations on end-user privacy.[689] In 2008, the Article 29 Working Party issued an official opinion as to the application of European data protection law to the context of search engines. Data retention periods for individual search log data were of particular concern. The Article 29 Working Group also noted the impact of detailed processing of end-users, at an individual level, on the fundamental right to privacy as enshrined in Article 8 ECHR and the right to access information freely, in particular without surveillance by public authorities, as enshrined in Article 11 of the European Charter of Fundamental Rights. The Article 29 Working Party pointed out that detailed profiles were being stored and possibly used by third parties and governments, as follows:

> An individual's search history contains a footprint of that person's interests, relations, and intentions. These data can be subsequently used both for commercial purposes and as a result of requests and fishing operations and/ or data mining by law enforcement authorities or national security services.[690]

It can be argued that the user's privacy is a precondition for the fundamental right to search, access and receive information and ideas freely. Free information-seeking behavior can be quite negatively affectedif the main available options to find information online entail comprehensive surveillance and storage of end-user behavior without appropriate guarantees in view of intellectual freedom.[691] Chapter 10 will address the protection of user privacy from the perspective of the right to freedom of expression in more detail.

8.7.   CONCLUSION

The aim of this chapter has been to develop a general theory for the implications of the right to freedom of expression for the governance of search engines, a theory denoted by 'search engine freedom'. The analysis of Chapters 5–7 clearly showed that the implications of freedom of expression were informed by the dominant normative conceptualization of the societal role being fulfilled by the press, the

---

688. For a discussion, see section 10.4.2.
689. See 28th International Data Protection and Privacy Commissioners' Conference 2006.
690. Article 29 Data Protection Working Party 2008.
691. Compare the privacy discussion with regard to the Google book settlement http://michaelzimmer. org/2009/09/08/google-book-search-privacy-policy-mirrors-web-search/.

Internet access provider and the library respectively. Hence, one of the underlying aims of this chapter was to demonstrate the way such a role for search media in the public networked information environment could be conceptualized. By comparing search media's function in the networked information environment with the functions of the entities studied before, a number of conclusions could be drawn.

Search media combine a passive (conduit/access) and active (editorial/selective) role in their production of meta-information. The search engines' role is related to the *relative accessibility* of information and ideas online. They do not, like publishers, produce content themselves, and compared to traditional editorial media they are more passive. At the same time, however, search media are inherently more active in their mediation than a passive conduit, such as for instance an Internet access provider. It is not the role of search engines to facilitate access to everything equally. After having established an index, search engines rank and select information and destinations online in return to user input in ways which, if anything, resemble editorial media like the press, albeit in respect to a much larger variety of information.

When looking deeper into the societal role of search engines, two conflicting ideals emerged: the ideal of universal access on the one hand and the ideal of information quality on the other hand. The first ideal for search engines is to help end-users navigate the entire Web, by crawling and ordering it and making the material in the index transparent and the underlying sources of online information accessible. The second ideal is to prioritize valuable information and ideas over less valuable ones. The analysis showed how the general purpose search engine, by definition, has to reconcile these conflicting ideals in its operations and that much of the regulatory debate about the responsibility of search media could be explained with reference to the tension between these different ideals.

The tension between information quality and information access that exists in the public networked information environment did not exist in the same manner in the public information environment predating the Web, in which the organization of access to information for the public tended to be separated from the organization of basic levels of quality and legal permissibility. Access was restricted to everything 'fit to print' and their editorial freedom and responsibility was seen as an essential element of a functioning free press and democracy. Likewise, the public library first selects the sources it will subsequently make accessible and applies information quality criteria in this context. After having established a collection, a transparent accessibility infrastructure, informed by professional principles for the organization of knowledge, it would ensure access to the materials that had been selected. For access providers to such a relatively controlled information environment, most of the discussion about liability and filtering in Chapter 6 would have been unnecessary.

Web search engines help establish the relative accessibility of information and ideas in the networked public information environment. This led Dutch philosophers of science Marres and De Vries to make the claim that the societal legitimization of knowledge in the networked information environment takes place through processes of opening up, understood as the process of connecting information and ideas online to their societal use. If one follows this logic, the overarching public interest in the legal governance of Web search engines, from the ideals underlying the right to freedom of expression, lies in the establishment of a rich and robust societal infrastructure for the opening up of the Web.

This characterization of the public interest in the governance of accessibility of the Web is attractive precisely because it captures both perspectives, i.e. access *and* quality, which arguably lie at the core of search engine governance. This reasoning also clarifies that search engine providers have to make non-trivial choices with regard to the balance between quality and access. In the networked information environment, publicity is no longer restricted to entities that offer a priori legitimacy to the information and ideas they make public. And the choices are non-trivial and of a political nature, and involve the complex balancing of different public and private interests, including the interests of end-users and information providers who depend on search engines as well.

When looking at the specific implications of the right to freedom of expression on the governance of search, the analysis showed that under Article 10 ECHR, the search engine should be able to claim protection for its publication of references on its website as well as the process of crawling that makes it possible to offer a search engine in the first place. The protection of the search engine's selection, meaning the selection of a set of relevant websites related to a specific query and ranking decisions under the right to freedom of expression may be one of the most interesting legal questions discussed in this chapter. In the United States, there is some early case law which establishes First Amendment protection for selection and ranking decisions by search engines. In *SearchKing*, a U.S. District Court applied the editorial freedom standards as developed by the Supreme Court in decisions such as *Miami Herald* and *Sullivan* to the freedom of search engines to decide freely how to rank and select references in response to user queries.

Considering the fact that operating a search engine logically implies a fundamental choice about the way to value online resources, there is much to be said for this part of the Court's conclusion. In other words, the choice of search engine operators regarding how to select, rank and present should be considered an editorial process, which deserves protection under the right to freedom of expression. The predominantly technological nature of the way these choices are expressed says less about the nature of this underlying process than about the massiveness of the index and the way technological innovation has offered new ways to organize and provide access to digital information collections. A proper understanding of the societal role of search media points in the same direction; by curating the relative accessibility of information in their index, Web search engines reconcile the ideal of universal access and navigation of the entire Web with the ideal of information quality.

Notably, accepting that a search engine provider's decisions on how to select, rank and present would be protected by the right to freedom of expression does not imply, at least not in the European context, that such freedom would be unlimited or could not be restricted in view of other fundamental values. The conclusion that there may not be and should not be 'one correct way' to select and rank search results does not logically imply that there cannot be any legally impermissible ways to do so when offering search media online. First, one can imagine certain editorial choices by search engine operators that could be unlawful in and of themselves, such as the choice to implement algorithms that are specifically directed at causing harm or that cause harm while having no justifiable purpose. Second, the right to freedom of expression as enshrined in Article 10 ECHR is not absolute and may be restricted in the interests and freedoms of others. It is possible to imagine legitimate restrictions being imposed on search engine operators, dominant search engines in particular, which aim to ensure that the fundamental interests of information providers and end-users remain sufficiently respected. This question, which points to a possible positive role of the State to safeguard the right to freedom of expression in the governance of search, will be more thoroughly addressed in the next and final part of this thesis.

Of special importance in the European context is the question about the duties and responsibilities of search engines which are tied to the exercise of the right to freedom of expression. The duties and responsibilities under Article 10 ECHR are tied to the exercise of one's expressive liberties, and need to be interpreted in the present-day conditions with regard to the new media environment, in which, in the Court's view, they have taken on an added importance. The potential impact of the medium and the nature of the content that can be found through a search engine will play a role in the determination of its possible duties and responsibilities. In other words, it is likely that major general purpose search engines such as Google, which have a particularly strong impact on the public information environment, could have enhanced duties and responsibilities based on their widespread use. In this context, it is worth noting that the Court's case law seems to imply that the more a communicator does to abide by professional standards with regard to quality and the mode of communicating, the more it will be able to defend itself against interferences. Most search engines do fairly little to guarantee a threshold minimum quality of the information they provide references to. In general, the lack of editorial control with regard to the actual content referred to and the lack of professional oversight over the inclusion of references could weaken a search engine's protection under Article 10 ECHR.

But there are other arguments in favor of less stringent duties and responsibilities as regards the quality of references in search engines. Arguably, duties and responsibilities should cut both ways. On the one hand, they can be argued to imply a professional responsibility on Web search providers to care about the quality of their references. On the other hand, they could be argued to entail a duty on search engine providers to be comprehensive and not to exclude references too lightly. In fact, an important normative principle in the Court's case law (*Open Door*) is that a communicator that leaves the decision to act upon its communications to the receiver cannot—in principle—be blamed for those decisions. The more facilitative the search engine would be with respect to the decisional autonomy of its users, the more protection it would receive against interferences which seek to prevent a certain reaction by the audience.

The protected interests of information providers under the right to freedom of expression can be best understood as the freedom to be present in the search engine's index and thereby to find their way to an audience. What is at stake for information providers in the context of dominant general purpose search engines could also be formulated in terms of representation. Hence, de-indexing by a dominant search engine is particularly problematic from the perspective of legitimate information providers. Legal issues related to the de-indexing of websites will be discussed in Chapter 9. The same may be said about an unfavorable treatment through selection and ranking decisions. However, it is impossible to argue that all information providers could have a legal claim to enter a dominant general purpose search engine index, as well as receive a favorable treatment by selection and ranking algorithms. Besides being impossible in practice, this claim would overlook a variety of legitimate grounds which a search engine could have for de-indexing or unfavorable ranking, including grounds directly related to the protection of search engines' providers under the right to freedom of expression and the interests of the end-users.

With regard to search engine users, ultimately, their interest under the right to freedom of expression in the context of search may be best understood as a right to inform themselves freely by exploring the Web to its full potential, using available search technologies and services which enhance the findability of information, ideas and resources in the public networked information environment. The use of search engines has become a daily activity for end-users. They rely on search engines to find news and other resources, to inform themselves about products, political candidates, diseases, and to reach destinations and other online services. The user's freedom obviously implies a right to be able to choose which available navigational media to use. In addition, the user has a general interest in navigational media of high quality. In Chapter 10, the question will be explored as to what extent these interests of end-users could inform additional legal and regulatory involvement directed at the search engine market.

Part III

Search Engine Freedom: Access and Quality

Chapter 9

Search Engine Access: Content Regulation and Intermediary Liability

9.1. INTRODUCTION

This chapter will discuss the legal liability of search engine providers for their role in facilitating access to information and ideas online. More specifically, it will address the way the law and regulatory frameworks for access to content online implicate search engines with the aim to prevent access to illegal, unlawful, as well as harmful content. The capacity of search engines to open up not only legal or uncontroversial publications but also illegal as well as controversial or allegedly harmful material has resulted in legal and regulatory pressure on search engines to adopt a variety of measures to restrict access to content through their services. These measures range from the removal of websites from the index and the monitoring of the index for illegal material to the filtering of search results for country-specific search services and the blocking of keywords to prevent certain usage of the service.

As was discussed in detail in the previous chapter, search engines have to reconcile two conflicting ideals relating to the accessibility of online material, namely the ideal to facilitate access to all the material that is available online on the one hand, and the ideal of facilitating access to the material online which is valuable for the user on the other hand. An important question from the perspective of the right to freedom of expression is whether this balance should also involve the removal of websites from search engines for legal reasons. As will be discussed in more detail below, search engines do remove illegal websites from their index due to legal reasons. In addition, in some jurisdictions, search engine providers have entered into self-regulatory and co-regulatory frameworks, which entail the voluntary proactive removal and filtering of websites to satisfy a public policy demand.

While search engines are involved in content regulation frameworks, it is also recognized, both in the United States and to some degree in Europe, that search engines, like other online intermediaries, should not be held fully liable for third-party material. First of all, search engines should be treated fairly under existing general liability standards. They should not be treated as the publisher of the content they merely refer to. Second, too strict liability standards could render it legally impossible to offer these essential services for the networked information environment. In particular, strict liability standards for search engines could have significant chilling effects under the right to freedom of expression, as they would incentivize search engine providers to monitor their index for possibly illegal material and remove lawful material from the index to avoid becoming the subject of litigation.

On the basis of the concerns over too strict intermediary liability (or third-party liability) for search engines, in some jurisdictions special 'safe harbors' for search engines apply, alongside similar safe harbors for other intermediaries like hosting providers or access providers.[692] In addition, search engines have played a role in the broader self-regulatory frameworks that are aimed at dealing with access to illegal and harmful content online and have been developed within the boundaries set by the safe harbor framework. As will become apparent in this Chapter, in comparison with access providers, the legal position search engine providers find themselves in (in the European context) is much less clear. The intermediary liability standards for search engines are not the same in Europe and the United States. In the United States, the safe harbor depends on the type of third-party liability, rendering search engines immune to defamation and similar unlawful content in search results (CDA 230),[693] while putting them under notice and takedown obligations in the context of references to copyright infringements on third-party websites. Although early case law of the European Court seems to point to the conclusion that search engines may invoke the protection of the hosting safe harbor, it remains questionable whether search engines fall under the safe harbor regime from the e-commerce directive in the first place.

Ultimately, the question addressed in this chapter is whether the existing legal governance of access to illegal and/or harmful content through search engines is consistent with the right to freedom of expression and in what ways the legal framework could be improved from the perspective of the right to freedom of expression. The chapter will first address some of the self-regulatory frameworks which lead to the removal of online material from search engines (section 9.2). The censorship of the online environment though the removal of references by search engines in China will be addressed first, because of its impact on the general debate about freedom of expression and search engine governance. Thereafter, the focus will be placed on examples of self-regulatory content regulation frameworks for search engines in Europe, specifically in Germany and the United Kingdom (section 9.2.3). After a discussion of these self-regulatory frameworks, the issue of

---

692. For a discussion of the U.S. and EU safe harbor for access providers, see section 6.4.
693. See section 6.4.4.

intermediary liability of search engines for referring users to unlawful publications on the Web (section 9.3) will be addressed, comparing the state of affairs in Europe with that in the United States. Section 9.4 brings together the findings of sections 9.2 and 9.3 and addresses the question about the consistency of the current legal framework from the perspective of the right to freedom of expression and evaluates possibilities for improvement. Section 9.5 concludes.

9.2. SEARCH ENGINES AND CONTENT REGULATION: CENSORSHIP OR SELF-REGULATION?

9.2.1. SEARCH ENGINE CENSORSHIP IN CHINA

Of all issues related to access to information and Web search engines, the most publicly debated one relates to a non-Western, namely Chinese context.[694] Google's decision to start a country-specific search engine in China *google.cn* next to its Chinese language version of *google.com* is famous in the debate about Internet content regulation. The search company was strongly criticized for adhering to the undemocratic demands of the Chinese government to censor access to content for Chinese citizens. It has come to serve as the paradigm case of undue government interference with the right to freedom of expression in the debate about content regulation and the Internet.

It seems that the bad accessibility of google.com in China, due to the Chinese government's interference with access to online material by the 'Great Firewall of China', was one of reasons for Google to start its Chinese operations.[695] This government-imposed Internet filtering at the network level interfered with the accessibility of *google.com* for Chinese Internet users on a regular basis, sometimes making the site completely inaccessible, and constantly interfered with access to specific content by blocking specific websites or resetting the browser of Chinese users in reaction to specific keywords. To be clear, Google was and remains only one of the many foreign information services affected by the Great Firewall. Many others, such as the BBC's news site, face similar challenges in making information available to a China-based audience.[696]

By moving into China, Google chose to make a compromise in terms of the governance of its index. To be able to operate an online information service, such as a search engine, in China, service providers need to obtain a license from the Chinese government. This license includes an agreement to self-regulate. More specifically, search companies have to agree not to provide access to certain types of content, including prohibited political or cultural expression. Other companies

---

694. See Levy 2011, 267–314; Mueller, Networks and States, 2010, 189–190. Deibert et al. 2007; Halavais 2009, 118.
695. For a discussion of Google's operation of a search engine in China, see Levy 2011, 267–314. See also Thompson 2006.
696. See e.g. BBC 2010.

had already obtained similar licenses; Yahoo! had moved into China years before, and Chinese companies, such as Baidu, were subject to similar restraints.

Thus, by obtaining the license to operate google.cn on Chinese soil, Google agreed to suppress the findability of political speech, in other words the type of information and ideas which lay at the core of the value of freedom of expression in western democratic societies. Online material covering the 1989 protests, the Falung Gong movement, political speech relating to Tibet, and opposition or political mobilization against the regime more generally, was somehow to be made invisible to the users of google.cn. It is important to note that the Chinese government does not provide readily usable blacklists to do so. The information providers themselves are expected to proactively monitor and exclude content on their services in view of vague standards about acceptable speech by the government. The absence of such official blacklists is shown by empirical research on the suppression of content by search providers in China.[697] There is no consistency in the suppressed references between the three major Western search engine providers in China (Google, Yahoo! and Microsoft).

The compromise that Google, Yahoo! and others[698] made not only led to public controversy, but also to legislative proposals. In the United States, several proposals were made to guarantee that U.S. companies would respect human rights while conducting business abroad.[699] Similar laws have been called for in the context of the European Union.[700] None of these proposals have yet been signed into law. Instead, a self-regulatory framework, the Global Network Initiative, consisting of industry (Google, Yahoo! and Microsoft), non-governmental organizations (Center for Democracy & Technology, Electronic Frontier Foundation) and research institutions (Harvard's Berkman Center for Internet & Society), has taken the lead in formulating an answer to the questions raised by 'the China problem'.[701]

In the beginning of 2010, the 'China problem' entered a third phase, after Google announced its unwillingness to continue censoring its google.cn index in reaction to a cyber attack originating from China.[702] Only a week later, U.S. Secretary of State Hillary Clinton publicly denounced China's interference with

---

697. See Villeneuve 2008.
698. Yahoo! was the subject of criticism because it handed over personal data of a user of its email service, a Chinese political activist, to the Chinese government, which resulted in the activist's arrest and incarceration. Yahoo! later faced litigation in the United States relating to the infringement of the activist's privacy. Microsoft deleted the content of a blog by a Chinese user even though the hosting service in question was not based in China. Cisco was heavily criticized for providing technology and knowledge to build the 'Great Firewall of China'. See Thompson 2006.
699. See U.S. Congress, H.R. 275 [110th]: Global Online Freedom Act of 2007, 2d sess., Rep 110-481, February 22, 2008. For a discussion, see Maclay 2010.
700. See Reuters 2009.
701. See Global Network Initiative http://globalnetworkinitiative.org/.
702. Since early 2010, Google no longer operates a search engine in China, but redirects its search traffic to its service in Hong Kong. Notably, Google did manage to renew its Internet Content Provider license to operate a website in China after it agreed to end automatic redirects for

the free flow of information in a public speech on Internet freedom,[703] showing how high-profile the issue had become. It has placed the issue firmly on the global Internet politics agenda for the current decade.[704]

A discussion of the actual political and regulatory environment for search engines in China goes well beyond the scope of this research. A legal comparison is difficult to make, considering the absence of a rule of law tradition in China, the differences in the protection of freedom of expression, the absence of general freedom to operate information services without a license, and the problems relating to the Chinese language, culture and its history. Yet, it is possible to use an important practical similarity between search engine operations in China and Western countries as a bridge to the discussion of search engines and content regulation in the West, namely the proactive blacklisting of online material or keyword-triggered filtering in search engines for legal or public policy reasons. Whereas the motives for, and the intensity and implementation of such interferences, may be quite different, search engines regularly suppress access to content through their services in constitutional democracies as well. In the remainder of this section, first the general regulatory background of such interferences in Europe and the United States will be discussed. After which, the types of content search engines typically suppress will be discussed, as well as the methods that are used to do so.

9.2.2.   SELF-REGULATORY REMOVAL OF REFERENCES: THE GERMAN
FSM FRAMEWORK

As was discussed in Chapter 6, the regulation of, and protection against, illegal and harmful information on the Internet tends to follow the self- and co-regulatory paradigm, introduced in the European context by the 1998 Council Recommendation.[705] Since the mid-1990s, several non-governmental agencies (hotlines) have been founded to deal with the issue of illegal content on the Web, child pornography in particular.[706] More often than not, search engines are not systematically addressed in these legal frameworks, which vary across the Member States and tend to focus on hosting and access intermediary responsibilities. In some Member States, such as the Netherlands, search engines are not (yet) specifically addressed at all. In other Member States, such as Germany and France, major search engine providers, together with public authorities, have adopted specific co-regulatory frameworks for the removal of illegal or harmful references in search engines. An important example of such a co-regulatory framework can be found in Germany, which will be discussed below. In other Member

---

google.cn to *google.com.hk*. The google.cn website now contains a link to the Google Hong Kong website. See Drummond (Google) 2010.

703.   United States Department of State 2010.
704.   For a discussion of the international law and human rights framework in the context of Internet content filtering, see Rundle & Birdling 2008, 73–102.
705.   Council Recommendation 98/560, 1998 OJ (L 270), 48 (EC).
706.   For a discussion, see e.g. Mueller 2010.

States, such as the United Kingdom, there are similar initiatives, which also involve search engine providers, but no formal government involvement.

Some of the voluntary frameworks for search engines in Europe entail the proactive removal of references and blocking of material in country-specific services. To complicate matters from a legal perspective, the voluntary frameworks exist alongside possible existing legal obligations to block or remove content from search engines.[707] In Europe, it is generally assumed that providers of general purpose search engines do not have a legal obligation to proactively monitor and remove references to illegal and/or harmful material from their services. However, there may be some specific exceptions to this general rule that search engines do not have a preventive duty of care as regards third-party material. Upon notice, search engines will typically fall under a legal obligation to remove references to illegal content.[708] These exceptions will be discussed in the context in which they typically arise, i.e. the context of third-party liability (section 9.3).

In some European countries, specific administrative government authorities have traditionally been assigned the task of the protection of the youth against dangerous or harmful content. In Germany, the *Bundesprüfstelle für jugendgefährdende Medien* (BPjM) (Federal Department for Media Harmful to Young Persons) administers a blacklist of illegal and harmful content. The BPjM does not itself monitor the media but can add media objects, including Internet sites, to its list of media considered dangerous or harmful to minors, after having received and reviewed a complaint.

After a debate in Germany about the availability of illegal and harmful material on the Internet and the resulting accessibility in search engines, major search engine providers, under the umbrella of the FSM *Freiwillige Selbstkontrolle Multimedia-Diensteanbieter* (FSM) (The Association for the Voluntary Self-Monitoring of Multimedia Service Providers), adopted a specific code of conduct in 2004. This code, the 'Subcode of Conduct for Search Engine Providers' (VK-S), was meant to prevent access to illegal and dangerous material through their German services. The FSM is a non-governmental association founded in 1997 by important players in the German Internet industry for the voluntary self-control of the Internet. The FSM is part of a European network of industry hotlines for illegal and harmful content which developed since the 1990s. According to the website of the FSM, all major search engines operating in Germany are signatories to the VK-S. The VK-S and other codes of the FSM are part of the general German framework of 'regulated self-regulation' (co-regulation) of the media, introduced by the German Federal Human Dignity and Child Protection Law.[709]

The FSM's 'Subcode of Conduct for Search Engine Providers' (VK-S) introduces a number of voluntary obligations for its search engine signatories, including

---

707. See e.g. Schulz & Held 2007.
708. See Spindler & Verbiest 2007, 69–71.
709. Staatsvertrag über den Schutz der Menschenwürde und den Jugendschutz in Rundfunk und Telemedien (Jugendmedienschutz-Staatsvertrag—JMStV).

the removal of references on a government-administered (BPjM) blacklist.[710] The blacklist is made available to search engine providers through a special technical tool (BPjM-Modul), which is meant to prevent the further dissemination of the BPjM blacklist. In practice, the German Subcode of Conduct for Search Engine Providers can result in reports about illegal material by members of the FSM to the BPjM and the removal of BPjM-blacklisted references from Germany-specific Web search engines, such as Yahoo.de or Google.de. These actions have a basis in Article § 2(5) of the VK-S. Article § 2(5)(a), provides that complaints about references to websites shall be forwarded to the BPjM and lists the categories of content that may lead to successful complaints. Listed are the following categories of content:

> Propaganda and insignia of unconstitutional organizations [. . .], Racial demagoguery and Holocaust disavowal [. . .], Incitement or inducement to criminal acts [. . .], Depictions of violence [. . .], Child, animal and violent pornography [. . .], Explicit sexual depictions involving minors [. . .], Content glorifying war [. . .], Degradations of human dignity.

Article § 2(5)(b), of the VK-S, provides that the signatories:

> agree to remove and not to show respectively any URLs which are indicated by the BPjM, insofar as they have access to the URL and insofar as the commercial expense is reasonable.[711]

It is notable that the BPjM also receives complaints from organizations apart from FSM signatories. The German child protection law grants several German governmental and non-governmental organizations the legal right to make an official complaint about a media object. The Kommission für Jugendmedienschutz (KJM) is an example of a governmental organization that operates hotlines and actively monitors online media in view of content possibly dangerous for minors. The BPjM has the legal obligation to review such complaints.

It is doubtful whether more than symbolic value can be attributed to the FSM framework for search engine providers. The impact of the scheme on the information practices of German users is unclear and remains undocumented. What is clear, however, is that it remains easy to find references to content in German-specific search services that under German law should clearly be considered dangerous for minors.[712] Moreover, due to the restriction of the framework to German-specific services, the filtered websites also remain easily accessible for German Internet users. The filtered websites are typically not one, but two clicks

---

710. See FSM 2004.
711. *Ibid.*
712. The FSM itself implicitly acknowledges this in its Frequently Asked Questions about the code of conduct for search engine providers: "Wenn man bei Suchmaschinen Begriffe mit eindeutig jugendgefährdendem Inhalt eingibt, erhält man trotzdem zahlreiche Treffer. Nützt das BPjM-Modul überhaupt etwas?". See FSM, FAQ Selbstkontrolle Suchmaschinen, http://fsm.de/de/FAQs_Selbstkontrolle_Suchmaschinen.

away, with the use of search services not specifically targeted at a German audience such as google.com.

An important example of a website that is filtered in Germany but remains accessible through non-German-specific versions of search engines is the right-wing extremist website *stormfront.org*.[713] However, the treatment of this website, which hosts an active white supremacist forum, by the various members of FSM is inconsistent and confusing. Both Google and Microsoft remove results to the domain from their search services directed at Germany. Their statements about the reasons of the removal are inconsistent with the information provided by the FSM. Whereas the FSM emphasizes the voluntary nature of the decision to remove websites such as stormfront.org, Google and Microsoft consistently state legal reasons for the removal. Google refers to an external partner, *chilllingeffects.org*, for more information about the removal of search results.[714] Google does not remove the site from its 'international' search engine, *google.com*, which can also be accessed through a German language interface at *www.google.com/de*.[715]

When conducting a search for the domain stormfront.org on *bing.com/?cc=de*, no results are shown. The link to the 'help' section that is shown does lead to a list of links about the service, one of which links to a general notice about the possible removal of references. This notice states that Bing excludes results that "local laws, regulations, or policies (such as copyright laws and local definitions of offensive content) require us to omit."[716] Elsewhere, Microsoft further addresses the production and possible removal of references, mentioning intellectual property rights, defamation, child abuse content or laws specific to individual countries. Apparently, the removal of stormfront.org must be placed in the last category. For these types of removals, however, Bing claims to interpret local laws as narrowly as possible.[717] This implies that Microsoft considers the FSM obligations a restatement of German law and directly contradicts the voluntary nature of the Code. With regard to child abuse material, Microsoft claims "to remove these

---

713. For the purpose of this study, these searches were (last) carried out on August 15, 2011.
714. On August 15, 2011, the search [site:stormfront.org] on *google.de* produces no results accompanied by a notice that reads "Aus Rechtsgründen hat Google 478 Ergebnis(se) von dieser Seite entfernt. Weitere Informationen über diese Rechtsgründe finden Sie unter ChillingEffects.org." Google uses the same notice for the removal of content from its general index: "In response to a legal request submitted to Google, we have removed [N] result(s) from this page. If you wish, you may read more about the request at ChillingEffects.org."
715. See http://www.google.com/intl/de/. Google seems to redirect German visitors to google.com to google.de, but allows them to subsequently visit the google.com page through a link on the google.de start site. It is worth noting that Google responds to notices relating to some categories of material, such as child pornography, by complete de-indexing on a global level.
716. See Microsoft, 'Why some results have been removed' http://onlinehelp.microsoft.com/en-us/bing/ff808530.aspx.
717. See Microsoft, 'How Bing delivers search results' http://onlinehelp.microsoft.com/en-gb/bing/ff808447.aspx. ("When approached with a request for removal of search results by a governmental entity, we require proof of the applicable law and authority of the government agency, and an official request to require removal. If such proof is provided and we can verify it, then we may comply with the removal request. If we are required to implement the request, we will do so as narrowly as required by the law.")

types of links only when we are confident that the government or quasi-governmental agency providing the links [. . .] limits the scope of its work to illegal child abuse content."[718] This is rather puzzling considering the fact that neither the BPjM, nor the FSM restricts itself to child abuse material.[719] Yahoo.de does not provide any specific information that references have been removed, even though the FSM code includes a transparency obligation. While earlier FSM member Ask did not filter the website from its German-specific service, in August 2011 it did not show any results for stormfront.org.[720]

It is clear that the various inconsistencies mentioned above, and the lack of transparency as regards the functioning of the self-regulatory framework in practice more generally, show room for improvement. The most important practical short-coming is the absence of a demonstrable impact on the German information eco-system. The easy accessibility of the blacklisted material for German Internet users raises the question of whether the current framework is redundant in the first place. It is possible that the framework reduces the risk of minors being exposed to the material considered inappropriate under German media child protection standards. But the framework is applied regardless of the age of search engine users and in the absence of empirical evidence that minors would actually find it harder to obtain access to blocked material, the effectiveness from the policy aim remains equally doubtful.

The questionable merit of the framework in terms of its success in preventing access to illegal and harmful material also raises a question about the proportionality of the framework under the right to freedom of expression as protected by Article 10 ECHR. If a measure interferes with the right to freedom of expression but does not contribute to the stated goal, the proportionality is questionable from the start. As was discussed in Chapter 6 as well as Chapter 8, Article 10 ECHR requires that a ban on certain illegal material has to be consistent. The ECtHR considered a restraint on publication to be disproportional if the material is still legally available through import. Likewise, in the context of search engines and the Internet, the restraint is inconsistent if public authorities, such as German public authorities, pressurize internationally operating search engine providers to remove certain material from one part of their offering *google.de*, but allow them to facilitate accessibility of the same material to the German population in the rest of their offering *google.com*.

In addition, self-regulatory frameworks for the removal or blocking of online content in which public authorities play a facilitative role can be problematic because of the informal nature of government pressure and the possible lack of substantive and procedural guarantees that would apply in case of proper legal

---

718. See Microsoft, 'How Bing delivers search results' http://onlinehelp.microsoft.com/en-gb/bing/ff808447.aspx.

719. The blacklist used by Lycos Germany was obtained and subsequently published by Wikileaks 2009. See Wikileaks 2009. For a discussion, see Schäfers 2009.

720. This could be the result of the fact that Ask is (reportedly) no longer producing its own search results. See also section 2.2.4.

obligations. There is a risk that the main difference between the two is that in the self-regulatory framework governments get to exert power over information flows without having to base its exercise on the law, a fundamental rule of law requirement and a specific requirement in Article 10 ECHR, second paragraph. In the German context, this requirement is usually taken seriously. In fact, the BPjM's blacklisting of websites is directly authorized by German law. Yet, there is a risk that self-regulatory agencies, such as the FSM, are not open to the same scrutiny as public agencies, based on a democratic legislative mandate. Of course, this may actually be a reason for the industry to prefer self-regulation over public regulation.

Moreover, the statements about the FSM framework by Google and Bing demonstrate significant ambiguity with regard to the voluntary nature of the framework and a lack of internalization by its members. What is the added value of a self-regulatory framework which involves the 'voluntary' removal of references from search engines if the obligations agreed to are actual legal obligations? In fact, the German 'voluntary' framework and the German legal framework seem to overlap: the stromfront.org website for instance is, in principle, illegal to link to in Germany,[721] as are publications of all the categories of content that are listed in Article § 2, paragraph 5(a) of the VK-S. Upon notice, not necessarily by a court, a search engine operating in Germany, or any other website publishing references, would normally have to remove these links.[722] As will be discussed in the next section, search engine liability for third-party material is not particularly clear in the European context. It is conceivable that search engines only adopted the FSM framework because of a lack of clarity about their legal obligations regarding references to illegal material and to prevent themselves from becoming the subject of specific regulation.

The lack of transparency in the functioning of the framework as applied in Germany, which results from the inconsistencies and the confusing statements from the various participants, is a final objection to the current framework. The FSM's code of conduct for search engines actually contains various transparency obligations, which, when taken seriously by the participants, could mitigate this concern. In its current form, however, the framework is not only ineffective in its aim to prevent access to illegal material for German Internet users through search engines, but may also fail to take account of the interference with the informational self-governance of end-users. As McIntyre and Scott explain:

---

721. It is notable that the German version of Wikipedia contains a lemma about the stormfront.org website, but it does not provide a hyperlink to the website itself, stating that it would be illegal under German law do so. See Wikipedia, 'Stormfront', http://de.wikipedia.org/wiki/Stormfront. ("Die Homepage von Stormfront wird von der deutschsprachigen Wikipedia aus rechtlichen Gründen nicht verlinkt.")

722. It can be argued that Article 10(2) ECHR would still require the act of notification by public authorities of illegal content to be taken down to be based on the law. See Schellekens et al. 2007, 17.

where [. . .] it is not clear what is being blocked, why, or by whom, the operation of mechanisms of accountability—whether by way of judicial review, media scrutiny, or otherwise—is greatly reduced.[723]

9.2.3.   PROACTIVE KEYWORD BLOCKING

There is one other field of self-regulatory activity targeting the accessibility of illegal and harmful content in search engines, namely through restrictions on the available choice of keywords.[724] Compared to the removal of references in search engines, this is not as widespread and is a rather murky field of regulatory activity, so it is not possible to go into as much factual detail. It is instructive to start with an example.

In 2008, U.S. media reported that a government-funded health care search engine was blocking all searches for the query [abortion].[725] The search engine, which claimed to be the world's largest database on reproductive health, was run by the John Hopkins Medical School of Public Health and funded by the U.S. federal agency for foreign aid, USAID.[726] The reason for the blocking of the keyword 'abortion' was related to an official government policy not to fund organizations that perform abortions, or that "actively promote abortion as a method of family planning in other nations."[727] After reports in the media about the blocking of the search term, a university official explained that the search engine administrators seemed to have overreacted. USAID had complained about two references in the search engine to websites which were one-sided in favor of abortion rights. The search engine operators had subsequently decided to block the entire keyword. The USAID official defended the complaints against the specific websites with reference to the government policy mentioned above.[728]

In Europe, the most famous example of the idea of keyword blocking is the proposal by former European Justice and Home Affairs Commissioner Franco Frattini. In 2007, Frattini told Reuters he planned the following:

---

723. See McIntyre & Scott 2008.
724. Since search engines are no longer just waiting for end-users to enter their own search terms but are assisting them in formulating their queries, regulatory action with regard to the choice of keyword also implicates these value-added services of major search engines.
725. See Stirland 2008a.
726. USAID is in charge of providing foreign aid, including health care funding, to developing nations.
727. The so-called Mexico City Policy was upheld after a First Amendment challenge due to a lack of standing of foreign NGOs (the policy only applied to foreign organizations) in *Center for Reproductive Law and Policy v. Bush*, 304 F.3d 183 (2nd Cir. 2002) (arguing, as in the case of mandatory Internet filters in libraries, that the government's choice not to fund was not a justiciable issue and that all organizations remained free not to apply for funding). President Obama overturned the policy in the first month of his presidency. See Obama 2009.
728. See Stirland 2008b.

to carry out a clear exploring exercise with the private sector [. . .] on how it is possible to use technology to prevent people from using or searching dangerous words like bomb, kill, genocide or terrorism.[729]

The plan to have search engines or other services block 'dangerous words' never seems to have materialized but was not as out of touch with reality as some commentators in the media might have thought it was. In 2005, for instance, the U.K. Home Office published a recommendation on good practices for search service providers, which contained the same proposal. The official government document stipulated the following:

> [T]he IWF maintains a list of key words or combinations of words which, whilst not illegal in themselves, can be used to search for illegal material. Search providers should consider using this list to prevent abuse of their services by individuals seeking illegal material.[730]

The Internet Watch Foundation (IWF), is the U.K. hotline for child abuse material online. More precisely, it is a private-public partnership with the aim of combating child pornographic material online (worldwide) and criminally obscene and incitement to racial hatred content (in the United Kingdom).[731] The IWF administers the blacklist used in the so-called CleanFeed system, which entails the blocking of child pornographic material by major U.K. access providers.[732] The IWF blacklist of *potentially criminal URLs related to child sexual abuse content on publicly accessible websites* is provided to all members of the IWF, which include all major search engine providers operating in the United Kingdom.

Search engine providers and other relevant members and partners not only receive the list of URLs filtered through the CleanFeed system but also the list of keywords mentioned above. According to the IWF, this is a *list of words and phrases commonly used by those seeking out child sexual abuse and criminally obscene adult content*, which can "help search engine providers to improve the quality of search returns."[733] It is unclear whether (and if so, how) search engines actually use the list to monitor, rank or block particular search results. One of the ways such lists are possibly being used is in the context of search query 'suggest' and 'auto-complete' functionalities. For words leading to certain predictably offensive queries, the search 'suggest' functionality does not auto-complete or trigger any suggested queries.[734] The search 'suggest' functionality has already led to some legal developments in other countries. In Italy, for instance, Google

---

729. Melander 2007.
730. Home Office UK 2005.
731. See Edwards 2010.
732. For a technical discussion of the CleanFeed system, see Clayton 2005.
733. See Internet Watch Foundation, Services, Keywords http://www.iwf.org.uk/services/keywords.
734. See e.g. Google.com, Web Search, Help Articles, Autocomplete, http://www.google.com/support/websearch/bin/static.py?hl=en&page=guide.cs&guide=1186810&answer=106230&rd=1. ("While we always strive to neutrally and objectively reflect the diversity of content on the web (some good, some objectionable), we also apply a narrow set of removal policies for

was held liable for suggesting queries which a Court held to be defamatory.[735] Furthermore, the music industry has successfully lobbied Google to incorporate changes to its search 'suggest' functionality. It will now "prevent terms that are closely associated with piracy from appearing in Autocomplete."[736] The Paris Court of Appeal dismissed liability for suggesting words such as 'torrent' or destinations such as RapidShare.[737]

While the removal of a reference from search results only blocks access to the specific website through the search service, the blocking of keywords goes much further. This is a direct result of the way search engines produce a set of relevant references in response to a search query. The search engine would typically select all the documents in the index containing the search query terms as could be possibly relevant for the user. Hence, a restriction on providing references in response to a certain search query consisting of certain keywords would function like a prior restraint on search media to refer to any material containing the allegedly dangerous keywords. As a result, filtering all references for a keyword is likely to prevent effective access to a host of lawful material as well. From the perspective of the right to freedom of expression, legal requirements to use such lists by general purpose search engines to block searches are likely to be disproportionate. Considering the strict requirements related to prior restraints, such legal requirements would be highly questionable under the right to freedom of expression as protected by Article 10 ECHR.[738]

The fact that certain terms could be used to search for unlawful material does not imply that there are no legitimate uses of the terms in search engines. In fact, controversy about a certain issue may actually imply there are strong reasons to gain access to information about the issue in question. For a keyword such as 'genocide' which was included in Frattini's proposal, it is actually hard to imagine how a search for said term could have any causal connection to genocide or illegal material relating to genocide. In fact, a ban on searches for 'genocide' would be similar to a ban on searches for 'holocaust' because of the existence of holocaust denial online. If we consider a possible search term such as 'child pornography', it could be true that people interested in finding child pornographic material use general purpose search engines and similar search queries to find this type of illegal material. In fact, child pornography laws typically make such attempts to access child pornography a crime and all search engines readily respond to requests to remove references to actual child abuse material from their index. If the keyword is

---

pornography, violence, hate speech, and terms that are frequently used to find content that infringes copyrights.")

735. Meyer 2011. Tribunale di Milano, March 24, 2011 (*Google suggest*).
736. See Walker (Google) 2010.
737. See Jasserand 2011.
738. In Europe, the keyword blocking proposals also arise in another regulatory context, namely the protection of data privacy. By opening up the Web, search engines facilitate access to personal data posted online including sensitive data such as credit card data or social security numbers. The European Data Protection Authorities have advised that search engines should remove these sensitive data on request. See Article 29 Data Protection Working Party 2008.

blocked instead, others who want to access information about the *phenomenon* of child pornography would be barred from using one of the most effective means available to inform themselves or could be chilled from looking further because of the blocking of these words. It can also prevent people from learning more about what their government is actually doing against child pornography.

Another question is whether search engines are, or should be, legally allowed to voluntarily block the use of certain keywords. Surely, keyword blocking based on lists of controversial words and phrases could be seen as one of the most economical ways for search engines to deal with the risks that they may facilitate access to illegal content. At the same time, they would risk harming their value for users as well as being accused of censoring the Web. In the United States, voluntary keyword blocking by search engines would be protected by the Communications Decency Act, section 230. In Europe, there are no specific rules protecting or preventing search engines from keyword blocking. It is doubtful that voluntary blocking of keywords to prevent access to illegal content could be argued to be unlawful. Under highly specific circumstances, including the type of search engine and its market power, the context, the reasons for blocking a keyword and the particular keywords that are being blocked, there could arguably be a positive obligation on the State under Article 10 ECHR to prevent certain negative effects of keyword blocking on access to lawful content. At the same time, the predictable negative and disproportionate impact of keyword blocking on access to information for end-users implies that it should not be promoted by the government as a proper way for search engines to deal with access to illegal or possibly harmful content in the first place.

9.3. INTERMEDIARY LIABILITY AND SEARCH ENGINES

9.3.1. DISCUSSION OF INTERMEDIARY LIABILITY REGULATION FOR SEARCH ENGINES

As already mentioned in the previous section, the discussion of proactive involvement of search engines in preventing access to illegal and harmful material through their services cannot be separated from their legal responsibility as regards the findability of illegal third-party content. There are a variety of laws that can make the publication of references in search engines legally problematic: data protection law, defamation and general tort law, criminal law, copyright law, trademark law and the law of trade secrets. The typical lack of editorial control with regard to the legality of material in the index means that search engines will normally contain some references that are unlawful themselves or link to unlawful material. The question is to what extent search engines can be held legally accountable for references containing or referring to unlawful information. When are search engines liable for such *unlawful references*? Is it possible and if so, under which circumstances are search engines themselves operating unlawfully because of their facilitative role as regards illegal material online? And more specifically, can there be a legal obligation to remove unlawful references and, if so, under what circumstances?

In general, this is a question about intermediary liability for which specific legislation has been adopted both in the United States and the European Union. In the next section, the position of search engines in the intermediary liability framework in the EU and the United States will be discussed. After concluding that a clear search engine specific safe harbor for search engines is absent at the European level, in contrast to U.S. law, the implications of this absence for the legal liability of search engines for third-party content will be discussed from the perspective of the right to freedom of expression.

9.3.2.   INTERMEDIARY LIABILITY OF SEARCH ENGINES AND THE
         DIRECTIVE ON ELECTRONIC COMMERCE

The liability of online intermediaries has been on the European legislative agenda since the late 1990s.[739] However, search engines have hardly been addressed in this debate.[740] The core result of European legislative efforts is the Directive on Electronic Commerce (2000/31/EC).[741] The objective of the Directive on Electronic Commerce (in short: Directive or ECD) is "to contribute to the proper functioning of the internal market by ensuring the free movement of information society services between the Member States."[742] In recital 40, it is noted that "both existing and emerging disparities in Member States' legislation and case law concerning liability of service providers acting as intermediaries prevent the functioning of the internal market, in particular by impairing the development of cross-border services and producing distortions of competition."[743]

The Directive aims to solve these internal market problems by introducing safe harbors for certain types of intermediaries. To be precise, the section in the Directive on the liability of information society services[744] acting as intermediaries does four things. First, it defines three categories of intermediaries, namely 'mere conduit' (Article 12), 'caching' (Article 13) and 'hosting' (Article 14). Second, for each of these categories it contains a conditional liability exemption. Third, it explicitly leaves open the possibility for a court or administrative authority to

---

739. Notable contributions to the discussion about online intermediary liability from a European perspective include Spindler & Verbiest 2007; Koelman 2000; Koelman 1997; Julia-Barceló 2000; Peguera 2009. See also section 6.4.

740. Two noteworthy early exceptions are Julia-Barceló 2000 and Verbiest 1999. For an extensive resource on hyperlink and search engine liability see the online collection by German legal scholar Stephan Ott at Links & Law http://www.linksandlaw.com.

741. Council Directive 2000/31, 2000 OJ (L 178) 1 (EC).

742. *Ibid.*, Article 1(1).

743. *Ibid.*, Preamble § 40.

744. Article 2(a) ECD refers to Directive 98/34, 1998 OJ (L 204) 37 (EC), *amended by* Directive 98/48, 1998 OJ (L 320) 54 (EC) for a definition of 'information society service': "any service normally provided for remuneration, at a distance, by electronic means and at the individual request of a recipient of services."

require the provider to terminate or prevent an infringement. In particular, the safe harbors do not restrict the possibility of obtaining injunctive relief, for instance a court order on an online intermediary to remove a certain piece of unlawful material from their servers or to hand over identification data with regard to subscribers. Moreover, the exemptions do not affect the lawfulness of the processing of information by providers of any of these types of intermediary services. The lawfulness has to be determined by applying the relevant laws of the Member States. Finally, the Directive proscribes general obligations on the providers of services, covered by Articles 12–14, to monitor the information that they transmit or store or to seek facts or circumstances indicating illegal activity (Article 15).

An important result is that the exemptions do not protect the providers of exempted services against litigation, most notably in the form of injunctive relief, the availability of which will depend on the law of the Member States.[745] An early version of the ECD proposal did contain an EU level restriction on injunctive relief—for online intermediaries within the scope of Articles 12, 13 or 14 ECD—to prohibitory injunctions. As Koelman explains, this restriction could be interpreted to prevent court orders that would require affirmative steps to prevent future unlawful third-party activities.[746] The final text of the Directive, however, does not restrict injunctive relief. In fact, recital 45 clarifies that the Directive does *not affect the possibility of injunctions of different kinds.* The room for injunctive relief, which depends on the law of the Member States, should of course respect the demands of Article 10 ECHR and similar safeguards of the right to freedom of expression at the national level.

The question is how search engines fit into the EU's intermediary liability regulation. The European Court of Justice has recently started to interpret the scope of the safe harbors as applied to search services and the European Commission launched a consultation in 2010 that specifically addresses the issue of search engine intermediary liability. However, before discussing these more recent legal developments it is important to examine the legislative background of the intermediary liability framework in the EU, the U.S. and the EU Member States regarding the treatment of search engines.

The ECD does cover search engines as information society services, as can be seen in recital 18:

> [I]nformation society services are not solely restricted to services giving rise to on-line contracting but also, in so far as they represent an economic activity, extend to services which are not remunerated by those who receive them, such as those offering on-line information or commercial communications, or those providing tools allowing for search, access and retrieval of data [...].[747]

---

745. See Spindler & Verbiest, 20–23.
746. See Koelman 2000, 38–39, 48–68.
747. Council Directive 2000/31, 2000 OJ (L 178) 1 (EC), pmbl. § 18. See also ECJ March 23, 2010, Joined Cases C-236/08 to C-238/08 (*Google Adwords*), § 110.

Seen in its proper context, Article 21 ECD on the re-examination by the European Commission suggests that search engines (information location tools) and hyperlinks are not covered by the intermediary liability regime of the Directive. Article 21.2 ECD provides as follows:

> in examining the need for an adaptation of this Directive, the report shall in particular analyse the need for proposals concerning the liability of providers of hyperlinks and location tool services [...].[748]

This provision was added to the European Commission's proposal for the Directive as a result of an amendment by the European Parliament.[749]

The legislative history of the Directive does not clarify why search engines were not specifically included in the intermediary liability regime.[750] The safe harbors in the ECD are modeled on the safe harbors in the U.S. Digital Millennium Copyright Act, adopted two years earlier in the United States. The DMCA, however, does contain a specific safe harbor for hyperlinking and information location tools in 17 U.S.C. § 512(d). Apparently, it was not politically viable in the EU to extend the harmonized safe harbor regime to hyperlinks and search media. Surely, the regime of Articles 12–15 can be seen as a compromise between the interests of the major stakeholders involved in the preparatory stages of the legislative proposal.[751] Since search engines were less dominant players at the time of drafting and were predominantly U.S.-based, it is conceivable that they were not involved or considered in these preparatory stages. If anything, the EU safe harbor compromise in the ECD mostly settled intermediary liability for traditional access and hosting intermediary activities. Search engines, selection intermediaries more generally and other (more active) types of hosting intermediaries, such as online marketplaces, for instance eBay or user-created content aggregators such as YouTube, were not as developed as they are now. The extent to which these other intermediaries can assert a legislative safe harbor also remains the subject of intense debate and litigation at the national and European level.

9.3.3.　Intermediary Liability of Search Engines in the United States

If we look at the United States, for comparison, there are a number of interesting similarities and differences, particularly with regard to the position of search

---

748. Council Directive 2000/31, 2000 OJ (L 178) 1 (EC), Article 21(2).
749. European Commission 1999.
750. See also Spindler & Verbiest 2007, 86–99.
751. For the European Commission's reaction on a few of the amendments by the European Parliament to the proposed liability regime of the Commission, see European Commission 1999, 7 ('as regards amendments concerning the liability of intermediaries (45 to 49, 53 and 54) which is a very important and sensitive area [...] a particular effort was made in the original proposal, in close consultation with the interested parties, to achieve a reasonable compromise solution that takes due account of all interests at stake').

engines. As discussed in Chapter 6, the U.S. Congress introduced two separate branches of intermediary liability regulation in the first major round of Internet legislation at the end of the last century.[752] Unlike the European safe harbors discussed above, the U.S. safe harbor regime is therefore not horizontal, resulting in a complicated set of different liability exemptions for different types of laws. And unlike the EU safe harbors, both safe harbors extend to search engines and hyperlinks.

One set of safe harbors was introduced by the Digital Millennium Copyright Act (DMCA) of 1998 and can be found in 17 U.S.C. § 512.[753] The respective safe harbor for hyperlinking and search engines in section 512(d) introduces a reactive notice and takedown obligation as a condition for protection against monetary liability for copyright infringements by third parties, as follows:

17 U.S.C. § 512 (d) Information location tools.

A service provider shall not be liable for monetary relief, or, except as provided in subsection (j), for injunctive or other equitable relief, for infringement of copyright by reason of the provider referring or linking users to an online location containing infringing material or infringing activity, by using information location tools, including a directory, index, reference, pointer, or hypertext link, if the service provider—

(1) (A) does not have actual knowledge that the material or activity is infringing;
(B) in the absence of such actual knowledge, is not aware of facts or circumstances from which infringing activity is apparent; or
C) upon obtaining such knowledge or awareness, acts expeditiously to remove, or disable access to, the material;

(2) does not receive a financial benefit directly attributable to the infringing activity, in a case in which the service provider has the right and ability to control such activity; and

(3) upon notification of claimed infringement as described in subsection (c)(3), responds expeditiously to remove, or disable access to, the material that is claimed to be infringing or to be the subject of infringing activity, except that, for purposes of this paragraph, the information described in subsection (c)(3)(A)(iii) shall be identification of the reference or link, to material or activity claimed to be infringing, that is to be removed or access to which is

---

752. For a recent discussion of safe harbors in the United States, see Lemley 2007. Lemley argues for an integration of existing safe harbors into one safe harbor with horizontal effect. With regard to the European safe harbors, he concludes that they have been a failure: "While the EC's 2000 Electronic Commerce Directive provides for some safe harbors, they do not appear to have been working, at least as implemented in national legislation and the courts." *Ibid.*, 22–23.

753. For a discussion of the application of the DMCA safe harbors to search engines, see Walker 2004.

to be disabled, and information reasonably sufficient to permit the service provider to locate that reference or link.[754]

Subsection (j) restricts the availability of injunctive relief, for mere conduit, hosting and other intermediaries. For search engines, injunctive relief is restricted by 17 U.S.C. § 512(j)(1)(A)(iii) to relief that:

> the court may consider necessary to prevent or restrain infringement of copyrighted material specified in the order of the court at a particular online location, if such relief is the least burdensome to the service provider among the forms of relief comparably effective for that purpose.

In addition, 17 U.S.C. § 512(j)(2) lists four specific considerations a court has to account for when considering injunctive relief on intermediaries that fall within the safe harbor framework. In particular, the consideration in 17 U.S.C. § 512(j)(2)(C) seemingly takes into account concerns related to the right to freedom of expression. Under U.S. law, Courts have to take the following into account:

> whether implementation of such an injunction would be technically feasible and effective, and would not interfere with access to noninfringing material at other online locations.

As mentioned above, similar restrictions on injunctive relief are absent in the Directive on Electronic Commerce.

For other types of illegal content, such as for defamation, the safe harbor for intermediaries is provided by the Communications Decency Act (CDA) (47 U.S.C. § 230). The scope of CDA, Section 230 can be found in 230(e), which provides that Section 230 is superior to State law and has no effect on criminal law, intellectual property law and communications privacy law. As was discussed in Chapter 6, CDA 230 provides a safe harbor to a broad class of intermediaries, defined as interactive computer services, ranging from access providers to discussion boards and search engines.[755] The case law about the scope of the safe harbor has followed the Fourth Circuit's conclusion in *Zeran* that "[b]y its plain language, § 230 creates a federal immunity to any cause of action that would make service providers liable for information originating with a third-party user of the service".[756]

The legislative purpose of CDA section 230 was also to take away legal incentives for intermediaries not to interfere with illegal and harmful third-party content, indecency in particular, hence its title the 'Good Samaritan Defense'.[757] Furthermore, the immunity provided by CDA 230 is absolute in the sense that it

---

754. 17 U.S.C. § 512(d). There is a growing body of case law interpreting the safe harbors in the DMCA, including section (d). See e.g., *Capitol Records, Inc. v. MP3Tunes, LLC*, 2011 WL 3667335 (S.D.N.Y. August 22, 2011).
755. CDA, Section 230(c)(1).
756. *Zeran v. AOL*, 129 F.3d 327 (4th Cir. 1997), at 330, Certiorari denied, 524 U.S. 937 (1998).
757. See *Zeran v. AOL*, 129 F.3d 327 (4th Cir. 1997) ("in enacting § 230, Congress sought 'to encourage service providers to self-regulate the dissemination of offensive material over their services' and to remove disincentives to self-regulation").

does not include a notice and takedown obligation. Even after obtaining knowledge about specific instances of third-party illegal material on its service, a search engine would not be liable if it decided *not* to remove it or prevent access to it. Hence, CDA 230 not only protects interactive computer services from being treated as publishers but also protects them against being treated as distributors.[758] Finally, although CDA 230 does not cover liability based on criminal law, it is generally interpreted to protect against all State laws, including State criminal laws and also against civil law claims based on federal criminal statutes. The remaining space for criminal liability of search engines and intermediaries more generally is probably limited.[759] Electronic communications privacy legislation is also excluded and has its own rules regarding the responsibility of electronic communications' service providers for the use of their services for harassment or similar problems.

The two branches of intermediary liability regulation in the United States do not provide the complete framework for search engine intermediary liability. Trademark infringement is neither covered by the DMCA, nor by the Communications Decency Act. For trademark liability, the Lanham Act contains what could be called a safe harbor in section 1114(2) for the category of 'innocent infringers'. This category could include search engines.[760]

9.3.4.   SEARCH ENGINE INTERMEDIARY LIABILITY IN EUROPE
          AT THE NATIONAL LEVEL

To complete the picture of search engine liability regulation from the European perspective, it is necessary to say something about the treatment of search engine intermediary liability at the level of the various Member States. The absence of a search engine specific safe harbor at the EU level from the intermediary liability regulation in the ECD has led to divergent treatment of search engines by legislatures and the judiciary in the various Member States of the EU. It is important to note that the ECD does not provide for full harmonization of intermediary liability exemptions. There were amendments in this direction by the European Parliament, but they are not included in the final text of the ECD.[761] Therefore, the ECD has left room for the Member States to extend the safe harbors to search engine

---

758. A Court of Appeal's decision that argued otherwise (namely that CDA 230 does not affect common law distributor liability standard for defamation) was subsequently struck down by the Californian Supreme Court in *Barret v. Rosenthal*. See *Barrett v. Rosenthal*, 40 Cal. 4th 33, 146 P.3d 510 (Cal. 2006).
759. In 2011, Google settled for USD 500 million with the U.S. Department of Justice in a criminal accomplice liability case against Google, involving the advertisement, targeting and sales of pharmaceuticals to U.S. citizens though the AdWords program. See Henning 2011.
760. See Lemley 2007. See also JOLT 2005.
761. See European Parliament 1999, 26 ('The limitations on liability established by Articles 12, 13 and 14 are exhaustive') and European Parliament 1999, 58, 82 (Amendments 22 and 16 by the Committee on Economic and Monetary Affairs and Industrial Policy and the Committee on Culture, Youth, Education and the Media respectively).

providers and other intermediaries. According to the European Commission's first report on the application of the ECD, this room has been used by a few Member States, including Spain, Portugal, Austria and EEA-member Liechtenstein.[762] The new EU Member States, Hungary and Poland, also extended the limitation on liability for providers of hosting services to information location tools.[763] Some national courts have, similar to the ECJ, applied the hosting safe harbor to search engines.[764] The absence of a search engine-specific safe harbor at the EU level also means that Article 15 ECD does not obviously apply in the context of search engines. This would mean that EU law does not stand in the way of national legal preventive duties of care or duties to monitor on search engine providers. It is to be noted that it is quite possible that Article 15 is merely a restatement of general legal principles which are already recognized at the national level. The same is actually true for Articles 12–14 ECD.[765]

In the remainder of this section, some notable developments in different European countries with regard to search engine intermediary liability regulation will be addressed, as well as the more recent case law of the ECJ about the scope of the hosting safe harbor. The latter is significant for the legal framework for search engines as the ECJ leaves room for the view that search engines are within the scope of Article 14 ECD.

The overview of national developments is far from comprehensive.[766] Instead, it functions as an overview to allow for a subsequent discussion about the merits of the legislative and different legal solutions from the perspective of freedom of expression. First, the choice of some legislatures to explicitly extend the safe harbors from the Directive to search engines will be discussed. After which, some notable case law in the Member States in which search engine liability was left unaddressed in the implementation of the Directive on Electronic Commerce will be addressed. The section will conclude with a discussion of more recent developments at the EU level, namely the European Commission review of the Directive and the case law of the ECJ about the scope of Article 14 ECD.

---

762. See European Commission 2003.
763. See 2001. évi CVIII Törvény az elektronikus kereskedelmi szolgáltatások, valamint az információs társadalommal összefüggő szolgáltatások egyes kérdéseiről [Act CVIII of 2001 on Electronic Commercial Services and Certain Legal Aspects of Information Society Services] (promulgated December 24, 2001), Magyar Közlöny [Hungarian Gazette] 2001/153; Ustawa z dnia 18 lipca 2002 r. o świadczeniu usług drogą elektroniczną [Law of July 28, 2002 Concerning the Provision of Electronic Services] (entered into force March 10, 2003), Dziennik Ustaw [Official Journal] 2002, no. 144, item 1204, available at http://www.nowemedia.home.pl/nuke/modules.php?name=Sections&op=viewarticle&artid=6 (Poland).
764. See section 9.3.5.
765. ECJ, Opinion Advocate-General Jääkinen, December 9, 2010, C-324/09 (*eBay*), § 136.
766. It does not include a discussion of the (complicated) situation in France. For a discussion, see Joslove & Krylov 2005. For example, a French court has concluded that Digg-like selection intermediaries can be held liable for third-party references to unlawful third-party publications. T.G.I. Paris, March 26, 2008. See also Spindler & Verbiest 2007.

Austria has adopted a search engine liability exemption modeled on the mere conduit safe harbor of Article 12 ECD.[767] It is interesting to note that in the Austrian government's initial proposal, the safe harbor was modeled on the hosting exemption of Article 14, which is similar to the safe harbor for search engines in the DMCA. Various stakeholders responded to the initial choice of the Austrian government with a range of arguments against treating search engine providers as hosting providers. It was argued that search engines are not the source of the information they link to and are not in the position to remove it from the Web.[768] The Austrian legislature changed the proposal into the mere conduit regime.

The Spanish legislature chose to adopt the hosting regime of Article 14 for unlawful results of search engine providers.[769] The Spanish law contains one provision for providers of hosting and search engine services. A hosting or search engine provider is not held liable for resulting damages if it does not have knowledge of the illegal nature of the information. The exemption requires that it act expeditiously if it obtains such knowledge. The Spanish implementation has been praised for providing legal certainty for search engines.[770]

However, the safe harbor does not protect search engines against administrative orders and litigation seeking injunctive relief. In 2011, for instance, the Spanish Data Protection Authority, which is charged with overseeing compliance with the EU Privacy Directive (95/46/EC), ordered Google to stop referencing to allegedly defamatory Spanish newspaper articles.[771] Google has challenged the administrative order to remove a hundred links in Spanish court, which has reportedly led to referral to the ECJ.[772] Most remarkably, the articles themselves, some of which are authored by major Spanish newspaper *El Pais*, and others, including official government reports published in the interest of transparency, are not the subject of litigation and are not proven to be defamatory or privacy-infringing in court. In fact, the Spanish Data Protection Authority has no power to request their removal from the sites themselves but merely seeks to limit the alleged damage of the allegedly defamatory articles through obscuring their existence in search engines.[773] In its defense against the order, Google explicitly refers to the profound chilling effect of the order on the right to freedom of expression. Spanish

---

767. Bundesgesetz: Regelung bestimmter rechtlicher Aspekte des elektronischen Geschäfts- und Rechtsverkehrs [E-Commerce Gesetz—ECG] [Law on Electronic Commerce] Bundesgesetz-blatt [BGBl] I No. 152/2001 (Austria).
768. For a discussion of the Austrian debate about the proper safe harbor in Austria, see van Hoboken 2009.
769. See Article 17 of Law 34/2002 on Information Society Services and Electronic Commerce (Ley 34/2002 de Servicios de la Sociedad de la Información y de Comercio Electronicó) of July 12, 2002 (B.O.E. 2002, 166) (Spain). For a short overview of the Spanish implementation of the Directive on Electronic Commerce, see Julia-Barceló 2002. See also Peguera 2009.
770. See Julia-Barceló 2002.
771. See Halliday 2011a.
772. See Halliday 2011b. See also Fleischer 2011. The court still had to make the actual reference at the time this study was finalized.
773. For a discussion, see section 8.5.4.

authorities, in turn, claim that the respective individuals have a right to be forgotten, a concept which has been made central in the review of the EU Privacy Directive by the European Commission.[774] However, the idea that search engines could be ordered to remove material from their index while the actual publication of this material should be considered legal is not consistent with the freedom of search engine providers to publish references as protected by Article 10 ECHR and the protected interests of information providers to freely find their way to an audience through search engines.[775]

In Germany, the ECD is implemented through the federal Telemediengesetz (TMG), amended in 2007. Articles 8–10 of the TMG do not contain limitations on liability for hyperlink and location tool providers, similar to the initial law implementing the Directive on Electronic Commerce, the Teledienstegesetz of 2002. Search engines, through the FSM, have expressly asked to extend the framework to search engines and to adopt the Austrian solution, but the German legislature has not acted on this industry plea (which explicitly refers to the value of a search engine specific safe harbor for the realization of the right to freedom of expression).[776] As a consequence, the liability of search engines is governed by general laws, applied by German courts in an increasingly complex body of case law.[777] Of special concern in the debate in Germany has been the question of the possibility of preventive duties of care on search engines, imposed on the basis of the German tort law doctrine of 'accessory liability' (*Störerhaftung*), which could result in obligations on search engines to filter or actively monitor specific unlawful references they might refer to.

The Dutch legislature transposed Articles 12–15 almost literally into the Dutch Civil Code.[778] In the absence of legislation and in view of the different outcomes of legal proceedings, the liability of search engines is a difficult, possibly open, issue in Dutch law.[779] Until today, the Dutch government or Parliament has not discussed the issue of hyperlink or search engine liability. Case law with regard to search engine (secondary) liability is scarce.[780] Dutch courts deal with questions about search engine liability and possible duties of care to remove references through general tort law principles, which tends to lead to a standard amounting to a safe harbor similar to that of hosting providers. Only after obtaining knowledge

---

774. OUT-LAW.COM 2011. See also Reding 2011, 4; Werro 2009.
775. See section 8.5.4.
776. See FSM 2007.
777. For an overview and discussion of search engine liability in Germany, see Spindler & Verbiest 2007, Annex D (Germany). See also Sieber & Liesching 2007; Ruess 2007; Ott 2008, Ott 2009.
778. Aanpassingswet richtlijn inzake elektronische handel [Implementation Law Directive on Electronic Commerce], Stb. 2004, 210 (Neth.). The limitations on civil liability can be found in the Dutch Civil Code, Article 6:196c.
779. For a discussion, see van Hoboken 2008.
780. Vzr. Rechtbank [District Court] Amsterdam April 26, 2007 (*Jensen*), Rechtbank [District Court] Haarlem May 12, 2004 (*Zoekmp3*), Gerechtshof [Court of Appeals] Amsterdam, June 15, 2006 (*Zoekmp3*).

from which the unlawfulness of a reference is apparent would there be a duty of care on search engines to remove the reference from the index.

The United Kingdom transposed the Directive on Electronic Commerce into national law in 2002 with the Electronic Commerce Regulations 2002 and did not insert additional exemptions for providers of hyperlinks and information location tools.[781] In the end of 2006, the U.K. government conducted a review of the intermediary liability regime specifically addressing the question of whether the existing safe harbors should be extended to providers of hyperlinks, location tools and content aggregation services.[782] The government received a predictably mixed response to its questionnaire and concluded that there was, at that point, insufficient evidence to justify an extension of the limitations on liability at the national level.[783] More specifically, the U.K. government concluded that the issue should be dealt with at the EU level by the European Commission in its review of the Directive.

9.3.5.   DEVELOPMENTS AT THE EU LEVEL AND THE ECJ

Article 21 of the Directive instructs the European Commission to conduct a biannual report on the application of the Directive. The report must contain an analysis of the need for proposals concerning the liability of providers of hyperlinks and location tool services.[784] In the report of 2003, concluding the first and only review thus far, the European Commission concluded that there was no reason to amend the existing intermediary liability rules with regard to search engines.[785] The Commission did note diverging legislative choices and wrote the following about legal developments with regard to search engine liability:

> It is encouraging that recent case-law in the Member States recognizes the importance of linking and search engines to the functioning of the Internet. In general, this case-law appears to be in line with the Internal Market objective to ensure the provision of basic intermediary services, which promotes the development of the Internet and e-commerce. Consequently, this case-law does not appear to give rise to any Internal Market concerns.[786]

Of course, the Directive was rather new and some Member States had not yet implemented it at the time of the review. The Commission subsequently placed the issue on the agenda of the next review. In 2010, the Commission finally launched a public consultation which will perhaps lead to an official review of the Directive.

---

781. Electronic Commerce Regulations, 2002, S.I. 2002/2013. For a critical discussion of the U.K. legislative choices with regard to intermediary liability, see Turner et al. 2003.
782. See DTI 2005.
783. See DTI 2006.
784. Article 21(2), Council Directive 2000/31, 2000 OJ (L 178) 1 (EC).
785. European Commission 2003, 22.
786. European Commission 2003, 13.

The consultation pays special attention to the question of intermediary liability, including the position of search engines in the EU safe harbor framework.[787]

The short overview in the previous section clarifies that there is significant divergence between the Member States with regard to the liability of search engines for unlawful references. This state of affairs has consistently led researchers to conclude that search engine liability in the EU is in a worrisome state and should be amended.[788] In fact, it is hard to disagree with Google's submission in response to the consultation:

> the law in this area is in tatters. Harmony across the EU is non-existent. There is no clarity for users, information society services or the courts.[789]

In the mean time, the European Court of Justice has started to answer prejudicial questions about the scope of the safe harbors in the ECD. However, it is unfortunate that the ECJ may have added to the confusion by concluding that search engines— at least with regard to sponsored links—could actually assert the protection of the hosting safe harbor, instead of concluding that the ECD does not harmonize search engine intermediary liability. In addition, the ECJ has restricted the EU safe harbors to intermediary activities of a *merely technical, automatic and passive nature*, a formula which is based on recital 42 of the Directive. A short review of the ECJ's main conclusions as well as the corresponding opinions of the Advocates General can be instructive to show the confusion about the scope of intermediary liability regulation at the EU level.

The first case touching on search engine liability to reach the ECJ was the Google AdWords case. This case was referred to the Court by the French *Cour de Cassation* in proceedings between Google France and Louis Vuitton. The case deals with the widely litigated question of whether a search engine can be held legally accountable for trademark infringements in sponsored search results.[790] Amongst the prejudicial questions was the question whether:

> the provider of the paid referencing service be regarded as providing an information society service consisting in the storage of information provided by the recipient of the service, within the meaning of Article 14 of [Directive 2000/31], so that that provider cannot incur liability before it has been informed by the trademark proprietor of the unlawful use of the sign by the advertiser?[791]

In his opinion, Advocate-General Maduro answers this question in the negative. As he rightly concludes, search engines do qualify as information society services. His analysis on this point is complicated somewhat by his consideration of the claim

---

787. European Commission 2010b. For instance, question 63 asks submitters to inform the European Commission about their experience with search engine liability in the Member States.
788. See e.g. Spindler & Verbiest 2007. See also van Hoboken 2009.
789. See Google 2010a.
790. See also ECJ March 26, 2010, C-91/09 (*EIS.de*), ECJ July 8, 2010, C-558/08 (*Portakabin*) and ECJ, Advocate-General Jääskinen, March 24, 2011, C-323/09 (*Interflora*).
791. ECJ March 23, 2010, Joined Cases C-236/08 to C-238/08 (Google Adwords).

that Article 21 ECD may be interpreted as meaning that search engines are not covered by the ECD at all. Usually, Article 21 ECD is used as evidence that the Directive does not provide for a search-specific safe harbor.[792] With regard to the question whether Google can assert the protection of the hosting safe harbor for its AdWords service, the Advocate-General relies on the nature of Google's relationship with advertisers to conclude that it cannot. In his opinion, Google is no longer a *neutral information vehicle* when providing the AdWords service, because it has a "direct interest in Internet users clicking on the ads' links."[793] The Advocate-General derives this neutrality requirement from Article 15 of the Directive, which is, in his view, "the very expression of the principle that service providers which seek to benefit from a liability exemption should remain neutral as regards the information they carry or host."[794] The opinion concludes that with regard to its organic results Google does, in fact, fulfill this neutrality requirement, on the basis of the following argument:

> [Google's] natural results are a product of automatic algorithms that apply objective criteria in order to generate sites likely to be of interest to the Internet user. The presentation of those sites and the order in which they are ranked depends on their relevance to the keywords entered, and not on Google's interest in or relationship with any particular site. Admittedly, Google has an interest—even a pecuniary interest—in displaying the more relevant sites to the Internet user; however, it does not have an interest in bringing any specific site to the Internet user's attention.[795]

Chapter 8 of this thesis concludes that search engines are not neutral by nature, since they actively match information providers and end-users and this active role with regard to the valuation of different online destinations for users is what helps make one search engine more valuable than another.[796] Since indifference to the value of information or an online destination offering goods or services would run contrary to the role of search engines for end-users, it would be wrong to use this as a criteria for a search engine liability safe harbor.

The ECJ does not follow this logic of the Advocate-General with regard to the scope of Article 14 of the Directive. The Court first explains that the hosting safe harbor in Article 14 ECD

> applies to cases "[w]here an information society service is provided that consists of the storage of information provided by a recipient of the service" and means that the provider of such a service cannot be held liable for the data which it has stored at the request of a recipient of that service unless that

---

792. See e.g. Spindler & Verbiest 2007. See also van Hoboken 2009a.
793. ECJ, Opinion Advocate General Maduro, September 22, 2009, Joined Cases C-236/08 to C-238/08 (*Google Adwords*), § 145.
794. *Ibid.*, § 143. It is notable that the word 'neutral' does not appear in the Directive at all. See also Walden 2010.
795. *Ibid.*, § 144.
796. See section 8.4.

service provider, after having become aware, because of information supplied by an injured party or otherwise, of the unlawful nature of those data or of activities of that recipient, fails to act expeditiously to remove or to disable access to those data.[797]

In the Court's view, the storage of *the keywords selected by the advertiser, the advertising link and the accompanying commercial message, as well as the address of the advertiser's site* on the request of the recipient of the service, i.e. the advertiser, falls within the scope of this provision.[798] The Court does not take into account Article 21 ECD. The ECJ then concludes that to profit from the safe harbors a service provider's conduct "should be limited to that of an 'intermediary service provider' within the meaning intended by the legislature in the context of Section 4 of that directive."[799] It then states that:

> it follows from recital 42 in the preamble to Directive 2000/31 that the exemptions from liability established in that directive cover only cases in which the activity of the information society service provider is "of a mere technical, automatic and passive nature", which implies that that service provider "has neither knowledge of nor control over the information which is transmitted or stored".
>
> 114. Accordingly [...], it is necessary to examine whether the role played by that service provider is neutral, in the sense that its conduct is merely technical, automatic and passive, pointing to a lack of knowledge or control of the data which it stores.[800]

While mentioning a number of circumstances that must be considered irrelevant—the mere fact that service is subject to payment—as well as some circumstances that must be considered relevant—the role of the search engine in drafting the message or the selection of keywords that trigger the advertisement—the ECJ concludes that the national courts are in the best position to make the final assessment whether the provider's conduct is actually protected by Article 14 ECD.

In the *AdWords* case, the ECJ does not address the question of the extent to which organic results would face a similar treatment and it avoids using the terms 'search engine' and 'information location tool' altogether. However, its conclusions directly imply that all EU safe harbors are conditional on the cited criteria of recital 42 ECD. Moreover, the Court's considerations directly impact the state of affairs of search engine liability in the Member States. National legislatures which assumed that the ECD did not affect search engine liability and provided for a specific safe harbor at the national level are confronted with the situation that search engines may end up being covered by the safe harbors at the EU level in a way their legislation did not anticipate. The same is true for national courts. In Germany, for instance, courts considered themselves unconstrained by the

---

797. ECJ March 23, 2010, Joined Cases C-236/08 to C-238/08 (*Google Adwords*), § 109.
798. *Ibid.*, § 111.
799. *Ibid.*, § 112.
800. *Ibid.*, §§ 113–114.

Directive in their interpretation of national legal rules with regard to search engine liability for third-party content.[801]

One explanation that the European Court's application of the wording of recital 42 in the context of the hosting safe harbor may have been a mistake has come from within the institution itself, namely from Advocate-General Jääskinen in the case between L'Oréal and eBay. The A-G points out that the safe harbors referred to in recital 42 solely concern the exemptions relating to 'mere conduit' and 'caching' and warns the Court against further attachment of recital 42 to the hosting safe harbor in Article 14.[802] In addition, he concludes that the 'neutrality' test is not the right test to decide on the scope of the hosting safe harbor in Article 14 ECD.[803] In its judgment, however, the ECJ does not follow this opinion and restates its conclusion in *Google AdWords* that an intermediary's service falls outside of the scope of the EU safe harbors, when it does the following:

> instead of confining itself to providing that service neutrally by a merely technical and automatic processing of the data provided by its customers, plays an active role of such a kind as to give it knowledge of, or control over, those data [...].[804]

Similar to the *Google AdWords* case, the ECJ adds a number of considerations which national courts have to take into account when answering this question. Amongst these considerations, of specific concern for search engine providers is the ECJ's conclusion that an intermediary service provider that has an active role in 'optimising the presentation of the offers for sale' would lose the protection of the hosting safe harbor.[805]

9.4. INTERMEDIARY LIABILITY REGULATION OF SEARCH ENGINES AND FREEDOM OF EXPRESSION

9.4.1. INTRODUCTION

What is at stake from the perspective of freedom of expression in the context of intermediary liability of search engines? Freedom of expression enters the considerations about appropriate third-party liability standards in a number of ways.[806] First, a clear legal framework for search engine providers for one of the most significant legal issues and related risks in operating a search service, namely third-party liability, facilitates a proper market for these services. Since search

---

801. See e.g. Schubert & Ott 2010, 85–88.
802. ECJ, Opinion Advocate General Maduro, September 22, 2009, Joined Cases C-236/08 to C-238/08 (*Google Adwords*), § 142. For a discussion, see Brömmekamp 2011; Van Eecke & Truyens 2011; Schubert & Ott 2010.
803. ECJ, Opinion Advocate-General Jääskinen, December 9, 2010, C-324/09 (*eBay*), § 146.
804. ECJ July 12, 2011, C-324/09 (*eBay*), at 113.
805. *Ibid.*, at 116.
806. See also the discussion of liability of Internet access providers in section 6.4.

engines are an essential element in the public information environment, the offering of such services should clearly not be hampered by legal uncertainty, but rather facilitated instead. Second, because of their facilitative role with respect to the communicative freedom of third parties, end-users and information providers in particular, the right to freedom of expression is inconsistent with extensive duties of care on search engines with regard to allegedly unlawful references, preventive duties of care to monitor unlawful content in particular. Such duties of care would incentivize search engine providers to restrict legal information flows to limit their legal risks of liability and would therefore have a predictable chilling effect on the effective enjoyment of the right to freedom of expression in the online environment. For these reasons, it is preferable to restrict the liability of search services to instances where a high level of fault can be established. The First Amendment standard developed in *Sullivan* for the press acting as an intermediary can serve as an excellent example of this generally accepted principle.[807] Finally, in the absence of clear legal standards regarding their proper legal obligations for the references in their indices, search engines could be incentivized to enter into restrictive self-regulation, for instance through filtering.[808]

The first aspect mentioned above should not be overlooked. Freedom of expression and communication is served by the freedom of communications and information service providers to actually provide their services online. The ECD also recognizes this in recital 9.[809] Proper legal certainty for, and the free movement of, search engine services in the European internal market would serve the right to freedom of expression because it would facilitate the actual offering of such services. The apparent confusion regarding third-party liability of search engines at the EU and Member State level can only be considered problematic from this perspective. In addition, a legal framework which would facilitate and stimulate the offering of a variety of search engines in the EU internal market could serve search engine choice and diversity. Dominant search engine providers such as Google are likely to be in a better position to deal with costly litigation or fulfill extensive duties of care imposed upon them.

As to the second aspect, the substance of the third-party liability standard for search engine providers, it is generally accepted that liability for third-party material can lead to chilling effects on lawful communications. A search engine provider has an economic incentive to minimize legal liability. The best evidence of the chilling effect on search engine providers is provided by studies of the way search engines respond to notices of unlawful references under the DMCA safe harbor. This safe harbor requires that unlawful references are removed upon obtaining knowledge thereof through specific notifications, a requirement that major U.S.-based search engines adhere to on a global level. Empirical evidence shows that search engine

---

807. Tushnet 2008. See also section 5.3.2.
808. See sections 9.2.2 and 9.2.2.
809. See section 6.4.6.

providers may overreact to notices of unlawful references.[810] The search provider has to make a determination of the merits of the notification: is the reference truly unlawful? This determination is not easy and involves a prediction of what a judge would ultimately rule on the merits. The provider has to strike a balance between the risk of being too responsive to notices, thereby obstructing legal information flows and diminishing the social utility of its service, and the risk of being too restrictive in responding to such notices, thereby not fulfilling the condition of the safe harbor and becoming liable.

Preventive duties of care not to provide references to unlawful material ever would basically mean that search engines would have to take strict editorial responsibility for the references provided by their services. The only way providers could be able to escape continuing risks of third-party liability would be to review every reference in their index. The typical open governance of search engines, in which reliance is placed on billions of third-party signals, would be impossible. Moreover, search engines would probably start to use Internet content filters and additional human review of every reference. In view of the number of websites that are typically included in the index of general purpose search engines, this could mean that the index of general purpose search engines would be drastically reduced. And the dynamic nature of websites would pose an additional problem, possibly leading to whitelisting instead of general indexing of the Web. In short, general purpose search engines, as we know them, would be made legally impossible.

It is also clear that in the case of search engines' services, some balance needs to be struck between the freedom of expression interests addressed in detail in this study and the need to enforce copyright law, defamation and privacy law and other laws imposing restrictions on information flows. It seems safe to assume that Web publishing will remain free and the barriers to entry will remain low. Prior restraints on the mere possibility to start a website are themselves unacceptable from the perspective of freedom of expression. At the same time, it is hard to argue against the assumption that some end-users will use this freedom to publish illegal or unlawful material online. General purpose search engines will subsequently crawl such websites and make them more widely available for a worldwide audience. Hence, a balance has to be struck between compromising information retrieval for the Web and the Internet more generally on the one hand and accepting access to unlawful references in search engines on the other hand.

It is clear that when deciding on the proper boundaries of search engine liability for third-party material the right to freedom of expression is not the only concern. As was mentioned above, there are a variety of reasons why references might be legally problematic and their removal from search engines may be argued to be desirable. Search engines do, as a result of the way they operate, provide references to material that may cause harm to a variety of third parties. To better understand the way a balance is and could be struck, it is important to understand the reasons for requiring search engines to remove such references in the first place. To arrive at this understanding, the next section will discuss the liability

---

810. Urban & Quilter 2006.

of search engines for references to unauthorized copies of creative works on the one hand and the liability of search engines for referring users to defamatory content and unlawfully published private information on the other hand.

9.4.2.   SEARCH ENGINE LIABILITY, FREEDOM OF EXPRESSION
            AND COPYRIGHT INFRINGING MATERIAL

The Internet and the Web facilitate the unlawful dissemination of copyright-protected works in various ways, a full discussion of which is far beyond the scope of this study.[811] What is clear, however, is that the effectiveness of the various dissemination models for creative content partly relies on the availability of an effective system to provide for findability of the content that is actually available for sharing. The World Wide Web (in combination with search engines) is uniquely qualified to facilitate access to creative works. If a band publishes one of their songs on their website, it becomes available to a global audience. The same is true, however, if someone other than the copyright owner posts an unauthorized copy of a song online. Leaving aside the possible constraints on bandwidth of the respective website, the only thing that could stand in the way of a global audience having effective access to the unlawfully published material is the absence of an effective means to find it: a search engine. Hence, search engines typically end up facilitating the accessibility of unlawfully published creative works, such as movies, music and written material.

To strike a balance between the need for effective information location tools and the interests of rights holders, the U.S. Congress provided for the specific safe harbor for information location tools in the DMCA, discussed in the previous section.[812] In contrast, such a specific safe harbor for information location tools in the context of intermediary liability for copyright infringements was not adopted at the European level. Instead, the legal responsibility for carrying references to unauthorized copies of copyright-protected material depends on the law of the Member State. In practice, the lack of a harmonized legal standard with respect to copyright infringements in the EU is compensated by the fact that all major general purpose search engines do not restrict their DMCA policies to the U.S. context but comply with all notices about copyright infringement, as if the DMCA safe harbor were applicable on a global level.

Hence, in practice, notifications to general purpose search engines such as Google or Bing of references linking to copyright infringing material will usually lead to their removal. The fact that there has been no well-publicized case law in Europe about intermediary liability of general purpose search engines for references linking to copyright infringing material is evidence of a generally accepted status quo between rights holders and dominant search engines that is in line with the policy prescribed by the DMCA.

---

811.   See e.g. Stamatoudi 2010; Huygen et al. 2009.
812.   Section 9.3.3.

From the European perspective, it is important to reflect on the question of whether the DMCA is the lowest common denominator, or whether general purpose search engines based in the United States are exporting a free speech-friendly standard to the rest of the world. The absence of a safe harbor at the European level implies that national law has to be as strict in its treatment of search engines as U.S. law. Dutch law maximally requires general purpose search engines to remove references to infringing material, if they are 'unmistakably infringing'.[813] It can be argued that this allows for a less responsive treatment of notifications of copyright infringement by general purpose search engines as required under the DMCA, which does not include similar wording 'unmistakably' to prevent legal content from being removed. And this is certainly the case under Austrian law, which treats search engines as mere conduits for the content of third parties. Hence, leaving aside the issue of jurisdiction which obviously complicates matters considerably, it is possible that from the perspective of the law of certain European Member States general purpose search engines are removing too much.

Of specific concern in the context of search engines and copyright infringements is the existence of specialized search engines for certain types of material on the Web, for instance for music files, movies, software or for the so-called torrent files which make the exchange of such material over peer-to-peer networks possible. In this context, the current status quo may more aptly be called an arms race. This arms race continues to result in plenty of litigation directed at specialized search tools, both in the United States and in Europe, with different results, a full discussion of which goes beyond the scope of this study. For instance, in the Netherlands, a Dutch Court of Appeals found search engine *Zoekmp3* to have acted unlawfully.[814] This case involved a dispute between rights holders and a provider of a crawler-based search engine specialized in links to music files on the Web. In the initial judgment, the District Court in Haarlem imposed a duty of care on *Zoekmp3* similar to the safe harbor for hosting providers. *Zoekmp3* had to remove 'unmistakably unlawful' references upon receiving notice. However, the Dutch Court of Appeals in Amsterdam ruled that the service was acting unlawfully, based on general Dutch tort law principles. The court concluded that the search engine was making its money by *structurally exploiting the availability of unauthorized mp3-files on the World Wide Web*, finding Zoekmp3 had not taken the interests of rights holders sufficiently into account.[815] The conclusion logically implies a duty for similar (vertical) search engines under Dutch law to actively prevent unlawful references from showing up in their service.[816]

---

813. See Vzr. Rechtbank [District Court] Amsterdam April 26, 2007 (*Jensen*).
814. For a discussion, see van Hoboken 2009a.
815. Gerechtshof [Court of Appeals] Amsterdam, June 15, 2006 (*Zoekmp3*).
816. The same reasoning was recently applied by the Dutch District Court of Utrecht to the popular torrent directory *Mininova*. For a discussion, see van Hoboken 2009d.

9.4.3.   SEARCH ENGINE LIABILITY, FREEDOM OF EXPRESSION AND THE
          PROTECTION OF PRIVATE LIFE AND REPUTATION

Another important reason to pressurize search engines to remove of references is the protection of privacy and the reputation of individuals. Without having to consider precise empirical evidence, it is clear that defamatory publications are posted on the Web on a daily basis and the Web is a significant source of unlawfully published personal data.[817] Search engines retrieve and include information and statements as related to natural persons in their lists of references. It is important to note that the actual harm that results from these publications typically manifests itself in the context of search results of popular search services such as Google.

It is in this context of defamation and privacy infringements through search engines that there are significant differences in the legal treatment of search engine liability between European states on the one hand and the United States on the other hand. In the United States, the absolute safe harbor for search engines in CDA 230 has resulted in a situation in which plaintiffs have no proper legal redress when confronted with unlawful information in search results. In Europe, the absence of a search engine specific safe harbor for intermediary liability implies that the legal obligations of search engines for these kinds of references will depend on the law of the Member State, while on a more fundamental level these obligations, as for the press and other types of media, will have to reflect a proper balance between the right to freedom of expression and the legally protected interests of the aggrieved person, including the right to private life as protected by Article 8 ECHR.

Consider a hypothetical example of defamation in search results, for instance an untrue statement on an online forum that 'X is an alcoholic.' The initial publication of this statement would typically be unlawful. If the online forum hosting the statement is crawled by search engines, the statement will normally show up as a reference in the search results for the query 'X'. This will become a problem if there are not many people bearing the name 'X' and the reference is prominently ranked in popular search engines.

If X were to notify the search engine provider of the unlawful reference, what should the search engine provider do? Under U.S. law, CDA section 230(c)(1) immunizes search engine providers for carrying the statement and showing the reference. The search engine could voluntarily decide to, but does not have to, remove the reference.[818] If it would remove the reference CDA section 230(c)(2) also immunizes the search engine against possible legal claims from third parties, including the website and the author of the statement.

---

817. For a discussion of the responsibility of search engines under EU data protection law, see Article 29 Data Protection Working Party 2008. See also Fleischer (Google) 2008.
818. See e.g. *Murawski v. Pataki*, 2007 WL 2781054 (S.D.N.Y. September 26, 2007).

A growing number of U.S. commentators considers the blanket immunity provided by CDA section 230 problematic.[819] Neither the provider of the discussion forum, nor the hosting service of that discussion forum, nor a provider of a search engine that would refer to the forum would be under an obligation to remove the statement.[820] As is obvious, the problems for X worsen if the website allows for anonymous postings—e.g. by not logging or registering any information, such as IP addresses, about users—and refuses to delete the statement after notification by X. There are several documented cases with this background, the most well-known cases involving the websites JuicyCampus and AutoAdmit and the defamation, harassment and threatening of two female Yale Law School students.[821] AutoAdmit provided an unedited discussion forum, did not log any information about the users of its service, and let search engines freely crawl the content on the website.

The absence of any legal duty of care on Internet intermediaries as regards damages resulting from defamation, even after specific notification of apparently unlawful speech, is exceptional. It can be interpreted as a combination of the exceptional value that is placed on the value of free speech in U.S. law,[822] combined with so-called cyberspace exceptionalism, i.e. the idea that legal governance online does not have to correspond to legal governance offline.

The situation under U.S. law, in which the victim of a privacy infringement or an act of online defamation is left without any legal remedy to get the content removed from the search engine or the platform where it is posted is quite unthinkable in Europe. In the European context, there is a clear need to strike a balance, as identified by the English court in *Metropolitan* discussed further below. This stands in stark contrast with the blanket immunity which is granted under U.S. law to a range of intermediaries. The precise duty of care of search engines, however, will depend on the national law of the Member States. Under Austrian law, search engine providers carrying the statement would be treated as mere conduits and exempted from monetary relief, even if they would have obtained knowledge of the unlawful nature of the statement. However, European safe harbors leave open the possibility of injunctive relief, which could also entail the removal of the statement from the search engine's index. Other European countries have provided for an explicit safe harbor, comparable to the safe harbor for hosting providers. In these jurisdictions, search engine providers would have to remove the website containing the defamatory statement from their indices after being specifically notified. A complicating factor in this regard is that search engine providers are not in a very good position to evaluate the defamatory nature of online

---

819. See e.g. Solove 2011.
820. Even if the author itself were to ask the website provider carrying its statement to remove it, the provider could refuse to do so. See *Sturm v. eBay, Inc.*, No. 1-06-CV-057926 (Cal. S. Ct. July 27, 2006). This seems to imply that search engines could continue carrying unlawful statements in their index even after they have been removed from the original website.
821. For a discussion, see Leiter 2011. See also Solove 2007, 149–160; Gasser & Palfrey 2010, 107; Citron 2008; Citron 2010.
822. See section 4.3.3.

content, while the massiveness of their index will have implications for their ability to respond to requests about problematic references.

A different category of search engine liability cases relating to privacy and reputation involves the manipulation of search results to attract an audience. These cases are intricately linked to the operation of search engines and their central role in the 'attention economy'. There are a number of cases which involve the manipulation of search results to attract an audience, for instance by providers of pornography websites. This manipulation typically consists of the use of popular search queries, such as the name of well-known persons in websites' text, or in their metadata. The providers (spammers) use the popularity of celebrities to manipulate search results and attract traffic. This practice is commonly referred to as spamdexing.[823]

One of such cases, in the Netherlands, involved a television hostess who complained to Google about the search results for her name.[824] A reference, titled *Urmia Jensen naakt* (Urmia Jensen naked), suggested the availability of nude material on the Web, even though no such nude material of the television hostess was available on the websites. The Dutch Court of First Instance in Amsterdam ruled out the possibility of preventive duties of care for search engine providers as regards the content of search engine results and the content of the websites referred to. It also did not consider it the duty of care of Google to remove the material from its index if, after being notified, it was not found to be 'manifestly unlawful'. A similar standard, using the wording 'unmistakably unlawful', had been developed for hosting providers in Dutch online intermediary liability case law with regard to hosting before the implementation of the ECD. Ultimately, the court concluded that Google had not been in the position to determine the unlawfulness of the reference and therefore, it did not have to block the results in question after being notified.[825]

In Germany, there was a similar case with a different result. In the German case, the court ordered the search engine to block the results and to install a filter that would prevent any future references with the combination of the plaintiff's name and the word *nackt* (naked) from showing up in its search results.[826] This type of keyword blocking is the type of preventive measure that was discussed in the previous section. These preventive measures, because of their overbroad

---

823. For an early discussion of the practices and legal problems related to spamdexing, see Nathenson 1998.
824. See Vzr. Rechtbank Amsterdam [District Court Amsterdam] April 26, 2007 (*Jensen*).
825. This is remarkable, because the mere fact that no nudity of the plaintiff was available on the website, which is quite easy to check, even for a search engine provider, arguably makes the content of the reference unlawful (under Dutch law). Furthermore, the Court did recognize that Google itself had removed the websites because of the manipulation of its search results. It is hard to see how such manipulation would not imply that the reference in question was unlawful with respect to the proper subject of manipulation, i.e. the television hostess. For a discussion, see Van Hoboken 2007.
826. LG Berlin [District Court Berlin], February 22, 2005, AZ 27 O 45/05.

character, should probably be considered inconsistent with the right to freedom of expression as applied to the search engine context.

This case seems an outlier in German case law. In general, German courts have been more receptive of the public freedom of expression interests associated with the operation of search engines and have called for a careful balancing of the right to freedom of expression and information with competing interests such as the right to respect for privacy and integrity of the person.[827] Perhaps the most important German court ruling relating to search engine and hyperlink liability is the *Paperboy* ruling of the German Supreme Court (BGH). In its report on the ECD, the European Commission took specific note of this judgment's consideration of the public interests in the functioning of search engines and hyperlinks, which it considered encouraging.[828]

The *Paperboy* judgment affirmed the permissibility of the use of hyperlink technologies by crawler-based search engines with a decision referring both to the social utility of selection intermediaries and the fundamental right of freedom of expression and information.[829] In a more recent ruling, the Court of Appeals in Hamburg built on the BGH's reasoning in *Paperboy*, concluding that the normal liability standard for publications would be too strict in the case of the publication of references by search engines.[830] The Hamburg Court of Appeals concludes that the normal liability standard requires an exception in the case of search engines, as follows:

> This follows from the required balancing between the general personality right and the freedom to impart and receive information, which is called for by a search engine decisively. That is to say, without the operation of search engines the practical application of the informational abundance on the World Wide Web would not be possible. In light of the tremendous amount of websites to be gathered, an automatic process is the only option for the gathering, extraction and presentation.[831]

In other words, the court argued that the liability of search engines for possibly unlawful expressions in their references—the result of the automatic reproduction of possibly unlawful information from the billions of websites on the Web—should be lowered because of the significance of search engines for the freedom of expression and information.[832] The Court nullified a ruling of the Hamburg Court of First Instance which had ruled that search engines start to become liable for the reproduction of unlawful publications of third parties in their references as soon as they become aware of them. In addition, the provider, in the lower court's view, would

---

827. For a discussion, see Spieker 2005.
828. European Commission 2003, 13.
829. BGH [German High Court] July 17, 2003, I ZR 259/00 (*Paperboy*). The *Paperboy* case addressed the permissibility of hyperlinking and deep linking by a German search engine for press articles under German copyright law and unfair completion law.
830. OLG Hamburg [Court of Appeals Hamburg], February 20, 2007, AZ. 7 U 126/06.
831. *Ibid.* (translation provided by the author).
832. For a discussion of this case, see also Ott 2008.

have to take preventive measures to ensure that similar infringements of the rights of others were not to take place in the future.[833] The Court of Appeals disagreed with the Court's conclusion. First, it considered that the snippets in question were not necessarily infringing, because of the automated nature of their composition and publication. The particular snippets were ambiguous and the average user could not interpret them in a way that would entail an infringement of the rights of the plaintiff.[834] The Court did leave open the possibility that a duty to remove unlawful references as well as a subsequent duty to prevent similar references from showing up in the future, could exist in a different context, for example if the content of the search results were to be unambiguously unlawful.

In the United Kingdom, there is a recent case, *Metropolitan*, which concerns the duty of care of search engines through the proper application of common law standards for defamation to search engine results at length.[835] The High Court Judge in London decided that the defendant search engine could not be considered the publisher of the defamatory statements, neither in the search results nor on the underlying websites, before receiving specific notice. Nor could it be considered the publisher between the moment that it received notice and the moment it decided to remove the respective website from its index. The ruling draws specific attention to the state of search engine third-party liability for defamation on websites across Europe, with numerous references to implementations of the Directive on Electronic Commerce and the case law in other Member States. In addition, the Court pays attention to the requirements of Article 10 ECHR. First, the Judge accepts that he should "*develop the law*, in so far as it is necessary to do so, in a manner which is compatible with Article 10 [ECtHR]."[836] In this context, he points to "the principle now recognized in English law (and, for that matter, in Strasbourg jurisprudence) that no one Convention right is to be regarded as taking automatic precedence over any other [...]."

The Judge then points out that he has to draw a balance between the right to sue effectively for defamation and the interference with the right to freedom of expression; the interference needs to be proportionate and necessary, ex Article 10 ECHR. The Judge summarizes this balance in the context of this case as follows:

> I am invited here [...] to come to the conclusion that it is neither necessary nor proportionate to impose potential liability for defamation on the owners or operators of a search engine in respect of material thrown up automatically on

---

833. LG Hamburg [District Court Hamburg], April 28, 2006—Az.: 324 O 993/05.
834. Differently, Gerechtshof Amsterdam [Court of Appeals Amsterdam] July 26, 2011 (*Zwartepoorte*).In this case, the court orders a webmaster to adjust the content on its website to prevent an certain combination of text to appear in the snippet alongside its reference in Google. It is notable that the content itself was perfectly lawful. The snippet combination, however, in the Court's view, suggested that the company was bankrupt which caused damage to the plaintiff. The 'damaging' snippet would only show up for a query with the company's name in combination with the Dutch word for bankrupt, 'failliet': [Zwartepoorte failliet].
835. *Metropolitan International Schools Ltd. v. Designtechnica Corp* [2009] EWHC 1765 (QB) (July 16, 2009).
836. *Ibid.*, § 42.

any of their 'snippet' search results. It is to be borne in mind that in cases where there is a genuine need for compensation or vindication the relevant complainant would (at least in theory) have a remedy, somewhere, against the person(s) who put the original article on the Web, to which the search engine has merely drawn attention.[837]

The Judge concludes that "the purpose of Article 10 is to protect not merely the right of free expression but also, correspondingly, the right on the part of others to receive information sought to be communicated."[838]

The need to strike the balance, as identified by the English court in *Metropolitan* lies at core of European intermediary liability law. This stands in stark contrast with the blanket immunity which is granted under U.S. law to a range of intermediaries. It can be argued that the ECHR would not even permit European Member States to adopt a provision similar to CDA 230, since it would be at odds with the requirement that a proper balance must be struck between the right to an effective remedy for infringements of Article 8 ECHR.[839] This requirement is most recently addressed by the ECtHR in the case *K.U. v. Finland*. In this case, an unknown person placed an online solicitation for a sexual relationship under the name of a young boy, listing the boy's name, phone number, date of birth and picture. A second person contacted the boy and was later identified and prosecuted for this act. In addition, the notice was taken down, but the publisher of the notice remained unknown except for the IP address at the time the notice was placed. The victim tried to identify the publisher with the help of law enforcement agencies through the access provider that had issued the IP address. At that time, however, Finnish law did not give the police the authority to order the access provider to hand over the data to the police, because of the low punishment for the crime of acting under a fake identity. Finnish courts affirmed this impossibility. The complainant in *K.U. v. Finland* subsequently claimed that Finnish law did not give him an effective remedy (Article 13 ECHR) under the Convention with regard to an infringement of his private life (Article 8 ECHR).

In answering the complaint under the Convention, the Court pointed to the positive obligation under Article 8 ECHR in the sphere of the relations of individuals between themselves. It concludes that the Member States:

> have a positive obligation inherent in Article 8 of the Convention to criminalise offences against the person, including attempted offences, and to reinforce the deterrent effect of criminalisation by applying criminal-law provisions in practice through effective investigation and prosecution [. . .].

Subsequently, it emphasizes the need to identify and prosecute offenders on the Internet:

---

837. *Ibid.*, § 43.
838. *Ibid.*, § 44.
839. Leaving aside the question of he extent to which the right to one's 'reputation' is protected under the right to protection of one's private life under Article 8 ECHR. See ECtHR April 28, 2009, *Karakó v. Hungary*.

It is plain that both the public interest and the protection of the interests of victims of crimes committed against their physical or psychological well-being require the availability of a remedy enabling the actual offender to be identified and brought to justice, in the instant case the person who placed the advertisement in the applicant's name, and the victim to obtain financial reparation from him.

In line with this reasoning, the ECtHR concludes that the legal barrier under Finnish law to get access to the personal data held by the access provider, which blocked the identification and prosecution of the perpetrator, was an infringement of the Convention.

An effective investigation could never be launched because of an overriding requirement of confidentiality. Although freedom of expression and confidentiality of communications are primary considerations and users of telecommunications and Internet services must have a guarantee that their own privacy and freedom of expression will be respected, such guarantee cannot be absolute and must yield on occasion to other legitimate imperatives, such as the prevention of disorder or crime or the protection of the rights and freedoms of others. Without prejudice to the question of whether the conduct of the person who had placed the offending advertisement on the Internet can attract the protection of Articles 8 and 10, having regard to its reprehensible nature, it is nonetheless the task of the legislator to provide the framework for reconciling the various claims which compete for protection in this context.

As is clear, a blanket immunity for Internet intermediaries to continue carrying publications which entail severe infringements of the right to private life would run contrary to the demands of a proper balance between Articles 8 and 10, as stated by the ECtHR in this case.[840] Although the ECtHR does not specifically address the question of the need to have an effective remedy to get references to unlawful material removed from search engines, the Court's reasoning seems to point in the direction of a positive obligation on the State under the Convention to provide for some kind of effective remedy to get material ultimately removed from search engines. The question is if, and how, this remedy can be constructed in a way that is both compatible with the freedom of expression and communication of Internet users and the rights and freedoms of third parties.

9.4.4.   THE FUTURE OF SEARCH ENGINE INTERMEDIARY LIABILITY
           IN THE EU: A RECOMMENDATION

Any third-party liability imposed on search engines, for instance in the form of a safe harbor, conditional on a reactive duty of care to remove references to

---

840. For a discussion of the possibility of aligning intermediary liability for defamation in the United States and EU, see Rustad & Koenig 2005.

infringing, unlawful or illegal content, would have some negative effects on robust findability of online material. This last section of this Chapter will identify the legal option as regards search engine intermediary liability that best takes into account the right to freedom of expression while still observing the overarching need to strike a balance between the competing interests which are at stake in this context.

As has been demonstrated, there is currently no clear answer to the question of search engine liability for third-party material at the European level, and even at the level of the Member States much remains unclear. Since search engines are amongst the core services that make the online information environment work for everyone, there is quite obviously a good case for harmonization at the European level. Harmonization would strengthen the internal market for search engine providers, enhance the free movement of search engine services and provide the legal certainty which is currently missing.

The initial reasoning of the European legislator not to harmonize was based on a combination of a lack of understanding of the significance of search engines for the online information environment and a willingness to wait for legal developments in the Member States. This has, quite obviously, led to a situation in which search engines, the most important of which are typically operating at a transnational level, are presented with a variety of legislative choices across Member States and continuing legal uncertainty in terms of complex legal developments in the case law of the Member States.

The recent case law of the ECJ has not improved the situation. Its emphasis on the standard from recital 42 ECD that intermediaries need to be neutral, as well as passive, merely technical and automatic in nature, may have further worsened the current state of affairs. Existing EU intermediary liability regulation is already under continuous pressure. Introducing proposals for new exemptions will be difficult in an environment that seems to lean towards extended duties of care for intermediaries. However, the necessary discussion at the EU level about the need for an extension of intermediary liability regulation to hyperlinks and selection intermediaries should not start from the assumption that the current status quo is the result of a full discussion of the subject. Search engine liability was, for the most part, ignored in the process leading to the ECD and ultimately stalled in Article 21 ECD. The question is what form a search engine specific safe harbor at the EU level should have and under what circumstances and conditions a search engine provider could be legally required to remove unlawful references from its index.[841]

---

841. More generally, the safe harbor framework in the ECD has not always functioned adequately, neither from the perspective of the services that have asserted their protection, nor from the perspective of third parties, including government, that have sought to the assistance of Internet intermediaries to prevent (access to) infringing or unlawful content or activities. See also Ch. 6. A discussion of the open issues in EU intermediary liability regulation more generally is beyond the scope of this research.

Regardless of the type of safe harbor that would be applied to search engines, it is important that the obligation on Member States in Article 15 ECD not to impose general obligations to monitor third-party content for illegal or unlawful communications on Internet intermediaries would be extended to search engine providers. Such general obligations could easily result in overly restrictive indexing practices by search engine providers, thereby resulting in serious obstacles to the right to freedom of expression online. At present, the relevance of Article 15(1) ECD for search engine providers depends on the question of whether search engines can assert the protection of one of the safe harbors in Article 12–14 ECD, since Article 15 ECD only applies to activities of information society services covered by the definitions of hosting, caching or mere conduit.

In addition, the application of the requirement derived from recital 42 ECD in the ECJ's case law that intermediary service provider's activity should be "neutral, in the sense that its conduct is merely technical, automatic and passive, pointing to a lack of knowledge or control of the data which it stores"[842] should be revisited. For search engines this requirement, when not specifically restricted to unlawful references could be particularly problematic, since the value of their intermediary activity in the public networked information environment is directly related to their lack of neutrality with regard to the value of the content for end-users. Moreover, the condition that its activity must remain technical and automatic could incentivize search engines to choose a hands-off approach with regard to the manual adjustment of problematic, low quality or possibly harmful search results.[843] In fact, search engines do manually interfere with search results on a regular basis to enhance the quality of their services. The requirement that a search engine should remain passive could also have undesirable implications for innovation and improvements in the field of search result quality. It is clear that any conditions tied to a search engine specific safe harbor should leave room for search engine providers to develop new methods to enhance the quality of their service for end-users and to optimize their service as platforms for information providers to compete for an audience.

When choosing between the current safe harbors in the Directive of Electronic Commerce, perhaps the most logical, and probably the most politically viable option for a search engine specific safe harbor, would be the hosting safe harbor. This would lead to a situation for search engines under EU law which is comparable to the legal situation for search engines in U.S. law under the DMCA, section 512(d). As discussed before, several European Member States have already chosen to adopt a similar search engine specific safe harbor as for hosting providers in their national implementations of the Directive on Electronic Commerce. Due to the current policies of dominant search engine providers, this choice would also not have any practical impact on search engine governance in the context of online

---

842. ECJ March 23, 2010, Joined Cases C-236/08 to C-238/08 (*Google Adwords*).
843. This is precisely the dilemma that led to the enactment of the Communications Decency Act, section 230. For a discussion, see Chapter 6, section 6.4.4.

copyright infringements,[844] and it would clarify the duties of care in the context of other interests such as defamation and privacy infringements.

However, it can be argued that from the perspective of the right to freedom of expression the hosting safe harbor is too strict for a number of reasons. First, research on the impact of the DMCA safe harbor on the practices of major search engines shows that search engine providers may end up removing allegedly unlawful material upon notice without conducting a proper review of the merits of the claim. In fact, search engines may not be properly equipped to make the required legal assessment in the first place. Second, the condition which is typically tied to the hosting provision, to remove unlawful content once the provider has obtained knowledge of the unlawful nature of the content, could also be too strict. It could easily result in the removal of references while the original content remains on the Web. As was concluded in Chapter 8, the matter-of-fact availability of material online should be taken into account when assessing the permissibility of a legal obligation not to refer to this material. It is notable that the hosting safe harbor is based on the standard for the duty of care of distributors.[845] It may make sense to treat the hosting providers of (the publications on) websites as distributors. Search engines, however, are not the distributors of online material. They merely assist in the effective distribution of material that is already present. They are not in a proper position to remove it. Due to the properties of the World Wide Web and the Internet, search engines, like any other publisher of hyperlinks to online material, do have the capacity to provide end-users with direct access to the actual material. This should not lead to the conclusion that search engines should be considered everyone's sole distributor.

It may make more sense to treat search engines similar to mere conduits, as with Internet access providers.[846] As was discussed above, search engines currently have the status of mere conduits under Austrian law, and, not surprisingly, this is also the preferred legal status of search engines themselves.[847] And as was discussed in the context of effective legal remedies against references to online publications that qualify as infringements of Article 8 ECHR, a mere conduit safe harbor for search engines could not be absolute, such as CDA section 230 in the United States. Even in the case of a mere conduit safe harbor for search engines, there should be room for an effective remedy against certain unlawful references in search results. If the safe harbor would leave open the possibility for "a court or administrative authority, in accordance with Member States' legal systems, of requiring the service provider to terminate or prevent an infringement,"[848] as all the safe harbors in the ECD currently do, there is arguably such a legal remedy available.

---

844. If the safe harbor would also contain an exception for 'abuse', i.e. search engine services which are specifically and predominantly tailored to profit from or advertised in terms of the findability of unlawful material.

845. See section 6.4.

846. *Ibid.*

847. See Google 2010a; Yahoo! Europe 2010.

848. Article 12(3) ECD.

In a strict sense, this would mean that everyone who is negatively affected by unlawful material in search engine results and who seeks a remedy would depend upon a court or administrative authority to order the removal of this material from the search engines' indices or the voluntary removal on request by the search engine. Existing self-regulation as discussed in section 9.2.2, if continued, would acquire a more voluntary character. Search engines would not be liable for monetary relief, even after obtaining knowledge of the unlawful nature of the material, but they would still be subject to litigation (seeking injunctions) and possible administrative orders, if provided for under national law. As can be predicted in such litigation, search engines would not be treated completely the same way as Internet access providers, since search engines can actually remove the references to unlawful material, whereas Internet access providers do not have an index to remove anything from.[849] Similar to hosting providers, courts and administrative authorities could maximally order search engine providers to remove the material if it is unlawful. The idea that search engines could also be ordered to remove material from their indices of which the actual publication online should be considered lawful is not consistent with the right to freedom of expression in the first place. An obligation on information providers to prevent references to lawful publications from showing up in search engines, for instance through the mandatory use of the robots.txt protocol, is similarly problematic.[850]

If one were to accept that search engines have a duty of care to remove unlawful references as soon as they become aware of them, the law would need to clarify what it means for a search engine provider to 'become aware'. The knowledge requirement in the hosting safe harbor has usually been understood as requiring actual knowledge of specific unlawful material.[851] A sufficiently clear notice to a search provider pointing to the specific unlawful material on a specific website could typically function as proof that the provider had knowledge of the unlawful nature of the material. To prevent a situation in which search providers err in favor of complaints regarding allegedly unlawful but actually perfectly lawful online publications, it would be preferable to restrict a reactive notice and takedown obligation of search engine providers to material that is manifestly or unmistakably unlawful. More generally, notice and takedown obligations on intermediaries could be codified in a way that guarantees due process with regard to the communicative interests of information providers and end-users and transparency and accountability with regard to the removal of content in particular. The guidelines relating to transparency and accountability in the CoE recommendation on freedom of expression and Internet filters, discussed in Chapter 6, can be useful in this context.

The existing safe harbor model which comes closest to striking a proper balance between the societal interest in the freedom of expression and information

---

849. This would change as soon as access providers would install the technical possibility to filter Internet access. See section 6.5.
850. See section 9.3.4. See also section 8.5.
851. See e.g. Helberger et al. 2008.

in the context of search engines on the one hand and the interests to prevent access to illegal and unlawful material on the other hand, is the safe harbor for proxy caching services, the most obscure of the three safe harbors in the ECD. Proxy caching is an activity of network and access providers which involves the storage of popular online material closer to the end-user. The role of proxy caching is to enhance the accessibility of online material, but the material remains accessible regardless of whether it is cached by the particular network or access provider. The caching safe harbor in Article 13 ECD provides that information society services which provide transmission services are not liable for proxy caching if a number of conditions are satisfied. In particular, the content should not be modified, while conditions on access must be observed, as well as industry standards on the updating of and recording of data on cached content. Most importantly, the provider has to act in the following manner:

> expeditiously to remove or to disable access to the information it has stored upon obtaining actual knowledge of the fact that the information at the initial source of the transmission has been removed from the network, or access to it has been disabled, or that a court or an administrative authority has ordered such removal or disablement.[852]

This condition on a search engine specific safe harbor would, on the one hand, reflect the reality that search engines, in their intermediary role, are merely facilitating access to online material and are not able to remove the material for end-users. On the other hand, it would provide some room for the legal requirement of search engines to remove references to illegal and unlawful material once the material is no longer available, or once a proper judicial authority, under applicable legal safeguards, has acquired a legal order to remove the actual material at its source.

9.5. CONCLUSION

This chapter has addressed the existing position of search engines in content regulation as well as their legal liability for referencing to third-party material from the perspective of the right to freedom of expression. It has been shown that self-regulation by general purpose search engines, as it currently exists in a number of European Member States is problematic from the perspective of freedom of expression. It is somewhat symbolic, and ineffective in addressing the underlying concerns. The analysis shows that these self-regulatory frameworks confuse the legal reasons for the proactive involvement (to escape liability and further regulatory pressure), and the possible genuine willingness to address the concerns of public authorities about the facilitative role of search engines to open up illegal and unlawful content on the Web. Various examples show how public authorities and officials pressurize search engines informally to block and remove

---

852.   Article 13(1)(e) ECD.

websites from their indices, and to pursue other strategies to prevent access to content, in a way that would be overbroad and therefore inconsistent with the right to freedom of expression if turned into a legal obligation.

A complicating factor is the lack of clarity on the legal responsibility of search engines for facilitating access to illegal and unlawful content online. Due to the connection between self-regulatory frameworks and actual legal responsibility, the analysis of self-regulation of access to illegal and harmful content in search engines leads to an analysis of the actual legal responsibility of search engines for the illegal publications of third parties.

The analysis of the position of search engine services in the regulation of Internet intermediary liability shows that search engines are inadequately addressed in these regimes, at least from a European perspective. The safe harbors for Internet intermediaries in Articles 12–14 ECD, as well as the prohibition to impose general duties of care on Internet intermediaries, do not clearly extend to providers of search engines. This stands in stark contrast to the legal situation of search engine providers under U.S. law, which not only contains safe harbors for the same categories of intermediaries which are exempted by the European Directive, but also provides for limited liability of search engines. As shown by the analysis, the absence of a harmonized safe harbor as regards intermediary liability of search engines, does not lead to strict liability at the level of the Member States, but instead a patchwork of legislative choices in some Member States to extend the safe harbors in different ways to search engines and complex legal developments in the case law of other Member States.

The overview of intermediary liability of search engines in the Member States shows that freedom of expression, in particular the interests of end-users to access and use effective means to find online material, is often taken into account by the national courts when addressing the liability of search engines for third-party material. However, the analysis also shows that there are many inconsistencies. Because of the general lack of certainty in the European context, the legal framework as regards intermediary liability for search engines can only be called unfavorable. In the meantime, the lack of legislative clarity on the status of search engines and other intermediaries under the EU safe framework has started to produce case law at the European level. The analysis of this case law shows that the ECJ may have added to the confusion by concluding that search engines could actually assert the protection of the hosting safe harbor, instead of concluding that the ECD does not harmonize search engine intermediary liability. In addition, the fact that the ECJ has restricted the EU safe harbors to intermediary activities of a *merely technical, automatic and passive nature*, may be problematic for search engines, considering the nature of the media.

From the European legal perspective, it is clear that intermediary liability for search engines and possible additional alternative regulation of search engine access need to strike a balance between the freedom of expression interests addressed in this study and the need to enforce laws imposing restrictions on information flows, such as defamation and privacy law or copyright law. A choice for blanket immunity, as imposed by the Communications Decency

Act, section 230, has been shown to be inconsistent with fundamental European legal principles, particularly the right to respect for private life (Article 8 ECHR). In that sense, Europe will have to formulate its own proper answer to the complex issue of intermediary liability of search engines.

The final part of this chapter addressed the most obvious possible ways in which intermediary liability of search engines could be harmonized at the European level. From the perspective of freedom of expression, it is argued that a safe harbor, as is currently applied to hosting services, would be sub-optimal, because of the tendency of search engines to be too responsive to legal notices in the context of a legal regime similar to that imposed by the DMCA. Either the current mere conduit or the caching safe harbor should be taken as the starting point in formulating a proper safe harbor for search engines. This safe harbor should also take into account the communicative interests of end-users and information providers in transparency and due process, when websites are being removed for legal or self-regulatory reasons. The current legal framework and actual search engine practices in regard to the removal of references for legal reasons do not sufficiently address these concerns.

Chapter 10

Search Engine Quality: Pluralism, Bias, Transparency and User Surveillance

10.1. INTRODUCTION

It is generally agreed that the introduction of Google in the late 1990s had a significant positive impact on search engine quality. The leap in quality was mostly attributed to its better selection and ranking algorithms, discussed in Chapter 3.[853] Apart from its successful implementation of the PageRank algorithm,[854] which improved search result rankings significantly, Google's success from the perspective of search engine quality was also related to its extremely user-friendly and clean search interface. Google was not caught up in distracting portal integration strategies and in the first years it did not incorporate any kind of advertising, let alone the types of distracting banner advertising that were commonly found on existing search engines at that time.

But in general, what does it mean to say that a search engine is of high quality? The scientific literature on the subject has addressed a variety of subjects in this context. Since the 1950s, the information retrieval literature has developed quality measures for information retrieval systems in terms of recall and precision and such relevance measures, as well as the actual ranking models, have been steadily improved.[855] Information scientists developed sophisticated theories about user-computer interaction and expectation of users which have helped the industry adapt their services to the users' needs. From the perspective of commercial search engine providers, search engine quality will most often be defined as end-user satisfaction, which can be used to substantiate the often used, more technological

---

853. See section 2.2.2.
854. Brin & Page 1998. See also Langville & Meyer 2006.
855. See Baeza-Yates & Ribeiro-Neto 2011.

term 'relevance'.[856] It is notable that in both cases, search engine quality is defined from the perspective of end-users and not from the perspective of information providers or advertisers.

Broadly speaking, in this chapter the question of search engine quality will be seen as the question of the way fundamental notions relating to the quality of the public information environment are affected by the way search engines value, select, rank and prioritize information and communication streams. As is obvious, the notion of quality will depend on the perceived purposes and role of search engines in general: quality will have to be seen in relation to that role and those purposes. Instead of discussing the notions of search engine quality from the field of information retrieval,[857] which is primarily focused on developing scientific models and tools to conceptualize and build better search engines, this chapter will focus on search engine quality from a regulatory and policy perspective. As search engines have become essential for the fulfillment of fundamental societal demands of general public interest, such as the free flow of and access to information and ideas, or consumer freedom in the market (not the specific focus of this study), it becomes essential to discuss how well the current offering of search engines is actually fulfilling these demands.

This chapter will build on the conclusions about the role of search engines in the public networked information environment, conceptualized in more depth in the preceding chapters, and focus on a number of selected regulatory notions and issues that implicate search engine quality in particular. The discussion will be limited to a discussion of three main regulatory issues relating to search engine quality and freedom of expression. First, the question will be addressed whether and how the regulatory notions of diversity and pluralism in the public information environment could be used as normative signposts in the context of search engine governance. Diversity and pluralism are amongst the most fundamental normative starting points for the regulation of the public information environment, which leads to the question of how these starting points can inform the regulatory debate in the context of search. To what extent do search engines impact diversity and pluralism of the public networked information environment? On the basis of existing evidence, what would be the main concerns when addressing search engines from this perspective and what is needed if legislators or regulatory agencies were to move forward from this perspective, which is after all a fundamental concern for them on the basis of Article 10 ECHR?

Second, the regulatory debate related to the lack of transparency in the selection and ranking of search results, the possibility of various forms of (possibly hidden) bias, and more concretely, the legal and policy issues relating to the advertisement-based business model of search engines and its impact on the quality of organic search results will be discussed. The question will be addressed regarding the extent to which the advertisement-based business model entailing the sales and production of sponsored search results could entail incentives on search engine

---

856. See van Couvering 2010, Ch. 6.
857. See e.g. Lewandowski 2007.

providers that would negatively impact search engine quality. More specifically, the way the law and specific regulatory agencies have responded to concerns about search engine monetization through advertising with labeling obligations will be addressed, as well as the merits of this response in view of the quality of search engines as mediators of the public information environment.

The chapter will conclude with an analysis of the legal issues relating to user data processing and its impact on the selection and ranking of search results from the perspective of the right to freedom of expression. The amount and nature of the user data processed by search engine providers, the increased personalization of search engine output as well as the lack of transparency in these practices pose some difficult regulatory problems. In the final section, the question will be addressed as to how data protection regulation and the right to privacy can be seen as a prerequisite for intellectual freedom of search engine users as well as the way the current legal regime incorporates this concern. Moreover, end-users may be served by extensive user data processing and profiling, since it would lead to higher search quality through more precisely tailored search results or advertisements. At the same time, for users it may be hard to assess the actual trade-off that is taking place in the absence of proper information about the end-user modeling and user data processing that is taking place and the impact it has on search engine output. Consequently, the question will be addressed as to whether the way search engines impact information consumption as a result of user data processing and personalization leads to undesirable outcomes from the perspective of the ideals underlying the right to freedom of expression more generally. These issues will be addressed in the final part of this chapter. In particular, it will explore the way data protection law, through its various rights and obligations relating to the accountability for the processing of personal data, could contribute to the establishment of informational autonomy of end-users in their relation with search engine providers.

10.2.   SEARCH ENGINE QUALITY: PLURALISM,
            DIVERSITY AND BIAS

10.2.1.   THE IMPACT OF SEARCH ENGINES ON PLURALISM
            AND DIVERSITY: A SHORT OVERVIEW

Considering the opportunities offered by current networked communications technologies and services, taking issue with diversity and pluralism in the networked information environment may need some clarification.[858] The World Wide Web and networked communications more generally have both diminished and altered the power of traditional media and knowledge institutions to control the public information environment significantly. Because of the World Wide Web and shifting societal information practices, citizens no longer need traditional mass media

---

858.   On the meaning of pluralism and diversity, see section 10.2.2.

to be able to make their ideas available to a broad audience. And because of the Web and search engines in particular, it may no longer matter a great deal whether or not a library selects a publication for their collection.

This much celebrated 'disintermediation' or even 'democratizing' effect of networked communications, however, typically emphasized the potential of the new environment in comparison with some of the drawbacks of the old environment in terms of control over public information flows. This effect was a blessing from the perspective of pluralism and diversity, at least if these notions were understood to relate to entry barriers to information access, production and distribution. It is in this vein that a recent Communication of the European Commission on 'A Digital Agenda for Europe' notes the following:

> The Internet is also a driver of greater pluralism in the media, giving both access to a wider range of sources and points of view as well as the means for individuals—who might otherwise be denied the opportunity—to express themselves fully and openly.[859]

But as the networked information environment matures, it has started to produce new bottlenecks, mediating institutions and apparent biases. On the one hand, the ease with which information and ideas can now be published may have solved some of the issues relating to pluralism and diversity in the context of content production and dissemination. On the other hand, the abundance of information and ideas online implies sharply increased competition for audiences, leading to what is often denoted as an 'attention economy'.[860]

In particular, the findability of information and ideas, as determined by the economical, institutional and increasingly complex technological infrastructure for the opening up of the public networked information environment, has sharply increased in importance. In the networked information society, it is simply not enough to publish one's views to effectively participate in online debate. Winners and losers, from the perspective of effective dissemination of information and ideas, are partly determined by successful representation in search engines and related selection intermediary services. In particular, the impact of search engines and the algorithms they deploy for the prioritization of the publicity of certain sources of information over others have become an important issue in the debate about the effective dissemination of information and ideas, both from the perspective of information providers as well as end-users.

Central to the critique of the assumption of the positive impact of the Web on diversity and the equalizing impact on information access and production, is the following observation. In the public networked information environment, it is not decisive whether information and ideas are accessible or retrievable, but whether they are visible and likely to be encountered by Internet users.[861] This observation

---

859. European Commission 2010c.
860. See Goldhaber 1997.
861. See Karppinen 2009, 175–161. See also Hargittai 2000; Hargittai 2007a; Hindman et al. 2003; Hindman 2009.

leads Hindman and others to specifically consider the impact of dominant search engine Google on pluralism and diversity. On the basis of an analysis of the structure of the Web, they claimed the following:

> Rather than "democratizing" the dissemination of information, the prospect of googlearchy suggests that citizens may continue to get their political information from only a few sources, even on the apparently limitless information vistas of cyberspace.[862]

This led them to conclude that there is a need for a careful consideration of the impact of dominant search engines on the visibility and relative accessibility of information and ideas.

Some authors have addressed the actual impact of the selection and ranking mechanisms of various search engine services on the visibility of online information for end-users. An early example is the paper by Lawrence and Giles, who warned that "not only are the engines indexing a biased sample of the web, but new search techniques are further biasing the accessibility of information on the web."[863] However, since it is arguably the role of search engines to prioritize certain sources of information over others, this argument does not persuade to the extent that it is based on the assumption that search engines could or should actually facilitate equal accessibility of sources of information in search engines.

The question is what normative standard should be used to evaluate search engine selection and ranking choices and their impact on the dissemination of and access to information and ideas. As Introna and Nissenbaum and others have observed, dominant search engines may be expected to adopt ranking technology which emphasizes popularity over objective quality standards.[864] If taken to the extreme, this could lead to a situation in which information and ideas, worthy of effective representation and worthy of being found, could be doomed to relative obscurity. While the analysis of linking to pages already reflected an equation of relevance and popularity, the apparent focus of search engine providers on end-user satisfaction has made the label 'popularity engines' for dominant search services such as Google even more appropriate.

And not surprisingly, considerable attention has been paid to the dominance of Google in the search engine market, and the possible influence this might have on access to information and ideas and the formation of opinion by end-users. Google's market share—in terms of search engine users—is well above 90% in many European countries, including the Netherlands and Germany.[865] Although this might make some worried about the impact of one commercial enterprise on the dissemination of information and ideas online,[866] it is a largely an open

---

862. Hindman et al. 2003, 4.
863. See e.g. Lawrence & Giles 1999, 107–109.
864. Introna & Nissenbaum 2000, 169–185. See also Finkelstein 2008, 104–120; Marres & De Vries 2002.
865. See Table 2.1, section 2.2.1.
866. See e.g. European Commission 2007a, 16.

question as to how the dominance of Google should be qualified in terms of the values of diversity and pluralism in the networked information environment.[867] This issue will be further addressed in the next section.

While a strict focus on end-user satisfaction may already favor information popularity over information quality,[868] the ways in which search engines monetize traffic may present additional issues from the perspective of search engine quality. In short, due to their monetization strategies commercial search engine providers can be expected to be at least as interested in providing value for their advertisers as in providing high quality search results for their end-users. End-user data processing and modeling in particular can be expected to be structured to provide value to potential advertisers, and the same can be expected of the optimization of search result pages, in particular the distribution and balance between organic and sponsored search results.[869] More generally, the commercial nature of dominant search engines might imply that existing services are more interested in optimizing the satisfaction of specific information needs of end-users, in particular the information needs of a commercial nature.[870] The amount and satisfaction of search engine users who are looking to buy a product or purchase a service will have a significant positive impact on the ability of search engines to make money, while at the same time having a possible negative impact on the satisfaction of other information needs.

Apart from the critiques of dominant commercial search engines in terms of their undoing of the promised equalizing potential of the Web, and the impact of the commercial business model on search result quality, there are more positive accounts of the impact of search engines on diversity.[871] One argument for search engines having a positive impact on diversity and pluralism would point to their impact on the visibility of information and ideas in otherwise heavily censored countries. In countries where certain minorities are not free to publish their views openly, or are not offered the same opportunities to speak openly in government-controlled or heavily censored media outlets, the Internet in combination with search engine services has had quite a dramatic impact on access to information and ideas that would otherwise have remained inaccessible. The facilitative role of search engines in accessing information and ideas from or about such minority views led to fast responses by public authorities in countries such as China, which push search engines to de-list certain websites, for instance relating to the Falung Gong movement. As was discussed in the last chapter, search engines have responded to certain government demands to filter out information, but at the

---

867. For an in-depth analysis of the power of Google as well as a discussion of the different concepts of power used in search engine scholarship, such as the gatekeeper concept, see Röhle 2010.
868. While popularity can be a sign of quality, it is taken for a given here that information quality and popularity are different properties that do not necessarily align. For instance, a false news report may be quite popular.
869. See e.g. Röhle 2006. See also Yang & Ghose, 2010, 602–623; Muthukrishnan 2009, 1–12.
870. See sections 3.3.2, 3.3.3.
871. See Fortunato et al. 2006. See also Lev-On 2008, 135–149.

same time they have refused to cater too much to the demands of repressive regimes to filter out information.

Another such positive account, by Yochai Benkler, concludes that Google's specific decentralized mechanism for assigning relevance actually promotes diversity.[872] Benkler takes Google's PageRank algorithm, which de facto allows all web publishers to express their views on the relevance of other sources of online information through the act of hyperlinking, as an example of the positive effects of peer-production in the networked information environment on individual autonomy.[873] He observed, with a small empirical overview of search results for the search 'Barbie', that Google's rankings seemed to treat critical information and ideas relatively favorably and concluded that Google may positively impact information diversity for end-users. Benkler conceptualizes diversity as a measure of the range of different information and ideas end-users are presented with when searching the Web. In particular, he sees diversity as a measure of the extent to which end-users will be capable of making a meaningful critical assessment of the value of the sources of information they retrieve.[874] Notably, this concept goes further than a measure of mere accessibility of information and takes into account the observation discussed earlier that what ultimately matters is the sources of information which individuals are likely to encounter.

Benkler's claim about Google's rankings may be somewhat anecdotal and his empirical findings may be outdated. Most importantly, however, it points in the same direction as identified by Hindman, Nissenbaum or others: The need for a careful study of the impact of selection and ranking practices of (dominant) search engines as mediators between information and ideas and Internet users, and a debate about the extent to which search engines do and should contribute to over-arching fundamental societal interests related to the dissemination of and access to information and ideas, pluralism and diversity in particular.

It is important to note that due to the interactive nature of search engines, search engine quality and access to information and ideas for Internet users more generally depends a great deal on end-users. Above, the observation was discussed that diversity and pluralism in the public networked information environment depend on findability and actual visibility of information and ideas for end-users. This points to the need for empirical as well as normative evaluations of the mechanisms behind search engine selection and ranking mechanisms. At the same time, there is an equal need to understand actual end-user behavior. It is clear that the findability of information and ideas in search engines greatly depends on end-users' behavior and sophistication. The importance of end-user skills and education is positive for those who have them and negative for those do not. An experienced end-user remains quite powerful and in control of the search process, even when a search service prioritizes certain sources of information over others in

---

872. Benkler 2006, 285–294.
873. On the conditions for quality to emerge in peer-produced information environments, see Duguid 2006.
874. Benkler 2006, 285–294. For more theoretical background, see Benkler 2001.

ways that do not directly serve the interests of end-users. This means that on the one hand, end-user skills and education are crucial for the overall quality of the search process. On the other hand, this means that some end-users do not have the appropriate skills to navigate the Web with the use of search engines effectively.[875] Some research has already been done on the use of search engines and access to information and ideas by different groups in society. Of particular interest in this context is the work of Eszter Hargittai. In a series of articles, she presents empirical evidence of search engine use, warning against assumptions about the positive state of access to information and ideas online, in particular for the less well-off in the networked information society.[876]

A final critique of the way search engines impact access to information and ideas is focused on their increased personalization of search results and the negative impact this may have on pluralism and diversity. Slowly but steadily, dominant search engines have moved towards increasingly personalized search results, for organic as well as sponsored listings. This personalization of the search process—and information services online more generally—has led to another critique relating to pluralism and diversity in the networked information environment, namely the related critiques of the 'daily me' and the 'filter bubble'. The 'daily me' refers to the idea of personalized media, made possible by digital information technologies which better and more directly reflect the actual interests of the Internet user than traditional media outlets.[877] Such personalization of media, Cass Sunstein warns, could lead to so-called information cocoons. Internet users would only access information and ideas they are already interested in and would not be confronted with other topics or perspectives. This could, amongst other effects, damage an important prerequisite for democratic debate: a shared platform to communicate about societal issues.[878] It could even lead to a situation in which extreme positions are amplified further, for instance, if personalization would respond to and amplify anti-social, sexist or even racist character traits of end-users. Sunstein has consistently called attention to these possible drawbacks of a heavily personalized information environment and argued for the value of independent selection by shared societal institutions such as the press and libraries.[879] It must be noted that neither Sunstein, nor Eli Pariser, whose more recent warning against 'filter bubbles' is discussed below, provide much empirical backing for their claims that existing personalization developments are actually having the effects on democracy they warn against. As a result, their arguments can be best understood as a contribution to the discussion about the normative ideals that should inform selection practices by mediating institutions in the public information environment.

---

875. See section 8.6.2.
876. See e.g. Hargittai 2007b. See also Halavais 2009.
877. The possibility and benefits of personalized media were explored by Bill Gates in the 1990s. See Gates 1995.
878. See also Karppinen 2009, 161–165.
879. See. Sunstein 2002, 44–50. See also Sunstein 2007.

Sunstein's warning against the downside of personalization has been expanded by others, such as Eli Pariser in his critique of the 'filter bubble'.[880] Pariser adds an element to the discussion by specifically addressing the way a range of Web-based services have started to personalize their services based on various types of end-user data processing and modeling which are not transparent to users.[881] He finds this is the case for selection intermediaries, search engines and social networks in particular, which are precisely the services which have a significant impact on actual information consumption. Pariser concludes that end-users have come to experience the effects of a 'daily me' type of personalization in a range of online services. In addition, he notes that end-users may not be in control or even aware of the type of personalization that is taking place. This is despite the fact that such personalized selecting, filtering and re-ranking has started to have a major impact on the process of finding different sources of information and ideas online.

The short overview of the various arguments related to the impact of search engine ranking and selection practices on pluralism and diversity clarifies a number of things. Many of the warnings of search engine bias may be better understood as a critique of overly positive assumptions about the democratizing effect of public networked communications. These assumptions may indeed be unjustified or overstated when looking at the actual exposure to information and ideas online. At the same time, however, it is questionable whether the normative framework for search engine quality should include the standard that search engines should facilitate access to information and ideas 'equally'. From the perspective of information quality and the role of search engines in the information environment, search engines should prioritize certain information and ideas over others. At the same time, as was argued at more length in Chapter 8, search engines should be allowed to make their selection and ranking decisions in relative free-dom, due to the editorial nature of the ranking and selection aspects of the search medium, which should be protected by the right to freedom of expression of search engine providers.

While it is important from the perspective of the right to freedom of expression to recognize that certain forms of search engine bias may be legitimate and not the proper subject of legal or regulatory interference, it is equally important to arrive at a proper understanding of the way search engines should be evaluated from the perspective of pluralism and diversity. The discussions that could eventually lead to such a framework are in still in their infancy. The next section will discuss some of the initial regulatory developments and explore the possibility of reaching such a framework for the assessment of pluralism and diversity in the context of search engines. In particular, it will take into consideration the positive obligation on the State to guarantee pluralism under Article 10 ECHR, on the one hand, and freedom of expression as a negative right protecting against government interference on the other hand.

---

880. See Pariser 2011. See also Morozov 2010; Pasquale 2010; Zuckerman 2008.
881. See also sections 10.3 and 10.4.

10.2.2.   Pluralism and Diversity in the Context of Search: Legal and Regulatory Background

The related legal and regulatory concepts of pluralism and diversity in the context of the media are broad and contested. According to a recent independent EU study on media pluralism, which also focuses on new types of media and dissemination of content in general, pluralism can be understood to implicate the following:

> the diversity of media supply, use and distribution, in relation to (1) ownership and control, (2) media types and genres, (3) political viewpoints, (4) cultural expressions and (5) local and regional interests.[882]

As this specific study also notes, pluralism and diversity are contested concepts. It points out that there are generally two underlying but conflicting views on pluralism and diversity. One view focuses on freedom of choice in a marketplace of information and ideas. The other view places more emphasis on diversity in a shared platform for public discourse, focusing on the public interest that society is served with various political views and cultural values.[883] These two underlying views of pluralism and diversity also inform and reflect different regulatory approaches towards the media.[884] In the former view, which is dominant in the United States, pluralism is a measure of free access and choice in the market, and would encourage media policies that focus on facilitating competition. In the latter view, the public interest with regard to pluralism and diversity suggests more active involvement with, and regulation of, the media environment to promote access of a broad range of information and ideas.

While the concept of media pluralism is strongly related to concerns over media concentration, the latter is not the only concern. Pluralism and diversity can be internal as well as external in nature. From an internal point of view, the demand of pluralism would require that a wide range of social, political and cultural values, opinions, information and interests can find their expression within one media organization. From an external point of view, pluralism would require that this process is facilitated through a number of media organizations, each expressing a particular point of view.[885]

It is important to note that the legal and regulatory dimension of media pluralism is linked to the positive obligation of the State to promote it under Article 10 ECHR. As was noted in Chapter 5, in the second half of the twentieth century it became accepted that the State does have a role in preventing too much concentration in the press and media in general. In the interest of pluralism, mass media, including the print media, are usually not only subject to general competition law, as any other commercial undertaking, but also to special media concentration and cross-ownership rules and policies.[886] Concentration of media outlets in the hands

---

882. See Valcke et al. 2009.
883. See *ibid.*, 5–6.
884. See also discussion of regulatory frameworks for public libraries, sections 7.3.1 and 7.3.2.
885. See e.g. European Commission 1992.
886. See section 5.2.

of a few would undermine pluralism, of which, according to the European Court of Human Rights, the State is the ultimate guarantor.[887] Therefore, a press and media policy aimed at preserving the conditions necessary for a pluralist media environment is a reflection of the right to freedom of expression and not an interference with the media's constitutionally protected freedom. In the broadcasting context, in which pluralism has had particularly strong regulatory history, special measures to promote pluralism in this traditionally heavily regulated environment were considered appropriate. These measures include broadcasting licensing criteria, must-carry obligations and rules about the types of programming that should be made available to the public.[888]

In the European context, pluralism is, in other words, a regulatory concept which informs, explains and legitimizes the role of government with regard to the media. Because of the broadness of both concepts, pluralism and freedom of expression might be seen as two sides of the same coin. In this European context, in which active media policies to promote pluralism still play an important role, pluralism also reflects the idea that government has an active role to play in guaranteeing certain qualitative aspects of the public information environment related to the diversity of viewpoints finding their expression through the media. As was noted in previous chapters, the State's obligation to promote pluralism under Article 10 ECHR is too broad and vague to be used to effectuate specific rights and/or obligations in specific contexts that may require government involvement to promote pluralism.[889] Member States have considerable leeway to make choices in the way they fulfill this obligation to promote pluralism.

The Council of Europe has played an important role in shaping the contours of the legal and regulatory concept of pluralism and the way Member States could or should fulfill their positive obligation to promote it. Apart from the case law of the ECtHR, several Recommendations of the Council of Europe Committee of Ministers pay attention to pluralism or are specifically dedicated to it, in particular focusing on print and broadcasting media.[890] In its most recent recommendations on media pluralism, the Committee of Ministers has started to develop the notion of media pluralism in relation to the digital networked information environment. The recommendation on freedom of expression and Internet filters contains safeguards in relation to the undue interference with the free dissemination of and access to information and ideas over the Internet.[891] The Committee of Ministers'

---

887. See section 5.2.
888. See Valcke 2004.
889. See sections 4.4.1 and 5.5.1.
890. See CoE, Recommendation (2007)2 of the Committee of Ministers to Member States on media pluralism and diversity of media content, January 31, 2007; see also CoE, Rec(99)1 of the Committee of Ministers to Member States on measures to promote media Pluralism, January 19, 1999.
891. For a discussion, see section 6.5.4.

Recommendation (2007)2 states that Member States should guarantee fair access to electronic communication networks for content providers.[892] Moreover, the same recommendation on media pluralism contains a broad reference to promoting pluralism and diversity in the context of new media. It states the following:

> Member States should encourage the development of other media capable of making a contribution to pluralism and diversity and providing a space for dialogue. These media could, for example, take the form of community, local, minority or social media. The content of such media can be created mainly, but not exclusively, by and for certain groups in society, can provide a response to their specific needs or demands, and can serve as a factor of social cohesion and integration. The means of distribution, which may include digital technologies, should be adapted to the habits and needs of the public for whom these media are intended.[893]

The Council of Europe may issue additional recommendations on pluralism and diversity in the context of the public networked information environment, considering the emergence of a range of new types of services, search engines and other selection intermediaries in particular, which impact the actual dissemination of and access to the variety of information and ideas online encountered by Internet users. At this point, the Council of Europe does not offer any specific guidance on the issue of search engines from the perspective of pluralism and diversity. However, future recommendations may specifically address the role of search engines from this perspective.[894]

In the context of the EU, it was already noted in Chapter 5 that pluralism is one of the single subject matters related to the press in which European institutions have taken an interest. Following the developments of convergence and the digital transition of (news) publishing, this interest has extended to pluralism in the electronic media environment. This interest has translated into a 2007 European Commission working paper and the independent report on media pluralism indicators mentioned above. Both the European Commission's working paper as well as the independent study note the apparent relevance of search engines when analyzing media pluralism and diversity.[895]

The EC's working paper shortly discusses and dismisses some warnings that search engines could be a problem from the perspective of pluralism. It does mention a concern that search engines could be manipulating users to visit specific sources of information, in particular those of their advertisers. This would obstruct users from navigating the Web freely. In reply to these concerns, the working paper asserts, without references, that "there are commercial incentives for offering an

---

892. CoE, Rec(2007)2 of the Committee of Ministers to Member States on media pluralism and diversity of media content, January 31, 2007.
893. *Ibid.*
894. Since 2010, the Council of Europe's Committee of Experts on New Media (MC-NM) has been working on a Draft Recommendation on the protection of human rights with regard to search engines. This Draft Recommendation was opened for public consultation in early 2011.
895. See European Commission 2007a, 16–17; Valcke et al. 2009.

objective search facility. The business model for search engines is based on the provision of clearly separated advertising links, derived from contextual analysis of a particular search."[896] Second, the working paper expresses its optimism with regard to the availability of and competition between different search engines from the perspective of pluralism on the Internet and notes that "there are no fundamental technical limitations on the number of search engines that the Internet could support."[897] Moreover, the paper touches on the aspect of competition between various selection and ranking systems, as applied by different search engines, when it notes, optimistically, that "there will be new search algorithms in [the] future, able to search multimedia content, a topic supported by EU Research projects. Through sophisticated indexing, cataloguing and filtering algorithms, these enable users to access wider news content than they would otherwise have access to."[898]

The independent EU study on pluralism indicators does recognize that new media of all types play a role from the perspective of pluralism. With reference to a discussion of technological and economic developments in the context of networked electronic communications, including the emergence of search engines, it notes that traditional indicators of pluralism may have become obsolete.[899] At the same time, it points out that these developments may open up new avenues to ensure or promote pluralism. With regard to search engines, specific reference is made to the importance of user education about the functioning of search engines, the question of the existence of regulatory safeguards for the editorial independence of search engines, the possibility of including indicators on search engine ownership and the role of search engines in providing access to local content.[900] However, the extent to which media pluralism policies should lead to an in-depth consideration of the specific impact of search engines on pluralism, and in what ways, remains somewhat unclear.

It goes beyond the scope of this research to develop an actual framework for the assessment of pluralism and diversity in the context of search engines. In view of the various early perspectives on pluralism, diversity and search engines, as well as the early regulatory responses discussed above, it is, however, possible to discern at least two dominant issues relating to pluralism and diversity, which deserve special attention. These are the question about the impact of the ownership structure of dominant search engines and the current market consolidation on the one hand, and the question about the diversity of references end-users are exposed to when using specific search engines, on the other hand.

First, the dominance of Google in the search engine market quite intuitively raises the question about the impact of the search engine market structure on pluralism and diversity. The question of the extent to which there is actual evidence

---

896. European Commission 2007a.
897. *Ibid.*
898. *Ibid.*
899. Valcke et al. 2009.
900. Valcke et al. 2009.

of a negative impact will be evaluated below as well as the rather difficult question about the way concentration in the search engine market should be scrutinized from the perspective of pluralism and diversity. Second, there seems to be general agreement amongst those who have considered search engines from the perspective of pluralism that an evaluation of pluralism in the networked information environment requires an assessment of the relative accessibility of content. This agreement points to a central focus on the services which affect the visibility and findability of content and actual search engine user behavior. Although pluralism remains an issue in the context of the production of information and ideas, pluralism in the networked information environment, characterized by abundance, cannot be separated from the question of whether or not it will become accessible and visible for Internet end-users.

10.2.3.   MARKET CONCENTRATION

The market for general search is dominated by a small number of firms.[901] If we look at the European and American markets, the large majority of search requests is currently handled by two firms, Google and Microsoft. Yahoo!, once the market leader with its famous directory, remains a competitor in the field of search traffic monetization, but it no longer produces its own search results and uses those of Bing instead.

There are a variety of reasons that can be given for this market consolidation, a full discussion of which goes beyond the scope of this research. Amongst the more plausible ones are (1) the current scale of the World Wide Web and the number of users (billions of online destinations, billions of users and queries); (2) the knowledge and human capital that is needed to design and operate a general purpose Web search engine of competitive quality (dominant firms guard such knowledge as trade secrets and heavily compete for scarce engineering talent); (3) the existence of patents in search technology and intellectual property rights restricting competition; (4) the general satisfaction of users with the current supply (the market leader Google may simply offer the highest quality search results); (5) the lack of price competition for search engine users and the subsidization of the distribution of organic and paid search results through third-party arrangements by dominant search providers (meta-search engines, portals, third-party sites and browsers, mobile operating systems); (6) the need for an extensive user base and large amounts of user data to improve search engine selection and ranking and innovative features such as search 'suggest'; (7) the dependencies in the two-sided market for advertisers and end-users (advertisers may choose the platform with the most users); (8) the effective integration of search services into and with a variety of other information services provided by the same company that provide a soft 'lock-in' for users.

---

901.   For a discussion of market developments and figures on market share, see sections 2.2.3 and 2.2.4.

It is clear that a highly concentrated market for general purpose search engines implies that the impact of such dominant services on the visibility of content for Internet users becomes stronger. The de-indexing of content by a dominant search service will have a particularly strong impact, since the removed source will not be visible at all to its users. These issues relating to access have been discussed in Chapter 9. Whereas de-indexing has a clear impact on the findability of content for search engine users, it is much harder to assess the impact of the selection and ranking mechanisms of particular search services and the related implications of market consolidation for pluralism and diversity.

Even though the dominance of Google may intuitively suggest otherwise, it is wrong to rush to the conclusion that Google's dominant position in terms of user market share is detrimental to pluralism and diversity. In fact, there seem to be a number of arguments which warrant skepticism regarding this claim. First of all, it is possible that Google respects pluralism and diversity much more than any of its competitors.[902] Second, it is also possible that existing commercial general purpose search engines are converging in terms of the visibility of different kinds of content, implying that it does not matter—from the perspective of pluralism and diversity—which of them users choose. Third, and perhaps most importantly, search services are interactive. Their selection and ranking algorithms do not carve the findability of sources of information in stone. Their output depends heavily on user input and perceived user expectations. The ranking and selection of organic results are strongly influenced by the online environment as a whole and by webmasters in particular. This even raises the question, whether one general purpose search engine service for the Web could be sufficient, from the perspective of diversity and pluralism of the public networked information environment.

In its review of the agreement between Yahoo! and Microsoft in 2009, which led to a reduction of different sources of organic search result listings, the European Commission explicitly considered the possible negative impact on users by a loss of variety.[903] The agreement meant that Yahoo! would no longer produce its own index and search results but would use the organic search results of Microsoft's search service, Bing, instead. Although both companies had very low market shares in the EU relative to Google and the combined market shares of Yahoo! and Microsoft were well below the safe harbor in the horizontal merger guidelines,[904] the possible impact on search quality, however, seems to have been the reason the European Commission investigated further as follows:

> given that competition in this market takes place in terms of quality and innovation, and the entry barriers are high, the Commission undertook a

---

902. For example, Benkler argued that Google, in comparison with other search engines, had an actual positive impact on diversity. See section 10.2.2. Although Benkler might be overly optimistic, the reverse claim might be overly pessimistic.
903. European Commission, Case No. Comp/M.5727—Microsoft/Yahoo! Search Business, February 18, 2010, § 202.
904. *Ibid.*, § 130.

thorough analysis of the possible effects of the transaction on the search market.[905]

The European Commission investigated whether the agreement would impact the incentive to innovate, whether lessened competition could incentivize lowering the quality of organic results (to increase click-through rates for advertisements), and whether users would be harmed by a loss of variety. It concluded that none of these effects risked occurring. Moreover, the European Commission concluded that "it is possible that due to the transaction some benefits will materialise due to larger scale of the merged entity."[906]

Considering the high entry barriers, the current market structure is unlikely to change much in the near future. And with its market share of 90% or more for Internet searches which are being reported, Google is obviously important from the perspective of findability of information and ideas online. As mentioned above, this raises the question about the impact of Google on pluralism and diversity, and on the way pluralism can be supported internally. This question will be addressed in the next section.

However, it is important to note that Google still exists in a broader context of other information services and electronic publishers that have an impact on the relative accessibility of information and ideas for end-users. In the general purpose Web search market, in the strict sense, there is still competition in European and the United States, most notably from Microsoft. In some local markets, such as those in the Czech Republic, Russia and China, there are strong local market players and leaders.[907] In addition, there are numerous vertical search engines which positively contribute to the findability of specific types of information. Furthermore, there are publicly funded search engine services, which may have little or negligible market share but can contribute to the quality and diversity of the online search environment. There is a variety of other dominant information services, including Facebook and Twitter, which provides different types of selection and recommendation mechanisms for users to access content in the networked information environment. Through the use of hyperlinking, electronic publishing in general also contributes to the findability of information and ideas on the Web. And finally, traditional media formats such as print and broadcasting have to be taken into account as well.

To sum up, the intuitive claim that consolidation in the market for general purpose search engines is detrimental to pluralism and diversity would need more empirical backing to be taken seriously. This is especially the case from a historical perspective on access to publishing opportunities and access to information and ideas. Search engines must be seen in their proper context: they are important for the relative accessibility of information and ideas but exist in a broader environment that includes a variety of services which also affect accessibility, such as publishers, directories, social networks and microblogging services, as well as

---

905. *Ibid.*, § 118.
906. *Ibid.*, § 226.
907. See section 2.2.4.

offline media. Moreover, the search engines addressed in this study operate with respect to the World Wide Web. It is quite likely that the democratizing, equalizing and disintermediation effects of the Web for access to audiences on the one hand and access to information and ideas, on the other hand, have been enthusiastically overstated. Yet, it is arguably the most open and diverse platform for the dissemination of information and ideas in human history.[908]

10.2.4. DIVERSITY IN THE CONTEXT OF PARTICULAR SEARCH SERVICES

As was discussed in the last section, an important question is how to assess specific search engines, the market leader Google in particular, from the perspective of pluralism and diversity. Google handles the large majority of global Internet search queries and almost all of them in many European countries. Like other issues related to search engine governance, the question of diversity of search results in the context of a specific search engine can be addressed from the perspective of all three stakeholders: the end-user, the information providers and the search engine itself.

From the information provider's perspective, the question of diversity is one about their level of representation in search results. Can they be found in a specific search engine at all, and if so, how easily? For end-users, the question of diversity is, first of all, an issue of being able to find information through search engines. But more specifically, and considering one of the conclusions in section 10.2.1, there is the question of the extent to which users are being confronted with a diverse set of search results, in terms of language, geographic location, source, viewpoint and other characteristics, and the extent to which users have an impact on the answer to this question. As research has shown, and search engines have adapted to the reality, most users will not look beyond the first page of search results. Thus, this question is of special relevance with regard to the first set of search results. From the search engine's perspective, the question about pluralism and diversity may be best framed in terms of the set of values that ultimately determines the design and thus the functioning of its service. In addition, the question remains as to what extent search engines have incentives to promote or diminish diversity and whether they actually do.

As was discussed in more detail in the preceding chapters, information providers depend on search engines to find a way to an audience, but have a range of options to optimize their exposure to users online. It seems that the simplest way to optimize one's ranking in search engines is to actually provide information that directly satisfies the information needs of users.[909] Wikipedia is an excellent example in this regard. For informational queries, it provides an easily accessible first source of encyclopedic information for Internet users. In fact, this most probably explains the prominent ranking of Wikipedia articles in Google's search results.

---

908. See e.g. Rogers 2004; Benkler 2006.
909. See e.g. Cutts 2006.

However, it is naïve to think that the optimization of search results would be limited to the creation of useful content for users. In fact, perhaps the biggest obstacle for information providers to gain a competitive ranking is the effort and money it takes to actually optimize their representation in search results effectively. SEO is a thriving industry and involves a variety of widely accepted and more controversial practices. Since SEO helps establish winners and losers in search engine results, it is conceivable that search engine rankings will—to some extent—reflect the economic means of underlying information providers as well as their willingness to engage in less acceptable optimization practices. This state of affairs could be considered problematic from the perspective of pluralism and diversity. In addition, since not only sponsored results but also organic results are important platforms for commercial communications, the question of the impact of marketing on diversity of search results is of particular importance. The issue of the impact of advertising on search engine quality will be addressed in more detail in section 10.3.

While it may already be considered problematic that search engine rankings could partly reflect publishers' financial means to optimize relevant search results, the possibility for information providers to optimize their rankings also leads to the spamming and manipulation of search engine results with wholly irrelevant sources of online information. There are various examples that show the feasibility of manipulating access to information for end-users through search engine optimization campaigns. Most famous are the so-called Google bombs that result in amusing or politically motivated search results for certain queries. The query 'miserable failure' would for some time return the official website of former president G.W. Bush as a first result and the Dutch query 'raar kapsel' (weird haircut) would return the website of former Dutch Prime Minister Balkenende.

The Google bomb technique was based on the use of the anchor texts of incoming hyperlinks to websites, meaning that a website would rank well for a particular search term if incoming hyperlinks included that term. Google has eventually found a specific algorithmic solution for these highly visible instances of external influence on search engine results.[910] The reasons Google gave for ultimately fixing these Google bombs was that it wanted to correct the perception that Google actually endorsed the opinion implied by the prominence of these search results, as well as that Google had hard-coded these specific results themselves into their search result pages.[911]

Google bombing, however, is only the tip of the iceberg and the algorithmic solution to defuse them does not prevent information providers from influencing search result selection and ranking more generally. Consider for instance the services that are offered to natural persons or businesses to push away unfavorable search results. As it may be quite hard in practice and legally difficult to have certain search results removed that negatively reflect on someone's reputation, a typical strategy pursued to minimize exposure to negative publicity is to optimize

---

910. See Sullivan 2007.
911. See Moulton & Carattini (Google) 2007.

the ranking of more favorable results and author additional favorable content to fill up the first page of Google's search results. Google reputation management strategies include the strategic creation of websites, blogs and social network profiles in ways that have a high chance of ending up on the top of the list of search results for relevant queries. Remarkably, considering the possible negative impact of the overall quality of search results, Google itself has endorsed this strategy, giving the following advice on the company website:

> If you can't get the content removed from the original site, you probably won't be able to completely remove it from Google's search results, either. Instead, you can try to reduce its visibility in the search results by proactively publishing useful, positive information about yourself or your business. If you can get stuff that you want people to see to outperform the stuff you don't want them to see, you'll be able to reduce the amount of harm that that negative or embarrassing content can do to your reputation.[912]

Hence, Google seems happy to grant information providers considerable power to influence rankings and seems unwilling to entertain the possibility that its algorithms will be unable to guarantee that negative or controversial information and ideas, which must be considered truthful or valuable from the perspective of end-users, could be effectively hidden from the public.

From the perspective of the ideals underlying the right to freedom of expression, the issue can be best framed as a question about the robustness of the search medium.[913] It is clear that the use of billions of third-party signals and the lack of traditional editorial control, in terms of what enters their indices and how well it ranks in search results, poses a risk to the ability of search engines to resist undue interference with their rankings. All major search engines are fighting these ongoing attempts to manipulate their search results, since they can easily deteriorate the value of their service for end-users. However, paradoxically, search engines also depend on these attempts to influence their rankings, which may partly explain Google's endorsement of the practice of reputation management discussed above. To a considerable extent, the signals that are provided by information providers in the form of content, hyperlinks or otherwise, are necessary to make the service work in the first place.

Optimistically speaking, search engines such as Google will be able to balance the different third-party signals with each other and to develop sophisticated technology and organizational strategies to combat undue interference with their service. In practice, however, search engines' dependence on third-party signals for the ranking of search results will predictably cause the service to produce some search results that no human editor would have selected as a relevant result for the query entered. And quite possibly, some third parties will be able to diminish the diversity

---

912. See Moskwa (Google) 2009.
913. In the sense of the word 'robust' in the U.S. Supreme Court's conclusion in *Sullivan* that the First Amendment requires that public debate should be *uninhibited, robust and wide-open*. See *New York Times v. Sullivan*, 376 U.S. 254.

of viewpoints that are present in the first set of search results, thereby negatively affecting exposure diversity for end-users. Apart from search engine optimization of organic results, another way this may happen is through the crowding out of organic results through advertising on search result pages. The optimization of organic results in combination with bidding on sponsored search results can effectively push other sources of information away from the users' view.[914]

For search engine providers, the first question to ask is how much they actually value diversity in the design of the service and how much of a priority it is for them in comparison with other values such as popularity or user satisfaction. Some of the relevant criteria with regard to the diversity mentioned above, such as geographic location and language, can be rather easily dealt with by existing technology. Hence, search engines could actively promote diversity by incorporating these aspects into their ranking algorithms. They could, for instance, aim to always include local results when available and more generally maximize the diversity of results in terms of their geographic location. In fact, Google currently offers its users the choice to specifically focus on local results and its offering of automatic translation tools has expanded the informational horizon of Internet users quite drastically.

For more content-related aspects of diversity, such as particular viewpoints on different societal issues, it may be harder for search engines to actively promote diversity directly and they may, for various reasons, be reluctant and unwilling to do so. Yet, it is possible to imagine that search engines would try to discern viewpoints on particular subjects in their indices, for example with regard to the greenhouse effect, but doing so is much harder than detecting geographic location.[915] It is easier for search engines to prioritize diversity, directly or indirectly, with regard to certain types of sources of information such as official government websites that provide relevant information on the one hand, or new phenomena such as Wikipedia and user-generated content such as Internet discussion forums on the other hand. As can be predicted, these types of sources of information will provide search engine users with different possible perspectives, even though the search engine would not have selected those different viewpoints directly as traditional editorial media would have.

There is one important aspect of operating a search engine that gives search engine providers room and possibly an incentive to promote diversity of search results. Because of the size of many user queries, which often consist of only a word or two, search engines are constantly making informed guesses about what their users are actually looking for. Consider, as a simplified example, the query 'New York'. The user could be interested in many things, including reading about

---

914. A good example of these practices from the United States is the reputation management strategy of the company Lifestyle Lift to obscure legitimate consumer complaints in search results by creating and optimizing a variety of new websites themselves. For a discussion, see Levy 2008.
915. On possible tools for the analysis of online political dynamics with regard to specific issues online, see Rogers 2004.

New York's history or culture, obtaining the lyrics of a song by Frank Sinatra, or booking a flight or hotel room for a holiday or business trip. These different types of information are all available on the Web, and the search engine's ranking algorithms will have a direct or indirect impact on the types of information that it presents to its users. It makes sense for search engines to discern these different types of information in their index and adapt their search result selection and ranking practices accordingly. Yahoo!, for instance, used to offer a special user interface that allowed users to re-rank search results on a scale between commercial and research.[916] Google has recently included a similar choice for users in its new advanced search tools. In the absence of other information or knowledge of user preferences, it would make sense for search engine providers to try to include all these possibilities in its search results. In other words, to the extent that it finds the means to do so, a dominant search engine such as Google is likely to continue to be relatively inclusive and try to satisfy minority interests, because it could lose market share to competitors and possible new verticals otherwise. Therefore, dominant general purpose search engine providers could be expected to try to optimize the diversity of their search result pages to cater to as many different information needs as possible.[917]

At the same time, a commercial search engine's focus on optimizing advertising revenues may entail incentives to focus on some specific user needs rather than others. In particular, search engine providers, such as Google or Microsoft, may be strongly biased towards consumer aspects of the end-user, since their revenues directly relate to the quality of the search process for searchers who are shopping. A strong focus on these information needs may be necessary in their competition for end-users. Otherwise, they could lose their users to destinations which are completely specialized in shopping, such as certain vertical search engines or e-commerce services such as Amazon. It is interesting to note that Microsoft's CEO Steve Ballmer made it clear in 2008 that their efforts in Web search would be mostly focused on search with 'high consumer intent'.[918] Microsoft halted their efforts to develop a book search and academic search service, and instead it started to focus on integrated commercial verticals such as for travel.

Major search engines have also developed other strategies to cater to different types of users. First of all, major search providers offer country- and language-specific search engines. Second, they typically offer a range of search services for special types of material or information, including image and video search, geographic search, news search, academic search, book search and blog search. And finally, the general Web search service has evolved into 'universal search', integrating these different types of material into one search result page. While the inclusion of some of these types of specific search results might be driven by a

---

916. This tool to re-rank results was called Yahoo! Mindset and was released by Yahoo! Research Labs in 2005. It is no longer available. See Yamomoto et al. 2007.
917. Similarly, van Couvering 2010.
918. See Sullivan 2008.

desire to foreclose competition,[919] these strategies could also impact diversity in the context of search, both favorably and unfavorably.

When addressing the question about diversity of search results, it is also interesting to look at the ways in which search engines have dealt with legal but indecent, offensive or controversial sources of information. Such search results could alienate certain search engine users from specific search engines. They can also lead to societal pressure on search engine providers to change their search engine algorithms. Therefore, dominant search engines may have external incentives to prioritize non-controversial information.

For certain types of controversial information, nudity and pornography in particular, the reaction of search engines has been to prevent accidental access through the application of filtering, which can be turned on or off by the user and is typically on by default. The references remain accessible, but only for those users who actively indicate that they are willing to find them by changing their default search settings. In general, however, a search engine such as Google seems to reflect the relative abundance of controversial information on the Web quite well in its search results. In general, the comprehensiveness of search engines' indices seems to carry more weight than the possible negative impact of confronting their users with sources of information they strongly disagree with or find offensive.[920]

Illustrative is the discussion about Google's treatment of the query 'jew'.[921] As is predictable, various flagrantly anti-Semitic information providers, such as 'Jew Watch News', have used the Web as a platform to communicate. Search engines have generally not decided to remove those sites from their index, and, on top of that, sites such as *jewwatch.com* even received very prominent rankings for the query 'jew'. Initially, Google responded to complaints about the prominence of anti-Semitic websites in its search results by arguing that these results were simply based on its neutral ranking algorithms, such as PageRank; the algorithms were applied without regard to the actual content. Eventually, Google decided to add a specific hard-coded notice (as a search result and for google.com also in the form of a self-sponsored link) to the search results for this particular query in its search service, explaining the prominent ranking of the website *jewwatch.com*. This statement now explains that the relative high ranking of anti-Semitic websites for the query 'jew' can partly be attributed to the fact that the word 'Jew' itself is typically used in a pejorative sense on anti-Semitic websites. Non-anti-Semitic websites tend not to use the word 'Jew' at all, but 'Jewish person' instead.[922] In short, Google's algorithms are argued to simply reflect both the availability of such information online and the typical meaning of the query 'jew'. Hence, one

---

919. See section 3.3.1.
920. Some entrepreneurs have identified this as a market opportunity and have developed search services that aim to prevent certain information from showing up. For a discussion of some of these services and their quality, see Hopkins 2010.
921. See also section 8.5.1.
922. See Google, 'An explanation of our search results' http://www.google.com/explanation.html.

could argue that Google prefers to confront its users with the fact that such websites exist than to hide the controversy from its users' sight.[923] This state of affairs does depend on the country-specific service and regulatory context. For the Germany-specific search service google.de, all results for the website jewwatch.com have simply been removed. The removal is comparable to the removal of the storm-front.org website for users of google.de, discussed in detail in the Chapter 9.

Returning to the need for search engines to match a typically weak signal of a user's information need with a very large set of possibly relevant search results, one of the most important ways in which search engines currently deal with the ambiguity of search queries is to analyze historic user behavior and evaluate and improve their results accordingly. The resulting user profiling and personalization combined with a strong focus on user satisfaction could be considered worrying from the perspective of pluralism and diversity in the online information environment. First, this combination could undo the incentive to confront users with as many relevant perspectives on a query as possible to increase the possibility of matching the user's information need. Second and related, it could lead to the biased information bubbles of which some have warned with detrimental effects on the possibility of an informed and shared debate about matters of public concern.[924]

However, the empirical evidence that personalization of search results does, in fact, cause such harm to our societies is not yet convincing.[925] It is possible that personalization of search results makes search engines somewhat less diverse. Yet, even in case of strong personalization search engines may keep confronting users with different stories or viewpoints on the same topic and search engines are hardly the only place where users encounter information and ideas online. In addition, search engines may also develop algorithms that satisfy the value of serendipitous encounters for end-users. Due to the interactive nature of search engines, much of the impact that personalization has will depend on the behavior of actual users. As regards the user's interest, the lack of transparency and control over personalization may be considered more problematic from the perspective of the informational autonomy of users than the mere fact that personalization is taking place.

It is clear that search quality is strongly related to the quality of interaction with search engine services, which to a considerable degree has to be shaped by the users themselves. The choice of the specific service, the knowledge of different languages, the ability to formulate and reformulate effective search queries and use advanced search options has considerable impact on the quality of the search experience. A search engine's choices may have an impact on the ease with which a user finds a variety of information and ideas, but it will hardly help

---

923. It is notable that it could be argued that the fact that search engines are directing users to hate speech is, in a different and possibly more fundamental way, detrimental to pluralism. This question will not be further addressed.
924. See sections 7.4.4 and 10.2.1.
925. At present, the most comprehensive case is made by Eli Pariser 2011. For the positive impact of personalization on the problem of bias more generally, see Goldman 2006.

low-educated users who have no experience with search engine querying and know no alternative services to navigate the Web effectively. Hence, for end-users the quality of their search experience—for instance in terms of the diversity of views they are presented with—will depend on their knowledge and user sophistication. A dedicated, skilled search engine user will be able to reformulate queries to find different points of view and sources of information. It is clear that many users will not take the time or will lack the skill to do so.[926]

The considerations above may be enough reason to conclude that currently there is not enough evidence that specific search engines, Google in particular, pose significant risks from the perspective of information diversity and pluralism. In fact, there are a range of arguments pointing in the opposite direction, since Google does help end-users access and navigate the abundant variety of information and ideas that are available online. However, considering the centrality of search media in the networked information environment, whether or not this is actually the case should be the subject of more thorough empirical research. The structural pressure on diversity by information providers which is inherent in the design of major search engines deserves special attention, as well as the ways in which end-users interact with search services and how the search experience depends on user knowledge, skills and education. The increased personalization of interaction between users and search engines does warrant special attention. While personalization may also have a positive impact on search engine quality, the way personalization is structured and the lack of transparency and control in this context is problematic from the perspective of end-users. The final section of this chapter will discuss the way data protection and privacy could be instrumental in dealing with this negative impact on informational autonomy of end-users.

Finally, it would help if search engines were more explicit about their underlying criteria for evaluating their search result pages. Does Google value pluralism and diversity, and if so, in what way?[927] Moreover, how can we hold a search engine such as Google accountable for acting in line with their stated preferences about the ranking and selection of their search results? It can be argued that the position of Google as the market leader comes with an increased responsibility to clarify its views on this issue, which is from a broader perspective of fundamental importance for our society and the functioning of our democracies. This leads to the subject of the next section, namely the way more transparency in ranking and selection could enhance search engine quality and promote the interests of end-users.

---

926. See e.g. Hargittai 2007b.
927. Since 2008, Google has published a range of articles specifically addressing search quality on *The Official Google Blog*. These articles are directed at a general audience and together provide quite some information about search quality issues in general and a good picture of Google's views on the issues involved. See e.g. Manber (Google) 2008; Singhal (Google) 2008; Singhal (Google) 2008b; Gomes (Google) 2008a; Gomes (Google) 2008b; Huffman (Google) 2008; Dembo (Google) 2008; Baker (Google) 2010; Aula & Rodden (Google) 2009; Cutts (Google) 2011; Champaneria & Yang (Google) 2011.

10.3.   SEARCH ENGINE QUALITY, TRANSPARENCY
          AND MARKETING

As was stated in the beginning of this chapter, search engine quality is addressed in this chapter as related to the way search engines value, select, rank and prioritize information and communication streams. From a legal and regulatory perspective, the relative opacity of industrial search engine ranking technology can be problematic and is typically seen as one of the central issues in the debate about search engine accountability, in particular with respect to Google. What is actually at work when Google selects and ranks its search results? What goals does it pursue and which strategies does it deploy? What hidden biases, deliberate or accidental, impact the relative accessibility of information and ideas for end-users and the possibility to reach an audience for information providers? Without some level of transparency in what is actually taking place, it is hard to arrive at any judgment about the way search engines rank and select search results.

In general, the actual selection and ranking practices of major search engines is best described as a grey box. Some may even call it a black box because search engines such as Google do not disclose (all) the algorithms that are used, but this is too simplistic. Most providers do make various credible statements about the technology and software that is used to provide the search service. Google, for instance, explains that it now uses more than two hundred different signals to determine the proper ranking of a search result and some of those signals are explicitly confirmed.[928] In addition, computer science provides general and specific knowledge about the ways in which general web search engines are or could be designed and operated.[929] Furthermore, part of the research and product development that goes on at industrial search engines such as Google, Microsoft or Yahoo!, is openly shared with the scientific community.[930] Finally, the SEO and SEM industry harbors a lot of knowledge about the selection and ranking practices of search engines based on continuous practical experimentation as part of their services to their customers.

This section will address two of the regulatory issues related to the lack of transparency in selection and ranking of search results that have arisen in the last decade and discuss them from the perspective of search engine quality and freedom of expression. First, the typical business model of commercial search engines involves the sales of sponsored search results. This raises a number of issues relating to the transparency in search engines' motives to produce certain search results and the proper level of disclosure of the mechanisms behind search engine result page composition. Section 10.3.1 will review and critically reflect on the

---

928. One of them is PageRank, although the PageRank algorithms may no longer be used in the form it was described by Google's founders in their 1998 scientific paper, Brin & Page 1998.
929. For a comprehensive overview of the state of the art in information retrieval from a computer science and engineering perspective, see e.g. Baeza-Yates & Ribeiro-Neto 2011. Baeza-Yates is working for Yahoo! Research.
930. For a discussion, see e.g. Tunkelang 2010.

regulatory debate about search advertising and discuss some of the more fundamental structural complexities of transparency in search engine advertising. More specifically, the analogy between search media and traditional commercial mass media that underlies the current separation and labeling of organic and sponsored results will be critically discussed, drawing on an analysis of the dynamics of search media on the one hand and the discussion about the press in Chapter 5 on the other hand. In particular, some of the more structural limitations relating to the possibility of freedom from advertiser and third-party influence for commercial search engine providers will be discussed, limitations which result from their relatively weaker distributed editorial process and their status of meta-media.

Second and related, the impact of the business model of dominant search engines on search engine quality has not been fully understood as well as the strategies search engines pursue to optimize their income more generally. Search engines have been accused of unlawfully manipulating the ranking of certain websites on various legal grounds, such as unfair competition. Some notable examples of this were already addressed in Chapter 8, and there are various other similar examples of such accusations, resulting, amongst other legal developments, in antitrust investigations into Google search in the EU as well as in the United States.[931] On a fundamental level, these accusations raise the question of the extent to which search engines should or could be forced to disclose their business strategies and specific decisions about ranking and selection of search results and the extent to which they should be allowed to freely determine the composition of their search result pages. These issues will be discussed in section 10.3.2.

10.3.1.   SEARCH ENGINE MARKETING: THE LABELING
           OF SPONSORED RESULTS

Search engines have become one of the most attractive marketing platforms in the networked information environment. Search engines are amongst the most popular and heavily used online services. They process billions and billions of search queries and each query presents the service with an opportunity to sell targeted user attention to the highest, or more precisely, the most profitable bidder.[932] As discussed in previous chapters, all dominant general purpose search engines now monetize their services through the sales of sponsored search results through complex auctioning systems. The organic results are separated from these specially labeled 'sponsored results', which offer advertisers the opportunity to market their products, services or points of view more prominently to users. This practice is also

---

931. See Dakanalis and van Rooijen 2011. See also Sterling 2010, Consumer Watchdog's Inside Google 2010; Euractiv 2010, Catan & Efrati 2011; Singhal (Google) 2011; Heise Online 2011; Pollock 2010.

932. When optimizing their income, advertising platforms such as Google AdWords do not sell to the highest bidder. Google's revenue through AdWords is not only related to the willingness to pay a certain price per click but also to the actual click-through rates of specific sponsored results. See e.g. Varian 2009 and cited references.

referred to as paid placement. In addition, some search services offer paid inclusion, meaning that they guarantee certain service levels with regard to the crawling and inclusion of a website in the search engine's index in return for a fee. The case of meta-search engines or the integration of vertical search engines into general search engines could be seen as a special case of paid inclusion.[933]

Both paid placement and inclusion have led to regulatory debate about the appropriateness and lawfulness of these monetization strategies, as end-users may be misled about the composition of search result pages. More generally, the monetization of search engine traffic through paid placement has led to an ethical debate in the search engine industry about these practices.[934]

In 2002, the U.S. Federal Trade Commission reacted to a consumer organization complaint about deceptive practices by search engines in terms of paid placement and inclusion, by outlining its views on the permissibility of these practices. In a recommendation to the industry, the FTC argued as follows with regard to paid placement:

> search engines should clearly and conspicuously disclose that certain Web sites or URLs have paid for higher placement in the display of search results. [. . .] The failure to disclose paid placement adequately within search results deviates from the established deception principle of clearly distinguishing editorial content from advertising content. The purpose of such a demarcation is to advise consumers as to when they are being solicited, as opposed to being impartially informed.[935]

Most search engine providers had already started to act in line with this guidance offered by the FTC and this recommendation has quickly become an industry standard practice, also in Europe.[936] Hence, it is worth taking a closer look at the reasoning and premises behind this standard of clearly demarcating sponsored results from organic results. In particular, from a regulatory perspective it is worth taking a closer look at the implicit underlying analogy with commercial editorial media and the value of demarcating editorial content from advertising in that context.

In Europe, the Directive on Electronic Commerce contains a specific obligation for an information society service to be transparent about commercial communications. Notably, search engines do, in principle, fall under the scope of this directive, as they are information society services.[937] Article 6 contains a specific

---

933. See also section 2.2.
934. For a discussion of Google's early struggle with the question about ethical advertising strategies, see Douglas Edwards 2011, Kindle edition, location 1253–1305.
935. Federal Trade Commission 2002.
936. In Germany, for instance, see e.g. W. Schulz et al. 2005b, 1419–1433.
937. See Article 2 sub (a) of Directive 2000/31/EC juncto Article 1(2) of Directive 98/34/EC as amended by Directive 98/48/EC. See also ECJ March 23, 2010, Joined Cases C-236/08 to C-238/08 (Google Adwords), at 110.

transparency obligation with regard to commercial communications in information society services. This provision reads as follows:

Article 6—Information to be provided

In addition to other information requirements established by Community law, Member States shall ensure that commercial communications which are part of, or constitute, an information society service comply at least with the following conditions:

(a) the commercial communication shall be clearly identifiable as such;
(b) the natural or legal person on whose behalf the commercial communication is made shall be clearly identifiable [...]⁹³⁸

When applied to search media this provision seems to call, like the recommendation of the FTC, for a clear demarcation of sponsored and organic results. The ECD entails a broad, technology-neutral definition of commercial communications in Article 2(f) as "any form of communication designed to promote, directly or indirectly, the goods, services or image of a company, organization or person pursuing a commercial, industrial or craft activity or exercising a regulated profession."⁹³⁹ Article 2(f) ECD contains two exceptions, both of which are relevant in the context of search. The first exception is for "information allowing direct access to the activity of the company, organization or person, in particular a domain name or an electronic-mail address."⁹⁴⁰ As long as search results can be seen as purely navigational, this exception could apply. In reality, however, both organic as well as sponsored search results tend to contain promotional information and offers for specific goods or services which would make these results fall outside the exception. The second exception is for "communications relating to the goods, services or image of the company, organization or person compiled in an independent manner, particularly when this is without financial consideration."⁹⁴¹

Hence, organic results in search media are probably not commercial communications affected by the obligations in Article 6 ECD; as long as providers are acting independently or simply do not receive compensation for their presentation. In other words, this interpretation of Article 6 and the definition of commercial communications of the ECD lead to a similar legal obligation in the European context with regard to the demarcation of organic and sponsored search results which the FTC recommends. Sponsored search results are commercial communications under European law and need to be clearly identifiable. In addition, the entity behind the communication should be clearly identifiable.⁹⁴²

---

938. Directive 2000/31/EC.
939. *Ibid.*
940. *Ibid.*
941. *Ibid.*
942. Notably, this last obligation was taken into account in the ECJ's judgment on Google AdWords, in which the Court concluded that a company is not allowed, under trademark law, to use trademarks of others as keywords, if Internet users would be confused about

Upon a closer look, however, it is questionable whether the stated goals of the FTC's recommendation can be achieved with the labeling of sponsored search results as has become industry practice and is expected from a regulatory perspective. The difference between commercial and other types of communications under European law may not so easily overlap with the difference between organic and sponsored search results.

Turning back to the FTC recommendation, which unlike Article 6 ECD explicitly focuses on search engines and advertising transparency, it is important to note that it is based on search engine user expectations. Search engines could, because of the inclusion or placement of advertisements in search results without disclosing these practices to their users, deceive their users about the reason behind the inclusion and ranking of certain results. At the time of the FTC complaint, reports claimed that a majority of search engines users were unaware of paid placement in search engines.[943] The solution to require more transparency in regard to these practices seems logical. However, for such transparency to make sense in terms of possible deception of users regarding the value of search results, one first has to ask what justified expectations end-users may have about the selection and ranking of search results in the first place.

In the recommendation, the FTC argued, that because search engines:

> historically displayed search results based on relevancy to the search query, as determined by algorithms or other objective criteria, the staff believes that consumers may reasonably expect that the search results displayed by individual search engines are ranked in accordance with this standard industry practice—that is, based on a set of impartial factors.[944]

There are a number of obvious and less obvious problems with this reasoning. First, labeling of different types of search results presupposes a level of knowledge of the functioning of search engines in general, which is arguably absent. Second, the user expectations that the ranking and selection of organic search results is objective, impartial or independent of third-party influence may not be justified. Third, the value of current labeling practices itself breaks down due to the functional similarities between sponsored and organic results for end-users as well as for information providers.

As discussed before, search engine users typically do not have a good idea of how search engines actually select and rank their results. Search engines are and have been secretive about the precise particularities of their selection and ranking practices. And the above-mentioned end-users who are unaware of advertising practices in search engines can be expected to understand even less about the

---

that company's identity. See ECJ March 23, 2010, Joined Cases C-236/08 to C-238/08 (Google Adwords), at 99.

943. See Princeton Survey Research Associates 2002. A later study from the Pew Internet & American Life project confirmed these results; 62% of searchers in the U.S. market were found to be unaware of the distinction between paid and unpaid results. See Fallows 2005, 17.

944. Federal Trade Commission 2002.

selection and ranking of organic search results more generally. It requires expert knowledge to understand even a little of the actual functioning of search engines and the reasons why certain search results may have been selected and ranked highly in response to a particular query.[945]

Moreover, the way search engines select and rank online destinations in their organic search results leaves room for the deception which the demarcation is aiming to prevent. It might simply be the case that end-users cannot justifiably expect the selection and ranking of search results to be based on an independent, objective and impartial valuation by search engine providers, but will have to make their own valuation instead. In other words, search engines may rely too much on third-party signals and do not—and probably cannot on the scale at which they operate—exercise the amount of editorial control which could be considered the prerequisite of a claim to objectivity, independence and impartiality. Some of these choices with regard to organic results could entail the prioritization of commercial communications. And more generally, providers might themselves deploy ranking algorithms that are not based on 'scientific' criteria to objectively assess the 'relevancy' of certain sources of information in respect to specific queries, but rather on their own undisclosed commercial or ideological motivations and editorial choices with regard to the selection and ranking of search engine results more generally.[946]

Hence, information providers have too much control over the ranking and selection of organic search results for the demarcation to make sense for end-users. This may be best illustrated by the fact that SEO of organic results is considered an effective strategy to market products and services, and even a substitute for advertising in sponsored search results.[947] Therefore, the FTC's statement that "any Web sites [. . .] that have paid to be ranked higher than they would be ranked by relevancy, or other objective criteria, should be clearly labeled as such using terms conveying that the ranking is paid for" is confused and arguably naïve in its trust of objectivity and impartiality of organic search results.[948] The application of the provisions from the Directive on Electronic Commerce on the search medium discussed above suffers from the same deficit, by substituting the requirement *without financial consideration* for the requirement *in an independent manner*.[949]

It is ironic that one of the reasons for the effectiveness of the optimization of organic search results might be that some end-users unjustifiably expect that these

---

945. For instance, even relative experts are still confused about the question if Google sells access to higher placement in organic results. In a recent higher educational guide on using search engines, including Google, for research, the writer states: "As is known, you end up higher in Google's search results if you pay for it—that is how the search engines makes its money. For instance when one types: books Willem Bilderdijk (number of results 129.000), gets two references to bol.com on the top (and these are no advertisements (Translation by the author)." See Sanders 2011, 13.
946. See also section 8.4.3.
947. See Yang & Ghose 2010, 2. See also Arnold et al. 2011.
948. Federal Trade Commission 2002.
949. See Article 2(f) Directive 2000/31/EC.

results are delivered free from commercial influences.[950] In a similar vein, end-users may undervalue sponsored search results as proper answers to their queries for the mere reason that they are labeled as sponsored links. However, the fact that end-users use search engines in the context of e-commerce implies that advertisements can be quite relevant or even more relevant than non-commercial communications from the perspective of end-users. In fact, the willingness to pay, measured through an advertisement auction, is a perfectly objective measure to rank advertisements and can be used as one of the signals to assess the relevance of an online destination for end-users.

Finally, there are some conceptual problems with the application of the traditional demarcation between editorial content and advertising in editorial media to the context of search media. On a functional level, search media—and other selection intermediaries such as Twitter for instance—may be an example, and perhaps even the main driver, of convergence of information retrieval, recommendation and advertising systems, in a way that cannot be disentangled by the mere labeling of so-called sponsored results.[951] Organic links and sponsored links are the same type of targeted reference: a link, a title and a short explanation, none of which tend to be written by the search engine provider.[952] Search media are not editorial with respect to their organic search results in the way that newspapers ideally are. Search media typically include everything in their index anyway and allow information providers to control what ends up being indexed or not. Advertisers do not participate in the sponsored results programs of major search engines to be included at all, as would typically be the case with advertising in editorial media. They participate to acquire relatively more prominence and subsequent attention of end-users. As a result, sponsored links will typically supplement organic results to the same information provider, and these two types of links to the same destination can be very similar and do not tend to provide different perspectives for the end-user. Paradoxically, the sponsored results are more heavily editorialized than the organic ones: they typically have to follow editorial guidelines for search advertisements, while, in principle, no such editorial guidelines exist for organic results.[953] The distinction between organic and sponsored links breaks down even more, because the ranking and selection of sponsored links, as is the case for organic results, heavily depends on the relevancy of the underlying content with respect to the search query entered by the user, as well as their success in terms of click-through rates, and not merely the advertisers' willingness to pay.[954]

---

950. See Jansen & Spink 2009.
951. On this new type of convergence, see Garcia-Molina et al. 2011.
952. See section 3.2.
953. One could consider the guidelines for permissible SEO of organic results to be editorial guidelines. Such guidelines include a ban on the sales of outgoing links, hidden links and the development of shadow domains or doorway pages. See Google 2010b.
954. Thus, a lack of relevance leads to lower rankings (or even removal) of the sponsored link, but can be compensated in a willingness to pay more per click in the auction.

In the context of the press, the labeling of advertising is only a small part in a more general best practice of the treatment of advertising and special interests and the protection of the press' and journalistic independence and impartiality. Considering that the model of editorial media has helped shape their treatment of paid inclusion programs, the search engine industry could adopt some of the related best practices in the field of editorial media. Search engines could, for instance, structure their internal operations in such a way as to prevent direct profit considerations from having a negative impact on the quality of their search results.[955] They could adopt codes of conducts about the way they deal with the various incentives which arise from their advertisement-based business model. While some search engine providers, including Google, would claim that they are already acting in line with such recommendations, the problem is that they have not yet developed a framework that makes their statements verifiable for the general audience. In one way or another, more transparency and disclosure will be needed for the labeling of search results to become really meaningful. For instance, more meaningful self-regulatory practices would include some kind of independent audits to verify the truthfulness of the stated practices.

To sum up, while the demarcation between sponsored links and organic results was meant to prevent end-users from being deceived about the mechanism behind the composition of search result pages, its logic is too simplistic to capture what is really going on. In reality, end-users' expectations with regard to organic results cannot justifiably be in line with the FTC's premise. Instead, end-users should be, or be made, aware of the many ways in which organic search results are, in fact, shaped by different forms of external pressure, including not only pressure from advertisers but also from other special interests. Search engines should complement the existing practice of labeling with additional internal policies and strategies to prevent the crowding out of objectively valuable, non-commercial references in their index. They should also make themselves publicly accountable for adhering to these policies. In the absence of such additional safeguards, search engine users may be better off not having any expectation of impartiality, objectivity of any type of search result. In that case, they will have to simply rely on their own judgment about the value of the references that are provided to them.

10.3.2.   SEARCH ENGINE ADVERTISING, QUALITY AND TRANSPARENCY

While the labeling of sponsored search results at least clarifies that search media engage in paid placement strategies, the monetization of search traffic raises other issues with regard to the ranking and selection of search results and search engine quality more generally, which have yet to be fully understood. For instance, an important question is what the impact is of the monetization of search engine traffic

---

955.   See van Couvering 2010. Van Couvering's interviews in the search engine industry show this to be considered an issue internally and to the extent that the different perspectives of information retrieval engineers and marketers lead to internal tension.

on the overall quality of search media and the willingness of search engines to innovate and improve the quality of their search results. Transparency in the strategies of existing search media in the context of ranking and selection to optimize their income is lacking. If anything, commercial search media can be expected to optimize their income through the optimization of clicks on sponsored search results. This could have adverse effects on the quality of search media seen as information retrieval systems from the perspective of end-users. At the very least, the business interests of commercial search engines to monetize as much traffic as possible implies that any statements of search media that present their selection and ranking strategies as merely directed at satisfying information needs of end-users should be critically assessed.

As discussed in the previous section, until now regulators such as the FTC cited above have been rather uncritical in following search engines' claims about independence, relevance and objectivity. In a similar vein, the ECJ's Advocate-General was happy to state the following:

> natural results are selected and ranked according to their relevance to the keywords. This is done through the automatic algorithms underlying the search engine program, which apply purely objective criteria.[956]

The uncritical adoption of these premises about the functioning and goals of commercial search engine providers is also the basis of the current labeling of sponsored search results, which, as argued in the previous section, falls short in providing real value for end-users. While the values of independence and impartiality in search engine ranking and selection practices could surely contribute to search engine quality for end-users, selection and ranking practices of dominant search media currently depend too heavily on third-party signals to be characterized as such.

On the one hand, the ranking and selection practices of major search media are a complicated, mostly opaque and automated set of decisions about the 'value' and 'relevance' of sources of information in view of a particular understanding of information needs of end-users. As argued in Chapter 8, the realization that selection and ranking involve a variety of subjective decisions about the relevance and value of information also offers search engine providers a freedom of expression defense to freely decide which choices to make in this context. As the Financial Times concludes, summarizing various critiques of the supposedly objective nature of search engine rankings, as follows:

> By changing its mathematical formula to modify the results returned to a particular query, Google's engineers are making judgments very similar to the editorial decisions made at a more traditional media organization [. . .].[957]

On the other hand, the judgments about the ranking and selection of search results may be primarily aimed to advance the business interest of the search medium.

---

956. ECJ, AG Opinion, Joined Cases C 236/08, C 237/08 and C 238/08 (*Google Adwords*).
957. Waters 2010.

In fact, the advertisement-based business model has some obvious implications for the incentives on search engine operators to make certain choices rather than others. Search engines are in the business of matching information needs of end-users and the offer and willingness to communicate of information providers. It is important to realize that this is exactly what advertisers have been doing all along, although with one particular mindset.

Ultimately, the question about search engine quality is a question about the values and goals of search engine providers and the compatibility of those values with societal interests that go beyond their direct business interest. And since end-user attention is scarce, the question is, ultimately, what kind of end-user information needs a search engine decides to satisfy: those that it considers, on the basis of some idea about the scientific, societal or political value of information and ideas, most worthy of finding satisfaction or those that would be most profitable? It would be quite unconvincing to argue that these perspectives will always overlap. And again, the question is how search engines will deal with the fact that information providers' willingness to find the attention of end-users, whether expressed through advertising in search engines or through SEO, does not necessarily reflect their value as sources of information.

The negative impact of advertising on broadcasting quality is well documented: commercial media can, in general, be expected to produce the level of quality of programming that is necessary to keep people watching.[958] This is used as one of the reasons for the subsidization of public broadcasting and the regulation of advertising in broadcasting. Will commercial search engines act similarly and produce the minimum level of quality of results which ensures that people will not switch to a competitor? Should regulators respond with public service search engines or search engine regulation? More specifically, can Google, as the market leader, be expected, and allowed if it does so, to mainly focus on sponsored links' prominence and quality? And in view of their business model, how important is it for major search engines to preserve or improve the quality of their organic listings, considering that clicks on organic links can be seen as missed opportunities for them to monetize attention? In the context of commercial search engines, the functional overlap between sponsored and organic search results further increases the pressure on the quality of organic search results. Both organic and sponsored search results are avenues in which information providers can influence their prominence.

At present, it is still easier to ask these questions than to answer them properly, and regulators have only quite recently started to address some of these issues more seriously, most notably in the competition law context and possible abuse of market power of industry leader Google. The European Commission addressed the possible impact of advertising on organic search quality in its review of the deal relating to organic search listings between Microsoft and Yahoo.[959] In general, the

---

958. See e.g. Baker 2002; Benkler 2006, 176–212.
959. European Commission 2010a.

Commission is quite optimistic about the current levels of innovation in terms of search engine quality:

> Search engines spend enormous efforts in order to continuously improve the search algorithm and their ability to match users and advertisers. [...] The high degree of innovation in these markets is proven by the rate at which new innovation has been introduced in the past (for example intro- duction of the auction mechanism, quality rank, analytics, spell check, etc.) and by constant experimentations that search engines undertake daily on several fronts.[960]

Further on, the Commission explains what kind of possible market behavior could be expected and considered negative for the quality of search engines for end- users, as follows:

> Theoretically, the rationale for possibly degrading the organic search stems from the trade off that search platforms appear to face between the incentive to provide relevant organic and paid results. The trade off arises because when a platform tries to attract more users through greater relevance on the organic search it runs the risk of losing revenues on the advertising side (i.e. less clicks on ads) due to users clicking predominantly on the organic side (especially if both types of clicks would bring the user to the same kind of information). [...]
> [P]latforms might have an incentive to dedicate a smaller part of the result page to organic results in favour of search advertising links [] thereby providing proportionally more advertising links. Alternatively, the platforms may rank the sponsored and organic search results in a way that firms offering competing products to the sponsored links are ranked, from the user's per- spective, on the organic side lower than optimally.[961]

In its actual analysis of the impact of the merger on the search engine market, the Commission does not come to the conclusion that this behavior takes place.[962] Due to the nature of competition law, it merely draws the conclusion that the deal under review would not worsen the situation. It does so on the basis of four arguments, namely that (1) users would be responsive with respect to variations to the rele- vance provided and be able to switch to alternatives, that (2) there was very limited switching of end-users between the two parties under review, that (3) other search engines (Ask or local ones) and competing verticals could still be expected to exercise a constraint on the main competing platforms not to degrade their service, and that (4) the improved scale of organic traffic for Microsoft would allow it to

---

960. *Ibid.*
961. *Ibid.*
962. At present, there seems to be no hard evidence of such practices taking place in the major search engines operating in Europe and the U.S. The current complaints at the European Commission, when reviewed, could provide more information.

actually improve the quality of its search results, thereby keeping up pressure on search quality for Google as well.[963]

From the perspective of competition law, these conclusions seem reasonable. Competition law can be expected to provide some constraints on search engine quality for end-users, but its role is necessarily limited for several reasons. First, from a market perspective it is difficult to address the impact of search engine market dynamics on end-users, since they (or rather, their attention and targeted navigation) are the product being sold instead of the paying customers. The Commission addresses this issue by using the economic theory of two-sided platforms. However, its analysis remains simplistic. In particular, it does not address the trade-offs between the participants on the two sides of the market. What could be considered harmful for end-users from the perspective of search engine quality, such as more and more space reserved for sponsored results,[964] can be expected to be beneficial for advertisers. Competition law does not answer which sets of competing harms and benefits are preferable.[965] In addition, advertisers are competing with other information providers for attention. It is hard to imagine how competition law can address the trade-offs between the interests of advertisers and other sources of information worthy of representation in search results, or the trade-offs between different types of users.

While this analysis of the European Commission did not directly target the business practices of Google, in 2010 both the European Commission and the U.S. antitrust authorities started to investigate complaints about possible anticompetitive ranking and selection practices of Google.[966] Amongst other complaints and accusations of abuse of dominance, the investigations are focusing on the anticompetitive effects of vertical integration of general purpose search engines and the possible preferential treatment of Google's own services in Google's search results.

Considering the complexities of the underlying markets, the result of these investigations can be expected to be of major significance for the future of the search engine industry. In addition, the investigations go to the heart of the question about the freedom of (dominant) search engine providers to rank and select search results and the proper limitations on such freedom in view of possible harm to third parties. Consider, for instance, the claim that Google harms competition by degrading

---

963. European Commission 2010a, §§ 219–223.
964. The European Commission does qualify this as a possible harm for search engine users, but concludes that the deal between Yahoo! and Microsoft is unlikely to provide both parties with additional incentives in this direction, considering the dominance of Google and the lack of competition between the parties under review. It does not discuss this harm in relation to possible benefits for the advertisers.
965. It is notable that some have complained about Google's emphasis on non-commercial results in its organic listings, such as Wikipedia, which pushes commercial information providers to participate in Google Adwords. See also Edelman 2009. There are also rumors that Google would rather have websites that run AdSense, hence other than Wikipedia, rank more favorably but that it feels a similar change would harm its credibility. The source for this rumor adds that Google-watching is like 'Kremlinology'.
966. European Commission 2010d. See also Bartz 2011. See also Mayer (Google) 2010.

the ranking of search results to competing verticals' search engines and directories. While it may be questionable whether this behavior takes place, and if it takes place, whether it should be considered an abuse of market power, it also raises the question of the extent to which the law could and should limit the freedom of search engines to decide that verticals and directories are simply inferior destinations from the perspective of search engine quality. In other words, the right to freedom of expression and the editorial freedom it arguably offers search engines with respect to the choices of which selection and ranking practices to engage in, should be taken into account in these investigations by competition authorities.

Under the current legal framework, and apart from the specific labeling obligation discussed in the previous section, transparency in ranking and selection is provided voluntarily and encouraged through self-regulation. There are no general legal disclosure requirements for search engines about their ranking and selection practices, which also typically enjoy protection as trade secrets. Some argue that it will be necessary to impose specific transparency obligations on major search engine providers. The most sophisticated proposals in this direction have proposed to install special oversight committees to prevent general disclosure to the public and competitors, while still providing the benefits from the perspective of accountability.[967']

While everything may seem to point in the direction of the value of more transparency in ranking and selection practices, it is important to note that there are some arguments against disclosure requirements for search engine ranking and selection practices. First of all, search engine providers would argue that disclosure might decrease search engine quality to the detriment of end-users, as it would allow interested parties to game their systems.[968] The production of search engine results takes place in a continuous competition for Internet traffic, search engine optimization and marketing. The current levels of disclosure and transparency are, at least to some extent, tailored to address the negative impact of this ongoing competition.

Second, and more fundamentally, the nature of the information that would have to be disclosed goes to the heart of the editorial aspect of the search medium. The observation that decisions about ranking and selection of search engines are editorial decisions implies that the law should not too easily impose restrictions on the freedom to decide how to rank and select search results. And it can be argued that the protection of the search engine provider's freedom to select and rank search results, based on a theory of editorial freedom, should also involve a limitation on requirements to disclose the precise practices, since such a requirement could result in chilling effects and provide search engine providers with incentives not to engage in certain selection and ranking practices. As a comparison, one would not imagine similar obligations on traditional editorial media. No one would propose to legally and generally require publishers to factually disclose the actual decisions that are made in the editorial room. This kind of regulation would be

---

967. See e.g. Bracha & Pasquale 2008, 1201.
968. See e.g. Grimmelmann 2007; Van Couvering 2010.

considered an infringement of the freedom of the press. In sum, from the perspective of the right to freedom of expression, it is preferable that transparency would be offered through self-regulation.

Another feasible approach would be the more systematic monitoring of the industry and the funding of independent research into the incentives search engines have with regard to the interplay between the quality of their organic search results and the optimization of income through sponsored search listings.[969] In addition, in the absence of sector-specific regulation of search engines, competition law may be expected to continue to provide some insights into the selection and ranking practices of dominant search engine providers. In particular, the regular reviews of commercial agreements and the recent investigations into the complaints about the abuse of market power involving or relating to Google's search business by competition authorities will help provide some transparency in the functioning of the search engine market, the possibilities and realization of abuse, and the motives behind the production of particular search result orderings.

10.4.	SEARCH ENGINE QUALITY AND USER DATA: PRIVACY, PERSONALIZATION AND INTELLECTUAL FREEDOM

This final section will address the regulatory issues relating to search engine quality and the processing of user data by search engines. High quality user data could be considered the holy grail of search engine providers (and most other commercial Web services for that matter). In his book on Google and the importance of search, John Battelle called Google's collection of user data 'the database of intentions'.[970] It goes well beyond the scope of this research to fully discuss the practices of user data processing by major web search providers such as Google. In the next section, a short overview will be provided, after which some of the legal issues relating to the processing of user data by search engine providers will be discussed from the perspective of the right to freedom of expression. More specifically, section 10.4.2 will address the way the observance of the right to privacy and data protection laws can be seen as a prerequisite to intellectual freedom of search engines users as well as the way the current legal regime incorporates this concern. Section 10.4.3 will discuss the way EU data protection law, as interpreted by the Article 29 Working Party, could in theory contribute to the informational autonomy of search engine users, if it were to be applied more rigorously on current data processing practices.

---

969. The incentives this produces is a complex question in search engine economics. See e.g. White 2008; Yang & Ghose 2010, 2. See also Arnold et al. 2011; Chan et al. 2011.

970. Battelle 2006. Since then, Battelle has extended the database of intentions, for which major Web services compete, to include the social environment, the status of action, as well as the location of individuals. See Battelle 2010.

10.4.1.   SEARCH ENGINE USER DATA PROCESSING: BACKGROUND

Search engines rely on complex, sophisticated processing of massive amounts of user data in many aspects of their service. Many users may only be aware of providing one relevant data point to search engine providers, namely the search query. But search engine user input consists of a range of data, over significant amounts of time. Some of these data are also directly provided by the user, such as search preferences, which are typically stored through the use of Web cookies, a file on the users' computer that helps individualize end-users. In addition, data relating to a search will be registered and processed, such as the date and time a search query was entered, as well as subsequent user actions such as a click on a search result. A lot of other data are provided by the users as a result of them interacting with the Web search service, such as their IP address, the operating system, the browser and its settings. Users are typically tracked over many sessions of use with so-called cookies containing unique identifiers. Whereas the IP address might not mean much to the average Internet user, these data allow web services to reveal something about someone's geographic location, when combined with other data sources. Similar combinations can subsequently be made with other data sets, such as demographics connected to ZIP codes.[971]

User data is an essential ingredient for the monetization of search, and competition in the search engine and Web services market more generally is strongly focused on the ability to collect user data.[972] The advertisement-based business model of search engines essentially turns around user data as every click by a user on a sponsored result is a micropayment from the advertiser to the service. These user clicks are registered and optimized in view of the profitability of the service. And in view of the interests of paying customers, these clicks need to be legitimate and not fraudulent. In addition, the more user data search engines have, or perhaps better, the more search engines can infer with some degree of statistical relevance, and the more targeted the advertisements that are displayed can be. The level of targeting increases the value of their product for advertisers, thereby increasing the profits of the search engine provider.[973]

User data collections also allow search engine providers to do research on user behavior.[974] Amongst other things, this research involves machine learning on large user data sets. The goal of such research could be to develop new statistical qualifiers to improve ranking and selection and sponsored result placement. User data can be analyzed in view of relevance and user satisfaction, particular patterns of user behavior can be predicted to be possibly fraudulent and search queries in general can be better understood. User data can also be used to innovate and develop new services, an often cited example of which is the 'suggestion' function that corrects spelling mistakes and suggests possible improvements of the search query.

---

971. See e.g. Weber & Castillo 2010.
972. See Bermejo 2007; Röhle 2007b. See more generally, Elmer 2004.
973. See generally Turow 2006.
974. See e.g. Baeza-Yates & Ribeiro-Neto 2011, 185 et seq.

Finally, user data can be used to personalize the service, in the sense that search engine providers will select and rank their search results on the basis of that user's history of interaction with the service or other data related to that specific user.[975] Any of the more simple data mentioned above, such as the IP address or language preference can be used to personalize results, but other and more sophisticated signals could be used as well, such as historic preference for certain media formats, for instance video or link navigation speed. Personalization can also be based on specific combinations of signals and rich data collections available from other services, such as email, social networks or video on demand. Since 2009, Google personalizes both its organic and sponsored results for all its users.[976] For authenticated users, it promotes websites that have been visited before, shows how many visits took place, and more generally seems to develop a kind of profile of interests which has an impact on the user's search results.[977] As mentioned, Google personalizes search results on the basis of a variety of criteria, most of which are unknown. It is clear that the possibilities to personalize further are only just being explored and can be expected to become the subject of intense competition between dominant Web services.

The regulatory debate about the processing of user data by search engines has been channeled through data protection and the right to privacy and confidentiality topics. Early commentators' worries about the amount and sensitivity of data being registered by search engines were publicly confirmed in 2006 when AOL released a set of user data for research purposes.[978] The data set consisted of a large number of search histories of AOL users, in which the IP addresses had been replaced by a unique number. The release was generally considered a mistake because of the sensitivity of the data. The New York Times showed in their report 'A Face is Exposed for AOL Searcher No. 4417749' that the search history could be used to identify an actual Internet user.[979]

The regulatory debate intensified in the years after the release of the AOL search logs. Most notably, European data protection authorities started an investigation into the processing of user data from a European data protection law perspective, first addressing only Google and later addressing the Web search industry at large. This investigation was concluded in 2008 in the form of an official opinion by the Article 29 Data Protection Working Party on 'data protection issues related to search engines'.[980] In the United States, the FTC looked into

---

975. See Pariser 2011; Feuz et al. 2011; Zuckerman 2011. See also Stalder & Mayer 2009.
976. See Sullivan 2009.
977. See Feuz et al. 2011.
978. On the importance of access to search logs for the research community and the negative impact of the public outcry about the release for information retrieval research, see Bar-Ilan 2007.
979. See Barbaro & Zeller 2006. See also Lenssen 2006. The data release has had a major impact on search engine privacy policy discussions and has been used by legal scholars, computer scientists and artists. See e.g. Tene 2008; Cooper 2008. Dutch artists and documentary makers Lernert & Sander made the movie 'I Love Alaska' about someone's queries. See Lernert & Sander 2008.
980. Article 29 Data Protection Working Party 2008.

search engine user data processing in the context of its recommendations about data privacy safeguards (in the form of self-regulation) with regard to behavioral advertising.[981]

As mentioned above, the scrutiny of the processing of search log data processing has mostly taken place through the lens of data protection and privacy law and regulation. As a consequence, the regulatory debate has placed particular emphasis on data privacy-related issues, such as the anonymization of user data and the retention period of individual search queries in non-aggregate form, the question of third-party access to search query data and the legitimacy of the goals underlying the processing of so much user data by search engine providers in the first place. Apart from these issues, the question about the proper application of jurisdictional provisions of the EU Privacy Directive (95/46/EC) to Web search engines operating from outside the EU and the question of whether or not the user data in search logs should be qualified as 'personal data' under the Privacy Directive have been important in the legal debate about the proper application of EU law in this context.

Much less attention has been paid to the question of how individual user data processing has shaped, and continues to shape, access to information by Internet users. In line with the focus of this study on the right to freedom of expression in the context of search, this section will specifically address this perspective by addressing two of the issues at the interplay of data protection, search engine user privacy and freedom of expression. First, in section 10.4.2, the question will be discussed as to how the current privacy and data protection framework for search engine user data processing takes into account the freedom of expression interests of users to seek and access information and ideas freely. In general, the instrumental value of privacy for the right to freedom of expression is well accepted.[982] For instance, this value lies in the possible chilling effect of the absence of appropriate privacy safeguards on expressive conduct, including the search for and the access to information and ideas online.[983] In the context of networked communications, the free exercise of the right to freedom of expression takes place in a new environment and with the use of new types of services, such as Web search engines. When data processing practices by new intermediaries do not go hand in hand with appropriate data protection and privacy safeguards, they may not only impact the right to privacy and data protection but also profoundly impact the enjoyment of the right to freedom of expression.

In section 10.4.3, the question will be addressed regarding if and how European data protection law could promote accountability in the context of search from a user's perspective, in particular with regard to the impact that search engine user data has on the selection and ranking of organic as well as sponsored search results. Building on the conclusion of European data protection authorities that much of the processing of user data by search engine providers amounts to the

---

981. See Federal Trade Commission 2007. See also Federal Trade Commission 2009.
982. See also sections 7.4.7 and 8.6.4.
983. See Solove 2009a, 193.

processing of personal data—processing which therefore falls under the scope of EU data protection laws—the question will be explored as to what ways data protection law could contribute to transparency and accountability in the context of search engine ranking and selection practices. This question has grown in relevance due to the increased personalization of search results. It will be shown that in theory, EU data protection law may indeed promote the informational autonomy of end-users in the context of search, but that until now data protection compliance and enforcement levels have been wanting in delivering this potential.

10.4.2.   INTELLECTUAL FREEDOM AND SEARCH ENGINE USER SURVEILLANCE

As was noted in Chapter 8, the search engine user's privacy can be seen as a condition for the fundamental right to search, access and receive information and ideas freely. Information-seeking behavior could be seriously chilled if the main available options to find information online entail comprehensive surveillance and storage of end-user behavior without appropriate guarantees that such information will not be used to one's disadvantage.

Historically, libraries have had the most experience with the need to guarantee the privacy of their patrons and the confidentiality of their reading habits.[984] In Chapter 7, it was shown how public libraries consider user privacy a fundamental concern, since it is instrumental in preserving the intellectual freedom of their patrons.[985] In some countries and in several states in the United States, access to library records by government agencies is restricted in view of the interest of privacy of library patrons. It must be noted that public libraries also process more and more user data in the context of electronic library products. User data can also be beneficial in view of the possibility to better serve the library user's needs through better targeted recommendations.

For other institutions such as the press, the processing of user data at the current scale is a new phenomenon. For some political publications subscriber records, if they did exist, were considered a sensitive matter. However, the scale in which electronic online media can and do process data on their readers or viewers is unprecedented. In addition, more and more electronic publishers allow end-users to make contributions as well. Typically, on these users additional data will be collected. The publishing sector at large has yet to show serious signs of reflecting on the possible need to balance the benefits of the processing of user data, such as personalization and targeted advertising, with the intellectual freedom of their users.

---

984. On comparing privacy in the context of libraries with the context of search engines, see Nissenbaum 2010, 194–195.
985. See cross-reference, Ch. Ch. 7. In particular, the question of how and whether new digital library services such as Google Books respect the user's privacy to the same extent as used to be the ideal in the traditional library setting is an important question. For a discussion, see Zimmer, September 8, 2009.

In the context of electronic communications service providers, such as Internet access providers, the individual's interests in communications privacy and confidentiality of the contents of communications are both protected by the right to respect for private life in Article 8 ECHR and safeguarded through specific legal · norms at the EU and the national level. The e-Privacy Directive at the EU level (2002/58/EC) provides that Member States have to ensure the confidentiality of electronic communications through legislation and restricts the permissibility of the processing of traffic and location data relating to communications. The e-Privacy Directive can, like the general EU Privacy Directive, be seen as an instance of the Member States acting under their positive obligation to protect communications privacy in horizontal relations.

In the context of information services such as search engines, there are no sector-specific rules for the protection of the privacy of users. General privacy and data protection laws, the EU Privacy Directive (95/46/EC) in particular, provide the legal framework for the processing of personal data of users by information society services, such as electronic publishers or search engine providers.

It could be argued that European data protection authorities have been somewhat successful in addressing the collection and processing of user data by search engines through an application of European data protection laws. The Article 29 Working Party's opinion on search engines and data protection clarifies that major search engine providers are subject to general data protection law and it outlines the way the EU Privacy Directive guarantees the fair processing of personal data in the context of Web search engines.[986] More specifically, the Article 29 Working Party concludes that search engine user data can typically be considered personal data, can only be processed for legitimate purposes and must be deleted or irreversibly anonymized afterwards.[987] In addition, search engine providers have to inform their users about the processing of their data and their rights to access, inspect or correct their data.

The regulatory debate about search engines' obligations under European data protection law has not been settled. The industry has been somewhat reluctant to recognize the application of EU data protection law, arguing on the one hand that most of the data cannot be considered personal data and on the other hand consistently avoiding stating their policies in terms of European data protection rules. The possible resulting lack of compliance will be addressed in the next section.

From the perspective of the right to freedom of expression, an important downside of the European data protection framework as applied to the processing of user data by search engine providers, or other information services such as the electronic press, is that it does not contain provisions that specifically recognize the

---

986. Article 29 Data Protection Working Party 2008.
987. There has been extensive debate about the threshold for anonymization of search logs to be meaningful. See e.g. Soghoian 2008. More fundamentally, computer scientists have shown that it may be theoretically impossible to anonymize a rich data set, since any information that distinguishes one person from the other can be used to re-identify data. See Shmatikov & Narayanan 2010, 22–26.

special nature of the data involved. As searching the Web has become a primary means for members of the information society to find and/or access information and ideas, and the provision of the services that satisfy those needs involves the processing of massive amounts of user data relating to one's interests and intentions, this could be reason for reflection on the need to include specific legal norms relating to the processing of data relating to an individual's information-seeking and information-accessing behavior.

The Article 29 Working Party does recognize the importance of search engines as first points of access to information online in its opinion on search engines. First, it notes that search logs contain a footprint of a user's interests, relations and intentions and explains that these logs may be used commercially or become the subject of requests by law enforcement and national security agencies. It than expresses its opinion as follows:

> Search engines play a crucial role as a first point of contact to access information freely on the Internet. Such free access to information is essential to build one's personal opinion in our democracy. Therefore, Article 11 of the European Charter of Fundamental Rights is of special relevance because it provides that "information should be accessible without any surveillance by public authorities, as part of freedom of expression and information".[988]

However, there are no specific rules in the EU Privacy Directive that acknowledge this fundamental concern related to the processing of user data by search engine providers. The way the Privacy Directive recognizes the special nature of certain categories of personal data is through the special regime for 'sensitive data'. Article 8 of the Privacy Directive contains a number of special categories of personal data, namely "data revealing racial or ethnic origin, political opinions, religious or philosophical beliefs, trade-union membership, and the processing of data concerning health or sex life."[989] For the processing of this data, stricter rules apply. The processing of these special categories of data is forbidden outside the circumstances listed in Article 8 of the Privacy Directive. If the processing of sensitive data is based on the data subject's consent, such consent needs to be explicit, which is a stricter standard than unambiguous (Article 8(2)(a) Privacy Directive).

While some may argue that search queries reveal sensitive types of information about an individual, the assumption that a direct link exists between data subjects' information access behavior and their proper characteristics as individuals is itself highly problematic. Notably, Article 29 Working Party did not address this question in its opinion on search engines. It is true that search engine user data, the user's queries and subsequent navigation in particular, could be used to infer certain information about end-users, such as information about diseases, political

---

988. Article 29 Data Protection Working Party 2008, 8.
989. These categories of data are based on Article 6 of the Council of Europe, Convention for the Protection of Individuals with regard to Automatic Processing of Personal Data Strasbourg, January 28, 1981.

viewpoints or religious beliefs. A user's search history may reveal an interest in a special heart disease, a certain political party or a particular religion. It may even be possible to statistically predict the ethnicity of the users on the basis of their search history and other data accessible to the search engine provider.[990] The possibility that search engines themselves do profile their users and personalize their offerings in these ways could be an additional argument for treating search user data that relates to these special categories as sensitive data themselves.

However, it is problematic to conclude that end-users who search for information about a disease, viewpoint or belief actually have that disease, viewpoint or belief. This may actually go to the heart of the value of privacy and intellectual freedom in the context of access to information and ideas. While the end-user uses the search engine to search for information and ideas, search engines are using the data users leave behind as an opportunity to predict more and more about the end-users' proper characteristics. As a consequence, particular patterns in information-seeking and information-accessing behavior lead to the attribution of certain characteristics to the individual. However, even if search engines process a user's data to predict that user's future interests, this does not necessarily mean that the search engine equals someone's interests with the person's proper characteristics. Search engines may actually not be interested at all in identifying their users. They may merely be interested in optimizing the chance of satisfying a user's query as well as monetizing it.[991] Yet, this behavior by search engines could have a chilling effect on the use of search engine services.[992] To conclude, while search engine user data may reveal information that relates to sensitive types of information, the special regime for the processing of sensitive data does not seem to fit the processing of search engine user data.

At the same time, the fact that so much information can be statistically predicted on the basis of search engine user data is the reason search engine providers work hard to obtain more and more user data and are actively exploring new ways to use and analyze them. Search engine providers use this data to improve the quality of the search service, increase the granularity of their targeted advertising programs or develop new and search-related products, such as the search 'suggest' functionality. In addition, there are numerous ways in which the analysis of search engine user data collections, on the scale that a search engine provider such as Google has access to, could be used in contexts completely unrelated to access to information and ideas or the optimization of marketing.

Google, for instance, has indirectly advocated the benefits of its extensive user surveillance and the research it enables through its Google Trends tools and Google

---

990. Recent research at Yahoo! shows that search engines may be able to predict (with some statistical accuracy) ethnic origin on the basis of query analysis. See Weber & Castillo 2010.
991. See also Stalder & Mayer 2009, 112.
992. Data protection, seen as the right to informational self-determination, can be more generally understood as protecting data subjects interests to develop themselves freely in a democratic and pluralist society. See BVerfGE 65,1—Volkszählung. For a discussion, see Fischer-Hübner, Hoofnagle et al. 2011.

Flu Trends in particular.[993] This service harvests aggregate search data to give an indication of geographic flu activity. It shows how search query analysis can be useful to predict various other events of general public interest and to further our understanding of the world more generally.[994] The following claim by Microsoft researcher Matthew Richardson summarizes the potential of search engine user data collections:

> With the advent of Web search engines, a new source of data about people and the world has become available. Every time a person queries a search engine, he provides a small window into his life, his interests, and the world around him. Taken as a whole, across millions of users, these queries constitute a measurement of the world and humanity through time.[995]

This leads him to advocate against limitations on the retention period of search engine user logs, claiming that the potential to use these data would be severely reduced by doing so. Search engines have an obvious business interest in establishing more and more legitimate purposes for this data, thereby solidifying the legitimacy of the processing of large amounts of user data in the first place.

Most problematic from the perspective of intellectual freedom of end-users, are the signs that government agencies and search engine providers may be coming into agreement on the need for extensive processing of search engine user data for the purposes of investigating or preventing crime.[996] Without a doubt, specific search engine user data may sometimes be helpful in the context of a criminal investigation. But as soon as the collection of user data by search engine providers becomes instrumental for the purposes of preventing and combating crime, intellectual freedom will be greatly sacrificed.

A similar sacrifice was made by the European legislature when it enacted the Data Retention Directive (2006/24/EC) in the context of electronic communications data. This directive mandates the retention of traffic and location data of publicly available electronic communications networks and services in view of their usefulness for law enforcement and national security agencies. More recently, proposals have been made in the European Parliament to extend data retention obligations to search engine providers in view of the combat of sexual harassment, pedophilia and child pornographic material.[997] In other words, the collection of user data by search engines would become instrumental, a priori, to the objectives of governmental agencies, in particular law enforcement and national security agencies.

Libraries, in particular, have been vocal opponents of attempts to access records of their patrons. Search engine providers have a mixed record. On the

---

993. See Google Flu Trends http://www.google.org/flutrends/about/how.html. For a discussion, see Carneiro & Mylonakis 2009.
994. See Richardson 2008.
995. Richardson 2008, 2.
996. See generally, Birnhack & Elkin-Koren 2003.
997. See McNamee 2010.

one hand, they have sometimes opposed access to their user data by government agencies. In 2006, Google scored a victory in a U.S. court over government attempt to gain access to individual search records.[998] Google often cites this legal victory as an example of its effective efforts to protect its users' privacy, also noting it was the only one resisting the attempt to gain access.[999] In general, however, major search providers are responsive to lawful government request to access user records.[1000] Moreover, Google has repeatedly defended its retention of user data by claiming that they could be necessary data for law enforcement agencies to track down criminals.[1001] Google's CEO, Eric Smith, publicly stated the following:

> If you have something that you don't want anyone to know, maybe you shouldn't be doing it in the first place.[1002]

Interesting in this context are the court proceedings between Google and Viacom, in the United States, about Google's liability for copyright infringement on You-Tube. In 2009, Viacom secured a court ruling which ordered Google to hand over the complete log related to its YouTube service, an enormous record of the viewing history of all visitors.[1003] The court dismissed Google's opposition, which was referring to its users' privacy and also specifically relied upon Video Privacy Protection Act (18 U.S.C. section 2710), with the following statement:

> [. . .] defendants cite no authority barring them from disclosing such infor-mation in civil discovery proceedings, and their privacy concerns are specu-lative. Defendants do not refute that the "login ID is an anonymous pseudo-nym that users create for themselves when they sign up with YouTube" which without more "cannot identify specific individuals" [. . .] and Google has elsewhere stated:
>
> > We . . . are strong supporters of the idea that data protection laws should apply to any data that could identify you. The reality is though that in most cases, an IP address without additional information cannot.[1004]

---

998. See *Gonzales v. Google, Inc.*, 234 F.R.D. 674 (N.D. Cal 2006).
999. See Cutts June 11, 2007; For a discussion of the way Google talks about privacy, see Hoofnagle 2009.
1000. See e.g. Google, March 14, 2007.
1001. See Soghoian, an end to privacy theatre, 2010, 194. More specifically, Soghoian refers to the interview by Robert Siegel with Eric Schmidt, Google's CEO, on National Public Radio, Octo-ber 2, 2009, available at http://www.npr.org/templates/story/story.php?storyId=113450803. In this interview, Schmidt states the following: '[T]he reason we keep [search engine data] for any length of time is one, we actually need it to make our algorithms better but more importantly, there is a legitimate case of the government, or particularly the police function or so forth, wanting with a federal subpoena and so forth—being able to get access to that information.' Former Google employee Edwards describes how after 9/11, Google employees tried to help, voluntarily, identifying the terrorists on the basis of their logs. See Edwards 2011, 233–235.
1002. See Tate 2009.
1003. For a discussion and further references, see Hoofnagle 2009.
1004. See *Viacom International* et al. *v. Youtube* et al., 07–CIV–2103 (S.D.N.Y. July 1, 2008).

In other words, the court concluded that there was no law that provided for the protection of user records against third-party access, and in view of Google's own treatment of and opinion on user data, the Judge dismissed Google's defense in view of user privacy. Hence, the protection of privacy for end-users under U.S. law is dependent on the views and policies of the service provider, and the privacy policies of dominant players in the market do not (unambiguously) provide end-users with reasonable expectations of privacy.[1005] Seen against this background, European data protection law may better serve the interests of end-users since data protection laws apply independent of the willingness of service providers to take their users' privacy seriously.

At the same time, the EU Privacy Directive itself does not recognize the special nature of the data which is being processed by search engine providers. It does not ensure the intellectual freedom of search engine users by preventing, or setting special standards on, access to this data by third parties once the data has been collected. Lawful access by third parties, including law enforcement and national security agencies, is a matter of the law of the Member States. Until now, no special restrictions have been adopted with regard to the processing of and access to search engine user data. Whereas Article 8 ECHR is an important legal safeguard, the scale of user data processing in the context of search may warrant specific norm-setting at the legislative level to ensure the fundamental interest of end-users to search for and access information freely in the online environment.

10.4.3.   ACCOUNTABILITY FOR USER DATA PROCESSING

The processing of user data has a real impact on the selection and ranking of search results in response to a query.[1006] Beyond queries and site navigation, one's geographic location and a range of other data are, and can be, used and interpreted by search engines to tailor the service to specific end-users. In practice, there are more questions than answers about the way user data is actually being used by search engine providers, as they tend to give only general information about the actual data processing that is taking place. Hence, personalization presents end-users with a problem in terms of their informational autonomy.[1007] Search engines tailor their offering on the basis of some kind of picture of who their end-users are, without actually giving end-users the capacity to determine whether they agree with that picture and the impact on the recommendations of online sources of information it implies.

Considering that European data protection law does apply to the processing of user data, following the Article 29 Data Protection Working Party's opinion on search engines, it is worth looking at the question of the extent to which data

---

1005.   This is, from a legal perspective, not a big surprise. See Solove 2004, 201–209.
1006.   For a discussion, see 10.4.1.
1007.   See Feuz et al. 2011; Zuckerman 2011; Rotenberg 2007.

protection laws could help make search engines more accountable from a user's perspective for their impact on informational autonomy.[1008] This would suit the nature of data protection law, which does little to prevent the processing of personal data and, more often than not, is a means to support other fundamental legal interests relating to the freedom of the individual in a technology- and information-driven society, interests that are different from the right to private life in the strict sense.[1009] More specifically, European data protection law contains a number of provisions relating to the transparency in the processing of personal data by controllers, in view of the possibility to exercise control over data processing by data subjects.

According to Articles 10 and 11 of the EU Privacy Directive, data controllers have a general obligation to provide information about the processing of personal data that is taking place, the recipients of this data, the purposes of processing, the categories of personal data that have not been obtained from the data subject itself and the existence of the rights of data subjects. Corresponding to this, data subjects have a right to gain access to their personal data (Article 12), "without constraint at reasonable intervals and without excessive delay or expense."[1010] This right of access of data subjects, includes the right to receive the following:

- confirmation as to whether or not data relating to him are being processed and information at least as to the purposes of the processing, the categories of data concerned, and the recipients or categories of recipients to whom the data are disclosed;
- communication to him in an intelligible form of the data undergoing processing and of any available information as to their source;
- knowledge of the logic involved in any automatic processing of data concerning him at least in the case of the automated decisions referred to in Article 15 (1).[1011]

Article 15 of the Data Protection Directive contains a strengthened transparency obligation in view of the fundamental interests of data subjects in relation to automated decision-making on the basis of personal data. Article 15(1) grants data subjects a right

not to be subject to a decision which produces legal effects concerning him or significantly affects him and which is based solely on automated processing of data intended to evaluate certain personal aspects relating to him, such as his performance at work, creditworthiness, reliability, conduct, etc.[1012]

1008. See also Rotenberg 2007.
1009. See Gutwirth 2002.
1010. Privacy Directive (95/46/EC).
1011. *Ibid.*
1012. *Ibid.*

Article 15(2) contains an exception to this general rule for automated decisions that are as follows:

> (a) [. . .] taken in the course of the entering into or performance of a contract, provided the request for the entering into or the performance of the contract, lodged by the data subject, has been satisfied or that there are suitable measures to safeguard his legitimate interests, such as arrangements allowing him to put his point of view; or

> (b) is authorized by a law which also lays down measures to safeguard the data subject's legitimate interests.[1013]

Finally, consideration (41) of the EU Privacy Directive contains another reference to the right of access of the data subject and the right to know the logic involved in the automated processing of data concerning him, clarifying that its purpose is particularly that data subjects can "control the accuracy of the data and the lawfulness of the processing."[1014] It is important that the Directive here also notes that on the one hand, these rights of the data subject "must not adversely affect trade secrets or intellectual property and in particular the copyright protecting the software" and on the other hand, states that "these considerations must not, however, result in the data subject being refused all information."[1015]

If we look at the processing of user data by Web search engines, in practice, the first question that arises is whether the user data that is being processed can be qualified as personal data. It is beyond the scope of this research to address this much-debated issue in detail. We will simply rely on the Article 29 Working Party's conclusion on this subject that search engines generally process a wide variety of user data which qualify as personal data, in case of both authenticated and non-authenticated users.[1016] It is important to note that this conclusion is not legally tested. It remains to be seen what the proper status of search engine user data is under the data protection directive. It is clear that this will depend on the precise practices of specific search engines with regard to user data.

It is important to note that the question of whether search engine logs qualify as personal data cannot be reduced to the question about the status of IP addresses under the definition of personal data, which is currently one of the issues most prominently debated in this context. Even if IP addresses of end-users, as processed by information service providers, may not in and by themselves be regarded as personal data, search engines tend to process such a wide variety of user data in a form relating to specific individuals that the question about the identifiability of the underlying end-user does not depend upon the status of one specific type of data. More fundamentally, it should be noted that the question about identification of end-users in an online context may need to be addressed a little differently. Providers of free services do rely on a range of individual user data to single out individuals

---

1013. *Ibid.*
1014. *Ibid.*
1015. *Ibid.*
1016. See Article 29 Data Protection Working Party 2008, 8–9, 27.

for specific treatment. In the online world, the basic identifiers of the offline world, such as name and home address, are typically less meaningful, especially if the service is provided for free.[1017]

Thus, when following the Article 29 Working Party, the transparency obligations and the data subject's right to access and correction typically apply to the user data as processed by search engine providers. This has a number of interesting consequences for the accountability of search engines for their personalized search results, consequences which in practice have not fully materialized. First, search engines may need to provide users with a lot more information about the data that is being processed and the purposes of such processing of user data. Second, end-users have a right to access all personal data relating to them as they are processed by search engines. Third, data protection law provides data protection authorities with various regulatory means to ensure public oversight as regards the veracity of the information as provided by search engine providers in their privacy policies.

Data controllers tend to comply with the obligation to inform data subjects about the processing of personal data through privacy policies. All major search engines have such privacy policies, including Google, the policy of which will be taken as an example to show a seeming lack of compliance with EU data protection rules.[1018] The following is meant as an illustration of the possible unfulfilled potential of EU data protection laws in the context of search, rather than an in-depth discussion of the question of whether Google's data processing policy and practices are in compliance with EU law.

Google's privacy policy seems to systematically inform end-users of the ways in which different user data is being collected and processed. But at a closer look, many of the statements are quite vague and may not be in full compliance with the recommendations of the Article 29 Working Party. First, Google systematically refrains from providing information in a form which makes it legally accountable under European data protection law. In particular, it does not use the word 'personal data' even once in any of its privacy policies, but instead uses the term 'personal information'. It defines 'personal information' as "information that you provide to us which personally identifies you, such as your name, email address or billing information, or other data which can be reasonably linked to such information by Google."[1019] This definition is clearly more restricted than the definition of personal data in European data protection law. In particular, it does not include data which is not provided by the end-user itself, or data which indentifies an individual indirectly. By failing to clarify which of the information it processes must be considered personal data, the value of Google's privacy policy from the perspective of European data protection law is limited from the start.

As is implicit, Google's choice to use its own definition of 'personal information' makes it clear that it is ready to defend the position that much of the user

---

1017. See Article 29 Data Protection Working Party 2007, 16.
1018. Google's privacy policy is a moving target. The discussion here is based on Google's privacy policy of October 3, 2010. See Google 2010c.
1019. See Google Privacy FAQ.

data that it processes in the context of its Web search service should not be considered personal data and hence does not implicate data protection obligations. In its main privacy policy, it explicitly states that it offers "a number of services that do not require you to register for an account or provide any personal information to us, such as Google Search."[1020] In its response to the Article 29 Working Party addressing the opinion on search engines, it notes on the one hand that "Google has always taken the view that IP addresses should be regarded as confidential information that deserves a very high standard of protection" but, on the other hand, it states that "there is significant debate as to whether an IP address should be considered 'personal data' for purposes of data protection obligations. Legal analysis of the potential status of IP addresses as personal data should be as rigorous as possible."[1021]

Second, the information Google provides about the purposes of the processing of user data in the context of its search engine may be too general. One of those purposes, namely *developing new services* is overbroad from the perspective of Article 6(1)(b), which provides that new purposes must be compatible. Often the information provided could be much more specific, for instance the information about the purposes of processing IP addresses in view of geographic location of end-users. Google understates the granularity of the geo-location information it processes, by stating that an "IP address can often be used to identify the country from which a computer is connecting to the Internet."[1022]

Google also generally informs end-users that it processes personal information in view of "the display of customized content and advertising."[1023] Apart from the fact that much of the information that is mentioned in Google's policy, such as logs, files, links and cookie data, are not defined as personal information, it is unclear which information is used and how it is used to customize the content and advertising in Google's services. Consider the statement about the processing of query log data, the historic search records of every single user of Google Search over lengthy periods of time. Google explains as follows:

> Logs data also helps us improve our search results. If we know that users are clicking on the #1 result, we know we're probably doing something right, and if they're hitting next page or reformulating their query, we're probably doing something wrong.[1024]

Does this mean that query logs are used to develop an understanding of the interests of specific end-users? If so, what kind of understanding is Google trying to develop? Does Google remember the types of links its individual users follow in its universal search product, such as news, entertainment, video or blogs?

1020. See Google 2010c.
1021. Fleischer (Google) 2008.
1022. Compare the information (implying more granular targeting), for AdWords customers. See Google Adwords Help.
1023. See Google 2010c.
1024. Google Privacy FAQ.

Does Google try to develop an understanding of more specific topics of interests of individual end-users to tailor search results and advertising, such as its 'interest-based advertising' product which it developed for its advertising network for Web publishers? And how exactly does this have an impact on the selection and ranking of future search results?

Third, the right to access personal data as processed by Google or any other search engine provider may provide some answers to the pressing questions outlined above. In its privacy policy, Google seems to provide for the right to access personal data. However, its narrow definition of 'personal information' means that for some of the data which would qualify as 'personal data' under European data protection law, this policy does not apply. Google does provide access to some of the user data it collects on individual users through its search history service. This service, however, is only available for end-users who use the search engine while logged into a personal account. For these authenticated users, Google offers an overview of some of the data stored in connection to an account and the various Google products being used.

In sum, European data protection law, at least as interpreted by the Article 29 Working Party in its opinion on search engines, clearly provides a framework of obligations and rights that could help address some of the accountability deficits in the context of the search engine data processing and its impact on informational autonomy of end-users. If European Data Protection Authorities were to seriously enforce the law as they have interpreted it in their opinion on search engines, the result would be that end-users and the public at large would be much better informed about the way search engines operate and have an impact on the information we end up finding while using their services.

The recent episode in which German data protection authorities decided to use their legal powers to investigate personal data processing of Google, in light of its collection of data for the controversial Street View service, shows how effective an actual audit can be in ensuring compliance with the law. Through the audit, it was concluded that Google had been collecting and storing information about, and communications sent over, personal wireless networks of European citizens.[1025] Subsequently, Google has been fined and has had to stop these practices and destroy the data collected. The search engine market may need to be addressed in a similar manner to ensure full compliance with data protection law. The public oversight as provided for in the data protection framework may also be a solution for the problem that full disclosure of data processing practices and purposes may infringe on the trade secrets and intellectual property rights of search engine providers or be harmful for end-users, in view of the possible manipulation of search results upon full public disclosure. Data protection authorities may present the findings pursuant to an audit of user data processing in the context of search engine operations to the general public, without having to disclose specific trade secrets or

---

1025.   See Federal Commissioner for Data Protection 2004.

infringe on the legitimate business interests of search engine providers in other ways.

10.5. CONCLUSION

This chapter has addressed a number of regulatory issues relating to search engine quality from the perspective of freedom of expression. The first section considered search engines from the perspective of pluralism and diversity. After a short overview on early perspectives on diversity and pluralism in the online information environment, the role of search engines and a discussion of some of the early regulatory responses addressing diversity and pluralism, a general starting point and a number of concerns were identified and further discussed.

The starting point is that in an online information environment characterized by abundance, an analysis of pluralism and diversity should take special account of search engines and selection intermediaries more generally, as they have a large impact on the information and ideas that individuals will encounter. Moreover, and in relation, in this context characterized by abundance an analysis of diversity and pluralism should also emphasize on exposure to information and ideas, instead of merely addressing what is available online.

A first possible concern is the consolidation of the search engine market, which could have negative effects on pluralism and diversity. Ultimately, the conclusion is drawn that there is not enough evidence of a negative impact from the current market structure, and attention was drawn to a number of arguments that warrant skepticism with regard to claims of such an impact. It can be argued that many of the critiques of search engines and their possible bias can be best understood as the debunking of overly optimistic assumptions about the equalizing, democratizing and disintermediating effects of the Internet and the Web. To the extent that such assumptions were simply unrealistic or untenable, such as the idea that search engines would facilitate access to information and ideas equally, these critiques are rather unsurprising, and can hardly serve as a starting point for a further analysis.

To be able to address the question about the impact of search engines on diversity and pluralism properly, much more research will need to be done on the impact of market competition on search engine quality. On the one hand, search engines may end up trying exactly the same approaches in their competition for users. On the other hand, a lack of competition could diminish incentives to innovate on search engine quality for end-users. Other open questions that need to be addressed in this context are the specific impact of dominant players on diversity and pluralism, as well as the way other players in the public networked information environment more generally could alleviate possible concerns following from market concentration in the search engine market.

The analysis of the way individual market participants could have an impact on diversity and pluralism followed three perspectives: the end-users, the information providers and the search engine itself. The analysis shows that search engine providers have a number of incentives to promote diversity of their search results, since it increases the chances of one or more of these results fulfilling the information needs of their end-users. At the same time, the search engine business model implies that search engines may be particularly interested in optimizing their offering in view of particular information needs of end-users of a commercial nature, since this optimizes their attractiveness as a marketing platform for advertisers. This could lead to a reduction of diversity of search results that satisfy other interests of end-users. Personalization of search results could become problematic from the perspective of diversity and pluralism, but the question whether that is actually the case depends on the values and principles underlying such personalization and warrants further research. On a more practical level, search engines could be more forthcoming about the value they attribute to diversity and how this impacts their decisions of how to select and rank search results for end-users.

When focusing on information providers, most problematic is the impact certain information providers could have on the diversity of search results and the overall robustness of the search medium. Because of the reliance on third-party signals, the opportunities for the optimization of search result rankings for information providers and the editorial model of search more generally, some information providers may be effectively pushing legitimate and valuable sources of information out of the end-users' view. It is remarkable that this is, to some extent, a practice endorsed by the market leader Google. Search results can be expected to be biased towards information providers with sufficient financial and/ or organizational means to participate in the ongoing competition for favorable rankings, which can be expected to have a negative impact on diversity and pluralism.

From the perspective of end-users, it is clear that search quality, to a considerable degree, has to be shaped by the users themselves. Due to the interactive nature of search engine services, the quality of the search experience, in terms of the diversity of information and ideas users are presented with, will depend upon the users' knowledge, sophistication and critical engagement. The choice of the specific service, the knowledge of different languages, the ability to formulate and reformulate effective search queries and use advanced search options all have a considerable impact on the quality of the search experience. Hence, the control of end-users over the search process warrants special attention. It is clear from empirical research about search engine users that search engine quality depends on the skills, the level of education and background of specific end-users.

Some of the questions relating to search engine quality and the search engines' advertisement-based business model were discussed in more detail in section 10.3, which specifically focused on transparency obligations in regard to sponsored search results, as well as the way optimization of revenue more generally could negatively impact search engine quality. First, the discussion of the obligation to delineate organic and sponsored listings showed that this obligation may be too simplistic to deliver real value to the quality of the search medium. This conclusion is based on the observation that search engines do not operate in a manner that can provide the independence and information quality guarantees for organic listings that the obligation assumes. The underlying assumption that a parallel can be drawn to traditional editorial media simply breaks down upon a closer look. Search engine users may be better off being informed about the various ways in which search engine results are being influenced through targeted campaigns and optimization strategies of specific information providers.

This points to the need for increased transparency in the way search engines operate, which currently is only provided voluntarily. This voluntary nature of transparency in the context of search has some obvious drawbacks. Search engines such as Google claim to engage in a number of best practices with regard to search engine quality, but a proper mechanism for verifying those claims is still lacking. In contrast, transparency obligations could also be considered problematic. On a practical level, they could impact the ability of search engines to resist manipulation. More fundamentally, strict transparency obligations could be at odds with the right to freedom of expression as applied to the choices of search engines to rank and select in relative freedom. Competition law can be expected to be one of the drivers for increased transparency as regards search engine selection and ranking practices by Google, as several complaints of monopolistic abuse are pending at the European Commission, national competition authorities in Europe, and in the United States. These investigations may also, at some point, have to come to terms with the question about the editorial freedom of search engine providers to rank and select search results.

The final section focused on two regulatory issues related to the massive processing of user data by search engine providers from the perspective of freedom of expression, privacy and data protection. The analysis showed that concerns underlying the right to freedom of expression can be reason enough to reflect on the possibility of enacting specific legal rules for the processing of user data about information accessing and seeking behavior. The current legal framework does not recognize the special role or status of these activities in the information society. At present, the processing of user data by search engine providers is covered by general data protection law, which in the view of European data protection authorities provides the legal framework through which search engines are made accountable for the processing of user data.

Data protection law could be of great value in view of the impact user data has on search engine operations. Increased personalization, in combination with a lack of transparency in end-user modeling, poses a real threat to informational autonomy of end-users. Data protection law contains a number of provisions which guarantee transparency in the processing of the user data that can be considered personal data. If data protection authorities are right in their interpretation of how European data protection law applies to search engines and will prove more successful in imposing this view on the market, this framework could also be instrumental in restoring some balance between end-users and search engine providers.

Chapter 11
Summary, Analysis and Conclusions

11.1.   INTRODUCTION

This final chapter summarizes and analyses the main findings of this thesis in order to answer the main research question:

> What are the implications of the right to freedom of expression for search engine governance and government involvement with regards to search?

This question was born from the observation that the Web search engine has emerged as a central intermediary in the public networked information environment, but that the implications of one of the fundamental legal principles which should inform the legal governance of Web search engines were far from understood. It is clear that the available technologies, services and online practices that constitute the infrastructure for the opening up of the Web—understood as the process of connecting information and ideas online to their societal use—are of considerable economic, cultural and political significance. This is particularly true for dominant search engine providers such as Google.

Search engines have been at the heart of some of the most important legal and regulatory developments with regard to the proper governance of information flows on the Internet. They are essential for information providers to connect to audiences and are amongst the primary means for Internet users to navigate the Web and inform themselves freely. This thesis addresses the way freedom of expression should and can inform the legal governance of Web search engines. It discusses the role of search engines in the public information environment from the perspective of freedom of expression doctrine and explores the regulatory issues in which freedom of expression can play a particularly important role.

The first part of this thesis (Chapters 2 and 3) provides insight into the history and emergence of the search medium in relation to the Internet and the World Wide

Web. It gives an overview of the market developments that have led to the currently available search media. It explains the basic inner workings of Web search engines, their position in the networked communications environment and the value chains on the Internet as well as their relation and function from the perspective of information providers and end-users.

The second part (Chapters 4–8) proceeds in three steps. Chapter 4 discusses freedom of expression doctrine in general, as well as the specific legal provisions the analysis is focuses on, namely Article 10 ECHR and the First Amendment. While the focus in this thesis is placed on a legal analysis from a European perspective, First Amendment doctrine has been introduced as a comparative legal element to reflect on the conclusions about the implications of Article 10 ECHR for search engine governance.

Chapters 5–7 provide the broader historical and contextual foundation for the general research question by discussing the implications of the right to freedom of expression for the governance of the press, the Internet access provider and the public library. These chapters share a similar structure and logic while seeking to do justice to the particular nature of each of these institutions.

Chapter 8 addresses the general question about the implications of the right to freedom of expression for the legal governance of Web search engines, with an emphasis on the development of a theory of the protection accorded to search media under the right to freedom of expression, as well as the way the said right of end-users and information providers should further inform a theory of search engine freedom. It discusses the societal role of search engines from a normative perspective, by making a comparison with, and drawing on, the societal role of the press, the access provider and the public library as informed by freedom of expression doctrine.

The final part of the thesis (Chapters 9 and 10) moves from the protection of communicative freedoms in the search engine context to a number of specific regulatory issues with regard to the governance of information flows through search engines. It addresses issues that have a strong link to the right to freedom of expression. The results of the second part of the thesis and the conclusions in Chapter 8 are used to discuss the extent to which the right to freedom of expression has been and could be properly taken into account in the legal and regulatory practices addressed in this final part of the thesis.

Chapter 9 addresses regulatory issues related to the governance of access in search engines and the legal issues related to search engine intermediary liability for potentially opening up illegal, unlawful as well as harmful material online. Chapter 10 deals with three regulatory issues related to search engine quality. First, the notions of diversity and pluralism are discussed in the context of search media. Second, the value of transparency in the ranking and selection of search results is addressed as well as the regulatory practice of separation between sponsored and organic results in search engine result pages. Third, Chapter 10 discusses issues of user privacy and data protection, while focusing specifically on the instrumental nature of privacy and data protection laws with regard to the intellectual freedom and informational autonomy of search engine users.

11.2.   SEARCH ENGINES IN THE PUBLIC NETWORKED
         INFORMATION ENVIRONMENT

The starting point for the analysis of freedom of expression and search engine governance is an understanding of the current role of search media in the public networked information environment. To that effect, Chapter 2 first analyzes the history and market developments related to Web search engines. Chapter 3 offers conceptual models for the Web search engine's information architecture and the way it can be positioned in the online information environment as a whole.

The historical analysis shows that the search engine has its origins in the scientific developments relating to the organization of digital information collections. Around fifty years ago, visionaries of the digital age, such as Vannevar Bush and Licklider, imagined the way information technology could be used to strengthen the effective organization of the access to knowledge in our societies. Notably, their thinking placed particular emphasis on how accessibility and navigation could be improved.

The history of the current Web search engines begins soon after the successful launch of the hypertext standards for online publication, the World Wide Web. It is important to note that the Web's design purposely left the actual organization of online material to its users. The idea was that effective navigation of online material would emerge as a result of linking by Web users. In that respect, the Web's design was different from another contemporary system for Internet publishing, Gopher, which entailed a more rigid model for the organization of materials in its design.

The revolutionary rise of the Web as a universal platform for online publication resulted in a strong demand for navigational media and services to help users find valuable online material. Most of the first Web search engines were developed in the academic realm. Later on, the business opportunities related to search engines, which proved to be among the most attractive in the Internet industry, became an important driver for the further development of the search engine industry and the innovations that have taken place since then, such as the dominant pay-per-click advertisement-based business model.

From a regulatory perspective, the gradual consolidation of the search engine market is the most significant market development since the end of the 1990s and most notably, the dominance of Google. Chapter 2 presents some of the major elements and historical factors that contributed to this consolidation, such as the evolving user expectations, the growing complexities of operating a general purpose search engine and the dynamics of the digital media and ICT industries.

Although Google's dominance raises concerns, this study argues and shows that it remains important to look beyond it. Chapter 2 supports this argument on the basis of a short exploration of remaining competition and alternative models for the production of Web search functionality in the broad sense. The amount of research and commercial activity focused on improving and facilitating the findability of online information gives little reason to be pessimistic about the question of reliance on a single company. Semantic web projects are also of interest in this context. While they would allow all search engines to improve their offerings, they could also diminish some of the power of dominant search engines—the part which is based on their *exclusive* understanding of the material on Web—by opening up improved meta-data to the Internet community as a whole.

Chapter 3 finds that search engine providers are Internet 'users' like anybody else. Search functionality and the organization of content are built on top or, to be precise, on the borders of the network like any other service or application. This means that from a technical perspective there is, in principle, nothing special or essential about the position of Google as a referencing service. From the perspective of end-users as well as information providers, there is a variety of alternatives to Google. These alternatives may take place on a much smaller scale on the one hand, or in different contexts such as the newer phenomena of online social networking and microblogging services such as Twitter, on the other hand.

By looking at the position of search media in the layered model of networked communications, Chapter 3 clarifies that search engines map both to the top of the applications/services layer as well as to the content layer of the layered model of networked communications. On the one hand, Web search engines are complex systems of software, typically server-based, made accessible for users of the network through their Web browsers. On the other hand, search engines have a rather unique link with the content layer as well. First, search engines can be argued to consume and produce 'content' of their own, namely information *about* information—shortly—meta-information. Second, Web search engines derive their functionality from the existence of publicly accessible content elsewhere on the Web. Without the open and unstructured dynamics of content creation on the Web, search engines would not play the role that they do today. The complexities with regard to the proper legal treatment of the production and proliferation of this kind of 'meta-information' or 'meta-content' are a key element in the legal issues arising in the context of Web search engine governance.

A representation of the search engine in view of the essential value chains in the public networked information environment offers more insight into the critical position of search media in practice. The first value chain in which the search engine plays an important role is the flow of knowledge, information, data, news and commercial offers from all sorts of online information and service providers to end-users. The second value chain, which is of particular importance from the business perspective of Web services, represents the flow of user attention and activity, in the form of their page views, clicks, purchases and personal data. In both of these value chains search media, and selection intermediaries more generally, have established themselves as one of the central mediating institutions. Search media such as Google are uniquely situated to negotiate between the interests of the various stakeholders involved in these value chains.

Chapter 3 concludes with a discussion of search media from a functional perspective, first from the perspective of users and subsequently from the perspective of information providers and advertisers. The discussion of Web search media from the perspective of users draws upon the models of users' needs in information retrieval. These models clarify that in comparison to traditional information retrieval systems, in which the information needs of users were typically only *informational*, Web search media tend to serve two additional types of user needs, namely *navigational* and *transactional*.

Navigational queries are the type of queries with which users aim to reach specific online destinations which they know or simply assume exist. By satisfying navigational queries, such as returning the website of the University of Amsterdam 'UvA' as the first result in return to the query 'uva', search engines help Internet users to speedily reach the home page of various institutions, organizations, companies or persons. From the perspective of the user, navigational queries have only one right answer. The search engine, however, will have to speculate intelligently, for instance on the basis of other information available about the user such as his location, what the real information need of the user is and whether it should actually return the website of the University of Virginia instead (UVa).

Informational queries represent the need of a user to learn about a certain topic. For Italian users, the query 'uva' could, for instance, express an informational need to learn about grapes. These kinds of queries, which range from the political and the educational to the medical and the cultural, do not implicate a clear right answer. It is in this context that the questions about search engine quality discussed in Chapter 10 are most pertinent. Is the way search engines rank, select and present search results serving the users' right to inform themselves freely? What is the impact of search engines on pluralism and diversity and what are the implications of the advertisement-based business model and the lack of transparency in and general complexity of ranking and selection practices by dominant search providers?

Transactional queries represent the type of user needs which are directed at reaching a destination where the user will be able to use, buy or consume a resource. The Web is a tremendous (marketing) platform for these resources provided by millions of information and service providers, sometimes for free. The fact that users use search engines to gain access to resources makes search engines particularly attractive marketing platforms. It also helps explain the integration of specific types of search, for instance for videos, geographic information, scholarly articles or pictures, into the offering of general purpose search engines and has informed the vertical integration of search engines into the markets for certain attractive resources.

In sum, the search engine is much more than as a simple telephone directory or yellow page service for the World Wide Web. They help users with a large variety of quite different information needs by actively selecting and ranking lists of online destinations. These information needs range from the political, medical and educational to the navigational, commercial, domestic and recreational. This shows not only the societal breadth of the function of search engines in our public networked information environment but also hints at the large variety of public and private interests that are tied to their operation. In addition, this leads to a conclusion about how search engines which end up selecting and ranking results for their users can be qualified. It can be seen as the expression of a range of underlying judgments about the relevance of various kinds of information and destinations in relation to the relative importance of the perceived needs of their users.

11.3.   IMPLICATIONS OF FREEDOM OF EXPRESSION FOR
          MEDIA AND COMMUNICATIONS SERVICES

Since the aim of this thesis is to understand the proper role of government with
regard to a specific medium under freedom of expression doctrine, the question
was studied as to what extent this role depends on the type of medium or communications services. Hence, the analysis of the implications of freedom of expression for the press, the Internet access provider and the library studied the way the
right to freedom of expression has informed the legal and regulatory environment
of these institutions. In particular, Chapters 5–7 paid close attention to the way the
different interests of the stakeholders in the communicative processes facilitated by
these entities, seen as functional intermediaries between users and information
providers, were legally sanctioned by the right to freedom of expression. Taken
together, this analysis of the implications of freedom of expression provides a rich
picture of the normative value of the right to freedom of expression for different
entities in the public networked information environment and their legal
governance.

11.3.1.   PRESS FREEDOM

Both the European Court of Human Rights and the U.S. Supreme Court have
dedicated some of their most significant judgments to press freedom. What stands
out is that the press is considered to have a particular role in constitutional democracies. The right to freedom of expression sanctions the freedom of the press partly
because of its role in informing the public and contributing to the free dissemination of information and ideas, which are important ideals underlying freedom of
expression doctrine. Hence, the communicative interests of the primary stakeholders in the communicative process are instrumental for the way the right to
freedom of expression operates in the press context. Notably, the press can claim
the highest available protection under the Convention and the First Amendment.
However, it does not have a specially protected status that is unavailable to others
who are not part of the organized press but still contribute to the publication and
dissemination of matters of public concern in a similar manner. Since the organized
press is subject to disruptive developments which are partly the result of convergence, digitization and the entry of new players such as search engines, news
aggregators and 'amateur' journalists, this conclusion is significant. It illustrates
the need to conceptualize the values *underlying* the freedom of the press, as well as
the need to identify the various entities in the public networked information
environment that could have similar claims to protection under freedom of
expression standards.

    The press must be free to contribute to the interests of speakers and readers,
but this 'instrumental' aspect of press freedom is limited by the protection of the
press versus government interference, its editorial freedom in particular. Freedom
of expression implies that the regulatory role of the State with regard to the affairs

of the press is minimal and press governance is mostly a matter of self-regulation, professional ethics and the proper application of general applicable laws. Neither the ECtHR nor the U.S. Supreme Court rules out the permissibility of prior restraints, an absolute restriction on editorial freedom, but both do apply heavy presumptions against its permissibility under the right to freedom of expression. The protection of the press under the right to freedom of expression also limits the ways in which the State can actively promote the ideals underlying press freedom as mentioned above. More specifically, an agenda for positive government involvement, such as indiscriminatory subsidization, media concentration rules and media pluralism policies more generally, can be permissible means to promote a healthy media environment, but these policies all have to be carefully drafted in light of press freedom as a constraint on interference by public authorities.

Under U.S. law, the editorial freedom of the press with respect to the selection of possible speakers is absolute, as follows from *Tornillo*. In this seminal decision, the Supreme Court referred to editorial freedom as the exercise of editorial control and judgment. It includes discretion about the choice of material to go into a newspaper, the decisions made as to limitations on the size and content of the newspaper and their treatment of (public) issues. Under the ECHR, the editorial freedom of the press is also strongly protected but it is possible that certain interferences with its freedom to decide what to print can be legitimate, for instance with reference to the rights and freedom of others, such as in a right to reply which is available in some European countries. In addition, the press has to exercise its editorial freedom in accordance with the duties and responsibilities mentioned in the text of Article 10 ECHR itself. The self-regulation of the media, the ethics of journalism, the impact and the technical means used for communicating ideas and information are relevant in this context. In *Stoll* and other recent judgments, the Court has made it clear that it takes these duties and responsibilities seriously. In the Court's view, the media has to ensure accuracy, precision, reliability and sometimes even prudence and reasonableness. The duties and responsibilities need to be interpreted in light of the present-day conditions of the media environment, in which, as per the ECtHR's view, they have taken on an added importance.

The First Amendment law contains a number of additional interesting doctrinal elements which reflect on the protected interests of potential speakers to reach an audience and the interests of the audience with regard to receiving information freely. First, under the First Amendment overbreadth doctrine the Supreme Court can scrutinize the effects of legal restrictions on unprotected speech on the free flow of protected matter. The possibility of chilling effects of unprotected speech regulation on protected speech can make a restriction impermissible. The regulation of speech to protect against unwilling exposure of a captive audience can be legitimate due to the protection of what can be seen as the informational self-governance of the audience. Finally, the First Amendment also contains a heavy presumption in favor of the rationality of the audience, which is illustrated most clearly in its case law about the protected status of commercial communications and the public's right to receive them.

11.3.2.   ISP Freedom

In stark contrast with the regulatory model for the press, there has traditionally been extensive regulation of communications network providers. However, content regulation tends to be absent or minimal in this context and raises issues under the right to freedom of expression. In vertical relations, the owners of the means of communications such as Internet access providers can assert their own right to 'freedom of expression' against government interference, and this right includes the right to access, receive and transmit. Even more than in the case of the press, these rights are informed by the communicative interests of the users of such communications networks.

The interests in communicating freely with the use of steadily improving communications techniques (postal mail, telegraphy, telephony and now the Internet) were clearly served by a practice in which the network owners would not restrict communications over the network. In that respect, the regulatory concepts of 'common carrier' and 'universal service', which have helped shape the regulatory models for communications network providers, can also be seen as informed by the right to freedom of expression. Universal service requirements acknowledge the way access to communications networks is essential to societal participation. The common carrier requirement guarantees equal treatment of users of the networks, thereby limiting the discretion of network providers to restrict lawful information flows. The discussion about net neutrality involves a discussion of the application of similar obligations on Internet access providers.

It is clear that convergence has complicated the regulatory environment for electronic communications services, such as Internet access providers, significantly. Internet users can use one and the same Internet connection to correspond privately, watch 'television', and broadcast their views or the data they have stored on their devices to a global audience. The facilitating role of Internet access providers with regard to the *public* networked information environment means that the normative role of the right to freedom of expression for the governance of communications networks has increased in importance. Traditionally, the constitutional rights to privacy and confidentiality of private correspondence, as is protected by Article 8 ECHR, were of relatively greater importance. This is not to say that the right to confidentiality of private communications is no longer relevant. On the contrary, pressure on Internet access providers to interfere with unlawful communications, business strategies related to price discrimination between different kinds of content and communications on their network and the availability of technical means such as deep packet inspection to actually monitor the communications of end-users show the lasting importance of Article 8 in the context of access providers.

In Chapter 6, the regulatory answer towards access providers in view of the public flow of illegal or unlawful content over the network was used to study the implications of the right to freedom of expression in this context. This regulatory framework was shown to consist of safe harbors that set the legal boundaries for the liability of access providers for third-party communications on the one hand, in combination with an emphasis on further self- and co-regulatory action on the other hand. The case law relating to these laws as well as their legislative history show that freedom of expression has been taken into account in this framework but the extent to which this has been done properly remains questionable and debated.

Legal obligations on access providers to prevent the use of their communications networks for illegal purposes or to prevent the possibility to access illegal material lead to clear problems under the right to freedom of expression. Such general obligations could only be adhered to with the use of Internet filters, the mandatory application of which is more than constitutionality doubtful. Although the pressure to move towards stricter legal responsibility of Internet access providers remains, and proposals to require blacklisting by access providers have been debated in European Parliament and elsewhere, the right to freedom of expression is an important reason why these kinds of proposals have mostly not materialized into actual laws.

In general, public policy aimed at having access providers restrict the accessibility of content and information flows on the Internet has not focused on command-and-control types of regulation but instead has minimized the official role of the State while, at the same time, aiming to achieve more restrictive practices. This self-regulatory paradigm can partly be viewed as a positive thing, as in the case of the governance of the press, precisely because of the right to freedom of expression. However, the relation between access providers and Internet users is quite different from that of the press with its readers and sources. Whereas for the press the freedom to select information and ideas for publication is sanctioned by the right to freedom of expression *because* of the importance of editorial freedom of the press, the legal protection of exclusion or blocking of communications by access providers is hard to harmonize with the ideals underlying freedom of expression.

This leads to one of the more complex and controversial issues touched upon in Chapter 6: how should the current legal framework for the horizontal relations between access providers and Internet users be evaluated from the perspective of the right to freedom of expression? Or to put it differently, what are the proper implications of the right to freedom of expression for the legal discretion of ISPs to restrict communication over their networks? Two different general points of view in this debate emerge in the analysis, a debate which has reached a climax in the United States in the context of ongoing litigation over the FCC's net neutrality obligations.

The first perspective, which may best be called 'the user freedom theory', tends to equate the right to freedom of expression in these potential conflicts of interests between access providers and users to the communicative interests of Internet users. In this theory, if freedom of expression legally requires anything with regard to the legal governance of these horizontal relations, it would be that government must safeguard the user's interest against undue interference by Internet access providers. Such safeguards might include the establishment of net neutrality, new types of common carrier and universal service rules or the establishment of due process guarantees in case of specific legitimate interferences with the flow of content or use of the network. In other words, the law should be aimed at the realization of the free exercise of the right to freedom of expression by Internet users. Council of Europe recommendations touching upon these issues testify to this perspective in European freedom of expression doctrine. Within the boundaries of this theory, much debate remains about the nature of the implications of the right to freedom of expression in the context of access to communications networks, in particular whether there is a real obligation for the State to act—which is generally hard to defend—or if it is better to speak of freedom of expression in this context as a regulatory principle that can inform or legitimize legislative action.

The second perspective, for which support is more common in the United States, tends to equate the right to freedom of expression with the discretion over the use of communicative means as established by the free market. This theory may be best called 'the ownership discretion theory of freedom of expression'. From this perspective, the right to freedom of expression protects the owners of the means of communications and media more generally against legal interferences with the freedom to decide how to use those means in the free market. The result of this theory is that government regulation aiming to safeguard the users' interests of having free, equal and indiscriminatory access to the Internet, would be restricted by the right to freedom of expression of access providers, more specifically their First Amendment right not to transmit or to exclude.

Chapter 6 concludes that Article 10 ECHR does not support a freedom of expression claim of an access provider to interfere with traffic on their networks. Instead, any claim in favor of interference would have to be based on the provider's market freedoms and its right to private property. In the safe harbor framework for Internet service providers in the Directive on Electronic Commerce, the right to freedom of expression can also be shown to be understood by the EU legislature to relate to the communicative interests of Internet users. The way freedom of expression has been internalized into the EU intermediary liability regime leaves room for criticism. No due process guarantees have been prescribed, such as those in the U.S. Digital Millennium Copyright Act, the room for injunctions is left wide open, and the hosting safe harbor, the scope of which is less clear than ever, has been shown to incentivize intermediaries to restrict lawful communications. In addition, the role of public authorities in the design of self-regulation has been questionable. Moreover, the right to freedom of expression has not demonstrably informed the way public authorities have sought cooperation with the industry with the aim of establishing more policing by access providers of communications on their network.

Looking at the United States, the analysis of how the right to freedom of expression has been accounted for in the legal framework for the responsibility of access providers for communications over the network and the safe harbors in particular shows a mixed picture. Some elements in the regulatory framework sanction the discretion of ISPs to disregard the interests of information providers and end-users in horizontal relations. Section 230 of the Communications Decency Act, also applicable to search engines, is perhaps most striking in this regard. It not only shields against liability but its 'Good Samaritan Defense' also provides far-reaching discretion for 'interactive computer services' with regard to third-party communications.

A study of the background of this provision enacted in 1996 shows that this provision has, in many ways, prevented First Amendment doctrine from having a further impact on the proper legal regime for various kinds of ISPs in the United States, including search engines. The different legal standards for carrier, distributor and publisher liability as they applied in defamation cases before the Internet, and the way editorial freedom and control played a role in the formation of these standards in a rich set of court decisions, have been replaced by a double-edged sword for Internet intermediaries: a shield against liability on the one hand, and the legal discretion to block various kinds of illegal and objectionable content, not excluding constitutionally protected communications, on the other hand. From the perspective of freedom of expression of Internet users, as well as the public interests underlying the notion of common carriage, this solution can be seen as sub-optimal.

The two theories mentioned above reflect perspectives on the right to freedom of expression with implications that go well beyond the context of Internet access providers or search engines. In the networked communications environment, a variety of new models and technological means to control communication flows have provided the means for traditionally passive conduits to be more actively involved in the selection and prioritization of content flows on the network. At the same time, those that tended to be more actively involved, such as news media, may have gained the means to be more 'passive', allowing third-party contributions to the publication, selection and the valuation of news. Chapter 6 sheds some light on the fundamental questions this raises about the way freedom relates to discretion and control relates to responsibility, and the way those answers should ultimately find their ways into properly informed legal treatment for various mediating entities in the public networked information environment.

11.3.3.   LIBRARY FREEDOM

Chapter 7 gives an overview of the ways in which freedom of expression has informed the legal governance of the library, one of the oldest societal institutions dealing with the organization of knowledge, information and ideas. Between European countries and the United States, there is considerable divergence with regard to the understanding of freedom of expression in the context of public libraries. In general, in the American public library context more emphasis is placed on individual rights and freedom of speech. This is probably best illustrated with the fact that many public libraries have an actual bill of rights. Historically, this can be explained by a strong cultural adherence to free speech values as individual rights in the United States in combination with the continuing pressure on American libraries to suppress controversial materials, such as books containing homosexuality.

In Europe, library policy tends to be part of general education, culture and welfare policy. Freedom of expression, fundamental rights and the social welfare state have blended together into a mix of publicly funded culture, media and information access support in which the public library still occupies an important position. The enabling role of government with regard to providing basic access to knowledge and culture stands to the fore, and as a result legal scholars tend to argue that by funding public libraries the State is acting under its positive obligation to promote basic levels of access to (high quality) information. However, the publicly funded library institutions are to remain independent with regard to their collection policies, which are informed by library practices.

In the United States, the Supreme Court is not willing to accept any such positive obligations for the State to promote the substantive liberties of its citizens or interpret State funding to promote access to information in this light. In fact, in its last ruling on public libraries, which involved the constitutionality of a condition on public library funding to install Internet content filters, the Supreme Court ruled that public libraries do not have a "role that pits them against the Government, and there is no comparable assumption that they must be free of any conditions that their benefactors might attach to the use of donated funds or other assistance."[1026] It is striking that precisely in the United States, where individual political liberties have had and continue to have a significant impact on library governance, the political independence of libraries from the State is thus constitutionally disregarded.

By looking at some of the normative principles underlying library governance and relating to the freedom of expression, Chapter 7 also clarifies some of the specific ways in which freedom of expression has informed collection management and access to library material. Public libraries are supposed to provide their constituencies with a collection that respects the principle of diversity. As such, they will sometimes confront library users with material they would not have selected themselves, for instance because they find it offensive. The negative reaction of a part of the constituency to this practice has been one of the main drivers for library censorship, understood as the undue suppression or removal of material. It is important to note that due to the nature of library collection management which implies selection of materials in the first place, the suppression of material can sometimes be hard to distinguish from legitimate selection decisions.

From the perspective of free access to information, the unmonitored access to library materials is of particular concern for the governance of libraries. The increased possibilities of personal data processing due to digital access, and automation of library management systems more generally, has made the privacy of public library users a present concern. At the same time, such data processing can contribute to the ideal of better serving the needs of library patrons. The analysis clarifies how the right to privacy of library users can be understood as instrumental to the exercise of their right to freedom of expression. In light of the amount of user data being collected by Web search engines about information access behavior, this conclusion establishes an interesting analogy to the search engine context.

1026. *United States v. American Library Association*, 539 U.S. 194 (2003).

11.4. FREEDOM OF EXPRESSION AND SEARCH ENGINE GOVERNANCE

As the analysis in Chapters 5–7 shows, the implications of freedom of expression in these contexts are informed by the dominant normative conception of the societal role being fulfilled by the press, the Internet access provider and the library respectively. Hence, one of the underlying aims of this thesis has been to explore the way such a role for search media in the public networked information environment can be described. Moreover, by comparing the search medium's role in the networked information environment with the role of these institutions, a number of interesting conclusions can be drawn.

11.4.1. THE SOCIETAL ROLE OF SEARCH ENGINES

Search media combine a passive (conduit/access) and active (editorial/selective) role in their production of meta-information, which is ultimately directed at the relative accessibility of information and ideas online. In their role as search engines, they do not, like publishers, produce content themselves, and compared to traditional editorial media they therefore play a much more 'passive' role. In contrast, however, search media are intrinsically more 'active' than a passive conduit such as an Internet access provider. The value of search engines is directly related to the ways in which they actively rank and select information and destinations online in response to the user's input. This process can be compared both to the editorial selection of the press and to the active organization of information and ideas by libraries.

In relation to this, when looking deeper into the societal role of search engines two conflicting ideals emerge: the ideal of universal access on the one hand and the ideal of information quality on the other hand. The first ideal for search engines is to help Internet users navigate the entire Web by ordering it and making the material that is available universally accessible. The second ideal is to prioritize the publicity of valuable, relevant and attractive information and ideas over lesser ones. The general purpose search engine, by definition, has to reconcile these conflicting ideals in its operations. Much of the debate about the proper role and responsibility of search media could be explained with reference to the tension between these two different ideals.

This tension between information quality and information access that exists in the public networked information environment did not exist, in the same manner, in the information environment predating the Web. Traditionally, the organization of access to information for the public was separated from the organization of basic levels of quality and legal permissibility. Hence, access in the context of the press was restricted, in principle, to everything 'fit to print'. Likewise, the public library first selects the sources which it subsequently makes accessible. Libraries apply their information quality criteria in the context of these selection decisions. After having established a collection, a transparent accessibility infrastructure informed by professional principles for the organization of knowledge ensures universal access to the materials that have been selected. For access providers to such a relatively controlled information environment, a discussion about the responsibility to prevent access to certain information and ideas, which is an ongoing discussion for Internet access providers, would mostly have been inconceivable.

The conflicting ideals of access and quality lie at the core of many of the debates about the governance of information flows on the Internet. The Internet and the Web, and the possibility of self-publication unrestricted by traditional knowledge institutions, has broken down the institutional encirclement of certain sources of information deemed fit by professionals for societal consumption. This 'disintermediation' has often been presented as one of the central promises of the Internet and the Web, with particular reference to values related to freedom of expression. By others it is seen as a central flaw, since they would place more emphasis on the value of a shared platform for debate in which the circulation of information and ideas is restricted by minimal levels of quality, or on the need to restrict access to illegitimate, illegal and potentially harmful information flows more generally.

The above leads Dutch philosophers of science, Marres and De Vries, to the claim that the societal legitimization of knowledge in the networked information environment takes place through processes of opening up. In practice, to a significant extent the governance of information quality on the Web no longer takes place through control over what is actually available on the network, but through processes that determine the relative accessibility of information and ideas. Web search engines, in particular, help establish the relative accessibility of information and ideas in the networked public information environment.

Following this logic, the overarching public interest in the legal governance of Web search engines, seen from the ideals underlying the right to freedom of expression, lies in the establishment of a rich and robust societal infrastructure for the opening up of the Web, understood as the process of connecting information and ideas to their societal use. This characterization of the public interest in the governance of relative accessibility of the Web captures both perspectives, access *and* quality, which lie at the core of search engine governance. This also clarifies that search engine providers have to make non-trivial choices with regard to the balance between quality and access. In the networked information environment, publicity is no longer restricted to entities that offer a priori legitimacy to the information and ideas they make public. And the choices are not only non-trivial, but also of a political nature and involve the complex balancing of different public and private interests, including the interests of end-users and information providers who depend upon search engines as well.

11.4.2.   WHOSE FREE SPEECH?

Whose freedom of expression should one talk about when addressing the implications of the right to freedom of expression for the governance of search engines?

The conclusion of this thesis is that all three primary stakeholders in the communicative process mediated by the Web search engine have reasonable claims under the right to freedom of expression, some of which are directly actionable. For example, the analysis showed that under Article 10 ECHR, the search engine can claim protection for its publication of references to information online. The user can claim protection for the free use of online search media. And the information provider can claim protection for allowing its information offering to end up in a search engine and being referred to Internet users.

In addition to these somewhat trivial examples, there are cases in which search engine providers can be argued to have a strengthened claim under Article 10 ECHR because of the way they serve the freedom of expression interests of information providers and end-users. A good example would be the claim of a search engine, under Article 10 ECHR, against a hypothetical legal obligation to actively monitor the index for unlawful or illegal content. The predictably negative impact such monitoring would have on the freedom of expression interests of search engine users to navigate the online environment, as well as the role of search engines as a forum for online information providers, could both be decisive in the establishment of the impermissibility of this interference.

There are also a variety of legal contexts, however, in which the interests of search media, end-users and information providers in the legal governance of Web search media do not align. This poses the question of which interests should prevail from the perspective of the right to freedom of expression. For instance, the possible—but, in practice and for legal reasons beyond the scope of the analysis, unlikely—decision of Web search engines to ignore no-crawling instructions with respect to lawful and publicly accessible information which the search engine deems valuable for its users. In the legal conflict that could arise from this decision by the search engine provider, it could arguably defend its decision under Article 10 ECHR with reference to its own right to access and analyze publicly accessible information online as well as the interests to access information of its end-users.

Considering the above, the answer to *whose freedom of speech?* cannot be answered categorically in the search engine context. Furthermore, it is not feasible to provide a detailed analysis of the way freedom of expression would apply to all the possible legal conflicts that could arise with respect to the governance of information flows by a Web search medium. Instead, a different approach was chosen in this thesis, namely to arrive at a proper understanding of the typical protected interests of search engines, end-users and information providers, and to provide a general framework for the ways in which these interests should be balanced against each other in certain selected instances. The analysis of the freedom of expression implications for the press, the ISP and the library, as well as the conception of the societal role of search engines provided the foundation for this endeavor which continues in the third part of the thesis.

The legally protected interest of the search engine user under the right to freedom of expression is best understood as the right to inform oneself freely by exploring the Web to its full potential, using available search technologies and services that enhance the findability of information, ideas and resources in the public networked information environment. End-users rely on search engines to find news and other resources, to inform themselves about products, culture, political candidates and diseases, and to reach destinations and other online services. The user's freedom obviously implies a right to be able to choose which available navigational media to use. In addition, the user has a general interest in navigational media of high quality, but this interest cannot be understood as an actionable legal claim. Instead, this interest of the end-user is an aspect of the right to freedom to expression that can inform legal and regulatory involvement directed at the search engine market and the promotion of robust findability more generally.

The protected interests of information providers under the right to freedom of expression can be best understood as the freedom to be included in the search engine's index and to find their way to an audience. What is at stake for information providers can also be formulated in terms of representation. The inclusion into a search engine's index is a prerequisite for being found in the first place. If no search engine includes a particular source of information, this would deprive it of the possibility of acquiring attention and legitimacy. Hence, de-indexing by a dominant search engine is particularly problematic from the perspective of information providers. The same may be said about an unfavorable treatment through selection and ranking decisions. However, it is impossible to argue that all information providers could have a legal claim to be in a dominant general purpose search engine index, or to receive favorable treatment by selection and ranking algorithms. Besides being unattainable in practice, this claim would overlook a variety of legitimate grounds a search engine may have for the de-indexing of information providers or for an unfavorable ranking, grounds directly related to the protection of search engine providers under the right to freedom of expression and the interests of end-users. The best possible outcome from the perspective of information providers is that they would have a claim to be treated fairly and that interferences by dominant search engine providers to effectively reach an online audience would need to be reasonable and justified.

While discussing the respect for the communicative interests of information providers in their relation with search engines, it is important to acknowledge the extent to which they are actually in control of their indexing and ranking. This control is substantial and leads to the continuing manipulation of search results. It also leads to the de-indexing of lawful information in particular search engines through the use of robots.txt instructions. More problematic from the perspective of the right to freedom of expression may be the legal pressure to adopt such instructions, with the aim of negating the impact of certain lawful information that may be considered harmful, damaging or too sensitive. The effectiveness of search engines such as Google to actually open up the networked information environment may explain the pressure on information providers to adopt these practices. The result can hardly be called favorable for the interests of end-users in navigating the Web and informing themselves.

Search engine providers have a larger variety of legal claims under the right to freedom of expression. First, their basic operations which together provide the basis for publishing referencing information clearly fall under its scope, which is the crawling of online references and the operation of a publicly accessible website that publishes references to online material in response to user queries. The weight that should be attached to these claims can be strengthened because of the way they contribute to the free flow of information on the Web in general and to the communicative interests of Internet users and information providers in particular.

It is important to recognize that freedom of expression doctrine, as in the case of press freedom, should focus on protecting the way search engines contribute to the ideals underlying freedom of expression and the functioning of the networked information environment as a whole. More fundamentally, the grounds for protecting Web search engines' right to operate freely ultimately lie in the public interest of a rich and robust infrastructure for the societal process of the opening up of the World Wide Web. This is another argument to look beyond Google. The societal process mentioned above is a complex phenomenon in which Google may play an important role, but to which a large variety of organizations, services, practices and technologies contribute. Moreover, the way this process is organized is still relatively open, reflecting design principles of the World Wide Web discussed in Chapter 2, and strongly depends on the potential input of the entire collection of Web authors and users in general.

The legal protection of the search engine provider's freedom to rank and select under the right to freedom of expression is one of the most interesting questions dealt with in this thesis. Chapter 8 looks at early U.S. case law about the way the discretion of search engines to apply the selection and ranking of their choice, specifically in conflicts with information providers over unfavorable rankings, was considered to be protected as an editorial choice. In *SearchKing*, an Oklahoma Court applied the editorial freedom standards as developed by the Supreme Court in decisions such as *Miami Herald* and *Sullivan* to the freedom of search engines to decide freely how to rank and select references in response to user queries.

Since operating a search engine implies choices of how to value online resources and how to serve the different information needs of individuals and the public, there is much to be said for this part of the Oklahoma Court's conclusion. The choice of search engine providers regarding how to select, rank, and present can be considered an editorial process, which deserves protection under the right to freedom of expression. The predominantly technological nature of the way these choices materialize says less about the nature of the underlying process than about the massiveness of the index and the way technological innovation has offered new ways to organize and provide access to digital information collections. A proper understanding of the societal role of search media points in the same direction: by prioritizing the publicity of certain information and ideas in their index, Web search engines help reconcile the ideal of universal access and navigation of the entire Web with the ideal of information quality.

Notably, accepting that a search engine provider's decisions on how to select, rank and present would be protected by the right to freedom of expression, does not imply, at least not in the European context, that such freedom would be unlimited, nor that it could not be restricted. The conclusion that there may not be and should not be 'one correct way' to select and rank search results does not logically imply there cannot be any legally impermissible ways to do so. Under Article 10 ECHR, proportional restrictions remain possible, for instance in the context of the application of general laws such as unfair competition law, tort law or antitrust laws. Moreover, one can imagine certain editorial choices by search engine operators that could be unlawful in themselves, such as the choice to implement algorithms that are specifically directed at causing harm or that cause harm while having no justifiable purpose. Second, the right to freedom of expression as enshrined in Article 10 ECHR is not absolute and may be restricted in the interests and freedoms of others. It is possible to imagine legitimate restrictions being imposed on dominant search engine providers with the aim of ensuring that the communicative interests of information providers and end-users remain sufficiently respected.

Of special importance in the European context is the question about the duties and responsibilities of search engines which are tied to the exercise of the right to freedom of expression. The duties and responsibilities under Article 10 ECHR are tied to the exercise of one's expressive liberties and need to be interpreted in light of the present-day conditions of the media environment, in which as per the ECtHR's view, they have taken on an added importance. The potential impact of the medium and the nature of the content that can be found through a search engine will play a role in the determination of its possible duties and responsibilities. In other words, it is likely that major general purpose search engines such as Google, with a particularly strong impact on the public information environment, could have enhanced duties and responsibilities based on their widespread use. In this context, it is worth noting that the ECtHR's case law seems to imply that the more a communicator does to abide by professional standards with regard to quality and the mode of communicating, the more it will be able to defend itself against interferences.

In general, the lack of editorial control with regard to the actual content referred to and the lack of oversight over the inclusion of references could weaken a search engine's protection under Article 10 ECHR. But there are other arguments in favor of less stringent or different types of duties and responsibilities as regards the quality of references in search engines. Arguably, duties and responsibilities should cut both ways. On the one hand, they could be argued to imply a professional responsibility on Web search providers to promote and care for the quality of their references. On the other hand, they could be argued to entail a duty on search engine providers to be comprehensive and not exclude references too lightly. In fact, an important normative principle in the Court's case law (*Open Door*) is that a communicator that leaves the decision to act upon its communications to the receiver cannot, in principle, be blamed for those decisions. The more facilitative the search engine would be with respect to the decisional autonomy of its users, the more protection it would receive against interferences that seek to prevent a certain reaction by the audience.

11.5. THE ROLE OF GOVERNMENT: REASONS FOR RESTRAINT AND ROOM FOR ACTION

Based on the above, it is also possible to discuss the ways in which the right to freedom of expression impacts the proper role of government with regard to search engine governance. This discussion is also important for the final part of this thesis, which studies the question of how specific legal and regulatory involvement with search engine governance should be evaluated. It is useful to discern, as in Chapter 4, the general normative implications of the right to freedom of expression on the basis of the different modalities of State and regulatory involvement. These implications depend, on the one hand, on the character of the legal relation: vertical or horizontal. On the other hand, they depend on the question of whether the involvement of the State in different instances should be characterized as an interference with, or whether it could be seen as promoting the right to freedom of expression of, one or more of the stakeholders involved. Together, these questions allow for the construction of a diagram of modalities of State involvement in which the various ways in which the right to freedom of expression is implicated in the governance of search engines can be visualized (see Figure 11.1).

The legal issues arising from the legal governance of search engines discussed in this thesis can be mapped onto this quadrant. For instance, the protection of commercial search engine providers under Article 10 to publish references to third-party material without undue government interference should be placed in the upper left quadrant. The issue of whether too strict intermediary liability rules for search engines could incentivize them to not reference certain lawful Internet content is an example that fits into the upper right quadrant. The public funding of search engines for end-users in view of their interests in accessibility to content and high-quality search tools could be placed in the lower left quadrant. And finally, the way government regulation could try to promote accessibility and diversity for end-users are examples that fit into the lower right quadrant.

The character of the right to freedom of expression changes if one moves from the upper left corner to the lower right corner of this diagram. Most importantly, freedom of expression as a legal right is strongest in the upper left quadrant, with corresponding fundamental legal obligations on public authorities not to interfere and actionable rights of affected private parties against such interference. When moving downwards and to the right this character changes and it may, at some point, be more appropriate to speak of a fundamental legal and regulatory principle instead of a fundamental right.

In addition, in horizontal relations the different fundamental interests under the right to freedom of expression of search engines conceptualized in the previous section need to be balanced. Of course, such balancing will typically involve other fundamental legally protected interests. When acting under its positive obligation under Article 10 ECHR, or when acting to promote freedom of expression more generally, the State has considerable legal leeway in shaping its specific involvement. Such positive interference with regard to search engine governance has to take into account the protection of search engine providers under freedom of expression as a negative right.

Figure 11.1: Search Engine Governance and Freedom of Expression

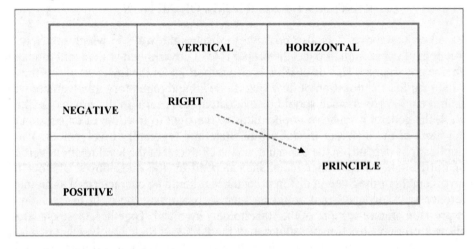

When focusing on the proper governance of search in horizontal relations, the way a balancing of interests ultimately must take place and the extent to which a certain positive role of government may be considered desirable will depend on the specific circumstances as well the larger context. A first factor that is important in this regard is the extent to which basic levels of effective exercise of the right to freedom of expression of end-users or information providers may be threatened. The market structure, as well as an analysis of the actual practices of dominant market players, may play an important role in answering this question.

The third part of this thesis explores and illustrates the ways in which legal and regulatory involvement related to access and quality in the context of search can be further informed by a proper understanding of the implications of the right to freedom of expression. The main findings of these last chapters are put into perspective here, also taking into account the conclusions presented above. More specifically, the sections below present the conclusions of Chapters 9 and 10 about the way freedom of expression could be used to improve existing laws and regulatory practices in the field of search engine governance.

It must be mentioned here that on the basis of the analysis of the concerns addressed in this thesis, there is no reason to recommend a general sector-specific approach to the regulation of search engines as they exist, for instance, for Internet access providers or audio-visual media. The justified claims under the right to freedom of expression for search engine providers imply that a specific framework of legal obligations with respect to the governance of information flows by Web search engines would be problematic and self-regulation in the sector would be preferable. Of course, the quality of self-regulation can still be considered a regulatory concern and with regard to specific issues, legal rules may be adopted that specifically address the search engine context. Sector-specific regulation of most of the issues discussed in this thesis would be hard, however, due to the heterogeneity and differences in scale of the various actors and services that contribute to the societal role of search engines and that perform similar actions.

11.5.1. SEARCH ENGINE INTERMEDIARY LIABILITY AND CONTENT CO-REGULATION

Amongst the most pressing legal issues for search engine providers in Europe is the question about third-party liability. By opening up the Web, general purpose search engines make illegal, unlawful or harmful information published online more easily accessible for Internet users. This state of affairs, which actually reflects the accomplishments of search engine providers in facilitating access to information for end-users, raises the question of the extent to which search engine providers can be held legally responsible for their role in facilitating such access. This question has not been answered clearly in the European context.

In the United States, intermediary liability rules for the Internet provide specific exceptions for search engine providers. The same type of rules has been adopted in the EU's Directive on Electronic Commerce, but this framework of safe harbors for intermediaries does not provide for a specific safe harbor for search engines. In addition, the EU safe harbor framework does a relatively poor job in internalizing the freedom of expression interest in the free flow of information through intermediaries more generally. The character of the Directive on Electronic Commerce, which harmonizes national rules related to information society services and e-commerce, may also have stood in the way of properly addressing these concerns of a non-economic nature.

The result of the lack of a specific safe harbor for search engines has been a complex patchwork of different legal approaches in the various Member States for search engine intermediary liability. Recent case law of the ECJ with regard to third-party liability for trademark infringement has added to the confusion by leaving room for the application of the existing EU safe harbor for hosting activities to search engines, as long as the activity of the search engine remains *merely technical, automatic and passive in nature*. This standard was not written with search engine activity in mind and does not fit with the understanding of the functioning and role of search engines as intermediaries in this thesis.

The legal uncertainty with regard to third-party liability for search engines, in combination with continuous litigation and regulatory pressure by public authorities is problematic from the perspective of freedom of expression. It incentivizes search engine providers to respond too willingly to legal notices of illegal or unlawful content in their index, which can harm the communicative interests of end-users and information providers in the governance of search. It also makes it harder to operate a search engine in Europe in the first place, thus having a negative impact on the development of a robust and diverse infrastructure for the opening up of the Web.

The second review of the Directive on Electronic Commerce, launched towards the end of 2010, provides an opportunity to reflect on the position of search engines in the EU safe harbor framework. Again, the nature of the Directive may imply an emphasis on the economic aspects of the governance of the online environment. In addition, the subject of search engine liability may be considered too controversial. It is clear, however, that an EC position on search engine liability would minimally need to reflect a balance between the freedom of expression interests that are at stake and the need to enforce intellectual property laws, defamation law, privacy law and other legal restrictions on communications. When looking for appropriate safe harbors for search engines, it can be argued that a safe harbor that implies a notice and takedown obligation is sub-optimal in consideration of the role of search engines in opening up the Web. It would wrongly conflate the search engine with a distributor. On the other hand, the kind of blanket immunity for third-party defamation and privacy infringements that is offered to search engine providers by the Communications Decency Act section 230 in the United States would be inconsistent with fundamental European legal principles, in particular the right to respect for private life (Article 8 ECHR). Europe will have to formulate its own answer to the complex issue of intermediary liability of search engines.

The lack of certainty about the actual legal responsibility with regard to third-party material also makes voluntarily participation in self-regulatory frameworks more problematic. From the perspective of freedom of expression, the self-regulatory paradigm which is also prevalent in the governance of the press should come together with a clarification of the actual legal responsibilities of search engine providers for illegal or unlawful content. At present, the willingness to give in to extra-legal pressure on search engines to self-regulate—in the form of blocking of references or on the basis of blacklists—can hardly be seen as voluntary. The informalized role of public authorities in these frameworks is also problematic from the perspective of freedom of expression, due to the fundamental legal requirement under Article 10 ECHR that interferences with the right to freedom of expression have to be 'prescribed by law'.

11.5.2.   SEARCH ENGINE QUALITY: DIVERSITY, TRANSPARENCY
             AND ACCOUNTABILITY TOWARDS END-USERS

Chapter 10 of this thesis addresses three selected issues in the regulatory debate about search engines with regard to search engine quality, in particular with regard to the way search engines rank, select and present search results. In the literature on the impact of search engines on the public information environment, much thought has been put into the possible biases of dominant commercial search media and the ways in which they may not be serving the public's right to receive information and ideas freely. This line of thought suggests a more positive agenda for government involvement in the search engine market, aimed at safeguarding the freedom of expression interests of end-users and information providers in the governance of search. The consolidation of the search engine market, and the dominance of Google in particular, has been the reason for concerns about the impact of search engines on the accessibility of information and ideas and the values of diversity and pluralism in the public networked information environment.

In an online information environment characterized by abundance, a proper analysis of pluralism and diversity must take special account of search engines and selection intermediaries more generally. They have a considerable impact on the information and ideas that Internet users are confronted with. Moreover and in relation, in an environment characterized by abundance an analysis of diversity and pluralism should emphasize the exposure to information and ideas, instead of merely addressing what is available online. Some researchers who have studied the impact of search engines on exposure diversity and the quality of search inter-mediation have warned against certain forms of search engine bias. Chapter 10 concludes that some of the critiques of search engines' biases may be best under-stood as the demystification of utopian assumptions about the equalizing, democ-ratizing and disintermediation effects of the Internet and the World Wide Web. To the extent that such assumptions were simply unrealistic, untenable or actually undesirable, such as the idea that search engines should facilitate access to infor-mation and ideas completely equally, these critiques are rather unsurprising and can hardly serve as a starting point for further analysis.

When addressing the offerings of search engines in the European context from the perspective of diversity and pluralism, a first possible concern is the consol-idation of the search engine market and a second possible concern is the impact of the dominant search engine on the European market, Google. This thesis concludes that there is not enough evidence for a negative impact of the current market structure on diversity and pluralism to warrant specific regulatory action. On a general level, the mere existence of general purpose search engines can be con-sidered positive for pluralism and diversity for end-users, due to the underlying diversity of information and ideas on the World Wide Web. There also remain a variety of alternatives to search engines—and to Google—which help users find, or be confronted with, information and ideas that may not necessarily show up prom-inently in major search engines' rankings.

However, to be able to address the question about the impact of search engines on diversity and pluralism properly, more research needs to be done on the impact of market competition on search engine quality. On the one hand, commercial search engines may end up trying to do exactly the same things in their competition for users. On the other hand, a lack of competition could diminish incentives to innovate on search engine quality for end-users. Other open questions that need to be addressed in this context are the specific impact of dominant players in the industry on diversity of search results as well as the way other players in the public networked information environment could alleviate possible concerns following from market concentration in the search engine market.

This thesis concludes that search engines could be more forthcoming about the value they attribute to diversity of search results and the fair representation of different information providers. The analysis shows that general purpose search engines actually have a number of incentives and possibilities to promote diversity. At the same time, the search engine business model implies that search engines may be particularly interested in optimizing their offerings in view of particular information needs of end-users of a commercial nature, and in view of them being marketing platforms for advertisers. This can, and does, result in the reduction of diversity of the first set of search results and decreases the number of results that satisfy other information needs of end-users. Personalization of search results could also become problematic from the perspective of diversity and pluralism, but the question of whether that is actually the case depends on the values and principles underlying such personalization and warrants further research.

The most problematic aspect in the context of pluralism and diversity is the impact that certain online information providers have on the quality of search results and the overall robustness of the search medium. Search engine 'optimization', while also fulfilling legitimate functions, effectively pushes legitimate sources of information out of the end-users' view. As is troublesome, these practices are not considered problematic and are even endorsed by search engine providers such as Google. More generally, because of the opportunities to optimize search engine rankings or participate in sponsored search result programs, search results can be expected to be biased towards information providers with sufficient financial and organizational means to participate in the ongoing competition for favorable rankings. This is a concern that deserves specific attention from the perspective of ongoing efforts to monitor, promote and enhance diversity and pluralism, and of the development of the public networked information environment more generally.

Search engine quality, to a considerable degree, is shaped by the users themselves. Due to the interactive nature of search engine services, the quality of the search experience, in terms of the diversity of information and ideas users are presented with, will depend upon a user's general knowledge, sophistication and critical engagement with the search interface. The proper choice for a suitable search service, the awareness of alternatives, the ability to formulate and reformulate search queries effectively and the use of advanced search options are amongst the things that significantly impact the quality of the Internet user's search experience. It is clear from empirical research that expectations of user skill should not be unrealistic and that even users who do have the skills will often accept easy answers. The concerns this raises with regard to the impact of a search engine such as Google are not new, and are ultimately best solved through education.

Chapter 10 also addresses the question of whether the search engines' advertisement-based business model is a concern from the perspective of the end-users' interest in high-quality search engines. An analysis of the current labeling obligations with regard to the delineation of sponsored and organic search results, which is aimed at protecting the users' interest, shows them to be inadequate. As is noticeable, this delineation is based on the traditional distinction found in traditional editorial media. However, general purpose search engines do not operate in a manner that can provide the independence and information quality guarantees for organic listings that the labeling obligation assumes. The parallel with editorial media further breaks down upon closer examination and the value the labeling provides to end-users is questionable due to the convergence of organic and sponsored search results and their optimization.

This points to the general lack of transparency in the functioning of search engines, information regarding which is currently provided voluntarily. This voluntary nature of transparency in the context of search has some obvious drawbacks. Search engines such as Google claim to engage in a number of best practices with regard to search engine quality, but a proper mechanism for verifying their · claims independently is lacking. In contrast, transparency obligations could also be considered problematic. On a practical level, they could impact the ability of search engines to resist manipulation. More fundamentally, strict transparency obligations could be at odds with the right to freedom of expression as applied to the choices of search engines to rank and select in relative freedom.

Competition law can be expected to be one of the drivers for increased transparency in regard to the selection and ranking practices of dominant market players, as several complaints of monopolistic abuse are pending at the European Commission, national competition authorities, and in the United States. These investigations will also have to come to terms, at some point, with the question about the editorial freedom of search engine providers to rank and select search results.

The final sections of Chapter 10 address the concerns related to the massive amounts of user data that search engines collect, process and analyze from the perspective of data protection, user privacy and the right to freedom of expression. European data protection authorities consider the processing of user data by search engine providers to be covered by general data protection law. The current legal framework, however, does not specifically recognize the special role or status of data about information-seeking and information-accessing behavior in the digital information environment. Search services have strong incentives to compete for more and more user data. These data collections are unprecedented in scale and, once collected, are valuable for a range of other purposes unrelated to facilitating access to information and ideas or even marketing. They are typically stored in undisclosed locations outside the control of end-users and are accessible by law enforcement and national security agencies under a range of applicable local laws. The possible chilling effects on information-seeking of a lack of privacy in the search engine context and the need to protect intellectual freedom more generally are reason to reflect on the need to adopt specific rules to safeguard intellectual freedom of search engine users.

Increased personalization and the lack of transparency in end-user modeling can be seen as a threat to the informational autonomy of search engine users. European data protection law already contains a number of provisions which can enhance transparency in, and accountability for, these types of user data processing if the user data can be considered personal data. If data protection authorities were right in their interpretation of how European data protection law applies to search engines, and will prove more successful in imposing this view on the market, this framework could be instrumental in establishing the interest in informational autonomy of end-users in the search engine context.

11.06. CONCLUSION

Web search and the organization of information and ideas inherent in its operation is a new phenomenon with technological, cultural, economic and political dimensions. While not providing the final answer, this thesis makes an important contribution to the legal and regulatory debates on the proper governance of Web search engines from the basis of a heretofore underdeveloped perspective, being that of the right to freedom of expression.

The conceptual and institutional approach of studying freedom of expression in better understood and functionally related contexts proves valuable, helping develop a well-informed general framework of implications of freedom of expression for the governance of search. This study shows how roles in the public information environment are shifting and that a re-articulation of the values underlying the right to freedom of expression is at stake. In the networked information environment, a fundamental shift has taken place from the governance of access to the governance of accessibility. While the Internet may treat censorship as damage and route around it as some claim, the intermediaries that control the relative accessibility of information and ideas may route around important conversations as a result of legal or regulatory interference or as a result of the dynamics inherent in the operations of search media.

Considering the centrality of search in an information environment characterized by abundance, the importance of critical engagement with search media from a user perspective, as well as on a regulatory level, cannot be understated. This engagement, however, must come hand in hand with an acknowledgement of the value search engines provide for users and information providers, the importance of search media performing their editorial and organizational practices in freedom, and the technological and economic realities of search. Rather than seeing law and regulation as a potential means to restrict certain practices, this thesis shows that there is room for a positive and enabling role of the State in the European context. This role is to ensure that the services, technologies and societal infrastructure for the opening up of the Internet can be and remain uninhibited, robust and wide-open.

References

2600, 'Seized!', August 1985, http://72.52.208.92/~gbpprorg/2600/seized.txt ('2600' 1985)

28th International Data Protection and Privacy Commissioners' Conference, 'Resolution on Privacy Protection and Search Engines', London, United Kingdom, November 2 and 3, 2006 (28th International Data Protection and Privacy Commissioners' Conference 2006).

Janet Abbate, *Inventing the Internet*, Cambridge/London: The MIT Press, 2000 (Abbate 2000).

G. Scott Aikens, 'The democratization of Systems of Public Opinion Formation,' *International Symposium on Technology and Society, Technical Expertise and Public Decisions*, Princeton: Princeton University Press, 1996 (Aikens 1996).

American Library Association, 'Library Bill of Rights', Adopted June 18, 1948, amended February 2, 1961, and January 23, 1980, inclusion of "age" reaffirmed January 23, 1996, by the ALA Council (American Library Association 1996).

David A. Anderson, 'Libel and Press Self-Censorship', 53 *Texas Law Review* 422, 1975 (Anderson 1975).

Nate Anderson, 'Google relents, adds privacy link to Spartan homepage', *Ars Technica*, July 7, 2008, http://arstechnica.com/old/content/2008/07/google-relents-adds-privacy-link-to-spartan-homepage.ars (Anderson 2008).

Christina Angelopoulos, 'Filtering the Internet for Copyrighted Content in Europe', *IRIS-plus (Supplement to IRIS—Legal Observations of the European Audiovisual Observatory)*, 2009-4 (Angelopoulos 2009).

F. Anklesaria et al., 'The Internet Gopher Protocol (a distributed document search and retrieval protocol)', *IETF, Request for Comments (RFC) 1436*, March 1993, http://tools.ietf.org/html/rfc1436 (Anklesaria et al. 1993).

David S. Ardia, 'Free Speech Savior or Shield for Scoundrels: An Empirical Study of Intermediary Immunity Under Section 230 of the Communications Decency Act', 43 *Loyola of Los Angeles Law Review* 373, 2010 (Ardia 2010).

References

J.C. Arnbak, J.J. van Cuilenburg, E.J. Dommering, et al., *Verbinding en Onvlechting in de Communicatie, Een studie naar toekomstig overheidsbeleid voor de openbare elektronische informatievoorziening*, Amsterdam: Otto Cramwinckel, 1990 (Arnbak et al. 1990).

Stephen E. Arnold, 'Could Google Become the Semantic Web?', *Semantic Universe*, 2010 (Arnold 2010).

Michael Arnold, Eric Darmon & Thierry Penard, 'To Sponsor or Not to Sponsor: Sponsored SearchAuctions with Organic Links and Firm Dependent Click-Through Rates', June 1, 2011, ftp://193.196.11.222/pub/zew-docs/veranstaltungen/ICT2011/Papers/Darmon.pdf (Arnold et al. 2011).

Article 29 Data Protection Working Party, 'Opinion 4/2007 on the concept of personal data', WP 148, June 20, 2007 (Article 29 Working Party 2007).

Article 29 Data Protection Working Party, Opinion 1/2008 on data protection issues related to search engines, WP 148, Brussels, April 4, 2008 (Article 29 Working Party 2008).

Lester Asheim, 'Not Censorship but Selection', *Wilson Library Bulletin*, September 1953 (Asheim 1953).

AT Internet, 'Baromètre des moteurs—Mars 2011', 2011, http://www.atinternet.com/ (AT Internet 2011).

Anne Aula & Kerry Rodden, 'Eye-tracking studies: more than meets the eye', *The Official Google Blog*, February 6, 2009, http://googleblog.blogspot.com/2009/02/eye-tracking-studies-more-than-meets.html (Aula & Rodden (Google) 2009).

Ken Auletta, *Googled: The End of the World As We Know It*, New York: The Penguin Press, 2009 (Auletta 2009).

Ricardo Baeza-Yates & Berthier Ribeiro-Neto, *Modern Information Retrieval, The concepts and technology behind search*, Second Edition, Harlow: Pearson Education Limited, 2011 (Baeza-Yates & Ribeiro-Neto 2011).

C. Edwin Baker, *Human Liberty and Free Speech*, New York: Oxford University Press, 1989 (Baker 1989).

C. Edwin Baker, 'Turner Broadcasting, Content-Based Regulation of Persons and Presses', 1994 Supreme Court Review 57, 1994 (Baker 1994).

C. Edwin Baker, *Media, Markets, and Democracy*, Cambridge (U.K.): Cambridge University Press, 2002 (Baker 2002).

C. Edwin Baker, 'The Future of News Part One', January 21, 2009, *Balkinization*, http://balkin.blogspot.com/2009/01/future-of-news-part-one-problem.html (Baker 2009a).

C. Edwin Baker, 'The Future of News Part Two', January 22, 2009, *Balkinization*, http://balkin.blogspot.com/2009/01/future-of-news-part-two-solutions.html (Baker 2009b).

Steven Baker, 'Helping computers understand language', *The Official Google Blog*, January 19, 2010, http://googleblog.blogspot.com/2010/01/helping-computers-understand-language.html (Baker (Google) 2010).

Robert Baldwin & Martin Cave, *Understanding Regulation: Theory, Strategy and Practice*, Oxford University Press, 1999 (Baldwin & Cave 1999).

Jack M. Balkin, 'Some Realism about Pluralism. Legal Realist Approaches to the First Amendment', 1990 Duke Law Journal 375, 1990 (Balkin 1990).

Jack M. Balkin, 'Digital Speech and Democratic Culture: A theory of Freedom of Expression for the Information Society', 79 *New York University Law Review* 1, 2004 (Balkin 2004).

Derek E. Bambauer, 'Orwell's Armchair', *University of Chicago Law Review*, Forthcoming 2011 (Bambauer Forthcoming 2011).

Michael Barbaro & Tom Zeller Jr., 'A Face Is Exposed for AOL Searcher No. 4417749', *The New York Times*, August 9, 2006, http://www.nytimes.com/2006/08/09/technology/09aol.html (Barbaro & Zeller 2006).

Eric Barendt, *Freedom of Speech*, Second Edition, Oxford University Press, 2005 (Barendt 2005).

John Perry Barlow, *A Declaration of the Independence of Cyberspace*, Davos, Switzerland, February 8, 1996 (Barlow 1996).

Jarome A. Barron, "The Telco, The Common Carrier Model and the First Amendment—The 'Dial-A-Porn' Precedent," 19 *Rutgers Computer & Technology Law Journal* 371, 1993 (Barron 1993).

Jerome A. Barron, 'Access to the Press. A New First Amendment Right', 80 Harvard Law Review 1641, 1966 (Barron 1996).

Judit Bar-Ilan, 'Position Paper: Access to Query Logs—An Academic Researcher's Point of View', *WWW 2007*, http://citeseerx.ist.psu.edu/viewdoc/download?doi=10.1.1.104.1866&rep=rep1&type=pdf (Bar-Ilan 2007).

Diane Bartz, 'FTC, Justice Dept mull Google antitrust probe', *Reuters*, April 5, 2011, http://www.reuters.com/article/2011/04/05/us-google-ftc-idUSTRE7340L520110405 (Bartz 2011).

Abraham A. Bass, 'Redefining the "gatekeeper" concept: a U.N. Radio case study', 46 *Journalism Quarterly* 59, 1969 (Bass 1969).

John Battelle, *The Search. How Google and Its Rivals Rewrote the Rules of Business and Transformed Our Culture*, New York: Portfolio, 2006 (Battelle 2006).

John Battelle, The Database of Intentions is Much Larger Than I Thought', *John Battelle's Search Blog*, March 5, 2010, http://battellemedia.com/archives/2010/03/the_database_of_intentions_is_far_larger_than_i_thought.php (Battelle 2010).

BBC, 'Nobel: China Blocks Foreign Websites Ahead of Ceremony', December 9, 2010, http://www.bbc.co.uk/news/world-asia-pacific-11962520 (BBC 2010).

Benjamin et al. 2006: Stuart M. Benjamin et al., *Telecommunications Law and Policy*, Durham (NC): Carolina Academic Press, 2006.

Yochai Benkler, 'From Consumers to Users: Shifting the Deeper Structures of Regulation toward Sustainable Common and User Access', 52 *Federal Communications Law Journal* 561, 2000 (Benkler 2000).

Yochai Benkler 'Siren Songs and Amish Children: Autonomy, Information, and Law', 76 *New York University Law Review* 23, 2001 (Benkler 2001).

Yochai Benkler, *The Wealth of Networks—How Social Production Transforms Markets and Freedom*, New Haven and London: Yale University Press, 2006 (Benkler 2006).

References

Yochai Benkler, 'A Free Irresponsible Press: Wikileaks and the Battle over the Soul of the Networked Fourth Estate', *Harvard Civil Rights—Civil Liberties Law Review*, Spring 2011 (Benkler 2011).

Isaiah Berlin, 'Two Concepts of Liberty', in: I. Berlin, *Four Essays on Liberty*, London: Oxford University Press, 2002 (Berlin 2002).

Berlin Group, 'Common Position on Data Protection and search engines on the Internet', Hong Kong, April 15, 1998, updated Washington D.C., April 6–7, 2006 (Berlin Group 2006).

Jerry Berman & Daniel J. Weitzner, 'Abundance and User Control: Renewing the Democratic Heart of the First Amendment in the Age of Interactive Media', 104 Yale Law Journal 1619, 1995 (Berman & Weizner 1995).

Fernando Bermejo, *The Internet Audience, Constitution and Measurement*, New York: Peter Lang, 2007 (Bermejo 2007).

Tim Berners-Lee & Robert Cailliau, 'WorldWideWeb: Proposal for a HyperText Project', November 12, 1990, http://www.w3.org/Proposal.html (Berners-Lee & Cailliau 1990).

Tim Berners-Lee, *Weaving the Web: The Original Design and Ultimate Destiny of the World Wide Web by its Inventor*, New York: HarperOne, 2000 (Berners-Lee 2000).

Tim Berners-Lee, James Hendler & Ora Lassila, 'The Semantic Web', *Scientific American*, March 17, 2001, http://www.scientificamerican.com/article.cfm?id=the-semantic-web (Berners-Lee et al. 2001).

June M. Besek & Phillippa S. Loengard, 'Maintaining the integrity of digital archives', 31 *Columbia Journal of Law & the Arts* 267, 2008 (Besek & Loengard 2008).

Lillian BeVier, 'An informed Public, An Informed Press: The Search for a Constitutional Principle', 68 California Law Review 482, 1980 (Bevier 1980).

Lillian Bevier, 'United States v. American Library Association: Whither First Amendment Doctrine', 55 *Supreme Court Review* 163, 2003 (Bevier 2003).

Michael D. Birnhack and Niva Elkin-Koren. 'The Invisible Handshake: The Reemergence of the State in the Digital Environment', 8 *Virginia Journal of Law & Technology* 6, 2003 (Birnhack & Elkin-Koren 2003).

Hugo L. Black, 'The Bill of Rights', 35 *New York University Law Review* 865, 1960 (Black 1960).

Margaret A. Blanchard, 'The American Urge to Censor: Freedom of Expression Versus the Desire to Sanitize Society—From Anthony Comstock to 2 Live Crew', 33 *William & Mary Law Review* 741, 1992 (Blanchard 1992).

Hans Blokland, *Wegen naar vrijheid, Autonomie, emancipatie en cultuur in de westerse wereld*, Meppel: Boom Amsterdam, 1995 (Blokland 1995).

Uki Bonim, 'Can a Soccer Star Block Google Searches?', *Time Magazine*, November 14, 2008, http://www.time.com/time/world/article/0,8599,1859329,00.html (Bonim 2008).

Haig A. Bosmajian, *Censorship, Libraries and the Law*, New York: Neal-Schuman Publishers, 1983 (Bosmajian 1983).

Geoffrey C. Bowker & Susan Leigh Star, *Sorting Things Out. Classification and its Consequences*, Cambridge (MA): The MIT Press, 2000 (Bowker & Leigh Star 2000).

Oren Bracha and Frank Pasquale, 'Federal Search Commission? Access, Fairness, and Accountability in the Law of Search', 93 *Cornell Law Review* 1149, 2008 (Bracha & Pasquale 2008).

Sergey Brin and Larry Page, 'The Anatomy of a Large-Scale Hypertextual Web Search Engine', *Computer Networks and ISDN Systems*, 30 (1–7), 1998, 107–117 (Brin & Page 1998).

Andrei Broder, A Taxonomy of Web Search, *SIGIR Forum*, 36(2), 2002, 3–10 (Broder 2002).

Birgit Brömmekamp, 'Der Fall L'Oréal gegen eBay: Prüfstein für die Informationsgesellschaft, *Wettbewerb in Recht und Praxis*, 2011-3, 306–316 (Brömmekamp 2011).

Vannevar Bush, 'As We May Think', *The Atlantic,* July 1945, http://www.theatlantic.com/magazine/archive/1969/12/as-we-may-think/3881/ (Bush 1945).

Alexandre Caldas, Ralph Schroeder, Gustavo S. Mesch & William H. Dutton, 'Patterns of Information Search and Access on the World Wide Web: Democratizing Expertise or Creating New Hierarchies?', 13 *Journal of Computer-Mediated Communications* 769, 2008 (Caldas et al. 2008).

Robert Cannon, 'The Legislative History of Senator Exon's Communications Decency Act- Regulating Barbarians on the Information Superhighway', 49 *Federal Communications Law Journal* 51, 1996 (Cannon 1996).

Herman Anthony Carneiro & Eleftherios Mylonakis, 'Google Trends: A Web-Based Tool for Real-Time Surveillance of Disease Outbreak', 49 *Clinical Infectious Diseases* 1557, 2009 (Carneiro & Mylonikas 2009).

Lionel Casson, *Libraries in the Ancient World*, New Haven: Yale University Press, 2001 (Casson 2001).

Stephen L. Carter, 'Technology, Democracy, and the Manipulation of Consent', 93 *Yale Law Journal* 581, 1984 (Carter 1984).

Thomas Catan & Amir Efrati, 'Feds to Launch Probe of Google', *The Wall Street Journal*, June 24, 2011, http://online.wsj.com/article/SB10001424052702303339904576403603764717680.html (Catan & Efrati 2011).

Z. Chafee Jr., Book Review, 'Free Speech and Its Relation to Self-Government, by A. Meiklejohn', 65 *Harvard Law Review* 891, 1948 (Chafee 1948).

Amay Champaneria & Beverly Yang, 'Hide sites to find more of what you want', *The Official Google Blog*, March 10, 2011, http://googleblog.blogspot.com/2011/03/hide-sites-to-find-more-of-what-you.html (Champaneria & Yang (Google) 2011).

David X. Chan, Yuan Yuan, Jim Koehler, Deepak Kum, (Google Inc.), 'Incremental Clicks Impact Of Search Advertising', 2011, http://www.gstatic.com/ads/research/en/2011_Search_Ads_Pause.pdf (Chan et al. 2011).

Jennifer A. Chandler, 'A Right to Reach an Audience: An Approach to Intermediary Bias on the Internet', 35 *Hofstra Law Review* 1095, 2008 (Chandler 2008).

Remy Chavannes, 'Brein/KPN: het gevaar van een bagatel?', *Mediaforum* 2007-6, 174–178 (Chavannes 2007).

Checkit.nl, 'Nationale Search Engine Monitor', June 2010 (Checkit.nl 2000).

Berkman Center for Internet & Society, Chilling Effects Clearinghouse, http://www.chillingeffects.org/ (Chilling Effects).

Jacques Chirac, 'Déclaration de M. Jacques Chirac, Président de la République, sur les priorités de la politique industrielle, notamment en matière d'innovation et de recherche', Paris, April 25, 2006, http://discours.vie-publique.fr/notices/067001499.html (Chirac 2006).

Marjorie Heins, Christina Cho & Ariel Feldman, Internet Filters, A Public Policy Report, Second Edition, Brennan Center for Justice, 2006 (Heins et al. 2006).

Angelique Chrisafis, 'Chirac unveils his grand plan to restore French pride', *The Guardian*, April 26, 2006, http://www.guardian.co.uk/technology/2006/apr/26/news.france (Chrisafis 2006).

Danielle Citron, 'Cyber Civil Rights', 89 *Boston University Law Review* 61, 2009 (Citron 2009).

Danielle Citron (ed.), *DU Porcess: Cyber Civil Rights Symposium Papers*, March 3, 2010, http://www.concurringopinions.com/archives/2010/03/du-process-cyber-civil-rights-symposium-papers.html (Citron 2010).

Richard Clayton, *Anonymity and traceability in cyberspace*, University of Cambridge: Computer Laboratory, November 2005, http://www.cl.cam.ac.uk/techreports/UCAM-CL-TR-653.pdf (Clayton 2005).

Richard Clayton, 'Failures in a hybrid content blocking system', in: Danezis and Martin (eds.), *Privacy Enhancing Technologies*, Lecture Notes in Computer Science, Springer 2006 (Clayton 2006).

Richard Clayton, 'The IWF Blocking List Recent UK Experiences', lides, INEX, Dublin, June 30, 2009, http://www.cl.cam.ac.uk/~rnc1/talks/090630-inex.pdf (Clayton 2009).

Julie E. Cohen, 'A Right to Read Anonymously: A Closer Look at "Copyright Management" in Cyberspace', 28 *Connecticut Law Review* 981, 1996 (Cohen 1996).

Ronald K. L. Collins & David Skover, *The Death of Discourse*, Westview Press, 1996 (Collins & Skover 1996).

Committee on Internet Navigation and the Domain Name System, *Signposts in Cyberspace: The Domain Name System and Internet Navigation*, Washington D.C.: The National Academic Press, 2005 (Committee on Internet Navigation 2005).

CommonCrawl, http://www.commoncrawl.org (CommonCrawl) comScore, 'comScore Releases July 2011 U.S. Search Engine Rankings', RESTON, VA, August 10, 2011 (Comscore 2011).

Consumer Watchdog's Inside Google, 'Google using search engine to muscle into Internet businesses, study finds' (Press Release), June 2, 2010, http://insidegoogle.com/2010/06/google-using-search-engine-to-muscle-into-internet-businesses-study-finds-2/ (Consumer Watchdog's Inside Google 2010).

Alissa Cooper, 'A survey of query log privacy-enhancing techniques from a policy perspective', *ACM Transactions on the Web (TWEB)*, Vol. 2, Issue 4, 2008, http://dl.acm.org/ft_gateway.cfm?id=1409222&type=pdf& CFID=62051225&CFTOKEN=90918461 (Cooper 2008).

Elizabeth van Couvering, *Search Engine Bias, The Structuration of Traffic on the World-Wide Web*, A thesis submitted to The Department Media and Communications, London School of Economics and Political Science, London, December 2009 (van Couvering 2009).

Florian Cramer, Personal Website, http://cramer.pleintekst.nl:70/ (Cramer).

Matt Cutts, 'SEO Advice: Writing useful articles that readers will love', *Matt Cutts: Gadgets, Google, and SEO*, August 21, 2006, http://www.mattcutts. com/blog/seo-advice-writing-useful-articles-that-readers-will-love/ (Cutts 2006).

Matt Cutts, 'Why I disagree with Privacy International', *Matt Cutts: Gadgets, Google, and SEO*, June 11, 2007, http://www.mattcutts.com/blog/privacy-international-loses-all-credibility/ (Cutts 2007).

Matt Cutts, 'Google search and search engine spam', *The Official Google Blog*, January 21, 2011, http://googleblog.blogspot.com/2011/01/google-search-and-search-engine-spam.html (Cutts (Google) 2011).

Daniel J. Czitrom, *Media and the American Mind*, Chapel Hill: University of Carolina Press, 1982 (Czitrom 1982).

H. K. Dai, et al., 'Detecting online commercial intention', *WWW2006*, 2006, 829–837 (Dai et al. 2006).

Dimos Dakanalis & Aswin van Rooijen, 'EU: Google under Antitrust Scrutiny', 2011 *Computer Law Review International* 29, 2011 (Dakanalis and van Rooijen 2011).

Robert Darnton, 'The Library in the Information Age, 6000 Years of Script', in: K. Becker & F. Stalder (eds.), *Deep search: the politics of search beyond Google*, Innsbruck: Studienverlag, 2009, 32–44 (Darnton 2009).

Ronald Deibert, John Palfrey et al. (ed.), Access Denied: The Practice and Policy of Global Internet Filtering, Cambridge MA: The MIT Press, 2007 (Deibert et al. 2007).

Daphne Dembo, 'Our international approach to search', *The Official Google Blog*, November 21, 2008, http://googleblog.blogspot.com/2008/11/our-international-approach-to-search.html (Dembo (Google) 2008).

Lothar Determann, 'Case Update: German CompuServe Director Acquitted on Appeal', 23 *Hastings International & Comparative Law Review* 109, 1999 (Determann 1999).

Eberhard P. Deutsch, 'Freedom of the Press and of the Mails', 36 *Michigan Law Review* 703 (1938) (Deutsch 1938).

Jos van Dijk, 'Seks, religie en boeken vol krassen: censuur door de bibliotheekgebruiker', Bibliotheek en samenleving, vol. 22, no. 3, 1994, 12–15 (van Dijk 1994).

P. van Dijk, et al. (eds.), *Theory and Practice of the European Convention on Human Rights*, 4th edition, Antwerpen: Intersentia, 2006 (van Dijk et al. 2006).

References

Bart Dingemans, 'Censuur en/in de openbare bibliotheek.' *Bibliotheek & Samenleving* 1980, no. 9, 271–276 (Dingemans 1980).

Cory Doctorow, 'Metacrap', Version 1.3: August 26, 2001, http://www.well.com/~doctorow/metacrap.htm (Doctorow 2001).

E.J. Dommering and L. Asscher (eds.), *Coding Regulation: Essays on the Normative Role of Information Technology*, The Hague: The T.M.C. Asser Press, 2006 (Dommering & Asscher 2006).

E.J. Dommering, 'Filteren is gewoon censuur, en daarmee basta', *Tijdschrift voor Internetrecht* 2008-5, 124–125 (Dommering 2009).

David Drummond, 'An Update on China', The Official Google Blog, June 28, 2010, Updated on July 9, 2010, http://googleblog.blogspot.com/2010/06/update-on-china.html (Drummond (Google) 2010).

DTI, DTI Consultation Document on the Electronic Commerce Directive: the Liability of Hyperlinkers, Location Tool Services and Content Aggregators, June 2005, http://www.berr.gov.uk/files/file13986.pdf (DTI 2005).

DTI, DTI Consultation document on the electronic commerce directive: the liability of hyperlinkers, location tool services and content aggregators—Government response and summary of responses, December 6, 2006, http://www.berr.gov.uk/files/file35905.pdf (DTI 2006).

Paul Duguid, 'Limits of Self-organization', First Monday, Vol. 11, No. 10, October 2, 2006 (Duguid 2006).

Paul Duguid, Search Before Grep. A Progress from Open to Closed?, in K. Becker & F. Stalder (Eds.), *Deep search: the politics of search beyond Google* (13–31). Innsbruck: Studienverlag, 2009 (Duguid 2009).

Dutch Data Protection Authority, 'Guidelines for the Publication of personal data on the Internet', December 2007 (Dutch Data Protection Authority 2007).

Rae Earhshaw & John Vince (eds.), *Digital Convergence—Libraries of the Future*, London: Springer, 2008 (Earhshaw & Vince 2008).

Ben Edelman, 'How Google and its Partners Inflate Conversion Rates and Increase Advertisers' Costs, *Benedelman.org*, May 13, 2009, http://www.benedelman.org/news/051309-1.html (Edelman 2009).

Lillian Edwards, 'Content Filtering and the New Censorship', *2010 Fourth International Conference on Digital Society, IEEE*, 2010, 317–322 (Edwards 2010).

Douglas Edwards, *I'm Feeling Lucky: The Confessions of Google Employee Number 59*, New York: Houghton Mifflin Harcourt, 2011, Kindle Edition (Edwards 2011).

Patrick van Eecke, Maarten Truyens, 'L'Oréal v. eBay: Is the Tide Finally Turning for Hosting Providers', Cri 2011-1, 1–8 (van Eecke & Truyens 2011).

Nico van Eijk, "Search Engines: Seek and Ye Shall Find? The Position of Search Engines in Law," *IRIS Plus Legal Observations*, 2006-2 (van Eijk 2006).

Nico van Eijk, 'Search engines, the new bottleneck for content access', in: B. Preissl, J. Haucap & P. Curwen (eds.), *Telecommunication markets: drivers and impediments,* Heidelberg: Physica-Verlag, 2009, 141–156 (van Eijk 2009).

Elizabeth L. Eisenstein, *The Printing Press as an Agent of Change, Communications and cultural transformations in early-modern Europe*, Volumes I and II, New York: Cambridge University Press, 1979 (Eisenstein 1979).

Niva Elkin-Koren, 'Let the Crawlers Crawl: On Virtual Gatekeepers and the Right to Exclude Indexing', 26 University of Dayton Law Review 180, 2001 (Elkin-Koren 2001).

Greg Elmer, *Profiling Machines*. Cambridge (MA): MIT Press, 2004 (Elmer 2004).

Thomas I. Emerson, 'The Doctrine of Prior Restraint', 20 *Law & Contemporary Problems* 648, 1955 (Emerson 1955).

EurActiv, 'EU regulators keeping close eye on Google', *Euractiv.com*, July 8, 2010, http://www.euractiv.com/infosociety/eu-regulators-keeping-close-eye-on-google-news-496130 (Euractiv 2010).

European Commission, Pluralism and Media Concentration in the Internal Market. An Assessment of the Need for Community Action, Green Paper, COM (92) 480 final, December 23, 1992 (European Commission 1992).

European Commission, Green Paper on Copyright and Related Rights in the Information Society, COM(95) 382, Brussels July 19, 1995 (European Commission 1995).

European Commission, Follow-up to the Green Paper on Copyright and Related Rights in the Information Society, COM(96) 0568, Brussels, November 20, 1996 (European Commission 1996a).

European Commission, Communication on illegal and harmful content on the Internet, COM(96) 487 final, Brussels, October 16, 1996 (European Commission 1996b).

European Commission, 'Green Paper on the Protection of Minors and Human Dignity In Audiovisual and Information Services', COM (96) 483 Final, Brussels, October 16, 1996 (European Commission 1996c).

European Commission, A European Initiative in Electronic Commerce, COM(97) 157, April 15, 1997 (European Commission 1997a).

European Commission, Working Document, Consultations on the Green Paper, protection of minors and human dignity in audiovisual and information services, SEC (97) 1203, Brussels, June 13, 1997 (European Commission 1997b).

European Commission, Amended proposal for a European Parliament and Council directive on certain legal aspects of electronic commerce in the Internal Market, COM (99) 427 final, Brussels, August 17, 1999 (European Commission 1999).

European Commission, 'Report on the Public Lending Right in the European Union', COM(2002) 502 final, Brussels, September 12, 2002 (European Commission 2002).

European Commission, 'First Report on the application of Directive 2000/31/EC', COM/2003/0702 final, Brussels, November 21, 2003 (European Commission 2003).

References

European Commission, 'Media Pluralism in the Member States of the European Union', Brussels, January 16, 2007, SEC (2007) 32 (European Commission 2007a).

European Commission, 'State aid: Commission endorses €120 million aid for German R&D project THESEUS', IP/07/1136, Brussels, July 19, 2007, http://europa.eu/rapid/pressReleasesAction.do?reference=IP/07/1136 (European Commission 2007b).

European Commission, 'A European approach to media literacy in the digital environment', COM (2007)833 final, Brussels, December 20, 2007 (European Commission 2007c).

European Commission, 'State aid: Commission authorises aid of €99 million to France for QUAERO R&D programme', IP/08/418, Brussels, March 11, 2008, http://europa.eu/rapid/pressReleasesAction.do?reference=IP/07/1136 (European Commission 2008a).

European Commission, 'Proposal for a Council Framework Decision on combating the sexual abuse, sexual exploitation of children and child pornography, repealing Framework Decision', 2004/68/JHA, 2009 (European Commission 2009).

European Commission, Case No. Comp/M.5727—Microsoft/Yahoo! Search Business, February 18, 2010 (European Commission 2010a).

European Commission, 'Public consultation on the future of electronic commerce in the internal market and the implementation of the Directive on electronic commerce (2000/31/EC)', April 7, 2010 (European Commission 2010b).

European Commission, Communication from the Commission to the European Parliament, the Council, the European Economic and Social Committee and the Committee of the Regions, A Digital Agenda for Europe, COM/2010/0245 final, Brussels, May 19, 2010 (European Commission 2010c).

European Commission, 'Antitrust: Commission probes allegations of antitrust violations by Google', IP/10/1624, Brussels, November 30, 2010, http://europa.eu/rapid/pressReleasesAction.do?reference=IP/10/1624 (European Commission 2010d).

European Commission, Digital Agenda: high-level group to discuss freedom and pluralism of the media across the EU', Press Release, IP/11/1173, October 11, 2011, http://europa.eu/rapid/pressReleasesAction.do?reference=IP/11/1173 (European Commission 2011).

European Digital Rights, 'The Slide of "Self-Regulation" to Corporate Censorship', discussion paper prepared by Joe McNamee, January 2011, http://www.edri.org/files/EDRI_selfreg_final_20110124.pdf (European Digital Rights 2011).

European Parliament, Committee on Legal Affairs and Citizens' Rights, Report on the proposal for a European Parliament and Council Directive on certain legal aspects of electronic commerce in the internal market, COM (98) 0586, Brussels, April 23, 1999 (European Parliament 1999).

European Union Ministers, Bonn Declaration, Bonn, July 6–7, 1997 (European Union Ministers 1997).

Deborah Fallows, 'Search Engine Users. Internet searchers are confident, satisfied and trusting—but they are also unaware and naïve', *Pew Internet & American Life Project,* Washington, January 23, 2005, http://www.pewinternet.org/~/media//Files/Reports/2005/PIP_Searchengine_users.pdf.pdf (Fallows 2005).

Federal Commissioner for Data Protection and Freedom of Information, 'Google-Street-View tours also used for scanning WLAN-networks', April 23, 2004, http://www.bfdi.bund.de/cln_134/sid_74A4D9FE1F85492D36F74BB3443-C41EA/EN/PublicRelations/PressReleases/2010/GoogleWLANScan.html (Federal Commissioner for Data Protection 2004).

Federal Communications Commission, Notice of Proposed Rulemaking, In the Matter of Preserving the Open Internet Broadband Industry Practice GN Docket No. 09-191, WC Docket No. 07-52, Washington, D.C., October 22, 2009 (Federal Communications Commission 2009).

Federal Trade Commission, 'Re: Complaint Requesting Investigation of Various Internet Search Engine Companies for Paid Placement and Paid Inclusion Programs', June 27, 2002, http://www.ftc.gov/os/closings/staff/commercialalertletter.shtm (Federal Trade Commission 2002).

Federal Trade Commission, 'FTC Staff Proposes Online Behavioral Advertising Privacy Principles', Press release, December 20, 2007, http://www.ftc.gov/opa/2007/12/principles.shtm (Federal Trade Commission 2007).

Federal Trade Commission, 'FTC Staff Revises Online Behavioral Advertising Principles', Press Release, January 12, 2009, http://www.ftc.gov/opa/2009/02/behavad.shtm (Federal Trade Commission 2009).

Martin Feuz, Matthew Fuller and Felix Stalder, 'Personal Web Searching in the Age of Semantic Capitalism: Diagnosing the Mechanisms of Personalization', *First Monday*, Vol. 16, No. 2, February 7, 2011 (Feuz et al. 2011).

P.M. Figliola et al., U.S. Initiatives to Promote Global Internet Freedom: Issues, Policy, and Technology, Congressional Research Service, April 5, 2010 (Figliola et al. 2010).

Seth Finkelstein, 'Google, Links, and Popularity versus Authority', in: Joseph Turow & Lokman Tsui (eds.), *The Hyperlinked Society*, The University of Michigan Press, 2008, 104–120 (Finkelstein 2008).

Simone Fischer-Hübner, Chris Hoofnagle, et al. (eds.), 'Online Privacy: Towards Informational Self-Determination on the Internet', *Dagstuhl Manifestos*, Vol. 1, Issue 1, 2011, 1–20 (Fischer-Hübner et al. 2011).

Owen M. Fiss, *Liberalism Divided: Freedom of Speech and the Many Uses of State Power*, Boulder: WestviewPress 1996 (Fiss 1996).

Peter Fleischer (Google), 'Response to the Article 29 Working Party Opinion On Data Protection Issues Related to Search Engines', December 8, 2008 (Fleischer (Google) 2008).

Peter Fleischer, '"The right to be Forgotten", seen from Spain', September 5, 2011, http://peterfleischer.blogspot.com/2011/09/right-to-be-forgotten-seen-from-spain.html (Fleischer 2011).

Tom Foremski, 'Inside Track: Google spins web of success', *Financial Times*, London, England, July 6, 2000 (Foremski 2000).

References

Fortunato et al., 'The Egalitarian Effect of Search Engines', August 23, 2006, http://arxiv.org/abs/cs/0511005 (Fortunato et al. 2006).

Dorothy Ganfield Fowler, *Unmailable: Congress and the Post Office*, Athens, GA: The University of Georgia Press, 1977 (Fowler 1977).

The FSM, Subcode of Conduct for Search Engine Providers of the Association of Voluntary Self-Regulating Multimedia Service Providers ("Freiwillige Selbstkontrolle Multimedia-Diensteanbieter"—FSM) (VK-S), December 21, 2004, http://fsm.de/en/SubCoC_Search_Engines (FSM 2004).

FSM, Stellungnahme der FSM zu den Haftungsregelungen des Telemediengesetzes, September 11, 2007, http://www.fsm.de/inhalt.doc/Stellungnahme_2007-09-11_TMG.pdf (FSM 2007).

FSM, FAQ Selbstkontrolle Suchmaschinen, http://fsm.de/de/FAQs_Selbstkontrolle_Suchmaschinen (FSM).

Susan Freiwald, 'Comparative Institutional Analysis in Cyberspace: The case of Intermediary Liability for Defamation', 14 *Harvard Journal of Law & Technology* 569, 2001 (Freiwald 2001).

David F. Gallagher, TECHNOLOGY; AOL Shifts Key Contract To Google, *The New York Times*, May 2, 2002, http://www.nytimes.com/2002/05/02/business/technology-aol-shifts-key-contract-to-google.html (Gallagher 2002).

Hector Garcia-Molina, Georgia Koutrika and Aditya Parameswaran, 'Information Seeking: Convergence of Search, Recommendations and Advertising', *Communications of the ACM*, Vol. 54, No. 11, 2011 (Garcia-Molina et al. 2011).

Stephen Gardbaum, 'The "Horizontal Effect" of Constitutional Rights', 102 *Michigan Law Review* 3, 2003 (Gardbaum 2003).

Stephen Gardbaum, 'The Myth and Reality of American Constitutional Exceptionalism', 106 *Michigan Law Review* 391, 2008 (Gardbaum 2008).

R.K. Gardner, Library *Collections: Their Origin, Selection, and Development*, New York: McGraw-Hill, 1981 (Gardner 1981).

Urs Gasser, 'Regulating Search Engines: Taking Stock and Looking Ahead', 8 *Yale Journal of Law and Technology* 201, 2006 (Gasser 2006).

Urs Gasser and John Palfrey, *Born Digital: Understanding the First Generation of Digital Natives*, Basic Books 2010 (Gasser & Palfrey 2010).

Bill Gates, 'The Road Ahead', *Newsweek Magazine*, November 26, 1995, http://www.thedailybeast.com/newsweek/1995/11/26/the-road-ahead.html (Gates 1995).

Susan Gerhart, 'Do Search Engines Suppress Controversy?', *First Monday*, Vol. 9, No. 1, 2004 (Gerhart 2003).

Dan Gilmore, *We the Media. Grassroots Journalism by the People, for the People*, O'Reilly Media, 2004 (Gilmore 2004).

Jane C. Ginsburg, 'Separating the Sony Sheep from the Grokster Goats: Reckoning the Future Business Plans of Copyright-Dependent Technology Entrepreneurs', *Columbia Public Law Research Paper* No. 08-166, February 16, 2008 (Ginsburg 2008).

George Gladney, 'How editors and readers rank and rate the importance of eighteen traditional standards of newspaper excellence', 73 *Journalism & Mass Communication Quarterly* 319, 1996 (Gladney 1996).

Global Network Initiative, http://globalnetworkinitiative.org/ (Global Network Initiative).

Michael Goldhaber, 'The Attention Economy: The Natural Economy of the Net', First Monday Vol. 2, No. 4, 1997 (Goldhaber 1997).

Eric Goldman, 'Search Engine Bias and the Demise of Search Engine Utopianism', 8 Yale Journal of Law & Technology 188, 2006 (Goldman 2006).

Jack Goldsmith & Tim Wu, *Who controls the Internet? Illusions of a borderless world*, Oxford University Press, 2006 (Goldsmith & Wu 2006).

Ben Gomes, 'Search quality, continued', *The Official Google Blog*, August 1, 2008, http://googleblog.blogspot.com/2008/08/search-quality-continued.html (Gomes (Google) 2008a).

Ben Gomes, 'Search experiments, large and small', *The Official Google Blog*, August 26, 2008, http://googleblog.blogspot.com/2008/08/search-experiments-large-and-small.html (Gomes (Google) 2008b).

Google, Inc., 'Google Log Retention Policy FAQ', March 14, 2007, available at http://www.seroundtable.com/google_log_retention_policy_faq.pdf (Google 2007a).

Google Inc., 'Google Guidelines for Quality Raters', Document Version: 2.1, April 6, 2007 (on file with the author) (Google 2007b).

Google Inc., 'An explanation of our search results', *Internet Archive, WayBack-Machine*, April 6, 2007, http://web.archive.org/web/20070406232706/http://www.google.com/explanation.html (Google 2007c).

Google Inc., 'An explanation of our search results', *Internet Archive, WayBack-Machine*, May 6, 2007, http://web.archive.org/web/20070506172153/http://www.google.com/explanation.html (Google 2007d).

Google Inc., 'Google contribution to the public consultation on the future of electronic commerce in the internal market and the implementation of the on electronic commerce (2000/31/EC)', 2010, http://ec.europa.eu/internal_market/consultations/2010/e-commerce_en.htm (Google 2010a).

Google, Inc., 'Search Engine Optimization Starter Guide', 2010, http://static.googleusercontent.com/external_content/untrusted_dlcp/www.google.com/en//webmasters/docs/search-engine-optimization-starter-guide.pdf (Google 2010b).

Google, Inc., *Google Privacy Center, Archive*, Privacy Policy, October 3, 2010, http://www.google.com/intl/en/privacy/archive/20101003.html (Google 2010c).

Google Inc., Privacy FAQ, http://www.google.com/intl/en/privacy_faq.html#toc-terms-urls (Google Privacy FAQ).

Google Inc. 'Web Search, Help Articles, Autocomplete', http://www.google.com/support/websearch/bin/static.py?hl=en&page=guide.cs&guide=1186810&answer=106230&rd=1 (Google Web Search Help Articles).

References

Google.org, 'Google Flu Trends', http://www.google.org/flutrends/about/how.html (Google Flu Trends).

Google Inc., 'An explanation of our search results', http://www.google.com/explanation.html (Google, An explanation of our search results).

Google Inc., 'How do I Target a specific geographic location', *Adwords Help*, http://adwords.google.com/support/aw/bin/answer.py?hl=en&lev=answer&cbid=1v49swmjnxrg0&answer=113247&src=cb (Google Adwords Help).

James Grimmelmann, 'Note, Regulation by Software', 114 *Yale Law Journal* 1719, 2005 (Grimmelmann 2005).

James Grimmelmann, 'The Structure of Search Engine Law', 93 *Iowa Law Review* 1, 2007 (Grimmelmann 2007a).

James Grimmelmann, 'Information Policy for the Library of Babel', *Maryland Journal of Business and Technology Law*, 2007, 29–40 (Grimmelmann 2007b).

James Grimmelmann, 'The Google Dilemma', 53 *New York Law School Law Review* 939, 2008 (Grimmelmann 2008).

James Grimmelmann, 'The Unmasking Option', Denver University Law Review Online, January 2010: 23, http://works.bepress.com/james_grimmelmann/29 (Grimmelmann 2010a).

James Grimmelmann, 'Some Skepticism About Search Neutrality', in: Berin Szoka & Adam Marcus (eds.), *The Next Digital Decade: Essays on the Future of the Internet*, Washington D.C.: TechFreedom, 2010, 435–460 (Grimmelmann 2010b).

David Gugerli, *Suchmaschinen. Die Welt als Datenbank*, Frankfurt am Main: Suhrkamp Verlag, 2009 (Gugerli 2009).

Serge Gutwirth. *Privacy and the Information Age*, Lanham: Rowman & Littlefield Publishers, 2002 (Gutwirth 2002).

Ian Hacking, *The Social Construction of What?*, Cambridge (MA): Harvard University Press, 1999 (Hacking 1999).

K. Hafner & M. Lyon, *Where Wizards Stay Up Late. The origins of the internet*, New York: Simon & Schuster Paperbacks, 1996 (Hafner & Lyon 1996).

Alexander Halavais, *Search Engine Society*, Cambridge: Polity, 2009 (Halavais 2009).

Robert Hale, 'Coercion and Distribution in a Supposedly Noncoercive State', 38 *Political Science Quarterly* 470, 1923 (Hale 1923).

Josh Halliday, 'Google to Fight Spanish Privacy Battle', *The Guardian*, January 16, 2011, http://www.guardian.co.uk/technology/2011/jan/16/google-court-spain-privacy (Halliday 2011a).

Josh Halliday, 'Europe's highest court to rule on Google privacy battle in Spain', *The Guardian*, March 1, 2011, http://www.guardian.co.uk/technology/2011/mar/01/google-spain-privacy-court-case (Halliday 2011b).

Daniel C. Hallin, *The Uncensored War. The Media and Vietnam*, Oxford University Press, 1986 (Hallin 1986).

Daniel. C. Hallin & Paolo Mancini, Comparing *Media Systems. Three Models of Media and Politics,* New York: Cambridge University Press, 2004 (Hallin & Mancini 2004).

Steven E. Halpern, 'Harmonizing the Convergence of Medium Expression and Functionality: A study of the Speech Interest in Computer Software', 14 *Harvard Journal of Law & Technology* 139, 2000 (Halpern 2000).

C.J. Hamelink, *The politics of world communication : a human rights perspective,* London; Thousand Oaks (CA): Sage Publications, 1994 (Hameling 1994).

Hans-Bredow-Institut, *Study on Co-Regulation Measures in the Media Sector,* Study for the European Commission, Final Report, June 2006 (Hans-Bredow Institut 2006).

Eszter Hargittai, 'Open Portals or Closed Gates Channeling Content on the World Wide Web', *Poetics (Journal of Empirical Research on Culture, the Media and the Arts),* Vol. 27, Nr. 4, 2000, 233–254 (Hargittai 2000).

Eszter Hargittai, 'The Changing Online Landscape: From Free-for-All to Commercial Gatekeeping', in: P. Day and D. Schuler (eds.), *Community Practice in the Network Society: Local Actions/Global Interaction,* Routledge, 2004, 66–76 (Hargittai 2004).

Eszter Hargittai & A. Hinnant, 'Toward a Social Framework for Information Seeking'. In: Amanda Spink and Charles Cole (eds.), *New Directions in Human Information Behavior,* New York: Springer, 2005, 55–70 (Hargittai & Hinnant 2005).

Eszter Hargittai, 'Content Diversity Online: Myth or Reality?', In: Philip Napoli (ed.), *Media Diversity and Localism: Meaning and Metrics,* Mahwah, NJ: Lawrence Erlbaum, 2007, 349–362 (Hargittai 2007a).

Eszter Hargittai, 'The Social, Political, Economic and Cultural Dimensions of Search Engines', *Special Section of the Journal of Computer Mediated Communication,* vol. 12, no. 3, 2007 (Hargittai 2007b).

Joe Haugney (Major USAF), 'ARPANET Newsletter', September 15, 1981, available at http://www.rfc-editor.org/rfc/museum/ddn-news/ddn-news.n8.1 (Haugney 1981).

Marti A. Hearst, *Search User Interfaces,* Cambridge, MA: Cambridge University Press, 2009 (Hearst 2009).

Heise Online, 'Gutachten: Rechtliche Bedenken gegen Internet-Sperren', February 8, 2009, http://www.heise.de/newsticker/Gutachten-Rechtliche-Bedenken-gegen-Internet-Sperren—/meldung/127095 (Heise Online 2009).

Heise Online, 'Französischer Suchmaschinenbetreiber verklagt Google auf Schadensersatz', June 28, 2011, http://www.heise.de/newsticker/meldung/Franzoesischer-Suchmaschinenbetreiber-verklagt-Google-auf-Schadensersatz-1269174.html (Heise Online 2011).

Natali Helberger, *Controlling Access to Content, Regulating Conditional Access in Digital Broadcasting,* The Hague: Kluwer Law International, 2005 (Helberger 2005).

Natali Helberger, 'The Media-Literate Viewer', in: N.A.N.M. van Eijk & P.B. Hugenholtz (eds.), *Dommering-bundel: Opstellen over informatierecht aangeboden aan prof. mr. E.J. Dommering*, Amsterdam: Otto Cramwinckel Uitgever, 2008, 135–148 (Helberger 2008).

Joan Hemels, *Op de Bres voor de Pers, De strijd voor de klassieke persvrijheid*, Assen: Van Gorcum & Comp. N.V., 1969 (Hemels 1969).

D.G. Hendry and E.N. Efthimiadis, 'Conceptual Models for Search Engines', in: A. Spink and M. Zimmer (eds.), *Web Searching: Interdisciplinary Perspectives*, Dordrecht: Springer, 2008, 277–307 (Hendry & Efthimiadis 2008).

Peter J. Henning, Behind Google's $500 Million Settlement with U.S., *The New York Times*, August 30, 2011, http://dealbook.nytimes.com/2011/08/30/behind-googles-500-million-settlement-with-u-s/ (Henning 2011).

Mark Y. Herring, *Fool's Gold: Why the Internet is no substitute for a library*, Jefferson: McFarland, 2007 (Herring 2007).

Matthew Hindman et al., "'Googlearchy': How a few heavily-linked sites dominate politics on the web." In: *Annual Meeting of the Midwest Political Science Association*, 2003 (Hindman et al. 2003).

Matthew Hindman, *The Myth of Digital Democracy*, Princeton and Oxford: Princeton University Press, 2009 (Hindman 2009).

Wouter Hins, 'Het ijzeren geheugen van internet', *Ars Aequi* 2008-07/08, 558–564 (Hins 2008).

Hitwise, 'Top Search Engines—Volume', May 14, 2011, http://www.hitwise.com/uk/datacentre/main/dashboard-7323.html (Hitwise 2011).

Joris van Hoboken, Case Note, Rb. Amsterdam, April 26, 2007 (Jensen / Google), *Mediaforum* 2007-6, 205–208 (Van Hoboken 2007).

Joris van Hoboken, 'Zoekmachines en de Wbp: over de grens van onze digitale horizon', *Privacy & Informatie* 2008-6, 210–216 (Van Hoboken 2008a).

Joris van Hoboken, 'New Dutch Notice-And-Take-Down Code Raises Questions', *EDRi-gram* 6.20, October 22, 2008, http://www.edri.org/edri-gram/number6.20/notice-take-down-netherlands (van Hoboken 2008b).

Joris van Hoboken, 'De aansprakelijkheid van zoekmachines: uitzondering zonder regels of regels zonder uitzondering?', *Computerrecht*, 2008-1, 15–22 (van Hoboken 2008c).

Joris van Hoboken, 'Freedom of expression implications for the governance of search', in: S. Nikoltchev (ed.), *Searching for audiovisual content (IRIS special)*, Strasbourg: European Audiovisual Observatory, 2008, 49–62 (van Hoboken 2008d).

Joris van Hoboken, 'Legal Space for Innovative Ordering. On the Need to Update Selection Intermediary Liability in the EU', *International Journal of Communications Law & Policy*, No. 13, 2009 (van Hoboken 2009a).

Joris van Hoboken, Case Note, ECtHR March 10, 2009, *Times Newspapers v. United Kingdom, Mediaforum*, 2009-4, nr. 11, 167–169 (van Hoboken 2009b).

Joris van Hoboken, 'Search engine law and freedom of expression: a European perspective'. In K. Becker & F. Stalder (Eds.), *Deep search: the politics of search beyond Google* (85–97). Innsbruck: Studienverlag, 2009 (van Hoboken 2009c).

Joris van Hoboken, 'Torrent Website Has to Remove All Torrents for Copyright Protected Works', IRIS 2009-9: 15/23, http://merlin.obs.coe.int/iris/2009/9/article23.en.html (van Hoboken 2009d).

Nadine Höchstötter & Dirk Lewandowski, 'What users see—Structures in search engine results pages', Information Sciences 179, 2009, 1796–1812 (Höchstötter & Lewandowski 2009).

Home Office Task Force on Child Protection on the Internet, 'Good practice guidance for search service providers and advice to the public on how to search safely', United Kingdom, December 2005 (Home Office UK 2005).

Chris Hoofnagle, 'Beyond Google and Evil: How Policy Makers, Journalists and Consumers Should Talk Differently About Google and Privacy', *First Monday*, Vol. 14, No. 4-6, 2009 (Hoofnagle 2009).

Curt Hopkins, 'What Would Jesus Search?', *Read Write Web*, September 14, 2010, http://www.readwriteweb.com/archives/people_of_the_search_engine_parsing_the_web_with_t.php (Hopkins 2010).

Scott Huffman, 'Search evaluation at Google', *The Official Google Blog*, September 15, 2008, http://googleblog.blogspot.com/2008/09/search-evaluation-at-google.html (Huffman (Google) 2008).

P.B. Hugenholtz, 'Copyright and Freedom of Expression in Europe', in: Dreyfuss, Zimmerman & First (eds.), *Expanding the Boundaries of Intellectual Property*, Oxford: Oxford University Press, 2001 (Hugenholtz 2001).

Annelies Huygen, Joost Poort, Nico Van Eijk, et al., 'Ups and downs. Economic and cultural effects of file sharing on music, film and games', TNO, SEO, IViR, February 2009 (Huygen et al. 2009).

Frank Huysmans, 'De betere bibliotheek. Over de normatieve grondslagen van het openbaar bibliotheekwerk in het internettijdperk', Inaugurele Rede, Universiteit van Amsterdam, June 23, 2006 (Huysmans 2006).

IFLA/UNESCO, *Public Library Manifesto*, 1994 (IFLA/UNESCO 1994).

IFLA, Statement on Libraries and Intellectual Freedom, prepared by IFLA/FAIFE and approved by The Executive Board of IFLA, The Hague, The Netherlands, March 25, 1999 (IFLA 1999).

John Ince, 'Inside Search Engines', *Upside*, May 2000 (Ince 2000).

Infoseek, Press Release, 'Infoseek Launches First One-Stop Internet Source for Information', February 13, 1995, http://web.archive.org/web/19970216144951/info.infoseek.com/doc/PressReleases/SearchLaunch.html (Infoseek 1995).

H.A. Innis, P. Heyer and D. J. Crowley, *The Bias of communication*, 2nd Edition, University of Toronto Press, 1991 (Innis et al. 1991).

Internet Watch Foundation, 'Keywords', http://www.iwf.org.uk/services/keywords (Internet Watch Foundation).

Lucas D. Introna and Helen Nissenbaum, 'Shaping the Web, Why the Politics of Search Engines Matters', *The Information Society* 16(3), 2000, 1–17 (Introna & Nissenbaum 2000).

Karol Jakubowicz, 'A New Notion of New Media', Council of Europe, April 2009 (Jakubowicz 2009).

References

Bernard J. Jansen, Danielle L. Booth, and Amanda Spink, 'Determining the informational, navigational, and transactional intent of Web queries', *Information Processing and Management* 44, 2008, 1251–1266 (Jansen et al. 2008).

Bernard J. Jansen, Amanda Spink, 'Investigating customer click through behaviour with integrated sponsored and nonsponsored results', *International Journal of Internet Marketing and Advertising*, Vol. 5, No. 1/2, 2009 (Jansen & Spink 2009).

Catherine Jasserand, 'Google Suggest: no copyright liability for suggesting words like Torrent, Megaupload and Rapidshare', *Kluwer Copyright Blog*, May 13, 2011, http://kluwercopyrightblog.com/2011/05/13/google-suggest-no-copyright-liability-for-suggesting-words-like-torrent-megaupload-and-rapidshare/ (Jasserand 2011).

Jean-Noel Jeanneney, *Google and the Myth of Universal Knowledge: A View from Europe*, London: University of Chicago Press, 2007 (Jeanneney 2007).

Rikke Frank Jørgensen, *Framing the Net—How Discourse Shapes Law and Culture*, PhD dissertation submitted at Roskilde University Department of Communication, Business and Information Technologies, September 2011, Copenhagen (Jørgensen 2011).

Richard R. John, *Spreading the News: the American postal system from Franklin to Morse,* First Harvard University Press paperback edition, 1998 (John 1998).

Recent Developments, *Making Your Mark on Google*, 18 *Harvard Journal of Law & Technology* 486, 2005 (JOLT 2005).

Bradley L. Joslove and Andréi V. Krylov, 'Dangerous Liaisons. Liability in the European Union for Hypertext and search engine services', 2005 Computer Law Review International 33, 2005 (Joslove & Krilov 2005).

Rosa Julia-Barceló, 'On-Line Intermediary Liability Issues: Comparing EU and US Legal Frameworks', 22 European Intellectual Property Review 106, 2000 (Julia-Barceló 2000).

Rosa Julia-Barceló, 'Spanish Implementation of the E-Commerce Directive: Main features of the Implementation of the E-Commerce directive in Spain', 2002 *Computer Und Recht International* 112, 2002 (Julia-Barceló 2002).

Harry Kalven Jr., 'The Metaphysics of the Law of Obscenity', 1960 Supreme Court Review 1, 1960 (Kalven 1960).

Kari Karppinnen, 'Rethinking Media Pluralism and Communicative Abundance', *Observatorio Journal*, Vol. 3, No. 4, 2009, 151–169 (Karppinen 2009).

Orin Kerr, 'Legal Responses to "Cyber-Bullying"', *The Volokh Conspiracy*, April 16, 2007, http://volokh.com/posts/1176705254.shtml (Kerr 2007).

David Knight, *Ordering the World. A History of Classifying Man*, London: Burnett Books, 1981 (Knight 1981).

Neesha Kodagoda & B.L. William Wong, 'Effects of low & high literacy on user performance in information search and retrieval', *BCS-HCI '08 Proceedings of the 22nd British HCI Group Annual Conference on People and Computers: Culture, Creativity, Interaction*, Vol. 1, 2008 (Kodagoda & Wong 2008).

K.J. Koelman, *Liability for on-line intermediaries*, Report to Imprimatur, 1997 (Koelman 1997).

K.J. Koelman, *Online Intermediary Liability*, in: P.B. Hugenholtz (ed.), *Copyright and Electronic Commerce*, Information Law Series-8, The Hague: Kluwer Law International, 2000, 7–58 (Koelman 2000).

Donald P. Kommers, *The Constitutional Jurisprudence of the Federal Republic of Germany*, Second Edition, Durham and London: Duke University Press, 1997 (Kommers 1997).

Thomas G. Krattenmaker & L. A. Powe, 'Converging First Amendment Principles for Converging Communications Media', 104 *Yale Law Journal* 1719, 1995 (Krattenmaker & Powe 1995).

Seth F. Kreimer, 'Technologies of Protest- Insurgent Social Movements and the First Amendment in the Era of the Internet', 150 *University of Pennsylvania Law Review* 119, 2001 (Kreimer 2001).

Seth F. Kreimer, 'Censorship by Proxy: The First Amendment, Internet Intermediaries, and the Problem of the Weakest Link', University of Pennsylvania Law Review, Vol. 155, No. 11, 2006 (Kreimer 2006).

Judica I. Krikke, *Het bibliotheekprivilege in de digitale omgeving*, ITeR-29, 1999 (Krikke 1999).

James F. Kurose & Keith W. Ross, *Computer Networking: A Top-Down Approach*, 5th edition, New York: Addison Wesley, 2009 (Kurose & Ross 2009).

David L. Lange, 'The Role of the Access Doctrine in the Regulation of the Mass Media: A Critical Review and Assessment', 52 *North Carolina Law Review* 1, 1973 (Lange 1973).

David L. Lange, 'The Speech and the Press Clause', 23 UCLA Law Review 77, 1975 (Lange 1975).

A. Langville & C.D. Meyer, *Google's PageRank and Beyond. The Science of Search Engine Rankings*, Princeton and Oxford: Princeton University Press, 2006 (Langville & Meyer 2006).

S. Lawrence and C.L. Giles, 'Accessibility of information on the web', Nature, No. 400, 1999, 107–109 (Lawrence & Giles 1999).

Linda Lawson, *Truth in Publishing: federal regulation of the press's business practices, 1880–1920*, Carbondale: Southern Illinois University Press, 1993 (Lawson 1993).

Rick A. Lawson, 'Confusion and Conflict? Diverging Interpretations of the European Convention of Human Rights is Strasbourg and Luxembourg', in: R.A. Lawson & M. de Blois (eds.), *The Dynamics of the Protection of Human Rights in Europe—Essays in Honour of Professor Henry G. Schermers*, 1994, 219–252 (Lawson 1994).

Brian Leiter, 'Cleaning Cyber-Cesspools: Google and Free Speech', in: Saul Levmore, Martha C. Nussbaum (eds.), *The Offensive Internet*, Harvard University Press, 2011, Kindle Edition (Leiter 2011).

Mark A. Lemley, 'Rationalizing Internet Safe Harbors', 5 *Journal on Telecommunications and High Technology Law* 101, 2007 (Lemley 2007).

Philipp Lenssen, AOL Shared Private Search Queries, *Google Blogoscoped*, August 7, 2006, http://blogoscoped.com/archive/2006-08-07-n22.html (Lenssen 2006).

References

Lernert & Sander, 'I Love Alaska', a film by Lernert & Sander, Commissioned by Submarine Channel for minimovies.org, 2008, http://www.lernertandsander. com/index.php?/projects/i-love-alaska/ (Lernert & Sander 2008).

Michael Lesk, 'The Seven Ages of Information Retrieval, UDT Occasional Paper #5, *IFLANET*, June 17, 1995, http://archive.ifla.org/VI/5/op/udtop5/udtop5. htm (Lesk 1995).

Lawrence Lessig, *Code and Other Laws of Cyberpace*, New York: Basic Books, 1999 (Lessig 1999).

John Lettice, 'When algorithms attack, does Google hear you scream?', *The Register*, November 19, 2009, http://www.theregister.co.uk/2009/11/ 19/google_hand_of_god/ (Lettice 2009).

Azi Lev-On, 'The Democratizing Effects of Search Engine Use: On Chance Exposures and Organizational Hubs', in: A. Spink & M. Zimmer (eds.), *Web Search: Multidisciplinary Perspectives*, Springer, 2008, 135–149 (Lev-On 2008).

Leonard W. Levy, *Emergence of a Free Press*, New York: Oxford University Press, 1985 (Levy 1985).

Paul Alan Levy, 'Using Misleading Keyword Advertising to Draw Consumers Away from Actual Complaint Web Sites', *Public Citizen Consumer Law & Policy Blog*, December 17, 2008, http://pubcit.typepad.com/clpblog/2008/12/ using-misleading-keyword-advertising-to-draw-consumers-away-from-actual-complaint-web-sites.html (Levy 2008).

Steven Levy, *In the Plex: How Google Thinks, Works, and Shapes Our Lives*, New York: Simon & Schuster, 2011 (Levy 2011).

Dirk Lewandowski, 'Mit welchen Kennzahlen lässt sich die Qualität von Suchmaschinen messen?', in: M. Machill &M. Beiler (eds.), Die Macht der Suchmaschinen/The Power of Search Engines, Köln: Herbert von Halem Verlag, 2007, 243–258 (Lewandowski 2007).

S. von Lewinski, 'Public lending right: A general and comparative survey of the existing systems in law and practise' (Droit de pret public: Etude comparative des systemes actuels sur les plans juridique et pratique), *Revue Internationale du Droit d'Auteur*, 1992-154, 3–83 (von Lewinski 1992).

Judith Lichtenberg, 'Foundations and Limits of Freedom of the Press', *Philosophy & Public Affairs*, Vol. 16, No. 4, 1987 (Lichtenberg 1987).

Doug Lichtner & Eric Posner, 'Holding Internet Service Providers Accountable', in: M. Grady & F. Parisi (eds.), *The Law and Economics of Cybersecurity*, Cambridge and New York: Cambridge University Press, 2006 (Lichtner & Posner 2006).

J.C.R. Licklider, *Libraries of the Future*, Cambridge (MA): MIT Press, 1969 (Licklider 1969).

Walter Lippmann, *Liberty and the News*, New York: Harcourt, Brace and Howe, 1920 (Lippmann 1920).

Walter Lippmann, *Public Opinion* (1922), Free Press, 1997 (Lippmann 1922).

Geert Lovink, 'The society of the query and the Googlization of our lives. A tribute to Joseph Weizenbaum', *Eurozine*, 2008 (Lovink 2008).

Nicola Lucchi, 'Access to Network Services and Protection of Constitutional Rights: Recognizing the Essential Role of Internet Access for the Freedom of Expression', *Cardozo Journal of International and Comparative Law*, Vol. 19, No. 3, 2011 (Lucchi 2011).

Clifford A. Lynch, 'When Documents Deceive: Trust and Provenance as New Factors for Information Retrieval in a Tangled Web', Journal of the American Society for Information Science and Technology, 52(1), 2001, 12–17 (Lynch 2001).

Gerald C. MacCallum, 'Negative and Positive Freedom', 3 *The Philosophical Review* 312, 1967 (MacCallum 1967).

Marcel Machill & Markus Beiler (eds.), *Die Macht der Suchmaschinen/The Power of Search Engines*, Cologne: Herbert von Halem 2007 (Machill & Beiler 2007).

Marcel Machill & Markus Beiler, 'Die Bedeutung des Internets für die journalistische Recherche', Media Perspektiven, Vol. 10, 2008, 516–531 (Machill & Beiler 2008).

Colin M. Maclay, 'Protecting Privacy and Expression Online: Can the Global Network Initiative Embrace the Global Character of the Net', in: R. Deibert, et al. (eds.), *Access Controlled*, The MIT Press, 2010, 87–108 (Maclay 2010).

Cédric Manara, 'HADOPI du bon sens!', *Juriscom.net*, March 31, 2009, http://www.juriscom.net/actu/visu.php?ID=1125 (Manara 2009).

Udi Manber, 'Introduction to Google Search Quality', *The Official Google Blog*, May 20, 2008, http://googleblog.blogspot.com/2008/05/introduction-to-google-search-quality.html (Manber (Google) 2008).

Christopher D. Manning, Prabhakar Raghavan & Hinrich Schütze, *Introduction to Information Retrieval*, Cambridge University Press, 2009 (Manning et al. 2009).

N. Marres & G.H. de Vries, 'Tussen toegang en kwaliteit. Legitimatie en contestatie van expertise op het Internet', in: H. Dijstelbloem & C.J.M. Schuyt (eds.), *De Publieke Dimensie van Kennis*, WRR Voorstudies en Achtergronden, Sdu Uitgevers, Den Haag, 2002, 171–247 (Marres & de Vries 2002).

M.E. Maron and J.L. Kuhns, 'On relevance, probabilistic indexing and information retrieval', *Journal of the Association for Computing Machinery*, Vol. 7, No. 3, 1960, 216–224 (Maron & Kuhns 1960).

M.E. Maron, 'An Historical Note on the Origins of Probabilistic Indexing', 44 *Information Processing and Management 971*, 2008 (Maron 2008).

Franz Matscher &Herbert Petzold (eds.), *Protecting Human Rights: The European Dimension, Studies in Honour of Gerard J. Wiarda*, Köln: Carl Heymanns Verlag KG, 1988 (Matscher & Petzold 1988).

Marissa Mayer (Google), Do Not Neutralize the Web's Endless Search, Ft.com Financial Times, June 14, 2010, http://www.ft.com/intl/cms/s/0/0458b1a4-8f78-11df-8df0-00144feab49a.html#axzz1crmvPBlE (Mayer (Google) 2010).

Ben McGrath, 'Search And Destroy: Nick Denton's Blog Empire', *The New Yorker*, October 18, 2010, http://www.newyorker.com/reporting/2010/10/18/101018fa_fact_mcgrath (McGrath 2010).

References

T.J. McIntyre & Colin David Scott, 'Internet Filtering: Rhetoric, Legitimacy, Accountability and Responsibility', in: R. Brownsword & K. Yeung (eds.), *Regulating Technologies*, Oxford: Hart Publishing, 2008 (McIntyre & Scott 2008).

Marshall McLuhan, *The Gutenberg Galaxy*, Toronto: University of Toronto Press, 1962 (McLuhan 1962).

Joe McNamee, 'Data Retention—Time For Evidence-Based Decision Making', *EDRi-gram*, 8.13, June 30, 2010, http://www.edri.org/edrigram/number8.13/data-retention-challange (McNamee 2010).

J.M. de Meij, *De vrije informatiestroom in grondwettelijk perspectief*, 2de druk, Otto Cramwinckel Uitgever, 1996 (De Meij 1996).

Alexander Meiklejohn, *Free Speech and Its Relation to Self-Government*, New York: Harpel & Brothers, 1948 (Meiklejohn 1948).

Alexander Meiklejohn, 'The First Amendment is an Absolute', 1961 Supreme Court Review 245, 1961 (Meiklejohn 1961).

John B. Meisel & Timothy S. Sullivan, 'Portals: the new media companies', *Info* 2-5, 477–486 (Meisel & Sullivan 2000).

I. Melander, 'Web search for bomb recipes should be blocked: EU', *Reuters*, September 10, 2007, http://www.reuters.com/article/InternetNews/idUSL1055133420070910 (Melander 2007).

David Meyer, 'Google loses autocomplete defamation case in Italy', *ZDNet UK*, April 5, 2011, http://www.zdnet.co.uk/news/regulation/2011/04/05/google-loses-autocomplete-defamation-case-in-italy-40092392/ (Meyer 2011).

Microsoft, 'Book search winding down', May 23, 2008, http://www.bing.com/community/blogs/search/archive/2008/05/23/book-search-winding-down.aspx (Microsoft 2008)

Microsoft, 'Why some results have been removed', 2011, http://onlinehelp.microsoft.com/en-us/bing/ff808530.aspx (Microsoft 2011a).

Microsoft, 'How Bing delivers search results', 2011, http://onlinehelp.microsoft.com/en-gb/bing/ff808447.aspx (Microsoft 2011b).

Francis L. Miksa & Philip Doty, 'Intellectual Realities and the Digital Library', In: J. L. Schnase et al. (eds.), *Proceedings of Digital Libraries '94: The First Annual Conference on the Theory and Practice of Digital Libraries*, 1994, 1–5 (Miksa & Doty 1994).

John Stuart Mill, *On Liberty*, 2nd edition, Boston: Ticknor and Fields, 1863 (Mill 1863).

John Milton, *Areopagitica*, In: *Areopagitica and other political writings of John Milton*, Indianapolis: Liberty Fund, 1999 (Milton 1999).

Viva R. Moffat, 'Regulating Search', 22 *Harvard Journal of Law & Technology* 475, 2009 (Moffat 2009).

Evgeny Morozov, 'Losing Our Minds to the Web', *Prospect*, Issue 172, June 22, 2010, http://www.prospectmagazine.co.uk/2010/06/losing-our-minds-to-the-web/ (Morozov 2010).

Susan Moskwa, Managing your reputation through search results, *The Official Google Blog*, October 15, 2009, http://googleblog.blogspot.com/2009/10/managing-your-reputation-through-search.html (Moskwa (Google) 2009).

Ryan Moulton & Kendra Carattini, 'A quick word about Googlebombs', *Google Webmaster Central Blog*, January 25, 2007, http://googlewebmastercentral. blogspot.com/2007/01/quick-word-about-googlebombs.html (Moulton & Carattini (Google) 2007).

Milton L. Mueller, Universal Service: Competition, Interconnection, and Monopoly in the Making of the American Telephone System, Cambridge, MA: The MIT Press, 1997 (Mueller 1997).

Milton L. Mueller, *Ruling the Root, Internet Governance and the Taming of Cyberspace*, Cambridge (MA): The MIT Press, 2004 (Mueller 2002).

Mueller, *Network and States. The Global Politics of Internet Governance*, The MIT Press, 2010 (Mueller 2010).

S. Muthukrishnan, 'Ad Exchanges: Research Issues', In: S. Leonardi (ed.): *WINE 2009*, 1–12 (Muthukrishnan 2009).

Michael I. Myerson, 'Authors, Editors and Uncommon Carriers: Identifying the "Speaker" within the New Media', 71 *Notre Dame L.aw Review* 79, 1995 (Myerson 1995).

Ira S. Nathenson, 'Internet Infoglut and Invisible Ink: Spamdexing Search Engines with Meta Tags', 12 *Harvard Journal of Law & Technology* 43, 1998 (Nathenson 1998).

NBD Biblion, 'Bezwaarprocedure aanschafinformatie', http://www.nbdbiblion.nl/ (NBD Biblion 2011).

Robert M. O'Neil, *The First Amendment and Civil Liability*, Bloomington: Indiana University Press, 2001 (O'Neil 2001).

John Nerone &Kevin G. Barnhurst, 'US newspaper types, the newsroom, and the division of labor, 1750-2000', *Journalism Studies*, 4:4, 2003, 435–449 (Nerone & Barnhurst 2003).

Aernoudt J. Nieuwenhuis, *Persvrijheid en Persbeleid*, Otto Cramwinckel Uitgever, 1991 (Nieuwenhuis 1991).

Aernoudt J. Nieuwenhuis, 'The concept of pluralism in the case-law of the European Court of Human Rights', European Constitutional Law Review 2007-3, 367–384 (Nieuwenhuis 2007).

Aernoudt J. Nieuwenhuis, 'Steun aan de pers: permanent in ontwikkeling?', *Mediaforum* 2009-3 (Nieuwenhuis 2009).

Melville Nimmer, 'Introduction—Is Freedom of the Press a Redundancy: What Does It Add to Freedom of Speech?', 26 Hastings Law Journal 639, 1975 (Nimmer 1975).

Melville B. Nimmer & David Nimmer, *Nimmer on Copyright: a treatise on the law of literary, musical and artistic property, and the protection of ideas*, New York: Metthew Bender looseleaf (Nimmer & Nimmer looseleaf).

Helen Nissenbaum, *Privacy in Context, Technology, Policy and the Integrity of Social Life*, Stanford: Stanford University Press, 2010 (Nissenbaum 2010).

Eli M. Noam, *Telecommunications in Europe*, New York/Oxford: Oxford University Press, 1992 (Noam 1992).

Note, 'The Chilling Effect in Constitutional Law', 69 *Columbia Law Review* 808, 1969 (Note 1969).

Note, 'First Amendment Overbreadth Doctrine', 83 *Harvard Law Review* 844, 1970 (Note 1970).

Dawn C. Nunziato, 'The Death of the Public Forum in Cyberspace', 20 *Berkeley Technology Law Journal* 1115, 2005 (Nunziatio 2005).

Dawn C. Nunziato, *Virtual Freedom and Free Speech in the Internet Age*, Stanford: Stanford University Press, 2009 (Nunziatio 2009).

Jeffrey D. Oldham & Fred Leach, 'The Presidential debate: Expanding the town hall', *The Official Google Blog,* October 8, 2008, http://googleblog.blogspot.com/2008/10/presidential-debate-expanding-town-hall.html (Oldham & Leach (Google) 2008).

Barack Obama, 'Mexico City Policy—Voluntary Population Planning', *The White House*, January 23, 2009, http://www.whitehouse.gov/the_press_office/MexicoCityPolicy-VoluntaryPopulationPlanning/ (Obama 2009).

Peter Olsthoorn, *De Macht van Google*, Utrecht: Kosmos Uitgevers, 2010 (Olsthoorn 2010).

Christopher Olston and Marc Najork, 'Web Crawling', *Foundations and Trends in Information Retrieval*, Vol. 4, No. 3, 2010. 175–246 (Olston & Najork 2010).

Charles B. Osburn & Ross Atkinson, *Collection Management: A New Treatise*, JAI Press, 1991 (Osburn & Atkinson 1991).

Stephan Ott, Links & Law, http://www.linksandlaw.com (Links & Law).

Stephan Ott, 'Die Entwicklung des Suchmaschinen- und Hyperlink-Rechts im Jahr 2007', *WRP* 2008-4, 393–414 (Ott 2008).

Stephan Ott, 'Die Entwicklung des Suchmaschinen- und Hyperlink-Rechts im Jahr 2008', *WRP* 2009-4, 351–372 (Ott 2009).

Out-Law.com, 'Spain orders Google to delete citizens' data from search engine results', August 8, 2011, http://www.out-law.com/page-12143 (Out-Law.com 2011).

Andrew K. Pace, *The Ultimate Digital Library, Where the New Information Players Meet*, Chicago: American Library Association, 2003 (Pace 2003).

Pandia Search Engine News, 'European search engine alliance to challenge Google', January 22, 2006, http://www.pandia.com/sew/162-europan-search-engine-alliance-to-challenge-google.html (Pandia Search Engine News 2006).

Mary-Rose Papandrea, 'Citizen Journalism and the Reporter's Privilege', 91 *Minnesota Law Review* 515, 2007 (Papandrea 2007).

Eli Pariser, *The Filter Bubble. What the Internet is Hiding From You*, Viking, Penguin Books, 2011, Kindle Edition (Pariser 2011).

Frank Pasquale, 'Rankings, Reductionism, and Responsibility', 54 *Cleveland Law Journal* 115, 2006 (Pasquale 2006).

Frank Pasquale, 'Asterisk Revisited: Debating a Right of Reply on Search Results', 3 *Journal of Business & Technology Law* 61, 2008 (Pasquale 2008).

Frank Pasquale, 'Dominant Search Engines: An Essential Cultural & Political Facility', in: B. Szoka & A. Marcus (eds.), *The Next Digital Decade: Essays on the Future of the Internet*, Washington D.C.: TechFreedom, 2010 (Pasquale 2010a).

Frank Pasquale, 'The Decline of Media Studies (and Privacy) in a Search Engine Society', *Concurring Opinions*, July 10, 2010, http://www.concurringopinions.com/archives/2010/07/the-decline-of-media-studies-and-privacy-in-a-search-engine-society.html (Pasquale 2010b).

M. Peguera, 'The DMCA Safe Harbors and Their European Counterparts: a comparative analysis of some common problems', 32 *Columbia Journal of Law & the Arts* 481, 2009 (Peguera 2009).

M. Peguera, 'Internet Service Providers' Liability in Spain: Recent Case Law and Future Perspectives', Journal of Intellectual Property, Information Technology and E-Commerce Law, Vol. 1, Nr. 3, 2010, 151–171 (Peguera 2010).

Henry H. Perrit, Jr. 'Tort Liability, the First Amendment, and Equal Access to Electronic Networks', 5 *Harvard Journal of Law & Technology* 65, 1992 (Perrit 1992).

Henry H. Perritt Jr., 'Tort liability, the First Amendment, equal access, and commercialization of electronic networks', *Internet Research*, Vol. 20, Issue 4, 2010, 436–460 (Perrit 2010).

Guy Pessach, 'The Role of Libraries in A2K: taking stock and looking ahead', 2007 Michigan State Law Review 257 (Pessach 2007).

Jeremy Peters, 'Some Newspapers, Tracking Readers online, Shift Coverage', *The New York Times*, September 5, 2010, http://www.nytimes.com/2010/09/06/business/media/06track.html (Peters 2010).

Rufus Pollock, 'Is Google the Next Microsoft: Competition, Welfare and Regulation in Online Search', 9:4 Review of Network Economics, Article 4 (2010) (Pollock 2010).

Monroe E. Price & Stefaan G. Verhulst, *Self-Regulation and the Internet*, Kluwer Law International, 2005 (Price & Verhulst 2005).

Princeton Survey Research Associates, 'A Matter of Trust: What Users Want From Web Sites', Results of a National Survey of Internet Users for Consumer WebWatch, January 2002, http://www.consumerwebwatch.org/pdfs/a-matter-of-trust.pdf (Princeton Survey Research Associates 2002).

Ulrich Prueb, 'The German Drittwirkung Doctrine and Its Socio-Political Background', in A. Sajó, R. Uitz (eds.), *The Constitution in Private Relations: Expanding Constitutionalism*, The Netherlands: Eleven International Publishing, 2005, 23–32 (Prueb 2005).

Maya Hertig Randall, 'Commercial Speech under the European Convention on Human Rights: Subordinate or Equal?', *Human Rights Law Review*, 6:1, 2006 (Randall 2006).

W. Boyd Rayward (ed.), *Selected Essays of Paul Otlet*, Amsterdam: Elsevier, 1990 (Rayward 1990).

Viviane Reding, 'The upcoming data protection reform for the European Union', *International Data Privacy Law*, Vol. 1, No. 1, 2011 (Reding 2011).

Martin H. Redish, *Money Talks. Speech, Economic Power and the Values of Democracy*, New York and London: New York University Press, 2001 (Redish 2001).

References

J.R. Reidenberg, 'Lex informatica: The Formulation of Information Policy Rules Through Technology', 76 *Texas Law Review* 553, 1998 (Reidenberg 1998).

Jorge Reinbothe & Silke Von Lewinski, *The EC Directive on Rental and Lending Rights and on Piracy*, London: Sweet & Maxwell, 1993 (Reinbothe & Von Lewinski 1993).

Reuters, 'EU media chief rules out Internet freedom law', February 3, 2009, http://www.reuters.com/article/2009/02/03/us-eu-Internet-idUS-TRE5124SB20090203 (Reuters 2009).

Neil M. Richards, 'Intellectual Privacy', 87 *Texas Law Review* 387, 2008 (Richards 2008).

Matthew Richardson, 'Learning about the World through Long-Term Query Logs', Microsoft Research, *ACM Trans. Web* 2, 4, Article 21, 2008 (Richardson 2008).

Bernhard Rieder, 'Democratizing Search? From Critique to Society-oriented Design', in: K. Becker and F. Stalder (eds.), *Deep Search: The Politics of Search Engines beyond Google*, Edison, NJ: Transaction, 2009, 133–151 (Rieder 2009).

Louise Robbins, 'Segregating Propaganda in American Libraries', *The Library Quarterly*, 1993-2 (63), 143–165 (Robbins 1993).

Theo Röhle, 'Desperately seeking the consumer: Personalized search engines and the commercial exploitation of user data', First Monday, Vol. 12, Nr. 9, 2006, http://firstmonday.org/htbin/cgiwrap/bin/ojs/index.php/fm/article/view/2008 (Röhle 2006).

Theo Röhle, 'Machtkonzepte in der Suchmaschinenforschung', in: Marcel Machill and Markus Beiler (eds.), Die Macht der Suchmaschinen. The Power of Search Engines. Köln: Herbert von Halem Verlag, 2007, 127–142 (Röhle 2007a).

Theo Röhle, '"Think of it first as an advertising system": Personalisierte Online-Suche als Datenlieferant des Marketings', *kommunikation@gesellschaft* 8, Beitrag 1, 2007 (Röhle 2007b).

Theo Röhle, Dissecting the Gatekeepers, Relational Perspectives on the Power of Search Engines, in K. Becker and F. Stalder (eds.), *Deep Search: The Politics of Search Engines beyond Google*, Edison, NJ: Transaction, 2009, 117–132 (Röhle 2009).

Theo Röhle, *Der Google Complex, Über Macht im Zeitalter des Internets,* Bielefelt: Transcript Verlag, 2010 (Röhle 2010).

Richard Rogers, *Information Politics on the Web*, Cambridge (MA): The MIT Press, 2004 (Rogers 2004).

Richard Rogers, 'The Googlization Question, and the Inculpable Engine', in: K. Becker and F. Stalder (eds.), *Deep Search: The Politics of Search Engines beyond Google*, Edison, NJ: Transaction, 2009, 173–184 (Rogers 2009a).

Richard Rogers, 'The End of the Virtual—Digital Methods', Inaugural Speech, Chair, New Media & Digital Culture, University of Amsterdam, May 8, 2009, http://www.govcom.org/rogers_oratie.pdf (Rogers 2009b).

Daniel E. Rose & D. Levinson, 'Understanding User Goals In Web Search', *Proceedings of the 13th International Conference on World Wide Web (WWW'04)*, 2004 (Rose & Levinson 2004).

Jay Rosen, 'Audience Atomization Overcome: Why the Internet Weakens the Authority of the Press', *Pressthink*, January 12, 2009, http://archive.pressthink.org/2009/01/12/atomization.html (Rosen 2009).

Boris Rotenberg, "Towards Personalised Search: EU Data Protection law and Its Implications for Media Pluralism", in: M. Machill & M. Beiler (eds.), *Die Macht der Suchmaschinen. The Power of Search Engines*, Köln: Herbert von Halem Verlag, 2007, 87–104 (Rotenberg 2007).

Peter Ruess, '"Just Google it?"—Neuigkeiten und Gedanken zur Haftung der Suchmaschinenanbieter für Markenverletzungen in Deutschland und den USA', 2007 *Gewerblicher Rechtsschutz und Urheberrecht* 198, 2007 (Ruess 2007).

M. Rundle & M. Birdling, 'Filtering and the International System: A question of Commitment', in: Deibert et al. (eds.), *Access Denied, The Practice and Policy of Global Internet Filtering*, Cambridge, MA: The MIT Press, 2008, 73–102 (Rundle & Birdling 2008).

Michael L. Rustad & Thomas H. Koenig, 'Harmonizing Cybertort Law for Europe and America', 5 *Journal of High Technology Law* 13, 2005 (Rustad & Koenig 2005).

A. Sajó & R. Uitz (eds.), *The Constitution in Private Relations: Expanding Constitutionalism*, The Netherlands: Eleven International Publishing, 2005 (Sajó & Uitz 2005).

Wolfgang Sakulin, *Trademark Protection and Freedom of Expression, An Inquiry into the Conflict between Trademark Rights and Freedom of Expression under European, German and Dutch Law*, Academisch Proefschrift, Oisterwijk, The Netherlands: Boxpress, 2010 (Sakulin 2010).

Ewoud Sanders, *Eerste Hulp Bij e-Onderzoek*, Amsterdam/Den Haag/Leiden: early dutch books online, 2011 (Sanders 2011).

M.A. Sanderson, 'Is Von Hannover v. Germany a Step Backwards for the Substantive Analysis of Speech and Privacy Interests?', 6 *European Human Rights Law Review* 631, 2004 (Sanderson 2004).

Søren Sandfeld Jakobsen, 'Danish Supreme Court Upholds Injunction to Block the Pirate Bay', *IRIS* 2010-8:1/24 (Jakobsen 2010).

Santa Clara County Library, Materials Selection Policy, http://www.santaclaracountylib.org/about/matselection.html (Santa Clara County Library).

Margaret Scammel, 'The Internet and Civic Engagement: the age of the citizen-consumer', 17 *Political Communication* 351, 2000 (Scammel 2000).

Thomas Scanlon, 'A Theory of Freedom of Expression', 1 *Philosophy and Public Affairs* 204, 1972 (Scanlon 1972).

Jörg-Olaf Schäfers, 'Wikileaks: Lycos Deutschland Zensurliste?', *Netzpolitik.org*, September 20, 2009, http://netzpolitik.org/2009/wikileaks-lycos-deutschland-zensurliste/ (Schäfers 2009).

Burkhard Schafer, 'The UK Cleanfeed system, Lessons for the German debate?', 34 *Datenschutz und Datensicherheit* 535, 2010 (Schafer 2010).

Bruce R. Schatz & Joseph B. Harding, 'NCSA Mosaic and the World Wide Web', Science, New Series, Vol. 265, No. 5174, 1994 (Schatz & Harding 1994).

Frederick Schauer, 'Fear, Risk and the First Amendment: Unraveling the Chilling Effect', 58 *Boston University Law Review* 685, 1978 (Schauer 1978).

Frederick Schauer, *Free Speech: a philosophical inquiry*, Cambridge: Cambridge University Press, 1983 (Schauer 1983).

Frederick Schauer, 'The Boundaries of the First Amendment', 117 Harv. L. Rev. 1765, 2004 (Schauer 2004).

Frederick Schauer, 'The Exceptional First Amendment', in: M. Ignatief (ed), *American Exceptionalism and Human Rights*, Princeton University Press, 2005 (Schauer 2005a).

Frederick Schauer, 'Freedom of Expression adjudication in Europe and the United States: a case study in comparative architecture', in: G. Nolte (ed.), *European and US Constitutionalism*, New York: Cambridge University Press, 2005, 49–69 (Schauer 2005b).

M.H.M. Schellekens, B.J. Koops and W.G. Teepe, 'Wat niet weg is, is gezien. Een analyse van art. 54a Sr in het licht van een Noticeand-Take-Down-regime', Cycris, TILT, November 2007 (Schellekens et al. 2007).

Tessie Schepman, Marian Koren, et al., 'Access With(out) Anonymity—Anonymity in Public Libraries in Modern Times', *BOBCATSSS 2008* (Schepman et al. 2008).

Barbara van Schewick, *Internet Architecture and Innovation*, The MIT Press, 2010 (van Schewick 2010).

Herbert I. Schiller, *Communication and Cultural Domination*, New York: International Arts and Sciences Press, 1976 (Schiller 1976).

Maximilian Schubert & Stephan Ott, 'Mehr Fragen als Antworten—die Google France Entscheidung des EuGH zum Keyword Advertising', *jusIT* 2010/36, 85–88 (Schubert & Ott).

G.A.I. Schuijt, *Vrijheid van Nieuwsgaring*, Den Haag: Boom Juridische Uitgevers, 2006 (Schuijt 2006)

Louis Michael Seidman, 'The *Dale* Problem, Property and Speech under the Regulatory State', 75 *Chicago Law Review* 1541, 2009 (Seidman 2009).

Pamela Shoemaker, *Gatekeeping*, Newbury Park: Sage Publications, 1991 (Shoemaker 1991).

Wolfgang Schulz, Thorsten Held & Arne Laudien, *Suchmaschinen asl Gatekeeper in der öffentliche Kommunikation*, Schriftenreihe Medienforschung der Landesanstalt für Medien Nordrhein-Westfalen, Band 49, Düsseldorf: Vistas verlag, 2005 (Schulz et al. 2005a).

W. Schulz, T. Held & A. Laudien, 'Search Engines as Gatekeepers of Public Communication: Analysis of the German framework applicable to Internet search engines including media law and anti-trust law', 6 *German Law Journal* 1419, 2005 (Schulz et al. 2005b).

Wolfgang Schulz & Thorsten Held, 'Der Index auf dem Index? Selbstzensur und Zensur bei Suchmaschinen', in: M. Machill & M. Beiler (eds.), *Die Macht der Suchmasxchinen / The Power of Search Engines*, Köln: Halem, 2007, 71–87 (Schulz & Held 2007).

David Segal, 'A Bully Finds a Pulpit on the Web', New York Times, November 26, 2010, http://www.nytimes.com/2010/11/28/business/28borker.html (Segal 2010).

Clay Shirky, *Here Comes Everybody: The power of organizing without organizations*, New York: The Penguin press, 2008 (Shirky 2008).

Vitaly Shmatikov & Arvind Narayanan, 'Myths and Fallacies of "Personally Identifiable Information"', *Communications of the ACM*, 53(6), 2010 (Shmatikov & Narayanan 2010).

U. Sieber and M. Liesching, 'Die Verantwortlichkeit der Suchmaschinenbetreiber nach dem Telemediengesetz', *Multimedia und Recht*, Issue 8/2007 (Sieber & Liesching 2007).

Ulrich Sieber & Malaika Nolde, 'Sperrverfügungen im Internet. Nationale Rechtsdurchsetzung im globalen Cyberspace?', *Criminal Law Research Reports*, vol. S 113, Berlin: Duncker & Humblot, 2008 (Sieber & Nolde 2008).

Amit Singhal, 'Modern Information Retrieval: A Brief Overview', IEEE Data Engineering Bulletin 24(4), 2001, 35–43 (Singhal 2001).

Amit Singhal, 'Introduction to Google Ranking', *The Official Google Blog*, July 9, 2008, http://googleblog.blogspot.com/2008/07/introduction-to-google-ranking.html (Singhal (Google) 2008a).

Amit Singhal, 'Technologies behind Google ranking', *The Official Google Blog*, July 16, 2008, http://googleblog.blogspot.com/2008/07/technologies-behind-google-ranking.html (Singhal (Google) 2008b).

Amit Singhal, 'Being bad to your customers is bad for business', The Official Google Blog, December 1, 2010, http://googleblog.blogspot.com/2010/12/being-bad-to-your-customers-is-bad-for.html (Singhal (Google) 2010).

Amit Singhal, 'Supporting choice, ensuring economic opportunity', *The Official Google Blog*, June 24, 2011, http://googleblog.blogspot.com/2011/06/supporting-choice-ensuring-economic.html (Singhal (Google) 2011).

Christopher Soghoian & Firuzeh Shokooh Valle, 'Adiós Diego: Argentine judges cleanse the Internet', *OpenNet Initiative*, November 11, 2008, http://opennet.net/blog/2008/11/adi%C3%B3s-diego-argentine-judgescleanse- internet (Soghoian & Valle 2008).

Chris Soghoian, 'Debunking Google's log anonymization propaganda', *CNET*, September 11, 2008, http://news.cnet.com/8301-13739_3-10038963-46.html (Soghoian 2008).

Christopher Soghoian, 'An End to Privacy Theater: Exposing and Discouraging Corporate Disclosure of User Data to the Government', 12 *Minnesota Journal of Law, Science & Technology* 191, 2010 (Soghoian 2010).

Ithiel de Sola Pool, *Technologies of Freedom: on free speech in an electronic age*, Cambridge (MA): Harvard University Press, 1983 (de Sola Pool 1983).

Daniel J. Solove, *The Digital Person: Technology and privacy in the digital age*, New York/London: New York University Press, 2004 (Solove 2004).

Daniel J. Solove, 'The First Amendment as Criminal Procedure', 82 N.Y.U. L. REV. 112, 114–15, 2007 (Solove 2007).

Daniel J. Solove, *The Future of Reputation: Gossip, rumor and privacy on the Internet*, New Haven and London: Yale University Press, 2007 (Solove 2007b).

Daniel J. Solove, Understanding Privacy, First Harvard University Press Paperback Edition, Cambridge (MA): Harvard University Press, 2009 (Solove 2009a).

Daniel J. Solove and Neil M. Richards, 'Rethinking Free Speech and Civil Liability', 109 Colum. L. Rev. 1650, 2009 (Solove 2009b).

Daniel J. Solove, 'Speech, Privacy and Reputation on the Internet', in: Saul Levmore, Martha C. Nussbaum, *The Offensive Internet*, Harvard University Press, 2011 (Solove 2011).

Lawrence B. Solum &Minn Chung, 'The Layers Principle: Internet Architecture and the Law', *University of San Diego Public Law Research Paper*, No. 55, 2003, http://papers.ssrn.com/sol3/papers.cfm?abstract_id=416263 (Solum & Chung 2003).

Robbert Sommer, 'The Ecology of Privacy', 36 *Library Quarterly* 234, 1966 (Sommer 1966).

Wes Sonnenreich & Tim Macinta, *Web Developers.com Guide to Search Engines*, New York: John Wiley & Sons, Inc., 1998 (Sonnenreich & Macinta 1998).

James B. Speta, 'The Shaky Foundations of the Regulated Internet', 8 Journal of Telecommunications and High Technology Law 101, 2010 (Speta 2010).

Oliver Spieker, 'Verantwortlichkeit von Internetsuchdiensten für Persönlichkeitsrechtsverletzungen in ihren Suchergebnislisten', *Multimedia und Recht* 2005, 727–732 (Spieker 2005).

Gerald Spindler & Thibaut Verbiest, *Study on the Liability of Internet Intermediaries*, Independent study prepared for the European Commission, MARKT/2006/09/E, November 12, 2007 (Spindler & Verbiest 2007).

Felix Stalder, 'The Failure of Privacy Enhancing Technologies (PETs) and the Voiding of Privacy', *Sociological Research Online,* vol. 7, no. 2, 2002 (Stalder 2002).

Felix Stalder & Christine Mayer, 'The Second Index. Search Engines Personalization and Surveillance', in: K. Becker & F. Stalder (Eds.), *Deep search: the politics of search beyond Google*, Innsbruck: Studienverlag, 2009, 98–116 (Stalder & Mayer 2009).

Konstantinos Sp. Staikos, The History of the Library in Western Civilization, Oak Knoll Press, 2004 (Staikos 2004).

Irini A. Stamatoudi (ed.), *Copyright Enforcement and the Internet*, Kluwer Law International, 2010 (Stamatoudi 2010).

Paul Starr, *The Creation of the Media, Political origins of modern communications*, New York: Basic Books, 2004 (Starr 2004).

Mark Stefik, *Internet Dreams. Archetypes, Myths, and Metaphors*, Cambridge (MA): The MIT Press, 1996 (Stefik 1996).

Greg Sterling, 'Admitting Role In Google Anti-Trust Complaints Microsoft Complains Of Google "Lock In"', *Search Engine Land*, February 27, 2010, http://searchengineland.com/admitting-role-in-google-anti-trust-complaints-microsoft-complains-of-google-lock-in-37009 (Sterling 2010).

Potter Stewart, "Or of the Press," 26 Hastings Law Journal 631, 1975 (Stewart 1975).

Sarah Lai Stirland, U.S. Funded Health Search Engine Blocks 'Abortion', Wired.com, April 3, 2008, http://www.wired.com/threatlevel/2008/04/a-government-fu/ (Stirland 2008a).

Sarah Lai Stirland, 'Overreaction to Bush Administration Complaint Prompted Block on "Abortion" Searches', Wired.com, April 4, 2008, http://www.wired.com/threatlevel/2008/04/administrators/ (Stirland 2008b).

W. Ph. Stol et al., 'Filteren van kinderporno op internet', Study for the Dutch Government, WODC, 2008 (Stol et al. 2008).

Geoffrey R. Stone, 'Fora Americana: Speech in Public Spaces', 1974 *Supreme Court Review* 233 (Stone 1974).

Geoffrey R. Stone, 'Revisiting the Patriot Act', *Chicago Tribune*, July 8, 2005 (Stone 2005).

Geoffrey R. Stone, et al., *The First Amendment*, Third Edition, Austin: Wolters Kluwer, 2008 (Stone et al. 2008).

Geoffrey R. Stone, Constitutional law, Sixth Edition, Aspen Publishers, 2009 (Stone 2009).

Geoffrey R. Stone, 'Privacy, the First Amendment and the Internet', in: S. Levmore, M. C. Nussbaum (eds.), *The Offensive Internet*, Harvard University Press, 2011, Kindle Edition (Stone 2010).

Paul Sturges, 'Gatekeepers and other Intermediaries', *Aslib Proceedings* 53-2, 2001 (Sturges 2001).

Kathleen M. Sullivan, 'Unconstitutional Conditions', 102 *Harvard Law Review* 1413, 1989 (Sullivan 1989).

Danny Sullivan, 'Google Kills Bush's Miserable Failure Search & Other Google Bombs', *Search Engine Land*, January 25, 2007, http://searchengineland.com/google-kills-bushs-miserable-failure-search-other-google-bombs-10363 (Sullivan 2007).

Danny Sullivan, 'Microsoft Burns Book Search—Lacks "High Commercial Intent"', *Search Engine Land*, December 23, 2008, http://searchengineland.com/microsoft-burns-book-search-lacks-high-consumer-intent-14066 (Sullivan 2008).

Danny Sullivan, Google Now Personalizes Everyone's Search Results, *Search Engine Land*, December 4, 2009, http://searchengineland.com/google-now-personalizes-everyones-search-results-31195 (Sullivan 2009).

Danny Sullivan, 'Google & Human Quality Reviews: Old News Returns', *Search Engine Land*, December 19, 2007, postscript July 14, 2010, http://searchengineland.com/google-human-quality-reviews-old-news-returns-12977 (Sullivan 2010a).

References

Danny Sullivan, 'Ask.com To Focus On Q&A Search, End Web Crawling', *Search Engine Land*, November 9, 2010, http://searchengineland.com/ask-com-to-focus-on-qa-search-end-web-crawling-55209 (Sullivan 2010b).

Cass R. Sunstein, *Democracy and the problem of free speech*, New York: The Free Press, 1993 (Sunstein 1993).

Cass R. Sunstein, 'Half-Truths of the First Amendment', 1993 *University of Chicago Legal Forum* 25, 1993 (Sunstein 1993).

Cass R. Sunstein, 'The First Amendment in Cyberspace', 104 *Yale Law Journal* 157, 1995 (Sunstein 1995).

Cass R. Sunstein, *Republic.com*, Princeton University Press, 2002 (Sunstein 2002).

Cass R. Sunstein, *Infotopia*, Oxford University Press, 2006 (Sunstein 2006).

Cass R. Sunstein, *Republic 2.0*, Princeton: Princeton University Press, 2007 (Sunstein 2007).

Damian Tambini, Danilo Leonardi & Chris Marsden, *Codifying Cyberspace. Communications Self-Regulation in the Age of Internet Convergence*, Oxon (U.K.): Routledge, 2008 (Tambini et al. 2008).

Ryan Tate, 'Google CEO: Secrets Are For Filthy People', *Gawker*, December 4, 2009, http://gawker.com/5419271/google-ceo-secrets-are-for-filthy-people (Tate 2009).

Omer Tene, 'What Google Knows, Privacy and Internet Search Engines', 4 *Utah Law Review* 1433, 2008 (Tene 2008).

The New York Times, 'The New York Times Semi-Sentenniel', Editor & Publisher, October 1, 1901 (The New York Times 1901).

THESEUS-Pressebüro, 'Was is THESEUS?', http://theseus-programm.de/was-ist-theseus (THESEUS).

Clive Thompson, 'Google's China problem (and China's Google problem)', *The New York Times Magazine*, April 23, 2006, http://www.nytimes.com/2006/04/23/magazine/23google.html (Thompson 2006).

Laurence H. Tribe & Thomas C. Goldstein, 'Proposed "Net Neutrality" Mandates Could Be Counterproductive and Violate the First Amendment', FCC.GOV, October 19, 2009, in: *Comments of Time Warner Cable Inc.*, GN Docket No. 09-191, WC Docket No. 07-52, Exhibit A, available at http://fjallfoss.fcc.gov/ecfs/document/view?id=7020375998 (Tribe & Goldstein 2009).

Daniel Tunkelang, 'Google and Transparency', *The Noisy Channel*, March 7, 2010, http://thenoisychannel.com/2010/03/07/google-and-transparency (Tunkelang 2010).

M. Turner, Mary Traynort & Herbert Smith, 'UK E-commerce liability, Ignorance is bliss', 19 *Computer Law & Security Report* 112, 2003 (Turner et al. 2003).

Joseph Turow, *Niche Envy. Marketing Discrimination in the Digital Age,* Cambridge, MA/London: The MIT Press, 2006 (Turow 2006).

Mark Tushnet, 'The Issue of State Action/Horizontal Effect in Comparative Constitutional Law', 1 *International Journal of Constitutional Law* 79, 2003 (Tushnet 2003).

Rebecca Tushnet, 'Power Without Responsibility: Intermediaries and the First Amendment', 76 *George Washington Law Review* 101, 2008 (Tushnet 2008).

UN Commission on Human Rights, 54th session, Report of the Special Rapporteur on the promotion and protection of the right to freedom of opinion and expression, 28/01/1998, E/CN.4/1998/40 (UN Commission on Human Rights 1998).

United Nations, 'Report of the Special Rapporteur on the promotion and protection of the right to freedom of opinion and expression', Frank La Rue, May 16, 2011, A/HRC/17/27 (United Nations 2011).

United States Department of State, Hillary Rodham Clinton, Secretary of State, 'Remarks on Internet Freedom', Washington D.C., January 21, 2010, http://www.state.gov/secretary/rm/2010/01/135519.htm (United States Department of State 2010).

J. Urban & L. Quilter, 'Efficient Process or "Chilling Effects"? Takedown Notices Under Section 512 of the Digital Millennium Copyright Act', 22 *Santa Clara Computer & High Technology Law Journal* 621, 2006 (Urban & Quilter 2006).

Siva Vaidhyanathan, *The Googlization of Everything (And Why We Should Worry)*, University of California Press, 2011 (Vaidhyanathan 2011).

Peggy Valcke, *Digitale Diversiteit—Convergentie van Media-, Telecommunicatie- en Mededingingsrecht* [*Digital Diversity—Convergence of Media, Telecommunications and Competition Law*]. Brussels: Larcier, 2004 (Valcke 2004).

Peggy Valcke & David Stevens, 'Graduated regulation of "regulatable" content and the European Audiovisual Media Services Directive: One small step for the industry and one giant leap for the legislator?', 24 *Telematics and Informatics* 285, 2007 (Valcke & Stevens 2007).

Peggy Valcke, 'In Search of the Audiovisual Search Tools in the EU Regulatory Frameworks', in: S. Nikoltchev (ed.), Searching for audiovisual content (IRIS special), Strasbourg: European Audiovisual Observatory, 2008 (Valcke 2008).

Peggy Valcke et al., *Independent Study on Indicators for Media Pluralism in the Member States,* KU Leuven et al., Prepared for the European Commission, 2009 (Valcke et al. 2009).

Hal R. Varian, 'Online Ad Auctions', American Economic Association, vol. 99(2), 2009, 430–434 (Varian 2009).

Thibault Verbiest, 'The liability, in French and Belgian Laws, of Search Tools on the Internet', 7 *International Journal of Law Information Technology* 238, 1999 (Verbiest 1999).

Anne-Lies Verdoodt, *Zelfregulering in de Journalistiek, De formulering en handhaving van deontologische standaarden in en door het journalistiek beroep,* Proefschrift, K.U. Leuven, 2007 (Verdoodt 2007).

Vereniging voor Nederlandse Bibliotheken, Statuut voor de Openbare Bibliotheek, 1990 (VNB 1990).

Vereniging voor Nederlandse Bibliotheken, Richtlijn voor basisbibliotheken, 2005 (VNB 2005).

Vereniging voor Nederlandse Bibliotheken, Statuut voor professionals in openbare bibliotheken 2007 (VNB 2007).

References

Nart Villeneuve, 'Search Monitor Project: Toward a Measure of Transparency', *Citizen Lab Occasional Paper* #1, 2008 (Villeneuve 2008).

David A. Vise & Mark Malseed, *The Google Story*, New York: Delacorte Press, 2005 (Vise & Malseed 2005).

Dirk Voorhoof, 'Krijgen Journalisten een streepje voor in Straatsburg?', *Mediaforum*, 2008-5 (Voorhoof 2008a).

Dirk Voorhoof, 'Seminar on the European Protection of Freedom of Expression: Reflections on Some Recent Restrictive Trends', Strasbourg, October 10, 2008, http://www-ircm.u-strasbg.fr/seminaire_oct2008/docs/Voorhoof_Final_conclusions.pdf (Voorhoof 2008b).

Dirk Voorhoof, 'Europees Mensenrechtenhof in de knoei met recht en journalistieke ethiek', Opinie, *Mediaforum*, 2008-11/12 (Voorhoof 2008c).

Ian Walden, 'Mine host is searching for a "neutrality" principle!', 26 *Computer Law & Security Review* 203, 2010 (Walden 2010).

Craig W. Walker, 'Application of the DMCA Safe Harbor Provisions to Search Engines', 9 V*irginia Journal of Law & Technology* 1, 2004 (Walker 2004).

J. Walker, 'Links and Power: The Political Economy of Linking on the Web', *Library Trends*, Vol. 53, No. 4, 2005 (Walker 2005).

Kent Walker, 'Making Copyright Work Better Online', Google Public Policy Blog, December 2, 2010, http://googlepublicpolicy.blogspot.com/2010/12/making-copyright-work-better-online.html (Walker (Google) 2010).

Stephen J. Ward, *The Invention of Journalism Ethics, The path to objectivity and beyond*, McGill-Queen's University Press, 2006 (Ward 2006).

Richard Waters, 'Unrest Over Google's Secret Formula', *FT.com Financial Times*, July 11, 2010, http://www.ft.com/cms/s/0/1a5596c2-8d0f-11df-bad7-00144feab49a.html#axzz1crmvPBlE (Waters 2010)

Ingmar Weber & Carlos Castillo, 'The Demographics of Web Search', SIGIR, ACM Press, 2010 (Weber & Castillo 2010).

Webhits, Nutzung von Suchmaschinen, May 18, 2011, http://www.webhits.de (Webhits 2011).

Websense Security Labs, 'State of Internet Security, Q1–Q2, 2009', A Websense White Paper, 2009, http://securitylabs.websense.com/content/Assets/WSL_Q1_Q2_2009_FNL.pdf (Websense Security Labs 2009).

David Weinberger, *Everything is Miscellaneous. The Power of the New Digital Disorder*, New York: A Holt Paperback, 2007 (Weinberger 2007).

Kevin D. Werbach, 'A Layered Model for Internet Policy', 1 *Journal on Telecommunications and High Technology Law* 37, 2002 (Werbach 2002).

Franz Werro, 'The Right to Inform v. The Right to be Forgotten: A Transatlantic Clash', in: A.C. Ciacchi, et al. (eds.), *Liability in the Third Millennium*, Baden-Baden, F.R.G., 2009 (Werro 2009).

David M. White, 'The Gatekeeper: A Case Study in the Selection of News', *Journalism Quarterly*, Vol. 27 No. 1, 1950, 383–390 (White 1950).

Alexander White, 'Search Engines: Left Side Quality Versus Right Side Profits', *Toulouse School of Economics Working Paper*, 2008, http://ssrn.com/abstract=1694869 (White 2008).

Wikileaks, Lycos Deutschland Suchmaschinen Zensurliste, September 19, 2009 (Wikileaks 2009).

Wikipedia, 'Stormfront' (German), http://de.wikipedia.org/wiki/Stormfront (Wikipedia).

Kevin M. Wilemon, 'The Fair Housing Act, the Communications Decency Act, and the Right of Roommate Seekers to Discriminate Online', 29 *Washington University Journal of Law & Policy* 375, 2009 (Wilemon 2009).

Hartmut Winkler, 'Suchmaschinen. Metamedien im Internet?', *Telepolis*, March 12, 1997, http://www.heise.de/tp/artikel/1/1135/1.html (Winkler 1997).

Alex Wright, *Glut. Mastering Information through the Ages*, Washington D.C.: Joseph Henry Press, 2007 (Wright 2007).

Alex Wright, 'The Web that Time Forgot', *The New York Times*, June 17, 2008 (Wright 2008).

Tim Wu, 'Network Neutrality, Broadband Discrimination', 2 *Journal of Telecommunications and High Technology Law* 141, 2003 (Wu 2003).

Tim Wu, *The Master Switch. The Rise and Fall of Information Empires*, New York: Alfred A. Knopf, 2010 (Wu 2010).

Yahoo! Europe, 'Yahoo! Europe Response to the European Commission Public Consultation on E-Commerce Google in EC Consultation', November 5, 2010, available through http://ec.europa.eu/internal_market/consultations/2010/e-commerce_en.htm (Yahoo! Europe 2010).

Takehiro Yamamoto, Satoshi Nakamura, and Katsumi Tanaka, 'An Editable Browser for Reranking Web Search Results', IEEE, 2007 (Yamamoto et al. 2007).

Sha Yang & Anindya Ghose, 'Analyzing the Relationship between Organic and Sponsored Search Advertising: Positive, Negative, or Zero Interdependence?' Marketing Science, vol. 29, no. 4, 2010, pp., 602–623 (Yang & Ghose 2010)

Christopher S. Yoo, 'Free Speech and the Myth of the Internet as an Unintermediated Experience', 78 George Washington Law Review 697, 2010 (Yoo 2010).

M. Zeco & W.B. Tomljanovich, 'The National and University Library of Bosnia and Herzegovina during the Current War', *The Library Quarterly* Vol. 66, No. 3, 1996, 294–301 (Zeco & Tomljanovich 1996).

Tom Zeller, 'Gaming the Search Engine, in a Political Season', The New York Times, November 6, 2006, http://www.nytimes.com/2006/11/06/business/media/06link.html (Zeller 2006).

Michael Zimmer, 'The Gaze of the Perfect Search Engine: Google as an Infrastructure of Dataveillance', In: A. Spink and M. Zimmer (eds.), Web Searching: Interdisciplinary Perspectives, Dordrecht: Springer, 2008, 77–99 (Zimmer 2008).

Michael Zimmer, 'Google Book Search Privacy Policy Mirrors Web Search, with One Hopeful, albeit Limited, Difference', Michael Zimmer.org, September 8, 2009, http://michaelzimmer.org/2009/09/08/google-book-search-privacy-policy-mirrors-web-search/ (Zimmer 2009).

References

Jonathan Zittrain, *The Future of the Internet. And How to Stop It*, New Haven/ London: Yale University Press, 2008 (Zittrain 2008).

Ethan Zuckerman, 'Homophily, serendipity, xenophilia', My heart's in Accra, April 25, 2008, http://www.ethanzuckerman.com/blog/2008/04/25/homophily-serendipity-xenophilia/ (Zuckerman 2008).

Ethan Zuckerman, 'In Soviet Russia, Google Researches You!', My heart's in Accra, March 24, 2011, http://www.ethanzuckerman.com/blog/2011/03/24/in-soviet-russia-google-researches-you/ (Zuckerman 2011).

Legal Texts and CoE Recommendations

United Nations Universal Declaration of Human Rights, adopted and proclaimed by General Assembly resolution 217 A (III) of December 10, 1948

United States Constitution, Adopted 1787

United States Constitution, Bill of Rights, Adopted 1791

Consolidated version of the Treaty on European Union, Official Journal C 325, December 24, 2002

Consolidated versions of the Treaty on European Union and the Treaty on the Functioning of the European Union, OJ C 83, March 30, 2010

Charter on Fundamental rights of the European Union, OJ 2000/C 364/01, December 18, 2000

Council Directive 92/100, 1992 OJ (L 346) 27 (EEC) (Directive on Rental and Lending Rights)

Council Directive 95/46, 1995 OJ (L 281), 31 (EC) (Privacy Directive)

Council Directive 98/34, 1998 OJ (L 204) 37 (EC)

Council Directive 98/48, 1998 OJ (L 320) 54 (EC)

Council Directive 2000/31, 2000 OJ (L 178) 1 (EC) (Directive on Electronic Commerce)

Council Directive 2002/22, 2002 OJ (L 108), 51 (EC) (Universal Service Directive)

Council Directive 2002/58, 2002 OJ (L 201), 37 (EC) (e-Privacy Directive)

Council Recommendation 98/560, 1998 OJ (L 270), 48 (EC) (1998 Recommendation on Protection of Minors)

European Parliament and Council Recommendation, 2006/952, 2006 OJ (L 378), 72 (EC) (2006 Recommendation on protection of Minors)

Council of Europe, Convention for the Protection of Human Rights and Fundamental Freedoms, November 4, 1950, Europ. T.S. No. 5

CoE, Convention for the Protection of Individuals with regard to Automatic Processing of Personal Data Strasbourg, ETS no. 108, January 28, 1981

CoE, Convention on Cybercrime, ETS no. 185, Budapest, November 23, 2001

CoE, Parliamentary Assembly, Resolution 1003 (1993) on the ethics of journalism

CoE, Committee of Ministers, Recommendation (99)1 of the Committee of Ministers to member states on measures to promote media Pluralism

CoE, Committee of Ministers, Recommendation (2004)16 of the Committee of Ministers to member states on the right of reply in the new media environment

CoE, Committee of Ministers, Recommendation Rec(2001)8 of the Committee of Ministers to member states on self-regulation concerning cyber content

CoE, Committee of Ministers, Declaration on Freedom of communication on the Internet, May 28, 2003

CoE, Committee of Ministers, Recommendation (2007)2 on media pluralism and diversity of media content, January 31, 2007

CoE, Committee of Ministers, Recommendation CM/Rec(2008)6 of the Committee of Ministers to member states on measures to promote the respect for freedom of expression and information with regard to Internet filters

Table of Cases

Table of Cases

ECtHR February 15, 2005, *Steel and Morris v. the United Kingdom*
ECtHR December 14, 2006, *Verlagsgruppe News Gmbh v. Austria*
ECtHR June 14, 2007, *Hachette Filipacchi Associees v. France*
ECtHR December 10, 2007, *Stoll v. Switzerland*
ECtHR July 29, 2008, *Flux v. Moldavia (No. 6)*
ECtHR December 2, 2008, *K.U. v. Finland*
ECtHR March 10, 2009, *Times v. United Kingdom*
ECtHR April 14, 2009, *Társaság a Szabadságjogokért v. Hungary*
ECtHR April 28, 2009 *Karakó v. Hungary*
ECtHR May 10, 2011, *Mosley v the United Kingdom*

United States

Ex Parte Jackson, 96 U. S. 727 (1878)
Davis v. Massachusetts, 167 U.S. 43 (1897)
Public Clearing House v. Coyne, 194 U.S. 497 (1904)
Masses Publishing Co. v. Patten, 244 F. 535 (S.D.N.Y. 1917)
Abrams v. United States, 250 U.S. 616 (1919)
Milwaukee Social Democratic Pub. Co. v. Burleson, 255 U.S. 407 (1921)
Leach v. Carlile, 258 U.S. 138 (1922)
Gitlow v. People, 268 U.S. 652 (1925)
Stromberg v. California, 283 U.S. 359 (1931)
Grosjean v. American Press Co., Inc., 297 U.S. 233 (1936)
Associated Press v. NLRB, 301 U.S. 103 (1937)
Lovell v. Griffin, 303 U.S. 444 (1938)
Hague v. CIO, 307 U.S. 496 (1939)
Chaplinsky v. New Hampshire, 315 U.S. 568 (1942)
Valentine v. Chrestensen, 316 U.S. 52 (1942)
Martin v. City of Struthers, 319 U.S. 141 (1943)
West Virginia State Board of Education v. Barnette, 319 U.S. 624 (1943)
Associated Press v. United States, 326 U. S. 1, 20 (1945)
Marsh v. Alabama, 326 U.S. 501 (1946)
Terminiello v. Chicago, 337 U.S. 1 (1949)
Kunz v. New York, 340 U.S. 290 (1951)
Smith v. California, 361 U.S. 147 (1959)
New York Times Co. v. Sullivan, 376 U.S. 254 (1964)
Freedman v. Maryland, 380 U.S. 51 (1965)
Lamont v. Postmaster General, 381 U.S. 301 (1965)
Griswold v. Connecticut, 381 U.S. 479 (1965)
Adderley v. Florida, 385 U.S. 39 (1966)
Curtis Publishing Co. v. Butts, Associated Press v. Walker, 388 U.S. 130 (1967)
Citizen Publishing Co. v. United States, 394 U.S. 131, (1969)
Stanley v. Georgia 394 U.S. 557 (1969)
Red Lion Broadcasting Co. v. FCC, 395 U.S. 367 (1969)
Rowan v. Post Office Department, 397 U.S. 728 (1970)

European Court of Justice

ECJ March 26, 2010, C-91/09 (*EIS.de*)
ECJ July 8, 2010, C-558/08 (*Portakabin*)
ECJ, Opinion Advocate-General Jääkinen, December 9, 2010, C-324/09 (*eBay*)
ECJ, Advocate-General Jääskinen, March 24, 2011, C-323/09 (*Interflora*)
ECJ, Conclusions of Advocate General M. Pedro Cruz Villalón, April 14, 2011, Case C-70/10 (*Scarlet v. SABAM*)
ECJ July 12, 2011, C-324/09 (*eBay*)

The Netherlands

Hoge Raad [Dutch High Court] November 9, 1960, NJ 1961, 206 (*Vestigingsbesluit leesbibliotheekbedrijf 1958*)
Hoge Raad [Dutch High Court] February 26, 1999, (*Antelecom*)
Hoge Raad [Dutch High Court] March 12, 2004, (*XS4all/Abfab*)
Gerechtshof [Court of Appeals] Amsterdam June 15, 2006 (*Zoekmp3*)
Gerechtshof [Court of Appeals] Amsterdam July 26, 2011 (*Zwartepoorte*)
Vzr. Rechtbank [District Court] Amsterdam April 26, 2007 (*Jensen*)
Rechtbank [District Court] Haarlem May 12, 2004 (*Zoekmp3*)

Germany

BGH July 17, 2003, I ZR 259/00 (*Paperboy*)
BVerfGE 7, 198 (*Lueth*)
BVerfG 65,1 (Volkszählung)
BVerfG January 14, 1998, 1 BvR 1861/93
OLG Hamburg, February 20, 2007—AZ.: 7 U 126/06
LG Berlin, February 22, 2005, AZ: 27 O 45/05
LG Hamburg, April 28, 2006, Az.: 324 O 993/05

United Kingdom

Metropolitan International Schools Ltd. V. Designtechnica Corp [2009] EWHC 1765 (QB) (July 16, 2009)

Belgium

District Court of Brussels, June 29, 2007, No. 04/8975/A, *SABAM v. S.A. Tiscali (Scarlet)*, published in CAELJ Translation Series #001 (Mady, Bourrouilhou, & Hughes, trans.), 25 Cardozo Arts & Ent. L. J., 2008

France

T.G.I. Paris, March 26, 2008 http://www.forumInternet.org/specialistes/veille-juridique/jurisprudence/IMG/pdf/tgi-par20080326.pdf

Italy

Tribunale di Milano, March 24, 2011 (*Google suggest*)

Index

Index

INFORMATION LAW SERIES

1. Egbert J. Dommering & P. Bernt Hugenholtz, *Protecting Works of Fact: Copyright, Freedom of Expression and Information Law*, 1991 (ISBN 90-654-4567-6).
2. Willem F. Korthals Altes, Egbert J. Dommering, P. Bernt Hugenholtz & Jan J.C. Kabel, *Information Law Towards the 21st Century*, 1992 (ISBN 90-654-4627-3).
3. Jacqueline M.B. Seignette, *Challenges to the Creator Doctrine: Authorship, Copyright Ownership and the Exploitation of Creative Works in the Netherlands, Germany and The United States*, 1994 (ISBN 90-654-4876-4).
4. P. Bernt Hugenholtz, *The Future of Copyright in a Digital Environment, Proceedings of the Royal Academy Colloquium*, 1996 (ISBN 90-411-0267-1).
5. Julius C.S. Pinckaers, *From Privacy Toward a New Intellectual Property Right in Persona*, 1996 (ISBN 90-411-0355-4).
6. Jan J.C. Kabel & Gerard J.H.M. Mom, *Intellectual Property and Information Law: Essays in Honour of Herman Cohen Jehoram*, 1998 (ISBN 90-411-9702-8).
7. Ysolde Gendreau, Axel Nordemann & Rainer Oesch, *Copyright and Photographs: An International Survey*, 1999 (ISBN 90-411-9722-2).
8. P. Bernt Hugenholtz, *Copyright and Electronic Commerce: Legal Aspects of Electronic Copyright Management*, 2000 (ISBN 90-411-9785-0).
9. Lucie M.C.R. Guibault, *Copyright Limitations and Contracts: An Analysis of the Contractual Overridability of Limitations on Copyright*, 2002 (ISBN 90-411-9867-9).
10. Lee A. Bygrave, *Data Protection Law: Approaching its Rationale, Logic and Limits*, 2002 (ISBN 90-411-9870-9).
11. Niva Elkin-Koren & Neil Weinstock Netanel, *The Commodification of Information*, 2002 (ISBN 90-411-9876-8).
12. Mireille M.M. van Eechoud, *Choice of Law in Copyright and Related Rights: Alternatives to the Lex Protectionis*, 2003 (ISBN 90-411-2071-8).
13. Martin Senftleben, *Copyright, Limitations and the Three-Step Test: An Analysis of the Three-Step Test in International and EC Copyright Law*, 2004 (ISBN 90-411-2267-2).
14. Paul L.C. Torremans, *Copyright and Human Rights: Freedom of Expression – Intellectual Property – Privacy*, 2004 (ISBN 90-411-2278-8).
15. Natali Helberger, *Controlling Access to Content: Regulating Conditional Access in Digital Broadcasting*, 2005 (ISBN 90-411-2345-8).
16. Lucie M.C.R. Guibault & P. Bernt Hugenholtz, *The Future of the Public Domain: Identifying the Commons in Information Law*, 2006 (ISBN 978-90-411-2435-7).

INFORMATION LAW SERIES

17. Irini Katsirea, *Public Broadcasting and European Law: A Comparative Examination of Public Service Obligations in Six Member States,* 2008 (ISBN 978-90-411-2500-2).
18. Paul L.C. Torremans, *Intellectual Property and Human Rights: Enhanced Edition of Copyright and Human Rights,* 2008 (ISBN 978-90-411-2653-5).
19. Mireille van Eechoud, P. Bernt Hugenholtz, Stef van Gompel, Lucie Guibault & Natali Helberger, *Harmonizing European Copyright Law: The Challenges of Better Lawmaking,* 2009 (ISBN 978-90-411-3130-0).
20. Ashwin van Rooijen, *The Software Interface between Copyright and Competition Law: A Legal Analysis of Interoperability in Computer Programs,* 2010 (ISBN 978-90-411-3193-5).
21. Irini A. Stamatoudi, *Copyright Enforcement and the Internet,* 2010 (ISBN 978-90-411-3346-5).
22. Wolfgang Sakulin, *Trademark Protection and Freedom of Expression: An Inquiry into the Conflict between Trademark Rights and Freedom of Expression under European Law,* 2011 (ISBN 978-90-411-3415-8).
23. Stef van Gompel, *Formalities in Copyright Law: An Analysis of their History, Rationales and Possible Future,* 2011 (ISBN 978-90-411-3418-9).
24. Nadezhda Purtova, *Property Rights in Personal Data: A European Perspective,* 2012 (ISBN 978-90-411-3802-6).
25. Brad Sherman & Leanne Wiseman, *Copyright and the Challenge of the New,* 2012 (ISBN 978-90-411-3669-5).
26. Ewa Komorek, *Media Pluralism and European Law,* 2012 (ISBN 978-90-411-3894-1).
27. Joris van Hoboken, *Search Engine Freedom: On the Implications of the Right to Freedom of Expression for the Legal Governance of Web Search Engines,* 2012 (ISBN 978-90-411-4128-6).

Lightning Source UK Ltd.
Milton Keynes UK
UKOW03n1641190114

224866UK00001B/30/P